MCSD CERTIFICATION TOOLKIT (EXAM 70-483)

MCSD Certification Toolkit (Exam 70-483)

MCSD Certification Toolkit (Exam 70-483):

PROGRAMMING IN C#

Tiberiu Covaci
Gerry O'Brien
Rod Stephens
Vince Varallo

wrox

A Wiley Brand

MCSD Certification Toolkit (Exam 70-483): Programming in C#

Published by
John Wiley & Sons, Inc.
10475 Crosspoint Boulevard
Indianapolis, IN 46256
www.wiley.com

ISBN: 9781118612095
ISBN: 978-1-118-61206-4 (ebk)
ISBN: 978-1-118-72950-2 (ebk)
ISBN: 978-1-118-72929-8 (ebk)
Manufactured in the United States of America

10 9 8 7 6 5 4 3 2 1

ABOUT THE AUTHORS

TIBERIU COVACI is an Independent trainer and mentor teaching C# and .NET in general, and ASP.NET and parallel computing in particular. He works closely with Microsoft Learning helping them develop new courses, conducting beta classes and doing technology reviews for the upcoming courses. He was part of the Microsoft Certified Trainer Advisory Council between 2010 and 2012.

Tiberiu is a popular speaker at industry conferences and user groups around the world. His sessions and workshops get good reviews from both the attendees and the organizers.

Tiberiu is a Microsoft Certified Trainer and holds almost all .NET certification from .NET 2.0 and forward. He is as well an IASA certified trainer, an ASP.NET Insider, and a Telerik Insider. He is an INETA Speaker Bureau member and IASA Speaker. For his dedication and passion, Microsoft and Telerik presented Tibi with the MVP Award.

Tiberiu is the husband of lovely Nicoleta and the proud father of Anna and Disa.

GERRY O'BRIEN currently works at Microsoft as a program manager in Microsoft Learning where he manages internal tools and platforms working with teams of developers and testers. Prior to the program manager role, Gerry worked as the Certification Product Planner for the developer and SQL Server audiences at Microsoft Learning. In that role, he planned the exam portfolio for these audiences, working with industry experts to define the exam content and manage the exam from envisioning through development, beta, and release. Prior to working at Microsoft, Gerry worked as a software development consultant and trainer.

ROD STEPHENS started out as a mathematician, but, while studying at MIT, discovered how much fun programming is and has been programming professionally ever since. During his career, he has worked on an eclectic assortment of applications in such fields as telephone switching, billing, repair dispatching, tax processing, wastewater treatment, concert ticket sales, cartography, and training for professional football players.

Rod is a Microsoft Visual Basic Most Valuable Professional (MVP) and has taught introductory programming at ITT Technical Institute. He has written more than two dozen books that have been translated into languages from all over the world, and more than 250 magazine articles covering Visual Basic, C#, Visual Basic for Applications, Delphi, and Java.

Rod's popular VB Helper website (`www.vb-helper.com`) receives several million hits per month and contains thousands of pages of tips, tricks, and example programs for Visual Basic programmers, as well as example code for this book. His C# Helper website (`www.csharphelper.com`) contains similar material for C# programmers.

You can contact Rod at `RodStephens@csharphelper.com` or `RodStephens@vb-helper.com`.

VINCE VARALLO has been developing applications using Microsoft technologies for the past 17 years. He began his career as a Visual Basic 3 developer and has worked with VB 4, 5, and 6 until the .NET Framework 1.0 was released. He was an early adopter of ASP.NET and C#, and has concentrated on line-of-business applications throughout his entire career. He is currently the director of Technology Solutions at a digital marketing agency where he works with a wide variety of technologies. He previously authored *ASP.NET 3.5 Enterprise Application Development with Visual Studio 2008* and contributed as an author for *Professional Visual Basic 6: The 2003 Programmer's Resource.*

ABOUT THE TECHNICAL EDITOR

ANDERS BRATLAND combines his two passions, programming and teaching other people how to program, by working as a freelance consultant, which gives him the chance to work both as a Microsoft Certified Trainer and as a developer.

Anders is a well-known speaker at conferences like TechDays, Scandinavian Developer Conference, and Developer Summit. Anders is also active as speaker in different user groups, such as DotnetForum, and also as one of the organizers in the largest Swedish user group, Swenug.

Anders has a strong commitment to techniques and methods that can help projects to be successful, especially by adopting agile values and disciplines.

Anders is a Microsoft ASP.NET MVP and a member of the Swedish Microsoft Extended Expert Team, MEET.

CREDITS

ACKNOWLEDGMENTS

I would like to thank my lovely wife Nicoleta and my daughters, Anna and Disa, for supporting me and putting up with me for the past three years. I know this was a long process, and I know you might have not liked it at times, but now that is done I hope that people will find it educational and then all of it was worth it.

I want to thank Bob Elliott for believing in me even when I didn't. I want to thank Jennifer Lynn and Rosemarie Graham for their help in making this book happen. I would like to thank Anders Bratland for lending his expertise and making sure that this book is technologically accurate. I would like to thank my co-authors Gerry O'Brien, Rod Stephens, and Vince Varallo for their hard work and devotion.

I would also like to thank Sergiu Damian for his help reviewing my chapters, Catalin Pop for helping me with his expertise on encryption, and Susan Ibach and Christopher Harrison for recommending me as author.

Last but not least I would like to thank my parents for making me who I am.

—Tiberiu Covaci

CONTENTS

INTRODUCTION

WHEN WE FIRST TALKED ABOUT WRITING THIS BOOK, our idea was to offer a way to our readers to learn to program using C#, and the byproduct of this process was for you to pass the 70-483 certification exam given by Microsoft. Being certified on specific technologies helps you in many ways. First, it helps you understand which parts are considered by the specialists to be important. Second, it helps you to understand a new technology by having a goal. Finally, it helps you in your career because certifications are recognized by employers, and this can give you advantage over other applicants.

WHO THIS BOOK IS FOR

Microsoft recommends that you have at least 1 year of experience programming in C# before attempting to take Exam 70-483. In addition, we recommend that you have some experience with other programming languages, although it is not necessary. If you are an experienced programmer, we recommend you to skim the chapters you are familiar with and read in detail those chapters you are not so confident about. If you are a novice programmer, we recommend you read the entire book, and make sure you understand all the chapter test questions and the study the Cheat Sheet at the end of every chapter.

WHAT THIS BOOK COVERS

This book covers C# language version 5.0 and .NET Framework version 4.5. We tried to cover all the skills measured by Exam 70-483, with each chapter focusing on specific key objectives. We provide, as well, many representative sample test questions that are similar to the ones used by Microsoft. You can find these questions at the end of every chapter.

HOW THIS BOOK IS STRUCTURED

Instead of following the test objectives as they were specified by Microsoft, this book follows a more natural approach to learning, where the knowledge base is built gradually.

In every chapter in this book you can find the following parts:

- ➤ A table showing how each chapter correlates to the test objectives
- ➤ Real-world case scenarios and code labs with solutions
- ➤ Advice, warnings, best practices, common mistakes, notes, and sidebars to point out important material
- ➤ Chapter test questions structured similar to how you will see questions on the exam
- ➤ Additional reading and resources

➤ Cheat Sheets

➤ Review of key terms

> **NOTE** *The chapter test questions and answers, the Cheat Sheet, and Review of Key Terms are also available on the website for you to download and print.*

Following is a breakdown of each chapter's focuses:

Chapter 1, "Introducing the Programming C# Certification Test": This chapter introduces you to the Microsoft certification process and to the specifics of the 70-483 Programming in C# certification.

Chapter 2, "Basic Program Structure": This chapter covers the topics necessary for you to be successful in understanding core functionality in the C# programming language. Key topics enable you to learn about statements in C#, both simple and complex. At the end of this chapter, you will understand how to create basic programs in C#.

Chapter 3, "Working with the Type System": This chapter covers the type system in C#. You learn about value and reference types, how to define them, and how to use them. You also learn the basic concepts of object-oriented programming.

Chapter 4, "Using Types": This chapter talks about how to work with types, convert between data types, and work with dynamic types. After that you explore different ways to work with strings.

Chapter 5, "Creating and Implementing Class Hierarchies": This chapter continues the discussion about object-oriented programming (started in Chapter 3), and describes how to create class hierarchies and classes that implement common .NET interfaces. It also covers the object's life cycle and how to handle unmanaged resources.

Chapter 6, "Working with Delegates, Events, and Exceptions": This chapter continues the discussion started in Chapter 3 about the type system and talks about two special data types: exceptions and delegates. After that, it discusses how to work with delegates to create and use events.

Chapter 7, "Multithreading and Asynchronous Processing": This chapter shows you how to improve the performance of your application by using threads, tasks, and the new asynchronous programming paradigm introduced in C# 5.0.

Chapter 8, "Creating and Using Types with Reflection, Custom Attributes, the CodeDOM, and Lambda Expressions": Reflection is the capability to analyze code dynamically, read, modify, and even invoke behavior dynamically. You learn how to define metadata for your code by using `Attribute` classes. You also learn how to create code generators using the CodeDOM. Finally, you learn how to query sets of data using expression- and method-based lambda expressions.

Chapter 9, "Working with Data": This chapter looks at different ways to work with data sets. It discusses arrays, collections, and technologies such as ADO.NET, ADO.NET Entity Framework, and WCF Data Services and how to work with the I/O system.

Chapter 10, "Working with Language Integrated Query (LINQ)": This chapter covers ways to query data by using the Language Integrated Query.

Chapter 11, "Input Validation, Debugging, and Instrumentation": This chapter starts by talking about different ways to validate data input. After that it continues to talk about ways to debug and instrument applications to minimize the errors.

Chapter 12, "Using Encryption and Managing Assemblies": This chapter covers two apparently unrelated technologies. First, you cover encryption to understand how to ensure data integrity and privacy. After that you cover ways to manage assemblies as deployment units.

WHAT YOU NEED TO USE THIS BOOK

To run the samples in the book, you need the following:

➤ A computer running Windows 7 or above

➤ Visual Studio 2012 Professional Edition or above. If you don't have this version, you can download a 90-day trial version from Microsoft (see http://www.microsoft.com/visualstudio/eng/downloads).

The source code for the samples is available for download from the Wrox website at www.wrox.com/remtitle.cgi?isbn=1118612094.

CONVENTIONS

To help you get the most from the text and keep track of what's happening, we've used a number of conventions throughout the book.

REAL-WORLD CASE SCENARIO Sample Scenario

The *Real-World Case Scenario* is an exercise similar to what may appear on the test. You should work through problems, following the text in the book.

Solution

After each *Real-World Case Scenario*, the example is explained in detail.

CODE LAB Sample Code Lab

The *Code Lab* focuses on code highlights discussed earlier. You must understand how and why this code is used for the purpose shown to pass the test.

Solution

After each *Code Lab*, the code and what it does is explained in detail.

COMMON MISTAKES

These boxes highlight mistakes you have made or seen others make. Here, you get a chance to learn from others' hard-learned lessons.

BEST PRACTICES

You are reading this book primarily to pass the MCSD Certification test. This feature covers topics highlighted because they are important for the test but also for common work practices.

ADVICE FROM THE EXPERTS

In these boxes you can find advice from the authors. We've been there before, and we want you to learn from what we've learned.

EXAM TIPS AND TRICKS

Here, you can find information that focuses on the Microsoft certification test or test-taking skills in general.

> **WARNING** *Warnings hold important, not-to-be-forgotten information directly relevant to the surrounding text.*

> **NOTE** *Notes point out important facts for you to remember.*

As for styles in the text:

➤ We *highlight* new terms and important words when we introduce them.

➤ We show keyboard strokes like this: Ctrl+A.

➤ We show filenames, URLs, and code within the text like so: `persistence.properties`

➤ We present code in two different ways:

```
We use a monofont type with no highlighting for most code examples.
```

We use bold to emphasize code that is particularly important in the present context or to show changes from a previous code snippet.

STUDY MATERIAL AND CODE ON THE WEBSITE

As you work through the examples in this book, you may choose either to type in all the code manually or to use the source code files that accompany the book. All the source code used in this book is available for download at `www.wrox.com`. Specifically for this book, the code download is on the Download Code tab at `www.wrox.com/remtitle.cgi?isbn=1118612094`.

You can also search for the book at `www.wrox.com` to find the code. Alternatively, you can go to the main Wrox code download page at `www.wrox.com/dynamic/books/download.aspx` to see the code available for this book and all other Wrox books.

At the beginning of each chapter, you can find the location of the major code files for the chapter. Throughout each chapter, you can also find references to the names of code files as needed in listing titles and text.

Most of the code on `www.wrox.com` is compressed in a ZIP, RAR archive, or similar archive format appropriate to the platform. After you download the code, just decompress it with an appropriate compression tool.

> **NOTE** *Because many books have similar titles, you may find it easiest to search by ISBN; this book's ISBN is 978-1-118-61209-5.*

In addition to the code, on the website you will also find the sample test questions and answers included in this book, as well as additional sample test questions and answers not included in this book to help you practice for the 70-483 certification exam.

ERRATA

We make every effort to ensure that there are no errors in the text or in the code. However, no one is perfect, and mistakes do occur. If you find an error in one of our books, such as a spelling mistake or faulty piece of code, we would be grateful for your feedback. By sending in errata, you may save another reader hours of frustration, and at the same time, you can help us provide even higher quality information.

To find the errata page for this book, go to www.wrox.com/remtitle.cgi?isbn=1118612094 and click the Errata link. On this page you can view all errata that has been submitted for this book and posted by Wrox editors.

If you don't spot "your" error on the Book Errata page, go to www.wrox.com/contact/techsupport .shtml and complete the form there to send us the error you have found. We'll check the information, and if appropriate post a message to the book's errata page and fix the problem in subsequent editions of the book.

P2P.WROX.COM

For author and peer discussion, join the P2P forums at http://p2p.wrox.com. The forums are a web-based system for you to post messages relating to Wrox books and related technologies and interact with other readers and technology users. The forums offer a subscription feature to e-mail you topics of interest of your choosing when new posts are made to the forums. Wrox authors, editors, other industry experts, and your fellow readers are present on these forums.

At http://p2p.wrox.com, you can find a number of different forums that can help you, not only as you read this book, but also as you develop your own applications. To join the forums, just follow these steps:

1. Go to http://p2p.wrox.com and click the Register link.

2. Read the terms of use and click Agree.

3. Complete the required information to join and any optional information you want to provide, and click Submit.

4. You will receive an e-mail with information describing how to verify your account and complete the joining process.

> **NOTE** *You can read messages in the forums without joining P2P, but to post your own messages, you must join.*

After you join, you can post new messages and respond to messages other users post. You can read messages at any time on the web. If you would like to have new messages from a particular forum e-mailed to you, click the Subscribe to This Forum icon by the forum name in the forum listing.

For more information about how to use the Wrox P2P, be sure to read the P2P FAQs for answers to questions about how the forum software works, as well as many common questions specific to P2P and Wrox books. To read the FAQs, click the FAQ link on any P2P page.

1

Introducing the Programming C# Certification

WHAT YOU WILL LEARN IN THIS CHAPTER

➤ Getting certified

➤ Understanding Microsoft certifications

➤ Understanding Microsoft certification exams

➤ Studying for the exam

This chapter is an introduction to Microsoft certifications in general and the Programming C# certification more specifically. In this chapter, you learn about the world of Microsoft certifications and why you might consider taking this exam and getting certified. The chapter also presents information on how exam questions are considered and written for Microsoft exams and describes how you can use this book to study for Exam 70-483.

A complete list of the topic areas that are covered on Exam 70-483 is also included to help you understand what to expect for objectives of each exam as you work toward your MCPD certification using the C# programming language.

Due to the nature of the content of Chapter 1, there are no code downloads for this chapter.

GETTING CERTIFIED

Certifications have been around for many years. Hardware manufacturers certify components, car dealers provide certified used cars, developers certify software to run on specific operating systems—and that's just to name a few.

What this basically means is that the term *certification* can have many different definitions depending on the context in which it is used. In this book, certification refers to Microsoft certifications. (Specifics about Microsoft certification are presented in the section "What Is MS Certification?" later in this chapter.) Like many other large companies in the IT industry, Microsoft has established and maintains a certification program to show developers' aptitude in designing and developing programs using Microsoft's products.

Although each organization, including Microsoft, has its own certification program, benefits, and requirements, there are still a lot of similarities among certifications. For example, most, if not all organizations, deliver their certification exams through an exam delivery partner (EDP). This has typically been through EDPs such as Prometric, Pearson Vue, and Certiport.

Each program requires that the candidate register in the program and take specific exams and meet certain requirements before the participant is awarded a certification. Some programs require one exam for a certification credential, and others require multiple exams. For example, Cisco, Microsoft, Adobe, Novell, and Oracle all have certifications you can earn by taking one knowledge-based exam. Some certifications are more difficult than others.

The more complex, multi-exam scenarios are found in the high-end certifications such as the Microsoft Certified Master (MCM), which is changing to Microsoft Certified Solutions Master (MCSM), or Cisco Certified Internetworking Expert (CCIE) certifications. These certifications and exams require much more than just a knowledge-based exam. These certifications require a candidate to complete lab-based portions, meaning that the participant performs actual tasks in either a real or emulated environment.

For the Cisco exam, you visit the testing center and configure the necessary network switches, routers, and firewalls according to a specification. The exam team then introduces bugs, or essentially breaks your configuration, and you have to troubleshoot the issues and fix it.

The MCM program has different requirements depending on the certification you are seeking. For most of the MCM certifications, you attend classroom training, take knowledge-based exams, and take a final lab-based exam over a 21-day period—that is, 21 days straight with no breaks in between. Some of the MCM programs permit the candidate to take training at different institutions and then take the requisite knowledge-based exams with a final performance-based lab-style exam at the end, hosted by Prometric.

Obviously, the more stringent the requirements for a certification, the more credibility the certification holds in the industry. It also means a higher cost, but with that rigorous certification in hand, you can also demand—and usually get—more money for consulting fees or a higher salary. But that is getting into the next section: why you should get certified.

Why Get Certified?

Obviously, if you purchased this book, you have already decided to get a certification, or at least take a certification exam. Of course you may also be just borrowing the book because you are curious about what might be involved in getting certified. Either way, this section describes some of the reasons why you might consider getting certified.

Having spent a lot of time pursuing certifications in the past, plus working as a Certification Product Planner, the reasons I have come across are varied and many. For the most part, to the reasons are summarized and rationalized for why certifications are good and why you may want to pursue them.

In the IT industry, especially in the realm of the developer world, most of the programmers who have been in the industry for some time came through academia and hold university degrees, typically in computer science. When you think about it, a Bachelor or Master's degree is a certification from a certain perspective. The degree shows the world that the person whose name is indicated on the degree certificate has met the requirements as set forth by a board of some sort, usually the university faculty and a governing body.

Not every programmer, database developer, database administrator, or other IT professional, however, has attended a four-year degree program at a university. Many have instead taken classes at two-year certificate programs. Whatever the institution or schooling background, upon successfully completing the program, students acquire a diploma, certificate, degree, or other named piece of documentation that indicates they have achieved some specific level of knowledge.

One of the problems that graduates face after completing these programs is that the knowledge they gained during the course of their schooling is actually outdated to a certain extent. You might think computer science concepts don't change at their core, and to a great extent, you are correct. But what does change are the technology and tools IT professionals use every day in their pursuit of the computer science career upon which they have embarked. A good example of this is how the Internet and the World Wide Web have changed your concept of what an application is. Just in the short lifespan of the web, you have seen the technology change from static pages with hyperlinks to pages supporting Cascading Style Sheets, JavaScript, ActiveX controls, server-side programming, state-management, and so on. None of these technologies or concepts were taught just a short time ago, yet they are relevant and important today.

Employers looking to hire programmers for developing websites that contain these technologies require some way to identify who has those skills. The Bachelor of Science document certainly doesn't indicate this. Actually, there isn't any way for an employer to know what courses a holder of a degree has actually taken unless the student provides a transcript. There isn't any way to show an employer what knowledge and skills were gained after attending a university either outside of a resume or perhaps a portfolio.

Industry certifications are a way to address some of these issues. When properly implemented, secured, and executed on, industry certifications are an effective way to show existing and potential employers some important information. Certifications can provide the person who holds the credential, the following benefits:

➤ Validation of knowledge

➤ Validation of skills

➤ A way to show continuing education

➤ A means to prove a commitment to maintaining skills

Whatever your reasons for pursuing a certification, you must understand the value of the certification you intend to acquire and perhaps even the process by which the certifications are developed and maintained. The next few sections present an insight into Microsoft certifications, including what certifications Microsoft makes available, how they fit into the overall certification portfolio for Microsoft, and an insider's view of how the certifications are planned, created, and delivered.

EXAM PIRACY AND BRAIN DUMPS

Many opponents to certifications cite reasons such as exam piracy and brain dumps for their opposition. Some indicate that employers don't value certifications, and therefore they aren't worth the money you would spend on them. Others, such as programmers, tell you that they don't work in a world of multiple choices, so a multiple-choice test isn't representative of their skills and knowledge.

Microsoft is not the only company affected by exam piracy and brain dumps. Any certification program is subject to these same issues. Although there are certain methods in existence to help deal with these problems, they can never be totally eradicated.

Microsoft is actively taking steps to counter some of these issues by performing exam analysis, in the form of statistical forensics, to help identify cheaters and exam centers that are at the heart of the problem. Over the past few years, it has been successful in shutting down testing centers that participate in exam piracy and websites that contribute to brain-dump activities. Because of the way the Internet works, however, it is impossible to completely stop all the brain-dump sites.

One of the best ways to help combat these issues is through the use of education and cooperation with certified professionals. Any time someone asks you for a brain dump or a way to cheat on a Microsoft exam, ensure that you explain the benefit of achieving the certification honestly and report any cheating activity to Microsoft. You can help drive the acceptance of your certifications and help to improve the reputation of these exams by helping to reduce exam piracy and cheating.

What Is MS Certification?

Microsoft certifications have evolved over the years. The exams have changed in their content, and the process for creating the exams has changed somewhat as well. Like most certification programs, the changes are based on customer feedback, changes in the industry, and standards board certifications.

Microsoft certifications are most commonly known as *MCP certifications*. MCP stands for Microsoft Certified Professional. To understand the Microsoft certification landscape, look at some terminology, what certifications are available from Microsoft, and how to obtain them.

Throughout this chapter, the terms *certification* and *credential* are used interchangeably. A certification is defined as a "title" that candidates can use after they complete the requirements set forth for that certification. Credential is another word for a certification. Again, it is a title that candidates can use after completing the requirements for that credential.

An example of a certification would be Microsoft Certified Solutions Associate (MCSA), Microsoft Certified Solutions Developer (MCSD), Microsoft Certified Solutions Expert (MCSE), or Microsoft Certified Solutions Master (MCSM). The following sections describe each of these designations.

Certification Changes

The MCSD and older Microsoft Certified Systems Engineer (MCSE) certifications served the industry well for many years. Like all programs, changes and improvements were a necessity. Some of these changes were brought about by the need to streamline requirements and simplify the program, whereas other driving reasons were employers and hiring managers.

As technology changes, IT professionals either keep their skills up to date or they do not. This can create a bit of an issue for hiring managers trying to discern qualifications from resumes submitted. For example, programmers could indicate that they hold an MCSD certification, but don't tell the hiring manager what programming language was used to achieve the credential. If the hiring manager is looking for a developer who could program using C++, the certification didn't actually tell them that. Also, what elective exam did candidates use? How much web experience did they have as opposed to Windows development experience?

Both candidates and hiring managers provided feedback to Microsoft, telling them that it was not easy to determine just what the certification name meant or what requirements were needed for a certification. The elective system made it difficult to determine qualifications. Other feedback indicated that one certification didn't necessarily map to the way the industry thought about job roles and skills qualifications.

As a result of this feedback and industry research, Microsoft made changes to the program and created new certifications and new exams to help address these issues and needs. It termed this new program the *New Generation of Certifications* and labeled the old system as *Legacy Certifications*. Then, just a few short years following that change, Microsoft introduced the current version of certifications, which is the third iteration of the certification, or cert, program. These changes are not designed to confuse you, but instead are intended to help ensure that your credentials have validity and meaning in the workforce.

The Initial Certifications (Version One)

The first iteration of the Microsoft certification program created a base credential known as MCP. This was the starting point for any of the higher certifications that consisted of:

- MCSE
- MCSD
- MCDBA (Microsoft Database Administrator)

These were the mainstream certifications that existed in version one of the Microsoft certification programs. They served Microsoft well for a number of years, and these three credentials became well known in the industry.

A New Generation of Certifications (Version 2)

As with any program, there is the potential not to meet the needs of every concerned party. Feedback to, and research by, Microsoft Learning resulted in some changes to the certification program. The changes were designed to address a couple of key areas: job roles and knowledge validation.

Both of these areas have some commonality. Hiring managers needed a way to identify which specific technologies a potential job candidate might have, and they needed a way to map the certifications to job roles. Only developer certifications are covered here.

Microsoft Certified Technology Specialist (MCTS)

For validating knowledge on a technical subject, Microsoft created the Microsoft Certified Technology Specialist (MCTS) credential. The MCTS certification is not considered to be an entry-level certification but is aimed at candidates who want to prove their knowledge and skills on a specific Microsoft technology.

To achieve an MCTS certification, the candidate would have to pass one or more exams. The MCTS certifications and exams also allowed Microsoft to provide a more valid way of testing candidates' knowledge and skills on a technology by permitting them to include more complete coverage of that technology. To explain this a little better, consider how the older MCSD certification focused on either web or Windows development, which is not bad, except that these two platforms encompass a lot of different programming skill sets.

By using the MCTS exam focus and the different technologies that Microsoft was releasing, adequate coverage of each different technology could now be included in a separate exam. This allowed Microsoft to provide sufficient coverage of a technology on an exam and also clearly state what that technology is. Candidates passing that exam would have proven their knowledge and skills on that technology. Hiring managers now had a way to determine what the job candidate was certified on.

Microsoft Certified Professional Developer (MCPD)

Microsoft also created another layer of certification known as the professional level. This credential is titled Microsoft Certified Professional Developer (MCPD). To achieve an MCPD credential, the candidate must pass any prerequisite MCTS certifications along with the MCPD exam.

The MCPD exams are designed to test a candidate's ability to work as a team lead or development lead and make decisions around application designs. There are also not as many MCPD credentials as there are MCTS credentials, and this is to support the fact that they are intended to focus on a job role as opposed to a breadth of technologies.

The Current Microsoft Certifications (Version 3)

The current version of Microsoft certifications changes the focus a bit more by looking at credentials such as Specialist and Solutions Experts or Solutions Developers. The changes made for the current set of credentials were designed to do the following:

- ➤ Reduce the number of entry points
- ➤ Reduce the number of certifications
- ➤ Clarify certification paths

➤ Enable single base certification to lead to multiple advanced certifications

➤ Streamline the program into a seamless process

Again, the reasons for changing the certification program were in response to industry feedback and research. As noted in the preceding list, the previous generations of certifications were still confusing due to the number of entry points into the program, with multiple paths and many different certifications and exams. The current program focuses on three levels of certification.

There are three main tiers in the latest certification program:

➤ **Solutions Associate level**: Designed to be the foundation for certifications in Microsoft proving technical skills.

➤ **Solutions Expert level**: Expands on the knowledge of those at the Associate level and requires more rigor in the exams and knowledge tested. Candidates at this level should be able to build solutions using multiple technologies including cloud computing.

➤ **Solutions Master level**: The top of the Microsoft certification program. Consists of certifications that require knowledge-based exams along with performance-based testing. Those who hold a Masters certification demand higher salaries.

Other Microsoft Certifications: The MTA

All the preceding certifications can be thought of as the technical certifications. Think of technical certifications as a set of exams and credentials intended to validate skills. There is another set of credentials that fall under the acronym MTA (Microsoft Technology Associate).

Actually, Microsoft is careful not to actually refer to the MTA as a certification. It is more of a certificate. The MTA is aimed at high school students and post-secondary institutions that offer two-year certificate programs; although, four-year universities can certainly deliver them as well.

Although the exams are technical in nature, they are designed to be entry level, and 80 percent of the content is intended to be knowledge level as opposed to implementation-specific. What that means is the questions are designed to test candidates on their understanding of the concepts, such as the following:

➤ What is a class in object-oriented programming(OOP)?

➤ What is a tuple in a database?

The MTA exams are used by some schools to augment their existing tests, and sometimes to replace them, for determining a student's knowledge of a subject area. These exams are also designed to serve a few more purposes, the most pertinent being that they provide students with a sense of achievement, helping them to realize their progression in their learning. Plus, they provide a means to introduce students to the world of certifications by exposing them to a Microsoft exam environment. If they pass the exam, they get access to the Microsoft Certified Professional community, where they can start preparing for the more technical certifications with the help of the MCP community and resources available there. The MTA has been well received by the academic community.

THINGS TO KNOW ABOUT THE TEST

For most developers and IT professionals outside of Microsoft, or even Microsoft Learning, the exam development process is a black box. For a developer, it's analogous to a Windows Communication Foundation (WCF) service. You know how to call it and get a result back, but you have no real insight into the algorithms that make it work. You can guess at it, but you're never quite certain.

It's always an eye-opening experience when someone steps into the process for the first time and sees what it takes to create these exams. The next section describes how the exam questions are written, but first it can help you to understand how an exam is created.

How the Test Is Created

At one time, Microsoft certification exams focused on product features. After all, it was the features of the product that developers were using to create their applications, and it was the features of the product that customers asked for, so it stood to reason that the features of the product were the important aspects to be testing on. Or does that logic make sense?

The history of these exams has shown that this methodology doesn't quite present a good testing experience, nor does it provide any validation that a candidate can actually use the features. It merely shows that developers can memorize what a feature is or does. The current process has been put in place to overcome these issues and to address some others as well. Psychometrics has been added to the certification exams. *Psychometrics* is a field of study dealing with the theories and techniques used to validate knowledge and skills through a measurement process. In this case, this measurement is a test. Before getting into how psychometrics is involved, first look at how the exam envisioning and design has changed to better address industry needs.

Microsoft releases new versions of software, on average, about every two years. A Product Manager and a Product Planner in Microsoft Learning work together to evaluate the changes in the next version of the product and how it will impact the industry. For example, a careful evaluation was made of all the technologies that make up Microsoft's .NET Framework to determine how the new features will be applied by developers in creating Windows or web-based applications. How have the data access mechanisms changed? What is new in WCF services?

After this information is evaluated, the Product Manager and Product Planner start to seek out developers in the industry who use these new technologies in their organization. As you can imagine, these developers will typically be early adopters who partner with Microsoft to gain access to early builds of the software. They also consist of Microsoft Most Valuable Professionals (MVPs) and Microsoft Certified Trainers (MCT). The criteria are clear. These developers must use the new software in real-world scenarios, and can describe how the new features are used and will be used by the industry.

Microsoft then hosts focus group sessions, typically in Redmond, Washington, with these industry experts to determine how the technologies are used. These sessions do not focus on features only. The sessions are designed to extract product-usage scenarios from these experts on how they use the technology, regardless of feature sets, in the real world. Obviously, there must be a focus on the new aspects of the software, or the exam becomes a rehash of the previous version.

The exam prep guide is the output of this focus group—well, sort of. The prep guide structure is explained a bit later in the section that details the objectives that this exam will test on, but for now, just know that the prep guide is the result of the focus group. The information taken from the focus group is formulated into the exam design document that gets a further validation pass by more industry experts. This validation step is known as a *blueprinting process*, where other industry experts who have never seen the list before and who did not participate in the focus group can look at each outlined objective and rate it based on relevancy, importance, and frequency. These values are fed into a spreadsheet that executes some magical psychometric formulas that spit out the number of required exam questions for each objective to appropriately measure the candidate's knowledge on the test. After the blueprinting is complete and the data is assembled, the exam question writing can begin. Note that as of the writing of this book, the exam questions are still in multiple choice or true/false format. Some newer items are being tested that consist of drag-and-drop or choosing code segments, but the bulk of the questions are multiple choice.

> **NOTE** Microsoft is committed to moving to a performance-based testing environment for all its certifications at some point. There are many hurdles to overcome before it is a reality, but that will change the face of Microsoft certifications considerably.

How Questions Are Written

Just how do the questions get written? Microsoft Learning works with various partners to create the content for the exams in a clear process that is guided and overseen by the Product Planners, the Content Development Managers, and the Project Managers at Microsoft.

Taking the exam design document and the blueprint values, a team of item writers is assembled to begin the process. These item writers must be industry experts as well, who work with the technology on a daily basis. They receive training on effective exam question writing.

This might sound a little strange at first. You may be saying to yourself, "Why would you need to have training on how to write a test question? If you know the technology, you can write a test question on it."

Although there is some truth to that thought, writing an effective exam question is not always an easy task. Here are the reasons why:

➤ The question must test the objective it maps to.

➤ The question must be worded in a technically accurate and correct form.

➤ Slang or nicknames cannot be used. (An example of this is in the IT world where in North America the acronym DMZ has been used to represent the perimeter network for security purposes. In certain other countries, DMZ has negative connotations.)

➤ Wording and terms must take into account translation into other languages.

➤ Each question must be legally defensible. That is to say, if the question is asking for one answer, there can be only one correct answer among the available answer choices. All other answers *must* be 100 percent incorrect.

➤ The writer cannot make up technologies or answers that do not exist in the product just to provide a wrong answer.

➤ Questions cannot be tricky with subtle wording that hides clues.

➤ Questions cannot be simply recall questions where a candidate would normally look up the answer in MSDN or use IntelliSense. An example would be writing a question that tests the order of parameters for a method call for a class in the base class library.

➤ One question on the exam cannot give away the answer to another question on the exam.

➤ Questions must be written to the correct cognitive level.

As you can see, there are quite a few rules involved in the acceptance criteria for the questions. Most writers think they will turn out their questions with minimal trouble because they know the technology so well, but they soon find out that good exam questions take hard work and careful thought.

After the questions have been written, the next formal part of the process is to hold an Alpha session. The Alpha session typically involves the lead item writer plus six to eight more subject matter experts who go over each written question. The original item writers are not involved in this process so that nobody's feelings get hurt when the questions are critically reviewed. It also helps the subject matter experts in the room to focus on being honest about the question's merits.

Any problematic questions either get fixed or completely rewritten during this five-day session. The output of this session is the set of questions included in the beta version of the exam. The beta version is where as many as 500 sets of eyes have a chance to evaluate the questions. Each beta candidate has the opportunity to provide comments and feedback on the items at the end of the exam. The feedback and comments are reviewed after the beta has completed, and a post-beta session is held where even more subject matter experts are involved. The task this time is to validate the comments and feedback, and then to set the passing score for the exam. At this stage, any questions that did not perform well on the exam or have technical issues are deleted from the final pool of exam questions.

This entire process can take anywhere from six to nine months from the design phase to release of an exam. The exam's planning process starts much sooner than that, of course, but the actual exam design, development, testing, and release portion can take this long.

> **EXAM TIPS AND TRICKS**
>
> Not every process is perfect, and even with this many subject matter experts looking at exam questions, some minor issues can escape notice. When you take the exam, remember there is a comment period at the end where you can submit your feedback on the exam or on individual questions. Don't be afraid to be brutally honest. At the same time, ensure that you provide usable feedback. Responses such as "This question stinks" are not actionable and do not identify issues with the question. The feedback can go a long way to help improve the quality of the exam questions.

HOW TO STUDY FOR THE EXAM USING THIS BOOK

And now you come back to the reason why you bought this book. Your objective is to study for and pass the exam, and you purchased this book to help you do that. Outside of the great information presented in this book, you gain advice on how you can use the book more effectively to help in your exam preparation.

Although there are many ways to start preparing for an exam, only a structured method helps to ensure success. Typically, when looking at exam preparation, a candidate faces a situation similar to an author staring at the first blank page for a book he is writing. Where do you start? Not only that, but you may also be thinking that preparing is going to be hard because you don't know what you don't know. You're not sure you want to study everything because you should already know most of the content that will be covered, but how do you know what to focus on? The following sections can help you determine just that.

Prep Guide

The first thing you should do is to focus on the exam prep guide that lists the objectives for the exam. (The objectives are included at the end of this chapter for your convenience, but you can also find them at `www.microsoft.com/learning/en/us/exam.aspx?ID=70-483`.) These objectives provide you with an idea as to what could be covered on the exam. There is a caveat that comes with the prep guides, however. You may notice the following wording under each objective that states,

"This objective may include but is not limited to...."

This text is an indication that the listed items after this text are the identified areas of coverage from the exam design sessions. The list is typically not complete for various reasons, such as not all topics were thought of during the design or complete coverage may not be possible.

Regardless of the reasons that there may not be complete coverage, the items are just indicators of what you may see a question written on. The other issue is that the exam designers and the item writers are, for the most part, different people. This means that the person writing the exam question was not present during the exam design and therefore was not privy to the conversations around this topic. They also have their own experiences that they bring to the process for what they will draw upon for writing the questions they have been assigned.

This doesn't mean there is a disconnect in the process or it is flawed. It is similar to the exams you took in school. You were expected to understand the subject to the extent that you could answer any question on the subject. You were not given explicit topic coverage on those exams either. These exams are similar in the prep guides in that they offer a little more information as to what may be covered, but as long as you fully understand the subject, you should be able to answer any question related to it.

Functional Groups

So step one is complete; you have reviewed the prep guide and evaluated the objectives, and now you have an idea what the exam questions will test on. Before you spend time studying topics, you should rate what you think your knowledge is for each of these objectives. Don't worry too much about the bolded items in the objectives listed here (the ones with the percentage ratings in parentheses). Those items are known as *Functional Groups*, and they are a convenient way to group related objectives. The percentage listed gives you an idea of how much of the exam a particular Functional Group will take up. You can use this value to determine where to focus your time studying if you want.

Practice Questions

After you have the objectives rated, turn your attention to practice questions. Practice test questions are a great way to evaluate your knowledge against what you think you know, and against reality. They are also a great way to focus your mind on how the exams are written and what the experience may be like when you take the actual exam. The other advantage you gain from the practice questions is the ability to identify your weak areas, allowing you to focus your study and maximizing your investment in preparation.

Preparation

The preparation part is primarily where this book comes in. The chapters of this book map directly to the exam objectives. This means that the book is focused training for the exam. This doesn't mean that it is a cheat sheet or a brain dump. To gain the most benefit, you need to read and understand the content of the chapters. You also then get to apply that understanding through the code labs in each chapter. These labs are designed to reinforce the theory presented in the chapter. Each chapter will also contain practice questions, Cheat Sheets, and Key Terms to help you focus on the right content.

The prep guide found on the Microsoft Learning Web site will help you to identify the key aspects of the exam itself along with the skills measured, a list of preparation materials such as courses or books, as well as a community section designed to provide resources from your fellow exam candidates and developers. The community can be a great study resource as well.

The authors of the book have done their best to evaluate the exam objectives and to provide you with material designed to help you prepare for the exam. Your study habits and how well you understand the content presented here will be factors in your success. The more experience you gain with the technology and the more you practice the labs in this book, the greater your chances to successfully pass the exam.

THE 70-483 OBJECTIVES

The following section lists the objectives for Exam 70-483, the topic of this book. The objectives are taken directly from the prep guides that you can find online at www.microsoft.com/learning under the Certifications tab.

Manage Program Flow (25 Percent)

Under this category, you will find topics that deal with threading, program flow, events, callbacks, and exception handling—all are important to managing how your application is executed.

Implement Multithreading and Asynchronous Processing

This objective may include but is not limited to use the Task Parallel library (ParallelFor, Plinq, and Tasks); create continuation tasks; spawn threads by using ThreadPool; unblock the UI; use async and await keywords; and manage data by using concurrent collections.

See Chapter 7, "Multithreading and Asynchronous Processing."

Manage Multithreading

This objective may include but is not limited to synchronize resources; implement locking; cancel a long-running task; and implement thread-safe methods to handle race conditions.

See Chapter 7, "Multithreading and Asynchronous Processing."

Implement Program Flow

This objective may include but is not limited to iterate across collection and array items; program decisions by using switch statements, if/then, and operators; and evaluate expressions.

See Chapter 2, "Basic Program Structure."

Create and Implement Events and Callbacks

This objective may include but is not limited to create event handlers; subscribe to and unsubscribe from events; use built-in delegate types to create events; create delegates; lambda expressions; and anonymous methods.

See Chapter 6, "Working with Delegates, Events, and Exceptions."

Implement Exception Handling

This objective may include but is not limited to handle exception types (SQL exceptions, network exceptions, communication exceptions, and network timeout exceptions); catch typed versus base exceptions; implement `try-catch-finally` blocks; throw exceptions; determine when to rethrow versus throw; and create custom exceptions.

See Chapter 6, "Working with Delegates, Events, and Exceptions."

Create and Use Types (24 Percent)

Creating and using types will take you into the world of C# data. It covers the built-in types that C# provides such as `int` and `string` but also delves into the more complex types such as structs, enums, and classes.

Create Types

This objective may include but is not limited to create value types (structs, enum), reference types, generic types, constructors, static variables, methods, classes, extension methods, optional and named parameters, and indexed properties; and create overloaded and overridden methods.

See Chapter 3, "Working with the Type System."

Consume Types

This objective may include but is not limited to box or unbox to convert between value types; cast types, convert types, and handle dynamic types; and ensure interoperability with unmanaged code, for example, dynamic keyword.

See Chapter 4, "Using Types."

Enforce Encapsulation

This objective may include but is not limited to enforce encapsulation by using properties, by using accessors (public, private, and protected), and by using explicit interface implementation.

See Chapter 3, "Working with the Type System."

Create and Implement a Class Hierarchy

This objective may include but is not limited to design and implement an interface; inherit from a base class; and create and implement classes based on `IComparable`, `IEnumerable`, `IDisposable`, and `IUnknown` interfaces.

See Chapter 5, "Creating and Implementing Class Hierarchies."

Find, Execute, and Create Types at Runtime Using Reflection

This objective may include but is not limited to create and apply attributes; read attributes; generate code at run time by using CodeDom and lambda expressions; and use types from the System. Reflection namespace (Assembly, PropertyInfo, MethodInfo, and Type).

See Chapter 8, "Creating and Using Types with Reflection, Custom Attributes, the CodeDOM, and Lambda Expressions."

Manage the Object Life Cycle

This objective may include but is not limited to manage unmanaged resources; implement IDisposable, including interaction with finalization; manage IDisposable by using the Using statement; and manage finalization and garbage collection.

See Chapter 5, "Creating and Implementing Class Hierarchies."

Manipulate Strings

This objective may include but is not limited to manipulate strings by using the `StringBuilder`, `StringWriter`, and `StringReader` classes; search strings; enumerate string methods; and format strings.

See Chapter 4, "Using Types."

Debug Applications and Implement Security (25 Percent)

This section focuses on aspects for understanding how you work with the tools and features of the .NET Framework to debug your applications and for implementing security in your code for encryption and validation.

Validate Application Input

This objective may include but is not limited to validate JSON data; data collection types; manage data integrity; evaluate a regular expression to validate the input format; use built-in functions to validate data type and content out of scope; and writing regular expressions.

See Chapter 11, "Input Validation, Debugging, and Instrumentation."

Perform Symmetric and Asymmetric Encryption

This objective may include but is not limited to choose an appropriate encryption algorithm; manage and create certificates; implement key management; implement the System.Security namespace; hashing data; and encrypt streams.

See Chapter 12, "Using Encryption and Managing Assemblies."

Manage Assemblies

This objective may include but is not limited to version assemblies; sign assemblies using strong names; implement side-by-side hosting; put an assembly in the global assembly cache; and create a WinMD assembly.

See Chapter 12, "Using Encryption and Managing Assemblies."

Debug an Application

This objective may include but is not limited to create and manage compiler directives; choose an appropriate build type; and manage programming database files and symbols.

See Chapter 11, "Input Validation, Debugging, and Instrumentation."

Implement Diagnostics in an Application

This objective may include but is not limited to implement logging and tracing; profiling applications; create and monitor performance counters; and write to the event log.

See Chapter 11, "Input Validation, Debugging, and Instrumentation."

Implement Data Access (26 Percent)

Most applications work with data in some form or another. Data may be stored in database systems, or it may be stored in flat files. Flat files may be text files, comma-separated value (CSV) files, or XML files. Knowing how to access this data for reading and writing is crucial for developers.

Perform I/O Operations

This objective may include but is not limited to read-and-write files and streams; read and write from the network by using classes in the System.Net namespace; and implement asynchronous I/O operations.

See Chapter 9, "Working with Data."

Consume Data

This objective may include but is not limited to retrieve data from a database; update data in a database; consume JSON and XML data; and retrieve data by using web services.

See Chapter 9, "Working with Data."

Query and Manipulate Data and Objects by Using LINQ

This objective may include but is not limited to query data by using operators (projection, join, group, take, skip, and aggregate); create method-based LINQ queries; query data by using query comprehension syntax; select data by using anonymous types; force execution of a query; and read, filter, create, and modify data structures by using LINQ to XML.

See Chapter 10, "Working with Language Integrated Query (LINQ)."

Serialize and Deserialize Data

This objective may include but is not limited to serialize and deserialize data by using binary serialization, custom serialization, XML Serializer, JSON Serializer, and Data Contract Serializer.

See Chapter 9, "Working with Data."

Store Data in and Retrieve Data from Collections

This objective may include but is not limited to store and retrieve data by using dictionaries, arrays, lists, sets, and queues; choose a collection type; initialize a collection; add and remove items from a collection; use typed versus nontyped collections; implement custom collections; and implement collection interfaces.

See Chapter 9, "Working with Data."

SUMMARY

This chapter provided an overview of the Microsoft certification program and what to expect from this book in preparing for the 70-483 Exam, which focuses on Windows Store applications development using C#.

This chapter explained the history of Microsoft certifications, how they have changed over the years, and why those changes were made. This will help you understand how the certification program is positioned in the industry, and what you can expect as a result of achieving a Microsoft certification.

The process of creating certifications and exams is a complex task that involves many participants, lots of research and planning, and an orchestrated set of procedures to create exams that are relevant in the industry and provide a good balance of feature and usage scenario coverage.

The list of objectives for the exam that you will take on your way to the MCSD certification will help you focus on key areas of coverage for your studies.

ADDITIONAL READING AND RESOURCES

Following are some additional useful resources to help you understand the topics presented in this chapter:

Training and certification resources and information
    `http://www.microsoft.com/learning`
Industry trends related to Microsoft developer tools and technologies
    `http://msdn.microsoft.com/en-us/aa497440`

> **NOTE** *As most developers who focus on the Microsoft tools and platforms are aware, the ultimate resource for news and information on developing on the Microsoft platform is MSDN. MSDN documentation can be installed on your local computer when you install Visual Studio. You can also get the latest developer documentation directly on the web at* `http://msdn.microsoft.com/en-us/`*. Microsoft categorizes developer topics into developer centers that focus on Visual Studio, Windows, Windows Phone, Windows Azure, and Office. All are reachable through the MSDN website.*

> **EXAM TIPS AND TRICKS**
>
> The Review of Key Terms and the Cheat Sheet for each chapter can be printed off to help you study. You can find these files in the ZIP file for each chapter at `www.wrox.com/remtitle.cgi?isbn=1118612094` on the Download Code tab. Due to the nature of the content in this chapter, no Cheat Sheet or Review of Key Terms is included.

Basic Program Structure

WROX.COM CODE DOWNLOADS FOR THIS CHAPTER

You can find the code downloads for this chapter at www.wrox.com/remtitle.cgi?isbn= 1118612094 on the Download Code tab. The code is in the chapter 02 download and individually named according to the names throughout the chapter.

Computer programming has certain foundational aspects that any programming language must incorporate. C# is no exception. Programming has basic concepts such as repetition structures that help you repeat certain tasks and decision structures that allow your code to execute a different branch of statements based on the outcome of comparisons. This chapter introduces you to the basics of programming in C# and covers the topics necessary for you to understand core functionality in the C# programming language so that you can successfully take the exam. These key topics enable you to learn about statements in C#, both simple and complex, and how they are used in a C# application to perform the actions necessary to complete the tasks your code is intended to perform. You will learn what statements are and how to construct them your code.

The chapter then focuses on giving you an understanding of some core programming structures that you can use to form the logic of your program code. As you develop applications, you can focus on writing algorithms. These algorithms are formed through logical program flow based on decisions and repetition.

Table 2-1 introduces you to the exam objectives covered in this chapter.

TABLE 2-1: 70-483 Exam Objectives Covered in This Chapter

OBJECTIVE	CONTENT COVERED
Implement Program Flow	*Iterate across collections.* This includes using looping structures such as `for`, `while`, and `do-while` loops for the iterations.
	Program using switch statements. This includes switch statement syntax describing the data types permitted as well as how to handle conditions in switch statements.
	Program using if/then. This includes using the decision structure to control program flow based on one or more conditions.
	Use operators. This includes using operators such as mathematical operators to perform math functions, assignment operators to assigning values to variables and comparison operators for use in decision structures.
	Evaluate expressions. This includes understanding how code behaves when boolean expressions are used.

WRITING YOUR FIRST PROGRAM

Most programming books that focus on teaching computer programming start with a simple application called *Hello World*. This book assumes you know the basic programming concepts and instead will focus on getting your knowledge on C# to the right level so that you can be successful on the exam. That's not to say this book provides you with explicit and focused information that guarantees a pass on the exam, but rather that it focuses on the knowledge while providing you with the opportunity to understand the concepts. Only through understanding can you be effective in applying the concepts learned. Microsoft will test you on the fundamentals of programming and the C# Language so you need to have a fresh understanding of the concepts.

You might be an experienced C# programmer looking to test on the latest certification exam, or you might be coming from another programming language and learning C#. In either case, a review of the fundamental language concepts is never a waste of time.

NOTE *C# was designed and developed at Microsoft to be an object-oriented programming language for the .NET platform. The concepts that you learn in this chapter are not new and are part of most other programming languages. This chapter will help you understand the concepts from the C# perspective.*

ADVICE FROM THE EXPERTS: Don't Skip This Chapter

If you have been programming in C# for some time, you may consider skipping this chapter. The exams are written by programmers that have years of programming experience and, as such, they typically write questions that will test your understanding of these core concepts, not just knowing what they are. Ensure you understand these concepts as opposed to just memorizing syntax. Remember, IntelliSense isn't available to you on the exam.

Exploring the Structure of the Program

Although the sections on C# statement types do not have a direct relationship to a section or objective on the exam, the concepts covered here are important in helping you understand the basic structure of a program in the C# language. As you start to learn the C# language and prepare for the exam, this foundational information can be helpful in understanding why the other aspects of the language, such as decision and repetition structures, work the way they do.

The remaining sections provide you with an understanding of the basic C# program structure that you can use in your applications. You can gain an understanding of controlling your program flow using repetition and decision structures. These are the core building blocks of an application written in C#, whether the application is a console-based app or one written with new Windows 8–style user interface (UI).

C# code is written using a series of statements. The language divides statements into two basic types: simple and complex. The following two sections provide you with an understanding of these statement types, enabling you to read C# code better and understand how to use the statement types in your own programs.

Understanding Simple Statements

In any programming language, *statements* are the code constructs that cause the application to perform an action. C# uses the concept of simple statements and complex statements. In C#, *simple statements* are those that end with a semicolon (;) and are typically used for program actions such as the following:

➤ Declaring variables (declaration statements)

➤ Assigning values to variables (assignment statements)

➤ Calling method in your code

➤ Branching statements that change program flow

> **NOTE** *Even a simple statement such as assigning a value to a variable can equate into many actual instructions to the CPU in the computer after the code is compiled.*

As a result of the rule that all statements end in a semicolon, you might come to the conclusion that simple statements will exist only on a single line. Although most do take up only a single line in your development editor because of the short length, you may find it necessary to continue a long statement on multiple lines for readability or screen resolution limits. In this case, the statement is still considered a simple statement, but it merely stretches across multiple lines. Only one semicolon is used at the end of the statement.

An example of simple statements follows. Don't worry about the data types such as int, float, and so on in these examples. Chapter 3, "Working with the Type System," introduces these and focuses on types.

```
//variable declaration statements
int counter;
float distance;
string firstName;

// assignment statements
counter = 0;
distance = 4.5;
firstName = "Bill";

// jump statements
break;
return;

// the empty statement consists of a single semicolon on a line by itself
// the statement does nothing and is merely a placeholder where a code
// statement is required but you don't want an action to take place.
// A good example of this is in a looping statement used in a delayed
// processing scenario

void SomeFunction()
{
        while (DoSomething())
        ;
}
```

Note that the last simple statement in the preceding code shows an empty statement. This is interesting in that it's not something you will use on a regular basis, but it demonstrates that C# recognizes a statement that contains no keywords but because the semicolon is present, C# recognizes it as a statement.

The *comment* section (a code line that starts with the // characters and is a way of helping to document the code) in the preceding code indicates that it might be used in a delayed processing scenario, but realistically, with the performance of computers today, delayed processing in this manner isn't that effective. Instead, you can use timer functions built into programming languages. This sample is just intended to show that you can use an empty statement to essentially take the place of one that might perform an action.

Understanding Complex Statements

C# also has complex statements. *Complex statements* are those that can or will enclose one or more simple statements into a code block surrounded by curly braces: {}. Typical complex statements are those that are covered in the section on loops and decision structures, such as foreach(), if(), switch, do(), and so on.

An example of using a complex statement might be iteration over an array of values and taking some action within the code using various statements. An example of such a use is shown here:

```
// check to see how many values in an array are even numbers
int[] numbers = {5, 24, 36, 19, 45, 60, 78};
int evenNums = 0;

foreach(int num in numbers)
{
        Console.Writeline(num);

        if(num % 2 == 0)
        {
                evenNums++;
        }
}
```

In this code sample, the first line declares an array, or collection, of integers. (Arrays are covered in Chapter 9, "Working with Data.") Arrays are merely a collection of similar types of data, in this case integers.

A variable called num is declared to be of type int so that you can use it in the foreach loop. (The foreach loop is covered in the "Using Loops" section later in this chapter, so don't worry too much about syntax right now.) The array declaration in line 1 and the variable declaration in line 2 are considered simple statements. (A *declaration* is used to create a variable in code.) The complex statement is the entire foreach loop that starts with the keyword foreach and ends with the final curly brace: }. Note that you actually have another complex statement within this complex statement. The if statement is another example of a complex statement.

The foreach loop looks at the array, and for every integer value it finds (for each), it writes the value to the console window. The if statement performs the mathematical modulus function on the value to see if it is an even number by checking for remainder after dividing by 2. If the result is 0, the number is even and the evenNums variable is *incremented* (increased by a certain value) by one.

Note that within each of these complex statements are simple statements. Console.Writeline(num); is a simple statement as is evenNums++;. So you might also say that complex statements are formed using multiple simple statements, but a structure is still required to contain the simple statements. With the exception of a few, complex statements do not end with a semicolon.

CONTROLLING PROGRAM FLOW

All applications require some program flow options. If you take a trip back in history and look at structured programming, you would notice that program flow was typically done in a top-down fashion with execution starting at the first line of code and continuing one line at a time until the end of the code sequence.

Often, this top-down approach didn't work well in helping to solve real-world problems that weren't computing-specific. In the real world, you iterate over a series of steps, but at some point, you might need to do something different depending on the outcome of some other action.

Consider a scenario in your code where a user is attempting to log in to a secure website. Your code will direct the user to the requested page in the site if they provide the correct username and password combination, or let the user know the login was not successful and offer them a chance to log in again.

This would equate to code branching. Code *branching* can be thought of as program flow moving to a different location in the code listing and then coming back to where it left off, or repeating lines of code to complete a set of tasks over and over.

Early attempts at program flow control used statements such as goto where labels were used in code and program flow was directed to code in a labeled section. In the days of BASIC, subroutines were commonly used, and the keyword GOSUB was a part of BASIC to provide code flow as well.

These code branching statements created *spaghetti code*, making it hard to debug and maintain application code because it forced the programmer to jump from one code location to another and back again to try to make sense of the logic often getting lost in the process. Why spaghetti? Next time you have a plate of spaghetti in front of you, try to follow one single noodle from one end to the other without pulling it out from the rest. You'll get the idea.

More detail on how these issues were overcome will be discussed in the book when functions are covered. The remainder of this chapter focuses on the various program components and aspects that enable you to make decisions in your program and control program flow based on those decisions. You might execute a piece of code, or do nothing. This chapter also takes a look at the components of C# that you use to repeat actions in code where necessary.

These sections can help you understand the exam objective "Implement Program Flow." The objective covers topics such as iterating over collections and arrays, making program decisions with switch statements, and if/then constructs. You can also gain an understanding of the operators used in evaluating expressions.

> **EXAM TIPS AND TRICKS: Understanding the Difference Between Exam Design and Question Writing**
>
> Exam design and exam question writing are two separate processes. The design session sets up the topic coverage, which is where the objectives come from. The authors who write the exam questions are typically not involved in the design session. As a result, you must understand all the concepts covered in an exam objective because you have no idea what an author has chosen to write the question about.

Conditional Instructions

Conditional instructions in C# are those that evaluate a condition and then execute an action, take no action, or choose between available actions to execute. To evaluate conditions, C# provides the following:

➤ Relational operators

➤ Boolean expressions

➤ Logical operators

➤ A conditional operator (ternary operator)

Conditions in your C# program enable you to compare values, typically held in variables but also constants and literals. A *variable* is a named location in memory that enables you to store a value for later use. It is called a variable because you can change the content in it whenever you want. A *constant* is like a variable in that it is a named memory location used to store a value, but you cannot change the value at will. It accepts a value when you declare it and keeps that value throughout the life of your program's execution time. *Literals* are values that, well, literally are what they are. Examples of literals are 1, 25, 'c', and "strings". You can't and don't assign other items to literals; you can assign literals only to variables of constants.

Your program execution can be controlled based on these comparisons. To effectively use these concepts in your programs, you need to understand the available comparison logical operators (*operators* perform an operation on values). These operators are listed in the Tables 2-2 and 2-3. Examples are included following each table.

TABLE 2-2: Relational Operators

OPERATOR	MEANING	SAMPLE
<	Less than	expr1 < expr2
>	Greater than	expr1 > expr2
<=	Less than or equal	expr1 <= expr2
>=	Greater than or equal	expr1 >= expr2
==	Equality	expr1 == expr2
!=	Not equal	expr1 != expr2

Now look at some examples to help clarify the meaning of these operators. The relational operators should be self-explanatory, but some simple examples help to solidify your understanding. An *expression* is an activity or code statement that returns a result.

The expression 2 < 3 checks to see if the value on the left is less than the value on the right. In this case, is 2 less than 3? If so, the evaluation returns true, which in this case it does.

The expression 2 > 3 checks to see if the left operand is greater than the right operand. In this case, 2 is not greater than 3, and the expression returns false.

The operators <= and >= check to see if the left operand is less than or equal to the right operand for the former and the opposite for the latter. For example, 2 < = 3 and 3 <= 3 both return true because 2 is less than 3, and in the second comparison, 3 is equal to 3. However 2 >= 3 would return false because 2 is neither greater than nor equal to 3.

Anytime time you see the = operator in C#, be certain you remember that it is an assignment operator and not a comparison operator. C# uses two = signs together (==) to denote equality. Therefore 2 = 2 is not the same as 2 == 2. The former is actually not legal in C# because it attempts to assign a literal to a literal, which is not possible. A literal in C# is an actual value as opposed to a variable. However, 2 == 2 is valid in C# and is evaluating whether the literal 2 is equal to the literal 2. In this case it is, and the result is a value of true for the comparison.

The final relational operator is the != operator, which means not equal. The expression 2 != 3 would return true because the literal value 2 is not equal to the literal value 3.

TABLE 2.3: Boolean (Boolean and Bitwise) Operators

OPERATOR	MEANING	SAMPLE
&	Unary variant returns the address of its operand. Binary variant is the bitwise AND of two operands.	& expr1 expr1 & expr2
|	The binary OR operator. True if one or both operand is true, false if both operands are false.	expr1 | expr2
^	The bitwise exclusive OR. Returns true if, and only if, one of the operands is true.	expr1 ^ expr2
!	Unary logical negation operator. Returns false if operand is true or vice versa.	! expr
~	The bitwise complement operator.	~expr
&&	Conditional AND that performs a logical AND operation on the bool operands. Capable of short circuit logic wherein the second operand is evaluated only if necessary.	expr && expr2
||	Conditional OR that performs a logical OR on the bool operands. Evaluates Only second operand if necessary.	expr1 || expr2
true	Used as a bool operator to indicate truth in an expression.	bool success = true;
false	Used as a bool operator to indicated untruth in an expression.	bool success = false;

For the boolean operators, you look only at samples of the most common operators that you can use in your decision making code. These are the and (&&), the or (||), and the bool values of true and false. (A *boolean* is a value that is represented as either true or false.)

The `&&` operator is used to evaluate multiple conditions. The most common use is to check if one value is true AND another value is true. True is returned only if both conditions are true. For example, if you are 21 years of age or older and you have ID to prove it, you can purchase alcohol:

```
if(age >= 21 && hasID == true)
```

The `&&` operator is also optimized for what is known as short-circuit evaluation. That is to say, because the expression returns only true if both conditions are true, you can also say that if the first condition is false, there is no need to evaluate the second condition. This is the short-circuit functionality, and although providing a small improvement in performance, it nevertheless eliminates some code work on the computer side.

To understand why requires that you know how the computer does comparisons. For each comparison that is made, the CPU must do the following:

1. Fetch the instruction and load it into memory.

2. Increment the instruction pointer.

3. Visit memory to get the first value and store that in a register.

4. Access memory for the second value and store that in a CPU register.

5. Perform the comparison and store the result in a CPU register.

6. Pop the stack for the instruction pointer to get back to where the code was executing before the comparison.

7. Return the value of the comparison to the code.

8. Continue execution at the next instruction.

For today's computers with fast CPUs, fast memory, various caching techniques, and hardware optimization, these small things can seem inconsequential, but enough of them combined can help make your programs more efficient.

The next boolean operator is the or (`||`) operator. This enables you to state that you want to know if one or the other condition is true. If so, the expression returns `true`; otherwise it returns `false`.

```
if(temperature < 60 || reaction == shivering)
      turn on heat
```

The values of `true` and `false` are considered to be of type `bool` in C#. To use these in code, you declare a variable of type `bool` and then assign the result of a comparison to that variable, for example:

```
// bool samples
bool result = true;   // always a good practice to assign
                      // a value to variables prior to using them
result = 2 < 3;       // result will contain the value true
result = 2 > 3;       // result will contain the value false
```

You can also flip the `bool` value through the use of the unary logical negation operator `!`. This can actually create some confusing code, but is also a unique way of "flipping" a `bool`:

```
// logical negation sample
bool result = true;        // result has the value true
result = !result;          // result has the value false
```

The final operator that C# offers for conditional logic is the conditional operator, also known as the *ternary operator*. This operator returns one of the two values included in the operator based on the evaluation of the boolean expression:

```
// example of using conditional operator
Random rnd = new Random();
int num = 0;
num = rnd.Next(100);    // generate a random number between 1 and 100
// and assign to num

// if the value in num mod 2 is equal to zero, the operator will return
// the string even indicating an even number, otherwise it will return
// the string false
string type = num % 2 == 0 ? "even" : "odd";
```

The preceding sample uses some of the C# built-in functionality for generating random numbers. `Random` is a class in .NET that is used here to generate a random number between 1 and 100. You assign that random number to the variable `num`.

The code then performs a little mathematical function known as modulus. *Modulus* returns the remainder of an integer division. For example, 5 divided by 2 is not an even number or an integer because it has a fractional part. The result is 2.5 in floating point math, but modulus works with integers (whole numbers with no decimals) so the value returned is actually 1 as far as modulus is concerned. Only even numbers divide by 2 will return a remainder of 0. As a result, the ternary operator checks for this by using the modulus operator in the condition portion. If 0 is returned, that means the number is an even number and the ternary operator returns a string indicating that, otherwise it returns the string value of `odd`.

The syntax of the ternary operator is:

```
condition ? value if true : value if false
```

Boolean Expressions

You have already seen an example of boolean operators in the previous section. This section describes what boolean expressions are and provides more detail on their use.

In the simplest of terms, a boolean expression in C# is an expression that results in a value of type `bool` being returned. In C#, the keyword `bool` is an alias for the `System.Boolean` type. `System.Boolean` has many methods but you are mostly concerned with the types that it uses. These are simply true and false. As a simple example, if you were asked whether or not 2 and 2 were the same number, you would likely reply yes, or you would say that is true. However, 2 and 3 are not the same number, and you would say that comparison is false.

In the past, programming languages that didn't implement a `bool` type used numeric values to represent boolean results such as 1 for true and 0 for false. They also used any non-zero value as true. This had the side-effect of causing confusion if programmers used more than one programming language. One application might be written in BASIC and another application written in COBOL. Programmers could forget which language implemented boolean values in which way and introduce subtle bugs in their code without knowing. Thankfully, you can use actual words with clear meaning in C#.

In C#, you form boolean expressions by comparison. These comparisons are made using the relational and boolean operators listed in the previous tables. The following code lab shows some uses of comparisons in boolean expressions in C#.

CODE LAB   Demonstrate the use of bool [Use of Bool Code Lab.txt]

```
// create a variable of type bool called result and assign it an initial
// value of false

bool result = false;

// check a simple comparison and assign the value to variable result
// in this case, we check if the literal 2 is equal to the literal 2
// the result of this comparison is true and the variable result will
// now contain the bool value true

result = 2 == 2;
Console.Writeline(result);  // will output the value true
```

Code Lab Analysis

The line `result = 2 == 2` might be a little foreign to you or perhaps hard to decipher at first glance. Although this book doesn't go into much detail on order or precedence, a small introduction here can help.

C# has a specific order of precedence. This determines what portions of a statement get evaluated first, then second, and so on. If you consider precedence in math, you know that multiplication and division have higher precedence than addition or subtraction. If the addition and subtraction are in the same expression, the one on the left is evaluated first.

In this code sample, comparison has a higher precedence than assignment, so the expression `2 == 2` is evaluated first. This results in a boolean, which in this case is true. That boolean is then assigned to the variable result. As a side note, you can change the precedence in C# as you can in math, through the use of parentheses.

Making Decisions in Code

Life involves decisions on a daily basis. What time do you set the alarm for waking in the morning? Do you buy milk and bread tonight or wait until tomorrow? If the light turns yellow, will you stop or should you race through the intersection before the light changes to red?

Programming is no different in this respect. Your code can execute simple tasks without the need for decisions, but at some point, your code needs to evaluate a condition and take an appropriate action based on the result of that condition. It might be the result of input by the user. It might stem from the fact that a disc is not in the drive when reading or writing files. You might need to check the presence of a network connection before sending requests to a server. All these scenarios require decision making in your program code, and C# provides the keywords and foundation for working with decisions in your code.

> **ADVICE FROM THE EXPERTS: Implementing Decision Types**
>
> As you go through these different decision types that follow, ensure you not only understand the syntax and how to use them, but also ensure you have gained the understanding of why one would be used over another. The exam tests your knowledge of how to implement these, but understanding when to use a specific decision structure can serve you well in your career as a programmer.

if Statements

The C# language provides the programmer with the ability to program decisions through the use of various decision structures. The first of these that you will look at is the `if` statement:

```
// single if statement syntax
if(condition)
    statement;
remaining code statements;
```

The `if` statement includes a conditional portion, in parentheses, and a statement or series of statements to execute. The `if` statement evaluates a boolean condition that is enclosed in the parentheses. If the boolean condition is `true`, the code immediately following the `if` statement is executed. If the return value is `false`, code execution skips the statement in the `if` clause and executes the remaining code statements following the `if` clause.

Note the indentation in the preceding code sample where `statement` is indented more than the rest of the code. Without this indentation it is difficult to know for certain which statements will execute as a part of the `if` statement. In the code sample, `statement;` executes only if the condition is true. The `remaining code statements;` executes regardless of the outcome of the `if` statement.

When coding `if` statements, it is recommended that you use curly braces to enclose the statements for each section of the `if` statement even when the structure includes only one statement. If you have multiple statements that need to be executed when the condition is `true`, you must use a statement block that is delineated with curly braces to include the set of statements that need to be executed. You cannot execute multiple statements for an `if` condition without using the statement block. The following sample uses the same statements as earlier with the exception of using curly braces to denote a statement block. Now it is clear which statements execute.

```
// single if statement syntax with a statement block
if(condition)
```

```
{
    statement;
}
remaining code statements;
```

So far you have seen only a single `if` statement, but you can also use nested `if` statements to help you deal with more complex decisions. For example, what happens if you want a piece of code to execute but only if another condition is also `true`? There are a couple of ways to do this, and the following sample shows two possible ways to accomplish this:

```
// nested if statement
if(condition1)
{
    if(condition2)
    {
        statement;
    }
    outer statement;
}
remaining code statements;

// if statement with logical operator
if(condition1 && condition2)
{
    statement;
}
```

In the first example, `condition1` is evaluated in the outer `if` statement. If the condition returns true, the inner `if` statement will execute and `condition2` will be evaluated. If `condition1` evaluates to false, `condition2` is never reached. Regardless of the evaluations in either of the `if` statements, the line with `remaining code statements;` will execute.

The second example depicts the use of the binary AND operator, `&&`. It simply states that if `condition1` is true AND `condition2` is true, then execute the statement. If either `condition1` or `condition2` is false, `statement;` will not be executed.

There is a subtle difference between these two uses. In the first example, the nested `if`, you check `condition1` and if true, you check `condition2`. Regardless of the outcome of `condition2`, outer `statement;` will execute. In other words, you can have multiple statements execute depending on a more complex set of evaluations in the nested `if` than you can with the second example where the conditions are evaluated in a single `if` statement. This is part of the reason why nested `if` statements can become confusing rather quickly.

You can nest `if` statements as deep as you want to, but it can quickly get unwieldy and become difficult to keep track of. Not to mention it is difficult to read when you nest deeper than even a low number of levels.

To help you gain a better understanding of each type presented so far, you create a small application that can help you understand the different `if` statements covered up to this point, as well as allowing you to see first-hand how the nested statements work.

Open Visual Studio on your computer, and create a new project using the C# template for a Console application. Name your application **using_if_statements**, or a name of your own choosing.

After the IDE loads the project, copy and paste, or type, the following code into the editor window. Note that Visual Studio creates some code for you automatically, such as the using statements, namespace, class, and main components, so you can either replace the entire code in your project with this code, or you can choose to include only the code within the static void main(string[] args) function.

```csharp
using System;
using System.Collections.Generic;
using System.Linq;
using System.Text;
using System.Threading.Tasks;

namespace using_if_statements
{
    class Program
    {
        static void Main(string[] args)
        {
            // declare some variables for use in the code and assign initial values
            int first = 2;
            int second = 0;

            // use a single if statement to evaluate a condition and output
            // some text
            // indicating the results

            Console.WriteLine("Single if statement");

            if (first == 2)
            {
                Console.WriteLine("The if statement evaluated to true");
            }
            Console.WriteLine("This line outputs regardless of the if condition");

            Console.WriteLine();

            // create an if statement that evaluates two conditions and executes
            // statements only if both are true
            Console.WriteLine("An if statement using && operator.");

            if (first == 2 && second == 0)
            {
                Console.WriteLine("The if statement evaluated to true");
            }
            Console.WriteLine("This line outputs regardless of the if condition");

            Console.WriteLine();

            // create nested if statements
```

```
        Console.WriteLine("Nested if statements.");

        if (first == 2)
        {
            if (second == 0)
            {
                Console.WriteLine("Both outer and inner conditions are true.");
            }
            Console.WriteLine("Outer condition is true, inner may be true.");
        }
        Console.WriteLine("This line outputs regardless of the if condition");

        Console.WriteLine();
    }
  }
}
```

Code Lab Analysis

After you have entered this code into your application, press Ctrl+F5, or choose Start Without Debugging from the Debug menu. This results in the code executing and generating output to the screen, as shown in Figure 2-1. Note that if you just press F5 and start the application without debugging, the output displays but the console window disappears as soon as the code finishes executing. By starting without debugging, the console windows remains open enabling you to view the output and then waiting for you press a key before stopping program execution.

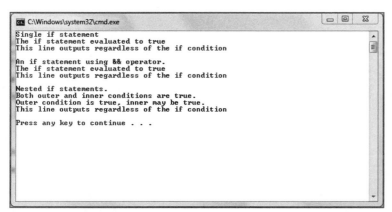

FIGURE 2-1: Output of code lab

In this initial setup, you have ensured that all paths return `true`, and as a result, all lines are output to the console window. Start changing the values of the two variables, and experiment with the results to see which lines get output based on the condition evaluations when both `true` and `false` are returned. Evaluate all possible values for each condition to ensure you understand how these `if` statements function.

As mentioned earlier, when executing an `if` statement, you evaluate a condition and then take action if that condition is `true`. If `false`, the code continues after the `if` statement. But what happens if you want to execute one set of code statements when the condition is `true` or another set of code statements if the condition is `false`, and then continue executing remaining code statements regardless of the outcome? You can use the `if-else` statement:

```
// if-else statement syntax
if (condition)
{
    statement1;
}
else
{
    statement2;
}
remaining code statements;
```

In this example, `statement1` is executed if the `condition` is true, otherwise the `else` clause will be entered and `statement2` will be executed. Regardless of the condition, the remaining code statements will execute after either the `if` or the `else` clause is executed.

You also saw an example of nested `if` statements for executing code only if the current and previous conditions evaluate to true. You can also choose to execute a code path based on multiple conditions by using the `if, else if` statement:

```
// if-else if statement syntax
if (condition1)
{
    statement1;
}
else if (condition2)
{
    statement2;
}
else if (condition3)
{
    statement3;
}
...
else
{
    statement4;
}
remaining code statements;
```

The ellipsis (. . .) in the preceding sample, just above the `else` statement, indicates that you can have as many `else if` portions as you want. Note that the `else` clause is also optional, as it is in the single `if` statement. What this code demonstrates is that you check `condition1` and if that is true you execute `statement1`. If `condition1` is not true, you skip `statement1` and check `condition2`. In this instance, `statement2` is executed if `condition2` is true; otherwise, you check `condition3` and so on. It's important to note that as soon as one condition evaluates to `true`, the statements for that condition are executed and the `if` statement then exits. None of the other conditions are evaluated, and the remaining code statements then get executed.

Beyond Basic if Statements

Now look at a simple application that demonstrates the use of these if statements. Copy and paste this code into Visual Studio in a C# console application. Change the values of the condition variables and execute the code to see how it affects the outcome. Again, run the code using different values for the boolean variables and watch how the output changes.

```csharp
using System;
using System.Collections.Generic;
using System.Linq;
using System.Text;
using System.Threading.Tasks;

namespace beyond_basic_if_statements
{
    class Program
    {
        static void Main(string[] args)
        {
            bool condition1;
            bool condition2;
            bool condition3;

            // single if statement
            condition1 = true;
            if (condition1)
            {
                Console.WriteLine("This statement prints if condition is true");
            }
            Console.WriteLine("This statement executes regardless of condition.");

            Console.WriteLine();

            //nested if statement
            condition1 = true;
            condition2 = true;
            if (condition1)
            {
                if (condition2)
                {
                    Console.WriteLine("This only prints if both conditions
                    are true.");
                }
            }

            Console.WriteLine();

            // if statement with logical operator
            condition1 = true;
            condition2 = true;
            if (condition1 && condition2)
            {
                Console.WriteLine("This only prints if both conditions are true.");
```

```
        }

        Console.WriteLine();

        // if-else statement
        condition1 = true;
        if (condition1)
        {
            Console.WriteLine("This statement prints if condition is true.");
        }
        else
        {
            Console.WriteLine("This statement prints if condition is false.");
        }
        Console.WriteLine("This statement executes regardless of condition.");

        Console.WriteLine();

        // if-else if statement
        condition1 = true;
        condition2 = false;
        condition3 = false;

        if (condition1)
        {
            Console.WriteLine("This statement prints if condition1 is true.");
        }
        else if (condition2)
        {
            Console.WriteLine("This statement prints if condition2 is true.");
        }
        else if (condition3)
        {
            Console.WriteLine("This statement prints if condition3 is true.");
        }
        else
        {
            Console.WriteLine("This statement prints if previous conditions
            are false.");
        }
        Console.WriteLine("This statement executes regardless of condition.");

        Console.WriteLine();
    }
  }
}
```

switch statements

In the preceding section, you saw examples of nested if statements and if, else if statements. Both of those sets of statements are hard to read when the number of nesting or if-else statements exceeds a certain number. C#, like other C-based programming languages, provides the switch statement to enable you to make multiple comparisons, executing code based on the condition, or conditions that return true. It is a much cleaner code construct than multiple `if-else` or nested `if` statements. Consider the following:

```
// switch statement syntax
switch (condition)
{
    case 1:
        statement1;
        break;

    case 2:
        statement2;
        break;

    case 3:
        statement3;
        break;

    default:
        defaultStatement;
        break;
}
```

The condition in a `switch` statement in previous languages, such as C, had to be of type `int`. C# allows you to compare any simple data type such as `int`, `string`, `float`, and even enumerations.

In the `switch` statement, the condition to evaluate is the value included in the opening `switch` phrase. The code then begins executing at the first `case` statement looking for a match. The code in the `case` statement that matches the condition is executed. Finally, the `break` statement causes the code to branch out of the `switch` statement and continue execution after the closing curly brace of the `switch` statement.

You can include as many `case` statements as you want, but keep in mind that no two `case` statements can include the same value. There is also an optional `default:` statement in the `switch`. If none of the `case` statements matches, the default statement is selected, if present. A sample follows:

```
// sample switch statement using a string comparison
string condition = "Hello";

switch (condition)
{
    case "Good Morning":
        Console.WriteLine("Good morning to you");
        break;

    case "Hello":
        Console.WriteLine("Hello");
        break;

    case "Good Evening":
        Console.WriteLine("Wonderful evening");
        break;

    default:
```

```
        Console.WriteLine("So long");
        break;
}
```

Another key feature of `switch` statements is that you can perform a single action in code, based on multiple conditions. To handle multiple conditions with a single action, you simply eliminate the `break` statements in each `case` section of the `switch` statement containing the conditions you want handled. A sample follows showing how you can do this:

```
// switch handling multiple conditions with a single action
int number;

switch (number)
{
    case 0:
    case 1:
    case 2:
        Console.Writeline ("Contained in the set of whole numbers.");
        break;
    case -1:
    case -10:
        Console.WriteLine ("Contained in the set of Integers.");
        break;
}
```

In the preceding example, the code checks to see if the value of number is either 0, 1, or 2. If so, it writes to the console that these values are contained in the mathematical set known as whole numbers. The `break` statement only comes after `case 2`, which means that the code will execute sequentially comparing number to 0, 1, or 2 allowing either condition to be `true`. If the value of number is either one of these numerical values, the statement is printed and then the `switch` statement is exited.

If the value of number is not 0, 1, 2, the `switch` statement continues to evaluate number to see if it is either -1 or -10. If so, it prints out the fact that these numbers are included in the mathematical set known as integers.

COMMON MISTAKES: Math Versus Programming Integer Types

Don't confuse the mathematical integer with the programming language integer data type. Programming language integer types have a specific range of values based on their size (16, 32, or 64 bit) whereas mathematical integers go from negative infinity to positive infinity, including zero.

Using Loops

Using looping structures in your code allows your applications to repeat a series of instructions to accomplish a task. (A *loop* is a repetition structure that repeats instructions.) You might need to calculate the average for a series of grades that are stored in a data structure such as an array, or you might need to iterate over a collection of items such as a dataset that stores records from a database.

C# provides four looping structures:

➤ `for` statements

➤ `foreach` statements

➤ `while` statements

➤ `do-while` statements

Deciding which one to use depends on your requirements, but ultimately, these structures all provide repetition functionality. The first looping structure you look at is the basic `for` structure.

for statements

The `for` statement looping structure in C# enables you to repeat a statement, or series of statements, until a specified condition is met. The `for` statement contains *initializer*, *condition*, and increment (*iterator*) components (an *iterator* is a portion of a loop that changes a value):

```
// for statement syntax
for(initializer; condition; iterator)
{
    statement(s);
}
```

In the preceding example, the `for` statement includes the components in parentheses that control the statement itself. The *initializer* is used to declare and/or *initialize* (set a starting value) a variable (counter) that will be used in the loop. The condition is used to determine what will cause the loop to stop, and the `iterator` portion is used to modify the `counter` variable. Note that each component is separated by a semicolon. An example follows:

```
// Count up to 10 in increments of 2
for(int counter = 0; counter <= 10; counter += 2)
{
  Console.WriteLine(counter);
}
```

In this example, the `for` statement initializes a loop counter variable conveniently named `counter`. You can use any variable name you choose for this portion of the `for` loop but keep the following in mind:

➤ You cannot use keywords for variable names.

➤ The variable declared here should not have the same name as a variable that you use for another purpose in the `for` loop.

➤ The variable used as the *initializer* can be used in the `for` loop. As you can see in the example, you output the value of `counter`.

➤ You cannot use this variable outside of the `for` loop due to variable scope.

The for statement then checks the condition to see if counter is less than or equal to 10. Because the loop hasn't executed yet, and you initialized counter to 0, this condition returns true and the loop statement Console.Writeline(counter); is executed.

The increment routine hasn't been forgotten. The increment portion will increment counter by 2 as a result of the += operator, but it executes only after the loop iterates over the statement block. You can use different aspects of counter modification in your for loops such as increment and decrement operators like ++, ==, +=, *=, and so on. Following is an explanation of the for loop execution.

To give you a better idea on this, you can visualize what happens by using the debugger and breakpoints in Visual Studio. The following screenshots show how the for loop functions.

In Figure 2-2, the code has just started the execution of the for loop, and counter has been initialized to zero. The image shows the code window with the breakpoint set and also shows the watch window where you can see the value counter. Note it is set at 0 and the highlight is on the Console.WriteLine(counter); line.

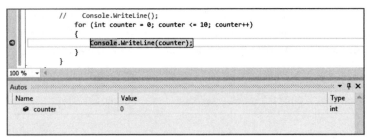

FIGURE 2-2: Counter Initialization

Figure 2-3 has stepped through the code to output the value to the console window, which is not shown here. Notice that the loop has executed the statement inside the curly braces, but now, Figure 2-3 shows the increment statement as highlighted. This is key to understanding how the for loop functions. The increment portion happens after the loop statements execute. However, because you haven't stepped into the next line, the value of counter in the watch window is still 0 indicating that the increment hasn't happened just yet.

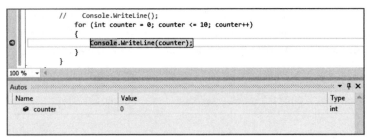

FIGURE 2-3: Counter prior to increment portion of loop

Figure 2-4 shows what happens when you step into the next line of code. The watch window shows that counter is now equal to 1, and the highlighted portion of the code shows the condition evaluation. In this way, you can see that the variable is incremented before the condition is next checked, but the initialization component is not performed again.

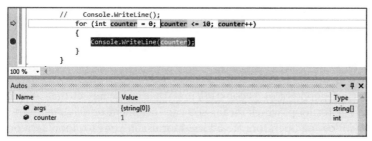

FIGURE 2-4: Counter has incremented.

The initialize portion happens only once; the first time the loop is executed. The condition portion is checked for each iteration of the loop including the first iteration. It happens prior to the increment and after the initialize. The loop statement block then executes, and finally the counter variable is acted on.

On each subsequent iteration of the loop, the condition is checked, and if it returns true, the loop executes the statement block and then increments the counter variable. After the condition returns `false`, the loop stops execution. The statements in the block are no longer executed, and the counter is not acted on any longer. Execution now continues at the next line after the for statement.

You should make use of the debugging features built into Visual Studio and use breakpoints throughout your code to see how these aspects of the C# language function. A picture truly is worth a thousand words here.

> **COMMON MISTAKES: Creating Infinite Loops**
>
> When writing your loop, ensure you have an exit condition for the loop. Failing to do so will result in an infinite loop. This is a loop that doesn't exit. Not only is this embarrassing, but also it can quickly lock up a computer by consuming memory and CPU resources depending on what the statements in the loop are doing. Unless of course you intend to create an infinite loop on purpose.

C# enables you to create an infinite loop if you choose to do so by simply creating the for loop without any of the values in the parentheses. You might decide to use an infinite loop in real-time applications where you want a continuous polling of inputs, or perhaps you want to stress test an application or server. Just ensure that you is a means to exit the loop, which is sometimes simply closing the application. Here is an example where there is no initializer, no condition, and no increment:

```
// infinite for loop in C#
for(;;)
{
    statement;
}
```

Another consideration when creating for loops is that your loop doesn't have to do anything. An empty statement block means that no code executes during the loop. The loop simply iterates until the condition is true:

```
// empty for loop
for(int counter = 0; counter >= 10; counter++)
{
    ;
}
```

Thus far, you have seen only the for loop iterator as counting up. You can use any of the C# increment operators in this portion of the for loop, which means you can increment or *decrement* (to decrease by a certain value). The following operators are all legal for use in your for loop iterator section:

➤ ++ is the increment operator where values are incremented by one.

➤ ~DH is the decrement operator where values are decremented by one.

➤ += is the operator that can be used with literals to change the step such as += 2, which increments by a value of 2 each time.

➤ -= is the decrement of the above operator.

➤ *= is the increment by a multiplication factor.

➤ /= is the decrement by a division factor.

Nested for Loops

As one final discussion topic on for loops, it's also important to note that you can nest for loops as well. This allows you to create more complex looping constructs that you might find useful in various applications. One that comes to mind immediately would be the lottery.

REAL-WORLD CASE SCENARIO   **Nested Loops for a Lottery Program**

Where I grew up, we had a lottery that was called 6/49. You could select six numbers from the range 1 to 49. My brother-in-law asked me to write a program for him to predict the winning numbers. Of course, I told him that wasn't possible because if it were, programmers much smarter than myself would be billionaires today. However, to appease him, I did create a small application that allowed him to randomly pick his numbers. Try to create this same application on your own. Take note that this code sample doesn't need to include logic to prevent duplicates.

Solution (lottery_program)

Here is the solution:

```
static void Main(string[] args)
{
    // used to set up a range of values to choose from
    int[] range = new int[49];

    // used to simulate lottery numbers chosen
```

```
int[] picked = new int[6];

// set up a random number generator
Random rnd = new Random();

// populate the range with values from 1 to 49
for (int i = 0; i < 49; i++)
{
    range[i] = i + 1;
}

// pick 6 random numbers
for (int limit = 0; limit < 49; limit++)
{
    for (int select = 0; select < 6; select++)
    {
        picked[select] = range[rnd.Next(49)];
    }

}
Console.WriteLine("Your lotto numbers are:");
for (int j = 0; j < 6; j++)
{
    Console.Write(" " + picked[j] + " ");
}
Console.WriteLine();
}
```

In this code, two arrays are set up to contain the values for the range (49) that can be chosen from and the count of values for a ticket (6). The random number generator is used to start a random sequence for choosing a random number from the 1 to 49 range. The first loop populates the range[] array with values from 1 to 49. The i + 1 is used because as you recall, arrays in C# start at 0, but 0 is not a valid number in the ticket choices.

The nested loop sets up the outer portion to iterate over all 49 possible values and pick a random value in the inner loop six times. This is not the cleanest possible method of doing this, but it serves to show a nesting example.

foreach statements

The for loop can be considered a sentinel controlled loop, one in which you determine when the loop terminates through the use of a counter. Typically, it's used when you know how you want to end the loop because you set up the condition in the loop. But what happens when you don't know how many iterations you need to loop over? This situation can arise when working with collections of items in your code where the quantity is not known at run time, such as dynamic allocations based on user input.

C# provides the foreach statement for iterating over collections of items. Collections are typically arrays but also other .NET objects that have implemented the IEnumerable interfaces. (IEnumerable is a code component in C# that supports iteration.)

You may have an array or collection that contains a known or unknown number of values. Although you can use the standard `for` loop for these collection types with known number of values, it's almost impossible to know how many values will be in a collection in all instances. For example, you might create a character array out of the individual characters of a text string entered by a user at run time. Other possibilities might be a dataset created after accessing a database. In both cases, you will not know the number of values at the time you write the code. Consider the following:

```
// foreach syntax
foreach(type in collection)
{
    statement;
}
```

In the this syntax example, `type` is a data type that the collection will contain. A simple example can demonstrate this. Assume you have an array that stores integer values for grades that a teacher may want to average, as shown in the following Code Lab.

CODE LAB   Using a foreach Loop [average_grades]

```
// foreach loop to average grades in an array
// set up an integer array and assign some values
int[] arrGrades = new int[] {78, 89, 90, 76, 98, 65};

// create three variables to hold the sum, number of grades, and the average
int total = 0;
int gradeCount = 0;
double average = 0.0;

// loop to iterate over each integer value in the array
// foreach doesn't need to know the size initially as it is determined
// at the time the array is accessed.
foreach(int grade in arrGrades)
{
    total = total + grade; // add each grade value to total
    gradeCount++;          // increment counter for use in average
}

average = total / gradeCount;   // calculate average of grades
Console.WriteLine(average);
```

Code Lab Analysis

In the preceding code sample, you know how many grades are in the array because you created the array at design time, but this is to simplify the example. You might have a scenario in which the user would enter grades, and you would dynamically create an array in your code.

You create three other variables:

➤   `total` is used to add the values of the grades

➤   `gradeCount` is used to keep track of how many grades were in the array, so you can calculate the average.

➤   `average` is declared as a double in the event you end up with a fractional value for the average.

The `foreach` loop declares an integer variable called `grade`. You have used an integer variable because the values in the array are integers. It's important to ensure that your variable in the `foreach` loop matches the data types expected in the collection. The variable `grade` is then used to iterate over each value in the array. The statements in the `foreach` loop then add the value in each integer in the array to the total variable.

You increment the `gradeCount` variable by one each time so that you can use the value in the average calculation. After the loop is finished, the average calculation is completed and output to the console window.

The `foreach` loop makes it easy for programmers to set up a means to iterate over the items in a collection without having to worry about knowing the number of items in advance.

while statements

The `while` statement acts in a similar fashion to the `for` statement in that it enables you to perform a statement or set of statements repeatedly until a condition is met (returns false). The easiest way to think of the `while` statement is to state it as, "while the condition remains true, execute the loop."

```
// while statement syntax
while(condition)
{
    statement;
}
```

The `while` statement starts with the keyword `while`, enclosed in parentheses is the condition to test. If the condition returns `true`, the statement or statements enclosed in the curly braces executes. When the condition returns `false`, the execution will fall to the line of code following the closing curly brace of the while statement. An example helps to demonstrate this concept:

```
// while statement example
int someValue = 0;

while(someValue < 10)
{
    Console.WriteLine(someValue);
    someValue++;
}
```

The preceding code sample sets the variable `someValue` to 0. The `while` loop tests a condition to see if `someValue` is less than 10. In this case 0 is less than 10, so the `while` loop executes and outputs the value of `someValue` to the console window. It then increments `someValue` by 1. The loop condition is checked again, and the loop executes because `someValue` is now equal to 1, which is still less than 10. Figure 2-5 provides a sample output from this code.

After `someValue` is incremented to the value of 10, the loop condition fails, and execution continues after the closing brace of the `while` loop. The value 10 is not printed due to the condition returning `false`. Some programmers new to the concept might think that the values up to and including 10 will be printed, but that is not the case.

FIGURE 2-5: Output of while loop

Note the differences between the `while` and `for` loops. The `for` loop sets up a variable, a condition, and an increment all within the `for` loop parentheses. The `while` loop relies on previously set variables and requires the increment to take place within the loop. Failure to increment in the loop could create an infinite loop here as well.

do-while statements

The last repetition structure to look at is the `do-while` loop. This looping structure operates in a similar fashion as the `while` loop with two distinct exceptions. First, the `do-while` loop executes the statement block at least once regardless of the condition. The reason for this comes from the second distinction, which is where the condition is evaluated in each structure. Second, the `while` loop checks the condition at the beginning, whereas the `do-while` loop checks the condition at the end.

```
// do-while loop syntax
do
{
    statement;
} while (condition);
```

As you can see from the preceding syntax, `statement;` will get executed first; then the `condition` is checked at the end in the `while` portion. Also important to note is the use of a semicolon at the end of the `while` portion even though it follows the closing brace. Forgetting this semicolon is considered a syntax error and results in the compiler generating an error with the message `; expected`.

> **EXAM TIPS AND TRICKS: Knowing the Difference Between Loops**
>
> Exam writers like to test your knowledge of the difference between loops. Ensure you watch for subtle things like the semicolon or where conditions are evaluated when reading the exam questions.

Take a moment to look at the previous `while` loop sample, converted to a `do-while` loop:

```
// do-while statement example
int someValue = 0;

do
{
    Console.WriteLine(someValue);
    someValue++;
} while (someValue < 10);
```

The preceding code sample produces the same output as the previous `while` statement (see Figure 2-6).

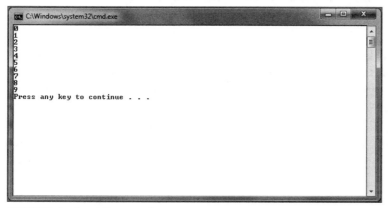

FIGURE 2-6: do-while execution

As a result, this sample doesn't actually depict the fact that these two loops behave differently, so you'll modify the code a bit to show how the `do` loop differs from the `while` loop:

```
// do-while statement example
int someValue = 10;

do
{
    Console.WriteLine(someValue);
    someValue++;
} while (someValue < 10);
```

What you have changed in this code sample is the initial value for the variable `someValue`. It is now set to 10. As a result, you might think that because the `while` condition tests for values less than 10, this loop will not execute the statements in the curly braces. However, the `do-while` loop will execute at least once, and as a result, Figure 2-7 shows the output from running this code sample.

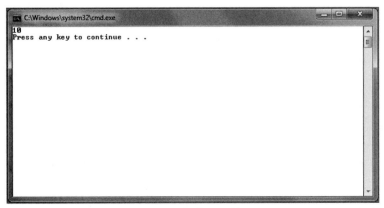

FIGURE 2-7: do-while after setting variable to 10

The output shows only a single value, 10. This was the initial value set in the variable, and it was output to the screen showing that the do-while executes the statement block at least once. When the condition is checked at the end of the loop, it returns false because someValue is not less than 10, and the loop no longer executes.

So why would you choose a do-while over a while? There could be many reasons for choosing one over the other, but a typical scenario is when you are expecting input from the user and need to ensure that input is taken in the loop as opposed to outside of the loop. An example helps to demonstrate:

```
// while statement example
char someValue;

do
{
    someValue = (char) Console.Read();
    Console.WriteLine(someValue);
} while (someValue != 'q');
```

This sample introduces some code you may not be familiar with yet, so don't fret too much over it. The variable declaration declares someValue to be of type char, which represents a single character. Inside the do loop, you set someValue equal to a character entered by the user when the program runs. The Console.Read() line is a method for the Console class that reads a single character from the console input. The (char) is merely an explicit cast that converts the input to a char value for use in the program.

The value input from the user is then echoed to the screen through the Console.WriteLine method. The while condition checks to see if the value entered by the user is the letter q. If so, the loop quits; otherwise, it continues until q is entered at the console. This type of loop control is known as a *sentinel*. The sentinel value causes the loop to stop. An example of the output is shown in Figure 2-8.

At this point, you might be anxious to try out some of these looping structures in code, so you can set up a sample that walks you through these different looping structures.

FIGURE 2-8: Using a sentinel to end a loop

CODE LAB   Working with Loops

Start a new C# console application in Visual Studio called **Loops.** After the code window opens for program.cs, paste or type this code into the main function:

```
// using a for loop to count up by one
Console.WriteLine("Count up by one");

for (int i = 0; i < 10; i++)
{
    Console.WriteLine(i);
}
Console.WriteLine();

// using a for loop to count down by one
Console.WriteLine("Count down by one");

for (int i = 10; i > 0; i~DH)
{
    Console.WriteLine(i);
}
Console.WriteLine();

// using a for loop to count up by 2
Console.WriteLine("Count up by two");

for (int i = 0; i < 10; i += 2)
{
    Console.WriteLine(i);
}
Console.WriteLine();

// using a for loop to increment by multiples of 5
Console.WriteLine("Count up by multiples of 5");

for (int i = 5; i < 1000; i *= 5)
{
```

```
            Console.WriteLine(i);
        }
        Console.WriteLine();

        // using a foreach loop with integers
        Console.WriteLine("foeach over an array of integers");

        int[] arrInts = new int[] { 1, 2, 3, 4, 5 };
        foreach (int number in arrInts)
        {
            Console.WriteLine(number);
        }
        Console.WriteLine();

        // using a foreach loop with strings
        Console.WriteLine("foreach over an array of strings");

        string[] arrStrings = new string[] { "First", "Second", "Third",
        "Fourth", "Fifth" };
        foreach (string text in arrStrings)
        {
            Console.WriteLine(text);
        }
        Console.WriteLine();

        // using a while loop
        int whileCounter = 0;

        Console.WriteLine("Counting up by one using a while loop");
        while (whileCounter < 10)
        {
            Console.WriteLine(whileCounter);
            whileCounter++;
        }
        Console.WriteLine();

        // using a do-while loop
        int doCounter = 0;

        Console.WriteLine("Counting up using a do-while loop");
        do
        {
            Console.WriteLine(doCounter);
            doCounter++;
        } while (doCounter < 10);
        Console.WriteLine();
```

Code Lab Analysis

This code sample can provide you with the opportunity to check out the different loop structures that were introduced in this chapter. You can use commenting to allow you to focus on individual sections and also make use of the debugging features in Visual Studio to place breakpoints in the code and step through the code to see how it operates.

SUMMARY

In this chapter you have learned some of the core foundational aspects of the C# programming language. C# enables you to build applications from statements. The language supports simple and complex statements. Simple statements are those that provide basic code functionality such as variable declarations, whereas complex statements include more structure around the components of the statement. Examples of complex statements are the `for` loop and the `switch` statement. All simple statements end with a semicolon; although, this is not a requirement for complex statements.

This chapter also looked at controlling program flow and how that is accomplished in C#. *Program flow* refers to the control of executing code within the program and allows you, the programmer, to determine which code or segment of code gets executed at any point in your program.

C# provides various program flow statements such as decision and repetition structures that allow the programmer to make decisions based on conditions and to iterate or repeat over code to accomplish necessary tasks.

Decision structures such as the if statement and the switch statement permit the programmer to compare values and direct code execution based on the result. These comparisons are typically the result of a `true` or `false` value returned using conditional operators such as less than (<), greater than (>), equal to (==), and so on.

Repetition in code enables you to iterate over collections or arrays to act on the items contained in those structures. Repetition also enables you to perform the same code statement or set of statements to perform various other actions until a certain condition is met. The `for`, `foreach`, `while`, and `do` loops all provide the repetition necessary in a C# program.

These foundational concepts can help you understand how to structure your C# code to achieve the output or program goal that you want. They are core to C# programming and will be found throughout the .NET Framework.

TEST QUESTIONS

Read each question carefully and select the answer or answers that represent the best solution to the problem. You can find the answers in Appendix A, "Answers to Sample Test Questions."

1. You want to declare an integer variable called `myVar` and assign it the value 0. How can you accomplish this?

    a.   `declare myVar as 0;`

    b.   `myVar = 0;`

    c.   `int myVar = 0`

    d.   `int myVar = 0;`

2. You need to make a logical comparison where two values must return true in order for your code to execute the correct statement. Which logical operator enables you to achieve this?

    a.   AND

    b. |

c. &

d. &&

3. What kind of result is returned in the condition portion of an `if` statement?

   a. Boolean

   b. Integer

   c. Double

   d. String

4. What are the keywords supported in an `if` statement?

   a. `if, else, else-if, return`

   b. `if, else, else if`

   c. `if, else, else if, break`

   d. `if, else, default`

5. In the following code sample, will the second if structure be evaluated?

   ```
   bool condition = true;

   if(condition)
       if(5 < 10)
           Console.WriteLine("5 is less than 10);
   ```

   a. Yes

   b. No

6. If you want to iterate over the values in an array of integers called `arrNumbers` to perform an action on them, which loop statement enables you to do this?

   a.
   ```
   foreach (int number in arrNumbers)
   {
   }
   ```

   b.
   ```
   for each (int number in arrNumbers)
   {
   }
   ```

   c.
   ```
   for (int i; each i in arrNumbers; i++)
   {
   }
   ```

   d.
   ```
   foreach (number in arrNumbers)
   {
   }
   ```

7. What is the purpose of `break;` in a switch statement?

    a. It causes the program to exit.

    b. It causes the code to exit the switch statement.

    c. It causes the program to pause.

    d. It causes the code to stop executing until the user presses a key on the keyboard.

8. What are the four basic repetition structures in C#?

    a. `for, foreach, loop, while`

    b. `loop, while, do-for, for-each`

    c. `for, foreach, while, do-while`

    d. `do-each, while, for, do`

9. How many times will this loop execute?

```
int value = 0;
do
{
   Console.WriteLine (value);
} while value > 10;
```

    a. 10 times

    b. 1 time

    c. 0 times

    d. 9 times

ADDITIONAL READING AND RESOURCES

Following are some additional useful resources to help you understand the topics presented in this chapter:

C# keywords

    `http://msdn.microsoft.com/en-us/library/x53a06bb.aspx`

C# Programming Guide

    `http://msdn.microsoft.com/en-us/library/kx37x362.aspx`

Developer Code Samples

    `http://code.msdn.microsoft.com/`

C# Corner

    `http://www.c-sharpcorner.com/`

CHEAT SHEET

This cheat sheet is designed as a way for you to quickly study the key points of this chapter.

Simple statements

➤ Will end with a semicolon.

➤ They typically exist on one line but may extend to more than one line.

➤ Commonly used for variable declarations.

➤ They are also used for assignment statements.

➤ Typical usage scenarios are to perform a simple task.

Complex statements

➤ May or may not end with a semicolon with the `do-while` loop being an example of ending with a semicolon.

➤ Typically contain simple statements within the curly braces.

➤ Complex statements use curly braces to enclose other statements.

➤ They have structures, such as parentheses, that support their function.

Boolean expressions

➤ These are used in comparisons.

➤ C# uses the `bool` values `true` and `false` rather than 1 and 0 as in some other languages.

➤ They can be considered logical operators.

➤ They can exist in both unary and binary forms.

➤ Unary operates on a single operand, such as logical negation `!`.

➤ Binary operates on two operands, such as `&&` and `||`.

if-then-else statements

➤ Used for decision making.

➤ Will execute a code path depending on condition.

➤ Returns either true or false from the condition check.

➤ Doesn't require curly braces but use is recommended to help clarify what is included in the statement.

➤ Can be nested within other `if-then-else` statements.

➤ The `else` clause is used to choose alternative path for a `false` condition.

➤ The `else if` clause is used to choose alternative path for a `true` condition.

switch statements

➤ Can check various data types in the condition in contrast to if statements.

➤ Uses case statements for each value to test against the condition.

➤ Switch statements are a cleaner code choice than nested if statements for code readability.

➤ Can use a default case when none of the cases return true.

➤ The break statement is used to end switch evaluation in a true case.

➤ They handle multiple conditions with a single set of instructions by removing the break from each case statement that holds the conditions to match.

for statements

➤ Create a simple repetition structure.

➤ Uses an initialize component, a condition, and iterator in parentheses.

➤ Makes use of a statement block to contain one or more statements for execution enclosed in curly braces.

➤ Can be nested to create more complex looping structures.

➤ The initialization portion executes only at the start of the loop and not for each iteration.

➤ The condition portion is checked at each iteration.

➤ The increment portion happens only after the statements are executed in each iteration.

➤ This loop does not end with a semicolon.

foreach statements

➤ They can be used for iterating over collections of items.

➤ They are best used when the number of values in collection is not known at design time.

➤ They work with any collection that implements `IEnumerable`.

➤ The declaration statement must use data types that are in the collection.

while statements

➤ These execute similar to a `for` loop.

➤ The initialization is not part of the `while` loop; it takes place before the loop.

➤ The condition is evaluated at the start and on each iteration.

➤ The increment is accomplished within the loop.

➤ These are more intuitive than the `for` loop in terms of readability.

do-while statements

➤ Similar to the `while` loop, requires initialization outside of the loop structure.

➤ The condition is evaluated at the end of the loop.

➤ The increment is accomplished within the loop.

➤ The loop will execute at least once, regardless of condition.

➤ This loop style does end with a semicolon.

REVIEW OF KEY TERMS

assignment Providing a value for a variable.

Boolean A value that is represented as either `true` or `false`.

branching Refers to changing code execution to a different path.

condition An evaluation of operands using logical operators.

conditional instructions Instructions that evaluate Boolean expressions and take action based on the outcome of the evaluation.

comment A code line that starts with the `//` characters and is a way of helping to document the code so that programmers can understand what the different code segments are intended to do.

complex statement A statement that can enclose one or more simple statements into a code block surrounded by curly braces `{}`. Typical complex statements are those used for repetition and decision structures such as `foreach()`, `if()`, `switch`, `do()` and so on.

constant A named value that is assigned at time of declaration and cannot be changed in code later.

declaration Used to create a variable in code.

decrement To decrease by a certain value.

expression An activity or code statement that returns a result.

IEnumerable A code component in C# that supports iteration.

increment To increase by a certain value.

initialize To set a starting value.

iterator A portion of loop that changes a value.

literal A notation used to indicate fixed values in code. Not the same as a constant. You cannot assign a value to a literal.

loop A repetition structure that repeats instructions.

modulus Remainder of integer division

operator Performs an operation on values.

program flow The logical execution of code.

sentinel A value used to signal the end for execution on a loop

simple statement A statement that ends with a semicolon and is typically used for program actions such as declaring variables, assigning values to variables, method calls, and code branching.

spaghetti code A term used to describe code that is complicated to follow and understand due to branching.

statement The code construct of the C# programming language that causes the application to perform an action.

ternary operator An operator that takes three arguments, a condition, a value for true, and a value for false.

variables Named values that can be changed in code.

EXAM TIPS AND TRICKS

The Review of Key Terms and the Cheat Sheet for this chapter can be printed off to help you study. You can find these files in the ZIP file for this chapter at www.wrox .com/remtitle.cgi?isbn=1118612094 on the Download Code tab.

3

Working with the Type System

WHAT YOU WILL LEARN IN THIS CHAPTER

- ➤ Using C# value types
- ➤ Understanding data structures
- ➤ Using enumerations
- ➤ Understanding C# reference types
- ➤ Working with reference types properties
- ➤ Understanding encapsulation
- ➤ Using generics

WROX.COM CODE DOWNLOADS FOR THIS CHAPTER

You can find the code downloads for this chapter at www.wrox.com/remtitle
.cgi?isbn=1118612094 on the Download Code tab. The code is in the chapter03
download and individually named according to the names throughout the chapter.

This chapter introduces you to the type system in C#, which provides the infrastructure necessary to model objects and handle the different types of data and information within a program.
As a result, the exam tests your abilities to create and consume types in the C# language.

To help you gain this understanding, you explore types in a sequenced and logical manner.
Value types are the simplest types in C#, and the chapter starts there. Not only are they the
basic core types you need to store values and data in your code, but they are also used to
maintain properties, which are components of C# classes. Class properties define characteristics of the classes you create.

Next, you look at reference types, which Microsoft defines as types that "store references to
the actual data." Another term for reference types is *classes*.

The key to working with reference types such as a C# class is the concept of encapsulation. Encapsulation enables a developer to create functionality in a class that is hidden from other developers who might use that class.

Table 3-1 introduces you to the exam objectives covered in this chapter.

TABLE 3-1: 70-483 Exam Objectives Covered in This Chapter

OBJECTIVE	CONTENT COVERED
Create types	*Create value types.* This focuses on creating and using the standard C# value type variables in your code.
	Create reference types. This includes creating and using class files in C#. Coverage of the components of the class files are covered in subsequent sections.
	Create generic types. This includes creating and using generic types in your code to represent unknown types at code creation time.
	Constructors. This includes defining constructors and how they are used in class files.
	Methods. This focuses on creating and using methods for the functionality in your code and class files.
	Classes. This includes defining and using class files in your code to represent real-world objects.
	Extension methods. This focuses on an understanding of how you can extend the functionality of existing classes without recompiling the class.
	Optional and named parameters. This includes discussion on the proper use of optional and named parameters in your methods.
	Indexed properties. This includes using indexed properties in a class to support enumerating the properties.
	Overloaded methods. This focuses on creating multiple methods with the same name that accept differing parameters and functionality depending on the need.
	Overridden methods. This discusses how to override virtual methods and to change the functionality of inherited methods in your classes.
Enforce encapsulation	*Properties.* This focuses on enforcing encapsulation of your class files through the use of properties to hide the member variables and provide a means to validate the values supplied to modify the member variables.
	Accessor methods. This topic focuses on the methods used to access member variables in your class files that are hidden through encapsulation.

CREATING VALUE TYPES

Exam 70-483 has an objective titled "Create types." Creating and consuming value types in C# is a core and fundamental skillset. Value types are the basis of all data types that you use in your C# programs.

C# divides value types into two distinct categories known as *structs* and *enumerations*. Structs are further divided into subcategories called *numeric types* (integral types, floating-point types, and decimals), *Boolean types* (bool), and *user-defined structs*. Enumerations, or enums, are formed as a set of types declared using the keyword enum. (More on enums later in the section on "Working with Enumerations.")

Understanding Predefined Value Types

Developer documentation from Microsoft refers to value types as intrinsic, simple, or built-in types. Value types identify specific values of data. This is a rather simple statement, but it is accurate. C# includes intrinsic data types that are present in many other programming languages and are used to store simple values. C# intrinsic data types have direct mappings to .NET Framework types that follow under the System namespace. The names listed in the type column in the following table are known as aliases for the .NET Types. All value types derive from System.ValueType.

Table 3-2 lists the basic value types that C# supports including the range of the data values that they support.

TABLE 3-2: C# Data Types

TYPE	VALUES	SIZE	.NET TYPE
bool	true, false	1 byte	System.Boolean
Byte	0–255	1 byte	System.Byte
char	0000–FFFF Unicode	16-bit	System.Char
decimal	$\pm 1.0 \times 10^{-28}$ to $\pm 7.9 \times 10^{28}$	28–29 significant digits	System.Decimal
double	$\pm 5.0 \times 10^{-324}$ to $\pm 1.7 \times 10^{308}$	15–16 digits	System.Double
enum	User-defined set of name constants		
float	$\pm 1.5 \times 10^{-45}$ to $\pm 3.4 \times 10^{38}$	7 digits	System.Single
int	−2,147,483,648 to 2,147,483,647	Signed 32-bit	System.Int32
long	9,223,372,036,854,775,808 to 9,223,372,036,854,775,807	Signed 64-bit	System.Int64
sbyte	−128 to 127	Signed 8-bit	System.SByte

continues

TABLE 3-2 *(continued)*

TYPE	VALUES	SIZE	.NET TYPE
short	−32,768 to 32,767	Signed 16-bit	`System.Int16`
struct	Includes the numeric types listed in this table as well as bool and user-defined structs		
uint	0 to 4,294,967,295	Unsigned 32-bit	`System.UInt32`
ulong	0 to 18,446,744,073,709,551,615	Unsigned 64-bit	`System.UInt64`
ushort	0 to 65,535	Unsigned 16-bit	`System.Uint16`

To work with these data types, you declare a variable to be of the specific date type. After a variable is declared, you can store the value directly in that variable through an assignment statement. Assignment can be included as part of the declaration as well. For example, the following code demonstrates both options:

```
// declare an integer variable
int myInt;

// and assign a value to it
myInt = 3;

// use declaration and assignment in one statement
int mySecondInt = 50;
```

The keyword `int` is used to indicate that the variable will be of type `int`, the alias for the `System.Int32` type. As a result, it can contain any value from negative 2,147,482,648 to positive 2,147,482,647.

> **ADVICE FROM THE EXPERTS: Don't Confuse C# Data Types**
>
> Do not confuse C# data types with similar names found in mathematical concepts. For example, the data type `int`, which is short for *integer*, is not the same as the mathematical integer concept. Integers in math can contain values from minus infinity to positive infinity. However, data types on C# are dependent on the number of bits used to contain the data type. In this case, `int` is 32-bits signed; 2 raised to the power of 32 provides you with a maximum of 4,294,967,296. Take away 1 bit to use for the signed portion, and you find the values listed in the preceding table for `int`.

You should be aware of a couple of restrictions with value types. You cannot derive a new type from a value type, and value types cannot contain a null value. Now, here is where the use of the alias for a value type and the .NET System type differ. Trying to use an alias with an unassigned variable in code will result in Visual Studio generating an error about the use of an unassigned variable. As mentioned, each value type has a corresponding .NET type in the System namespace, and you can use an unassigned version of this type. This is possible because the System types are essentially *classes* (reference types), are created through use of the new operator, and contain a default value. The following Code Lab shows an example of this.

CODE LAB   **Comparison of value types and their alias [value_type_alias]**

```
// create a variable to hold a value type using the alias form
// but don't assign a variable
int myInt;
int myNewInt = new int();

// create a variable to hold a .NET value type
// this type is the .NET version of the alias form int
// note the use of the keyword new, we are creating an object from
// the System.Int32 class
System.Int32 myInt32 = new System.Int32();

// you will need to comment out this first Console.WriteLine statement
// as Visual Studio will generate an error about using an unassigned
// variable.  This is to prevent using a value that was stored in the
// memory location prior to the creation of this variable
Console.WriteLine(myInt);

// print out the default value assigned to an int variable
// that had no value assigned previously
Console.WriteLine(myNewInt);

// this statement will work fine and will print out the default value for
// this type, which in this case is 0
Console.WriteLine(myInt32);
```

Code Lab Analysis

In the previous code sample, the myInt32 variable is created as a new object based on the System.Int32 .NET type. A value isn't provided in the statement System.Int32 myInt32 = new System.Int32();. As a result, Visual Studio calls the default constructor for this object and assigns the default value. (You learn more about constructors and their purposes later in this chapter under the section titled "Using Constructors" in "Creating Reference Types.")

A variable was created called myNewInt by using the keyword new. The .NET Framework recognizes this form of variable declaration as being the same as using the System.Int32 style of variable. Although the declaration of int myInt; does not allow you to output the value of this variable if it has not been assigned, the declaration of int myNewInt = new int(); does allow you to output the unassigned variable. This second version is not often used when dealing with simple types, however, but nothing is stopping you from using it.

The .NET Framework provides default values for all System value types created in this way. The default values for all the numeric types are equivalent to the value zero (0). Any of the floating point types such as decimal, double, or float will be 0.0. The default value for bool is false, char is '\0', enums are (E)0, and structs are set to null.

Another important aspect to understand about value types is in the way the values are managed. The .NET Framework stores value types on the stack rather than on the heap, in computer memory. The result of these types storing the value directly and being stored on the stack is that if you assign one value type to another, it will copy the value from the first to the second. Reference types copy a reference (memory address) as opposed to the actual values, which are discussed later in the section "Creating Reference Types." The following sample code shows the creation of two integer variables. A value is assigned to one of the variables and then one variable is assigned to another.

```
// assigning one value type to another
int myInt;
int secondInt;

// myInt will be assigned the value of 2
myInt = 2;

// secondInt will contain the value 2 after this statement executes
secondInt = myInt;

// output the value of the variables
Console.WriteLine(myInt);
Console.WriteLine(secondInt);
Console.WriteLine();
```

Although in the previous samples you have shown only the integer data type, you work with the other simple value types in a similar manner. Copy and paste, or type, this code into a new Console application in Visual Studio to see how to work with other value types.

CODE LAB Using value types [using_value_types]

```
// declare some numeric data types
int myInt;
double myDouble;
byte myByte;
char myChar;
decimal myDecimal;
float myFloat;
long myLong;
short myShort;
bool myBool;

// assign values to these types and then
// print them out to the console window
// also use the sizeOf operator to determine
// the number of bytes taken up be each type

myInt = 5000;
Console.WriteLine("Integer");
Console.WriteLine(myInt);
```

```
Console.WriteLine(myInt.GetType());
Console.WriteLine(sizeof (int));
Console.WriteLine();

myDouble = 5000.0;
Console.WriteLine("Double");
Console.WriteLine(myDouble);
Console.WriteLine(myDouble.GetType());
Console.WriteLine(sizeof(double));
Console.WriteLine();

myByte = 254;
Console.WriteLine("Byte");
Console.WriteLine(myByte);
Console.WriteLine(myByte.GetType());
Console.WriteLine(sizeof(byte));
Console.WriteLine();

myChar = 'r';
Console.WriteLine("Char");
Console.WriteLine(myChar);
Console.WriteLine(myChar.GetType());
Console.WriteLine(sizeof(byte));
Console.WriteLine();

myDecimal = 20987.89756M;
Console.WriteLine("Decimal");
Console.WriteLine(myDecimal);
Console.WriteLine(myDecimal.GetType());
Console.WriteLine(sizeof(byte));
Console.WriteLine();

myFloat = 254.09F;
Console.WriteLine("Float");
Console.WriteLine(myFloat);
Console.WriteLine(myFloat.GetType());
Console.WriteLine(sizeof(byte));
Console.WriteLine();

myLong = 2544567538754;
Console.WriteLine("Long");
Console.WriteLine(myLong);
Console.WriteLine(myLong.GetType());
Console.WriteLine(sizeof(byte));
Console.WriteLine();

myShort = 3276;
Console.WriteLine("Short");
Console.WriteLine(myShort);
Console.WriteLine(myShort.GetType());
Console.WriteLine(sizeof(byte));
Console.WriteLine();

myBool = true;
Console.WriteLine("Boolean");
Console.WriteLine(myBool);
```

```
Console.WriteLine(myBool.GetType());
Console.WriteLine(sizeof(byte));
Console.WriteLine();
```

Code Lab Analysis

This lab declares variables of various values types that are intrinsic to C#. Then each variable is used in a repeating set of code statements that:

➤ Assigns a value to the variable

➤ Outputs a line to the console indicating the value type

➤ Outputs the value that was assigned

➤ Outputs the System type associated with the value type

➤ Outputs the size of the value type in bytes

To gain a thorough understanding of these types, change the values in the assignment statements to different types or outside the range and see what the compiler returns for error messages.

An understanding of these simple types is necessary to represent the data that your applications will use to represent real-world problems. They also form the basis for the properties that you will create in your classes as you move into the next section on reference types.

> **BEST PRACTICES: Code Efficiency**
>
> Developers writing code today spend less and less time thinking about efficiency of code and the data types used, mostly due to the power and storage capacity of computers that are in use today. In the early days of the personal computer, thinking back to the Commodore VIC-20 era, memory was at a premium, and all code written was done in a way to conserve memory usage of the application.
>
> Understanding the data sizes helps you to choose the proper data type for your storage needs. Too large a data type can waste resources, while too small a data type range can cause overflow issues and sometimes wrap-around issues where incrementing an int value that is signed might go from 32,767 to –32,767, causing bugs that are hard to locate.

Working with Data Structures

Data structures, or simply *structs*, are value types that you can use for storing related sets of variables. Structs share some similarities with classes, but they also have certain restrictions.

The C# language provides numerous mechanisms for storing related data such as structs, classes, arrays, collections, and so on. Each has a specific set of requirements and restrictions that dictate how or where you can use them. Arrays and collections are covered in Chapter 9, "Working With Data," and classes will be covered later in this chapter in the section "Creating Reference Types." For now, you'll focus on an understanding of structs.

Consider some common uses of a struct to help better understand where you might use one, leading to the creation of structs and how to use them in code. If you consider an object in real-life that has a set of characteristics, you can understand how to model this object using a struct.

For a simple example, consider a student as a real-world object you want to model in your code. Yes, you could consider using a class for this, and realistically you would in all likelihood, but for this example, you will create a simple struct to model the student. To do so, think about the characteristics that you want to model. To put it into perspective, consider how you want to use the Student struct in your code. For this simple example, consider using the Student struct as a means to help a teacher calculate the student's average grade across a number of tests. Here are the characteristics to consider:

- ➤ First Name
- ➤ Middle Initial
- ➤ Last Name
- ➤ Test1 Score
- ➤ Test2 Score
- ➤ Test3 Score
- ➤ Test4 Score
- ➤ Test5 Score
- ➤ Average

Use a relatively simple set of characteristics where you limit the number of tests to only 5, provide a field to store the average of all tests, and fields for the Student's name. (A *field* is a variable that stores characteristic data for a class.) You could have used an array for the grades here as well but in the lab portion of this section, you get a chance to do so. For now, create this struct in code:

```
public struct Student
{
    public string firstName;
    public string lastname;
    public char initial;
    public double score1;
    public double score2;
    public double score3;
    public double score4;
    public double score5;
    public double average;
}
```

The Student struct created includes a set of properties represented by variables of simple value types. As you can see, a struct is a value type, but it is a complex value type because it can hold multiple differing value types as properties.

To use this struct in your code, you need to create a new instance of it. You cannot simply use `Student` as a new type in your code. The following code shows how to create a new instance of the `Student` struct in your code:

```
// create a new instance of the Student struct in code
Student myStudent = new Student();

// create a new instance of the Student struct without the new keyword
Student myOtherStudent;
```

After you create a new instance of the struct, you can then begin to assign or read values from the properties declared in the struct. The following code demonstrates creating a new struct of type `Student`, assigning values to the properties, and reading the values from the properties. It also demonstrates a small piece of code that attempts to use `Student` directly in code.

```
// create a new instance of the Student struct
Student myStudent = new Student();

// assign some values to the properties of myStudent
myStudent.firstName = "Fred";
myStudent.lastName = "Jones";
myStudent.score1 = 89;
myStudent.score2 = 95;

Console.Write("Student " + myStudent.firstName + " " + myStudent.lastName);
Console.Write(" scored " + myStudent.score1 + " on his/her first test. ");

// illegal statement, cannot use the type directly
// Visual Studio will indicate that an object reference is required
Student.firstName = "Fail";
```

Structs can contain more than just properties. They can include functions, constructors, constants, indexers, operators, events, and nested types and can implement interfaces. You must understand the use of constructors in structs because they differ slightly from classes. The following points about constructors in structs are worth noting:

➤   Constructors are optional, but if included they must contain parameters. No default constructors are allowed.

➤   Fields cannot be initialized in a struct body.

➤   Fields can be initialized only by using the constructor or after the struct is declared.

➤   Private members can be initialized using only the constructor.

➤   Creating a new struct type without the new operator will not result in a call to a constructor if one is present.

➤   If your struct contains a reference type (class) as one of its members, you must call the reference type's constructor explicitly.

The following code expands on the previous `Student` struct by adding a constructor that sets the `Student`'s name when the object is created:

```
// create a Student struct that uses a constructor
public struct Student
{
    public string firstName;
    public string lastname;
    private string courseName;

    public Student(string first, string last,string course)
    {
       this.firstName = first;
       this.lastName = last;
       this.courseName = course;
    }
}
```

In the preceding sample code, the struct is simplified just to show the use of the constructor. You have only two fields for first and last name, and use the constructor to supply those values to the fields when the object is created with the keyword `new`.

The next sample code snippet shows an illegal use of a constructor in a struct. The reason is that in a struct if you create a constructor, you must provide for each member field in the struct; otherwise, Visual Studio throws and error.

```
public struct Student
{
    public string firstName;
    public string lastName;
    public char initial;
    public double score1;
    public double score2;
    public double score3;
    public double score4;
    public double score5;
    public double average;

    public Student(string first, string last)
    {
       this.firstName = first;
       this.lastName = last;
    }
}
```

As stated before, a struct can contain functions as well. You would create functions or methods in your struct to allow it to perform some action on the data members it contains, or for other purposes you deem necessary. The following code snippet shows an example of the previous `Student` struct with a method added to calculate the `Student` average. The constructor code has been removed to keep the sample clean.

```
// Student struct that contains a method to calculate the Student average
public struct Student
{
```

```
        public string firstName;
        public string lastname;
        public char initial;
        public double score1;
        public double score2;
        public double score3;
        public double score4;
        public double score5;
        public double average;

        public void calcAverage()
        {
            double avg = ((score1 + score2 + score3 + score4 + score5) / 5);
            this.average = avg;
        }
    }
```

Coming from the perspective of efficient code, a programmer should always consider how best to use the available data structures in a language. To that end, you should consider whether a struct or a class is required when deciding how to store your application objects.

In the preceding sample code, the Student struct is simple and should be created as a struct to avoid the overhead necessary with class files. However, evaluate the scenario where you want to store a number of student objects in a collection, such as an array. Knowing that value types are passed by value, your memory consumption can grow rather quickly if you start passing around an array of Student structs. Remember, these are passed on the stack. Instead, consider using a class for the student, in which case an array of student objects will be filled with pointers (references) to the student objects rather than the whole student data structure.

Now that you have covered the core concepts of structs, get some practice in creating them in code.

REAL-WORLD CASE SCENARIO | **Creating structs**

Open Visual Studio and create a C# console-based application, naming it **bookStruct**. The book struct will contain the following properties:

➤ Title

➤ Category

➤ Author

➤ Number of pages

➤ Current page

➤ ISBN

➤ Cover style

➤ Methods to turn pages, called nextPage and prevPage

Implement the code based on the knowledge you have gained so far about structs. Use a constructor to initialize the properties. Using the main method in your console application, create a new struct for a

book you know about, such as this one, and assign the properties in the constructor. Using the `Console`
`.WriteLine` method, output each property to the console window, and then call the next and previous
page methods. These methods need to take into consideration only the current page, and then increment
or decrement that based on the method called.

Solution

The complete code is provided here:

```
public struct Book
{
    public string title;
    public string category;
    public string author;
    public int numPages;
    public int currentPage;
    public double ISBN;
    public string coverStyle;

    public Book(string title, string category, string author, int numPages, int
        currentPage, double isbn, string cover)
    {
        this.title = title;
        this.category = category;
        this.author = author;
        this.numPages = numPages;
        this.currentPage = currentPage;
        this.ISBN = isbn;
        this.coverStyle = cover;
    }

    public void nextPage()
    {
        if (currentPage != numPages)
        {
            currentPage++;
            Console.WriteLine("Current page is now: " + this.currentPage);
        }
        else
        {
            Console.WriteLine("At end of book.");
        }
    }

    public void prevPage()
    {
        if (currentPage != 1)
        {
            currentPage--;
            Console.WriteLine("Current page is now: " + this.currentPage);
        }
        else
        {
            Console.WriteLine("At the beginning of the book.");
```

```
        }
      }
   }

   static void Main(string[] args)
   {
      Book myBook = new Book("MCSD Certification Toolkit (Exam 70-483)",
         "Certification", "Covaci, Tiberiu", 648, 1, 81118612095, "Soft Cover");

      Console.WriteLine(myBook.title);
      Console.WriteLine(myBook.category);
      Console.WriteLine(myBook.author);
      Console.WriteLine(myBook.numPages);
      Console.WriteLine(myBook.currentPage);
      Console.WriteLine(myBook.ISBN);
      Console.WriteLine(myBook.coverStyle);

      myBook.nextPage();
      myBook.prevPage();
   }
```

This sample application enables you to see how structs can be used in an application by enabling you to create a struct using properties and methods. It shows you how to instantiate a struct in code and access its data members and methods.

You might notice that in the struct shown in the Real-World Case Scenario, the methods and properties were declared as `public`. Structs share a similar trait to classes for accessibility of the members of the struct. `Public` means that code has access to the members directly and can assign values and read values as well as call the methods. At times, you want to control access to your members. To do so, you can declare them as `private` instead of `public`. This allows you to create accessor methods for the properties.

Accessor methods are methods that are public and provide an interface to your struct. By using accessor methods, you can set your data member fields as private, which prevents writing or reading them directly. Instead, users of your struct must go through the accessor methods. In these methods, you can include code to check the validity of the data entered. For example, what happens if other developers use your struct in their code and attempt to input a string value for the ISBN number? This would result in a bug in the code. Instead, your code inside the struct could perform validation on the input value and return an error to the calling code if the value is not correct.

You can leave structs for now and move onto discussing enumerations; however, more on accessibility of data fields will be covered in the section on reference types. In that section, you learn to use accessor functions and can apply that knowledge to structs as well.

Working with Enumerations

Microsoft defines *enumerations* as "a distinct type that consists of a set of named constants called the enumerator list." Now break this down so you can make sense of the definition. First, an enumeration is known as a type. A distinct type means that it will be declared as a type in your code, and no other type can have that same name and be declared as an `enum`. Each `enum` in your code needs to be distinct.

A set of named constants merely indicates that the enum is a set, which is to say a grouping of like values. The values contained in the enumeration are given names, so you can easily identify them, and they are constants, meaning you cannot change the names or the values after the enumeration is created.

Even though you assign names to the members of the enum list, the compiler actually assigns integer values to the members of the list starting with 0 and incrementing by one for each successive member in the enum. This is the default behavior. You can initialize members with your own value to override the default behavior. (To *override* is to extend or modify the abstract or virtual implementation of an inherited method, property, indexer, or event.) A common example used to demonstrate enumerations is to use the months of the year as named constants. The following sample code demonstrates using an enum called Months that contains the 12 months of the year. The first sample uses the default starting point of 0, whereas the second changes that to start at 1.

```
// enum called Months, using default initializer
enum Months {Jan, Feb, Mar, Apr, May, Jun, Jul, Aug, Sept, Oct, Nov, Dec};

// enum call Months, using an overidden initializer
enum Months {Jan = 1, Feb, Mar, Apr, May, Jun, Jul, Aug, Sept, Oct, Nov, Dec};
```

> **BEST PRACTICES: Enumerator Names**
>
> Much like variable names, the names of your enumerators cannot contain spaces. If you want to use names that might require a space, consider using CamelCase notation or an underscore.

In the previous examples, the first sample uses the default initializer of 0 and therefore the values in the enum contain the values 0 through 11; Jan = 0, Feb = 1, Mar = 2, and so on. For the most part, you know the months as Jan = 1, Feb = 2, Mar = 2, and so on. To better maintain that numeric representation, you can choose the second sample in the preceding code and start the enum at 1 with each subsequent month containing the correct numeric representation.

By default, and in the sample code shown, the enum uses an underlying data type of int to represent the list values. You can choose to change that default underlying type if you want by following the name of the enum with a colon and the data type as the below code demonstrates.

```
// using a non-default data type for an enum
enum Months : byte {Jan, Feb, Mar, Apr, May, Jun, Jul, Aug, Sept, Oct, Nov, Dec};
```

You can use only certain data types for the underlying types on enums. The allowable value types are

➤ byte

➤ sbyte

➤ short

➤ ushort

➤ int

➤   `uint`

➤   `long`

➤   `ulong`

All these types are numeric types. So why would you want to choose a different underlying type than the default? It depends on your requirements for you enumeration values. For example, if you are truly concerned about memory conservation in your application, you might elect to use the `byte` type as previously shown for the `Months` enumeration to save on memory requirements. After all, an `int` is a 32-bit value, which means 4 bytes when compared with using the `byte` type for a single byte. It doesn't amount to a large savings in this one instance, but little bits can add up.

You do not need to rely on the incremental assignment of values either. You can assign each enumerator its own nonsequential value. For example, aircraft pilots deal with different air speeds to help them know when they can safely lower the landing gear and the flaps, or when they are about to aerodynamically stall the airplane. You can represent specific air speeds by their letter designators and then assign the proper airspeeds to those designators by using an enumeration.

```
// enumeration to depict airspeeds for aircraft
enum AirSpeeds
{
    Vx = 55,
    Vy = 65,
    Vs0 = 50,
    Vs1 = 40,
    Vne = 120
{
```

In this sample enumeration, you have established five enumerators to represent different airspeeds in an airplane. `Vx` is the best angle of climb speed; `Vy` is the best rate of climb; `Vs0` is the stall speed in a clean configuration; `Vs1` is the stall speed with flaps and gear extended; and `Vne` is the never exceed speed. As you can see, if you were to write code that used only the numeric values, the code would be hard to read because you couldn't easily decipher the meaning of the values. However, with an enumeration, programmers writing an application to handle air speeds would understand the named constants when encountered in code—assuming they knew the different airspeed designators that is.

In addition to making your code easier to read when using these constants, enumerations have a couple other distinct advantages, such as enabling other developers using your enumeration to know clearly what the allowable values are for that enumeration, and feeding the IntelliSense engine of Visual Studio. When you declare an enumeration and then create a new type that uses your enumeration, IntelliSense displays the allowable values, as shown in Figure 3-1.

Earlier you learned that each value type had its own equivalent System type, such as `System.Int32` or `System.Byte`. The enum type is no different because it is an instance of the `System.Enum` type. `System.Enum` contains a number of methods that you can use with your own enums. Refer to the MSDN documentation for a complete list of these methods, but following is some sample code that shows a couple of the methods available to you when working with your enumerations.

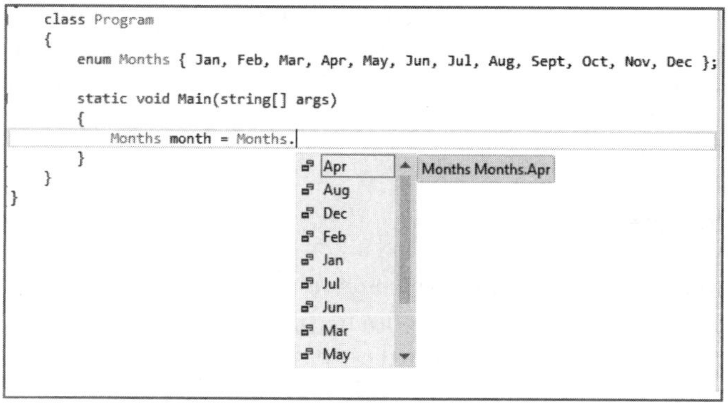

FIGURE 3-1: IntelliSense displaying enumeration list

CODE LAB   Using an enum [using_enums]

```
class Program
{
    enum Months { Jan = 1, Feb, Mar, Apr, May, Jun, Jul, Aug, Sept,
            Oct, Nov, Dec };

    static void Main(string[] args)
    {
        string name = Enum.GetName(typeof(Months), 8);
        Console.WriteLine("The 8th month in the enum is " + name);

        Console.WriteLine("The underlying values of the Months enum:");
        foreach (int values in Enum.GetValues(typeof(Months)))
        {
            Console.WriteLine(values);
        }
    }
}
```

Code Lab Analysis

The preceding code sample created an enumeration called Months that starts the values at 1 and increments the default value of 1 for each subsequent month. In the method main, you create a string variable called name and then used the GetName() method of System.Enum to get the eighth value from the enumeration, assign it to the variable name, and then output it to the console window.

Next, the code uses the fact that enumerations implicitly implement IEnumerable, and as such, you can iterate over them using foreach. The foreach loop uses the GetValues() method of the System.Enum class to pull the underlying values for the enumeration and print them to the console window.

This section has discussed the various value types that you can use in your code when building C# applications. Value types form the basis for the data that you can store in your application and are the simple data types that all programs use at some point. Understanding them and how to use them in your code gives you a solid foundation for moving onto the next section on reference types.

CREATING REFERENCE TYPES

In the previous section, you were introduced to value types, which represent the most basic data types you use in your applications. Early applications were actually written using only these basic data types. Although you can write a complete application with only these basic data types, attempting to create sophisticated applications that help users solve their real-world problems is incredibly complex. Object-oriented programming (OOP) was conceived to help developers deal with this complexity.

OOP enables the developer to model real-world objects in their code through the use of classes. Consider creating an application that might be used in a banking ATM. Your application would need to deal with objects such as customers, accounts, deposits, withdrawals, balances, and so on. It's much easier to write code to model these objects by creating a representation of such objects in your code and then assigning these code objects the same characteristics and functionality as the real-world objects. This is where class files come into play. A *class file* is a file that contains all the code necessary to model the real-world object. You create a class to act as a template for objects that will be created in code.

C# refers to classes as *reference types*. (Also included in the reference type category are interfaces and delegates. Interfaces are covered in Chapter 5, "Creating and Implementing Class Hierarchies" while delegates are found in Chapter 6, "Working with Delegates, Events, and Exceptions.") The reason these types are referred to as *reference types* is that the variable declared for the type holds only a reference to the actual object. A brief explanation of how C# deals with data types helps to clarify what this means.

In .NET code, there are two distinct, logical sections of computer memory used. They are called the *stack* and the *heap*. The *stack* is an area of memory reserved by the operating system for the executing application. This stack is where .NET stores simple data types. It is a relatively small amount of memory used for code execution. Mostly the simple data types will typically be created and destroyed rather quickly as the application executes, and therefore the stack can be kept somewhat clean during execution of the code. It is also the reason why you will receive out-of-memory exceptions if you have an infinite loop executing that is storing values on the stack.

The *heap* is a much larger area of memory that the .NET Framework uses to store the objects you create in your code based on classes. An object created from a class can require large amounts of memory depending on the size of the class. Classes contain simple data types to hold the values pertaining to the characteristics of the objects you are modeling. They also contain methods that provide the functionality that an object exhibits. An example might be a method for a game character to stand up, run, or talk.

As a result of an object potentially taking up a large amount of memory, the .NET Framework uses the reference for the object, which is its *memory address*. In this way, if the code requires copying or assigning the object to another variable, for example, memory is conserved because the compiler copies only the memory address and not the object itself. Classes are created with a specific syntax as shown here:

```
class MyClass
{
    // fields

    // properties

    // methods

    // events

    // delegates

    // nested classes
}
```

The preceding example doesn't dictate the order of the components of the class, but merely lists the items that a class can contain. Also, the listed items are not mandatory. The fields portion is where you would list the characteristics of the objects. If you were modeling a car, fields might consist of the model, make, color, year, number of doors, and so on. Fields are also commonly known as *members*, *data members*, and *data fields*.

Properties are directly related to the fields. Properties are used to allow controlled access to the fields in your class. Why this is important will be discussed more in the section on encapsulation, so you can leave the concept of properties for later.

Methods are used to provide the functionality for your objects. Real-world objects have functionality that needs to be modeled. Sticking with the car analogy, you know that a car can have the engine turned on or off and it can accelerate, slow down, stop, and so on. These are examples of methods that you might create within a car class.

Events are also functionality in your code, but in a different way. Think of events as things that happen as the result of some outside influence. For example, if a sensor in a car detects a problem, it raises an event and the computer in the car "hears" the event getting triggered. It can then take action or generate a warning about the issue. Essentially, events are a mechanism for objects to notify other objects when something happens. The object that raised the event is the *event publisher*, and the object that receives the event is the *event subscriber*.

Microsoft defines a delegate as "a type that references a method." Think of a delegate in terms of a political scenario, and you can gain an understanding of how a delegate functions. For example, a political delegate is someone who has been chosen to represent one or more other people. In C#, a delegate can be associated with any method that has a similar *signature* (argument types).

Nested classes are exactly what they sound like—one class file nested inside another class file. This book doesn't delve into nested classes too much because they are not necessary for passing the exam.

Understanding Modifiers

Before creating classes, you must understand the use of modifiers in C#. *Modifiers* are used in the declaration of types and the data members of your reference types. Table 3-3 lists the modifiers available in C# along with a description of what the modifiers do.

TABLE 3-3: C# Modifiers

MODIFIER	DESCRIPTION
public	An access modifier that declares the accessibility of the type it is assigned to. This is the most permissive level. Access outside the class body or struct is permitted. Reference and value types can be declared public. Methods can also be declared public.
private	An access modifier that declares the accessibility of the type it is assigned to. The least permissive, it enables access only with the body of the class or struct. Reference and value types can be declared private. Methods can also be declared private.
internal	An access modifier that declares the accessibility of the type it is assigned to. Allows access only within files in the same .NET assembly.
protected	A member access modifier. Members declared protected are accessible only from within the class and in derived classes.
abstract	Used for classes to indicate that this class cannot be instantiated but that it serves as a base class for other classes in an inheritance hierarchy.
async	Sets up the method or lambda expression it is applied to as an asynchronous method. This allows the methods to call long-running processes without blocking the calling code.
const	Applying this to a field indicates that field cannot be modified. Constants must be initialized at the time they are created.
event	Used to declare events in your code.
extern	Used to indicate that the method has been declared and implemented externally. You might use this with imported DLLs or external assemblies.
new	When used with class members, this modifier hides inherited members from the base class members. You would do this if you have inherited a member from a base class but your derived class needs to use its own version of that member.
override	Used when inheriting functionality from a base class that you want to change. Overriding is covered later in the chapter in the section "Abstract and Overriden Methods."
partial	Class files can exist across multiple files in the same assembly. This modifier tells the compiler that the class exists in another file or files in the assembly.
readonly	Read-only members can be assigned only during declaration or in a class constructor. No other means of changing or assigning a value to that member are permitted.
sealed	Applied to classes. Sealed classes cannot be inherited.

MODIFIER	DESCRIPTION
static	When applied to a class member, it means that the member belongs to the class only and not to specific objects created from the class. The .NET Framework has many examples of this such as the `Math` class or the `String` class.
unsafe	C# is managed code, which means that memory operations are handled in a protected manner. Using the `unsafe` keyword declares a context that is not safe in terms of memory management. C++ pointers are examples of unsafe memory operations. To use pointers in C#, you need to declare an unsafe context.
virtual	If you create a class and want to allow the method to be overridden in a derived class, you can use the `virtual` modifier.
volatile	When this modifier is applied to a field, the field can be modified by components other than your code. Examples might be the operating system.

When you look at encapsulation later in the section titled "Understanding Encapsulation," you start to apply some of the access modifiers to enforce encapsulation on your classes. You also explore some of the other modifiers as you look at creating and consuming classes.

Defining Fields

As discussed earlier in the section on reference types, you use fields to store the data that describes the characteristics of your classes. Fields are declared as variables within the class and can be any type including value and reference types.

Fields come in two basic types, instance and static, and a class can contain either or both. An instance field is one that you will use most often in your classes. *Instance fields* are those that are contained within each object you create from the class definition. Each instance field contains data specific to the object that it is assigned to. As an example, create a simple class file in code and then create two instances of the class file, setting different values for the fields in the class.

CODE LAB Student class depicting instance fields [student_class]

```
// create a class called Student
class Student
{
    public static int StudentCount;
    public string firstName;
    public string lastName;
    public string grade;
}

class Program
{
    static void Main(string[] args)
    {
        Student firstStudent = new Student();
```

```
    Student.StudentCount++;
    Student secondStudent = new Student();
    Student.StudentCount++;

    firstStudent.firstName = "John";
    firstStudent.lastName = "Smith";
    firstStudent.grade = "six";

    secondStudent.firstName = "Tom";
    secondStudent.lastName = "Thumb";
    secondStudent.grade = "two";

    Console.WriteLine(firstStudent.firstName);
    Console.WriteLine(secondStudent.firstName);
    Console.WriteLine(Student.StudentCount);
  }
}
```

Code Lab Analysis

This example is a simple example of creating and using a class, but it demonstrates some key points. The first portion of the code creates a simple class called Student. In this class, you create four variables. One is declared as a static variable of type int and is called StudentCount. You use this variable to keep track of how many Students you have created. Because it is static, it is a variable that is assigned to the class, not to an instance. (You see how this differs in the code later.)

Each of the remaining variables are instance variables and will be assigned values in each object (instance) of this class that you create. Again, these are just simple for the purpose of demonstration. You will get into more complex classes later when you start creating private fields, properties, and so on.

Inside your main method, you can create two instances of the Student class: one called firstStudent and one called secondStudent. You can do so by first indicating the type for the variable that you will use. In the same way that you created value types, use the type name followed by the variable name. In this case, the variable name is actually the name of an object of the class type that you create in code. The keyword new tells the compiler that you want to create a new instance of the class type Student. The new keyword is an instruction to the compiler to look at the class Student, identify the members and their data types, and then reserve enough memory to store the object and all its data requirements.

After you create each object, use the static variable in the Student class and increment it by one. This variable is only available in the class and not in the instance objects, so you must use the name of the class, Student, to access this variable.

After you have your instances created, like the structs earlier in the chapter, you can now assign values to the members. You must use the name of each instance to assign a value to the members of that instance. This is where the differentiation comes in for static and instance variables. After the assignments are done, you output values to the console window. In this case, you output only the first names of each Student instance just to show that the values actually are unique for each instance. You also output the count of Student objects using the class name as opposed to an instance name, again because StudentCount is a static class variable and not an instance variable.

Using Constructors

The previous section showed an example of creating a simple class and instantiating some objects of that class. The class was simple because it included only four data fields. Each of the data fields was assigned values after the class was instantiated in code. There is another way, and preferred by some, to assign values to the members of an object. This is through the use of a constructor.

A *constructor* is a method called whenever an object is instantiated. You can use constructors in your class files to allow you, or other programmers, to set initial values for some or all the data members in the objects you create from the class definition. In the previous code example, you didn't use a constructor because C# enables you to create your own constructor. If you don't provide a constructor of your own, C# creates a default constructor. The default constructor sets the values of each member variable to its default value. The default values were discussed earlier in the chapter.

Constructors have a specific syntax, as shown here:

```
// constructor syntax
public ClassName()
{
    optional initializing statements;
}

// constructor for the Student class
class Student
{
    public static int StudentCount;
    public string firstName;
    public string lastName;
    public string grade;

    public Student(string first, string last, string grade)
    {
        this.firstName = first;
        this.lastName = last;
        this.grade = grade;
    }

    public Student()
    {

    }
}
```

There are two constructors listed in the previous sample code. The top of the code listing shows the syntax for a constructor. Constructors use the `public` modifier because they must be accessible outside of the class. This is necessary to allow the object to be initialized when it is created. The constructor takes the same name as the class. Within the enclosing braces, the initialization statements are optional. A constructor is a method but includes no return type, not even void. To include a return type in a constructor is improper syntax and will generate a compiler warning.

In the `Student` class code, there are two constructors provided. One is a nondefault constructor that accepts three string values and uses them to initialize the member variables. The second is a default constructor that includes no statements and takes no arguments. This is the type of constructor that the compiler generates if no other constructors are created by the developer. This constructor initializes the member variables with their default values.

The compiler deals with constructors when there are multiple constructors in a class. When you create a new object from a constructor, you have the option of using any of the available constructors declared in the class, or none at all. In the previous Student class example, you can call the nondefault constructor, passing in the values for first and last names as well as the grade. If you don't provide any values, the default constructor will be called. Also, you cannot call the previous nondefault constructor with only some of the values. It's all or nothing.

> **NOTE** *Default constructors are used only when no other constructor is called or none exist.*

Defining Methods

Methods are the components in an application that enable you to break up the computing requirements of your application into smaller pieces of functionality. Good programming practice dictates that you create methods to perform discrete pieces of functionality in your code and that the method performs only that which is necessary to achieve the wanted outcome. Some argue that coding in this manner results in code that takes up more resources due to the need for the operating system to maintain instruction pointers and references for all the function calls, but it makes your code much easier to read and to maintain. If your program is generating errors, it's much easier to track down the method providing the offending functionality and debug that small piece of code.

In essence, a *method* is a construct in code that contains a name, a signature, a statement block enclosing a statement or set of statements, and an optional return statement. The syntax for a method follows:

```
// method syntax
modifier return type name(optional arguments)
{
    statements;
}
```

In the preceding syntax example, the modifier is one of the previously mentioned modifiers such as public, private, and so on. The return type can be any valid C# type (value or reference) but can also be the keyword void, which indicates the method does not return any value to the caller. The name is used to identify the method in code and is used when calling the method. The parentheses enclose optional arguments for the method. A method can have 0 or more arguments depending on the requirements of the method. Within the enclosing braces is where the functionality exists for the method in the form of statements. These statements can be any legal C# statement and can also include an optional return statement. The return statement is used only if the method declares a return type.

> **NOTE** *It is illegal to include a* `return` *statement in a method that declares the return type* `void`. *Also, a compiler warning will be generated if you omit a return statement or a method that indicates a return type other than* `void`.

Now look at some examples of methods that you might write to perform simple functionality in code. Continue to use the `Student` class example and create two simple methods in the code. One method retrieves the `Student` first and last name, concatenates them, and returns the name to the calling method. The calling method does not return a value but prints out the name to the console window.

CODE LAB   Methods in a class [student_class_with_methods]

```
class Student
{
    public static int StudentCount;
    public string firstName;
    public string lastName;
    public string grade;

    public string concatenateName()
    {
        string fullName = this.firstName + " " + this.lastName;
        return fullName;
    }

    public void displayName()
    {
        string name = concatenateName();
        Console.WriteLine(name);
    }
}

class Program
{
    static void Main(string[] args)
    {
        Student firstStudent = new Student();
        Student.StudentCount++;
        Student secondStudent = new Student();
        Student.StudentCount++;

        firstStudent.firstName = "John";
        firstStudent.lastName = "Smith";
        firstStudent.grade = "six";

        secondStudent.firstName = "Tom";
        secondStudent.lastName = "Thumb";
        secondStudent.grade = "two";

        firstStudent.displayName();
    }
}
```

Code Lab Analysis

This example demonstrates the use of methods both within the class and in the main method of the application. In the `Student` class, you added two methods. The first method is called `concatenateName()` and returns a string value. You have used the `public` modifier, listed the return type as `string`, named the method, and included a `return` statement. The method takes no parameters but simply declares a variable called `fullName` of type `string`. It then uses the string concatenation functionality in C# and combines the `firstName` variable with a space and the `lastName` variable to create the full name for the `Student`. It assigns this to the `fullName` variable and then you send it back to the calling function with the `return` statement.

The calling function for `concatenateName()` is another simple method that you created, called `displayName()`. Note that `displayName()` uses the return type `void`, which means it does not return a value and does not have a `return` statement in the statement block. It declares a string variable called `name` and uses the return value from the called method `concatenateName()` to assign to the name variable. It then writes the value to the console window.

Here is how this code functions. In the `main` method of the application, you added a new statement to the end of the method, `firstStudent.displayName();`. This statement uses the `firstStudent` object that you created in code and calls its `public` method `displayName()`. Execution shifts to this method in the object's code. The method creates a variable, and then in the assignment statement, it calls the `concatenateName()` method of the same object. Execution now passes to this method where the `fullName` variable is created and used in an assignment statement to be assigned the concatenated values of first and last name.

Because the statement `string name = concatenateName();` was responsible for calling this method, the compiler has kept track of this on the memory stack and knows where the return value needs to go. The return statement of `concatenateName()` ends that method and returns the value to the calling method where the value of the concatenated name is assigned to the `name` variable. The `displayName()` method can now output the full name to the console window.

One further aspect of methods not covered yet is the capability of the method to accept incoming values. This is possible through the use of parameters and arguments. The method signature that accepts values looks like this:

```
// method syntax for accepting values
modifier return type name (parameters)
{
   statements;
}
```

Unfortunately, the use of the terms parameters and arguments have been misused somewhat among programmers and even authors. When dealing with methods, the term *parameter* is used to identify the placeholders in the method signature, whereas the term *arguments* are the actual values that you pass in to the method. Now look at a method signature and a call to that method to put these terms in better focus:

```
// sample method signature to accept values
public int sum(int num1, int num2)
```

```
    {
        return num1 + num2;
    }

    int sumValue = sum(2, 3);
```

In the preceding example, the method `sum` is `public` and returns an integer value. But what you are interested in is how it accepts values. Within the parentheses you see `int num1, int num2`. These are correctly known as parameters to the method. You must indicate the type of data that will be expected in these parameters. This helps the compiler catch invalid assignments when the method is called. The names `num1` and `num2` are the actual parameters.

The last line in the sample code calls the `sum` method and passes in two values. These two values are correctly called the arguments of the method call. You can see now where confusion can come from and why these two terms are used interchangeably at times. To keep it straight, think of the parameters as the placeholders in the method signature, and the arguments as the values that are passed in to these placeholders.

The preceding example is also simple and passes in only value types. Methods support the ability to pass objects as well. An important distinction, however, is when passing value types, a copy of the value is passed to the method, but when passing reference types, a reference (memory address) to that type is passed and not the entire object. Remember, that could take up considerable memory if you passed an entire object to a method.

This brings up a unique characteristic of method calls and how they act on the arguments that are passed in. When using value types, the method acts only on a local copy of the variable and doesn't change the original value. When acting on a reference type being passed in, it does affect the original value. Another code example can demonstrate this.

CODE LAB   **Passing value types to methods [value_type_passing]**

```
class Student
    {
        public string firstName;
        public string lastName;
        public string grade;
    }

    class Program
    {
        static void Main(string[] args)
        {
            int num1 = 2;
            int num2 = 3;
            int result;

            Student firstStudent = new Student();

            firstStudent.firstName = "John";
            firstStudent.lastName = "Smith";
            firstStudent.grade = "six";
```

```csharp
        result = sum(num1, num2);
        Console.Write("Sum is: ");
        Console.WriteLine(result);   // outputs 5
        Console.WriteLine();

        changeValues(num1, num2);
        Console.WriteLine();
        Console.WriteLine("Back from changeValues()");
        Console.WriteLine(num1);   // outputs 2
        Console.WriteLine(num2);   // outputs 3

        Console.WriteLine();
        Console.WriteLine("First name for firstStudent is " +
          firstStudent.firstName);
        changeName(firstStudent);
        Console.WriteLine();
        Console.WriteLine("First name for firstStudent is " +
          firstStudent.firstName);

    }

    static int sum(int value1, int value2)
    {
        Console.WriteLine("In method sum()");
        return value1 + value2;
    }

    static void changeValues(int value1, int value2)
    {
        Console.WriteLine("In changeValues()");
        Console.WriteLine("value1 is " + value1);   // outputs 2
        Console.WriteLine("value2 is " + value2);   // outputs 3
        Console.WriteLine();
        Console.WriteLine("Changing values");

        value1--;
        value2 += 5;

        Console.WriteLine();
        Console.WriteLine("value1 is now " + value1);   // outputs 1
        Console.WriteLine("value2 is now " + value2);   // outputs 8
    }

    static void changeName(Student refValue)
    {
        Console.WriteLine();
        Console.WriteLine("In changeName()");
        refValue.firstName = "George";
    }
}
```

Code Lab Analysis

There is a lot going on here. The Student class is simplified for this example, and you have only three member fields. In the main method of the program, you declare four variables, three of type int and one of type Student. You assign values to num1, num2, and the members of the Student object called first-Student. The variable result will get assigned later in the code.

The first method you call is the sum method. You pass in num1 and num2 as arguments to the method. Inside sum(), write out a message to indicate that you are inside this method. This helps you keep track of where you are. Next, add the two values and return the result back to the caller where it is assigned to the variable result. Then output that to the window to show that the sum() method did indeed add the two values.

Next, show an example of how method calling with value types uses copies of the values. Call the changeValues() method passing in num1 and num2 again. Inside the method output the fact that you are inside changeValues() and you output the numeric values of the two parameters value1 and value2. This is to show that you indeed did pass in the same values for num1 and num2. Then indicate that you will change these values and decrement value1 by 1 and increment value2 by 5. Before leaving changeValues(), output the new values for value1 and value2. The method then ends.

Back in main, output the values for num1 and num2 again to show that these variables have not been changed by the changeValues() method. Only the local copies were changed, not the original values. This is how value types work in method calls.

To show how reference types are affected in method calls, now output the first name of the firstStudent object you created to show that its value is Fred, the value assigned to it early in the code. Then call another method called changeName(), which takes a reference variable of type Student, and pass firstStudent as the reference type to this method. Inside this method, change the first name of firstStudent to George. After returning from the method, output the first name of firstStudent and notice that it has indeed changed. This clearly shows that passing a reference variable to a method results in changing the original value—quite different from passing value types. Figure 3-2 shows the output from the previous code.

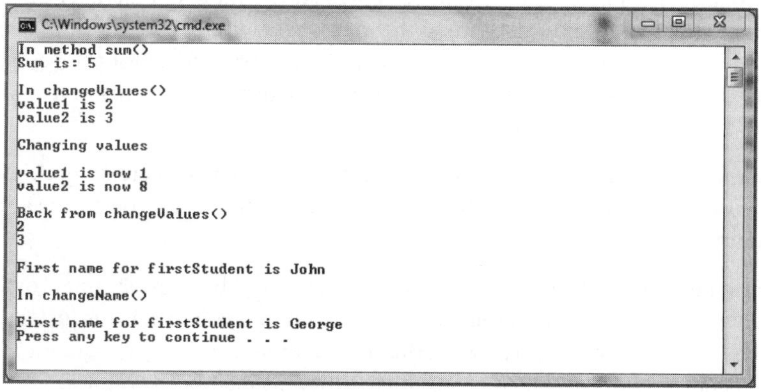

```
C:\Windows\system32\cmd.exe
In method sum()
Sum is: 5

In changeValues()
value1 is 2
value2 is 3

Changing values

value1 is now 1
value2 is now 8

Back from changeValues()
2
3

First name for firstStudent is John

In changeName()

First name for firstStudent is George
Press any key to continue . . .
```

FIGURE 3-2: Output of value_type_passing

Overloaded Methods

Methods are defined by the modifier, return type, name, and number and type of arguments. But a method also has a signature. The signature is what uniquely identifies the method from any other method with the same name. When you call a method in your code, the compiler looks for a method with the correct signature. The signature actually consists of the method name plus the data type and kind of the parameters in the method. You already know what the data types represent, but the kind or parameter in a method may be a value type, a reference type, or an output parameter. The return type is not a unique component of a method signature.

You might ask why you would want to create more than one method with the same name in your code. Wouldn't that surely introduce complications and make your code hard to read? To answer that question, consider that you might need to have a method name the same based on the action you want to take, but which performs its internal functionality differently depending on the data sent to method. Think about some simple mathematics as an example. You can calculate the area of various geometric shapes with each having a specific formula. Following are two sample methods to calculate the area of a circle and a rectangle:

```
// calculate the area of a circle
public double calcArea(double radius)
{
    double area = Math.Pi * (r*r);
    return area;
}

// calculate the area of a rectangle
public double calcArea(double length, double width)
{
    double area = length * width;
    return area;
}
```

Here you have two methods with the same name `calcArea`. The name explains the purpose of the method, to calculate the area. The difference between the two methods is in the signature. In the first, you set up the method to accept a single `double` type to represent the radius of a circle. The method then performs the correct calculation to determine the area of the circle whose radius is passed in. The second method is also called `calcArea()` but accepts two arguments for the `length` and `width` of a rectangle and performs the appropriate calculation to determine the area of a rectangle.

This is an example of *overloaded methods*. Overloading essentially means that you create multiple methods with the same name but with each having a different signature, intended to perform some action specific to the functionality wanted.

Another common use of overloaded methods is in constructors for classes. The overloading provides you the opportunity to initialize member variables selectively. Remember, a constructor is just a method without a return type. As a way of reinforcing overloaded methods, create the `Student` class again, this time with multiple constructors designed to initialize different member variables.

Overloading constructors

Oftentimes when working with classes in a program, you will need to provide multiple ways to initialize the class. The rationale is that at creation time in a program, you want to provide some flexibility to the users of the program and only require known information. An example would be completing a form in an application to establish new students in a system. At the time, the instructor may not know the student's class or the student will not necessarily have a grade. Overloading the constructor is the preferred mechanism to provide this functionality.

Start Visual Studio and create a C# console-based application. Create the `Student` class with the following member variables:

➤ `firstName` of type `string`

➤ `lastName` of type `string`

➤ `Grade` of type `int`

➤ `schoolName` of type `string`

In the `Student` class, create three constructors that will be overloaded. Create a default constructor that takes no arguments and doesn't initialize any member variables. Create a second constructor that accepts values for the `Students`' first and last names. Assign these to the member variables in the constructor. Use the last constructor to accept values for all the member variables and assign them in the constructor.

After you have the class created, using the main method in your console application, create three new `Student` objects. Call a different constructor on each `Student` object, watching the IntelliSense in Visual Studio to see how the different constructors are listed there. Provide the necessary values for each `Student` object to set the member values using the constructors.

Solution

Here is the solution:

```
class Student
{
    public string firstName;
    public string lastName;
    public int grade;
    public string schoolName;

    public Student()
    {
    }

    public Student(string first, string last)
    {
        this.firstName = first;
        this.lastName = last;
    }

    public Student(string first, string last, int grade, string school)
```

```
        {
            this.firstName = first;
            this.lastName = last;
            this.grade = grade;
            this.schoolName = school;
        }

    }

    class Program
    {
        static void Main(string[] args)
        {
            Student Student1 = new Student();

            Student Student2 = new Student("Tom", "Jones");

            Student Student3 = new Student("Mike", "Myers", 5, "My School");

        }
    }
```

As you can see from the preceding code, method overloading enables you to achieve some specific functionality in the constructors of your class. The constructor has three different versions. Each version is differentiated by the number of parameters in the constructor. This provides a fair bit of flexibility in how you create out objects in code by allowing you to assign values at the time you create an object, or defer the assignments until later.

Abstract and Overridden Methods

So far, you have taken a look at simple methods and at overloaded methods discussing the rationale for each and how to use them. Another key aspect in OOP is the use of abstract and overridden methods. First, take a look at abstract methods; then review overriding methods. The two are almost related.

If you look up the definition of abstract, you can find something such as, "not relating to concrete objects but expressing something that [can] be appreciated [only] intellectually." Bing.com's online dictionary gives you one more definition that is closer to what you will see when dealing with *abstract methods* in programming: "nonrepresentational: aiming not to depict an object but composed with the focus on internal structure and form."

In OOP concepts, an abstract method is one that declares a method signature but no implementation. It is also known as a *virtual method*, which means it isn't considered a real method because it has no implementation. So, how does it become useful if there is no implementation? Quite simply, it means that derived classes must implement the functionality in their code. This is also where overridden methods come into the picture. A derived class must override abstract classes through the implementation.

```
    // an abstract method inside a class
    public abstract class Student
    {
```

```
        public abstract void outputDetails();
    }
```

As you can see from this simple example, the method is declared with the `abstract` keyword and ends with a semicolon. It contains no implementation details. In other words, developers who derive a class from this `Student` base class must provide their own implementation of how to output the details for the `Student` objects they create.

> **WARNING** You cannot include an abstract method declaration in a nonabstract class.

You won't get to class inheritance until Chapter 5, but to understand abstract and overridden methods, you need to see an example here showing an abstract base class along with a derived class including the overridden method. The following code sample uses the same abstract `Student` class and method done previously, but shows the use of a derived class overriding the abstract method:

```
// an abstract method inside a class
public abstract class Student
{
    public abstract void outputDetails();
}

public class CollegeStudent: Student
{
    public string firstName;
    public string lastName;
    public string major;
    public double GPA;

    public override void outputDetails()
    {
        Console.WriteLine("Student " + firstName + " " + lastName +
            " enrolled in " + major + " is has a GPA of " + GPA);
    }
}
```

Again, keep in mind that these examples are kept simple to demonstrate the concepts without adding too much complexity around the actual implementations. In this example, the `Student` class becomes an abstract class that serves as the base class for other `Student` type classes. In this case, you create a new class to represent a college `Student`. The college `Student` class declaration names the class and follows it with : `Student`, which indicates that the `CollegeStudent` class inherits from the `Student` class. (Again, this is covered in Chapter 5 in more detail for inheritance.)

Inherited classes take on the characteristics of their base classes, but in this instance, you provided only an abstract method in the base class. This means that `collegeStudent` must implement that functionality by overriding this abstract method. The method simply concatenates the member variables into an output string to the console. Again, this isn't complex, but it does serve to illustrate the point of abstract methods. By creating an abstract class with abstract methods, you can enforce a specific structure on classes that are derived from the abstract base class but leave the implementation details to each derived class. That means that each derived class is free to implement this `outputDetails()` method in the way that makes the most sense for that class.

> **WARNING** *You cannot create an instance of an abstract class. If you attempt to do so, Visual Studio generates an error and your code does not compile. Abstract classes are meant to be base classes only.*

Extension Methods

Extension methods provide you the opportunity to extend an existing class or type by adding a new method or methods without modifying the original class or type and without recompiling that class or type. The reason you might want to do this is to add functionality to an existing type without extending the entire class or type. Prior to .NET 3.5 this was the only way to add functionality to existing types.

Extension methods can be applied to your own types or even existing types in .NET. An example might be adding some functionality to the `Math` class that .NET already includes. Yes, the existing `Math` class already provides quite a bit of functionality, but it doesn't cover all the mathematical functions or procedures you might want in your application. There is no need to create a new `Math` class, nor is there a need to inherit from the existing `Math` class just to add the functionality you want. You can use extension methods. In this section, you won't add extension methods to the `Math` class but rather extend the .NET `int` type to include a method for squaring numbers.

If your programmer wheels are churning around this, you might be thinking that you can just create your own lightweight class that has the methods you need and call those in your code. You might say that there is actually no need to create extension methods as a result because your own class can do what you need. And that would be correct as well, and you can certainly not even bother with extension methods if you don't want. However, .NET uses extension methods for the LINQ standard query operators to add functionality to existing types such as `IEnumerable`. This doesn't mean you need to use them, but understanding them can go a long way to helping you work with LINQ in your C# code as well—not to mention that the exam also covers them.

So, exactly how do you create extension methods? First, you need to include the extension method in a `public static` class, so first you must create that class. After the class is created, you define the method inside that class and make the method an extension method with the simple addition of the keyword `this`. Remember the keyword `this` refers to the specific instance of the class in which it appears. The following code example demonstrates how you might create an extension method to the .NET `int` type:

```
public static class MyExtendedMethods
    {
        public static int square(this int num)
        {
            int result = 0;
            result = num * num;
            return result;
        }
    }
```

The method must also be `static`. If you don't declare it as `static`, it does not display in the code IntelliSense window and is not available for you to call. Figure 3-3 shows an example of not declaring the method static, whereas Figure 3-4 shows the correctly implemented method and the IntelliSense result.

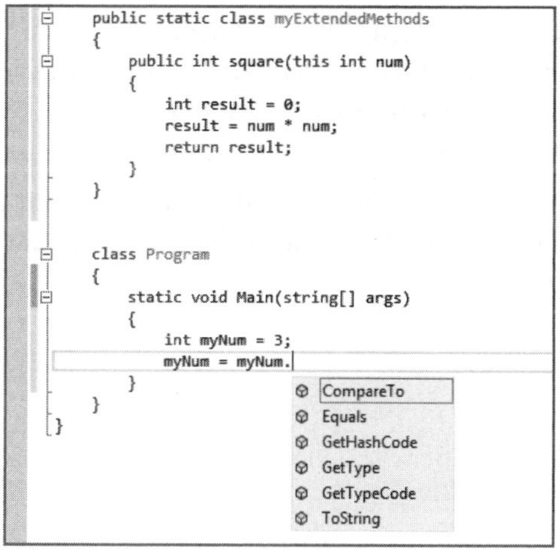

FIGURE 3-3: Built-in methods

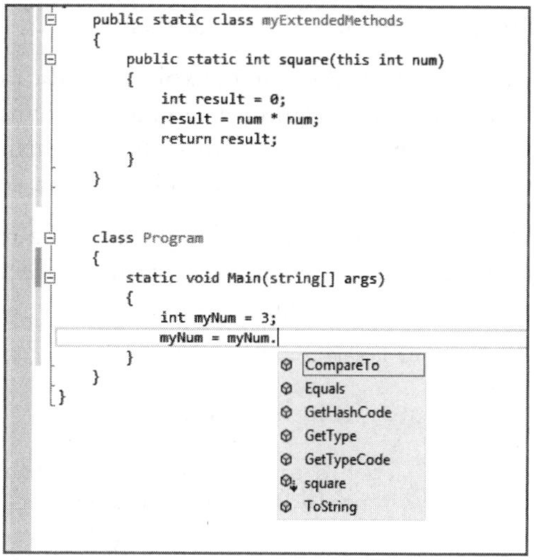

FIGURE 3-4: Extension method added

Note that absence of the `static` keyword and the `square` method in Figure 3-3. Figure 3-4 shows that the `static` keyword has been added to the method. And in the `Main` method call, you can now see the method `square` added to the IntelliSense window indicating that you have indeed extended the `int` type to include a method for squaring integers.

> **ADVICE FROM THE EXPERTS: Naming Extension Methods**
>
> If you create an extension method for a type, but that type already has a method with the same name as your extension method, the compiler will use only the type's method and not your extension method. Name your extension methods carefully.

> **WARNING** Creating extension methods on the type `Object` results in the extension method being available for every type in the framework. Your implementation must be carefully thought out and allow for correct operation on the different types it might be applied to.

Optional and Named Parameters

Typically, when calling a method that contains multiple parameters, you must pass in the arguments to the parameters in the order in which the parameters exist. The parameters are known as positional. IntelliSense aids greatly in this effort and enables you to see the method signature from the perspective of the parameters and the order. However, not all programmers use Visual Studio for their coding so IntelliSense may not be an option for them.

Named arguments enable you to explicitly indicate which parameter the argument is intended to be used for. Named arguments go hand-in-hand with named parameters. In other words, the parameter must be named first; then the argument you pass in can use that parameter name. But wait, your parameters are all named regardless, so one-half of the solution is already present.

As an example, consider calculating the area of a rectangle. The method includes parameters for the length and width of the rectangle. It performs the area calculation and returns the result. The call to the method uses named arguments.

```
class Program
{
    static void Main(string[] args)
    {
        double area = rectArea(length: 35.0, width: 25.5);
        Console.WriteLine(area);
    }

    public static double rectArea(double length, double width)
    {
        return length * width;
    }
}
```

In the call to the `rectArea()` method, you can pass in the two arguments required, but use the named arguments `length:` and `width:`. Failure to add the colon at the end of the argument name results in a compiler warning. The warning is not intuitive, unfortunately, and merely indicates the requirement for a closing parenthesis. This is simply because the compiler isn't quite sure what your intentions are for the label without the colon.

Another key advantage to using named arguments is in the readability of your code. Looking at the code sample, you can tell precisely which value is the length and which is the width of the rectangle you want to calculate the area of. This is also a quick-and-dirty form of debugging because it helps you to ensure you pass in the proper values. Bugs that result from these types of errors are known as logic errors and are often difficult to debug.

> **WARNING** Named arguments can follow positional arguments, but positional arguments cannot follow named arguments.

Optional parameters are a feature of methods that enables you to require only some arguments be passed in to a method while making others optional. Calling a method with optional parameters means that the caller must provide required parameters but can omit the optional parameters. Required parameters are those that are not declared optional.

Optional parameters are permitted in methods, constructors, indexers, and delegates. Each optional parameter also includes a default value to be used in the event a value is not provided in a call to that method. Default values can be

➤ A constant expression

➤ Value types including creating new types with the new keyword

Optional parameters are placed at the end of the parameter list in the method signature. All required parameters must be listed first in the method signature. Also, if you provide a value for an optional parameter, any optional parameters that precede this optional parameter must also be provided with a value.

```
// sample method with optional parameters
public void displayName(string first, string initial = "", string last = "")
{
    Console.WriteLine(first + " " + initial + " " + last);
}
```

In this simple example, you can create a method that outputs a name to the console window. It uses two optional parameters for the middle initial and last name. They are optional parameters because of the default values assigned to them. These default values are an empty string because you don't want to output arbitrary characters or strings if the caller chooses not to supply values for these. In this example, the caller must provide a value for the first parameter but can exclude the initial and last. However, if the caller provides a value for last, it must also provide a value for the initial. If a value for the initial is passed, a value for the last name is still optional, however.

> **WARNING** *Required parameters cannot exist after an optional parameter in a method signature.*

UNDERSTANDING ENCAPSULATION

In OOP, the term *encapsulation* is used to describe the concept of packaging the properties, methods, and any other members into a package called the class. But it does more than just package these components. Encapsulation is also used to refer to the "hiding" of the implementation details of the class functionality and also the protection of the class characteristics.

To get a better understanding of this, consider your MP3 player. When you look at the device, you see certain external characteristics such as the color, shape, size and so on. But there are other characteristics internally such as the amount and type of storage used along with the functionality such as playlists, play, pause, stop, shuffle, and such. You have no idea how the device functions internally, and you don't need to know that to use the MP3 player. You are provided a specific set of controls to operate the device. These controls are essentially the interface for interacting with the device.

Now take this to the class concept. If you create a class for a digital music player, you create certain characteristics for your software player in the form of member variables. You also provide some functionality in the class to open song files, display song information, shuffle the song lists, create playlists, play the song, pause, stop, add, delete, and more. This class defines your software version of a music player, and it might be a class that you want other developers to use in their code.

To ensure that the music player class can be used by other developers with minimal effort, and to ensure that the other developers do not get bogged down in the details of how your various methods work, you use encapsulation. The methods of your class merely expose the method signature for the class methods. As you know, the signature includes the method name, any return type, and required or optional parameters. Use of the class methods is limited to calling the method and accepting any return value back. The implementation details of how the play method works are not important to someone using the class. They need to provide only the arguments to the play method, which would likely be a song filename. Internally, the play method would have functionality to locate the song file provided, open a handle to that file, start playing the song, and perhaps call other methods to display the song details. The caller of this method could care less about how the method does these tasks; they simply want the song to play.

The "hiding" aspect of encapsulation comes into being when you explore the use of properties in a class. Your classes contain member variables to store the class characteristics. As mentioned earlier in the chapter, you can set access modifiers on these variables. So far, you have used the public access modifier to make all the member variables available outside the class. This was for ease of use. However, this style of class programming leads to a situation that can result in your application becoming unsafe or crashing more than you had hoped.

The reason for these mentioned issues is due to the way developers might use your classes. Allowing a member variable to be modified directly means that you have little to no control over validation of the value assigned to that member variable. This means that you might inadvertently assign a string value to a variable intended to hold only a numeric value. The compiler catches this at compile-time—maybe—and if not, it can result in your application crashing at run time, in a nongraceful manner. Another more serious consideration is in the form of hacking attempts such as SQL injection attacks where hackers take advantage of nonsecure code such as this to include characters in a SQL query string that you didn't anticipate.

The way to avoid these issues is to make your member variables private and expose them only through properties. The next section introduces you to properties, what they are, and how to use them in your classes.

Properties

Properties are public methods that you use for access to the private member variables. Making the member variables private means they cannot be accessed directly from outside of the class. So how do you access the values or set the values of these variables if they are private? You can do so through the use of the properties. Remember that public access means that the methods can be accessed outside of the class. Also, because the properties are members of the class, they have access to the private members of the class.

Properties can be modified by using access modifiers as well. You can assign the `public`, `private`, `protected`, `internal`, or `protected internal` access modifiers to a property. Properties can also be declared with the `static` keyword, which means that they can be called on the class without having to instantiate a new object.

Just like methods in a base class, you can also choose to make a property virtual, which enables derived classes to override the behavior code in the property to better suit the needs of the derived class. You may also use the `abstract` keyword when declaring a property, and it acts just like an abstract method, which requires an implementation in the derived class.

Even though properties can be considered as components of a class that represent object characteristics, they are not the characteristics by themselves. Properties rely on two key methods to access and modify the member variables. The first method is known as the `get` method. `get` is used to access the member variable the property represents. The second method is called `set`. As you might expect, this method is used to modify (set) the data of a member variable it represents. The syntax of a property for a class follows:

```
// sample propety syntax
class Student
{
    private firstName;

    public string FirstName
    {
        get {return firstName;}

        set { firstName = value;}
    }
}
```

Note the specific characteristics of the property syntax. First, in the class you declare the `firstName` property as `private`. The property follows including a return type and uses a name identical to the member variable except that it starts with an uppercase letter. This is not a strict syntax requirement, but is more of a recommended form of coding. The name should be as close as possible to the name of the member variable that it is intended to modify for code readability. Some developers prefer to also include the word `Property` in the name but this also is not a requirement.

Inside the property you see two methods called `get` and `set`. As you might expect, the `get` method returns the value from the corresponding member variable, and `set` is responsible for modifying the associated member variable. The `set` method uses a parameter called `value`. This is a component of the property method `set` and contains the value passed in to the method call.

You can create read-only properties and write-only properties by simply omitting either the `get` or `set`, respectively, in your property code. A write-only property is rare; however, and the most common are either read/write or read-only.

The two property methods enable you to control the values assigned or returned from your class. In this way, you can validate the data passed in to a property before assignment, and you can transform values being read prior to passing them to the caller, if necessary. The following section discusses how to enforce encapsulation through the use of properties.

Enforced Encapsulation by Using Properties

As stated earlier, encapsulation in OOP involves hiding data and implementation. Now see an example of this as you modify your `Student` class to take advantage of encapsulation through properties.

You create a `Student` class that contains numerous member variables but declare them as `private`. You permit access to them only through properties. Start Visual Studio and create a new console-based application, or use an existing `Student` class example if you have created one from earlier in this chapter. Add the following code to your application to create the `Student` class.

CODE LAB   Using properties [using_properties]

```
public class Student
{
    private string firstName;
    private char middleInitial;
    private string lastName;
    private int age;
    private string program;
    private double gpa;

    public Student(string first, string last)
    {
        this.firstName = first;
this.lastName = last;
    }

    public string FirstName
    {
        get { return firstName; }
        set { firstName = value; }
    }

    public string LastName
    {
        get { return lastName; }
        set { lastName = value; }
    }

    public char MiddleInitial
    {
        get { return middleInitial; }
        set { middleInitial = value; }
    }

    public int Age
    {
        get { return age; }
        set
        {
            if (value > 6)
            {
                age = value;
            }
            else
            {
                Console.WriteLine("Student age must be greater than 6");
```

```
                    }
                }
            }

        public string Program
        {
            get { return program; }
            set { program = value; }
        }

        public double GPA
        {
            get { return gpa; }
            set
            {
                if (value <= 4.0)
                {
                    gpa = value;
                }
                else
                {
                    Console.WriteLine("GPA cannot be greater than 4.0");
                }
            }
        }
    public void displayDetails()
        {
    Console.WriteLine(this.FirstName + " " + this.MiddleInitial + " " + this.LastName);
            Console.WriteLine("Has a GPA of " + this.GPA);
        }
    }
```

Code Lab Analysis

In this class, you declared a number of private data members. These are no longer accessible outside of this class unless the caller goes through the properties or the constructor. That's right; if you look at the code for the Student class, you can notice that the constructor can still directly access the private member variables. The constructor is part of the class, so it has access to the private members. Note that the constructor makes use of the keyword this to ensure that the values are applied to the instance variables of the instantiated class.

After the constructor, you start to create some properties for this class—one property for each private member variable. This is how your code can now access the member variables. Unlike standard methods, properties do not enclose parameters in parentheses. That is because you accept only one value for the property or return only one value. The parameter for a property is known as the value, as shown in the set portions of these properties.

You could have included substantially more code in each property for validation, such as including a check for length of values passed in to the name properties or ensuring the middle initial is only a single character. To keep the code simple while you gain an understanding of working with properties, you include only validation logic for the age and GPA values. But this is an example of how properties enable you to validate data prior to assigning it to a member variable.

The final piece of code in the Student class is a method called displayDetails(). In this method simply concatenate the name components and then include a text message about the Student's GPA. When code calls this method, it has no idea how the details are assembled to be output to the console window. In this way, you can change the implementation of this method at any time you want, as long as you don't change the signature, and callers of this method still function correctly and the details are still output.

Now, use the Student class in your program to see how the properties have now become the interface for the member variables. Before you enter the code to use the Student class, take note of the IntelliSense displayed in Figure 3-5, which shows the property names and not those of the member variables. This is due to the access modifiers used on the member variables making them private. The properties are public.

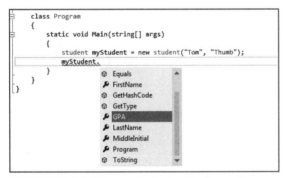

FIGURE 3-5: IntelliSense displaying the properties

Enter the following code in your application to make use of the Student class you created and access the properties by assigning values to them. After you have the code entered and working, change the values of the age and GPA to values outside the range and see the behavior.

CODE LAB   Accessing properties [accessing_properties]

```
class Program
{
    static void Main(string[] args)
    {
        Student myStudent = new Student("Tom", "Thumb");
        myStudent.MiddleInitial = 'R';
        myStudent.Age = 15;
        myStudent.GPA = 3.5;
        myStudent.displayDetails();
    }
}
```

Code Lab Analysis

In this sample code for using the `Student` class, you rely on the constructor to set the first and last names. Then you call on the properties to set the `middle initial`, `age`, and `GPA` values. Then you output the values to the console window to validate that they did indeed get set correctly.

Indexed Properties

Indexed properties, or *indexers*, behave a little differently from standard properties. The primary purpose of indexed properties is to allow "array-like access to groups of items," according to MSDN documentation. In other words, if you have classes that make use of arrays or other collection types, you should consider using indexers for accessing the values of these internal collections. The standard properties discussed so far are used to access single values in classes, whereas an indexed property will be used to encapsulate a set of values.

To demonstrate indexed properties, you need a simple example that illustrates the use of these types of properties in a class. One example might be for an application that deals with network addresses in an IP subnetting scenario. If you aren't familiar with TCP/IP v4 addressing, a brief explanation follows. For those who understand it, feel free to skip this portion.

IP addresses in version 4 of TCP/IP are 32-bit addresses. The bits can be set to either a 0 or a 1, giving you a total of 2 raised to the power of 32, which is the number of addresses available for use. You might want to create a class that contains an array of 32 values to store these addresses. Each array could represent a specific IP address by setting the array elements to either a 1 or a 0 and then used to represent an IP address. Now create an address class and create an indexed property inside the class to store the array of bits that will be used for the IP address.

```
public class IPAddress
{
    private int[] ip;

    public int this[int index]
    {
        get
        {
            return ip[index];
        }
        set
        {
            if (value == 0 || value == 1)
                ip[index] = value;
            else
                throw new Exception("Invalid value");
        }
    }
}

class Program
```

```
    {
        static void Main(string[] args)
        {
            IPAddress myIP = new IPAddress();

            // initialize the IP address to all zeros
            for (int i = 0; i < 32; i++)
            {
                myIP[i] = 0;
            }

        }
    }
```

Again, you created simple code samples to focus on the core principles. This class contains only one property, which is an indexed property to store the 32 bits of an IP address. The key differentiator that makes this an indexed property is the use of the keyword `this` in the property. Notice also that the property appears to accept a parameter, but in reality it is accepting an index for the `value` parameter.

Place this code into a C# console application and execute it as-is to populate the `int` array property in `IPAddress` with all zeros. To try out the code sample even further, add your own code to update the values of arbitrary index values and inspect the array through debugging to see how the values have been applied.

Here are some key points to keep in mind for indexed properties:

➤ They accept an index value in place of the standard property value parameter.

➤ They are identified through the use of the keyword `this`.

➤ Indexed properties can be created in classes or structs.

➤ Only one indexed property can exist in a single class or struct.

➤ They can contain get and set methods just like other properties.

UNDERSTANDING GENERIC TYPES AND GENERIC METHODS

Generics didn't always exist in C#; they were added only in version 2.0 of the C# language. The benefit of using generics is that you can now design your classes and the methods in those classes without specifying the types until declaration and instantiation. The advantage to doing so is a reduction in type casting or boxing and unboxing at run time. Generics work for both value types and reference types. Other advantages of generics can be found in code reuse, type safety, and efficiency.

Consider using different collection types in your code that act on objects. For example, consider the `Queue` class. You can store objects in the queue class using the `Enqueue()` method and remove them using the `Dequeue()` method. However, what happens if your queue is used to store items of different types such as `int` or `char`? Because the .NET `Queue` object is designed to hold reference types, you need to use boxing and unboxing for value types. If you are storing objects in the queue, you need to use explicit casts for those reference types when dequeuing. This can result in error-prone code.

Instead of dealing with the performance hit of converting types, you can use generic classes with a generic parameter that accepts a class type at run time. This also saves the need to create multiple classes that implement the same functionality for each type you need to support.

Defining Generic Types

Defining generic types is done through the use a generic type parameter enclosed in angle brackets, `<T>`. `T` is just the standard representation for generic types that is used in most documentation concerning generics. You can use the letter of your own choosing. An example of a generic `Queue` class follows:

```
// example of a generic style Queue
public class GenericQueue<T>
{
    public void Enqueue(T obj);
    public T DeQueue();
}
```

Although a class is demonstrated here called `GenericQueue<T>` to differentiate a queue from the .NET `Queue` class, you should look at the `System.Collection.Generic` namespace to determine if the .NET Framework already contains a generic class. Always reuse existing code where possible.

Your generic types act just like other reference types and can include constructors, member variables, and methods. The methods, including the constructor, can include type parameters as well.

Using Generic Types

Creating the `GenericQueue` class allows you to pass in the type of object that this class can store in the queue when you instantiate the object. An example of instantiating a `GenericQueue` object to store `Student` objects follows:

```
// generic queue that will be used to store Student objects
GenericQueue<Student> StudentQueue = new GenericQueue<Student>();

Student myStudent = new Student("Tom", "Thumb");

// store the myStudent object in the StudentQueue
StudentQueue.Enqueue(myStudent);

// retrieve the myStudent object from the StudentQueue
StudentQueue.Dequeue();
```

By using generics, this queue class can add and remove `Student` objects in the queue without the need for explicit casting because the reference type is specified during the instantiation.

Defining Generic Methods

Much as you might expect, generic methods will be declared with type parameters as well. This means that like the class signature, the method signature will use a placeholder for the type that will be passed in to the method. In the same way that generic classes are type-safe and don't require boxing/unboxing or explicit casts, generic methods also share this same characteristic. One of the simplest examples that exists on MSDN and in various other documentation samples is using a swap method. Swapping is a commonly used function in simple sorting algorithms. An example of a generic swap method follows:

```
// example of generic method with type parameters
public void Swap<T>(ref T valueOne, ref T valueTwo)
{
    T temp = valueOne;
    valueOne = valueTwo;
    valueTwo = temp;
}
```

Now take a moment to dissect this method to understand how it is designed. In the signature of the method, you still use access modifiers and return types. In this case, make this method public and set the return type as void. Then name the function as Swap, and similar to the generic class, use the angle brackets and a type placeholder <T>.

Here is where the generic method differs slightly from the nongeneric version. The parameters use the keyword ref and the type placeholder. The ref keyword means that the arguments passed in will be passed by reference. The method acts on the actual values passed in through the reference to the memory address for the arguments. The T placeholder means that the arguments will be of type T, based on the type used at the time the method is called. This can be value types or reference types.

Also notice that the local variable in the swap method called temp is also declared with type T. Thinking about this, it makes perfect sense because you need to use the same types during the swap process, and temp is just a local variable that can be used to temporarily store one value before assigning it to the second variable.

Using Generic Methods

When using generic methods, you simply pass the correct type into the method call, replacing the T parameter with the type you use for the swap. For this example, assume you have an array of values and want to call the swap method to help with sorting the array. The array can be of almost any type, but ideally if you are sorting, you would want it to be of types that can actually have a sorting value. The example here is designed to sort integer values:

```
class Program
{
    static void Main(string[] args)
    {
        int[] arrInts = new int[] {2, 5, 4, 7, 6, 7, 1, 3, 9, 8};
        char[] arrChar = new char[] { 'f', 'a', 'r', 'c', 'h' };

        // Sorting: integer Sort
        for (int i = 0; i < arrInts.Length; i++)
        {
            for (int j = i + 1; j < arrInts.Length; j++)
            {
                if (arrInts[i] > arrInts[j])
                {
                    swap<int>(ref arrInts[i], ref arrInts[j]);
```

```
                    }
                }
            }

            // Sorting: character Sort
            for (int i = 0; i < arrChar.Length; i++)
            {
                for (int j = i + 1; j < arrChar.Length; j++)
                {
                    if (arrChar[i] > arrChar[j])
                    {
                        swap<char>(ref arrChar[i], ref arrChar[j]);
                    }
                }
            }
        }

        static void swap<T>(ref T valueOne, ref T valueTwo)
        {
            T temp = valueOne;
            valueOne = valueTwo;
            valueTwo = temp;
        }
    }
```

You could certainly have written the swap functionality within the nested for loop because the swap is relatively simple. However, in this instance you want to demonstrate how you can use a type-safe, generic method that will accept any type of object where you can compare for greater or less than.

The first array consists of integers and the bubble sort works fine when you call the swap method and pass it in the int type. The second array consists of characters of the type char. When you call the swap method this time, pass in the char type as the type that will be acted on.

Okay, so you cheated a little bit because ultimately char values are compared using their numeric codes, which enable you to determine which character comes before another. But again, without complicating the concepts, it demonstrates how you can use generic methods with different types.

SUMMARY

The type system in C# is the foundation for the data that your application will work with. At the basic level are the value types providing the data structures for supporting basic data types for numeric and character data. To model real-world objects, the .NET platform provides object-oriented programming support in the form of classes.

Value types are the simplest to work with and can be used to store simple data or complex data through the use of structs and enumerations. Structs are similar to lightweight class files, whereas enumerations make code more readable through the use of named constants for related data.

Through the OOP principle of encapsulation, you can create class files that hide the details of the implementation for the methods that make up the class. Encapsulation means that a class can act similar to a black box. In other words, a public accessible interface exposes only the signatures of the methods with required and optional parameters while not exposing the details of how the class or methods perform their functions. This makes class files easier to use because the coding of objects based on these classes do not get written around the class implementation details.

With the inclusion of generics in C#, the platform supports the creation of classes with operations not specific to any particular data type. Generics include more than just classes because they also extend to interfaces, methods, and delegates. Generics provide the developer with the convenience creating type-safe classes and methods resulting in less error-prone code, but also in better performing code by taking away the need to do conversion on data types through boxing and boxing of value types.

CHAPTER TEST QUESTIONS

Read each question carefully and select the answer or answers that represent the best solution to the problem. You can find the answers in Appendix A, "Answers to Chapter Test Questions."

1. What is the maximum value you can store in an `int` data type?

   a. Positive infinity

   b. 32,167

   c. 65,536

   d. 4,294,967,296

2. True or false: `double` and `float` data types can store values with decimals.

3. Which declaration can assign the default value to an `int` type?

   a. `new int();`

   b. `int myInt = new int();`

   c. `int myInt;`

   d. `int myInt = new int(default);`

4. True or false: structs can contain methods.

5. What is the correct way to access the `firstName` property of a struct named `Student`?

   a. `string name = Student.firstName;`

   b. `string name = Student.firstName();`

   c. `string name = Student(firstName);`

   d. `string name = Student.(firstName);`

6. In the following enumeration, what will be the underlying value of Wed?

   `enum Days {Mon = 1, Tue, Wed, Thur, Fri, Sat, Sun};`

   a. 2

   b. 3

    c.   4

    d.   It has no numeric value.

7.   What are two methods with the same name but with different parameters?

    a.   Overloading

    b.   Overriding

    c.   Duplexing

    d.   Duplicate

8.   What is the parameter in this method known as?

```
public void displayAbsoluteValue(int value = 1)
```

    a.   Modified

    b.   Optional

    c.   Named

    d.   Default

9.   When you create an abstract method, how do you use that method in a derived class?

    a.   You must overload the method in your derived class.

    b.   You must override the method in your derived class.

    c.   Abstract methods cannot be used in derived classes.

    d.   You need to declare the method as virtual in your derived class.

10.   How do you enforce encapsulation on the data members of your class?

    a.   Create private data members.

    b.   Create private methods.

    c.   Use public properties.

    d.   Use private properties.

    e.   Use the protected access modifier on methods, properties, and member variables.

11.   Boxing refers to:

    a.   Encapsulation

    b.   Converting a value type to a reference type

    c.   Converting a reference type to a value type

    d.   Creating a class to wrap functionality in a single entity

12. What is one advantage of using named parameters?

    a. You can pass the arguments in to the method in any order using the parameter names.

    b. You can pass in optional arguments as long as you use the parameter names in your arguments.

    c. Named parameters make compiling much faster.

    d. Name parameters do not affect compile time.

13. What is an advantage of using generics in .NET?

    a. Generics enable you to create classes that span types.

    b. Generics enable you to create classes that accept the type at creation time.

    c. Generics perform better than nongeneric classes.

    d. Generics do not use optional parameters.

14. What does the `<T>` designator indicate in a generic class?

    a. It is the parameter for all arguments passed in to the class constructor.

    b. It is the parameter designator for the default method of the class.

    c. It is a placeholder that will contain the object type used.

    d. It is a placeholder that will serve as the class name.

15. How are the values passed in generic methods?

    a. They are passed by value.

    b. They are passed by reference.

    c. They must be encapsulated in a property.

    d. They are passed during class instantiation.

ADDITIONAL READING AND RESOURCES

Here are some additional useful resources to help you understand the topics presented in this chapter:

C# keywords

    `http://msdn.microsoft.com/en-us/library/x53a06bb.aspx`

The C# Programming Guide

    `http://msdn.microsoft.com/en-us/library/kx37x362.aspx`

MSDN Code Gallery

    `http://code.msdn.microsoft.com`

CHEAT SHEET

This cheat sheet is designed as a way for you to quickly study the key points of this chapter.

Value types

➤ Store the values directly.

➤ Are an alias for `System` types such as `int` for `System.Int32`.

➤ Are passed as a copy to methods.

➤ Framework includes standard data types most commonly required.

➤ Legal values are based on number of bits used to store the type.

Data structures

➤ Data structures involved structs, enumerations, and classes.

➤ Structs are lightweight data structures.

➤ Structs can contain member variables and methods.

➤ Structs are passed by value unlike reference types, which are passed by reference.

Enumerations

➤ Enumerations contain a list of named constants.

➤ They make code more readable.

➤ They use an underlying value for the named constant.

➤ Underlying values of type `int` start at 0 and increment by one unless otherwise indicated in the declaration.

Reference types

➤ Reference types are also commonly referred to as *classes*.

➤ Classes contain member variables to store characteristics.

➤ Classes contain member functions to provide functionality.

➤ Class files encompass data and functionality in one package.

Modifiers

➤ Modifiers are used to determine access for classes and class members.

➤ See Table 3-3 for a complete list of modifiers.

➤ Modifiers are listed first in declarations.

Fields

➤ Fields contain the data for classes.

➤ Fields are also known as *member variables*.

➤ They describe characteristics of the class.

➤ They should be marked private to avoid unwanted modification.

Constructors

➤ Use to initialize classes.

➤ Do not include a return type.

➤ Use the same name as the class.

➤ May contain no parameters (default constructor).

➤ If no constructor is defined, compiler generates a default constructor.

Methods

➤ Provide functionality for a class

➤ Can be used with modifiers

➤ Can return values or not (return type void)

➤ Can accept arguments through parameters in the signature

➤ Can use optional and named parameters

Overloaded methods

➤ Same method name with multiple instances for different functionality

➤ Defined by the signature (name, types, and kinds of parameters)

Abstract methods

➤ Do not define an implementation

➤ Can be declared in abstract classes only

➤ End with a semicolon

Overridden methods

➤ Hide the implementation of a method of the same name in the base class

➤ Provide a means to change method behavior in derived class

➤ Used for virtual and abstract methods in base class

Extension methods

➤ Can be applied to your own types or even existing types in .NET

➤ Extend existing classes by adding methods without recompiling

Optional parameters

➤ Enable you to choose which parameters are required in a method.

➤ Defined as optional by including a default value.

➤ The default value is used if none is passed by caller.

➤ Must exist after required parameters.

➤ If multiple optional parameters exist and a value is specified for one, all preceding optional parameters must also be supplied values.

Named parameters

➤ Allow for giving parameters in a method a name

➤ Increase code readability

➤ Enable you to pass arguments to a method in an order other than in the method signature

Encapsulation

➤ Also known as data hiding.

➤ Involves making member variable private.

➤ Data exposed through properties.

➤ Functionality and data are all enclosed as part of the class.

➤ Creates a "black box" concept.

Properties

➤ Present the public interface to your class

➤ Enforce encapsulation

➤ May be read/write, read-only, or write-only

➤ Can be used to perform data validation on incoming and outgoing data values

Indexed properties

➤ Allow array-like access to groups of items

➤ Must be access using an index in the same manner as arrays

Generic types

➤ Design classes without specifying the types at definition stage

➤ Design methods without specifying the types for parameters at definition stage

➤ Use a placeholder at definition stage that will be replaced by type during instantiation

➤ Enable type-safe coding

➤ Increases performance due to reduction in conversions, boxing/unboxing

REVIEW OF KEY TERMS

abstract method Indicates that the thing modified has a missing or incomplete implementation. The abstract modifier can be used with classes, methods, properties, indexers, and events. Use the abstract modifier in a class declaration to indicate that a class is intended to be only a base class of other classes.

accessor methods Methods used to access hidden member variables.

class files File that contain a C# class. Classes encapsulate data and functionality into one unit of code.

classes Coding components that enable you to create custom types that group together characteristics, methods, and events.

constructors Class methods executed when an object of a given type is created.

data structures Components in code that are used to store data within the program.

encapsulation The hiding of details around the implementation of an object so there are no external dependencies on the particular implementation.

enumerations A distinct type consisting of a set of named constants.

event publisher The object in code that will raise the event for the listener or subscriber.

event subscriber The object that listens for an event to be raised

fields Variables that store characteristic data for a class.

heap An area of memory used by the .NET compiler to store reference type variables

instance fields The same as fields but are known as instance fields because they relate to an instance of an object. In other words, their values are not shared among objects of the same class.

memory address An addressable location in computer memory that is used to store and retrieve values stored there.

methods Provide the functionality for a class.

modifiers Modify declarations of types and type members.

overloaded methods Methods with identical names for procedures that operate on different data types.

override To extend or modify the abstract or virtual implementation of an inherited method, property, indexer, or event.

properties Members that provide a flexible mechanism to read, write, or compute the values of private fields.

reference types Class files or other objects represented as references to the actual data (memory addresses).

signature In this case, a method signature. It is the unique identifying components of the method such as return type, name, and parameters.

stack An area of memory used by the .NET compiler to store value types during program execution.

EXAM TIPS AND TRICKS

The Review of Key Terms and the Cheat Sheet for this chapter can be printed off to help you study. You can find these files in the ZIP file for this chapter at www.wrox.com/remtitle.cgi?isbn=1118612094 on the Download Code tab.

Using Types

WHAT YOU WILL LEARN IN THIS CHAPTER

➤ Converting values from one data type to another

➤ Widening, narrowing, implicit, and explicit conversions

➤ Casting

➤ Converting values with help methods and classes

➤ Manipulating strings

➤ Formatting values

WROX.COM CODE DOWNLOADS FOR THIS CHAPTER

You can find the code downloads for this chapter at www.wrox.com/remtitle.cgi?isbn= 1118612094 on the Download Code tab. The code is in the chapter 04 download and individually named according to the names throughout the chapter.

Chapter 3, "Working with the Type System," introduces the C# type system. It explains how to create value types (data structures and enumerations) and reference types (classes). It also explains encapsulation, and generic types and methods. This chapter continues the discussion of types by explaining how to convert between different types, such as converting an `int` or `float` into a `string` for display to the user. It explains how to use types to interact with unmanaged code. It also explains how to manipulate `string`s to perform such operations as determining whether a `string` begins with a given prefix and extracting substrings.

Table 4-1 introduces you to the exam objectives covered in this chapter.

TABLE 4-1: 70-483 Exam Objectives Covered in This Chapter

OBJECTIVE	CONTENT COVERED
Create and Use Types	*Create types.* This includes boxing and unboxing value types, converting and casting between value types, handling dynamic types, and ensuring interoperability with unmanaged code.
	Manipulate strings. This includes understanding string methods, searching strings, formatting strings, and manipulating strings by using the `StringBuilder`, `StringWriter`, and `StringReader` classes.

CONVERTING BETWEEN TYPES

Many programs must convert data from one type to another. For example, a graphing program might use the `Math.Sin` and `Math.Cos` functions to calculate values for a graph, and then use the `Graphics` object's `DrawLines` method to draw the graph. However, `Math.Sin` and `Math.Cos` return values as `doubles`, and `DrawLines` represents points as `floats` or `ints`. At some point the program must convert the `double` values into `floats` or `ints`.

In addition to converting one data type into another, a program may need to convert text entered by the user into other data types such as `ints`, `floats`, or `DateTimes` so that it can manipulate those values.

The following sections discuss various ways a C# program can convert one data type to another:

➤ Casting

➤ Using the `as` operator

➤ Parsing

➤ Using `System.Convert`

➤ Using `System.BitConverter`

Using Widening and Narrowing Conversions

You can categorize conversions as either widening or narrowing. The code that performs a conversion can also be implicit or explicit.

In a *widening conversion*, the destination data type can hold any value provided by the source data type. In a *narrowing conversion*, the destination data type cannot hold all possible values held by the source data type.

For example, an `int` variable can hold integer values between –2,147,483,648 and 2,147,483,647. A `short` variable can hold integer values only between –32,768 and 32,767. That means converting from a `short` to an `int` is a widening conversion because an `int` can hold any value that a `short` can hold. A widening conversion always succeeds.

In contrast, converting from an `int` to a `short` is a narrowing conversion because a `short` cannot hold every possible value in an `int`. That doesn't mean a narrowing conversion from an `int` to a `short` will always fail, however. If an `int` variable happens to hold a value that can fit in a `short`, such as 100 or –13,000, the conversion succeeds. If the `int` holds a value that won't fit in a `short`, such as 70,000, the conversion fails.

By default, C# does not throw an exception if a narrowing conversion results in an error for integer or floating point types. For integers, it truncates the result and continues merrily along as if nothing had gone wrong. For floating point types, the program sets the result variable's value to `Infinity` if the value doesn't fit and again continues executing.

You can make C# throw an exception for invalid narrowing integer conversions in a couple ways. First, you can use a `checked` block as shown in the following code. (The cast operator `(short)` is described in the section "Casting" later in this chapter.)

```
checked
{
    int big = 1000000;
    short small = (short)big;
}
```

Within the `checked` block, the program throws an `OverflowException` if the conversion from the `int big` to the `short small` fails.

> **NOTE** A `checked` block does not protect code inside methods called within the block. For example, suppose the code inside a `checked` block calls the `CalculateTaxes` method. In that case the `checked` block does not protect the `CalculateTaxes` method if it performs a narrowing conversion. If `CalculateTaxes` tries to make a narrowing conversion that fails, the program does not throw an exception.

You can also make a program throw exceptions for invalid integer conversions by opening the project's Properties page, selecting the Build tab, and clicking the Advanced button to display the Advanced Build Settings dialog (see Figure 4-1). Make sure the Check For Arithmetic Overflow/Underflow box is checked, and click OK.

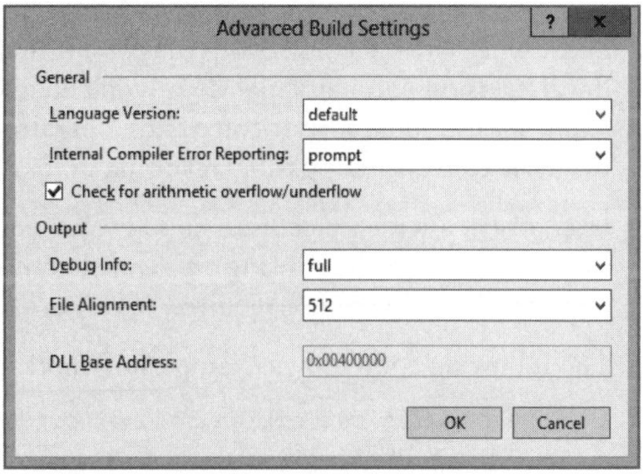

The `checked` block and Check for Arithmetic Overflow/Underflow setting throw exceptions only for integer operations. If a program saves a `double` precision value into a `float` variable, the code must explicitly check the result to see if it is set to `Infinity` to detect an overflow. The code should probably also check for `NegativeInfinity` to catch underflow conditions.

FIGURE 4-1: Use the Advanced Build Settings dialog to make the program check for integer overflow and underflow.

> **COMMON MISTAKES: Performing Narrowing Conversions That Result in Integer Overflows**
>
> Beginning programmers often don't realize that the program won't complain if it performs a narrowing conversion that results in an integer overflow or underflow. To avoid confusing bugs, make the program throw an exception in those cases.

The following code uses the `float` type's `IsInfinity` method to determine whether the narrowing conversion caused an overflow or underflow:

```
double big = -1E40;
float small = (float)big;
if (float.IsInfinity(small)) throw new OverflowException();
```

> **COMMON MISTAKES: Performing Floating Point Conversions That Result in Overflows**
>
> Beginning programmers often don't realize that the program will continue running if a floating point conversion or calculation results in an overflow or underflow. To avoid bugs, check the result for `Infinity` and `NegativeInfinity`.

Using Implicit and Explicit Conversions

An *implicit conversion* is one in which the program automatically converts a value from one data type to another without any extra statements to tell it to make the conversion. In contrast, an *explicit conversion* uses an additional operator or method such as a cast operator (described in the next section) or a parsing method (described in the section "Parsing Methods") to explicitly tell the program how to make the conversion.

Because narrowing conversions may result in a loss of data, a C# program won't perform a narrowing conversion automatically, so it won't enable an implicit narrowing conversion. The code must explicitly use some sort of conversion operator or method to make it clear that you intend to perform the conversion, possibly resulting in loss of data.

In contrast, a widening conversion always succeeds, so a C# program can make widening conversions implicitly without using an explicit conversion operator or method. You can use a conversion operator, but you are not required to do so.

The following code shows examples of implicit and explicit conversions:

```
// Narrowing conversion so explicit conversion is required.
double value1 = 10;
float value2 = (float)value1;

// Widening conversion so implicit conversion is allowed.
int value3 = 10;
long value4 = value3;
```

For reference types, converting to a direct or indirect ancestor class or interface is a widening conversion, so a program can make the conversion implicitly. The following section includes more about converting reference types.

Casting

A cast operator explicitly tells the compiler that you want to convert a value into a particular data type. To cast a variable into a particular type, place the type surrounded by parentheses in front of the value that you want to convert.

For example, the following code initializes the `double` variable `value1`, casts it into the `float` data type, and then saves the new `float` value in variable `value2`.

```
double value1 = 10;
float value2 = (float)value1;
```

> **NOTE** *Casting a floating point value into an integer data type causes the value to be truncated. For example, the statement* `(int)10.9` *returns the integer value* 10. *If you want to round the value to the nearest integer instead of truncating it, use the* `System.Convert` *class's* `ToInt32` *method (described in the section "System.Convert" later in this chapter) or the* `Math.Round` *method.*

As the previous section mentioned, converting a reference type to a direct or indirect ancestor class or interface is a widening conversion, so a program can make the conversion implicitly. For example, if the `Employee` class is derived from the `Person` class, you can convert an `Employee` object into a `Person` object:

```
Employee employee1 = new Employee();
Person person1 = employee1;
```

Converting a reference value to an ancestor class or interface does not actually change the value; it just makes it act as if it were of the new type. In the previous example, `person1` is a `Person` variable, but it references an `Employee` object. The code can use the variable `person1` to treat the object as a `Person`, but it is still an `Employee`.

Because `person1` is actually an `Employee`, you can convert it back to an `Employee` variable:

```
Employee employee1 = new Employee();
Person person1 = employee1;
Person person2 = new Employee();

// Allowed because person1 is actually an Employee.
Employee employee2 = (Employee)person1;
```

Converting from `Person` to `Employee` is a narrowing conversion, so the code needs the `(Employee)` cast operator.

This kind of cast operator enables the code to compile, but the program throws an `InvalidCastException` at run time if the value is not actually of the appropriate type.

For example, the following code throws an exception when it tries to cast a true `Person` object into an `Employee`:

```
Person person2 = new Person();

// Not allowed because person2 is a Person but not an Employee.
Employee employee3 = (Employee)person2;
```

Because programs often need to cast reference data from one class to a compatible class, as shown in the previous code, C# provides two operators to make that kind of casting easier: `is` and `as`.

The is Operator

The `is` operator determines whether an object is compatible with a particular type. For example, suppose the `Employee` class is derived from `Person`, and the `Manager` class is derived from `Employee`. Now suppose the program has a variable named `user` and it must take special action if that variable refers to an `Employee` but not to a `Person`. The following code uses the `is` operator to determine whether the `Person` variable refers to an `Employee` and takes a special action:

```
if (user is Employee)
{
    // Do something with the Employee...
    ...
}
```

If the `is` operator returns `true`, indicating the variable `user` refers to an `Employee`, the code takes whatever action is necessary.

The `is` operator returns `true` if the object is compatible with the indicated type, not just if the object actually *is* of that type. The previous code returns `true` if user refers to an `Employee`, but also returns `true` if user refers to a `Manager` because a `Manager` is a type of `Employee`. (`Manager` was derived from `Employee`.)

The as Operator

The previous code takes special action if the variable user refers to an object that has a type compatible with the `Employee` class. (In this example, that means user is an `Employee` or `Manager`.) Often the next step is to convert the variable into a more specific class before treating the object as if it were of that class. The following code casts user into an `Employee`, so it can treat it as an `Employee`:

```
if (user is Employee)
{
    // The user is an Employee. Treat is like one.
    Employee emp = (Employee)user;

    // Do something with the Employee...
    ...
}
```

The `as` keyword makes this conversion slightly easier. The statement `object as Class` returns the object converted into the indicated class if the object is compatible with that class. If the object is not compatible with the class, the statement returns `null`.

The following code shows the previous example rewritten to use the `as` operator:

```
Employee emp = user as Employee;
if (emp != null)
{
    // Do something with the Employee...
    ...
}
```

> **NOTE** *Whether you use the earlier version that uses* is, *or this version that uses* as, *is largely a matter of personal preference.*

One situation in which the `as` operator is particularly useful is when you know a variable refers to an object of a specific type. For example, consider the following `RadioButton` control's `CheckedChanged` event handler:

```
// Make the selected RadioButton red.
private void MenuRadioButton_CheckedChanged(object sender, EventArgs e)
{
    RadioButton rad = sender as RadioButton;
    if (rad.Checked) rad.ForeColor = Color.Red;
    else rad.ForeColor = SystemColors.ControlText;
}
```

This event handler is assigned to several `RadioButtons`' `CheckedChanged` events, but no matter which control is clicked, you know that the `sender` parameter refers to a `RadioButton`. The code uses the `as` operator to convert `sender` into a `RadioButton`, so it can then use the `RadioButton`'s `Checked` and `ForeColor` properties.

Casting Arrays

As the previous sections explained, casting enables you to convert data on one type to another compatible type. If the conversion is widening, you don't need to explicitly provide a cast operator such as `(int)`. If the conversion is narrowing, you must provide a cast operator. These rules hold for value types (such as converting between `int` and `long`) and reference types (such as converting between `Person` and `Employee`).

These rules also hold for arrays of reference values. Even the `is` and `as` operators work for arrays of reference values.

Suppose the `Employee` class is derived from the `Person` class, and the `Manager` class is derived from the `Employee` class. The CastingArrays example program uses the following code to demonstrate the casting rules for arrays of these classes:

```
// Declare and initialize an array of Employees.
Employee[] employees = new Employee[10];
for (int id = 0; id < employees.Length; id++)
    employees[id] = new Employee(id);

// Implicit cast to an array of Persons.
// (An Employee is a type of Person.)
Person[] persons = employees;

// Explicit cast back to an array of Employees.
```

```
    // (The Persons in the array happen to be Employees.)
    employees = (Employee[])persons;

    // Use the is operator.
    if (persons is Employee[])
    {
        // Treat them as Employees.
        ...
    }

    // Use the as operator.
    employees = persons as Employee[];

    // After this as statement, managers is null.
    Manager[] managers = persons as Manager[];

    // Use the is operator again, this time to see
    // if persons is compatible with Manager[].
    if (persons is Manager[])
    {
        // Treat them as Managers.
        //...
    }

    // This cast fails at run time because the array
    // holds Employees not Managers.
    managers = (Manager[])persons;
```

This code follows the previous discussion of casting in a reasonably intuitive way. The code first declares and initializes an array of Employee objects named employees.

It then defines an array of Person objects named persons and sets it equal to employees. Because Employee and Person are compatible types (one is a descendant of the other), this cast is potentially valid. Because it is a widening conversion (Employee is a type of Person), this can be an implicit cast, so no cast operator is needed and the cast will succeed.

Next, the code casts the persons array back to the type Employee[] and saves the result in employees. Again these are compatible types, so the cast is potentially valid. This is a narrowing conversion (Employees are Persons but not all Persons are Employees) so this must be an explicit conversion and the (Employee[]) cast operator is required.

The code then uses the is operator to determine whether the persons array is compatible with the type Employee[]. In this example, persons holds a reference to an array of Employee objects, so it is compatible and the program executes whatever code is inside the if statement. (This makes sense now but there's a counterintuitive aspect to this that is discussed shortly.)

Next, the program uses the as operator to convert persons into the Employee[] array employees. Because persons can be converted into an array of Employees, this conversion works as expected.

The code then uses the as operator again to convert persons into the Manager[] array managers. Because persons holds Employees, which cannot be converted into Managers, this conversion fails, so the variable managers is left equal to null.

The program then uses the `is` operator to see if `persons` can be converted into an array of `Managers`. Again that conversion won't work, so the code inside this `if` block is skipped.

Similarly, the explicit cast that tries to convert `persons` into an array of `Managers` fails. When it tries to execute this statement, the program throws an `InvalidCastException`.

COMMON MISTAKES: Casting Doesn't Make a New Array

All of this makes sense and fits well with the earlier discussion of casting and implicit and explicit conversions. However, there is one counterintuitive issue related to casting arrays. When you cast an array to a new array type, the new array variable is actually a reference to the existing array not a completely new array.

That is consistent with the way C# works when you set two array variables equal to each other for value types. For example, the following code makes two integer array variables refer to the same array:

```
int[] array1, array2;
array1 = new int[10];
array2 = array1;
```

This code declares two array variables, initializes `array1`, and then makes `array2` refer to the same array. If you change a value in one of the arrays, the other array contains the same change because `array1` and `array2` refer to the same array.

This can cause confusion if you're not careful. If you want to make a new array instead of just a new way to refer to an existing array, use `Array.Copy` or some other method to copy the array.

Now back to arrays of references. When the code sets the `persons` array equal to the `employees` array, `persons` refers to the same array as `employees`. It treats the objects inside the array as `Persons` instead of `Employees`, but it is not a new array.

You can see this in Figure 4-2 where IntelliSense is showing the values in the `persons` array right after setting `persons` equal to `employees`. At the top level, IntelliSense shows that `persons` is equal to `CastingArrays.Form1.Employee[10]`, which is an array of 10 Employee objects. When `persons` is expanded, IntelliSense

```
// Implicit cast to an array of Persons.
// (An Employee is a type of Person.)
Person[] persons = employees;

// Explicit cast back to an array of Employees.
// (The Persons in the arrat happen to be Employees.)
employees = (Employee[])persons;

                            persons  {CastingArrays.Form1.Employee[10]}
// Use the is operator.             [0] {Person: 0}
if (persons is Employee[])          [1] {Person: 1}
{                                   [2] {Person: 2}
    // Treat them as Employees.     [3] {Person: 3}
    //...                           [4] {Person: 4}
}                                   [5] {Person: 5}
                                    [6] {Person: 6}
// Use the as operator.             [7] {Person: 7}
employees = persons as Employee     [8] {Person: 8}
                                    [9] {Person: 9}
// After this as statement. managers is null.
Manager[] managers = persons as Manager[];
```

FIGURE 4-2: When you cast an array of reference values, the new variable still refers to the original array.

treats each of its members as if they were `Person` objects. That is possible because an `Employee` is a type of `Person` so, even though the array holds `Employees`, the `persons` array can treat them as if they were `Persons`.

Knowing that `persons` is actually a disguised reference to an array of `Employee` objects, it makes sense that the following statement fails:

```
persons[0] = new Person(0);
```

This code tries to save a new `Person` object in the `persons` array. The `persons` array is declared as `Person[]` so you might think this should work but actually `persons` currently refers to an array of `Employee`. You cannot store a `Person` in an array of `Employee` (because a `Person` is not a type of `Employee`), so this statement throws an `ArrayTypeMismatchException` at run time.

> **COMMON MISTAKES: Casting Reference Arrays into a New Type**
>
> Remember that a reference array cast into a new type doesn't actually have that new type. You can just treat the objects it holds as if they are of the new type.

In summary, you can cast arrays of references in a reasonably intuitive way. Just keep in mind that the underlying values still have their original types even if you're treating them as something else, as this example treats `Employee` objects as `Person` objects.

Converting Values

Casting enables a program to convert a value from one type to another compatible type, but sometimes you may want to convert a value from one type to an incompatible type. For example, you may want to convert the `string` value **10** to the `int` value 10, or you might want to convert the `string` value **True** to the `bool` value true. In cases such as these, casting won't work.

To convert a value from one type to an incompatible type, you must use some sort of helper class. The .NET Framework provides three main methods for these kinds of conversions:

➤ Parsing methods

➤ `System.Convert`

➤ `System.BitConverter`

Each of these methods is described in more detail in the following sections.

Parsing Methods

Each of the primitive C# data types (`int`, `bool`, `double`, and so forth) has a `Parse` method that converts a string representation of a value into that data type. For example, `bool.Parse` takes as an argument a string representing a boolean value such as `true` and returns the corresponding `bool` value `true`.

These parsing methods throw exceptions if their input is in an unrecognized format. For example, the statement `bool.Parse("yes")` throws a `FormatException` because that method understands only the values `true` and `false`.

When you use these methods to parse user input, you must be aware that they can throw exceptions if the user enters values with an invalid format. If the user enters **ten** in a TextBox where the program expects an int, the int.Parse method throws a FormatException. If the user enters **1E3** or **100000** where the program expects a short, the short.Parse method throws an OverflowException.

You can use a try-catch block to protect the program from these exceptions, but to make value checking even easier, each of these classes also provides a TryParse method. This method attempts to parse a string and returns true if it succeeds or false if it fails. If it succeeds, the method also saves the parsed value in an output variable that you pass to the method.

Table 4-2 lists the most common data types that provide Parse and TryParse methods.

TABLE 4-2: Data Types That Provide Parse and TryParse Methods

bool	byte
char	DateTime
decimal	double
float	int
long	sbyte
short	TimeSpan
uint	ulong
ushort	

The following code shows two ways a program can parse integer values that are entered in TextBoxes:

```
int quantity;
try
{
    quantity = int.Parse(quantityTextBox.Text);
}
catch
{
    quantity = 1;
}

int weight;
if (!int.TryParse(weightTextBox.Text, out weight)) weight = 10;
```

The code declares the variable quantity. Inside a try-catch block, the code uses int.Parse to try to convert the text in the quantityTextBox control into an integer. If the conversion fails, the code sets quantity to the default value 1.

Next, the code declares the variable `weight`. It then uses `int.TryParse` to attempt to parse the text in the `weightTextBox` control. If the attempt succeeds, the variable `weight` holds the parsed value the user entered. If the attempt fails, `TryParse` returns `false`, and the code sets `weight` to the default value 10.

> **BEST PRACTICES: Avoid Parsing When Possible**
>
> Sometimes, you can avoid parsing numeric values and dealing with invalid inputs such as **ten** by using a control to let the user select a value instead of entering one. For example, you could use a `NumericUpDown` control to let the user select the quantity instead of entering it in a `TextBox`.

Usually, the parsing methods work fairly well if their input makes sense. For example, the statement `int.Parse("645")` returns the value 645 with no confusion.

Even the `DateTime` data type's `Parse` method can make sense out of most reasonable inputs. For example, in U.S. English the following statements all parse to 3:45 PM April 1, 2014.

```
DateTime.Parse("3:45 PM April 1, 2014").ToString()
DateTime.Parse("1 apr 2014 15:45").ToString()
DateTime.Parse("15:45 4/1/14").ToString()
DateTime.Parse("3:45pm 4.1.14").ToString()
```

By default, however, parsing methods do not handle currency values well. For example, the following code throws a `FormatException` (in the U.S. English locale):

```
decimal amount = decimal.Parse("$123,456.78");
```

The reason this code fails is that, by default, the `decimal.Parse` method enables thousands and decimal separators but not currency symbols.

You can make `decimal.Parse` enable currency symbols by adding another parameter that is a combination of values defined by the `System.Globalization.NumberStyles` enumeration. This enumeration enables you to indicate special characters that should be allowed such as the currency symbols, a leading sign, and parentheses.

Table 4-3 shows the values defined by the `NumberStyles` enumeration.

TABLE 4-3: NumberStyles Enumeration Values

STYLE	DESCRIPTION
`None`	Enables no special characters. The value must be a decimal integer.
`AllowLeadingWhite`	Enables leading whitespace.
`AllowTrailingWhite`	Enables trailing whitespace.
`AllowLeadingSign`	Enables a leading sign character. Valid characters are given by the `NumberFormatInfo.PositiveSign` and `NumberFormatInfo.NegativeSign` properties.

STYLE	DESCRIPTION
AllowTrailingSign	Enables a trailing sign character. Valid characters are given by the `NumberFormatInfo.PositiveSign` and `NumberFormatInfo.NegativeSign` properties.
AllowParentheses	Enables the value to be surrounded by parentheses to indicate a negative value.
AllowDecimalPoint	Enables the value to contain a decimal point. If `AllowCurrencySymbol` is also specified, the allowed currency symbol is given by the `NumberFormatInfo.CurrencyDecimalSeparator` property. If `AllowCurrencySymbol` is not specified, the allowed currency symbol is given by the `NumberFormatInfo.NumberDecimalSeparator`.
AllowThousands	Enables thousands separators. If `AllowCurrencySymbol` is also specified, the separator is given by the `NumberFormatInfo.CurrencyGroupSeparator` property and the number of digits per group is given by the `NumberFormatInfo.CurrencyGroupSizes` property. If `AllowCurrencySymbol` is not specified, the separator is given by the `NumberFormatInfo.NumberGroupSeparator` property and the number of digits per group is given by the `NumberFormatInfo.NumberGroupSizes` property.
AllowExponent	Enables the exponent symbol `e` or `E` optionally followed by a positive or negative sign.
AllowCurrencySymbol	Enables a currency symbol. The allowed currency symbols are given by the `NumberFormatInfo.CurrencySymbol` property.
AllowHexSpecifier	Indicates that the value is in hexadecimal. This does not mean the input string can begin with a hexadecimal specifier such as `0x` or `&H`. The value must include only hexadecimal digits.
Integer	This is a composite style that includes `AllowLeadingWhite`, `AllowTrailingWhite`, and `AllowLeadingSign`.
HexNumber	This is a composite style that includes `AllowLeadingWhite`, `AllowTrailingWhite`, and `AllowHexSpecifier`.
Number	This is a composite style that includes `AllowLeadingWhite`, `AllowTrailingWhite`, `AllowLeadingSign`, `AllowTrailingSign`, `AllowDecimalPoint`, and `AllowThousands`.
Float	This is a composite style that includes `AllowLeadingWhite`, `AllowTrailingWhite`, `AllowLeadingSign`, `AllowDecimalPoint`, and `AllowExponent`.
Currency	This is a composite style that includes all styles *except* `AllowExponent` and `AllowHexSpecifier`.

continues

TABLE 4-3 *(continued)*

STYLE	DESCRIPTION
Any	This is a composite style that includes all styles *except* `AllowHexSpecifier`.

If you provide any `NumberStyles` values, any default values are removed. For example, by default `decimal.Parse` enables thousands and decimal separators. If you pass the value `NumberStyles.AllowCurrencySymbol` to the method, it no longer enables thousands and decimal separators. To allow all three, you need to pass the method all three values as in the following code:

```
decimal amount = decimal.Parse("$123,456.78",
    NumberStyles.AllowCurrencySymbol |
    NumberStyles.AllowThousands |
    NumberStyles.AllowDecimalPoint);
```

Alternatively, you can pass the method the composite style `Currency`, as shown in the following code:

```
decimal amount = decimal.Parse("$123,456.78",
    NumberStyles.AllowCurrencySymbol);
```

LOCALE-AWARE PARSING

Parsing methods are locale-aware, so they try to interpret their inputs for the locale in which the program is running. You can see that in the descriptions in Table 4-3 that mention the `NumberFormatInfo` class. For example, the allowed currency symbol is defined by the `NumberFormatInfo.CurrencySymbol` property, and that property will have different values depending on the computer's locale.

If the computer is localized for French as spoken in France, `DateTime.Parse` understands the French-style date "1 mars 2020," but doesn't understand the German version "1. März 2020." (It understands the English version "March 1, 2020" in either the French or German locale.)

Similarly, if the computer's locale is French, the `int.Parse` method can parse the text "123 456,78" but cannot parse the German-style value "123.456,78."

All literal values within C# code should use U.S. English formats. For example, no matter what locale the computer uses, a C# program would use a `double` variable to "0.05" not "0,05" inside its code.

COMMON MISTAKES: Parsing Currency Values

Many beginning programmers don't realize they can parse currency values. If a `TextBox` should hold currency values, parse it correctly so that the user isn't told "$1.25" has an invalid numeric format.

System.Convert

The `System.Convert` class provides more than 300 methods (including overloaded versions) for converting one data type to another. For example, the `ToInt32` method converts a value into a 32-bit integer (an `int`). Different overloaded versions of the methods take parameters of different types such as `bool`s, `byte`s, `DateTime`s, `double`s, `string`s, and so forth.

Table 4-4 lists the most useful data type conversion methods provided by the `System.Convert` class.

TABLE 4-4: Basic System.Convert Data Conversion Methods

ToBoolean	ToByte
ToChar	ToDateTime
ToDecimal	ToDouble
ToInt16	ToInt32
ToInt64	ToSByte
ToSingle	ToString
ToUInt16	ToUInt32
ToUInt64	

> ### BANKER'S ROUNDING
>
> The methods that convert to integral types (`ToByte`, `ToIntXX`, and `ToUIntXX`) use "banker's rounding," which means values are rounded to the nearest integer, but if there's a tie, with the value ending in exactly `.5`, the value is rounded to the nearest *even* integer. For example, `ToInt16(9.5)` and `ToInt16(10.5)` both return `10`.
>
> All these methods throw an exception if their result is outside of the range of allowed values. For example, `ToByte(255.5)` returns `256`, which is too big to fit in a `byte`, and `ToUInt32(-3.3)` returns `3`, which is less than zero, so it won't fit in an unsigned integer.
>
> The `Math.Round` method uses banker's rounding by default but also enables you to use parameters to indicate if it should round toward `0` instead. This method returns a result that is either a decimal or a double, so often code must use a cast to convert the result into an integral data type as in the following code:
>
> ```
> float total = 100;
> int numItems = 7;
> int average = (int)Math.Round(total / numItems);
> ```

The `System.Convert` class also provides a `ChangeType` method that converts a value into a new type determined by a parameter at run time. For example, `(int)Convert.ChangeType(5.5, typeof(int))` returns the integer `6`. Often it is easier to use one of the more specific methods such as `ToInt32` instead of `ChangeType`.

System.BitConverter

The System.BitConverter class provides methods to convert values to and from arrays of bytes. The GetBytes method returns an array of bytes representing the value that you pass to it. For example, if you pass an int (which takes up 4 bytes of memory) into the method, it returns an array of 4 bytes representing the value.

The System.BitConverter class also provides methods such as ToInt32 and ToSingle to convert byte values stored in arrays back into specific data types.

For example, suppose an API function returns two 16-bit values packed into the left and right halves of a 32-bit integer. You could use the following code to unpack the two values:

```
int packedValue;

// The API function call sets packedValue here.
. . .

// Convert the packed value into an array of bytes.
byte[] valueBytes = BitConverter.GetBytes(packedValue);

'// Unpack the two values.
short value1, value2;
value1 = BitConverter.ToInt16(valueBytes, 0);
value2 = BitConverter.ToInt16(valueBytes, 2);
```

After the API function sets the value of packedValue, the code uses the BitConverter class's GetBytes method to convert the value into an array of 4 bytes. The order of the bytes depends on whether the computer's architecture is big-endian or little-endian. (You can use the BitConverter's IsLittleEndian field to determine whether the value is big-endian or little-endian.)

The BitConverter class's methods are quite specialized, so they are not described further here. For more information, see "BitConverter Class" at http://msdn.microsoft.com/library/3kftcaf9.aspx.

Boxing and Unboxing Value Types

Boxing is the process of converting a value type such as an int or bool into an object or an interface that is supported by the value's type. *Unboxing* is the processing of converting a boxed value back into its original value.

For example, the following code creates an integer variable and then makes an object that refers to its value:

```
// Declare and initialize integer i.
int i = 10;

// Box i.
object iObject = i;
```

After this code executes, variable iObject is an object that refers to the value 10.

Boxing and unboxing take significantly more time than simply assigning one value type variable equal to another, so you should avoid boxing and unboxing whenever possible. If that's true, why would you ever do it?

Usually boxing and unboxing occur automatically without taking any special action. Often this happens when you invoke a method that expects an object as a parameter but you pass it a value. For example, consider the following code:

```
int i = 1337;
Console.WriteLine(string.Format("i is: {0}", i));
```

The version of the `string` class's `Format` method used here takes as parameters a format string and a sequence of `object`s that it should print. The method examines the `object`s and prints them appropriately.

The code passes the value variable `i` into the `Format` method. That method expects an `object` as a parameter, so the program automatically boxes the value.

Ideally, you could avoid this by making the `Format` method take an `int` as a parameter instead of an `object`, but then what would you do if you wanted to pass the method a `double`, `DateTime`, or `Person` object? Even if you made overloaded versions of the `Format` method to handle all the basic data types (`int`, `double`, `string`, `DateTime`, `bool`, and so on), you couldn't handle all the possible combinations that might occur in a long list of parameters.

The solution is to make `Format` take nonspecific `object`s as parameters and then use reflection to figure out how to print them.

Similarly, you could use nonspecific `object`s for parameters to the methods that you write and then use reflection to figure out what to do with the `object`s. For more information on reflection, see Chapter 8, "Using Reflection."

Usually, you'll get better performance if you can use a more specific data type, interface, or generic type for parameters. For more information on generic types and methods, see Chapter 3.

Even if you're willing to live with the performance hit, boxing and unboxing has a subtle side-effect that can lead to some confusing code. Consider again the following code:

```
// Declare and initialize integer i.
int i = 10;

// Box i.
object iObject = i;
```

After this code executes, variable `iObject` is an object that refers to the value `10`, but it's not the same value `10` stored in the variable `i`. That means if the code changes one of the values, the other does not also change. For example, take a look at the following code, which adds some statements to the previous version:

```
// Declare and initialize integer i.
int i = 10;

// Box i.
```

```
object iObject = i;

// Change the values.
i = 1;
iObject = 2;

// Display the values.
Console.WriteLine(i);
Console.WriteLine(iObject);
```

This code creates an integer variable i and boxes it with the variable iObject. It then sets i equal to 1 and iObject equal to 2. When the code executes the Console.WriteLine statements, the following results appear in the Output window:

```
1
2
```

The variable iObject seems to refer to the variable i but they are actually two separate values.

Incidentally, the Console.WriteLine method has many overloaded versions including one that takes an int as a parameter, so the first WriteLine statement in the previous code does not require boxing or unboxing. The second WriteLine statement must unbox iObject to get its current value 2.

The moral of the story is that you should avoid boxing and unboxing if possible by not storing references to value types in objects. If the program automatically boxes and unboxes a value as the string.Format method does, there's usually not too much you can do about it. Finally, you should not declare method parameters or other variables to have the nonspecific type object unless you have no other choice.

Ensuring Interoperability with Unmanaged Code

Interoperability enables a C# program to use classes provided by unmanaged code that was not written under the control of the *Common Language Runtime* (CLR), the runtime environment that executes C# programs. ActiveX components and the Win32 API are examples of unmanaged code that you can invoke from a C# program.

The two most common techniques for allowing managed programs to use unmanaged code are COM Interop and Platform invoke (P/invoke). COM Interop is discussed briefly in the following section. This section deals with P/invoke.

To use P/invoke to access an unmanaged resource such as an API call, a program first includes a DllImport attribute to define the unmanaged methods that will be used by the managed program. The DllImport attribute is part of the System.Runtime.InteropServices namespace, so many programs add that namespace in a using statement to make using the attribute easier.

The DllImport attribute takes parameters that tell the managed program about an unmanaged method. The parameters indicate such things as the DLL that contains the method, the character set used by the method (Unicode or ANSI), and the entry point in the DLL used by the method. (If you omit this, the default is the name of the method.)

The program applies the attribute to a `static extern` method declaration. The declaration includes whatever parameters the method requires and defines the method's return type. This declaration should be inside a class such as the class containing the code that uses the method.

For example, the following code fragment shows where the `using` statement and `DllImport` attribute are placed in the `ShortPathNames` example program (which is described shortly in greater detail). The `DllImport` statement is highlighted.

```
using System;
using System.Collections.Generic;
... Other standard "using" statements ...
using System.Runtime.InteropServices;

namespace ShortPathNames
{
    public partial class Form1 : Form
    {
        public Form1()
        {
            InitializeComponent();
        }

        [DllImport("kernel32.dll", CharSet = CharSet.Auto,
            SetLastError = true)]
        static extern uint GetShortPathName(string lpszLongPath,
            char[] lpszShortPath, int cchBuffer);

        ... Application-specific code ...
    }
}
```

The `DllImport` statement indicates that the method is in the kernel32.dll library, that the program should automatically determine whether it should use the Unicode or ANSI character set, and that the method should call `SetLastError` if there is a problem. If there is an error, the program can use `GetLastWin32Error` to see what went wrong.

The method's declaration indicates that the program will use the `GetShortPathName` method, which converts a full path to a file into a short path that can be recognized by Windows. (If the method uses the Unicode character set, the method's name usually ends with a "W" for "wide characters" as in `GetShortPathNameW`.) This method returns a `uint` and takes as parameters a `string`, `char` array, and `int`.

> **NOTE** Often the prefixes on the parameter names give you hints about the purposes of those parameters. In this example, `lpsz` means "long pointer to string that's zero-terminated" and `cch` means "count of characters." If you read the online help for the `GetShortPathName` API function, you'll find that those prefixes make sense.

The first parameter is the file path that you want to convert to a short path. When you call the method, P/Invoke automatically converts it into a null-terminated string. The second parameter should be a pre-allocated buffer where GetShortPathName can store its results. The third parameter gives the length of the buffer that you allocated, so GetShortPathName knows how much room it has to work with.

The method returns a uint indicating the length of the string that the method deposited in the lpszLongPath buffer.

You can figure out the syntax for this DllImport statement by staring at the method's signature in the online help, in this case at http://msdn.microsoft.com/library/windows/desktop/aa364989 .aspx. A much easier option, however, is to look up the method at http://www.pinvoke.net. This website contains DllImport statements for a huge number of Win32 API functions. It even sometimes includes examples, discussion, and links to the methods' online documentation. When you need to use a Win32 API function, this is a great place to start.

Having declared the method, the program can now use it. The ShortPathNames example program, which is available for download on the book's website, uses the method in the following code:

```
// Get the long file name.
string longName = fileTextBox.Text;

// Allocate a buffer to hold the result.
char[] buffer = new char[1024];
long length = GetShortPathName(
    longName, buffer,
    buffer.Length);

// Get the short name.
string shortName = new string(buffer);
shortNameTextBox.Text = shortName.Substring(0, (int)length);
```

This code gets a long file path entered by the user in the fileTextBox control and allocates a buffer of 1024 chars to hold the short path. It then calls the GetShortPathName method, passing it the long file path, the buffer, and the length of the buffer.

After the method returns, the program uses the buffer to initialize a new string. It uses the Substring method and the length returned by GetShortPathName to truncate the string to its proper length and displays the result.

Usually, the kind of DllImport statement shown earlier is good enough to get the job done. If you need more control over how values are converted between managed and unmanaged code, you can add the MarshalAs attribute to the method's parameters or return value.

The following code shows a new version of the DllImport statement for the GetShortPathName method that uses MarshalAs attributes:

```
[DllImport("kernel32.dll", CharSet = CharSet.Auto, SetLastError=true)]
static extern uint GetShortPathName(
  [MarshalAs(UnmanagedType.LPTStr)] string lpszLongPath,
  [MarshalAs(UnmanagedType.LPTStr)] StringBuilder lpszShortPath,
  uint cchBuffer);
```

The first `MarshalAs` attribute indicates that the first parameter is an `LPTStr` data type in the unmanaged code and should be treated as a `string` in the managed code.

The second `MarshalAs` attribute indicates that the second parameter is an `LPTStr` data type in the unmanaged code and should be treated as a `StringBuilder` in the managed code.

Of course, if you use this declaration, you need to change the code to use a `StringBuilder` for a buffer instead of an array of `char`.

Handling Dynamic Types

The `DllImport` and `MarshalAs` attributes described in the previous section enable you to tell the program where to find an unmanaged method, and what data types it uses for parameters and a return type. This enables the program to invoke unmanaged methods through P/invoke.

COM Interop provides another way a managed program can interact with unmanaged code. To use COM Interop, you need to give your program a reference to an appropriate library. To do that, look in the Solution Explorer, right-click the References entry, and select Add Reference. Find the reference that you want to add in the COM tab's Type Libraries section (for example, Microsoft Excel 14.0 Object Library), check the box next to the entry, and click OK.

Adding the library reference tells your program (and Visual Studio) a lot about the unmanaged COM application. If you open the View menu and select Object Browser, you can use the Object Browser to search through the objects and types defined by the library. (For the Excel library mentioned earlier, look in the Microsoft.Office.Interop.Excel assembly.)

The library gives Visual Studio enough information for it to provide IntelliSense about some of the library's members, but Visual Studio may still not understand all the types used by the library. C# 4.0 and later provide a special data type called `dynamic` that you can use in this situation. This is a static data type, but its true type isn't evaluated until run time. At design and compile time, C# doesn't evaluate the `dynamic` item's type, so it doesn't flag syntax errors for problems such as type mismatches because it hasn't evaluated the `dynamic` type yet. This can be useful if you can't provide complete information about an item's type to the compiler.

C# considers objects defined by the unmanaged COM Interop code to have the `dynamic` type, so it doesn't care at compile time what their actual types are. It skips checking the objects' syntax and waits until run time to see if the code makes sense.

The ExcelInterop example program, which is available for download on the book's website, uses the following code to make Microsoft Excel create a workbook:

```
// Open the Excel application.
Excel._Application excelApp = new Excel.Application();

// Add a workbook.
Excel.Workbook workbook = excelApp.Workbooks.Add();
Excel.Worksheet sheet = workbook.Worksheets[1];

// Display Excel.
excelApp.Visible = true;

// Display some column headers.
```

```
sheet.Cells[1, 1].Value = "Value";
sheet.Cells[1, 2].Value = "Value Squared";

// Display the first 10 squares.
for (int i = 1; i <= 10; i++)
{
    sheet.Cells[i + 1, 1].Value = i;
    sheet.Cells[i + 1, 2].Value = (i * i).ToString();
}

// Autofit the columns.
sheet.Columns[1].AutoFit();
sheet.Columns[2].AutoFit();
```

In this code the `dynamic` data type is used implicitly in a couple of places. Visual Studio doesn't actually understand the data type of `sheet.Cells[1, 1]`, so it defers type checking for that value. That lets the program refer to this entity's `Value` property even though the program doesn't know whether the cell has such a property. Actually, you could try to set `sheet.Cells[1, 1].Whatever = i` and Visual Studio won't complain until run time when it tries to access the `Whatever` property and finds that it doesn't exist.

Similarly, Visual Studio treats `sheet.Columns[1]` as having type `dynamic`, so it doesn't know that the `AutoFit` method exists until run time.

For an example that's more C#-specific, consider the following code, which is demonstrated by the CloneArray example program available for download on the book's website:

```
// Make an array of numbers.
int[] array1 = { 1, 2, 3, 4, 5, 6, 7, 8, 9, 10 };

// This doesn't work because array1.Clone is an object.
//int[] array2 = array1.Clone();

// This works.
int[] array3 = (int[])array1.Clone();
array3[5] = 55;

// This also works.
dynamic array4 = array1.Clone();
array4[6] = 66;

array4[7] = "This won't work";
```

This code initializes an array of integers. The commented out code tries to use the array's `Clone` method to make a copy of the array. Unfortunately, the `Clone` method returns a nonspecific `object`, so the code cannot save it in a variable that refers to an array of `int`. The next statement correctly casts the `object` into an `int[]` so that it works. The code then stores a new integer value in the array.

Next, the code declares `array4` to have the type `dynamic`. The program clones the array and saves the clone in variable `array4`. At run time the program can tell that the clone is actually an `int[10]` so that is the data type it assigns to `array4`.

The final statement tries to save a `string` in `array4[7]`. At design and compile time, Visual Studio doesn't try to validate this statement because `array4` was declared `dynamic`. At run time, however, this fails because `array4` is actually an `int[]` and cannot hold a `string`.

The `dynamic` data type enables you to avoid syntax errors when you do not know (or cannot know) the type of an object at compile time. Unfortunately, not understanding an object's type at design time also means Visual Studio cannot provide type checking or IntelliSense. That means you need to ensure that the methods you invoke actually exist, that you can assign specific values to a `dynamic` variable or property, and that you don't try to save a `dynamic` value in an incompatible variable. The program will complain about any mistakes at run time, but you won't get much help at design and compile time.

To prevent these kinds of errors at run time, you should avoid the `dynamic` data type and use more specific data types whenever possible.

REAL-WORLD CASE SCENARIO Order Entry Forms

Order entry forms similar to the one shown in Figure 4-3 are common in order processing applications. In this Real-World Case Scenario, you build a form similar to this one. You can make it a Windows Forms application, a Metro-style application, or even a Windows Phone application if you prefer.

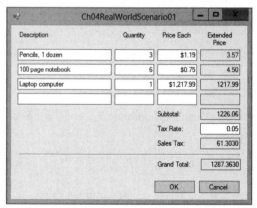

FIGURE 4-3: This order entry form parses numeric and currency values entered by the user.

When the user clicks the OK button, validate the form and calculate and display the appropriate values. (Don't worry about formatting output fields as currency. Just use the variables' `ToString` methods to display the text. You learn how to format values as currency in the section "Formatting Values.")

If all the values entered by the user are valid, display a message box telling the user that the order is okay and asking whether the program should continue. If the user clicks Yes on the message box, or if the user clicks the form's Cancel button, close the form.

Make the following validations:

➤ If any of the fields in a row is nonblank, then all the fields in that row must be nonblank.

➤ Quantity is an integer between 1 and 100.

➤ Price Each is a decimal between $0.01 and $100,000.00. (Be sure to allow values with a currency format.)

➤ Tax rate is a decimal between 0.00 and 0.20. (Don't worry about percentage values such as 7 percent now. You add that feature later after you learn about manipulating strings in the section "Manipulating Strings.")

Hint: Don't forget to add a using `System.Globalization` statement to make using `NumberStyles` easier.

As a follow-up question, can you improve the user interface to reduce the amount of data validation required?

Solution

Here is the solution:

1. There are several ways you can structure the program's code to make it easier to use and maintain. This isn't the focus of this chapter, however, so they aren't covered in detail here. You can download the chapter's code and look at the Ch04RealWorldScenario01 program for details. Briefly, however, you may want to consider writing the following methods:

   a. `DisplayErrorMessage` displays a standard error message and sets the focus to a `TextBox` that has a missing or invalid value.

   b. `ValidateRequiredTextBox` verifies that a particular `TextBox` has a nonblank value.

   c. `ValidateRow` validates a row of input consisting of Description, Quantity, and Price Each `TextBox`es.

2. To see if a `TextBox` has a blank value, compare its `Text` property to the empty string `""` or to `string.Empty`.

3. To get a value from a `TextBox`, use the appropriate `TryParse` method. For example, the following code shows how the program might read a Price Each value:

```
// Try to parse priceEach.
if (!decimal.TryParse(priceEachTextBox.Text, NumberStyles.Currency,
    null, out priceEach))
{
    // Complain.
    DisplayErrorMessage(
        "Invalid format. Price Each must be an currency value.",
        "Invalid Format", priceEachTextBox);
    return true;
}
```

This code uses `NumberStyles.Currency` to enable currency values.

4. Use if statements to determine whether values fall within their expected bounds. The following code shows how the program might validate a Price Each value:

```
// Make sure priceEach is between $0.01 and $100,000.00.
if ((priceEach < 0.01m) || (priceEach > 100000.00m))
{
    // Complain.
    DisplayErrorMessage(
        "Invalid Price Each. Price Each must be between $0.01 and $100,000.00",
        "Invalid Quantity", priceEachTextBox);
    return true;
}
```

5. Calculate and display the Extended Price, Subtotal, Sales Tax, and Grand Total values. The following code shows how the example solution processes the order form's first row:

```
subtotal = 0;
if (ValidateRow(descr1TextBox, quantity1TextBox, priceEach1TextBox,
    out quantity, out priceEach)) return;
extendedPrice = quantity * priceEach;
if (extendedPrice == 0m) extendedPrice1TextBox.Clear();
else extendedPrice1TextBox.Text = extendedPrice.ToString();
subtotal += extendedPrice;
```

This code calls the ValidateRow method to validate and get the first row's Description, Quantity, and Price Each values. If that method indicates an error by returning true, the code returns. If the row does not contain an error, the code calculates extendedPrice and displays its value in the appropriate TextBox. It then adds the row's extended price to the running subtotal value and continues to process the other rows.

Download the example solution to see the complete code.

Follow-up question: One obvious way to improve the user interface would be to remove the Quantity TextBoxes and replace them with NumericUpDown controls. Then the user can select a value within minimum and maximum allowed values. The user couldn't type in garbage and couldn't select values outside of the allowed range.

You can even use a NumericUpDown control for the Tax Rate by setting its properties Minimum = 0, Maximum = 0.2, Increment = 0.05, and DecimalPlaces = 2.

You could also use NumericUpDown controls for the Price Each fields but that control makes entering monetary values awkward.

In general it's better to let users select a value instead of entering one in a TextBox so that they can't enter invalid values.

MANIPULATING STRINGS

Strings are different from other data types. Programs usually treat them as if they were any other value-type piece of data but behind the scenes the string class is remarkably complex. You can ignore the extra complexity in most day-to-day programming, but it is important to understand how strings work so that you can handle special situations when they arise. For example, if you understand how strings are stored, you will know when it would be better to use the StringBuilder class instead of simply concatenating strings together.

> **NOTE** *In C# the keyword* string *is an alias for* System.String, *so when you create a* string *variable, you are actually creating a* String *object. Stylistically most C# programmers prefer to use* string, *but the following sections use* String *to emphasize that these are objects and not the simple value types they may appear to be.*

Behind the Strings

The .NET Framework represents characters as *Unicode* version UTF-16, a format that uses 16 bits to store each character. That enables a Unicode character to represent far more characters than are provided on a standard American keyboard. (The latest version of Unicode defines values for more than 110,000 characters in more than 100 scripts.)

A String is an object that uses a series of Unicode characters to represent some text. One of the more unusual features of Strings is that they are *immutable*. That means a String's content cannot be changed after the String has been created. Instead, methods that seem to modify a String's value, such as Replace and ToUpper, actually return a new String object that contains the modified value.

To conserve memory, the CLR maintains a table called the *intern pool* that holds a single reference to each unique text value used by a program. Any String variable that refers to a particular piece of text is actually a reference into the intern pool. Multiple Strings that represent the same value refer to the same entry in the intern pool.

All this requires some overhead, so working with Strings is not quite as fast as working with value types. If a program must perform a large number of concatenations, each one creates a new String instance that must be interned and that takes time. In that case, using the StringBuilder class might give better performance. The StringBuilder class is described further in the section "StringBuilder."

String Constructors

Three of the most common ways to initialize a String variable are to:

➤ Set it equal to a string literal.

➤ Set it equal to text entered by the user in a control such as a TextBox or ComboBox.

➤ Set it equal to the result of a string calculation.

The last of these includes methods that format a variable to produce a String such as using the ToString method or the String.Format method. These techniques are described in the section "Formatting Values."

In addition to these methods, the String class provides several constructors that can sometimes be useful:

➤ One constructor initializes the String from an array of char.

➤ A second constructor uses only part of an array of char, taking as parameters the array, a start position, and the length of characters to use.

➤ A third constructor takes as a parameter a character and the number of times you want to repeat that character in the new String. This can be particularly useful if you want to indent a string by a certain number of spaces or tab characters. For example, the following code displays the numbers 1 through 10 on separate lines with each line indented four more spaces than the one before:

```
for (int i = 1; i <= 10; i++)
{
    string indent = new string(' ', 4 * i);
    Console.WriteLine(indent + i.ToString());
}
```

Most String values are created by string literals, text entered by the user, or the results of calculations, but String constructors can sometimes be useful.

String Fields and Properties

The String class provides only three fields and properties: Empty, Length, and a read-only indexer.

The Empty field returns an object that represents an empty string. You can use this value to set a String's value or to see if a String holds an empty value. (Alternatively, you can use the empty string literal " ".)

The Length property returns the number of characters in the string.

The read-only indexer returns the chars in the String. Because it is an indexer, you can get its values by adding an index to a String variable's name. For example, the statement username[4] returns character number 4 in the string username.

The indexer is read-only, so you can't set one of the String's characters with a statement such as username[4] = 'x'. If you need to do something like that, you can use the String methods described in the next section.

If it would be easier to treat the String as if it were a read/write array of characters, you can use the ToCharArray method to convert the String into an array of characters, manipulate them, and then create a new String passing the constructor the modified array. For example, the following code uses an array to make a string's characters alternate between uppercase and lowercase:

```
char[] characters = text.ToCharArray();
for (int i = 0; i < characters.Length; i++)
    if (i % 2 == 0) characters[i] = char.ToUpper(characters[i]);
    else characters[i] = char.ToLower(characters[i]);
text = new string(characters);
```

You can also use the indexer as a source of iteration in a `foreach` loop:

```
string text = "The quick brown fox jumps over the lazy dog.";

int[] counts = new int[26];
text = text.ToUpper();
foreach (char ch in text)
{
    if (char.IsLetter(ch))
    {
        int index = (int)ch - (int)'A';
        counts[index]++;
    }
}
```

This code makes a `String` object named `text`. It creates a `counts` array to hold counts for the 26 letters A to Z used in the string. Before processing the string, the code then converts `text` into uppercase.

Next, the code uses a `foreach` statement to loop over the characters in the string. For each character, the code uses the `char` class's `IsLetter` method to decide whether the character is a letter and not a space or punctuation mark. If the character is a letter, the code converts it into an integer and subtracts the value of "A" converted into an integer from it to get an index into the `counts` array. The letter A has index 0, B has index 1, and so forth. The code then increments the count for that index. When the code finishes, the `counts` array holds the number of times each character occurs in the string.

String Methods

The `String` class provides lots of methods that enable you work with strings. Table 4-5 describes the most useful static methods provided by the `String` class. Because these are static methods, a program uses the `String` class to invoke these methods. For example, to use the `Compare` method, the program uses a statement similar to if (`String.Compare(value1, value2) > 0) . . . .`

TABLE 4-5: Useful Static String Methods

METHOD	DESCRIPTION
Compare	Compares two `Strings` and returns −1, 0, or 1 to indicate that the first `String` should be considered before, equal to, or after the second `String` in the sort order. Overloaded versions of this method enable you to specify string comparison rules, whether to ignore case, and which culture's comparison rules to use.
Concat	Takes as a parameter an array of `Strings` or other objects and returns a `String` holding the concatenation of the objects. An overloaded version enables you to pass any number of arguments as parameters and returns the arguments concatenated. See also `Join`.
Copy	Returns a copy of the `String`. See also the `Clone` instance method in Table 4-6.

METHOD	DESCRIPTION
Equals	Returns true if two Strings have the same value. See also the Equals instance method in Table 4-6.
Format	Uses a format string and a series of objects to generate a formatted text string. See the "String.Format" section for more information.

IsNullOrEmpty	Returns true if the String holds a blank string "" or the String variable refers to null. The following code sets two variables equal to an empty string and a third variable to null:
	
	`string value1 = "";`
	`string value2 = String.Empty;`
	`string value3 = null;`
	
	There is a difference between an empty string and null. The IsNullOrEmpty method makes it easier to treat both values in the same way.

IsNullOrWhiteSpace	Returns true if the String variable holds a blank string, refers to null, or holds only whitespace characters. Whitespace characters are those for which Char.IsWhiteSpace returns true.

Join	Joins the values in an array of strings or other objects separated by a separator string. For example, the following code sets the variable allDays to hold the days of the week separated by commas:
	
	`string[] weekdays =`
	`{`
	`    "Monday", "Tuesday", "Wednesday",`
	`    "Thursday", "Friday", "Saturday",`
	`    "Sunday"`
	`};`
	`string allDays = string.Join(",", weekdays);`

Table 4-6 describes the most useful instance methods provided by the String class. Because these are instance methods, a program must use an instance of the String class to invoke these methods. For example, to use the CompareTo method, the program would use a statement similar to if (value1.CompareTo(value2) > 0) ....

TABLE 4-6: Useful String Instance Methods

METHOD	DESCRIPTION
Clone	Returns a new reference to the String. The behavior is a bit different from the Clone methods provided by most other classes because Strings are immutable. For this class, the new reference refers to the same value in the intern pool as the original String. Refer also to the static Copy method in Table 4-5.

continues

TABLE 4-6 *(continued)*

METHOD	DESCRIPTION
CompareTo	Compares the String to another String and returns −1, 0, or 1 to indicate that this String should be considered before, equal to, or after the other String in the sort order. If you want to specify string comparison rules, whether to ignore case, and which culture's comparison rules to use, use the static Compare method.
Contains	Returns true if the String contains a specified substring.
CopyTo	Copies a specified number of characters from a specified start position into a char array.
EndsWith	Returns true if the String ends with a specified substring. Overloaded versions enable you to specify string comparison type, whether to ignore case, and culture.
Equals	Returns true if this String has the same value as another String. Refer also to the static Equals method in Table 4-5.
IndexOf	Returns the index of the first occurrence of a character or substring within the String. Parameters enable you to specify the position in the String where the search should begin and end, and string comparison options.
IndexOfAny	Returns the index of the first occurrence of any character in an array within the String. Parameters enable you to specify the position in the String where the search should begin and end.
Insert	Inserts a String at a specific position within this String and returns the result.
LastIndexOf	Returns the index of the last occurrence of a character or substring within the String. Parameters enable you to specify the position in the String where the search should begin and end, and comparison options.
LastIndexOfAny	Returns the index of the last occurrence of any character in an array within the String. Parameters enable you to specify the position in the String where the search should begin and end.
PadLeft	Returns the String padded to a certain length by adding spaces or a specified character on the left. This makes it easier to align text in columns with a fixed-width font.
PadRight	Returns the String padded to a certain length by adding spaces or a specified character on the right. This makes it easier to align text in columns with a fixed-width font.

METHOD	DESCRIPTION
Remove	Removes the characters starting at a specified position either to the end of the String or for a certain number of characters and returns the result.
Replace	Replaces all instances of a character or string with another character or string and returns the result.
| Split | Returns an array holding the String's pieces as delimited by characters in an array. Overloaded versions enable you to indicate the maximum number of pieces to return and split options such as whether to remove empty entries. For example, the following code splits a series of numbers separated by commas and dashes, removing any entries that are empty:<br><br>```csharp
char[] delimiters = { ',', '-' };
string values = "12-21,,33-17,929";
string[] fields = values.Split(delimiters,
    StringSplitOptions.RemoveEmptyEntries);
``` |
StartsWith	Returns true if the String starts with a specified substring. Overloaded versions enable you to specify comparison type, whether to ignore case, and culture.
Substring	Returns a new String containing a substring of this String specified by a start position and length.
ToCharArray	Returns an array of char representing some or all the String's characters.
ToLower	Returns a copy of the String converted to lowercase.
ToString	Returns the String. Normally, you don't need to do this, but if you're treating the String as an object, for example if it is in a list or array of objects, it's useful to know that this object has a ToString method.
ToUpper	Returns a copy of the String converted to uppercase.
Trim	Returns a copy of the String with leading and trailing whitespace characters removed. An overloaded version enables you to specify which characters should be removed.
TrimEnd	Returns a copy of the String with trailing whitespace characters removed.
TrimStart	Returns a copy of the String with leading whitespace characters removed.

The String class's methods let a program perform all sorts of string manipulations such as parsing user input to get the pieces of an address, phone number, or other pieces of formatted information. Chapter 11, "Input Validation, Debugging and Instrumentation," has more about parsing and validating user input by using the String class's methods.
```

Handling Percentage Values

Modify the order entry form that you built for this chapter's first Real-World Case Scenario so that it can handle Tax Rate specified as a percentage. If the value entered by the user contains a % character, parse the value and divide it by 100.

Solution

The `decimal.TryParse` method cannot parse a string that contains the % character. To parse the value, the program must remove the % character if it is present, use `TryParse` to convert the result into a decimal value, and then divide by 100 if the original text contained the % character.

The following code snippet shows one way the program can do this:

```
// Get the tax rate as a string.
string taxRateString = taxRateTextBox.Text;

// Remove the % character if it is present.
taxRateString = taxRateString.Replace("%", "");

// Parse the tax rate.
decimal taxRate;
if (!decimal.TryParse(taxRateString, out taxRate))
{
    // Complain.
    DisplayErrorMessage(
        "Invalid format. Tax Rate must be a decimal value.",
        "Invalid Format", taxRateTextBox);
    return;
}

// If the original string contains the % character, divide by 100.
if (taxRateTextBox.Text.Contains("%")) taxRate /= 100;
```

Additional String Classes

The `String` class is intuitive and easy to use. You can use its methods to easily examine `Strings`, remove sections from `Strings`, trim a `String`'s start or end, and extract substrings.

The unusual way `Strings` are interned, however, makes them inefficient for some purposes. Figure 4-4 shows the permutations example program, which is available for download on the book's website. This program displays a big `String` holding all the permutations of a set of letters. In Figure 4-4, the program is showing permutations of the letters A through H.

There are 8! (or 5040 permutations of those eight letters) so the result is 5040 `Strings` concatenated together. To make matters worse, the program builds each permutation one character at a time, so each permutation requires building eight smaller `Strings`. That

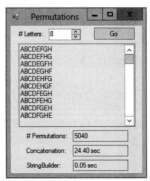

FIGURE 4-4: The permutations example program displays the permutations of a set of letters.

means the program builds 8 × 5040 = 40,320 `Strings` in all, each of which must be interned. As a result, the program is quite slow, taking approximately 23 seconds to produce these 5,040 permutations by using `String` concatenation.

For special cases such as this, when the `String` class is particularly inefficient, a program may get better performance by using the specialized string processing classes:

➤   `StringBuilder`

➤   `StringWriter`

➤   `StringReader`

Referring to Figure 4-4, you can see that the program took only 0.05 seconds to build the permutations when it used a `StringBuilder` instead of `String` concatenations. Each of these string processing classes is described in the following sections.

StringBuilder

The `StringBuilder` class represents a mutable, noninterned string. It stores character data in an array and can add, remove, replace, and append characters without creating a new `String` object or using the intern pool.

Normally, a program uses a `StringBuilder` to build a string in a long series of steps and then calls the `StringBuilder`'s `ToString` method to convert the result into a normal `String`.

For example, the following code uses a `StringBuilder` to build a string holding a series of employee names on separate lines:

```
string[] employeeNames =
{
    "Able",
    "Baker",
    "Charley",
    "Davis",
};
StringBuilder allNames = new StringBuilder();
foreach (string name in employeeNames)
{
    allNames.Append("[" + name + "]" + Environment.NewLine);
}
employeeTextBox.Text = allNames.ToString();
```

The code starts by defining an array of employee names. It then creates a `StringBuilder` and loops over the names in the `EmployeeNames` array. For each name the code calls the `StringBuilder`'s `Append` method to add the name surrounded by brackets to the string. After it has processed all the names, the code calls the `StringBuilder`'s `ToString` method to convert it into a normal `String` and displays the result in the `employeeTextBox` control.

Table 4-7 describes the `StringBuilder` class's most useful properties.

TABLE 4-7: Useful StringBuilder Properties

PROPERTY	DESCRIPTION
Capacity	Gets or sets the number of characters that can be held by the StringBuilder. If the amount of text stored in the StringBuilder exceeds this amount, the object allocates more space. If you know the StringBuilder needs to hold at least a certain number of characters, you can use this property to make the object pre-allocate memory instead of allocating memory incrementally. Some overloaded versions of the class's constructor let you specify an initial capacity.
Length	Gets or sets the current number of the characters stored in the StringBuilder. If you set this value to less than the current length, the text in the StringBuilder is truncated.

The StringBuilder's indexer returns the characters stored in the object. A program can use the indexer to get and set character values. For example, the statement allNames[10] = 'X' sets character number 10 to X.

Table 4-8 describes the StringBuilder class's most useful methods.

TABLE 4-8: Useful StringBuilder Methods

METHOD	DESCRIPTION
Append	Appends a string representation of an object to the end of the StringBuilder's text
AppendFormat	Formats a series of objects and appends the result to the end of the StringBuilder's text
EnsureCapacity	Ensures that the StringBuilder has at least a given capacity
Insert	Inserts a string representation of an object at a given position in the StringBuilder's text
Remove	Removes a range of characters from the StringBuilder's text
Replace	Replaces all instances of a character or string with a new character or string
ToString	Returns a normal String representation of the StringBuilder's text

The StringBuilder class does add some overhead to a program and sometimes makes the code harder to read, so you should generally use it only if you perform a large number of string operations. In one set of tests, simple String concatenation was faster than creating and using a StringBuilder for fewer than approximately seven concatenations.

Also keep in mind that the times involved for a few `String` operations are small. Using a `StringBuilder` to concatenate 10 strings may be slightly faster than performing 10 simple `String` concatenations, but the total amount of time saved is measured in milliseconds. Unless the program repeats that operation many times or makes much longer concatenations, it may be better to sacrifice a few milliseconds to keep the code easier to understand.

StringWriter

The `StringWriter` class provides an interface that makes it easier in some cases to build a string on an underlying `StringBuilder`. The `StringWriter` class provides methods that make it easier to sequentially write values into a string.

Table 4-9 describes the `StringWriter`'s most useful methods.

TABLE 4-9: Useful StringWriter Methods

METHOD	DESCRIPTION
Flush	Flushes any buffered data into the underlying `StringWriter`.
ToString	Returns the object's current contents as a `String`.
Write	Appends an item to the string data. Overloaded versions append `char`, `string`, `int`, `double`, and many other data types.
WriteAsync	Asynchronously appends a `char`, `string`, or array of `char` to the end of the string data.
WriteLine	Appends an item to the string data much as `Write` does and then adds a new line.

`StringWriter` can be useful when you want to append values only to a string. `StringWriter` also implements a `TextWriter` interface, so it can be useful when other classes require a `TextWriter` to produce output and you want to store that output in a string. For example, the `XmlSerializer` class's `Serialize` method sends output to a `TextWriter`. If you want to serialize into a string, you can send the output to a `StringWriter` and then use the `StringWriter`'s `ToString` method to get the result. If you need to manipulate the underlying string data in other ways, such as removing or replacing characters, `StringBuilder` provides more flexibility.

StringReader

The `StringReader` class provides a `TextReader` implementation that reads pieces of data taken from an underlying `StringBuilder`. It provides methods that make it easier to sequentially read pieces of text from a string.

Table 4-10 describes the `StringReader`'s most useful methods.

TABLE 4-10: Useful StringReader Methods

METHOD	DESCRIPTION
Peek	Returns the next character in the data but does not advance to the following character.
Read	Returns the next character in the data and advances to the following character. An overloaded version can read a block of characters.
ReadAsync	Asynchronously reads characters from the StringReader into a buffer.
ReadBlock	Reads up to a maximum number of characters from the StringReader into a buffer beginning at a specified index.
ReadBlockAsync	Asynchronously reads up to a maximum number of characters from the StringReader into a buffer beginning at a specified index.
ReadLine	Reads characters from the StringReader until it encounters the end of the line.
ReadLineAsync	Asynchronously reads characters from the StringReader until it encounters the end of the line.
ReadToEnd	Returns the remaining text from the StringReader as a String.
ReadToEndAsync	Asynchronously returns the remaining text from the StringReader as a String.

The StringReader class provides access to a StringBuilder's data at a relatively low level. Often a program uses a StringReader only because it needs to pass information to a predefined method that requires a StringReader or TextReader as a parameter.

REAL-WORLD CASE SCENARIO **Using StringBuilder**

Using only StringBuilders (no Strings), write a program that displays all the initial subsequences of the letters of the alphabet A, AB, ABC, and so forth in a TextBox, as shown in Figure 4-5.

Solution

The following code does the job:

```
private void Form1_Load(object sender, EventArgs e)
{
    // Make a StringBuilder holding the ABCs.
    StringBuilder letters =
        new StringBuilder("ABCDEFGHIJKLMNOPQRSTUVWXYZ");

    // This one holds the next line of letters.
```

```
        StringBuilder line = new StringBuilder();

        // Create the result StringBuilder.
        StringBuilder result = new StringBuilder();

        // Loop over the letters.
        for (int i = 0; i < 26; i++)
        {
            // Add the next letter to line.
            line.Append(letters[i]);

            // Add line to the result.
            result.AppendLine(line.ToString());
        }

        // Display the result.
        stringBuilderTextBox.Text = result.ToString();
        stringBuilderTextBox.Select(0, 0);
    }
```

The code first builds a `StringBuilder` holding the letters of the alphabet. It makes a second `StringBuilder` to hold a line of output and a third to hold the final result.

Next, the code loops over the numbers 0 through 25. For each value of `i`, the code appends the `i`th character in `letters` to the value in `line`. It then appends the new value of `line` to the result, following it with a new line.

When the code finishes its loop, it displays the result.

In this example it's not clear whether using `StringBuilder` is faster than using simple `String` concatenations. In one test that executed this code and similar code that performed `String` concatenations 100,000 times, the `StringBuilder` version took approximately 54 percent as long, so there is a time-savings, but the result for a single execution is negligible.

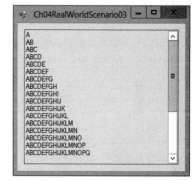

FIGURE 4-5: This program uses StringBuilders to list initial sequences of the alphabet.

FORMATTING VALUES

Formatting a value for display is a particularly important type conversion. Until you convert a `DateTime`, `decimal`, or `double` into some sort of `String`, you can't display it to the user.

Two of the most useful methods for formatting values as strings are the `ToString` and `String.Format` methods described in the next two sections. Both of those methods use formatting strings, which are described in the section after those.

ToString

The `object` class provides a `ToString` method that every other class inherits. By default this method returns an object's type name as a `String`, but most classes for which it makes sense override this method to return the object's value as a `String`.

For example, if a `float` variable holds the value `1.23`, its `ToString` method returns the value "`1.23`" as a string. In contrast, if you define an `Employee` class, by default its `ToString` method returns the name of the class, which is similar to `WindowsFormsApplication1.Employee`.

If you use a variable's `ToString` method without parameters, you get a default representation of its value.

The `ToString` method can also take as parameters a format provider, a formatting string, or both. By using the formatting string, you can customize the resulting text. For example, if the variable cost is a `float`, the statement `cost.ToString("0.00")` produces a string holding the value of `cost` displayed to 2 decimal places.

String.Format

The `ToString` method enables you to convert a single variable's value into a `String`. The `String` class's static `Format` method enables you to build a `String` that may contain the values of many variables formatted in different ways.

The `String.Format` method has a few overloaded versions, but the most common takes as parameters a formatting string and one or more arguments that are used to fill in items within the formatting string.

Each format item in the formatting string has the following *composite format* syntax:

```
{index[,length][:formatString]}
```

Here, *index* is the zero-based index of a parameter that follows the formatting string that should be used for this item; *length* is the minimum length of the result for the item; and *formatString* is a standard or custom format string for the item. If *length* is negative, the value is left-aligned within its length.

Stating this formally makes it sound confusing but it's actually not too bad. The following code shows a simple example.

```
int i = 163;
Console.WriteLine(string.Format("{0} = {1,4} or 0x{2:X}", (char)i, i, i));
```

The code defines an `int` variable named `i` and sets it equal to 163. It then uses `string.Format` to format a line that it writes to the Output window.

The format string is `{0} = {1,4} or 0x{2:X}`. This string has three format items that mean:

➤ `{0}` displays argument 0 with default formatting

➤ `{1,4}` displays argument 1 in a field at least four characters wide

➤ `{2:X}` displays argument 2 with format string X (which displays an integer in hexadecimal)

The other characters inside the formatting string (=, and or 0x) are included in the output as they appear in the formatting string.

The parameters that come after the formatting string are the arguments that should be used with the formatting string. The first argument casts the integer i into a char. The second and third arguments are simply the variable i.

The result is that this line displays the value 163 converted into a character, then as a decimal value, and then in hexadecimal. The following shows the result:

```
£ =  163 or 0xA3
```

An argument does not need to be used in the formatting string. Arguments can also be used in any order and may be used repeatedly, so the following statement is valid:

```
string text = string.Format("{1} {4} {2} {1} {3}",
    "who", "I", "therefore", "am", "think");
```

Whether you use String.Format or concatenate a series of statements together to produce output is largely a matter of personal preference.

Formatting Strings

Both the ToString and String.Format methods can take formatting strings as parameters to tell them how to format a value. For String.Format this refers to the formatting string within format items. For example, in the statement string.Format("0x{0:X}", 90), the formatting string is the X inside the braces.

Formatting strings fall into two broad categories:

➤ *Standard formatting strings* enable you to determine how you want a value displayed at a high level. The standard formatting strings are locale-aware, so they let the program produce an output that is appropriate for the computer's locale. For example, the "d" date format string indicates a short date pattern and produces a result similar to 3/14/2014 in the United States or 14/03/2014 in France.

➤ *Custom formatting strings* enable you to build formats that are not provided by the standard formatting strings. For example, the following statement produces a result similar to It is now 14 o'clock.

```
Console.WriteLine(string.Format("It is now {0:HH} o'clock", DateTime.Now));
```

You can use custom formatting strings to produce results that are similar to those produced by the standard strings, but you should use the standard strings whenever possible so that you get appropriate changes if your program runs on a computer that is configured for a different locale.

The ToString and String.Format methods understand hundreds of standard and custom formatting strings. Some are so seldom used that listing them all here would waste a lot of space. The following two tables list the most useful standard formatting strings for numeric and DateTime values. For complete lists of the allowed standard and custom formatting strings, see the URLs in the "Additional Reading and Resources" section.

Tables 4-11 describes the most useful standard numeric formatting strings.

TABLE 4-11: Standard Numeric Format Strings

FORMAT	DESCRIPTION	EXAMPLE
C or c	Currency	$12,345.67
D or d	Decimal (integer types only)	12345
E or e	Scientific notation	1.234567E+004
F or f	Fixed-point	12345.67
G or g	General (fixed-point or scientific, whichever is shorter)	12345.67
N or n	Number (with decimal and thousands separators)	12,345.67
P or p	Percent (multiplied by 100 and % added)	0.12 becomes 12.00 %
X or x	Hexadecimal (integer types only)	3039

Some of these formats can take an optional precision specifier that controls the number of digits displayed. For most of these types, the precision specifier indicates the number of digits to display after the decimal point. For example, if value is 12345.67 then value.ToString("C4") produces $12,345.6700.

For scientific notation the precision specifier indicates the number of digits after the decimal point in the mantissa. For example, if value is 12345.67, then value.ToString("E2") produces 1.23E+004.

Tables 4-12 describes the most useful standard DateTime formatting strings.

TABLE 4-12: Standard DateTime Format Strings

FORMAT	DESCRIPTION	EXAMPLE
d	Short date	3/14/2014
D	Long date	Friday, March 14, 2012
f	"Full" with short time	Friday, March 14, 2012 2:15 PM
F	"Full" with long time	Friday, March 14, 2012 2:15:16 PM
g	"General" with short time	3/14/2014 2:15 PM
G	"General" with long time	3/14/2014 2:15:16 PM
m or M	Month/day	March 14

FORMAT	DESCRIPTION	EXAMPLE
t	Short time	2:15 PM
T	Long time	2:15:16 PM
y or Y	Year/month	March, 2014

In addition to these standard formats, the `DateTime` structure provides four methods that produce output similar to the d, D, t, and T format specifiers. These methods are `ToShortDateString`, `ToLongDateString`, `ToShortTimeString`, and `ToLongTimeString`.

For more information on these and other formatting strings, see the URLs in the "Additional Reading and Resources" section.

REAL-WORLD CASE SCENARIO Displaying Currency Values

Modify the order entry form that you built for this chapter's second Real-World Case Scenario (Handling Percentage Values) so it displays Extended Price, Subtotal, Sales Tax, and Grand Total in currency format.

Solution

The program already uses the `ToString` method to display those values. The only change needed is to pass the currency formatting string "C" to those calls to `ToString`. For example, the following code shows how the program displays the Grand Total in currency format:

```
grandTotalTextBox.Text = grandTotal.ToString("C");
```

SUMMARY

This chapter explained how to work with types. It explained how to convert from one type to another using both implicit and explicit conversions. It explained how to use classes such as `System.Convert` and `System.BitConverter` to perform more specialized data type conversions.

This chapter also explained how to use the `String` class to manipulate strings, and how to use the `String.Format` and `ToString` methods to convert values into text for display.

One of the many kinds of type conversion a program can make is between classes. For example, if the `Employee` class is derived from the `Person` class, then you can implicitly convert an `Employee` into a `Person` and, in some cases you can explicitly cast a `Person` into an `Employee`. The next chapter explains how you can build the class hierarchies that enable these sorts of conversions.

TEST QUESTIONS

Read each question carefully and select the answer or answers that represent the best solution to the problem. You can find the answers in Appendix A, "Answers to Chapter Test Questions."

1. To parse a string that might contain a currency value such as $1,234.56, you should pass the `Parse` or `TryParse` method which of the following values?

   a. `NumberStyles.AllowCurrencySymbol`

   b. `NumberStyles.AllowThousands`

   c. `NumberStyles.Currency`

   d. A combination of all `NumberStyles` values

2. Which of the following statements is true for widening conversions?

   a. Any value in the source type can fit into the destination type.

   b. The conversion will not result in loss of magnitude but may result is some loss of precision.

   c. An explicit cast is optional.

   d. All of the above.

3. Which of the following statements is true for narrowing conversions?

   a. The conversion will not result in loss of magnitude but may result is some loss of precision.

   b. The source and destination types must be compatible.

   c. An explicit cast is optional.

   d. A cast can convert a `string` into an `int` if the `string` holds numeric text.

4. Assuming `total` is a `decimal` variable holding the value `1234.56`, which of the following statements displays `total` with the currency format $1,234.56?

   a. `Console.WriteLine(total.ToString());`

   b. `Console.WriteLine(total.ToCurrencyString());`

   c. `Console.WriteLine(total.ToString("c"));`

   d. `Console.WriteLine(Format("{0:C}", total);`

5. Which of the following statements generates a string containing the text `"Veni, vidi, vici"`?

   a. `String.Format("{0}, {1}, {2}", Veni, vidi, vici)`

   b. `String.Format("{1}, {2}, {3}", "Veni", "vidi", "vici")`

   c. `String.Format("{2}, {0}, {3}", "vidi", "Venti", "Veni", "vici")`

   d. `String.Format("{Veni, vidi, vici}")`

6. If `i` is an `int` and `l` is a `long`, which of the following statements is true?

   a. `i = (int)l` is a narrowing conversion.

   b. `l = (long)i` is a narrowing conversion.

   c. `l = (long)i` could cause an integer overflow.

   d. The correct way to copy `i`'s value into `l` is `l = long.Parse(i)`.

7. Which of the following methods is the best way to store an integer value typed by the user in a variable?

   a. `ToString`

   b. `Convert`

   c. `ParseInt`

   d. `TryParse`

8. The statement `object obj = 72` is an example of which of the following?

   a. Explicit conversion

   b. Immutable conversion

   c. Boxing

   d. Unboxing

9. If `Employee` inherits from `Person` and `Manager` inherits from `Employee`, which of the following statements is valid?

   a. `Person alice = new Employee();`

   b. `Employee bob = new Person();`

   c. `Manager cindy = new Employee();`

   d. `Manager dan = (Manager)(new Employee());`

10. Which of the following is not a `String` method?

   a. `IndexOf`

   b. `StartsWith`

   c. `StopsWith`

   d. `Trim`

11. Which of the following techniques does not create a `String` containing 10 spaces?

   a. Set a `String` variable equal to a literal containing 10 spaces.

   b. Use a `String` constructor passing it an array of 10 space characters.

   c. Use a `String` constructor passing it the space character and 10 as the number of times it should be repeated.

   d. Use the `String` class's `Space` method passing it 10 as the number of spaces the string should contain.

12. Which of the following statements can you use to catch integer overflow and underflow errors?

    a. `checked`

    b. `overflow`

    c. `watch`

    d. `try`

13. Which of the following techniques should you use to watch for floating point operations that cause overflow or underflow?

    a. Use a `checked` block.

    b. Use a `try-catch` block.

    c. Check the result for the value `Infinity` or `NegativeInfinity`.

    d. Check the result for `Error`.

ADDITIONAL READING AND RESOURCES

Following are some additional useful resources to help you understand the topics presented in this chapter:

Explanation of Big Endian and Little Endian Architecture
> `http://support.microsoft.com/kb/102025`

Convert Class
> `http://msdn.microsoft.com/library/system.convert.aspx`

BitConverter Class
> `http://msdn.microsoft.com/library/3kftcaf9.aspx.)`

Standard Date and Time Format Strings
> `http://msdn.microsoft.com/library/az4se3k1.aspx`

Custom Date and Time Format Strings
> `http://msdn.microsoft.com/library/8kb3ddd4.aspx`

Standard Numeric Format Strings
> `http://msdn.microsoft.com/library/dwhawy9k.aspx`

Custom Numeric Format Strings
> `http://msdn.microsoft.com/library/0c899ak8.aspx`

Standard TimeSpan Format Strings
> `http://msdn.microsoft.com/library/ee372286.aspx`

Custom TimeSpan Format Strings
> `http://msdn.microsoft.com/library/ee372287.aspx`

Enumeration Format Strings
> `http://msdn.microsoft.com/library/c3s1ez6e.aspx`

Understanding the Dynamic Keyword in C# 4
> `http://msdn.microsoft.com/en-us/magazine/gg598922.aspx`

CHEAT SHEET

This cheat sheet is designed as a way for you to quickly study the key points of this chapter.

Conversion Basics

➤ Implicit conversion doesn't use a cast operator.

➤ Explicit conversion uses a cast operator.

➤ Widening conversions always succeed and a cast is optional. Magnitude is never lost but precision may be.

➤ Narrowing conversions do not always succeed, and a cast or other conversion method is required.

➤ Integer operations (including casting) that result in overflow or underflow are ignored unless you use a `checked` block or the Advanced Builds Settings dialog.

➤ Floating point operations that result in overflow or underflow are ignored. Check the result for the value `Infinity` or `NegativeInfinity` to see if overflow or underflow has occurred.

➤ You can cast arrays of references but be aware that the new array refers to the same array and not a new one.

The is and as Operators

➤ Use the `is` operator to determine if a variable is compatible with a certain type.

➤ Use the `as` operator to convert an object into a compatible type (or null if the object isn't compatible with the type).

➤ The `as` operator is particularly useful if you know an object's type, for example in an event handler.

Parsing

➤ Use the `Parse` method to parse text into a value. You must protect `Parse` method calls with `try-catch` blocks.

➤ Use the `TryParse` method to attempt to parse text and see if there is an error. `TryParse` returns `true` if it succeeds and `false` if there is an error.

➤ Use the `System.Globalization.NumberStyles` enumeration to allow `Parse` and `TryParse` to understand special symbols such as thousands separators, decimal points, and currency symbols.

➤ Some useful `NumberStyles` values include `Integer`, `HexNumber`, `Number`, `Float`, `Currency`, and `Any`.

Specialized Conversions

➤ The `System.Convert` class provides methods that convert from one data type to another.

➤ System.Convert methods include ToBoolean, ToDouble, ToSingle, ToByte, ToInt16, ToString, ToChar, ToInt32, ToUInt16, ToDateTime, ToInt64, ToUInt32, ToDecimal, ToSByte, and ToUInt64.

➤ The System.BitConverter class converts data to and from arrays of bytes.

➤ Boxing occurs when you convert a value type into a reference type as in object obj = 72. This is slow, so you should avoid it if possible.

➤ Unboxing occurs when you convert a reference type back into a value type.

➤ The dynamic type is a static type, but its value isn't evaluated until run time.

Strings

➤ Strings are immutable.

➤ The intern pool holds an instance of every unique String.

➤ StringBuilders are mutable and can be more efficient than Strings for performing a long series of concatenations.

➤ The StringWriter and StringReader classes provide methods for writing and reading characters and lines with an underlying StringBuilder object.

Formatting

➤ The ToString and String.Format methods convert values into strings.

➤ String.Format uses composite format strings that can specify argument numbers, field widths, alignments, and format strings. Field indexes start at 0.

➤ Standard format strings are locale-aware so you should use them whenever possible.

➤ Useful standard numeric formatting strings include C/c (currency), D/d (decimal), E/e (exponential), F/f (fixed point), G/g (the shorter of E or F), N/n (number, as in 1,234.56), P/p (percent), and X/x (hexadecimal).

➤ Useful standard DateTime formatting strings include d (short date), D (long date), f ("full" with short time), F ("full" with long time), g ("general" with short time), G ("general" with long time), M or m (month/day), t (short time), T (long time), and Y or y (year/month).

REVIEW OF KEY TERMS

boxing Boxing is the process of converting a value type such as int or bool into an object or an interface supported by the value's type. This enables a program to treat a simple value as if it were an object. See also unboxing.

Common Language Runtime (CLR) A virtual machine that manages execution of C# (and other .NET) programs.

composite format A format item used by `String.Format` to indicate how an argument should be formatted. The basic syntax is `{index[,length][:formatString]}`.

custom formatting string Enable you to build formats that are not provided by the standard formatting strings.

explicit conversion In an explicit conversion, the code uses an operator (such as a cast) or method (such as `int.Parse`) to explicitly tell the program how to convert a value from one type to another.

immutable A data type is immutable if its value cannot be changed after it has been created. The `String` class is immutable. `String` methods that seem to modify a `String`, such as `Replace` and `ToUpper`, actually replace the `String` with a new value containing the modified contents.

implicit conversion In an implicit conversion, the program automatically converts a value from one data type to another without any extra statements to tell it to make the conversion.

intern pool The CLR maintains a table called "intern pool" that contains a single reference to every unique string used by the program.

interoperability Interoperability enables managed code (such as a C# program) to use classes provided by unmanaged code that was not written under the control of the CLR.

narrowing conversion A narrowing conversion is a data type conversion where the destination type cannot hold every possible value provided by the source data type. Converting from a `long` to an `int` is a narrowing conversion because a `long` can hold values such as 4,000,000,000 that cannot fit in an `int`. Narrowing conversions must be explicit.

standard formatting string Enables you to determine how you want a value displayed at a high level.

unboxing Unboxing is the processing of converting a boxed value back into its original value type value. See also boxing.

Unicode Unicode is a standard for encoding characters used by scripts in various locales around the world. It enables a program to display English, Chinese, Kanji, Arabic, Cyrillic, and other character sets. The .NET Framework uses the UTF-16 encoding, which uses 16 bits to represent each character.

widening conversion A widening conversion is a data type conversion where the destination type can hold any value provided by the source data type; although, some loss of precision may occur. For example, converting from an `int` to a `long` is a widening conversion.

EXAM TIPS AND TRICKS

The Review of Key Terms and the Cheat Sheet for this chapter can be printed off to help you study. You can find these files in the ZIP file for this chapter at www.wrox .com/remtitle.cgi?isbn=1118612094 on the Download Code tab.

5

Creating and Implementing Class Hierarchies

WHAT YOU WILL LEARN IN THIS CHAPTER

➤ Deriving one class from another

➤ Calling base class constructors

➤ Defining and implementing interfaces

➤ Using important interfaces such as `IComparable`, `IEquatable`, and `IEnumerable`

➤ Managing resources by implementing `IDisposable` and providing destructors

WROX.COM CODE DOWNLOADS FOR THIS CHAPTER

You can find the code downloads for this chapter at www.wrox.com/remtitle.cgi?isbn=1118612094 on the Download Code tab. The code is in the chapter05 download and individually named according to the names throughout the chapter.

Chapter 4, "Using Types," explains how you can convert data between various data types. Some of the conversions are between primitive types such as converting a `float` value into an `int` or converting a `DateTime` value into a `string`.

Some of the most interesting type conversions, however, are between one object type and another. For example, if the `Employee` class inherits from the `Person` class, you can convert a reference to an `Employee` into a reference to a `Person` because an `Employee` is a kind of `Person`.

This chapter explains how you can build hierarchies of classes such as the `Person-Employee` hierarchy. It also explains how to create and use interfaces, which provide another form of inheritance. Finally, this chapter explains how to manage an object's resources when the object is destroyed.

Table 5-1 introduces you to the exam objectives covered in this chapter.

TABLE 5-1: 70-483 Exam Objectives Covered in This Chapter

OBJECTIVE	CONTENT COVERED
Create and implement a class hierarchy	*Inherit from a base class*. This includes invoking constructors from a derived class's or the same class's constructors.
	Create and implement interfaces. This includes defining and using interfaces, and using standard interfaces such as `IComparable`, `IEquatable`, and `IEnumerable`.
Manage the Object Lifecycle	*Implementing* `IDisposable`. This includes working with managed and unmanaged resouirces, providing destructors, and using the `using` statement.

INHERITING FROM A BASE CLASS

The section "Creating Reference Types" in Chapter 3, "Working with the Type System," explains how to create classes. The following code shows the definition of a simple `Person` class and should be familiar to you:

```
public class Person
{
    public string FirstName { get; set; }
    public string LastName { get; set; }
    public Person(string firstName, string lastName)
    {
        // Validate the first and last names.
        if ((firstName == null) || (firstName.Length < 1))
            throw new ArgumentOutOfRangeException(
                "firstName", firstName,
                "FirstName must not be null or blank.");
        if ((lastName == null) || (lastName.Length < 1))
            throw new ArgumentOutOfRangeException(
                "lastName", lastName,
                "LastName must not be null or blank.");

        // Save the first and last names.
        FirstName = firstName;
        LastName = lastName;
    }
}
```

The `Person` class contains two auto-implemented `string` properties: `FirstName` and `LastName`. (A class used by a real application would probably have a lot more properties to hold information such as postal address, phone numbers, and e-mail addresses.) Its constructor takes first and last names as parameters, performs some validation, and saves the values in the `FirstName` and `LastName` properties.

Now suppose you want to create an `Employee` class that has `FirstName`, `LastName`, and `DepartmentName` properties. You could build this class from scratch, but it needs the same properties as the `Person` class and would need the same validations, so building it from scratch would require you to repeat all of that code.

A better solution is to derive the `Employee` class from the `Person` class so that it inherits that class's fields, properties, methods, and events. That makes sense logically, too. An employee is a kind of person, so it makes sense that an `Employee` should be a kind of `Person`. If an `Employee` is a kind of `Person`, there's no reason why the same code inside the `Person` class that works for `Person` objects shouldn't also work for `Employee` objects.

CLASS TERMINOLOGY

There is a lot of terminology surrounding class hierarchies.

When you *derive* one class from another class, the new class *inherits* all the code included in the original class. In this case, the original class is called the *parent class*, *base class*, or *superclass*. The new class is called the *derived class*, *child class*, or *subclass*. Deriving one class from another is called *subclassing*.

Some of the terminology of family trees also applies to inheritance hierarchies. For example, a parent class's children, their children, and so on are the parent class's *descendants*. Similarly a class's parent, the parent's parent, and so on are the class's *ancestors*. You can even define *sibling classes* to be classes that have a common parent.

To derive a class from another class, simply follow the class's name with a colon and then the name of the parent class. The following code shows an `Employee` class that is derived from the `Person` class.

```
public class Employee : Person
{
    public string DepartmentName { get; set; }
}
```

In this example, the `Employee` class inherits any fields, properties, methods, and events defined by the `Person` class. It also adds a new property, `DepartmentName`. Although a child class inherits most of the code in its parent class, it doesn't inherit the class's constructor.

At this point, a program could use the following code to create an `Employee` object without initializing its `FirstName` and `LastName` properties:

```
Employee employee = new Employee();
```

Because this code doesn't initialize the `Employee`'s `FirstName` and `LastName` properties, they have the values `null`, which defeats the purpose of the `Person` class's constructor. The solution is to give the child class constructors that call the parent class's constructors.

Calling Parent Class Constructors

To ensure that the `Person` class's constructor is called so it can validate the `Employee`'s first and last names, you need to give the `Employee` class a constructor, so you begin by creating a constructor for the `Employee` class. Then you follow the constructor's argument list with a colon, the keyword `base`, and any parameters that you want to pass to the base class's constructor.

In this example, the `Employee` constructor should pass the first and last names that it receives to the `Person` class's constructor. The highlighted code shows where the constructor calls the base class's constructor.

```
public class Employee : Person
{
    public string DepartmentName { get; set; }
    public Employee(string firstName, string lastName,
      string departmentName)
        : base(firstName, lastName)
    {
        // Validate the department name.
        if ((departmentName == null) || (departmentName.Length < 1))
            throw new ArgumentOutOfRangeException(
                "departmentName", departmentName,
                "DepartmentName must not be null or blank.");

        // Save the department name.
        DepartmentName = departmentName;
    }
}
```

If the base class has multiple constructors, the child class can use the `base` keyword to invoke any of them. The program uses the arguments that follow the `base` keyword to figure out which constructor to use.

> **NOTE** When a constructor uses the `base` keyword to invoke a base class constructor, the base class's constructor executes before the body of the child class's constructor executes.

If both the parent and child class have constructors, the child class's constructor *must* invoke one of the parent class's constructors. That means the highlighted `base` statement in the previous code snippet is required. If you remove that code, Visual Studio displays the error message "PersonHierarchy.Person Does Not Contain a Constructor That Takes 0 Arguments." (Here, `PersonHierarchy` is the namespace that contains the `Person` class.) The `Employee` class's constructor is implicitly trying to access a `Person` constructor that takes no parameters and it can't find one.

One oddity to this system is that you can make an `Employee` class with no constructors even though that allows the program to create an instance of the `Employee` class without invoking a `Person` class constructor. That means the following definition for the `Employee` class is legal:

```
public class Employee : Person
```

```
    {
        public string DepartmentName { get; set; }
    }
```

If you want to prevent the program from circumventing the parent class's constructors, you should give the child class at least one constructor.

Calling Same Class Constructors

Often, it's convenient to give a class multiple constructors to perform different kinds of initialization depending on what parameters are passed into the constructor. In that case, multiple constructors may need to perform the same tasks.

For example, suppose the Person class has FirstName and LastName properties, and you want to allow the program to create a Person object by specifying either first name only or both first and last names. The following code shows one way you could write the class with two constructors to handle these two options:

```
class Person
{
    public string FirstName { get; set; }
    public string LastName { get; set; }

    // Constructor with first name.
    public Person(string firstName)
    {
        FirstName = firstName;
    }

    // Constructor with first and last name.
    public Person(string firstName, string lastName)
    {
        FirstName = firstName;
        LastName = lastName;
    }
}
```

The first constructor takes a first name as a parameter and stores it in the FirstName property. The second constructor takes both first and last names as parameters and saves their values in the FirstName and LastName properties.

In this code, the second constructor begins by performing the same work that the first constructor does when it saves the first name. In this simple example, that's no big deal. In a more complicated scenario in which the constructors perform more difficult tasks, this repetition of code would be a problem. It would mean multiple copies of the same code for you to implement, debug, and maintain over time.

One way to avoid this duplication of code is to make one constructor call another. In this case you could rewrite the second constructor to make it call the first constructor so that it can handle the first name parameter.

You make one constructor invoke a second constructor much as you invoke a base class constructor except you use the `this` keyword instead of the `base` keyword. The following code shows how the `Person` class's second constructor can invoke its first constructor. The code that invokes the first constructor is highlighted.

```
// Constructor with first and last name.
public Person(string firstName, string lastName)
    : this(firstName)
{
    LastName = lastName;
}
```

> **NOTE** When a constructor uses the `this` keyword to invoke a second constructor in the same class, the second constructor executes before the body of the first constructor executes.

To take things one step farther, suppose you derive the `Employee` class from the `Person` class and the Employee class adds a `DepartmentName` property. You might want different `Employee` constructors that can take as parameters a first name, first and last names, or first and last name and department name.

Those constructors can use the same technique shown in this version of the `Person` class to make more complicated constructors invoke simpler ones. The `Employee` constructors can also use the base keyword described in the previous section to invoke the `Person` class constructors.

For example, the `Employee(firstName, lastName, departmentName)` constructor can use `this` to invoke the `Employee(firstName, lastName)` constructor and that constructor can use `base` to invoke the `Person(firstName, lastName)` constructor.

Figure 5-1 shows the ThisAndBase example program, which is available for download on the book's website. This program creates several `Person` and `Employee` objects and displays messages indicating when various constructors execute.

FIGURE 5-1: The ThisAndBase example program demonstrates constructors that invoke other constructors.

The following code shows the main form's `Load` event handler, which creates the `Person` and `Employee` objects.

CODE LAB | **Demonstrating Constructors That Invoke Other Constructors [ThisAndBase]**

```
public static string Results = "";

private void Form1_Load(object sender, EventArgs e)
{
    // Make some Persons.
```

```
        Results += "Making Person(Bea)" + Environment.NewLine;
        Person bea = new Person("Bea");
        Results += Environment.NewLine;

        Results += "Making Person(Al, Able)" + Environment.NewLine;
        Person al = new Person("Al", "Able");
        Results += Environment.NewLine;

        // Make some Employees.
        Results += "Making Employee(Carl)" + Environment.NewLine;
        Person carl = new Employee("Carl");
        Results += Environment.NewLine;

        Results += "Making Employee(Deb, Dart)" + Environment.NewLine;
        Person deb = new Employee("Deb", "Dart");
        Results += Environment.NewLine;

        Results += "Making Employee(Ed, Eager, IT)" + Environment.NewLine;
        Person ed = new Employee("Ed", "Eager", "IT");
        Results += Environment.NewLine;

        // Display the results.
        resultsTextBox.Text = Results;
        resultsTextBox.Select(0, 0);
    }
```

Code Lab Analysis

This code first defines a static string named `Results` that other parts of the program can write into to keep a log of what is happening. The event handler then creates a series of `Person` and `Employee` objects to demonstrate the classes' constructors. It adds a message to the `Results` string explaining what it is doing before it creates each object. After it finishes creating the objects, the code displays the `Results` string in the form's `TextBox`.

The following code shows the ThisAndBase program's `Person` class:

```
class Person
{
    public string FirstName { get; set; }
    public string LastName { get; set; }

    // Constructor with first name.
    public Person(string firstName)
    {
        Form1.Results += "  Person(" + firstName + ")" +
            Environment.NewLine;
        FirstName = firstName;
    }

    // Constructor with first and last name.
```

```
    public Person(string firstName, string lastName)
        : this(firstName)
    {
        Form1.Results += "  Person(" + firstName + ", " +
            lastName + ")" + Environment.NewLine;
        LastName = lastName;
    }
}
```

This class first defines `FirstName` and `LastName` properties. Its first constructor adds a message to `Form1.Results` to keep track of what's happening. The second constructor uses the `this` keyword to invoke the first constructor and then adds its own message to `Form1.Results`.

The following code shows the program's `Employee` class:

```
class Employee : Person
{
    public string DepartmentName { get; set; }

    // Constructor with first name.
    public Employee(string firstName)
        : base(firstName)
    {
        Form1.Results += "    Employee(" + firstName + ")" +
            Environment.NewLine;
    }

    // Constructor with first and last name.
    public Employee(string firstName, string lastName)
        : base(firstName, lastName)
    {
        Form1.Results += "    Employee(" + firstName + ", " +
            lastName + ")" + Environment.NewLine;
    }

    // Constructor with first name, last name, and department name.
    public Employee(string firstName, string lastName,
        string departmentName)
        : this(firstName, lastName)
    {
        Form1.Results += "    Employee(" + firstName + ", " +
            lastName + ", " + departmentName + ")" + Environment.NewLine;
        DepartmentName = departmentName;
    }
}
```

The class's first and second constructors take the same parameters used by `Person` class constructors, so they simply use the `base` keyword to invoke the corresponding `Person` constructors and they do nothing else (other than recording messages). The third constructor uses the `this` keyword to invoke the `Employee` constructor that takes first and last names as parameters and then saves the `DepartmentName` value.

If you look closely at Figure 5-1, you see that an invoked constructor executes before the constructor that invokes it. You can also follow the chain of invocation for each object's creation. For example, when the program creates the `Employee` Ed Eager, the sequence of constructor calls is:

1. `Employee(Ed, Eager, IT-12a)` uses `this` to invoke.

2. `Employee(Ed, Eager)` uses `base` to invoke.

3. `Person(Ed, Eager)` uses `this` to invoke.

4. `Person(Ed)`.

A constructor can directly invoke only one base class constructor or one same class constructor. However, a different same class constructor must invoke a base class constructor, so when you use `this` to invoke a same class constructor, you're indirectly invoking a base class constructor anyway. For example, the `Employee(firstName, lastName)` constructor invokes the `Person(firstName, lastName)` constructor.

BEST PRACTICES: Creative Constructors

If you want to invoke multiple constructors, you can move their code into separate methods and invoke those instead. For example, suppose you want the `Customer` class to have the constructors `Customer(email)`, `Customer(address)`, and `Customer(email, address)` where the `email` parameter is a string and the `address` parameter is an `Address` structure holding address information. In that case you might like to build the constructors using code similar to the following:

```
public Customer(string email)
{
    // Store the email address.
    ...
}

public Customer(Address address)
{
    // Store the postal address.
    ...
}

public Customer(string email, Address address)
    : this(email), this(address)
{
}
```

The prohibition against invoking multiple constructors prevents this. Fortunately, you can work around it by moving the interesting code into methods and then calling them instead:

```
public Customer(string email)
{
    StoreEmail(email);
```

continues

```
continued
    public Customer(Address address)
    {
        StoreAddress(address);
    }
    public Customer(string email, Address address)
    {
        StoreEmail(email);
        StoreAddress(address);
    }

    // Store the email address.
    private void StoreEmail(string email)
    {
        ...
    }

    // Store the postal address.
    private void StoreAddress(Address address)
    {
        ...
    }
```

REAL-WORLD CASE SCENARIO **Ellipses and Circles**

Make an `Ellipse` class that represents an ellipse. It should store the ellipse's size and position in a `Location` property of type `RectangleF` (defined in the `System.Drawing` namespace). Give it two constructors: one that takes a `RectangleF` as a parameter and one that takes X position, Y position, width, and height as parameters. Make the second constructor invoke the first, and make the constructors throw an exception if width or height is less than or equal to 0.

Then make a `Circle` class that inherits from `Ellipse`. Make its constructors invoke the appropriate base class constructors, and make them verify that width = height. (Hint: You should need to verify only height = width in one place.)

Don't worry about any other code that the classes would provide in an actual program such as methods to draw ellipses and circles.

Solution

The following `Ellipse` and `Circle` classes work:

```
class Ellipse
{
    public RectangleF Location { get; set; }

    // Constructor that takes a RectangleF as a parameter.
```

```csharp
    public Ellipse(RectangleF rect)
    {
        // Validate width and height.
        if (rect.Width <= 0)
            throw new ArgumentOutOfRangeException(
                "width",
                "Ellipse width must be greater than 0.");
        if (rect.Height <= 0)
            throw new ArgumentOutOfRangeException(
                "height",
                "Ellipse height must be greater than 0.");

        // Save the location.
        Location = rect;
    }

    // Constructor that takes x, y, width, and height as parameters.
    public Ellipse(float x, float y, float width, float height)
        : this(new RectangleF(x, y, width, height))
    {
    }
}

class Circle : Ellipse
{
    // Constructor that takes a RectangleF as a parameter.
    public Circle(RectangleF rect)
        : base(rect)
    {
        // Validate width and height.
        if (rect.Width != rect.Height)
            throw new ArgumentOutOfRangeException(
                "width and height",
                "Circle width and height must be the same.");
    }

    // Constructor that takes x, y, width, and height as parameters.
    public Circle(float x, float y, float width, float height)
        : this(new RectangleF(x, y, width, height))
    {
    }
}
```

DESIGNING AND IMPLEMENTING INTERFACES

Now that you know how to derive a child class from a parent class, you can build diagrams that use arrows to show the relationships among different classes. C# enables a class to have at most one parent class, so the result is a tree-like hierarchy. For example, Figure 5-2 shows a small hierarchy designed to model airline customers and personnel.

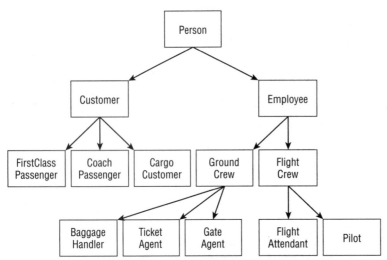

FIGURE 5-2: By deriving classes from each other, you can build class hierarchies.

Class hierarchies are sufficient for a wide variety of modeling problems, but occasionally it would be convenient to allow a class to inherit from multiple parent classes. For example, suppose you're writing an application to manage a university's students and personnel. Two important classes are Student, which represents people who take classes, and Faculty, which represents people who teach classes.

The problem arises when you try to add a Teaching Assistant class to represent teaching assistants who are students who also teach classes. Ideally, you would like to use *multiple inheritance*, where a class has more than one parent class, to make this class inherit from both the Student and Faculty classes, so it can take advantage of their code as shown in Figure 5-3. Unfortunately, C# does not allow multiple inheritance, so this isn't possible.

Although you can't use multiple inheritance in C#, you can use interfaces to simulate multiple inheritance, as described next.

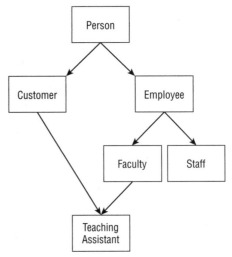

FIGURE 5-3: C# does not enable a class such as TeachingAssistant to inherit from more than one parent class.

> **NOTE** An interface requires a class to provide certain features much as a parent class does, except the interface doesn't provide an implementation. Because this is somewhat similar to inheritance without the implementation, it is sometimes called interface inheritance. A class can inherit from at most one parent class, but it can implement any number of interfaces.

Defining Interfaces

An interface is similar to a class that specifies properties, methods, and events, but it doesn't provide any code to implement them. It forms a contract specifying features that other classes can implement.

If a class implements an interface, it agrees to provide the features defined by the interface. That tells other parts of the program that the class has those features, so the code can invoke them.

This provides a kind of polymorphism that is similar to the way classes let a program treat an object as if it were of another class. For example, suppose the Employee class inherits from the Person class and implements the ICloneable interface. In that case a program could treat an Employee object as if it were an Employee, Person, or ICloneable object.

This may all seem a bit abstract, but an example should make it easier to understand. The following code shows a simple interface named IStudent that defines the features of a student:

```
public interface IStudent
{
    // The student's list of current courses.
    List<string> Courses { get; set; }

    // Print the student's current grades.
    void PrintGrades();
}
```

This interface defines a property named Courses that is of type List<string> and a method named PrintGrades. (In a real application, the interface would probably be more complicated and define many other features.)

> **NOTE** By convention, interface names begin with a capital letter I as in
> IStudent, IComparable, *and* ICloneable.

The following code shows the Student class:

```
public class Student : Person, IStudent
{
    // Implement IStudent.Courses.
    // The student's list of current courses.
    public List<string> Courses { get; set; }

    // Implement IStudent.PrintGrades.
    // Print the student's current grades.
    public void PrintGrades()
    {
        // Do whatever is necessary...
    }
}
```

This class inherits from the Person class, which provides the FirstName and LastName properties. It also implements the IStudent interface. The code inside the Student class must provide implementations for the features defined by the `IStudent` interface. In this example, it provides the `Courses` property as an auto-implemented property, and it includes code (which isn't shown here) to implement the `PrintGrades` method.

The following code shows the `TeachingAssistant` class. (Assume for now that the other classes shown in Figure 5-3 such as `Employee`, `Faculty`, and `Staff` have been defined.)

```
public class TeachingAssistant : Faculty, IStudent
{
    // Implement IStudent.Courses.
    // The student's list of current courses.
    public List<string> Courses { get; set; }

    // Implement IStudent.PrintGrades.
    // Print the student's current grades.
    public void PrintGrades()
    {
        // Do whatever is necessary...
    }
}
```

This class inherits from the `Faculty` class and implements the `IStudent` interface. Now the program can create a `TeachingAssistant` object and treat it as either a `Faculty` object or an object that implements `IStudent`.

Implementing Interfaces

Sometimes writing all the methods defined by an interface can be a lot of work. Unless the interface is well documented, even figuring out what properties, methods, and events are necessary can be hard.

Fortunately, Visual Studio provides a tool that creates code to implement an interface for you. To use the tool, write the class's declaration and specify the interface:

```
public class TeachingAssistant : Faculty, IStudent
{
}
```

At this point, Visual Studio knows you have not implemented the interface. Right-click the interface's declaration to display a context menu (in this example, `IStudent` in the class statement). Open the Implement Interface item, and select either Implement Interface or Implement Interface Explicitly to make Visual Studio insert code stubs that satisfy the interface.

The following code shows the result produced by this tool for the `TeachingAssistant` class if you pick the Implement Interface Explicitly item:

```
// Explicit implementation.
public class TeachingAssistant : Faculty, IStudent
{
    List<string> IStudent.Courses
    {
        get
        {
            throw new NotImplementedException();
        }
```

```
        set
        {
            throw new NotImplementedException();
        }
    }

    void IStudent.PrintGrades()
    {
        throw new NotImplementedException();
    }
}
```

If you select Implement Interface, the code doesn't include the `IStudent.` parts, shown highlighted in the previous code.

The new pieces of code simply throw exceptions when they are called. You need to edit the code to replace the default code with code that provides the needed features.

Aside from the difference in syntax, there is a functional difference between implicit and explicit interface implementation. If a class implements an interface explicitly, the program cannot access the interface's members through a class instance. Instead it must use an instance of the interface.

For example, suppose the `TeachingAssistant` implements the `IStudent` interface explicitly. Then the following code shows incorrect and correct way to call the `PrintGrades` method:

```
TeachingAssistant ta = new TeachingAssistant();

// The following causes a design time error.
ta.PrintGrades();

// The following code works.
IStudent student = ta;
student.PrintGrades();
```

If a class implements an interface implicitly, the program can access the interface members through either a class instance or an interface instance.

Delegating Interfaces

The `Student` and `TeachingAssistant` classes shown earlier both implement the `IStudent` interface, so they both include code to provide the interface's features.

> **BEST PRACTICES: Avoiding Dangerous Duplication**
>
> Seeing that duplicated code should have given you a bad feeling because it's never a good idea for a program to contain duplicated pieces of code. Duplicated code means you need to write and debug the code twice. Even worse, it means that you need to maintain the code in parallel over time. If you update the code in one place but forget to update it in another, you could hide bugs and the program may produce inconsistent results depending on which piece of code is executed.

You can avoid duplicating this code by delegating the work of implementing the interface to a `Student` object inside the `TeachingAssistant` class. Simply place a `Student` object inside the `TeachingAssistant` class. Whenever the `TeachingAssistant` object needs to perform some task specified by the `IStudent` interface, it makes its `Student` object do the work.

The following code shows the `TeachingAssistant` class delegating to a `Student` object:

```
// Delegate IStudent to a Student object.
public class TeachingAssistant : Faculty, IStudent
{
    // A Student object to handle IStudent.
    private Student MyStudent = new Student();

    public List<string> Courses
    {
        get
        {
            return MyStudent.Courses;
        }
        set
        {
            MyStudent.Courses = value;
        }
    }

    public void PrintGrades()
    {
        MyStudent.PrintGrades();
    }
}
```

The class defines a private instance of the `Student` class named `MyStudent`. To implement the `Courses` property, the class uses the `MyStudent` object's `Courses` property. To implement the `PrintGrades` method, the class calls the `MyStudent` object's `PrintGrades` method.

This may seem like extra work, but it lets you keep all the code to implement the interface in the `Student` class. Now if you need to change the code, you can do it in that one place.

IMPLEMENTING COMMON INTERFACES

The .NET Framework includes many interfaces that help Framework classes do their jobs. For example, if one of your classes implements the `IComparable` interface, the `Array.Sort` method can sort an array of that class.

The following sections explain how you can implement some of the most useful interfaces defined by the .NET Framework.

> **NOTE** The `IDisposable` *interface is another useful interface defined by the .NET Framework. It is described in the section "Implementing the IDisposable Interface."*

IComparable

If a class implements IComparable, it provides a CompareTo method that enables a program to compare two instances of the class and determine which belongs before the other in sorted order. For example, suppose you want to make a Car class to keep track of your favorite cars and you want to sort Car objects by their names. In that case you can make the Car class implement the IComparable interface, and then use Array.Sort to sort an array of Car objects.

The IComparable interface comes in two versions: a plain version and a generic version.

If you use the plain version, the CompareTo method takes two nonspecific objects as parameters, and the code must convert them into Car objects before comparing their names. The following code shows the Car class with this type of CompareTo method:

```
class Car : IComparable
{
    public string Name { get; set; }
    public int MaxMph { get; set; }
    public int Horsepower { get; set; }
    public decimal Price { get; set; }

    // Compare Cars alphabetically by Name.
    public int CompareTo(object obj)
    {
        if (!(obj is Car))
            throw new ArgumentException("Object is not a Car");

        Car other = obj as Car;
        return Name.CompareTo(other.Name);
    }
}
```

The CompareTo method first checks whether the obj parameter is a Car object and throws an exception if it is not. If obj is a Car, the method creates a Car variable to work with it and then compares the current object's Name property to the other Car's Name property.

The following code shows the Car class implementing the generic version of the IComparable interface:

```
class Car : IComparable<Car>
{
    public string Name { get; set; }
    public int MaxMph { get; set; }
    public int Horsepower { get; set; }
    public decimal Price { get; set; }

    // Compare Cars alphabetically by Name.
    public int CompareTo(Car other)
    {
        return this.Name.CompareTo(other.Name);
    }
}
```

In this version, the interface name is followed by a generic parameter telling the kind of object to which the class can compare itself, in this case `Car`. The `CompareTo` method's parameter is an object of that type, so `CompareTo` doesn't need to verify that the object is a `Car` and it doesn't need to convert the object into a `Car`.

COMMON MISTAKES: The Generic Version of IComparable

The generic version of `IComparable` is simpler than the nongeneric version and provides strong type checking, so you should use it. The nongeneric version is provided for compatibility with older versions of the .NET Framework. The strong type checking provided by the generic version prevents you from making the mistake of trying to compare objects of the wrong type. If you use the generic version, Visual Studio will flag the error at design time.

The IComparableCars example program, which is available for download on the book's website, uses this version of the `Car` class to display an array of `Cars`. The program uses the following code to display the array of `Cars` twice, first unsorted and then sorted:

CODE LAB   Comparing Cars [IComparableCars]

```
private void Form1_Load(object sender, EventArgs e)
{
    // Make some data.
    Car[] cars =
    {
        new Car() { Name="SSC Ultimate Aero", MaxMph=257,
            Horsepower=1183, Price=654400m},
        new Car() { Name="Bugatti Veyron", MaxMph=253,
            Horsepower=1001, Price=1700000m},
        ...
    };

    // Display the cars unsorted.
    DisplayCars(cars, unsortedListView);

    // Sort the array of cars.
    Array.Sort(cars);

    // Display the cars sorted.
    DisplayCars(cars, sortedListView);
}
```

Code Lab Analysis

After creating the `cars` array, the code calls the `DisplayCars` method, described shortly, to display the `Cars` in the `ListView` control named `unsortedListView`. It then calls `Array.Sort` to sort the cars array and calls `DisplayCars` again to display the sorted array in the `ListView` control named `sortedListView`.

The following code shows the `DisplayCars` method:

```
// Display the cars in the ListView control.
private void DisplayCars(Car[] cars, ListView listView)
{
    listView.Items.Clear();
    foreach (Car car in cars)
    {
        ListViewItem item = listView.Items.Add(car.Name);
        item.SubItems.Add(car.MaxMph.ToString());
        item.SubItems.Add(car.Horsepower.ToString());
        item.SubItems.Add(car.Price.ToString("C"));
    }
    foreach (ColumnHeader header in listView.Columns)
    {
        header.Width = -2;
    }
}
```

This method clears the items in the `ListView` control and then loops through the `cars` array. For each `Car` object, the code creates a `ListViewItem` displaying the `Car`'s `Name` property. It then gives that item subitems that display the `Car`'s `MaxMph`, `Horsepower`, and `Price` properties.

The method finishes by setting each `ListView` column's `Width` property to –2, which makes it size itself to fit its data.

Figure 5-4 shows the IComparableCars example program displaying its unsorted and sorted lists of cars.

Name	Max MPH	Horsepower	Price	Name	Max MPH	Horsepower	Price
Bugatti Veyron	253	1001	$1,700,000.00	SSC Ultimate Aero	257	1183	$654,400.00
Ferrari Enzo	217	660	$670,000.00	Bugatti Veyron	253	1001	$1,700,000.00
Jaguar XJ220	217	542	$650,000.00	Saleen S7 Twin-Turbo	248	750	$555,000.00
Koenigsegg CCX	245	806	$545,568.00	Koenigsegg CCX	245	806	$545,568.00
Lamborghini Murcielago LP640	211	640	$430,000.00	McLaren F1	240	637	$970,000.00
McLaren F1	240	637	$970,000.00	Ferrari Enzo	217	660	$670,000.00
Pagani Zonda F	215	650	$667,321.00	Jaguar XJ220	217	542	$650,000.00
Porsche Carrera GT	205	612	$440,000.00	Pagani Zonda F	215	650	$667,321.00
Saleen S7 Twin-Turbo	248	750	$555,000.00	Lamborghini Murcielago LP640	211	640	$430,000.00
SSC Ultimate Aero	257	1183	$654,400.00	Porsche Carrera GT	205	612	$440,000.00

FIGURE 5-4: The IComparableCars example program displays a list of Car objects unsorted on the left and sorted on the right.

IComparer

The IComparableCars example program described in the previous section used a `Car` class that implements `IComparable`, so it can sort an array of `Car` objects by their names, but what if you want to sort the `Cars` by maximum speed, horsepower, or price? The `CompareTo` method can sort on only one field at a time, so there isn't a good way to make the `Car` class sort on different properties.

The IComparer interface provides a solution. A class that implements the IComparer interface must provide a Compare method that compares two objects. For example, you could create a CarPriceComparer class that implements IComparer and that has a Compare method that compares Car objects by Price. You could then pass a CarPriceComparer object to the Array.Sort method, and it can use that object to sort an array of Car objects.

> **ADVICE FROM THE EXPERTS: Using the Generic Version of IComparer**
>
> Like the IComparable interface, IComparer has generic and nongeneric versions. The generic version is simpler and provides strong type checking so you should use it.

The CarPriceComparer class takes care of sorting by Price but still leaves the problem of sorting by maximum speed or other Car properties. You could make multiple Car comparer classes but there's an easier solution.

Make a single CarComparer class and give it a field that the program can set to tell it which Car field to use when comparing Car objects. The following code shows a CarComparer class that demonstrates this approach:

```
class CarComparer : IComparer<Car>
{
    // The field to compare.
    public enum CompareField
    {
        Name,
        MaxMph,
        Horsepower,
        Price,
    }
    public CompareField SortBy = CompareField.Name;

    public int Compare(Car x, Car y)
    {
        switch (SortBy)
        {
            case CompareField.Name:
                return x.Name.CompareTo(y.Name);
            case CompareField.MaxMph:
                return x.MaxMph.CompareTo(y.MaxMph);
            case CompareField.Horsepower:
                return x.Horsepower.CompareTo(y.Horsepower);
            case CompareField.Price:
                return x.Price.CompareTo(y.Price);
        }
        return x.Name.CompareTo(y.Name);
    }
}
```

The class begins with an enumeration that defines the kinds of sorting that this class can provide. Its SortBy field indicates the Car field that the class should use when sorting.

The Compare method examines the SortBy value and compares two Car objects appropriately.

The IComparerCars example program, which is shown in Figure 5-5 and available for download on the book's website, uses this CarComparer class to sort Car objects by Name, MaxMph, Horsepower, or Price.

The IComparerCars example program uses the following code to display its Car objects:

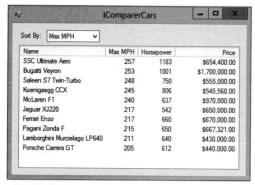

FIGURE 5-5: The IComparerCars example program displays a list of Car objects sorted by Name, MaxMph, Horsepower, or Price.

```csharp
// Display the cars in the ListView control.
private void DisplayCars()
{
    if (Cars == null) return;

    // Make the appropriate comparer.
    CarComparer comparer = new CarComparer();
    if (sortByComboBox.Text == "Name")
        comparer.SortBy = CarComparer.CompareField.Name;
    else if (sortByComboBox.Text == "Max MPH")
        comparer.SortBy = CarComparer.CompareField.MaxMph;
    else if (sortByComboBox.Text == "Horsepower")
        comparer.SortBy = CarComparer.CompareField.Horsepower;
    else
        comparer.SortBy = CarComparer.CompareField.Price;

    // Sort.
    Array.Sort(Cars, comparer);

    // If we're not sorting by name, reverse the array.
    if (sortByComboBox.Text != "Name") Array.Reverse(Cars);

    carListView.Items.Clear();
    foreach (Car car in Cars)
    {
        ListViewItem item = carListView.Items.Add(car.Name);
        item.SubItems.Add(car.MaxMph.ToString());
        item.SubItems.Add(car.Horsepower.ToString());
        item.SubItems.Add(car.Price.ToString("C"));
    }
    foreach (ColumnHeader header in carListView.Columns)
    {
        header.Width = -2;
    }
}
```

This method creates a `CarComparer` object and sets its `SortBy` value according to the value selected in the program's `sortByComboBox` control. It then calls `Array.Sort` passing it the array of `Car` objects and the `CarComparer`. To display the numeric `Car` values (`MaxMph`, `Horsepower`, and `Price`) in descending order, the program calls `Array.Reverse` if it is sorting by one of those values. Finally, the method displays the sorted `Car` data in a `ListView` control much as the previous example did.

IEquatable

If a class implements the `IComparable` interface, it provides a `CompareTo` method that enables you to determine how two objects should be ordered. Sometimes, you may not need to know how two objects should be ordered, but you need to know instead whether the objects are equal. The `IEquatable` interface provides that capability by requiring a class to provide an `Equals` method.

For example, the IEquatablePerson example program, which is available for download on the book's website, enables you to build a list of `Person` objects. If you try to create a `Person` with the same first and last name as a previously created `Person`, the program displays an error message.

The following code shows the program's `Person` class:

```
class Person : IEquatable<Person>
{
    public string FirstName { get; set; }
    public string LastName { get; set; }

    public bool Equals(Person other)
    {
        return ((FirstName == other.FirstName) &&
            (LastName == other.LastName));
    }
}
```

This class has two properties, `FirstName` and `LastName`, and a simple `Equals` method that returns true if the two `Person` objects have the same names.

The following code shows how the program adds a new `Person` to its list when you enter a first and last name in the `TextBoxes` and then click Add:

```
// The List of Persons.
private List<Person> People = new List<Person>();

// Add a Person to the List.
private void btnAdd_Click(object sender, EventArgs e)
{
    // Make the new Person.
    Person person = new Person()
    {
        FirstName = firstNameTextBox.Text,
        LastName = lastNameTextBox.Text
    };

    if (People.Contains(person))
    {
        MessageBox.Show("The list already contains this person.");
    }
```

```
    else
    {
        People.Add(person);
        firstNameTextBox.Clear();
        lastNameTextBox.Clear();
        firstNameTextBox.Focus();
    }
}
```

The btnAdd_Click event handler uses the value entered in the TextBoxes to create a new Person object. It then uses the list's Contains method to see if the Person is already in the list. If the Person is already in the list, the program displays a message. If the Person is not in the list, the program adds it.

The list's Contains method uses the fact that the Person class implements IEquatable to decide whether two objects are the same. If you comment out the : IEquatable part of the Person class's declaration, the class no longer implements IEquatable, so the list treats two different objects as different even if they happen to have the same first and last name values. (You don't even need to remove the Equals method from the Person class. If the class doesn't implement IEquatable, the Contains method won't use Equals.)

> **BEST PRACTICES: Provide Equatable**
>
> Generic collection classes such as List, Dictionary, Stack, and Queue provide Contains and other methods that compare objects for equality. Microsoft recommends that any class that you are likely to place in one of these generic collections should implement IEquatable.

ICloneable

A class that implements the ICloneable interface must provide a Clone method that returns a copy of the object for which it is called. For example, the following code shows a simple, cloneable Person class:

```
class Person : ICloneable
{
    public string FirstName { get; set; }
    public string LastName { get; set; }
    public Person Manager { get; set; }

    // Return a clone of this person.
    public object Clone()
    {
        Person person = new Person();
        person.FirstName = FirstName;
        person.LastName = LastName;
        person.Manager = Manager;
        return person;
    }
}
```

This class's `Clone` method simply creates a new `Person` object with the same `FirstName`, `LastName`, and `Manager` properties as the original and then returns the new object. Notice that the `Clone` method returns a nonspecific `object`, not a `Person`, so the calling code must cast the result into a `Person`.

The following code shows how the `ICloneablePerson` example program, which is available for download on the book's website, creates two `Person` objects and then clones one of them:

```
Person ann = new Person()
{
    FirstName = "Ann",
    LastName = "Archer",
    Manager = null
};
Person bob = new Person()
{
    FirstName = "Bob",
    LastName = "Baker",
    Manager = ann
};
Person bob2 = (Person)bob.Clone();
```

This code creates a `Person` named Ann Archer and another named Bob Baker. It then clones the Bob Baker `Person` to make a third `Person` object.

CLEVER CLONES

There are two kinds of clones: shallow clones and deep clones.

In a *shallow clone*, any reference values in the copy refer to the same objects as those in the original object. The `Person.Clone` method class described in this section is a shallow clone because it sets the clone's `Manager` property equal to the `Manager` property of the original object.

In a *deep clone*, the new object's reference values are set to new objects. The following code shows how the `Person` class could provide deep clones:

```
public object Clone()
{
    Person person = new Person();
    person.FirstName = FirstName;
    person.LastName = LastName;
    person.Manager = Manager;
    if (Manager != null)
        person.Manager = (Person)Manager.Clone();
    return person;
}
```

The `ICloneable` interface doesn't specify whether the `Clone` method should return a shallow or deep clone, so you must do what makes the most sense for your application. If you like, you can also make a second `Clone` method that takes as a parameter a boolean value that indicates whether the copy should be a deep clone.

IEnumerable

A class that implements the IEnumerable interface provides a method for a program to enumerate the items that the class contains. Its GetEnumerator method returns an object that implements IEnumerator.

The IEnumerator object provides a Current property that returns the current object in the enumeration. It also provides a MoveNext method that moves the enumerator to the next object in the enumeration and a Reset method that resets the enumerator to just before the beginning of the enumeration. Finally, the enumerator provides a Dispose method that lets it clean up any resources it is using when it is no longer needed.

The IEnumerableTree example program, which is shown in Figure 5-6 and available for download on the book's website, builds a tree and then enumerates over the nodes it contains.

FIGURE 5-6: The IEnumerableTree example program enumerates over the nodes in a tree.

The following code shows the TreeNode class that holds information for a node in a tree.

CODE LAB **Enumerating Tree Nodes [IEnumerableTree]**

```
class TreeNode : IEnumerable<TreeNode>
{
    public int Depth = 0;
    public string Text = "";
    public List<TreeNode> Children = new List<TreeNode>();
    public TreeNode(string text)
    {
        Text = text;
    }

    // Add and create children.
    public TreeNode AddChild(string text)
    {
        TreeNode child = new TreeNode(text);
        child.Depth = Depth + 1;
        Children.Add(child);
        return child;
    }

    // Return the tree's nodes in an preorder traversal.
    public List<TreeNode> Preorder()
    {
        // Make the result list.
        List<TreeNode> nodes = new List<TreeNode>();

        // Traverse this node's subtree.
        TraversePreorder(nodes);

        // Return the result.
```

```
            return nodes;
        }
        private void TraversePreorder(List<TreeNode> nodes)
        {
            // Traverse this node.
            nodes.Add(this);

            // Traverse the children.
            foreach (TreeNode child in Children)
                child.TraversePreorder(nodes);
        }

        public IEnumerator<TreeNode> GetEnumerator()
        {
            return new TreeEnumerator(this);
        }
        IEnumerator IEnumerable.GetEnumerator()
        {
            return new TreeEnumerator(this);
        }
    }
}
```

Code Lab Analysis

The class begins by defining the node's Depth in the tree and the Text value that the node holds. The Children field holds a list of the TreeNode objects that are the node's children in the tree. The class provides a single constructor that initializes the node's text.

To make building a tree easier, the AddChild method adds a new child to the node's Children list and returns the new child.

The Preorder method returns the tree's nodes in a preorder traversal. In a preorder traversal, each node displays before its children. The Preorder method builds a list of TreeNode objects to hold the traversal and then calls the TraversePreorder method to perform the actual traversal. The TraversePreorder method adds the current node to the list of nodes and then recursively calls each of the child nodes' TraversePreorder methods, so they can add themselves to the list. Figure 5-6 shows the preorder traversal for the tree built by the example program.

The rest of the TreeNode class's code is part of the IEnumerable interface. The two GetEnumerator methods, both of which are required, return an enumerator object. In this program, the object is of the type TreeEnumerator, a class that is described next.

The TreeEnumerator class defines objects that can enumerate over a tree made of TreeNode objects:

```
class TreeEnumerator : IEnumerator<TreeNode>
{
    // The tree's nodes in their proper order.
    private List<TreeNode> Nodes;

    // The index of the current node.
    private int CurrentIndex;
```

```
        // Constructor.
        public TreeEnumerator(TreeNode root)
        {
            Nodes = root.Preorder();
            Reset();
        }

        public TreeNode Current
        {
            get { return GetCurrent(); }
        }
        object IEnumerator.Current
        {
            get { return GetCurrent(); }
        }
        private TreeNode GetCurrent()
        {
            if (CurrentIndex < 0)
                throw new InvalidOperationException();
            if (CurrentIndex >= Nodes.Count)
                throw new InvalidOperationException();
            return Nodes[CurrentIndex];
        }

        public bool MoveNext()
        {
            CurrentIndex++;
            return (CurrentIndex < Nodes.Count);
        }

        public void Reset()
        {
            CurrentIndex = -1;
        }

        public void Dispose()
        {
        }
    }
```

The class begins with a list that holds the nodes in the traversal over which the TreeEnumerator can enumerate. The CurrentIndex field keeps track of the index of current TreeNode in the traversal.

The TreeEnumerator's constructor takes a TreeNode as a parameter, uses its Preorder method to get a traversal of the tree rooted at the TreeNode, and saves the result in the Nodes list. It then calls Reset (described shortly) to reset the enumerator to the beginning of the traversal.

The two Current methods return a reference to the current TreeNode object in the enumeration. Both of these methods call the GetCurrent method to get the object in position CurrentIndex in the list of TreeNode objects.

The MoveNext method simply adds 1 to CurrentIndex. If the new value of CurrentIndex is within the range of the Nodes list, MoveNext returns true to indicate that the current item exists and the enumerator hasn't finished enumerating all the items.

The Reset method sets CurrentIndex to –1. By convention the enumeration should begin (and reset to) one position before the first item, so the program must call MoveNext before using the first item.

The class finishes with the Dispose method. In this example, method doesn't need to do anything. See the section "Implementing the IDisposable Interface" for more information on the Dispose method and the IDisposable interface.

With the TreeNode class implementing IEnumerable and the TreeEnumerator class implementing IEnumerator, the main program can create and use enumerators to enumerate over a TreeNode's tree. The following code shows how the main example program builds and displays its tree:

```
// Build and display a tree.
private void Form1_Load(object sender, EventArgs e)
{
    // Build the tree.
    TreeNode president = new TreeNode("President");
    TreeNode sales = president.AddChild("VP Sales");
    sales.AddChild("Domestic Sales");
    sales.AddChild("International Sales");
    // Other tree-building code omitted.
    ...

    // Display the tree.
    string text = "";
    IEnumerator<TreeNode> enumerator = president.GetEnumerator();
    while (enumerator.MoveNext())
        text += new string(' ', 4 * enumerator.Current.Depth) +
            enumerator.Current.Text +
            Environment.NewLine;
    text = text.Substring(0, text.Length - Environment.NewLine.Length);
    treeTextBox.Text = text;
    treeTextBox.Select(0, 0);
}
```

The code starts by building a tree. It then uses the root node's GetEnumerator method to get an enumerator.

The code then enters a while loop that executes as long as the enumerator's MoveNext method returns true to indicate that there is a valid current record. Inside the loop, the code gets the enumerator's current TreeNode object and uses its Depth and Text fields to add the object to the text the program is building.

After the loop finishes, the code removes the new line at the end of the text and displays the result in a TextBox.

BEST PRACTICES: Making Enumerations Easy

Implementing the IEnumerable interface is a lot of work, requiring you to implement several methods plus making an IEnumerator helper class. If all the program wants to do is loop over a series of objects, there's an easier approach.

Give the class a method that returns an object of type IEnumerable<class> where class is the class you're working with. Have the method find the objects that should be in the enumeration and call yield return to place each in the enumeration. Make the method return or call yield break when it finishes building the enumeration.

The following code shows how the TreeNode class creates an enumeration in the TreeEnumerator example program, which is available for download on the book's website:

```
// Return an enumerator.
public IEnumerable<TreeNode> GetTraversal()
{
    // Get the preorder traversal.
    List<TreeNode> traversal = Preorder();

    // Yield the nodes in the traversal.
    foreach (TreeNode node in traversal) yield return node;
    yield break;
}
```

The code calls the Preorder method described earlier to get a list containing the tree's nodes. It then loops over the nodes in the list calling yield return to add each to the enumeration. It finishes the enumeration by calling yield break.

The following code shows how the main program uses the enumeration:

```
string text = "";
foreach (TreeNode node in president.GetTraversal())
{
    text += new string(' ', 4 * node.Depth) +
        node.Text +
        Environment.NewLine;
}
```

This code loops over the enumeration returned by the GetTraversal method to build a result string in the same way the previous version of the program did.

If you just want to use foreach to iterate over some items, using the yield keyword is a lot easier than implementing IEnumerable.

MANAGING OBJECT LIFE CYCLE

When a C# program instantiates a class, it creates an object. The program manipulates the object for a while, and at some point the object may no longer be needed. When the program loses its last reference to the object, either because all the references to it have been set to `null` or have gone out of scope, that object is no longer accessible to the program and becomes a candidate for *garbage collection* (the process of running the garbage collector to reclaim memory that is no longer accessible to the program).

At some later point, the *garbage collector* (GC) may decide the program is running low on memory and decide to start garbage collection. The GC marks all the memory that has been used by the program as currently *unreachable*. It then goes through all the references accessible to the program and marks the memory to which they refer as *reachable*. If a reference refers to an object that has its own references, the GC follows those references until it has visited every object that the program can reach.

When it finishes checking references, the GC examines any objects still marked as unreachable. If an object has a `Finalize` method (described in greater detail in the section "Providing Destructors" later in this chapter), the GC calls it to let the object perform any necessary cleanup chores. After calling `Finalize`, the GC at long last recycles the object's memory and makes it available for future use.

The process of calling an object's `Finalize` method is called *finalization*. Because you can't tell when the GC will call an object's `Finalize` method, this process is called *nondeterministic finalization*.

This process is reasonably straightforward for simple objects, but can become more complicated when an object has access to a resource that must be cleaned up somehow. For example, suppose a program creates an object that locks a file for writing, perhaps to log events. When the object goes out of scope, the object is a candidate for finalization, but you can't tell when the GC will get around to finalizing it. Meanwhile the file remains locked, possibly for a long time. Actually, if the program doesn't use too much memory, the GC might not run at all while the program executes, so it might not release the file until the program ends.

You can take two steps to help objects free their resources: implementing the `IDisposable` interface and providing destructors.

Implementing the IDisposable Interface

A class that implements the `IDisposable` interface must provide a `Dispose` method that cleans up any resources used by the class. The program should call the `Dispose` method (or use the `using` statement described in the section "Using the using Statement" later in this chapter) when an object is no longer needed so it can perform this cleanup.

The `Dispose` method's main purpose is to clean up unmanaged resources, but it can also clean up managed resources. If an object uses references to other objects that implement the `IDisposable` interface, it can call those objects' `Dispose` methods.

> **NOTE** *Managed resources are those under the control of the Common Language Runtime (CLR), the runtime environment that executes C# programs.*
>
> *Unmanaged resources are those outside of the control of the CLR. Unmanaged resources include such things as handles to windows, files, pens, brushes, and other objects the program is manipulating through API calls.*

For example, suppose a `Shape` object represents a drawn shape and has properties that are references to `Brush` and `Pen` objects. The `Brush` and `Pen` classes are managed classes, and they implement `IDisposable`, so the `Shape` class's `Dispose` method should call their `Dispose` methods to free their resources.

For another example, suppose the `ImageTransformer` class uses unmanaged code to manipulate bitmaps. It uses API calls to get a handle to a bitmap (HBITMAP) and other API calls to get a device context (DC) and to manipulate the bitmap. Because these handles were obtained by using API calls, they represent unmanaged resources. If an `ImageTransformer` object is destroyed without using other API calls to free those handles, their memory is lost. The `ImageTransformer` class's `Dispose` method should use the appropriate API calls to free those resources when they are no longer needed.

> **BEST PRACTICES: Reusing Objects**
>
> Microsoft recommends that a class provide `Close` and `Open` methods if a program might want to later reopen the object's resources. In contrast the `Dispose` method should be called only if the object will not be needed again later. Trying to use an object after its `Dispose` method has been called usually causes an exception.

By convention it should be safe to call an object's `Dispose` method more than once. You can give the class a boolean variable to indicate whether the method has been called before and make the method do nothing if it has already executed.

Unfortunately `IDisposable` is only half of the story. Before you see code for a class that implements `IDisposable`, you should learn about the rest of the solution for freeing resources: destructors.

Providing Destructors

The `Dispose` method frees resources if the program calls it, but if the program doesn't call `Dispose`, the resources are not freed. When the GC eventually gets around to destroying the object, it frees any managed resources, but unmanaged resources are not freed and are lost to the program. To handle this situation, you can give the class a destructor to free resources when the object is destroyed.

A *destructor* is a method with no return type and a name that includes the class's name prefixed by ~. The GC executes an object's destructor before permanently destroying it.

For example, the following code shows an empty destructor for the class named `DisposableClass`:

```
~DisposableClass()
{
}
```

Several rules apply to destructors that do not apply to other methods. The following list summarizes these rules:

➤ Destructors can be defined in classes only, not structures.

➤ A class can have at most one destructor.

➤ Destructors cannot be inherited or overloaded.

➤ Destructors cannot be called directly.

➤ Destructors cannot have modifiers or parameters.

DESTRUCTOR TO FINALIZER

The GC actually calls an object's finalizer, not its destructor. The destructor is converted into an override version of the `Finalize` method that executes the destructor's code and then calls the base class's `Finalize` method. For example, suppose the `Person` class includes the following destructor:

```
~Person()
{
    // Free unmanaged resources here.
    ...
}
```

This destructor is converted into the following `Finalize` method:

```
protected override void Finalize()
{
    try
    {
        // Free unmanaged resources here.
        ...
    }
    finally
    {
        base.Finalize();
    }
}
```

You cannot explicitly override the `Finalize` method in C# code. That's just as well because your code cannot call the base class's `Finalize` method directly. (See the preceding list of destructor rules.)

The GC calls the destructor before it permanently destroys the object so you have one last chance to clean up the object's mess.

When the destructor executes, the GC is probably in the process of destroying other objects, so the destructor's code cannot depend on other objects existing. For example, suppose the `Person` class contains a reference to a `Company` object. The `Person` class's destructor cannot assume that its `Company` object exists because it may have already been destroyed by the GC. That means the `Person` class's destructor cannot call the `Company` object's `Dispose` method (if it has one).

There's one final twist to the resource management saga. If an object has a destructor, it must pass through a *finalization queue* (a queue of objects that are ready to be finalized) before it is destroyed, and that takes extra time. If the `Dispose` method has already freed all the object's resources, there's no need to run the object's destructor. In that case, the `Dispose` method can call `GC.SuppressFinalize` to tell the GC not to call the object's finalizer (destructor) and to let the object skip the finalization queue.

The following list summarizes the resource management rules and concepts:

➤ If a class contains no managed resources and no unmanaged resources, it doesn't need to implement `IDisposable` or have a destructor.

➤ If the class has only managed resources, it should implement `IDisposable` but it doesn't need a destructor. (When the destructor executes, you can't be sure managed objects still exist, so you can't call their `Dispose` methods anyway.)

➤ If the class has only unmanaged resources, it needs to implement `IDisposable` and needs a destructor in case the program doesn't call `Dispose`.

➤ The `Dispose` method must be safe to run more than once. You can achieve that by using a variable to keep track of whether it has been run before.

➤ The `Dispose` method should free both managed and unmanaged resources.

➤ The destructor should free only unmanaged resources. (When the destructor executes, you can't be sure managed objects still exist, so you can't call their `Dispose` methods anyway.)

➤ After freeing resources, the destructor should call `GC.SuppressFinalize`, so the object can skip the finalization queue.

COMMON MISTAKES: Using Managed Versus Unmanaged Resources

To avoid confusion, a class should ideally not include both managed and unmanaged resources. If the class has unmanaged resources, it should manage only one resource.

The IDisposableClass example program, which is available for download, uses the following class to demonstrate the `IDisposable` interface and destructors:

```
class DisposableClass : IDisposable
{
    // A name to keep track of the object.
    public string Name = "";

    // Free managed and unmanaged resources.
    public void Dispose()
    {
```

```
            FreeResources(true);
    }

    // Destructor to clean up unmanaged resources
    // but not managed resources.
    ~DisposableClass()
    {
        FreeResources(false);
    }

    // Keep track if whether resources are already freed.
    private bool ResourcesAreFreed = false;

    // Free resources.
    private void FreeResources(bool freeManagedResources)
    {
        Console.WriteLine(Name + ": FreeResources");
        if (!ResourcesAreFreed)
        {
            // Dispose of managed resources if appropriate.
            if (freeManagedResources)
            {
                // Dispose of managed resources here.
                Console.WriteLine(Name + ": Dispose of managed resources");
            }

            // Dispose of unmanaged resources here.
            Console.WriteLine(Name + ": Dispose of unmanaged resources");

            // Remember that we have disposed of resources.
            ResourcesAreFreed = true;

            // We don't need the destructor because
            // our resources are already freed.
            GC.SuppressFinalize(this);
        }
    }
}
}
```

The class starts by defining a string property called Name. The example program uses Name to keep track of the objects that it creates. (You probably won't need this field in your classes.)

The Dispose method calls the FreeResources method described shortly to do all the work. It passes the method the value true to indicate that FreeResources should free managed resources.

The destructor also calls FreeResources to do the interesting work. It passes that method the value false to indicate that FreeResources should not free managed resources. Remember that managed objects may have already been destroyed when the destructor executes, so the FreeResources method should not try to do anything with them.

Next, the class declares the variable ResourcesAreFreed and sets it to false to indicate that the resources have not yet been freed.

The `FreeResources` method first writes a message in the Console window and then checks the variable `ResourcesAreFreed` to see if the resources have already been freed. If the resources have been freed, the method does nothing.

If the resources have not yet been freed, the `FreeResources` method checks its `freeManaged Resources` parameter to see if it should free managed resources. If `freeManagedResources` is true, the method frees its managed resources. (In this example, the code simply writes a message to the Console window, so you can see what's happening.)

Next, the `FreeResources` method frees the object's unmanaged resources. (In this example, the code writes another message to the Console window, so you can see what's happening.)

The code then sets `ResourcesAreFreed` to true so it knows the resources have been freed. That way if the program calls `Dispose` again later, the method doesn't do anything, so it's safe to call `Dispose` more than once.

Finally, the method calls `GC.SuppressFinalize` to let the object skip the finalization queue when it is destroyed.

The IDisposableClass example program has three buttons: one labeled Create & Dispose, a second labeled Create, and a third labeled Collect Garbage.

When you click the first button, the following code executes:

```
// Used to give objects different names.
private int ObjectNumber = 1;

// Create an object and dispose of it.
private void createAndDisposeButton_Click(object sender, EventArgs e)
{
    // Make an object.
    DisposableClass obj = new DisposableClass();
    obj.Name = "CreateAndDispose " + ObjectNumber.ToString();
    ObjectNumber++;

    // Dispose of the object.
    obj.Dispose();
}
```

This code creates a `DisposableClass` object, sets its `Name` property, and increments the variable `ObjectNumber` used to give the objects different names. It then calls the object's `Dispose` method to free its resources. In this example, the `Dispose` method merely displays messages in the Console window.

If you click the Create button, the following code executes:

```
// Create an object and do not dispose of it.
private void createButton_Click(object sender, EventArgs e)
{
    // Make an object.
    DisposableClass obj = new DisposableClass();
    obj.Name = "Create " + ObjectNumber.ToString();
    ObjectNumber++;
}
```

This is similar to the other button's code except it doesn't call the object's `Dispose` method.

You can use these two buttons to see when the objects you have created free their resources. For example, suppose you click the buttons in the following sequence and then close the program:

1. Create & Dispose

2. Create

3. Create

4. Create & Dispose

When you first click Create & Dispose, you see the following messages in the Console window:

```
CreateAndDispose 1: FreeResources
CreateAndDispose 1: Dispose of managed resources
CreateAndDispose 1: Dispose of unmanaged resources
```

When you then click Create twice, you do not see any new messages in the Console window because those objects have not been destroyed yet. The variables that refer to them are out of scope, so the objects are eligible for finalization but the GC has not destroyed them.

When you click Create & Dispose again, you see the following messages in the Console window as the program creates and disposes of another object:

```
CreateAndDispose 4: FreeResources
CreateAndDispose 4: Dispose of managed resources
CreateAndDispose 4: Dispose of unmanaged resources
```

Finally, when you close the program, you see the following messages in the Console window:

```
Create 3: FreeResources
Create 3: Dispose of unmanaged resources
Create 2: FreeResources
Create 2: Dispose of unmanaged resources
```

Notice that the final two objects aren't destroyed until the program ends and that their destructors are called in reverse order. In general you cannot assume that one object will be destroyed before another one.

Notice also that `FreeResources` was not called again for the first and fourth objects. Their `Dispose` methods were already called, so the call to `GC.SuppressFinalize` prevented their destructors from being called.

If you click the IDisposableClass program's Collect Garbage button, the following code forces the GC to immediately perform garbage collection:

```
// Force garbage collection.
private void collectGarbageButton_Click(object sender, EventArgs e)
{
    GC.Collect();
}
```

You can use the `GC.Collect` statement to test garbage collection and destructors, but you should not use it in the final program because it interferes with the GC's normal scheduling algorithm and may decrease performance.

Using the using Statement

If an object has a `Dispose` method, a program using it should call it when it is done using the object to free its resources. This is important but easy to forget. To make it easier to ensure that the `Dispose` method is called, C# provides the `using` statement.

The `using` statement begins a block of code that is tied to an object that implements `IDisposable`. When the block ends, the program automatically calls the object's `Dispose` method for you.

For example, the following code shows how the IDisposableClass example program described in the previous section could use `using` to allocate and dispose of an object:

```
using (DisposableClass obj = new DisposableClass())
{
    obj.Name = "CreateAndDispose " + ObjectNumber.ToString();
    ObjectNumber++;
}
```

The `using` block calls `Dispose` when it ends, even if the code inside it throws an exception. That makes the previous code equivalent to the following:

```
{
    DisposableClass obj = new DisposableClass();
    try
    {
        obj.Name = "CreateAndDispose " + ObjectNumber.ToString();
        ObjectNumber++;
    }
    finally
    {
        if (obj != null) obj.Dispose();
    }
}
```

The `using` statement has three syntactic forms:

```
// Version 1.
using (DisposableClass obj1 = new DisposableClass())
{
}

// Version 2.
DisposableClass obj2 = new DisposableClass();
using (obj2)
{
}

// Version 3.
DisposableClass obj3;
```

```
using (obj3 = new DisposableClass())
{
}
```

In the first version, the object that the `using` block disposes is declared and initialized inside parentheses after the `using` keyword. This method is preferred because it keeps the variable declaration and assignment together, and because it restricts the variable's scope to the `using` block.

The second and third methods both declare their variable outside of the `using` block, so the variable has scope that extends beyond the block. After the `using` block ends, however, the variable has already been disposed, so it probably can't be used unless it is reinitialized to another object.

REAL-WORLD CASE SCENARIO   Shape Resources

Suppose the `Shape` class has the properties `FillBrush` (of type `Brush`) and `OutlinePen` (of type `Pen`). The `Brush` and `Pen` classes are defined in the `System.Drawing` namespace and are managed classes. How would you manage the `Shape` class's `FillBrush` and `OutlinePen` resources? (Don't worry about any other code that the class should provide, such as methods to draw a shape.)

Solution

Because the `FillBrush` and `OutlinePen` properties are managed resources, the `Shape` class should implement `IDisposable` and not have a destructor. The following `Shape` class works:

```
class Shape : IDisposable, IComparable<Shape>
{
    // The FillBrush and OutlinePen properties.
    public Brush FillBrush { get; set; }
    public Pen OutlinePen  { get; set; }

    // Remember whether we've already run Dispose.
    private bool IsDisposed = false;

    // Clean up managed resources.
    public void Dispose()
    {
        // If we've already run Dispose, do nothing.
        if (IsDisposed) return;

        // Dispose of FillBrush and OutlinePen.
        FillBrush.Dispose();
        OutlinePen.Dispose();

        // Remember that we ran Dispose.
        IsDisposed = true;
    }
}
```

The class implements the `IDisposable` interface. Its `Dispose` method calls the `Dispose` methods for its two managed resources, `FillBrush` and `OutlinePen`. It also sets the boolean variable `IsDisposed` to true, so it knows that the `Dispose` method has executed.

This class does not need a destructor because it has no unmanaged resources. It doesn't need to call `GC.SuppressFinalize` because it has no destructor and therefore won't be put in the finalization queue anyway.

SUMMARY

This chapter explained how to work with classes and interfaces. It explained how to derive one class from another and how to define and implement interfaces.

It also explained how to implement some of the most useful interfaces defined by the .NET Framework: `IComparable`, `IComparer`, `IEquatable`, `ICloneable`, and `IEnumerable`. It explained how to use the `yield return` statement to make enumerations more easily than you can with the `IEnumerable` interface.

Finally, this chapter explained garbage collection and how to manage resources as objects that are created and destroyed. It explained how to use the `IDisposable` interface to free managed and unmanaged resources, and it explained how to use destructors to free unmanaged resources.

An interface specifies properties, methods, and events that a class must provide to implement the interface. A delegate is a bit like an interface in the sense that it specifies the characteristics of a method. It specifies the parameters that a method takes and the type of result it returns, if any. The next chapter explains delegates. It also explains events, which use delegates, and exceptions, which are useful in any program.

TEST QUESTIONS

Read each question carefully and select the answer or answers that represent the best solution to the problem. You can find the answers in Appendix A, "Answers to Chapter Test Questions."

1. Which the following statements about the `base` keyword is false?

    a. A constructor can use at most one `base` statement.

    b. A constructor cannot use both a `base` statement and a `this` statement.

    c. The `base` keyword lets a constructor invoke a different constructor in the same class.

    d. If a constructor uses a `base` statement, its code is executed after the invoked con-
        structor is executed.

2. Which the following statements about the `this` keyword is false?

    a. A constructor can use at most one `this` statement.

    b. A constructor can use a `this` statement and a `base` statement if the `base` statement
        comes first.

    c. The `this` keyword lets a constructor invoke a different constructor in the same class.

    d.   If a constructor uses a `this` statement, its code is executed after the invoked constructor is executed.

3.   Suppose you have defined the `House` and `Boat` classes and you want to make a `HouseBoat` class that inherits from both `House` and `Boat`. Which of the following approaches would not work?

    a.   Make `HouseBoat` inherit from both `House` and `Boat`.

    b.   Make `HouseBoat` inherit from `House` and implement an `IBoat` interface.

    c.   Make `HouseBoat` inherit from `Boat` and implement an `IHouse` interface.

    d.   Make `HouseBoat` implement both `IHouse` and `IBoat` interfaces.

4.   Suppose the `HouseBoat` class implements the `IHouse` interface implicitly and the `IBoat` interface explicitly. Which of the following statements is false?

    a.   The code can use a `HouseBoat` object to access its `IHouse` members.

    b.   The code can use a `HouseBoat` object to access its `IBoat` members.

    c.   The code can treat a `HouseBoat` object as an `IHouse` to access its `IHouse` members.

    d.   The code can treat a `HouseBoat` object as an `IBoat` to access its `IBoat` members.

5.   Which of the following is not a good use of interfaces?

    a.   To simulate multiple inheritance.

    b.   To allow the code to treat objects that implement the interface polymorphically as if they were of the interface's "class."

    c.   To allow the program to treat objects from unrelated classes in a uniform way.

    d.   To reuse the code defined by the interface.

6.   Suppose you want to make a `Recipe` class to store cooking recipes and you want to sort the `Recipes` by the `MainIngredient` property. In that case, which of the following interfaces would probably be most useful?

    a.   `IDisposable`

    b.   `IComparable`

    c.   `IComparer`

    d.   `ISortable`

7.   Suppose you want to sort the `Recipe` class in question 6 by any of the properties `MainIngredient`, `TotalTime`, or `CostPerPerson`. In that case, which of the following interfaces would probably be most useful?

    a.   `IDisposable`

    b.   `IComparable`

    c.   `IComparer`

    d.   `ISortable`

8. Which of the following statements is true?

   a. A class can inherit from at most one class and implement at most one interface.

   b. A class can inherit from any number classes and implement any number of interfaces.

   c. A class can inherit from at most one class and implement any number of interfaces.

   d. A class can inherit from any number of classes and implement at most one interface.

9. A program can use the `IEnumerable` and `IEnumerator` interfaces to do which of the following?

   a. Use `MoveNext` and `Reset` to move through a list of objects.

   b. Use `foreach` to move through a list of objects.

   c. Move through a list of objects by index.

   d. Use the `yield return` statement to make a list of objects for iteration.

10. Which of the following statements about garbage collection is false?

   a. In general, you can't tell when the GC will perform garbage collection.

   b. It is possible for a program to run without ever performing garbage collection.

   c. An object's `Dispose` method can call `GC.SuppressFinalize` to prevent the GC from calling the object's destructor.

   d. Before destroying an object, the GC calls its `Dispose` method.

11. Which of the following statements about destructors is false?

   a. Destructors are called automatically.

   b. Destructors cannot assume that other managed objects exist while they are executing.

   c. Destructors are inherited.

   d. Destructors cannot be overloaded.

12. If a class implements `IDisposable`, its `Dispose` method should do which of the following?

   a. Free managed resources.

   b. Free unmanaged resources.

   c. Call `GC.SuppressFinalize`.

   d. All of the above.

13. If a class has managed resources and no unmanaged resources, it should do which of the following?

   a. Implement `IDisposable` and provide a destructor.

   b. Implement `IDisposable` and not provide a destructor.

   c. Not implement `IDisposable` and provide a destructor.

   d. Not implement `IDisposable` and not provide a destructor.

14. If a class has unmanaged resources and no managed resources, it should do which of the following?

    a. Implement `IDisposable` and provide a destructor.

    b. Implement `IDisposable` and not provide a destructor.

    c. Not implement `IDisposable` and provide a destructor.

    d. Not implement `IDisposable` and not provide a destructor.

ADDITIONAL READING AND RESOURCES

Here are some additional useful resources to help you understand the topics presented in this chapter:

IEnumerable Interface
> `http://msdn.microsoft.com/en-us/library/system.collections.ienumerable.aspx`

Using IEnumerator and IEnumerable in the .NET Framework
> `http://www.codeproject.com/Articles/4074/`
> `Using-IEnumerator-and-IEnumerable-in-the-NET-Frame`

yield (C# Reference)
> `http://msdn.microsoft.com/library/vstudio/9k7k7cf0.aspx`

Garbage Collector Basics and Performance Hints
> `http://msdn.microsoft.com/library/ms973837.aspx`

Garbage Collection: Automatic Memory Management in the Microsoft .NET Framework
> `http://msdn.microsoft.com/magazine/bb985010.aspx`

Finalize Methods and Destructors
> `http://msdn.microsoft.com/library/0s71x931.aspx`

CHEAT SHEET

This cheat sheet is designed as a way for you to quickly study the key points of this chapter.

Inheritance

➤ C# does not enable multiple inheritance.

➤ Use the `base` keyword to make a constructor invoke a parent class constructor as in the following code:

```
public class Employee : Person
{
    public Employee(string firstName, string lastName)
        : base(firstName, lastName)
    {
        ...
    }
}
```

➤ Use the `this` keyword to make a constructor invoke another constructor in the same class as in the following code:

```
public class Person
{
    public string FirstName { get; set; }
    public string LastName { get; set; }

    public Person(string firstName)
    {
        FirstName = firstName;
    }

    public Person(string firstName, string lastName)
        : this(firstName)
    {
        LastName = lastName;
    }
}
```

➤ A constructor can invoke at most one base class constructor or one same class constructor.

➤ If a parent class has constructors, a child class's constructors must invoke them directly or indirectly.

Interfaces

➤ By convention, interface names begin with `I` as in `IComparable`.

➤ A class can inherit from at most one parent class but can implement any number of interfaces.

➤ Implementing an interface is sometimes called interface inheritance.

➤ If a class implements an interface explicitly, the code cannot use an object reference to access the interface's members. Instead it must use an interface instance.

➤ If a class implements an interface implicitly, the code can use a class instance or an interface instance to access the interface's members.

➤ An `IComparable` class provides a `CompareTo` method that determines the order of objects.

➤ An `IComparer` class provides a `Compare` method that compares two objects and determines their ordering.

➤ An `IEquatable` class provides an `Equals` method that determines whether an object is equal to another object.

➤ An `ICloneable` class provides a `Clone` method that returns a copy of an object.

➤ An `IEnumerable` class provides a `GetEnumerator` method that returns an `IEnumerator` object that has `MoveNext` and `Reset` methods for moving through a list of objects.

➤ A method can use the `yield return` statement to add objects to an `IEnumerator` result.

Destructors

➤ Destructors can be defined in classes only, not structures.

➤ A class can have at most one destructor.

➤ Destructors cannot be inherited or overloaded.

➤ Destructors cannot be called directly.

➤ Destructors cannot have modifiers or parameters.

➤ The destructor is converted into an override version of the `Finalize` method. You cannot override `Finalize` or call it directly.

Resource Management

➤ If a class contains no managed resources and no unmanaged resources, it doesn't need to implement `IDisposable` or have a destructor.

➤ If the class has only managed resources, it should implement `IDisposable` but it doesn't need a destructor. (When the destructor executes, you can't be sure managed objects still exist, so you can't call their `Dispose` methods anyway.)

➤ If the class has only unmanaged resources, it needs to implement `IDisposable` and it needs a destructor in case the program doesn't call `Dispose`.

➤ The `Dispose` method must be safe to run more than once. You can achieve that by keeping track of whether it has been run before.

➤ The `Dispose` method should free managed and unmanaged resources.

➤ The destructor should free only unmanaged resources. (When the destructor executes, you can't be sure managed objects still exist, so you can't call their `Dispose` methods anyway.)

➤ After freeing resources, the `Dispose` method should call `GC.SuppressFinalize` to prevent the GC from running the object's destructor and to keep the object out of the finalization queue.

➤ The `using` statement lets a program automatically call an object's `Dispose` method, so you can't forget to do it. If you declare and initialize the object in the `using` statement, this also limits the object's scope to the `using` block.

REVIEW OF KEY TERMS

ancestor class A class's parent, the parent's parent, and so on.

base class A class from which another class is derived through inheritance. Also known as a *parent class* or *superclass*.

child class A class derived from a parent class.

Common Language Runtime (CLR) A virtual machine that manages execution of C# (and other .NET) programs.

deep clone A copy of an object where reference fields refer to new instances of objects, not to the same objects referred to by the original object's fields.

derive To create one class based on another through inheritance.

derived class A child class derived from a parent class through inheritance.

descendant class A class's child classes, their child classes, and so on.

destructor A method with no return type and a name that includes the class's name prefixed by ~. The destructor is converted into a `Finalize` method that the GC executes before permanently destroying the object.

finalization The process of the GC calling an object's `Finalize` method.

finalization queue A queue through which objects with finalizers must pass before being destroyed. This takes some time, so you should not give a class a finalizer (destructor) unless it needs one.

garbage collection The process of running the GC to reclaim memory that is no longer accessible to the program.

garbage collector (GC) A process that executes periodically to reclaim memory that is no longer accessible to the program.

inherit A derived class inherits the properties, methods, events, and other code of its base class.

interface inheritance Using an interface to require a class to provide certain features much as inheritance does (except the interface doesn't provide an implementation).

managed resources Resources that are under the control of the CLR.

multiple inheritance Allowing a child class to have more than one parent class. C# does not allow multiple inheritance.

nondeterministic finalization Because you can't tell when the GC will call an object's `Finalize` method, the process is called *nondeterministic finalization*.

parent class A base class. Also known as a *superclass*.

reachable During garbage collection, an object is reachable if the program has a path of references that let it access the object.

shallow clone A copy of an object where reference fields refer to the same objects as the original object's fields.

sibling classes Classes that have the same parent class.

subclass A derived class.

subclassing The process of deriving a subclass from a base class through inheritance.

superclass A base class. Also known as a *parent class*.

unmanaged resources Resources that are not under the control of the CLR.

unreachable During garbage collection, an object is unreachable if the program has no path of references that let it access the object.

EXAM TIPS AND TRICKS

The Review of Key Terms and the Cheat Sheet for this chapter can be printed off to help you study. You can find these files in the ZIP file for this chapter at `www.wrox.com/remtitle.cgi?isbn=1118612094` on the Download Code tab.

Working with Delegates, Events, and Exceptions

WHAT YOU WILL LEARN IN THIS CHAPTER

➤ Understanding delegates and predefined delegate types

➤ Using anonymous methods including lambda expressions

➤ Publishing and subscribing to events

➤ Allowing derived classes to raise base class events

➤ Catching, throwing, and rethrowing exceptions

➤ Creating custom exceptions

WROX.COM CODE DOWNLOADS FOR THIS CHAPTER

You can find the code downloads for this chapter at www.wrox.com/remtitle
.cgi?isbn=1118612094 on the Download Code tab. The code is in the chapter11
download and individually named according to the names throughout the chapter.

Chapter 3, "Working with the Type System," explained data types including predefined types
(such as int and string), data structures, and enumerations. For example, the following code
snippet defines a Person structure that groups a person's name and address information:

```
struct Person
{
    public string FirstName, LastName, Street, City, State, ZIP;
}
```

This chapter explains delegates, data types that define kinds of methods. It also explains events (which use delegates), exceptions, and error handling.

Table 6-1 introduces you to the exam objectives covered in this chapter.

TABLE 6-1: 70-483 Exam Objectives Covered in This Chapter

OBJECTIVE	CONTENT COVERED
Manage program flow	*Create and implement events and callbacks.* This includes creating event handlers, subscribing and unsubscribing from events, using built-in delegate types to create events, creating delegates, using lambda expressions, and using anonymous methods.
	Implement exception handling. This includes handling different exception types, catching exceptions of specific and base types, implementing `try-catch-finally` blocks, throwing exceptions, creating custom exceptions, and determining when to throw or rethrow exceptions.

WORKING WITH DELEGATES

As you saw in the introduction to this chapter, a *delegate* is a data type that defines kinds of methods and explains events (which use delegates), exceptions, and error handling. A delegate is a data type much as a class or structure is. Those types define the properties, methods, and events provided by a class or structure. In contrast, a delegate is a type that defines the parameters and return value of a method. The following sections explain how you can define and use delegates.

Delegates

The following code shows how you can define a delegate type.

```
[accessibility] delegate returnType DelegateName([parameters]);
```

Here's a breakdown of that code:

➤ `accessibility`: An accessibility for the delegate type such as `public` or `private`.

➤ `delegate`: The delegate keyword.

➤ `returnType`: The data type that a method of this delegate type returns such as `void`, `int`, or `string`.

➤ `delegateName`: The name that you want to give the delegate type.

➤ `parameters`: The parameter list that a method of this delegate type should take.

For example, the following code defines a delegate type named `FunctionDelegate`.

```
private delegate float FunctionDelegate(float x);
```

This type represents methods that take a `float` as a parameter and returns an integer.

After you define a delegate type, you can create a variable of that type. The following code declares a variable named `TheFunction` that has the `FunctionDelegate` type:

```
private FunctionDelegate TheFunction;
```

Later you can set the variable equal to a method that has the appropriate parameters and return type. The following code defines a method named `Function1`. The form's `Load` event handler then sets the variable `TheFunction` equal to this method.

```
// y = 12 * Sin(3 * x) / (1 + |x|)
private static float Function1(float x)
{
    return (float)(12 * Math.Sin(3 * x) / (1 + Math.Abs(x)));
}

// Initialize TheFunction.
private void Form1_Load(object sender, EventArgs e)
{
    TheFunction = Function1;
}
```

After the variable `TheFunction` is initialized, the program can use it as if it were the method itself. For example, the following code snippet sets the variable `y` equal to the value returned by `TheFunction` with parameter `1.23`.

```
float y = TheFunction(1.23f);
```

At this point, you don't actually know which method is referred to by `TheFunction`. The variable could refer to `Function1` or some other method, as long as that method has a signature that matches the `FunctionDelegate` type.

CODE LAB   Using delegate variables [GraphFunction]

The GraphFunction example program, which is shown in Figure 6-1 and which is available for download on the book's website, uses delegates to graph one of three functions. When you select a function from the `ComboBox`, the program draws it.

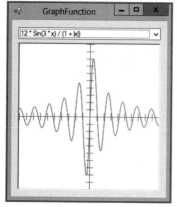

FIGURE 6-1: The GraphFunction example program uses a delegate variable to store the function that it should graph.

When you select a function from the program's `ComboBox`, the following code makes the program graph the selected function.

```
// Select the appropriate function and redraw.
private void equationComboBox_SelectedIndexChanged(
    object sender, EventArgs e)
{
    switch (equationComboBox.SelectedIndex)
    {
        case 0:
            TheFunction = Function1;
            break;
        case 1:
            TheFunction = Function2;
```

```
            break;
        case 2:
            TheFunction = Function3;
            break;
    }
    graphPictureBox.Refresh();
}
```

Code Lab Analysis

This code sets the variable `TheFunction` to one of three methods. It then refreshes the `graphPictureBox` control to make it repaint itself.

The `graphPictureBox` control's `Paint` event handler contains a lot of graphics code that isn't relevant to this discussion, so it isn't shown here. The following code shows the key part of the event handler that uses `TheFunction`:

```
// Generate points on the curve.
List<PointF> points = new List<PointF>();
for (float x = wxmin; x <= wxmax; x += dx)
    points.Add(new PointF(x, TheFunction(x)));
```

This code uses `TheFunction` to make a `List<PointF>`. It then loops over X-coordinate values and uses `TheFunction` to get the corresponding Y value for each X value. The code doesn't know which function `TheFunction` is at this point and it doesn't care. It simply uses `TheFunction` to get the appropriate Y coordinate value, makes a `PointF` representing the point, and saves it in the list.

After it has built the list, the program uses the list's `ToArray` method to convert the list into an array and then draws lines to connect the points. Download the example program to see the details.

To summarize, you can use a delegate much as you use any other type. First, use the `delegate` keyword to define the delegate type. Next, create variables of the delegate type, and set them equal to methods that match the delegate's parameters and return type. Finally, write code to invoke the variable, which calls the method referred to by the variable.

Delegate Details

Using a delegate is similar to using any other data type. The only confusing issue is that the values being manipulated are references to methods rather than some more concrete data type such as an `int` or `string`.

Addition and subtraction are even defined on delegate variables. Suppose `Method1` and `Method2` are two methods that take no parameters and return void, and consider the following code:

```
Action del1 = Method1;
Action del2 = Method2;
Action del3 = del1 + del2 + del1;
```

This makes `del3` a delegate variable that includes a series of other delegate variables. Now if you invoke the `del3` delegate variable, the program executes `Method1` followed by `Method2` followed by `Method1`.

You can even use subtraction to remove one of the delegates from the series. For example, if you execute the statement del3 -= del1 and then invoke del3, the program executes Method1 and then Method2.

There are also a few issues that are unique to delegates. The following sections describe differences between delegates that use static and instance methods, and the two concepts of covariance and contravariance.

Static and Instance Methods

If you set a delegate variable equal to a static method, it's clear what happens when you invoke the variable's method. There is only one method shared by all the instances of the class that defines it, so that is the method that is called.

If you set a delegate variable equal to an instance method, the results is a bit more confusing. When you invoke the variable's method, it executes in the instance that you used to set the variable's value.

CODE LAB   **Using static and instance delegates [StaticAndInstanceDelegates]**

The StaticAndInstanceDelegates example program, which is available for download on the book's website, demonstrates setting delegate variables equal to static and instance methods. The following example defines the following Person class:

```
class Person
{
    public string Name;

    // A method that returns a string.
    public delegate string GetStringDelegate();

    // A static method.
    public static string StaticName()
    {
        return "Static";
    }

    // Return this instance's Name.
    public string GetName()
    {
        return Name;
    }

    // Variables to hold GetStringDelegates.
    public GetStringDelegate StaticMethod;
    public GetStringDelegate InstanceMethod;
}
```

Code Lab Analysis

This class defines a public Name variable, so you can tell objects apart. It then declares the GetStringDelegate delegate type to be a method that takes no parameters and returns a string.

The class then defines two methods. The static method StaticName simply returns the string "Static." The GetName instance method returns the name of the instance on which it is running.

Finally, the class declares two variables of the GetStringDelegate type: StaticMethod and InstanceMethod.

When the program starts, the following Load event handler executes to demonstrate the delegates.

```
private void Form1_Load(object sender, EventArgs e)
{
    // Make some Persons.
    Person alice = new Person() { Name = "Alice" };
    Person bob = new Person() { Name = "Bob" };

    // Make Alice's InstanceMethod variable refer to her own GetName method.
    alice.InstanceMethod = alice.GetName;
    alice.StaticMethod = Person.StaticName;

    // Make Bob's InstanceMethod variable refer to Alice's GetName method.
    bob.InstanceMethod = alice.GetName;
    bob.StaticMethod = Person.StaticName;

    // Demonstrate the methods.
    string result = "";
    result += "Alice's InstanceMethod returns: " + alice.InstanceMethod() +
        Environment.NewLine;
    result += "Bob's InstanceMethod returns: " + bob.InstanceMethod() +
        Environment.NewLine;
    result += "Alice's StaticMethod returns: " + alice.StaticMethod() +
        Environment.NewLine;
    result += "Bob's StaticMethod returns: " + bob.StaticMethod();
    resultsTextBox.Text = result;
    resultsTextBox.Select(0, 0);
}
```

This code creates two Person objects named alice and bob. It sets alice's InstanceMethod variable equal to alice's GetName method and sets alice's StaticMethod variable equal to the Person class's static StaticName method.

The code then sets bob's GetName and StaticMethod variables equal to the same values.

Next, the code executes the methods stored in the delegate variables. The alice object's InstanceMethod variable invokes that object's GetName method and returns "Alice."

The bob object's InstanceMethod variable also refers to alice's instance of the GetName method, so it also returns "Alice."

Both objects' StaticMethod variables refer to the class's StaticName method, so both execute it, returning the value "Static."

Figure 6-2 shows the program's output.

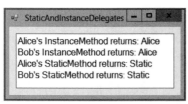

FIGURE 6-2: The StaticAndInstance-Delegates example program demonstrates delegates set to static and instance methods.

Covariance and Contravariance

Covariance and contravariance give you some flexibility when assigning methods to delegate variables. They basically let you treat the return type and parameters of a delegate polymorphically.

Covariance lets a method return a value from a *subclass* of the result expected by a delegate. For example, suppose the `Employee` class is derived from the `Person` class and the `ReturnPersonDelegate` type represents methods that return a `Person` object. Then you could set a `ReturnPersonDelegate` variable equal to a method that returns an `Employee` because `Employee` is a subclass of `Person`. This makes sense because the method should return a `Person`, and an `Employee` is a kind of `Person`. (A variable is called *covariant* if it enables covariance.)

Contravariance lets a method take parameters that are from a *superclass* of the type expected by a delegate. For example, suppose the `EmployeeParameterDelegate` type represents methods that take an `Employee` object as a parameter. Then you could set an `EmployeeParameterDelegate` variable equal to a method that takes a `Person` as a parameter because `Person` is a superclass of `Employee`. When you invoke the delegate variable's method, you will pass it an `Employee` (because the delegate requires that the method take an `Employee` parameter) and an `Employee` is a kind of `Person`, so the method can handle it. (A variable is called *contravariant* if it enables contravariance.)

CODE LAB   **Understanding covariance and contravariance
[CovarianceAndContravariance]**

The CovarianceAndContravariance example program, which is available for download on the book's website, uses `Person` and `Employee` classes to demonstrate covariance and contravariance. The following code shows how the program's `Load` event handler demonstrates covariance and contravariance:

```
// A delegate that returns a Person.
private delegate Person ReturnPersonDelegate();
private ReturnPersonDelegate ReturnPersonMethod;

// A method that returns an Employee.
private Employee ReturnEmployee()
```

```
    {
        return new Employee();
    }

    // A delegate that takes an Employee as a parameter.
    private delegate void EmployeeParameterDelegate(Employee employee);
    private EmployeeParameterDelegate EmployeeParameterMethod;

    // A method that takes a Person as a parameter.
    private void PersonParameter(Person person)
    {
    }

    // Initialize delegate variables.
    private void Form1_Load(object sender, EventArgs e)
    {
        // Use covariance to set ReturnPersonMethod = ReturnEmployee.
        ReturnPersonMethod = ReturnEmployee;

        // Use contravariance to set EmployeeParameterMethod = PersonParameter.
        EmployeeParameterMethod = PersonParameter;
    }
```

Code Lab Analysis

The program defines the `ReturnPersonDelegate` type to represent methods that take no parameters and return a `Person` object. It then defines a variable of that type named `ReturnPersonMethod`.

The program then defines the `ReturnEmployee` method, which returns a new `Employee` object.

Next, the program defines the `EmployeeParameterDelegate` type to represent methods that take an `Employee` as a parameter and return `void`. It then defines a variable of that type named `EmployeeParameterMethod`.

The program then defines the `PersonParameter` method, which takes a `Person` as a parameter and returns `void`.

The form's `Load` event handler demonstrates covariance and contravariance. It sets `ReturnPersonMethod` equal to `ReturnEmployee`. The method referred to by `ReturnPersonMethod` returns a Person. The `ReturnEmployee` method returns an `Employee`, which is a kind of `Person`, so covariance allows this.

The `Load` event handler sets `EmployeeParameterMethod` equal to `PersonParameter`. The method referred to by `EmployeeParameterMethod` takes an `Employee` as a parameter. The `PersonParameter` method takes a `Person` as a parameter. `Person` is a superclass of `Employee`, so contravariance allows this.

Built-in Delegate Types

The .NET Framework defines two generic delegate types that you can use to avoid defining your own delegates in many cases: `Action` and `Func`.

Action Delegates

The generic `Action` delegate represents a method that returns `void`. Different versions of `Action` take between 0 and 18 input parameters. The following code shows the definition of the `Action` delegate that takes two parameters:

```
public delegate void Action<in T1, in T2>(T1 arg1, T2 arg2)
```

The keyword `in` within the generic parameter list indicates that the `T1` and `T2` type parameters are contravariant.

Unless you need to define a delegate that takes more than 18 parameters, you can use the `Action` instead of creating your own delegates. For example, the code in the previous section defined an `EmployeeParameterDelegate` type that takes an `Employee` object as a parameter and returns `void`. The following code shows two ways you could declare variables of that type:

```
// Method 1.
private delegate void EmployeeParameterDelegate(Employee employee);
private EmployeeParameterDelegate EmployeeParameterMethod1;

// Method 2.
private Action<Employee> EmployeeParameterMethod2;
```

This code's first statement defines the `EmployeeParameterDelegate` type. The statement after the first comment declares a variable of that type. The statement after the second comment declares a comparable variable of type `Action<Employee>`.

Func Delegates

The generic `Func` delegate represents a method that returns a value. As is the case with `Action`, different versions of `Func` take between 0 and 18 input parameters. The following code shows the definition of the `Func` delegate that takes two parameters:

```
public delegate TResult Func<in T1, in T2, out TResult>(T1 arg1, T2 arg2)
```

The three types defined by the generic delegate represent the types of the two parameters and the return value.

The code in the previous section defined a `ReturnPersonDelegate` type that takes no parameters and returns a `Person` object. The following code shows two ways you could declare variables of that type:

```
// Method 1.
private delegate Person ReturnPersonDelegate();
private ReturnPersonDelegate ReturnPersonMethod1;

// Method 2.
private Func<Person> ReturnPersonMethod2;
```

This code's first statement defines the `ReturnPersonDelegate` type. The statement after the first comment declares a variable of that type. The statement after the second comment declares a comparable variable of type `Func<Person>`.

Anonymous Methods

An *anonymous method* is basically a method that doesn't have a name. Instead of creating a method as you usually do, you create a delegate that refers to the code that the method should contain. You can then use that delegate as if it were a delegate variable holding a reference to the method.

The following shows the syntax for creating an anonymous method.

```
delegate([parameters]) { code... }
```

Here's a breakdown of that code:

➤   `delegate`: The delegate keyword.

➤   `parameters`: Any parameters that you want the method to take.

➤   `code`: Whatever code you want the method to execute. The code can use a `return` statement if the method should return some value.

The following code stores an anonymous method in a variable of a delegate type.

```
private Func<float, float> Function = delegate(float x) { return x * x; };
```

This code declares a variable named `Function` of the type defined by the built-in `Func` delegate that takes a `float` as a parameter and that returns a `float`. It sets the variable `Function` equal to a method that returns its parameter squared.

The program cannot refer to this method by name because it's anonymous, but it can use the variable `Function` to invoke the method.

> **BEST PRACTICES: For One-time Use**
>
> Usually anonymous methods are used when a program needs a relatively simple piece of code in a single place. If the method is long or will be invoked in several places, most programmers make it a normal named method.

The previous line of code shows how you can make a delegate variable refer to an anonymous method. Two other places where programmers often use anonymous methods are defining simple event handlers and executing simple tasks on separate threads.

The following code adds an event handler to a form's `Paint` event:

```
private void Form1_Load(object sender, EventArgs e)
{
    this.Paint += delegate(object obj, PaintEventArgs args)
        {
            args.Graphics.DrawEllipse(Pens.Red, 10, 10, 200, 100);
        };
}
```

When the form receives a `Paint` event, the anonymous method draws a red ellipse.

The following code executes an anonymous method on a separate thread:

```
private void Form1_Load(object sender, EventArgs e)
{
    System.Threading.Thread thread = new System.Threading.Thread(
            delegate() { MessageBox.Show("Hello World"); }
        );
    thread.Start();
}
```

This code creates a new `Thread` object, passing it a reference to the anonymous method. When the thread starts, it executes that method, in this case displaying a message box.

Lambda Expressions

Anonymous methods give you a shortcut for creating a short method that will be used in only one place. In case that isn't short enough, lambda methods provide a shorthand notation for creating those shortcuts. A *lambda expression* uses a concise syntax to create an anonymous method.

> **NOTE** The examples here store lambda expressions in delegate variables because they are easy to describe that way. In many applications, lambda expressions are added to an event's event handler list, passed into methods that take delegates as parameters, or are used in LINQ expressions. Chapter 10, "Working with Language Integrated Query (LINQ)," discusses LINQ in detail.

Lambda expressions come in a few formats and several variations. To make discussing them a little easier, the following sections group lambda expressions into three categories: expression lambdas, statement lambdas, and async lambdas. Each of these has several variations, which are covered on the next section about expression lambdas.

Expression Lambdas

The following text shows an expression lambda's simplest form:

```
() => expression;
```

Here, `expression` is a single C# statement that should be executed by the delegate. The fact that this lambda expression has a single expression on the right side is what makes it an expression lambda.

The empty parentheses represent the empty parameter list taken by the anonymous method. The `=>` characters indicate that this is a lambda statement.

The following code snippet shows how you could use this kind of lambda expression:

```
Action note;
note = () => MessageBox.Show("Hi");
note();
```

BREAKPOINTS AND ANONYMOUS NAMES

You can set a breakpoint inside a lambda expression and execution stops at that point when the lambda expression's anonymous method runs. This can be rather confusing, however, so if you expect to spend a lot of time debugging a piece of code, you might want to use a named method instead.

If you pause execution inside an anonymous method, the Call Stack window enables you to discover its name. The following code shows the ungainly name that was given to one anonymous method that took a string as a parameter. (It appears on one line in the Call Stack window but is broken here to fit the page better.)

```
AnonymousMethods.exe!AnonymousMethods.
    Form1..ctor.AnonymousMethod__0(string m)
```

This code's first statement creates a variable named `note` of type `Action`, which the section "Built-in Delegate Types" earlier in this chapter explained is a delegate type representing methods that take no parameters and that return `void`.

The second statement sets `note` equal to the anonymous method created by a lambda expression. This expression executes the single statement `MessageBox.Show("Hi")`.

The code's final statement invokes the anonymous method referred to by the `note` variable.

BEST PRACTICES: Declare and Initialize

In this example, you could combine the first two lines in a single statement as in the following:

```
Action note = () => MessageBox.Show("Hi");
```

The previous example kept the lines separate to make them a little easier to read.

The previous example demonstrates the simplest kind of lambda expression, which takes no parameters and executes a single statement. You can also add parameters to lambda expressions as in the following example:

```
Action<string> note = (message) => MessageBox.Show(message);
```

This example creates an anonymous method that takes a `string` as a parameter and then displays that `string` in a message box.

> **NOTE** *If a lambda expression has exactly one parameter, you can omit the parentheses around it as in the following code.*
>
> ```
> Action<string> note = message => MessageBox.Show(message);
> ```
>
> *Including the parentheses makes the code slightly more readable, and lambda expressions are confusing enough already, so many programmers include them even though they are not required.*

Usually, Visual Studio can infer the data type of a lambda expression's parameters. In the previous code, for example, the note variable is declared to be of type Action<string>, so the parameter must be a string.

If Visual Studio cannot infer the parameters' data types, or if you want to make the code more explicit, you can include the parameters' data types as in the following version:

```
Action<string> note = (string message) => MessageBox.Show(message);
```

You can add as many parameters as you like to a lambda expression. The following example uses a lambda expression that takes four parameters:

```
Action<string, string, MessageBoxButtons, MessageBoxIcon> note;

note = (message, caption, buttons, icon) =>
    MessageBox.Show(message, caption, buttons, icon);

note("Invalid input", "Alert", MessageBoxButtons.OK,
    MessageBoxIcon.Asterisk);
```

In this code, the delegate type takes four parameters: two strings, a MessageBoxButtons enum value, and a MessageBoxIcon enum value.

This lambda expression uses the parameters to display a message box with a message and caption, displaying the indicated buttons and icon.

The last line of code displays a message box with message parameter "Invalid input" with caption parameter "Alert". The message box displays the OK button and the asterisk icon, as shown in Figure 6-3.

FIGURE 6-3: Lambda expressions can take any number of parameters.

In the examples shown up to now, the lambda expressions have returned void, but there's no reason why a lambda expression cannot return a value. An expression lambda can return a value by simply creating that value.

The following code shows a lambda expression that takes a float as a parameter and returns that value squared.

```
Func<float, float> square = (float x) => x * x;
float y = square(13);
```

The part of the expression on the right, x * x, creates the return value.

Working with Delegates | **221**

> **NOTE** *The fact that this type of the lambda expression returns the value defined by the statement on the right is what gives this form the name "expression lambda."*

For a more complicated example, the GraphFunction program shown in Figure 6-1 uses delegates to graph one of three functions. The following code shows a key `switch` statement that sets the delegate variable `TheFunction` equal to the function that the program should graph:

```
switch (equationComboBox.SelectedIndex)
{
    case 0:
        TheFunction = Function1;
        break;
    case 1:
        TheFunction = Function2;
        break;
    case 2:
        TheFunction = Function3;
        break;
}
```

Instead of setting `TheFunction` equal to a named method, the code could set it equal to an anonymous method created by a lambda expression. The following code shows the first `case` statement rewritten to use a lambda expression:

```
case 0:
    TheFunction = x => (float)(12 * Math.Sin(3 * x) / (1 + Math.Abs(x)));
    break;
```

This expression is about as complicated as you should probably get with an expression lambda. If it were much more complicated, reading it would be confusing.

Statement lambdas provide one way to make complicated lambda expressions a bit easier to read.

Statement Lambdas

A *statement lambda* is similar to an expression lambda except it encloses its code in braces. That makes it a bit easier to separate complicated lambda expressions from the code around them. It also enables you to include more than one statement in an anonymous method.

In addition to the braces, the other way in which statement lambdas differ from expression lambdas is that a statement lambda must use a `return` statement to return a value.

Figure 6-4 shows the AnonymousGraph example program, which is available for download on the book's website, graphing the function $Ax^6 + Bx^5 + Cx^4 + Dx^3 + Ex^2 + Fx + G$ for constants A, B, C, D, E, F, and G. (This program is similar to the GraphFunction example program described earlier except it uses anonymous methods instead of named methods for its functions.)

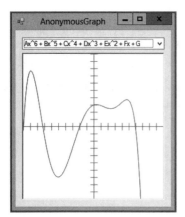

FIGURE 6-4: The equation for the GraphFunction program's third function shown here is easier to read in a statement lambda than in an expression lambda.

The function graphed in Figure 6-4 is a simple polynomial but it's long and would be messy if written out in an expression lambda. The following code shows how the program uses a statement lambda to save a reference to an anonymous method that evaluates this function:

```
TheFunction = (float x) =>
    {
        const float A = -0.0003f;
        const float B = -0.0024f;
        const float C = 0.02f;
        const float D = 0.09f;
        const float E = -0.5f;
        const float F = 0.3f;
        const float G = 3f;
        return (((((A * x + B) * x + C) * x + D) * x + E) * x + F) * x + G;
    };
```

Note the use of the braces and the `return` statement.

Async Lambdas

Chapter 7, "Multithreading and Asynchronous Processing," explains asynchronous processing and multithreading, but this topic is worth discussing briefly here in the context of lambda expressions.

Basically, you can use the keyword `async` to indicate that a method can be run asynchronously. You can then use the `await` keyword to make a piece of code call an asynchronous method and wait for it to return. Usually an asynchronous method is named, but you can use the `async` keyword to make lambda expressions asynchronous, too.

CODE LAB   Asynchronous lambdas [AsyncLambda]

The AsyncLambda example program, which is available for download on the book's website, uses the following code to demonstrate async lambdas.

```
// The number of times we have run DoSomethingAsync.
private int Trials = 0;

// Create an event handler for the button.
private void Form1_Load(object sender, EventArgs e)
{
    runAsyncButton.Click += async (button, buttonArgs) =>
    {
        int trial = ++Trials;
        statusLabel.Text = "Running trial " + trial.ToString() + "...";
        await DoSomethingAsync();
        statusLabel.Text = "Done with trial " + trial.ToString();
    };
}

// Do something time consuming.
async Task DoSomethingAsync()
{
    // In this example, just waste some time.
    await Task.Delay(3000);
}
```

Code Lab Analysis

This code starts by defining the variable `Trials` to keep track of the number of times the code executes.

When the form loads, its `Load` event handler installs an event handler for Run Async button's `Click` event. The event handler is defined by a statement lambda that begins with the keyword `async` to indicate that the anonymous method runs asynchronously.

The event handler's code increments `Trials`, displays a status message, and then calls the `DoSomethingAsync` method to perform some task. It uses the `await` keyword when it calls `DoSomethingAsync`, so the event handler's code blocks at that point until the call to `DoSomethingAsync` returns. Then the event handler continues to display another status message.

The example's `DoSomethingAsync` method simply pauses for 3 seconds. Note that the method's declaration begins with the `async` keyword, indicating that it also runs asynchronously. (In a real application, the `DoSomethingAsync` method would do something more useful, such as downloading a file from the Internet or generating a time-consuming report.)

WORKING WITH EVENTS

Events enable objects to communicate with a program to tell it when something interesting has happened. For example, an e-mail object could raise an event to tell the program that it has received a new message; a file transfer object could raise an event to tell the program that a download has completed, and a button object could raise an event to tell the program that the user clicked the button's graphical representation on the screen.

The object that raises an event is called the event's *publisher*. The class that catches an event is called its *subscriber*. Note that a given event may have many subscribers or no subscribers.

The following sections describe the code that is necessary to publish and subscribe to events.

Publishing Events

Before an object can raise an event, it must declare the event so that subscribers know what the event is called and what parameters it includes. The following shows the basic syntax for declaring an event:

```
accessibility event delegate EventName;
```

Here's a breakdown of that code:

➤ `accessibility`: The event's accessibility as in `public` or `private`.

➤ `event`: The `event` keyword.

➤ `delegate`: A delegate type that defines the kind of method that can act as an event handler for the event.

➤ `EventName`: The name that the class is giving the event.

For example, the `BankAccount` class might use the following code to define the `Overdrawn` event:

```
public delegate void OverdrawnEventHandler();
public event OverdrawnEventHandler Overdrawn;
```

The first line declares the `OverdrawnEventHandler` delegate, which represents methods that take no parameters and that return `void`.

The second line declares an event named `Overdrawn` that has the type `OverdrawnEventHandler`. That means subscribers must use a method that matches the `OverdrawnEventHandler` delegate to catch the event.

Later a `BankAccount` object can raise the event as necessary. For example, consider the following simple but complete `BankAccount` class:

```
class BankAccount
{
    public delegate void OverdrawnEventHandler();
    public event OverdrawnEventHandler Overdrawn;

    // The account balance.
    public decimal Balance { get; set; }

    // Add money to the account.
    public void Credit(decimal amount)
    {
        Balance += amount;
```

```
        }

        // Remove money from the account.
        public void Debit(decimal amount)
        {
            // See if there is this much money in the account.
            if (Balance >= amount)
            {
                // Remove the money.
                Balance -= amount;
            }
            else
            {
                // Raise the Overdrawn event.
                if (Overdrawn != null) Overdrawn();
            }
        }
    }
```

The class defines the OverdrawnEventHandler delegate and declares the Overdrawn event to be of that type. It then defines the auto-implemented Balance property.

Next, the class defines two methods, Credit and Debit, to add and remove money from the account. The Credit method simply adds an amount to the balance.

The Debit method first checks the account's Balance to see if there is enough money in the account. If Balance >= amount, the method simply removes the money from the account.

If there is not enough money in the account, the method raises the Overdrawn event. To raise the event, the code first checks whether the event has any subscribers. If the event has no subscribers, then the "event" appears to be null to the code. If the event isn't null, the code invokes it to notify its subscribers.

Predefined Event Types

The previous example used the following code to define an event delegate and create an event of that type:

```
public delegate void OverdrawnEventHandler();
public event OverdrawnEventHandler Overdrawn;
```

This delegate represents methods that take no parameters and that return void. The section "Built-in Delegate Types" earlier in this chapter described that the predefined Action delegate represents the same kind of method. That means you can simplify the previous code to the following:

```
public event Action Overdrawn;
```

Event Best Practices

Microsoft recommends that all events provide two parameters: the object that is raising the event and another object that gives arguments that are relevant to the event. The second object should be of a class derived from the EventArgs class.

For example, if a program uses several of the `BankAccount` objects described in the previous section, then the first parameter to the event handler can help the program figure out which account raised the `Overdrawn` event.

The fact that the event was raised tells the program that the account doesn't hold enough money to perform a debit, but it doesn't tell the program how large the debit is. The program can examine the `BankAccount` object to figure out the current balance, but it can't figure out how big the debit was. You can use the second parameter to the event handler to give the program that information.

To pass the information in the event handler's second parameter, derive a class from the `EventArgs` class to hold the information. By convention, this type's name should begin with the name of the event and end in `EventArgs`.

For example, the following code shows an `OverdrawnEventArgs` class that can pass information to the `Overdrawn` event handler:

```
class OverdrawnEventArgs : EventArgs
{
    public decimal CurrentBalance, DebitAmount;

    public OverdrawnEventArgs(decimal currentBalance, decimal debitAmount)
    {
        CurrentBalance = currentBalance;
        DebitAmount = debitAmount;
    }
}
```

This class holds a `BankAccount`'s current balance and a debit amount. It provides a constructor to make initializing a new object a bit easier.

Now the program can pass the `Overdrawn` event the object raising the event and an `OverdrawnEventArgs` object to give the program additional information about the event.

Because the event handler now takes two parameters, you need to revise the event declaration, so the delegate it uses reflects those parameters. You could create a new delegate but the .NET Framework defines a generic `EventHandler` delegate that makes this easier. Simply use the `EventHandler` type and include the data type of the second parameter, `OverdrawnEventArgs` in this example, as the generic delegate's type parameter.

The following code shows the revised event declaration:

```
public event EventHandler<OverdrawnEventArgs> Overdrawn;
```

This indicates that the `Overdrawn` event takes two parameters. The first is assumed to be the object that is raising the event, and the second is an object of type `OverdrawnEventArgs`.

The following code shows the `Debit` method revised to use the new event type:

```
// Remove money from the account.
public void Debit(decimal amount)
{
    // See if there is this much money in the account.
    if (Balance >= amount)
```

```
        {
            // Remove the money.
            Balance -= amount;
        }
        else
        {
            // Raise the Overdrawn event.
            if (Overdrawn != null)
                Overdrawn(this, new OverdrawnEventArgs(Balance, amount));
        }
    }
```

When the code raises the Overdrawn event, it passes the event the arguments this as the object raising the event and a new OverdrawnEventArgs object giving further information.

The BankAccount example program, which is available for download on the book's website, demonstrates this version of the BankAccount class.

Event Inheritance

While building Windows Forms classes and classes in the.NET Framework, Microsoft found that simple events such as those described so far don't work well with derived classes. The problem is that an event can be raised only from within the class that declared it, so a subclass cannot raise the base class's events.

The solution that Microsoft uses in the .NET Framework and many other class hierarchies is to give the base class a protected method that raises the event. Then a derived class can call that method to raise the event. By convention, this method's name should begin with On and end with the name of the event, as in OnOverdrawn.

For example, consider the BankAccount class described in the previous section. Its Debit method raises the Overdrawn event if the program tries to remove more money than the account holds. To follow the new event pattern, the class should move the code that raises the event into a new OnOverdrawn method and then call it from the Debit method, as shown in the following code:

```
// Raise the Overdrawn event.
protected virtual void OnOverdrawn(OverdrawnEventArgs args)
{
    if (Overdrawn != null) Overdrawn(this, args);
}

// Remove money from the account.
public void Debit(decimal amount)
{
    // See if there is this much money in the account.
    if (Balance >= amount)
    {
        // Remove the money.
        Balance -= amount;
    }
    else
    {
        // Raise the Overdrawn event.
```

```
            OnOverdrawn(new OverdrawnEventArgs(Balance, amount));
        }
    }
```

Now suppose you want to add a new `MoneyMarketAccount` class derived from the `BankAccount` class. When its code needs to raise the `Overdrawn` event, it invokes the base class's `OnOverdrawn` method.

The following code shows the `MoneyMarketAccount` class:

```
class MoneyMarketAccount : BankAccount
{
    public void DebitFee(decimal amount)
    {
        // See if there is this much money in the account.
        if (Balance >= amount)
        {
            // Remove the money.
            Balance -= amount;
        }
        else
        {
            // Raise the Overdrawn event.
            OnOverdrawn(new OverdrawnEventArgs(Balance, amount));
        }
    }
}
```

The new `DebitFee` method subtracts a fee from the account. If the balance is smaller than the amount to be subtracted, the code calls the base class's `OnOverdrawn` method to raise the `Overdrawn` event.

REAL-WORLD CASE SCENEARIO **Overdraft account**

Make an `OverdraftAccount` class that inherits from the `BankAccount` class. Give this class a `SavingsAccount` property that is a reference to another `BankAccount` object.

When the program tries to remove money from an `OverdraftAccount` object, if the object doesn't have a large enough balance, it can take additional money from the `SavingsAccount`.

If the `OverdraftAccount` and its `SavingsAccount` don't hold enough money between them for a debit, raise the `OverdraftAccount` object's `Overdrawn` event.

Build an interface similar to the one shown in Figure 6-5 so that you can test the new class.

Be sure to catch the `Overdrawn` events for both the `OverdraftAccount` object and its associated `SavingsAccount` object.

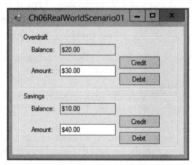

FIGURE 6-5: An OverdraftAccount object can remove money from its associated SavingsAccount object if necessary.

Solution

The following code shows the OverdraftAccount class:

```
class OverdraftAccount : BankAccount
{
    // The associated savings account.
    public BankAccount SavingsAccount { get; set; }

    // Remove money from the account.
    public new void Debit(decimal amount)
    {
        // See if there is this much money in the account.
        if (Balance + SavingsAccount.Balance < amount)
        {
            // Raise the Overdrawn event.
            OnOverdrawn(new OverdrawnEventArgs(Balance, amount));
        }
        else
        {
            // Remove the money we can from the overdraft account.
            if (Balance >= amount) Balance -= amount;
            else
            {
                amount -= Balance;
                Balance = 0m;

                // If there's still an unpaid amount, take it from savings.
                if (amount > 0m) SavingsAccount.Balance -= amount;
            }
        }
    }
}
```

The class inherits from the BankAccount class. It defines the new SavingsAccount property.

The new class can inherit the Balance property and the Credit method from the BankAccount class, but it needs to replace the Debit method with a new version so that it can take money from the SavingsAccount object if necessary. The OverdraftAccount's Debit method is declared with the new keyword to indicate that this version should replace the one defined by the BankAccount class.

The new version checks the money available in the overdraft account and its savings account. If there isn't enough money in both accounts to cover the debit, the code calls the inherited OnOverdrawn method to raise the Overdrawn event.

If there is enough money in the overdraft account to cover the debit, the code subtracts the money from that account.

If the overdraft account doesn't hold enough money to cover the debit, then the code subtracts what it can from that account and subtracts the rest from the associated savings account.

Subscribing and Unsubscribing to Events

There are several ways you can subscribe and unsubscribe to events depending on whether you want to do so in code or with a form or window designer. The following sections describe those two approaches.

Using Code to Subscribe to an Event

You can use code similar to the following to subscribe to an event:

```
processOrderButton.Click += processOrderButton_Click;
```

This adds the method named `processOrderButton_Click` as an event handler for the `processOrderButton` control's `Click` event.

> **NOTE** *The following code shows an alternative syntax for subscribing to an event:*
>
> ```
> processOrderButton.Click +=
>     new System.EventHandler(processOrderButton_Click);
> ```
>
> *This is an older syntax but it is still supported. You probably shouldn't use it in your code because it makes your code longer and more cluttered, but you should understand it if you see it.*

The following code shows an empty `processOrderButton_Click` event handler:

```
void processOrderButton_Click(object sender, EventArgs e)
{
}
```

The parameter list used by the event handler must match the parameters required by the event. In this case, the event handler must take two parameters, a nonspecific `object` and an `EventArgs` object.

You can write an event handler, or you can let Visual Studio's code editor generate one for you. If you enter the text `processOrderButton.Click +=`, the code editor displays the message shown in Figure 6-6. (This message is for a Windows Forms project, but you get a similar message if you write a XAML application.)

FIGURE 6-6: Visual Studio's code editor can insert the default event handler name for you.

If you press the Tab key, the code editor inserts the default name for the button, which consists of the button's name followed by an underscore and then the event's name, as in `processOrderButton_Click`.

At that point, if you have not already defined the event handler, the code editor displays the message shown in Figure 6-7. If you press the Tab key, the code editor creates an event handler similar to the following:

```
private void Form1_Load(object sender, EventArgs e)
{
    processOrderButton.Click += processOrderButton_Click;
}
                          Press TAB to generate handler 'processOrderButton_Click' in this class
```

FIGURE 6-7: Visual Studio's code editor can generate an event handler for you.

```
void processOrderButton_Click(object sender, EventArgs e)
{
    throw new NotImplementedException();
}
```

This initial event handler simply throws an exception to remind you to implement it later. You should delete that statement and insert whatever code you need the event handler to execute.

The following code shows how a program can unsubscribe from an event:

```
processOrderButton.Click -= processOrderButton_Click;
```

> **COMMON MISTAKES: Oversubscribed**
>
> If you subscribe to an event more than once, the event handler is called more than once. For example, if the program executes the statement `processOrderButton.Click += processOrderButton_Click` three times, when the user clicks the button, the `processOrderButton_Click` event handler executes three times.
>
> Each time you unsubscribe from an event, the event handler is removed from the list of subscribers once. For example, if the program executes the statement `processOrderButton.Click += processOrderButton_Click` three times and the statement `processOrderButton.Click -= processOrderButton_Click` once, if the user clicks the button, the event handler executes two times.
>
> If you unsubscribe an event handler that is not subscribed for an event, nothing happens and there is no error. For example, if a program executes the statement `processOrderButton.Click -= processOrderButton_Click` but that event handler has not been subscribed to the event, the program continues running normally.

Using Designer to Subscribe to an Event

If you write a Windows Forms application and the event publisher is a control or component that you have added to a form, you can use the form designer to attach an event handler to the event. Open the form in the form designer and select a control. In the Properties window, click the Events button (which looks like a lightning bolt) to see the control's events. Figure 6-8 shows the Properties window displaying a Form object's events.

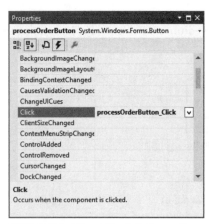

FIGURE 6-8: Visual Studio's Properties window enables you to select or create event handlers.

To subscribe an existing event handler to an event, click the event in the Properties window, open the drop-down to its right, and select the event handler.

To create a new empty event handler for an event, double-click the event in the Properties window.

To use the Properties window to unsubscribe from an event, right-click the event's name and select Reset.

The process for subscribing and unsubscribing events by using the Window Designer in a XAML application is similar to the process for a Windows Forms application. Some of the details are slightly different but the basic approach is the same.

One difference between Windows Forms and XAML applications is where the code is placed to subscribe the event. In a Windows Forms application, that code is normal C# code placed in the form's designer file, for example, `Form1.Designer.cs`.

In a XAML application, a `Click` element is inserted into the XAML code file. The following code snippet shows the definition of a button in a XAML file. The `Click` element subscribes the `processOrderButton_Click` event handler to the button's `Click` event:

```
<Button x:Name="processOrderButton" Content="Process Order"
    HorizontalAlignment="Left"
    VerticalAlignment="Top" Click="processOrderButton_Click" />
```

The previous sections dealt with events. Events trigger some sort of action and, no matter how carefully you write an application, an action can lead to errors. The sections that follow explain how you can use exception handling to catch errors so the program can take reasonable action instead of crashing.

COMMON MISTAKES: Undersubscribed

If you delete an event handler that was subscribed to an event by the Properties window, Visual Studio complains loudly. It won't let you run the application, and if you try to open the form in the form designer, you see an error similar to the one shown in Figure 6-9.

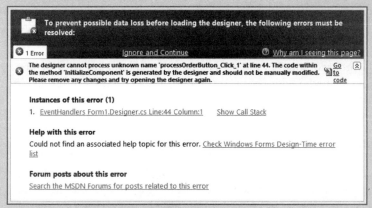

FIGURE 6-9: The form designer won't display a form if a subscribed event handler is missing.

To fix this problem, click the link on the form designer or double-click the error message in the Errors window to find the incorrect line in the designer's code file. If the form's name is Form1, this file is called `Form1.Designer.cs`.

The line causing the problem should be highlighted in the form designer's code, as shown in Figure 6-10. Delete the line that subscribes the missing event handler, and the form should be ready to run again.

```
//
// processOrderButton
//
this.processOrderButton.Location = new System.Drawing.Point(73, 63);
this.processOrderButton.Name = "processOrderButton";
this.processOrderButton.Size = new System.Drawing.Size(75, 23);
this.processOrderButton.TabIndex = 0;
this.processOrderButton.Text = "button1";
this.processOrderButton.UseVisualStyleBackColor = true;
this.processOrderButton.Click += new System.EventHandler(this.processOrderButton_Click);
```

FIGURE 6-10: Delete the line that subscribes the missing event handler to fix the form.

EXCEPTION HANDLING

No matter how well you design an application, problems are still inevitable. Users will enter invalid values, indispensable files will be deleted, and critical network connections will fail. To avoid and recover from these sorts of problems, a program must perform error checking and exception handling.

Error Checking and Exception Handling

Error checking is the process of anticipating errors, checking to see if they will occur, and working around them. For example, if the user must enter an integer in a text box, eventually someone will enter a non-numeric value. If the program tries to parse the value as if it were an integer, it will crash.

Instead of crashing, the program should validate the text to see if it makes sense before trying to parse it. The `int.TryParse` method does both, attempting to parse a text value and returning an error indicator if it fails.

> ### ADVICE FROM THE EXPERTS: Make Mistakes Impossible
>
> You can reduce the need for this kind of error checking by removing opportunities for the user to enter invalid values. For example, if the program uses a `NumericUpDown` or `TrackBar` control instead of a `TextBox`, the user cannot enter an invalid integer such as "ten" or "1.2."

Similarly, before opening a file or downloading a file across a network, the program can verify that the file exists and the network connection is present. If the program detects this kind of error, it can tell the user and cancel whatever operation it was attempting.

In contrast to error checking, *exception handling* is the process of protecting the application when an unexpected error occurs. For example, suppose the program starts downloading a file over a network and then the network disappears. There is no way the program can anticipate this problem because the network was present when the download started.

Even if you validate every value entered by the user and check every possible condition, unexpected exceptions can arise. A file may become corrupted; a network connection that was present may fail; the system may run out of memory; or a code library that you are using and over which you have no control may throw an exception.

If you can, it is generally better to proactively look for trouble before it occurs, rather than react to it after it happens. For example, it is better to check whether a file exists before opening it, rather than just trying to open it and handling an error if the file isn't there.

If you can spot a problem before it occurs, you usually have a better idea of what the problem is, so you can be more specific when you tell the user what's wrong. If you look for a file and it's missing, you can tell the user so. If you try to open a file and fail, you don't know whether the file is missing, corrupted, locked by another process, or unavailable for some other reason.

Generating exception information also adds some extra overhead to the program, so you'll usually get better performance if you anticipate errors before they happen.

Even if you validate user input, look for needed files and network connections, and check for every other error you can think of, the program may still encounter unexpected situations. In those cases, a program can protect itself by using `try-catch-finally` blocks.

try-catch-finally Blocks

The *try-catch-finally block* allows a program to catch unexpected errors and handle them. This block actually consists of three sections: a `try` section, one or more `catch` sections, and a `finally` section. The `try` section is required, and you must include at least one `catch` or `finally` section. Although, you don't need to include both, and you don't need to include any code inside the `catch` or `finally` section.

The `try` section contains the statements that might throw an exception. You can include as many statements as you like in this section. You can even nest other `try-catch-finally` sequences inside a `try` section to catch errors without leaving the original `try` section.

The following code shows the syntax for a `try` section:

```
try
{
    // Statements that might throw an exception.
    ...
}
```

The following shows the syntax for a `catch` section:

```
catch [(ExceptionType [variable])]
{
    Statements to execute...
}
```

If an exception occurs in the `try` section, the program looks through its list of `catch` sections in the order in which they appear in the code. The program compares the exception that occurred to each catch section's `ExceptionType` until it finds an exception that matches.

The exception matches if it can be considered to be of the `ExceptionType` class. For example, the `DivideByZeroException` class is derived from the `ArithmeticException` class, which is derived from the `SystemException` class, which is derived from the `Exception` class. If a program throws a `DivideByZeroException`, then a catch `section` could match the exception with any of the classes `DivideByZeroException`, `ArithmeticException`, `SystemException`, or `Exception`. All exception classes inherit directly or indirectly from `Exception`, so a `catch` section where `ExceptionType` is `Exception` will catch any exception.

When it finds a matching `ExceptionType`, the program executes that `catch` section's statements and then skips any remaining `catch` sections.

ADVICE FROM THE EXPERTS: Sort Exceptions

Because the program considers `catch` sections in the order in which they appear in the code, be sure to list them in order from most specific (or most derived) to least specific. For example, the `FormatException` class inherits from the `SystemException` class, which in turn inherits from the `Exception` class. Consider the following list of `catch` statements:

```
try
{
    Statements...
}
catch (SystemException ex)
{
    Statements...
}
catch (FormatException ex)
{
    Statements...
}
catch (Exception ex)
{
    Statements...
}
```

The `FormatException` class is more specific than the `SystemException` class, but its `catch` section comes after the one for `SystemException`. If a `FormatException` does occur, the first `catch` section will handle it because a `FormatException` is a type of `SystemException`. That means the second `catch` section will never execute.

The final `catch` section handles the `Exception` class, which is the ancestor of all exception classes. If any exception gets past the other `catch` sections, the final catch section will handle it.

If you omit the `ExceptionType`, the `catch` section catches every kind of exception. For example, consider the following code:

```
int quantity;
try
{
    quantity = int.Parse(quantityTextBox.Text);
}
catch
{
    MessageBox.Show("The quantity must be an integer.");
}
```

This code tries to parse the value in a `TextBox`. If the value isn't an integer, the `int.Parse` statement throws an exception, and the `catch` section displays a message box. In this case only one message is appropriate no matter what exception was thrown.

If you include the ExceptionType, then variable is a variable of the class ExceptionType that gives information about the exception. All exception classes provide a Message property that gives textual information about the exception. Sometimes you can display that message to the user, but often the message is technical enough that it might be confusing to users.

If you include the ExceptionType but omit variable, then the catch section executes for matching exception types, but the code doesn't have a variable that can give information about the exception.

The finally section executes its statements when the try and catch sections are finished no matter how the code leaves those sections. The finally section *always* executes, even if the program leaves the try and catch sections because of any of the following reasons:

➤ The code in the try section executes successfully and no catch sections execute.

➤ The code in the try section throws an exception and a catch section handles it.

➤ The code in the try section throws an exception and that exception is not caught by any catch section.

➤ The code in the try section uses a return statement to exit the method.

➤ The code in a catch section uses a return statement to exit the method.

➤ The code in a catch section throws an exception.

USING THE USING STATEMENT

The using statement actually behaves as a special-purpose try-finally sequence that calls the object's Dispose method in its finally section. For example, consider the following code:

```
using (Pen pen = new Pen(Color.Red, 10))
{
    // Use the pen to draw...
}
```

This is roughly equivalent to the following try-finally sequence:

```
Pen pen;
try
{
    pen = new Pen(Color.Red, 10);
    // Use the pen to draw...
}
finally
{
    if (pen != null) pen.Dispose();
}
```

This means the program calls the pen's Dispose method no matter how it leaves the using block. For example, if the statements within the block execute a return statement or throw an exception, the Dispose method is still called.

Note that only the code in the `try` section of a `try-catch-finally` block is protected by the block. If an exception occurs inside a `catch` or `finally` section, the exception is not caught by the block.

You can nest another `try-catch-finally` block inside a `catch` or `finally` section to protect the program from errors in those places. That can make the code rather cluttered, however, so in some cases it may be better to move the risky code into another method that includes its own error handling.

EXPECTED EXCEPTIONS

One common method for building `catch` lists for `try-catch-finally` blocks is to start with a series of `catch` statements that handle the exceptions you expect. Add a final `catch` section that looks for the `Exception` class, and set a breakpoint in that section. Now test the program thoroughly, causing as many exceptions as you can. Each time the code stops in the final `catch` section, add a specific `catch` section to the block. After you test the code thoroughly, you should look for a fairly comprehensive list of exceptions.

Leave the final `catch` block in the code, however, just in case you missed something.

Unhandled Exceptions

An *unhandled exception* occurs when an exception is thrown and the program is not protected by a `try-catch-finally` block. This can happen in two ways. First, the statement that throws the error might not be inside a `try` section of a `try-catch-finally` block. Second, the statement might be inside a `try` section, but none of the `try-catch-finally` block's `catch` sections may match the exception.

When a program encounters an unhandled exception, control moves up the call stack to the method that called the code that threw the exception. If that method is executing inside the `try` section of a `try-catch-finally` block, its `catch` sections try to match the exception. If the calling method is not inside the `try` section of a `try-catch-finally` block or if no `catch` section can match the exception, control again moves up the call stack to the method that called this method.

Control continues moving up the call stack until one of two things happens. First, the program may find a method with an active `try-catch-finally` block that has a `catch` section that can handle the exception. In that case, the `catch` section executes its code, and the program continues running from that point.

The second thing that can happen is control pops off the top of the stack and the program crashes. If you are running inside the Visual Studio environment, the program stops at the statement that caused the unhandled exception, and you see an error message similar to the one shown in Figure 6-11.

If a program is running outside of Visual Studio and encounters an unhandled exception, control unwinds up the call stack and a message similar to the one shown in Figure 6-12 appears.

Normally a program spends most of its time doing nothing while it waits for an event to occur. When an event occurs, for example if the user clicks a button or selects a menu item, the program takes some action. If that action causes an unhandled exception, the user sees the message shown in Figure 6-12.

FIGURE 6-11: If a program running inside Visual Studio encounters an unhandled exception, execution stops at the statement that threw the exception and this message box appears.

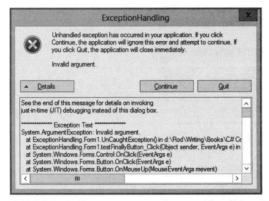

FIGURE 6-12: If a program running outside of Visual Studio encounters an unhandled exception, this message box appears.

If the user clicks Quit, the program ends. If the user clicks Continue, the program attempts to continue running. Normally that means it goes back to doing nothing while it waits for another event to occur.

ADVICE FROM THE EXPERTS: Bulletproofing

To protect the program from any possible exception, you need to put all the code inside every event handler inside a `try-catch-finally` block. In practice many programmers protect only code that they think might throw exceptions, regard other code as "safe," and rely on testing to flush out any unexpected exceptions that might occur.

Common Exception Types

The .NET Framework defines hundreds of exception classes to represent different error conditions. Figure 6-13 shows the hierarchy of some of the most common and useful exception classes defined in the System namespace. Table 6-2 describes the classes.

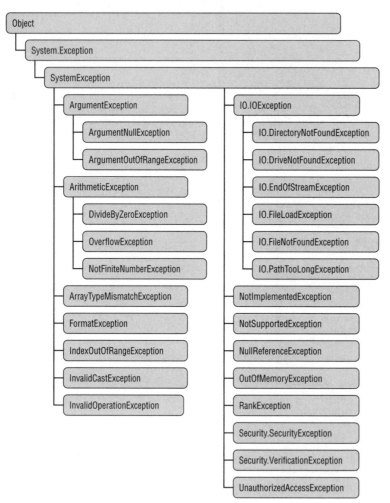

FIGURE 6-13: All of the exception classes in this hierarchy are descendants of the System.Exception class.

TABLE 6-2: Useful Exception Classes

CLASS	DESCRIPTION
Object	This class is the ancestor of all classes.
System.Exception	This is the ancestor class of all exception classes. It represents errors at a high level.

CLASS	DESCRIPTION
SystemException	This is the base class for exceptions defined in the `System` namespace.
ArgumentException	One of a method's arguments is invalid.
ArgumentNullException	An argument was `null` but `null` is not allowed.
ArgumentOutOfRangeException	An argument was outside of the allowed range of values.
ArithmeticException	An arithmetic, casting, or conversion error occurred.
DivideByZeroException	The program tried to divide an integral or decimal value by 0. This exception is not thrown for floating point operations. If a program divides a floating point value by zero, the result is the special value `Infinity`.
OverflowException	A checked arithmetic, casting, or conversion operation results in an overflow.
NotFiniteNumberException	A floating point operation gave a result that was infinity, negative infinity, or NaN (not a number).
ArrayTypeMismatchException	The program tried to store the wrong kind of item in an array.
FormatException	An argument has an incorrect format.
IndexOutOfRangeException	The program tried to access an array element with an index that is outside of the array.
InvalidCastException	A cast or conversion was invalid.
InvalidOperationException	A method call was invalid for an object's current state.
IO.IOException	An input/output error occurred.
IO.DirectoryNotFoundException	A part of a file or directory path was not found.
IO.DriveNotFoundException	The program tried to access a drive or network share that is not available.
IO.EndOfStreamException	The program tried to read past the end of a stream.
IO.FileLoadException	The program tried to load an assembly that is present but could not be loaded.
IO.FileNotFoundException	The program tried to access a file that could not be found.
IO.PathTooLongException	The program tried to use a path or filename that is too long.

continues

TABLE 6-2 *(continued)*

CLASS	DESCRIPTION
`NotImplementedException`	The program tried to access a feature that is not implemented. You can throw this exception to act as a placeholder for features that you have not yet implemented.
`NotSupportedException`	The program tried to invoke a method that is not supported. You can throw this exception to indicate a method that has been removed in recent versions of a library.
`NullReferenceException`	The program tried to access an object through a `null` reference.
`OutOfMemoryException`	There is not enough memory for the program to continue. It is hard to recover from this exception because there may not be enough memory to do anything useful.
`RankException`	The program passed an array with the wrong number of dimensions to a method.
`Security.SecurityException`	The program detected a security error.
`Security.VerificationException`	Security policy requires code to be type safe, and the code could not be verified as type safe.
`UnauthorizedAccessException`	The operating system denied access because of an input/output or security error.

In addition to these basic exceptions, the .NET Framework defines several other exception classes that have more specialized use. For example, SQL exceptions can occur when a program works with SQL Server databases.

The following sections describe some of the more common and useful of these specialized exception classes.

SQL Exceptions

SQL Server uses the single class `System.Data.SqlClient.SqlException` to represent all errors and exceptions. You can use the `SqlException` object's properties to determine what has gone wrong and how severe it is.

Table 6-3 describes some of the most useful `SqlException` class properties.

TABLE 6-3: Useful SqlException Properties

PROPERTY	DESCRIPTION
Class	A number between 0 and 25 giving the type of error. Values 20 through 25 are fatal and the database connection closes. The values indicate
	0–10: Information messages rather than errors.
	11–16: User problems that can be fixed by the user.
	17: SQL Server has run out of a configurable resource such as locks. The DBA may fix this.
	18: A nonfatal internal software problem.
	19: SQL Server has exceeded a nonconfigurable resource limit.
	20: A problem occurred in a statement issued by the current process.
	21: SQL Server encountered a problem that affects all processes in a database.
	22: A table or index has been damaged.
	23: The database is suspect.
	24: Hardware problem.
	25: System error.
LineNumber	Returns the line number within the T-SQL command batch or stored procedure that caused the error.
Message	Returns a message describing the problem.
Number	Returns the error number.
Procedure	Returns the name of the stored procedure or remote procedure call that caused the error.

The `System.Data.Common.DbException` class is the parent class of `SqlException` and three other classes that return similar information for other database types. The following list summarizes the three other child `DbException` child classes:

➤ `System.Data.Odbc.OdbcException`: Errors in ODBC databases

➤ `System.Data.OleDb.OleDbException`: Errors in OLE DB databases

➤ `System.Data.OracleClient.OracleException`: Errors in Oracle databases

All these classes provide a `Message` property that gives information about the exception, although they do not provide the `Class`, `LineNumber`, `Number`, and `Procedure` properties provided by the `SqlException` class.

Overflow Exceptions

By default, a C# program does not throw an exception if an arithmetic operation causes an integer overflow. If the operands are integral or `decimal`, the program discards any extra bits, returns a truncated result, and continues running as if nothing had gone wrong. In that case you might not be aware that the result is gibberish.

You can make the program throw an `OverflowException` either by using a *checked block* or by using the Advanced Build Settings dialog. For more information, see the section "Using Widening and Narrowing Conversions" in Chapter 4, "Using Types."

A C# program also doesn't throw an exception if a floating point operation causes an overflow or underflow, or if it produces the special value `NaN` (which stands for "not a number").

The floating point types define static properties `PositiveInfinity`, `NegativeInfinity`, and `NaN`. You can compare a floating point variable to the `PositiveInfinity` and `NegativeInfinity` values. However, if you compare a variable to `NaN`, the result is always false. (Even `float.NaN == float.NaN` returns false.)

Instead of trying to compare results to the special values, it is better to use the type's methods to determine whether a variable holds one of these special values. Table 6-4 describes these methods.

TABLE 6-4: Floating Point Special Value Methods

METHOD	DESCRIPTION
`IsInfinity`	Returns `true` if the value is `PositiveInfinity` or `NegativeInfinity`
`IsNaN`	Returns `true` if the value is `NaN`
`IsNegativeInfinity`	Returns `true` if the value is `NegativeInfinity`
`IsPositiveInfinity`	Returns `true` if the value is `PositiveInfinity`

Using the special value methods listed in Table 6-4 makes code easier to understand and protects the code in case the special values such as `PositiveInfinity` change in some later version of .NET, for example if the float data type moves to 64 bits.

REAL-WORLD CASE SCENARIO   Factorials

The factorial of a number N is written N! and is defined by N! = 1 × 2 × 3 × ... × N. Write a Factorial method that uses long integers to calculate a number's factorial. Watch for the following errors:

➤   N isn't an integer

➤   N < 0

➤   Overflow

➤   Other unexpected problems

Solution

The following code shows the basic `Factorial` method:

```
// Calculate a number's factorial.
private long Factorial(long n)
{
    long result = 1;
    for (long i = 2; i <= n; i++) result *= i;
    return result;
}
```

This code could have problems if it causes an integer overflow, which would not be detected by default, or if the input parameter n is less than 0. The following code shows the improved `Factorial` method:

```
// Calculate a number's factorial.
private long Factorial(long n)
{
    // Make sure n >= 0.
    if (n < 0) throw new ArgumentOutOfRangeException(
        "n", "The number n must be at least 0 to calculate n!");

    checked
    {
        long result = 1;
        for (long i = 2; i <= n; i++) result *= i;
        return result;
    }
}
```

Now if the input parameter is less than zero, the method throws an `ArgumentOutOfRangeException`.

The checked block makes the code throw an `OverflowException` if there is an integer overflow. Notice that this method does not catch that exception. The calling code should catch it. This method could catch the exception and throw a new one, but it couldn't actually add any meaningful new information beyond that an overflow occurred, so there's little point in doing that.

The following code shows how the program calls the `Factorial` method:

```
// Calculate the number's factorial.
private void calculateButton_Click(object sender, EventArgs e)
{
    resultTextBox.Clear();

    try
    {
        long n;
        if (!long.TryParse(nTextBox.Text, out n))
        {
            MessageBox.Show("The number must be an integer.");
            return;
        }
```

```
            resultTextBox.Text = Factorial(n).ToString();
    }
    catch (ArgumentOutOfRangeException)
    {
        MessageBox.Show("The number must be at least 0.");
    }
    catch (OverflowException)
    {
        MessageBox.Show("This number is too big to calculate its factorial.");
    }
    catch (Exception ex)
    {
        MessageBox.Show(ex.ToString());
    }
}
```

The code immediately enters a `try-catch-finally` block to protect itself against errors. Its first real statement clears the result `TextBox`, so it is cleared even if the following `TryParse` statement makes the event handler exit.

Next, it tries to parse the user's input value. If `TryParse` indicates that the user's input cannot be parsed, the event handler displays an error message and returns.

The program then calls the `Factorial` method and displays the result.

If any of that code throws an exception, control jumps to a `catch` section. If the exception is `ArgumentOutOfRangeException` or `OverflowException`, the program displays an appropriate error message.

If the program encounters some other kind of exception, it uses the exception's `ToString` method to display information about the unanticipated error. You can look at this information to determine what kind of exception this is so that you can add an appropriate `catch` section to the code.

Exception Properties

The `System.Exception` class, which is an ancestor of all other exception classes, defines several properties that a program can use to try to determine what is happening and to tell the user about the problem. Table 6-5 describes those properties.

TABLE 6-5: Exception Class Properties

PROPERTY	DESCRIPTION
Data	A collection of key/value pairs that give extra information about the exception.
HelpLink	A link to a help file associated with the exception.

PROPERTY	DESCRIPTION
HResult	A numeric code describing the exception.
InnerException	An Exception object that gives more information about the exception. Some libraries catch exceptions and wrap them in new exception objects to provide information that is more relevant to the library. In that case, they may include a reference to the original exception in the InnerException property.
Message	A message describing the exception in general terms.
Source	The name of the application or object that caused the exception.
StackTrace	A string representation of the program's stack trace when the exception occurred.
TargetSite	Information about the method that threw the exception.

The Message property doesn't tell exactly where the error occurred, but tells in general terms what went wrong. For example, an OverflowException object's Message property is Arithmetic Operation Resulted in an Overflow.

Many programs simply display an exception's Message to the user and let the user try to determine what went wrong. Although an exception's Message is correct, it isn't user-friendly and doesn't tell the user what calculation caused the exception or how to fix it. A better solution is for the program to catch the exception and display a more meaningful message to the user.

For example, suppose a program processes an order form and catches an OverflowException while multiplying quantity by price per unit for the third item on the form. Instead of telling the user, Arithmetic Operation Resulted in an Overflow, it would be better to say something like, "Quantity Times Price Is Too Large for Item Number 3. Please Enter Smaller Values for Those Amounts." (It would be even better to validate the quantity and price separately so that you could display a message such as Quantity Must Be Between 1 and 100.)

An exception's Message isn't quite specific enough to show a user, but it is sometimes enough to show developers during debugging. The Exception class's ToString method, however, provides even more useful information for developers. It includes the name of the exception's class, the Message property, and a stack trace. For example, an OverflowException object's ToString method might return the following text:

```
System.OverflowException: Arithmetic operation resulted in an overflow.
    at OrderProcessor.OrderForm.CalculateSubtotal() in
        d:\Support\Apps\OrderProcessor\OrderForm.cs:line 166
```

Using the class name included in this information, you can add a new catch section to the try-catch-block to look specifically for this exception and display a more user-friendly error message.

Throwing and Rethrowing Exceptions

A method can use a `try-catch-finally` block to catch exceptions. If that method interacts with the user, it can display a message to tell the user about the problem.

However, often a method should not interact directly with the user. For example, if you're writing a library of tools that will be called by other methods, your methods probably shouldn't interact directly with the user. Instead those methods should throw exceptions of their own to tell the calling code what went wrong, and then let that code deal with the problem. That code might display a message to the user, or it might handle the problem without bothering the user.

The question then becomes, "What exceptions should your method catch, what exceptions should it ignore, and what exceptions should it throw?" The following sections discuss some of the issues involved in catching, throwing, and rethrowing exceptions.

Using Exceptions and Return Values

A method can take some action and then return information to the calling code through a return value or through output parameters. Exceptions give a method one more way to communicate with the calling code. An exception tells the program that something exceptional has happened and that the method may not have finished whatever task it was performing.

There is some discussion on the Internet about when a method should return information through a return value or parameters, and when it should return information through an exception. Most developers agree that normal status information should be returned through a return value and that exceptions should be used only when there's an error.

The best way to decide whether to use an exception is to ask if the calling code should be allowed to ignore the method's status. If a method returns status information through its return value, the calling code can ignore it. If the method throws an exception, the calling code must include a `try-catch-block` to handle the exception explicitly.

For example, consider the following method that returns the factorial of a number:

```
// Calculate a number's factorial.
private long Factorial(long n)
{
    // Make sure n >= 0.
    if (n < 0) return 0;

    checked
    {
        try
        {
            long result = 1;
            for (long i = 2; i <= n; i++) result *= i;
            return result;
        }
        catch
        {
            return 0;
        }
    }
}
```

If the parameter is less than zero or if the calculation causes an integer overflow, the method returns the value 0. Because 0 is not a valid value for the factorial function, the calling code can detect that something went wrong.

There are two problems with this approach. First, the calling code could ignore the error and treat the value 0 as a number's factorial, giving an incorrect result. If the value is used in a complex calculation, the error might become embedded in the calculation. The program would produce an incorrect result that might be hard to notice and fix later.

The second problem is that the calling code cannot tell what went wrong. The return value 0 doesn't indicate whether the input parameter was less than 0 or whether there was an integer overflow. You could use multiple return values, so 0 means the parameter was less than 0, and −1 means an integer overflow, but that just creates more status values that the calling code can ignore.

A better solution is to throw appropriate exceptions when appropriate. The following version of the Factorial method, which was shown earlier in this chapter, uses exceptions:

```
// Calculate a number's factorial.
private long Factorial(long n)
{
    // Make sure n >= 0.
    if (n < 0) throw new ArgumentOutOfRangeException(
        "n", "The number n must be at least 0 to calculate n!");

    checked
    {
        long result = 1;
        for (long i = 2; i <= n; i++) result *= i;
        return result;
    }
}
```

If the parameter is less than zero, the code throws an exception. Because the calculations are enclosed in a checked block, if they cause an integer overflow, they will throw an OverflowException.

In contrast to the Factorial method, suppose the SendInvoice method sends an invoice to a customer. Depending on the customer's preferences, the method might send e-mail, send a fax, or print an invoice for mailing.

As long as this method sends an invoice, the calling code can probably ignore it. In that case the method could return a status value to indicate which method it used.

However, if the method failed to send an invoice for any reason, it should throw an exception, so the calling code knows the customer will not receive an invoice.

Catching, Throwing, and Rethrowing Exceptions

If a method can explain why an exception occurred rather than merely reporting that an exception did occur, or if it can add new information to make an exception more specific, then it should catch the exception and throw a new one that includes the new information.

For example, suppose a mapping program reads different files with obscure names such as D:\mparam .na.wv.map depending on which part of the world it needs to map. If a file is missing, the method receives a `FileNotFoundException` that includes the name of the file that is missing, but passing that name back to the calling code probably won't be helpful to the user. In this case it would make sense to catch the exception and throw a new `FileNotFoundException` with the message, "Could Not Find the Map File for West Virginia."

If you throw a new exception in this manner, it is good practice to include the original exception in the new exception's `InnerException` property so that the calling code has access to the original information if that would be helpful.

If a method cannot add any information to an exception, it should usually not catch it. Instead, it should let the exception move up the call stack and let the calling code handle it.

For example, if the `LoadParameters` method tries to load settings from file `C\parameters.txt` and receives a `FileNotFoundException`, there's no reason for it to catch the exception. The calling code knows which file wasn't found, so the method can't actually add any new information to the exception.

One time when you might want to break this rule is when you want the method to take some "private" action before allowing the exception to move up the call stack. For example, suppose you're writing a library of tools for other programmers to use. When a method encounters an exception, you may want it to save information about the exception in a log file so that you can fix the problem later. In that case, you might want the method to catch an exception, log the error, and then rethrow the exception so that it can move up the call stack normally.

To rethrow the current exception, use the `throw` statement without passing it an exception. The following code snippet demonstrates this technique:

```
try
{
    // Do something dangerous.
    ...
}
catch (Exception)
{
    // Log the error.
    ...

    // Re-throw the exception.
    throw;
}
```

Contrast this code with the following version:

```
try
{
    // Do something dangerous.
    ...
}
catch (Exception ex)
{
    // Log the error.
    ...

    // Re-throw the exception.
    throw ex;
}
```

The new version explicitly throws the same exception object that the `try-catch-finally` block caught. When the code throws an exception in this way, the exception's call stack is reset to the current location so that it refers to the line of code that contains the `throw` statement. That may mislead any programmers who try to locate a problem by making them look at the wrong line of code. The situation is even worse if the line of code that threw the exception was inside another method called by this one. If you rethrow the exception in this way, the fact that the error is in another method is lost.

In all cases a method should clean up as much as possible before throwing or rethrowing an exception. If the method opens a file or connects to a database, it should close the file or database connection before throwing an exception, leaving the calling code with as few side effects as possible.

> **ADVICE FROM THE EXPERTS: Throwing Away the Call Stack**
>
> There are still a few situations in which you might want to rethrow an exception like this to reset the call stack information. For example, if the method is in a library and you want to hide the details of the library from the calling code, you don't necessarily want the call stack to include information about private methods within the library. In that case, you could catch exceptions in the library's public methods and then rethrow them so that the call stack begins at those public methods.

Creating Custom Exceptions

When your code encounters a problem, it can throw an exception to tell the calling code about it. If possible, you should throw one of the exception classes defined by the .NET Framework. The predefined exception classes have specific meanings so, if you use one, other developers will have a good idea what the exception represents.

Sometimes, however, you may not find a predefined exception class that fits your situation well. In that case, you can create your own exception class.

Derive the new class from the `Exception` class. End the new class's name with the word `Exception`.

To make the new class as useful as possible, give it constructors that match those defined by the `Exception` class. The following code shows a simple `InvalidException` class that provides four constructors that take parameters similar to those used by the constructors defined in the `Exception` class:

```
[Serializable]
class InvalidProjectionException : Exception
{
    public InvalidProjectionException()
        : base() { }

    public InvalidProjectionException(string message)
        : base(message) { }

    public InvalidProjectionException(string message,
        Exception innerException)
        : base(message, innerException) { }
```

```
protected InvalidProjectionException(SerializationInfo info,
    StreamingContext context)
    : base(info, context) { }
}
```

Each of the constructors simply passes its parameters to the base class's constructors. The `SerializationInfo` and `StreamingContext` types are defined in the `System.Runtime.Serialization` namespace.

BEST PRACTICES: Serialization Required

An exception must be serialized and deserialized to cross `AppDomain` boundaries. To make the class as useful as possible, give it the `Serializable` attribute.

If the custom exception class provides specialized information, add the appropriate properties to the class, and add additional constructors if you like.

ADVICE FROM THE EXPERTS: Derive from Exception

Microsoft used to recommend that you derive new exception classes from `ApplicationException`, but it later decided that this just adds another level to the exception hierarchy without providing any actual benefit.

It doesn't matter whether you derive new exception classes from `Exception` or `ApplicationException`, but it's probably worth using `Exception` to be consistent with other developers who follow Microsoft's recommendations.

Making Assertions

The `System.Diagnostics.Debug` class provides an `Assert` method that is often used to validate data as it passes through a method. This method takes a boolean value as its first parameter and throws an exception if that value is false. Other parameters let you specify other messages to display to give you more information about where the assertion failed.

In a debug build, the `Assert` method halts execution and displays a stack trace. In a release build, the program skips the call to `Assert`, so it continues running even if the assertion is false.

A method can use `Assert` to verify that its data makes sense. For example, suppose the `PrintInvoice` method takes as a parameter an array of `OrderItem` objects named `items` and prints an invoice for those items. The method might begin with the following `Assert` statement to verify that the `items` array contains no more than 100 items:

```
Debug.Assert(items.Length <= 100)
```

If an order contains more than 100 items, the `Assert` statement halts execution, so you can examine the code to decide whether this is a bug or just an unusual order. If this is a valid but unusual order, you can change the statement to look for orders that contain more than 150 items.

In a release build, this `Assert` statement is ignored, so the program must be prepared to handle orders that contain many items, even if the `Assert` statement would not allow that in a debug build.

If a piece of data is invalid and the program cannot continue, throw an exception. If a piece of data is unusual and may indicate a bug but the program can meaningfully continue, use `Debug.Assert` to detect the unusual value during testing.

SUMMARY

This chapter described two methods that different parts of a program can use to communicate: events and exceptions.

Events enable an object to notify other parts of the application when some interesting event occurs. To define and raise an event, a program must use delegates, so this chapter explained delegates. It also explained anonymous methods and lambda expressions, which enable you to make methods that have no names but that can be stored in delegate variables and that can be used as event handlers.

Exceptions let a method tell the calling code that it has encountered a critical problem. This chapter explained how to use the `try-catch-block` to catch and handle exceptions. It also explained how and when your code can throw exceptions. It described some of the more useful predefined exception classes and explained how you can define new custom exception classes when none of the predefined classes fit your needs.

There are three kinds of lambda expressions: expression lambdas, statement lambdas, and async lambdas. This chapter described all three but only briefly mentioned async lambdas, which let a program indicate that the lamba expression will run asynchronously.

Chapter 7 explains asynchronous processing and multithreading in greater detail. It explains how a program can run processes on different threads to improve responsiveness and how to use asynchronous code such as that defined by async lambdas.

CHAPTER TEST QUESTIONS

Read each question carefully and select the answer or answers that represent the best solution to the problem. You can find the answers in Appendix A, "Answers to Chapter Test Questions."

1. Which of the following is a valid delegate definition?

    a. `private delegate float MyDelegate(float);`

    b. `private delegate MyDelegate(x);`

    c. `private delegate MyDelegate(float x);`

    d. `private delegate void MyDelegate(float x);`

2. Which of the following statements is *not* true of delegate variables?

  a. You need to use a cast operator to execute the method to which a delegate variable refers.

  b. A `struct` or class can contain fields that are delegate variables.

  c. You can make an array or list of delegate variables.

  d. You can use addition to combine delegate variables into a series of methods and use subtraction to remove a method from a series.

3. If the `Employee` class inherits from the `Person` class, covariance lets you do which of the following?

  a. Store a method that returns a `Person` in a delegate that represents methods that return an `Employee`.

  b. Store a method that returns an `Employee` in a delegate that represents methods that return a `Person`.

  c. Store a method that takes a `Person` as a parameter in a delegate that represents methods that take an `Employee` as a parameter.

  d. Store a method that takes an `Employee` as a parameter in a delegate that represents methods that take a `Person` as a parameter.

4. If the `Employee` class inherits from the `Person` class, contravariance lets you do which of the following?

  a. Store a method that returns a `Person` in a delegate that represents methods that return an `Employee`.

  b. Store a method that returns an `Employee` in a delegate that represents methods that return a `Person`.

  c. Store a method that takes a `Person` as a parameter in a delegate that represents methods that take an `Employee` as a parameter.

  d. Store a method that takes an `Employee` as a parameter in a delegate that represents methods that take a `Person` as a parameter.

5. In the variable declaration `Action<Order> processor`, the variable `processor` represents which of the following?

  a. Methods that take no parameters and return an `Order` object.

  b. Methods that take an `Order` object as a parameter and return `void`.

  c. Methods that take an `Order` object as a parameter and return an `Order` object.

  d. Methods provided by the `Action` class that take no parameters and return `void`.

6. In the variable declaration `Func<Order> processor`, the variable `processor` represents which of the following?

    a. Methods that take no parameters and return an `Order` object.

    b. Methods that take an `Order` object as a parameter and return `void`.

    c. Methods that take an `Order` object as a parameter and return an `Order` object.

    d. Methods provided by the `Action` class that take no parameters and return `void`.

7. Suppose `F` is declared by the statement `Func<float, float> F`. Then which of the following correctly initializes `F` to an anonymous method?

    a. `F = (float x) { return x * x; };`

    b. `F = delegate { return x * x; };`

    c. `F = float Func(float x) { return x * x; };`

    d. `F = delegate(float x) { return x * x; };`

8. Suppose the variable `note` is declared by the statement `Action note`. Then which of the following correctly initializes `note` to an expression lambda?

    a. `note = { return x * x; };`

    b. `note = () { return x * x; };`

    c. `note = () => MessageBox.Show("Hi");`

    d. `note = MessageBox.Show("Hi");`

9. Suppose the variable `result` is declared by the statement `Func<float, float> result`. Which of the following correctly initializes `result` to an expression lambda?

    a. `result = (float x) => x * x;`

    b. `result = (x) => return x * x;`

    c. `result = x => x * x;`

    d. Both a and c are correct.

10. Which of the following statements about statement lambdas is false?

    a. A statement lambda can include more than one statement.

    b. A statement lambda cannot return a value.

    c. A statement lambda must use braces, `{ }`.

    d. If a statement lambda returns a value, it must use a `return` statement.

11. Suppose the `MovedEventHandler` delegate is defined by the statement `delegate void MovedEventHandler()`. Which of the following correctly declares the `Moved` event?

    a. `public MovedEventHandler MovedEvent;`

    b. `public event MovedEventHandler MovedEvent;`

    c. `public event Action MovedEvent;`

    d. Both b and c are correct.

12. Suppose the `Employee` class is derived from the `Person` class and the `Person` class defines an `AddressChanged` event. Which of the following should you *not* do to allow an `Employee` object to raise this event?

    a. Create an `OnAddressChanged` method in the `Person` class that raises the event.

    b. Create an `OnAddressChanged` method in the `Employee` class that raises the event.

    c. Make the `Employee` class call `OnAddressChanged` as needed.

    d. Make the code in the `Person` class that used to raise the event call the `OnAddressChanged` method instead.

13. Which of the following statements subscribes the `myButton_Click` event handler to catch the `myButton` control's `Click` event?

    a. `myButton.Click += myButton_Click;`

    b. `myButton_Click += myButton.Click;`

    c. `myButton_Click handles myButton.Click;`

    d. `myButton.Click = myButton_Click;`

14. Suppose the `Car` class provides a `Stopped` event that takes as parameters `sender` and `StoppedArgs` objects. Suppose also that the code has already created an appropriate `StoppedArgs` object named `args`. Then which of the following code snippets correctly raises the event?

    a. `if (!Stopped.IsEmpty) Stopped(this, args);`

    b. `if (Stopped) Stopped(this, args);`

    c. `if (Stopped != null) Stopped(this, args);`

    d. `raise Stopped(this, args);`

15. Which of the following statements about events is false?

    a. If an object subscribes to an event twice, its event handler executes twice when the event is raised.

    b. If an object subscribes to an event twice and then unsubscribes once, its event handler executes once when the event is raised.

    c. If an object subscribes to an event once and then unsubscribes twice, its event handler throws an exception when the event is raised.

    d. In a Windows Forms application, you can use the Properties window to subscribe and unsubscribe events, and to create empty event handlers.

16. Which of the following statements about inheritance and events is false?

   a. A derived class can raise a base class event by using code similar to the following:

```
if (base.EventName != null) base.EventName(this, args);
```

   b. A derived class cannot raise an event defined in an ancestor class.

   c. A class can define an `OnEventName` method that raises an event to allow derived classes to raise that event.

   d. A derived class inherits the definition of the base class's events, so a program can subscribe to a derived object's event.

17. Which of the following statements about exception handling is true?

   a. You can nest a `try-catch-finally` block inside a `try`, `catch`, or `finally` section.

   b. A `try-catch-finally` block must include at least one `catch` section and one `finally` section.

   c. An exception is handled by the `catch` section that has the most specific matching exception type.

   d. The code in a `finally` section executes if the code finishes without an error or if a `catch` section handles an exception but not if the code executes a return statement.

18. Which of the following methods can you use to catch integer overflow exceptions?

   a. Use a `try-catch-finally` block.

   b. Use a `checked` block and a `try-catch-finally` block.

   c. Check the Advanced Build Settings dialog's overflow/underflow box, and use a `try-catch-finally` block.

   d. Either b or c.

19. Which of the following returns `true` if variable `result` holds the value `float.PositiveInfinity`?

   a. `result == float.PositiveInfinity`

   b. `float.IsInfinity(result)`

   c. `float.IsPositiveInfinity(result)`

   d. All of the above.

20. Which of the following statements about throwing exceptions is false?

   a. If you catch an exception and throw a new one to add more information, you should include the original exception in the new one's `InnerException` property.

   b. If you rethrow the exception ex with the statement `throw`, the exception's call stack is reset to start at the current line of code.

   c. If you rethrow the exception ex with the statement `throw ex`, the exception's call stack is reset to start at the current line of code.

   d. Before a method throws an exception, it should clean up as much as possible, so the calling code has to deal with the fewest possible side effects.

21. Which of the following should you *not* do when building a custom exception class?

    a. Derive it from the `System.Exception` class, and end its name with `Exception`.

    b. Give it event handlers with parameters that match those defined by the `System.Exception` class.

    c. Make it implement `IDisposable`.

    d. Give it the `Serializable` attribute.

ADDITIONAL READING AND RESOURCES

Here are some additional useful resources to help you understand the topics presented in this chapter:

Delegates (C# *Programming Guide*)
    http://msdn.microsoft.com/library/ms173171.aspx

Anonymous Methods (C# *Programming Guide*)
    http://msdn.microsoft.com/library/0yw3tz5k.aspx

Lambda Expressions (C# *Programming Guide*)
    http://msdn.microsoft.com/library/bb397687.aspx

Events (C# *Programming Guide*)
    http://msdn.microsoft.com/library/awbftdfh.aspx

How to: Raise Base Class Events in Derived Classes (C# *Programming Guide*)
    http://msdn.microsoft.com/library/hy3sefw3.aspx

Best Practices for Handling Exceptions
    http://msdn.microsoft.com/library/seyhszts.aspx

Exception Handling Best Practices in .NET
    http://www.codeproject.com/Articles/9538/
    Exception-Handling-Best-Practices-in-NET

SqlException Class
    http://msdn.microsoft.com/library/system.data.sqlclient.sqlexception.aspx

SystemException Class inheritance hierarchy
    http://msdn.microsoft.com/library/system.systemexception
    .aspx#inheritanceContinued

AppDomain Class
    http://msdn.microsoft.com/library/system.appdomain.aspx

CHEAT SHEET

This cheat sheet is designed as a way for you to quickly study the key points of this chapter.

Working with delegates

➤ A delegate is a type that represents a kind of method. It defines the method's parameters and return type.

➤ Often the name of a delegate type ends with `Delegate` or `Callback`.

➤ You can use + and – to combine delegate variables. For example, if a program executes the statement `del3 = del1 + del2`, then `del3` will execute the methods referred to by `del1` and `del2`.

➤ If a delegate variable refers to an instance method, it executes with the object on whose instance it was assigned.

➤ Covariance lets a method return a value from a subclass of the result expected by a delegate.

➤ Contravariance lets a method take parameters that are from a superclass of the type expected by a delegate.

➤ The .NET Framework defines two built-in delegate types that you can use in many cases: `Action` and `Func`. The following code shows the declarations for `Action` and `Func` delegates that take two parameters:

```
public delegate void Action<in T1, in T2>(T1 arg1, T2 arg2)
public delegate TResult Func<in T1, in T2, out TResult>
(T1 arg1, T2 arg2)
```

➤ An anonymous method is a method with no name. The following code saves a reference to an anonymous method in variable `function`:

```
Func<float, float> function = delegate(float x) { return x * x; };
```

➤ A lambda expression uses a concise syntax to create an anonymous method. The following code shows examples of lambda expressions:

```
Action note1 = () => MessageBox.Show("Hi");
Action<string> note2 = message => MessageBox.Show(message);
Action<string> note3 = (message) => MessageBox.Show(message);
Action<string> note4 = (string message) => MessageBox.Show(message);
Func<float, float> square = (float x) => x * x;
```

➤ An expression lambda evaluates a single expression whose value is returned by the anonymous method.

➤ A statement lambda executes a series of statements. It must use a `return` statement to return a value.

➤ An async lambda is a lambda expression that includes the `async` keyword.

Working with events

➤ Events have publishers and subscribers. A given event may have many subscribers or no subscribers.

➤ Use a delegate type to define an event, as in the following code:

```
public delegate void OverdrawnEventHandler();
public event OverdrawnEventHandler Overdrawn;
```

➤ You can use the predefined Action delegate type to define events, as in the following code:

```
public event Action Overdrawn;
```

➤ Microsoft best practice: Make the event's first parameter a sender object and the second an object that gives more information about the event. Derive the type of the object from the EventArgs class, and end its name with Args as in OverdrawnEventArgs.

➤ You can use the predefined EventHandler delegate type to define an event that takes an object named sender as a first parameter and an event data object as a second parameter, as shown in the following code:

```
public event EventHandler<OverdrawnEventArgs> Overdrawn;
```

➤ Raise an event, as in the following code:

```
if (EventName != null) EventName(arguments...);
```

➤ Classes cannot inherit events. To make it possible for derived classes to raise base class events, give the base class an OnEventName method that raises the event.

➤ A program can use += and -= to subscribe and unsubscribe from events.

➤ If a program subscribes to an event more than once, the event handler is called multiple times.

➤ If a program unsubscribes from an event more times than it was subscribed, nothing bad happens.

Exception handling

➤ Error checking is the process of proactively anticipating errors and looking for them. Exception handling is the process of protecting a program from unexpected errors. Error checking is usually more efficient than exception handling.

➤ A try-catch-finally block must have at least one catch section or a finally section.

➤ The finally section *always* executes no matter how the program leaves a try-catch-finally block.

➤ The most-specific (most-derived) catch sections must come first in a try-catch-finally block.

➤ You can include only an exception type and omit the exception variable in a `catch` section if you don't need to do anything with the exception.

➤ The `Exception` class is an ancestor of all exception classes, so `catch (Exception)` catches all exceptions.

➤ A `catch` section with no exception type catches all exceptions.

➤ A `using` statement is equivalent to a `try-catch-finally` block with a `finally` section that disposes of the object.

➤ If an exception is not handled, control moves up the call stack until either a `try-catch-finally` block handles it or the program crashes.

➤ An exception object's `Message` property gives information about the exception. Its `ToString` method includes the `Message` plus additional information including a stack trace.

➤ The `SqlException` class represents all SQL Server exceptions. Properties such as `Class` and `Message` give additional information about the error.

➤ By default, integer operations do not throw `OverflowExceptions`. Use a checked block or the Advanced Build Settings dialog to make overflows throw this exception.

➤ Floating point operations do not cause overflow. Instead they set the result to `PositiveInfinity`, `NegativeInfinity`, or `NaN`.

➤ Use the floating point methods `IsInfinity`, `IsInfinity`, `IsInfinity`, and `IsNaN` to determine whether a result is one of these special values.

➤ To rethrow the current exception, use the `throw` statement without passing it an exception object. To rethrow the exception `ex` while resetting its stack trace, use `throw ex`.

➤ To return noncritical status information, a method should return a status value. To prevent a program from ignoring a critical issue, a method should throw an exception.

➤ If a method cannot add useful information to an exception, it should not catch and rethrow it. Instead it should let it propagate up to the calling code.

➤ To create a custom exception, derive it from the `System.Exception` class and end its name with `Exception`. Mark it serializable and give it constructors that match those defined by the `Exception` class.

➤ You can use `Debug.Assert` to throw an exception in a debug build to find suspicious data. The statement is ignored in release builds, so the program must continue even if `Debug.Assert` would stop the program in a debug build.

➤ If you catch an exception and throw a new one to add extra information, include a reference to the original exception in the new one's `InnerException` property.

➤ Clean up as much as possible before throwing or rethrowing an exception so that the calling code faces as few side effects as possible.

REVIEW OF KEY TERMS

checked By default, a program doesn't throw `OverflowExceptions` when an arithmetic operation causes an overflow. A program can use a `checked` block to make arithmetic expressions throw those exceptions.

contravariance A feature of C# that enables a method to take parameters that are from a *superclass* of the type expected by a delegate. For example, suppose the `Employee` class is derived from the `Person` class and the `EmployeeParameterDelegate` type represents methods that take an `Employee` object as a parameter. Then you could set an `EmployeeParameterDelegate` variable equal to a method that takes a `Person` as a parameter because `Person` is a superclass of `Employee`. When you invoke the delegate variable's method, you will pass it an `Employee` (because the delegate requires that the method take an `Employee` parameter) and an `Employee` is a kind of `Person`, so the method can handle it.

contravariant A variable is contravariant if it enables contravariance.

covariance A feature of C# that enables a method to return a value from a subclass of the result expected by a delegate. For example, suppose the `Employee` class is derived from the `Person` class and the `CreatePersonDelegate` type indicates a method that returns a `Person` object. Then you could set a `CreatePersonDelegate` variable equal to a method that returns an `Employee` because an Employee is a kind of `Person`.

delegate A data type that defines a method with given parameters and return value.

error checking The process to anticipate errors, check to see if they occur, and work around them, for example, validating an integer entered by the user in a `TextBox` instead of simply trying to parse it and failing if the value is not an integer. See also *exception handling*.

exception handling The process to protect the application when an unexpected error occurs, for example, protecting the code in case a file downloads fails when it is halfway done. See also *error checking*.

expression lambda A lambda expression that has a single expression on the right side.

lambda expression A concise syntax for defining anonymous methods.

publisher An object that raises an event.

statement lambda Similar to an expression lambda except it encloses its code in braces and it can execute more than one statement. If it should return a value, it must use a `return` statement.

subscriber An object that receives an event.

try-catch-finally block The program structure used to catch exceptions. The `try` section contains the code that might throw an exception, `catch` sections catch different exception types, and the `finally` section contains code to be executed when the `try` and `catch` sections finish executing.

unhandled exception Occurs when an exception is thrown and the program is not protected by a `try-catch-finally` block, either because the code isn't inside a `try` section or because there is no `catch` section that matches the exception.

EXAM TIPS AND TRICKS

The Review of Key Terms and the Cheat Sheet for this chapter can be printed off to help you study. You can find these files in the ZIP file for this chapter at `www.wrox` `.com/remtitle.cgi?isbn=1118612094` on the Download Code tab.

Multithreading and Asynchronous Processing

WHAT YOU WILL LEARN IN THIS CHAPTER

- ➤ Understanding threads and thread pool
- ➤ Using the Task Parallel Library
- ➤ Using concurrent collections
- ➤ Implementing asynchronous methods

WROX.COM CODE DOWNLOADS FOR THIS CHAPTER

You can find the code downloads for this chapter at www.wrox.com/remtitle
.cgi?isbn=1118612094 on the Download Code tab. The code is in the chapter07
download and individually named according to the names throughout the chapter.

In 1967, Gordon Moore observed that the numbers of transistors that can be fit on the same
surface on a silicon chip is doubling every other year. Today, this doubling happens every one-
and-a-half years. Until 2005, this translated into several improvements such as doubling the
frequency and processing speed, doubling the capacity, cutting the size of the chip in half, and
so on. In 2005, the frequency a CPU could operate at reached a plateau. Although the hardware
manufacturers could still follow Moore's law, the frequency could not be increased without
major implications, mainly because of the huge heat that got generated by the processor, and
that heat needed to be taken care of. So to still benefit from technological advancement outlined
by Moore's law, the hardware manufacturer started to deliver more processing units per processor, known as *cores*, instead of increasing the speed. Developers now face the biggest challenge
of their careers because many are used to thinking and developing applications for machines
that have only one core. Fortunately, Microsoft realized that already, so it created new libraries
and introduced new paradigms into C# so life can be easier.

In this chapter, you will explore different options you have to improve the performance of your application. This chapter starts by discussing threads and the thread pool, then continues with a discussion about the `BackgroundWorker` class and how you can use it in WPF and Windows Forms applications. Next, you will look at the Task Parallel Library (TPL), as well as some applications of the TPL, like the `Parallel` class. After that the chapter covers the new asynchronous programming paradigm introduced by C# 5.0. The chapter then continues the discussion by describing synchronizing access to resources to ensure the correctness of your application and working with concurrent collections. Finally, the chapter by describes cancellations in .NET Framework.

Table 7-1 introduces you to the exam objectives covered in this chapter.

TABLE 7-1: 70-483 Exam Objectives Covered in This Chapter

OBJECTIVE	CONTENT COVERED
Implement multithreading and asynchronous processing	*Task Parallel Library (ParallelFor, Plinq, Tasks).* This includes creating new tasks and using them to increase the performance of your application.
	Create continuation tasks. This includes discussing techniques to work with task continuations.
	Spawn threads by using `ThreadPool`. This includes creating `Thread` objects and using threads from the thread pool.
	Unblock the UI. This includes using the `BackgroundWorker` class in order to create responsive applications.
	Use `async` *and* `await` *keywords.* This includes using the new `async` and `await` keywords to create responsive applications.
	Manage data by using concurrent collections. This includes using the classes from the `System.Concurrent.Collections`.
Manage multithreading	*Synchronize resources.* This includes using `ManualResetEvent` and `AutoResetEvent` classes.
	Implement locking. This includes discussing the `Monitor`, `Mutex`, and `Semaphore` classes.
	Cancel a long-running task. This includes using `CancellationTokenSource` and `CancellationToken`.
	Implement thread-safe methods to handle race conditions.

CREATING RESPONSIVE APPLICATIONS

The first computers were created following a logical design called "von Newmann architecture," which was developed by John von Newmann and other mathematicians in 1945. According to that design, a computer should have one processing unit, a control unit, memory, and an input and output system (IO). The processing unit and the control unit form the central processing unit (CPU). Because the design had only one processing unit, the programs needed to be written for that kind of design were sequential, and most of the programming languages were created to be used in a sequential manner, which is a practice still used in today's programming languages, including C#. The biggest disadvantage of creating such applications is that whenever your application had to wait for something to happen, the whole system would freeze, creating a very unpleasant user experience. Threads were introduced to minimize this kind of problem.

Working with Threads

Less than 20 years ago, most consumer operating systems (OS) could run one single process with one *thread* of execution. (A thread is the smallest unit of execution that can be independently scheduled by the OS.) In a single-threaded OS, the computer runs only one application at the time. There was normally a command-line interpreter that was interpreting the commands entered by the user. When a command was entered, the interpreter transferred the control to the processor to the application the command was referring to. When the application was done, it transferred the control back to the interpreter. If you think about it, this made a lot of sense, considering the fact that you had only one thread. The biggest problem was that the user could feel that the computer froze when an application did one of the following two things:

➤   Intensive calculations

➤   Fetched some data from the I/O

When your application had to do intensive calculations, there wasn't too much you could do except either using a quicker computer to decrease the time it took to do the calculation or splitting the problem into smaller ones and distributing it across several computers, both of which are expensive operations, and sometimes it might take longer to do the calculations.

When your application fetched data from the I/O, your CPU was waiting for the data to come, doing no processing in the meantime. To improve the responsiveness of your application, the notion of *multithreading* was introduced. In a multithreaded application, one thread would spawn another thread to do the fetching and waiting while the parent thread continued to do other work. When the data was needed, the parent thread was blocked waiting for the spawned thread to finish its work. This pattern is known as *fork-join pattern*.

ADVICE FROM THE EXPERTS: Understanding Threads

Although threads are not explicitly required for the exam, it is the authors' firm belief that a good understanding of how threads work in Windows can help you become a better programmer and understand this chapter. If you are already familiar with this subject, you can skip this section and jump to the next one, "Spawning New Threads by Using ThreadPool," after going through the code in this section.

Having one processor, it meant that only one thread could be run at any given time. This can be achieved in two different ways:

➤ **Collaboratively:** Every thread must give up the control so that another thread can execute.

➤ **Preemptively:** The operating system has a component called *scheduler* that makes sure that no thread monopolizes the CPU. This is how Windows is implemented.

The Windows scheduler works as follows:

1. Every thread gets a priority assigned when it is created. A created thread is not automatically started; you have to do that.

2. When a thread is started, it will be added on a queue with all the threads that can be run.

3. The scheduler takes the thread with the highest priority on the queue, and it starts to run it.

4. If several threads have the same priority, the scheduler schedules them in circular order (round robin).

5. When the time allotted is up, the scheduler suspends the thread, adding it at the end of the queue. After that, it picks up a new thread to run it.

6. If there is no other thread with higher priority than the one just interrupted, that thread executes again.

7. When a thread is blocked because it has to wait for an I/O operation, or for some other reasons such as locking (discussed later in this chapter in the "Synchronizing Resources" section), the thread will be removed from the queue and another thread will be scheduled to run.

8. When the reason for blocking ends, the thread is added back in the queue to get a chance to run.

9. When a thread finishes the work, the scheduler can pick another thread to run it.

There is one thread called *System idle process* that does nothing, except keeping the processor busy when there is no other thread to run. This process of time slicing creates the impression that your operating system can run several applications at the same time, including answering to the user interface (UI) commands you send, such as moving the mouse or moving windows around.

In .NET all applications have several threads. Following is a list with some of those threads:

➤ **Garbage Collector thread:** Responsible for the garbage collection.

➤ **Finalizer thread:** Responsible to run the Finalize method of your objects.

➤ **Main thread:** Responsible to run your main application's method.

➤ **UI thread:** If your application is a Windows Form application, a WPF application, or a Windows store application, it will have one thread dedicated to update the user interface.

Except for the main thread, all the threads mentioned so far are background threads. When you create a new thread, you have the option to specify if the thread should be a background thread.

When the main thread and all other nonbackground threads of a .NET application finishes, the .NET application finishes as well.

With the coming of the new multicore and many-core processors, the applications that are written in a multithreaded fashion will inherently benefit from those improvements, whereas the applications written sequentially will underuse the resources available while making the user wait unnecessarily.

> **NOTE** *Multicore and many-core are both used to describe systems with more than one core, but there is a difference between them. Multicore refers to CPUs that have several cores of the same type on the same silicon chip. Many-core refers to CPUs that have different kinds of specialized cores on the same silicon chip.*

To illustrate what happens when your application is compute-intensive but is written in a sequential manner versus if it were written in a concurrent manner with multiple cores in mind, analyze Figures 7-1 and 7-2.

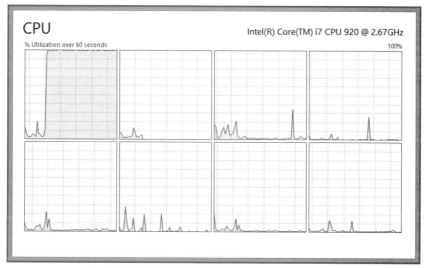

FIGURE 7-1: Single-threaded compute-intensive application

As you can see in Figure 7-1, the CPU on the top left is working at 100 percent load most of the time, whereas the other seven CPUs are idling most of the time. In some situations you might see that the load moves from one CPU to the other, but still there is only one CPU fully loaded by the application at any given time.

The same application in Figure 7-2 is loading all the CPUs to 100 percent. Although this might seem a bad thing in the eye of a system administrator, this is actually a good thing. The reason this might seem a bad thing for the system administrator is because historically a CPU loaded to 100 percent meant that one application entered an endless loop consuming all the resources, impeding other applications on the same machine from doing their job. In this case, you know that the application is compute-intensive and, therefore, is not waiting for any I/O to complete. The scheduler will do its job and ensure that all the threads having the same priority get a chance to run, so 100 percent in this situation just means that the computer is busy working. However, you need to tell your system administrator about your application so she won't mistake it for an erroneous application.

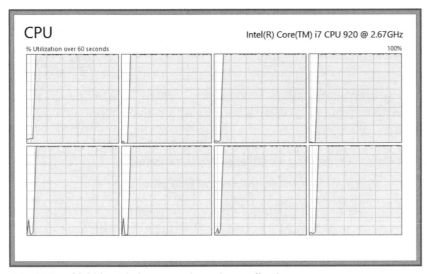

FIGURE 7-2: Multithreaded compute-intensive application

Following are some of the disadvantages of multithreaded applications:

➤ All threads are resource-intensive. They need a lot of memory (1 megabyte is standard), and every time the scheduler has to switch between threads, the processor will be busy saving the context of the suspending thread and restoring the context of the running thread.

➤ If your application creates too many threads, the context switching consumes a considerable amount of time.

➤ Because the thread needs so much memory, it usually takes a considerable amount of time for the system to create one tread and takes some time to destroy it as well.

In .NET threads are implemented in the `System.Threading.Thread` class. Because threads are not required for the exam, you can find more information about the `Thread` class in the "Additional Readings and Resources" section at the end of this chapter.

It is a straightforward process to work with threads:

1. Create a thread object.

2. Start the thread.

3. Do more work in the calling method.

4. Wait for the thread to finish.

5. Continue the work on the calling method.

Take a look at the following Code Lab.

CODE LAB **Using threads [Chapter7\SimpleApp\Program.cs]**

```csharp
class Program {

    static void Main(string[] args) {

        // We are using Stopwatch to time the code
        Stopwatch sw = Stopwatch.StartNew();

        // Here we call different methods
        // for different ways of running our application.
        RunSequencial();

        // Print the time it took to run the application.
        Console.WriteLine("We're done in {0}ms!", sw.ElapsedMilliseconds);
        if (Debugger.IsAttached) {
            Console.Write("Press any key to continue . . .");
            Console.ReadKey(true);
        }
    }

    static void RunSequencial() {

        double result = 0d;

        // Call the function to read data from I/O
        result += ReadDataFromIO();
        // Add the result of the second calculation
        result += DoIntensiveCalculations();

        // Print the result
        Console.WriteLine("The result is {0}", result);
    }

    static double ReadDataFromIO() {

        // We are simulating an I/O by putting the current thread to sleep.
        Thread.Sleep(5000);
        return 10d;
    }

    static double DoIntensiveCalculations(){

        // We are simulating intensive calculations
        // by doing nonsens divisions
        double result = 100000000d;
        var maxValue = Int32.MaxValue;
```

```
            for(int i=1; i < maxValue; i++){
                result /= i;
            }
            return result + 10d;
        }
    }
```

Code Lab Analysis

This code shows a program that must do two things: read data from I/O and do some intensive calculations. The implementation of the two methods is not important in this context; they simulate the intended behavior. In a real application the assumption is that the ReadFromIO method does real I/O operations, such as reading files or requiring data from the network, whereas DoIntensiveCalculations does calculations needed for the application. Running this application produces the following result:

```
The result is 20.
We're done in 10437ms.
```

Because the two methods are independent, you can improve the response time of this code by using threads. To do this, you need to modify the Main method accordingly to call RunWithThreads instead of RunSequencial.

```
        static void RunWithThreads() {

            double result = 0d;

            // Create the thread to read from I/O
            var thread = new Thread(() => result = ReadDataFromIO());

            // Start the thread
            thread.Start();

            // Save the result of the calculation into another variable
            double result2 = DoIntensiveCalculations();

            // Wait for the thread to finish
            thread.Join();

            // Calculate the end result
            result += result2;

            // Print the result
            Console.WriteLine("The result is {0}", result);

        }
```

You start by creating a new thread that will run the result = ReadDataFromIO() code. The thread is not started when it is created, so you have to start it by calling the Start() method. This queues this new thread for execution while continuing to run the code in the current method, in this case double result2 = DoIntensiveCalculations(). When the intensive calculation is done, you need to wait for the previously created thread to finish executing. You do that by calling the Join() method. Join blocks the current thread until the other thread is finished executing. When the other thread finishes, Join will return, and the current thread will be unblocked.

Please note that a new variable called `result2` has been introduced to hold the result from the second method, instead of using the `result` variable. (Why this was done is discussed later in this chapter in the "Synchronizing Resources" section.) When you run the application now, you get the following result:

```
The result is 20
We're done in 5370ms!
```

As you can see, this cuts the time it took to run the calculation by 5 seconds (the time it took for the I/O operation to complete). This improvement can be achieved for any number of cores. If both methods were doing calculations, you would have reduced the execution time only if you have had two or more cores.

This is a naïve take at the multithreading problem, but it illustrates the problem and the solution quite well.

The number of threads you can end up creating can be big, and because of the resource-intensive nature of the threads, sometimes it is better to have the threads already created.

Spawning New Threads by Using ThreadPool

As discussed in the previous section, threads are expensive resources, and to improve the overall performance of your application, you can choose to pre-create some threads. In .NET there is a class called `System.Threading.ThreadPool` used when you want to work with threads from the *thread pool*. This class contains only static methods that are useful when working with the `ThreadPool`. Table 7-2 lists some of the methods you normally need from that class.

TABLE 7-2: System.Threading.ThreadPool Methods

METHOD	DESCRIPTION
GetAvailableThreads	Returns the number of threads available in the thread pool. This represents the number of threads that can pick up work items from the queue.
GetMaxThreads	Returns the maximum number of threads that can be created by the thread pool.
GetMinThreads	Returns the minimum number of threads that will be available in the thread pool.
QueueUserWorkItem	Adds a request for execution to the thread pool queue. If there are available threads in the thread pool, then the request will execute right away.

continues

TABLE 7-2 *(continued)*

METHOD	DESCRIPTION
RegisterWaitForSingleObject	Registers a method to be invoked when either the WaitHandle specified as the first parameter gets signaled or when the timeout specified as fourth parameter will elapse. This method has four overloads, one for every mode, that the timeout can be expressed as: int, long, unsigned int, or TimeSpan.
SetMaxThreads	Sets the maximum number of threads that can be created in the thread pool.
SetMinThreads	Sets the minimum number of threads that will be available in the thread pool at any given time.

The preceding list is not complete, and from this list you are more likely to use only one method: QueueUserWorkItem. If you are interested in all the methods that the ThreadPool class has to offer, you can follow the link from the "Additional Reading and Resources" section at the end of this chapter.

The thread pool works in the following way. When you need a long running method to be run in a separate thread, instead of creating a new thread, you call the QueueUserWorkItem method to place a new work item in a queue managed by the thread pool. If there is a thread idle in the pool, it picks up the work item and runs it to completion like any thread will do. If there is no thread available and the total number in the pool is less than MaxThreads, the pool creates a new thread to run the work item; otherwise, the job work item waits in the queue for the first available thread.

SetMinThread is used to prepopulate the pool with threads to improve the performance of your application when you know that you will use the thread pool.

QueueUserWorkItem has two overloads:

➤   public static bool QueueUserWorkItem(WaitCallback callBack)

➤   public static bool QueueUserWorkItem(WaitCallback callBack, Object state)

The first parameter is of type System.Threading.WaitCallback, which is a delegate defined as follows:

public delegate void WaitCallback(Object state)

If you recall from Chapter 6, "Working with Delegates, Events, and Exceptions," this represents a method that takes one parameter of type Object and doesn't return any value.

Before looking at a code example, you need to know a bit about the differences between threads created manually and threads from the thread pool:

➤   All the threads from the thread pool are background threads, whereas the manually created threads are foreground threads by default and can be set as background threads as well.

➤ You can't abort or interrupt a thread from the thread pool.

➤ You can't join a thread from the thread pool. To achieve that, you must use some other mechanisms (discussed later in this chapter in the "Synchronizing Resources" section).

➤ Threads from the thread pool are reused when they finish their work, whereas the normal threads are destroyed.

➤ You can't control the priority of a thread from the thread pool.

More differences exist but are outside the scope of this book.

> **NOTE** *The maximum number of threads in the thread pool is different for different versions of .NET and should be treated as an implementation detail. In .NET 2.0 there were 25 threads per core, in .NET 3.5 there were 250, and in .NET 4 there are 1,023 threads for the 32-bit applications and 32,767 threads for the 64-bit applications.*

REAL-WORLD CASE SCENARIO   **Using the thread pool**

Now it's time to return to the problem. If you skipped the previous section, go back and take a look at the program proposed earlier. This scenario requires for you to create a method named RunInThreadPool that uses the thread pool to run the ReadDataFromIO method and call it from the Main method.

Solution

The RunInThreadPool looks like this:

```
static void RunInThreadPool() {

    double result = 0d;

    // Create a work item to read from I/O
    ThreadPool.QueueUserWorkItem((x) => result += ReadDataFromIO());
    // Save the result of the calculation into another variable
    double result2 = DoIntensiveCalculations();
    // Wait for the thread to finish

    // TODO: We will need a way to indicate
    // when the thread pool thread finished the execution

    // Calculate the end result
    result += result2;

    // Print the result
    Console.WriteLine("The result is {0}", result);

}
```

Calling the `ThreadPool.QueueUserWorkItem` method places the work item on the queue managed by the thread pool. When a thread from the pool is available, it picks up the item and runs it to completion. The only problem is that you don't know when the thread finishes its work. There is no `Join` method or something similar. To solve this problem, you need to use some kind of signaling mechanism. (Different signaling mechanisms are discussed later in the "Synchronizing Resources" section.)

If you run the application now, you get the correct result but only because the thread pool thread returns before the other method finishes its work. If you increase the value you send to `Sleep` to be higher than the total time it takes to run the other method, you will observe that the result will be 10 instead of 20, which is wrong.

Often you won't use the `ThreadPool` class directly. Instead you can use other technologies built on top of it, such as *Task Parallel Library* (TPL), *Asynchronous Pattern Model* (APM), *Event-based Asynchronous Pattern* (EAP), *Task-based Asynchronous Pattern Model* (TAP), or the new `async`/`await` keywords.

Unblocking the UI

One of the biggest problems mentioned earlier in this chapter was that your application might become unresponsive, giving the user the impression that the application is hung up. The reason for this is often because heavy work is placed on the thread responsible for updating the UI. To improve the perceived performance of the application, you can move this heavy work into another thread. To achieve that, you have to apply different asynchronous programming patterns. (You can find a detailed explanation of those patterns in the "Additional Reading and Resources" section.)

Windows forms or WPF applications have one thread responsible to update the UI. Any update to the UI should be done through this thread.

If your application targets .NET 4.5, the new `async`/`await` programming model (discussed later in this chapter in the "Programming Asynchronous Applications with C# 5.0" section) takes care of this for you. If you target a .NET version prior to 4.5, you must take care of this by yourself.

BackgroundWorker Class

.NET 2.0 introduced a class called `System.ComponentModel.BackgroundWorker` that abstracts away the thread creation and the usage of the thread pool. Tables 7-3, 7-4, and 7-5 show some of the methods, properties, and events that this class offers.

TABLE 7-3: System.ComponentModel.BackgroundWorker Methods

METHOD	DESCRIPTION
`RunWorkerAsync`	Registers a start request for the background operation
`ReportProgress`	Raises the `ProgressChanged` event
`CancelAsync`	Registers a cancellation request for the background operation

TABLE 7-4: System.ComponentModel.BackgroundWorker Properties

PROPERTY	DESCRIPTION
CancellationPending	Set to true if CancelAsync was called for this background operation.
IsBusy	Returns true after the RunAsync was called and before the background operation completed.
WorkerReportsProgress	Set this property to true if you want your background operation to report progress updates.
WorkerSupportsCancellation	Set this property to true if you want your background operation to support cancellation.

TABLE 7-5: System.ComponentModel.BackgroundWorker Events

EVENT	DESCRIPTION
DoWork	Triggers when RunWorkerAsync is invoked. This is where you call your long-running method.
ProgressChanged	Triggers when ReportProgress is invoked.
RunWorkerCompleted	Triggers when the background operation is done. It can be done either because the operation completed successfully, as a response to a cancellation request, or because of an unhandled exception.

> **NOTE** For a complete list of methods, properties, and events, refer to the "Additional Reading and Resources" section at the end of this chapter.

The workflow of using the BackgroundWorker class is as follows:

1. Create a method that follows the DoWorkEventHandler signature.

2. In this method call the long-running operation. When the operation finishes, assign the result of the operation to the Result property of the DoWorkEventArgs parameter.

3. Create a BackgroundWorker instance.

4. Use the method you created on the first step to subscribe to the DoWork event.

5. Create a method that follows the RunWorkerCompletedEventHandler signature.

6. In this method, get the result of the long-running operation and update the UI.

7. Use this method to subscribe to the RunWorkerCompleted event so that your code knows when the long-running operation is completed. Before reading the result, you must make sure that your long-running operation did not throw an exception by checking the Error property

of the `RunWorkerCompletedEventArgs` parameter. If the property is `null`, it means that no exception was thrown.

8. Optionally, create a method to be used to report progress, following the `ProgressChangedEventHandler` signature and subscribing this method to the `ProgressChanged` event.

9. Call the `RunWorkerAsync` method to start the background work.

10. If the work supports cancellation and you want to cancel the work, you can call the `CancelAsync` method.

> **BEST PRACTICES: Threading with BackgroundWork**
>
> The implementation of the `BackgroundWork` class ensures that in a Windows Forms or WPF application the `RunWorkerCompleted` event handler is run by a UI thread if the `RunWorkerAsync` is called by the UI thread. In other words, if you start the background work inside an event handler, the completion event will be run in the UI thread. You can see the implications of this in the next two sections.

Assume that you have a Windows Forms application that has a form with one label called `lblResult` and one button called `btnRun`. If you use the long-running method from the previous section together with `BackgroundWork`, the resulting code might look like this:

```
public partial class Form1 : Form {

    private BackgroundWorker worker;


    public Form1() {

        InitializeComponent();

        worker = new BackgroundWorker();
        worker.DoWork += worker_DoWork;
        worker.RunWorkerCompleted += worker_RunWorkerCompleted;
    }

    void worker_DoWork(object sender, DoWorkEventArgs e) {

        e.Result = DoIntensiveCalculations();
    }

    void worker_RunWorkerCompleted(object sender, RunWorkerCompletedEventArgs e) {

        lblResult.Text = e.Result.ToString());
    }

    private void btnRun_Click(object sender, EventArgs e) {

        if (!worker.IsBusy) {
            worker.RunWorkerAsync();
        }
```

```
    }

    static double DoIntensiveCalculations() {

        // We are simulating intensive calculations
        // by doing nonsens divisions
        double result = 100000000d;
        var maxValue = Int32.MaxValue;
        for (int i = 1; i < maxValue; i++) {
            result /= i;
        }
        return result + 10d;
    }
}
```

Multithreaded Windows Forms Applications

As mentioned earlier, both Windows Forms and WPF applications have dedicated threads that update the UI to avoid a situation that might arise in multithreaded applications, called *race conditions*. A race condition occurs when two or more threads access shared data, for writing, at the same time. (How to deal with race conditions is covered later in this chapter in the "Synchronizing Resources" section.) If you try to update the UI from another thread, .NET Framework throws an InvalidOperationException containing the following message: "Cross-thread operation not valid: Control 'ctrlName' accessed from a thread other than the thread it was created on." You might not get this exception every time, but this doesn't make your code correct. The code in the previous section works because you started the background worker from the UI thread. If the background worker would have been started from another thread, you would have gotten the exception mentioned earlier. To solve the problem, change the worker_RunWorkerCompleted method as follows:

```
void worker_RunWorkerCompleted(object sender, RunWorkerCompletedEventArgs e) {
    if (this.InvokeRequired) {
        this.Invoke(
            new Action<string>(UpdateLabel),
            e.Result.ToString());
    }
    else {
        UpdateLabel(e.Result.ToString());
    }
}

private void UpdateLabel(string text) {
    lblResult.Text = text;
}
```

This is what you had to do with the preceding code:

1. You moved the UI code in to its own method. In this case you called the method UpdateLabel.

2. In the worker_RunWorkerCompleted method, you now check the InvokeRequired property. This property is defined in the Control class, and as such is present on all the

controls on a page. `InvokeRequired` is set to false if you call it from the UI thread and true otherwise.

3. If you are in the UI thread, you just call the `UpdateLabel` method. If you are in another thread, you must call the `Invoke` method, which is defined on the `Control` class.

4. The `Invoke` method takes as the first parameter a delegate, meaning any method can be placed there. The *new Action<string>()* constructor call is used to make sure that you get a delegate. If your method has a different signature, you must change that constructor accordingly. The rest of the parameters of the `Invoke` method are sent directly to the method you want to run. `Invoke` places the method call in a queue to be picked up by the UI thread.

Multithreaded WPF Applications

Like with Windows Forms applications, WPF applications have a dedicated UI thread. Unlike Windows Forms, WPF has an extra thread responsible for rendering the UI. This second thread is private to WPF, and you don't have access to it from your application. For detailed information about the threading model in WPF, consult the "Additional Reading and Resources" section at the end of this chapter.

Now see how the application from the previous section looks in the WPF world. Start by assuming that you have a WPF application that has a main window. On that window you have a button called btnRun and a label called lblResult. A possible implementation of the `MainWindow` class that calls the `DoIntensiveCalculation` method can look as follows:

```
public partial class MainWindow : Window {

    private BackgroundWorker worker;

    public MainWindow() {
        InitializeComponent();
        worker = new BackgroundWorker();
        worker.DoWork += worker_DoWork;
        worker.RunWorkerCompleted += worker_RunWorkerCompleted;
    }

    void worker_RunWorkerCompleted(object sender, RunWorkerCompletedEventArgs e) {
        lblResult.Content = e.Result;
    }

    void worker_DoWork(object sender, DoWorkEventArgs e) {

        e.Result = DoIntensiveCalculations();
    }

    private void btnRun_Click(object sender, EventArgs e) {
        if (!worker.IsBusy) {
            worker.RunWorkerAsync();
        }
    }

    static double DoIntensiveCalculations() {
```

```
        // We are simulating intensive calculations
        // by doing nonsens divisions
        double result = 100000000d;
        var maxValue = Int32.MaxValue;
        for (int i = 1; i < maxValue; i++) {
            result /= i;
        }
        return result + 10d;
    }
}
```

As you can see, the code for the WPF application looks almost the same as the one for the Windows Forms application. The only difference is how you update the label—instead of the setting the `Text` property, you set the `Content` property. This solution suffers from the same issue that the Windows Forms solution suffered from. If the background worker is triggered from another thread than the UI thread, when you try to update the UI, the .NET Framework throws an `InvalidOperationException` with the message: `The calling thread cannot access this object because a different thread owns it`. The solution to this problem resembles the one in the previous section but is much simpler. The new `worker_RunWorkerCompleted` should look like the following:

```
void worker_RunWorkerCompleted(object sender, RunWorkerCompletedEventArgs e) {
    this.Dispatcher.Invoke(()=> lblResult.Content = e.Result);
}
```

As you can see it is enough to call the `Dispatcher.Invoke` method in all the situations. This call ensures that the lambda expression `()=> lblResult.Content = e.Result` is run by the UI thread, regardless from which thread the method is called.

> **BEST PRACTICES: Updating the UI**
>
> When you need to update the UI, make sure that you keep the non-UI work to a minimum. You should dispatch only the code that updates the UI (in the previous example, only the code that updates the label). If in your code, after you get the result from the background worker, you need to do some more processing before updating the UI, do that processing before you call the `Dispatch.Invoke` method for WPF applications or `Invoke` method for Windows Forms applications.

WORKING WITH THE TASK PARALLEL LIBRARY

One of the shortcomings of using threads is that they are resource-intensive. When you start a thread, that thread competes with other threads for the CPU in order to run. Sometimes a thread it is interrupted in the middle of an operation and must wait for its turn to run again to be able to complete that operation.

Most of the time you need to perform some work unitarily and get back the result. You don't care about the underlying implementation in the OS. This unit of work is called *task* and can be run independently. Microsoft introduced a new library, TPL, which is a collection of classes designed to abstract away the threads.

Introducing Task

With .NET 4 Microsoft introduced the Task class, which represents an asynchronous operation. The tasks are as well a way to abstract away the need for threads from the programmer. It uses threads from the thread pool but offers a great deal of flexibility and control over how the task is created. The Task class is defined under the System.Treading.Tasks namespace. There are two task classes: Task and Task<TResult>. The first one is used when you run a method as a task and you don't have or don't need the return value, and the second one is used when you run a function as a task and you want to use the return value.

The methods and properties used most often are described in Tables 7-6 and 7-7, respectively.

TABLE 7-6: System.Threading.Tasks.Task Methods

METHOD	DESCRIPTION
ContinueWith	Creates new task that will be started asynchronously when the current task completes.
Delay	This static method creates a task that is marked as completed after the specified delay.
Run	This static method adds a request for work on the thread pool and it returns a Task object.
Start	Starts the task represented by this instance.
Wait	Waits for the task represented by this instance to complete.
WaitAll	This static method waits for all tasks sent as parameters to complete.
WaitAny	This static method waits for any of the tasks sent as parameters to complete.
WhenAll	This static method creates a task that is marked as completed when all tasks sent as parameters complete.
WhenAny	This static method creates a task that is marked as completed when any of the tasks sent as parameters complete.

TABLE 7-7: System.Threading.Tasks.Task Properties

PROPERTY	DESCRIPTION
CurrentId	This read-only static property retrieves the ID of the currently executing task.
Exception	This read-only property retrieves the unhandled `AggregateException`, if any, that caused the task to end its execution.
Factory	This read-only static property returns a factory object that can be used to create a new task.
ID	This read-only property gets the ID of a particular task instance.
IsCanceled	This read-only property is set to `true` if the task completed because it was canceled.
IsCompleted	This read-only property is set to `true` when the task completes.
IsFaulted	This read-only property is set to `true` if the task completes because of an unhandled exception.
Status	This read-only property returns the status of the task.
Result	This read-only property gets the value returned by the asynchronous operation represented by this task.

For a complete list of methods and properties, refer to the "Additional Reading and Resources" section at the end of this chapter.

The static property `Factory` is of type `TaskFactory` and is used to create new tasks. Table 7-8 describes some of the most common methods.

TABLE 7-8: System.Threading.Tasks.TaskFactory Methods

METHOD	DESCRIPTION
ContinueWhenAll	Creates a task that starts when all the tasks sent as parameters complete.
ContinueWhenAny	Creates a task that starts when any of the tasks sent as parameters complete.
FromAsync	Several overloaded methods used to bring old APM code to the new TAP model by wrapping a task around the asynchronous call.
StartNew	Several overloaded methods used to create a task and start it.

For a complete list of methods and properties, refer to the "Additional Reading and Resources" section at the end of this chapter.

Creating Tasks

You can create a task in several ways:

➤ You can create an instance of `Task`. This method of creating is useful when you want to update code that uses threads to use tasks instead. The task is not started, so you must call the `Start` method.

➤ You call one of the overloads of the static method `TaskFactory.StartNew`. Those methods create and start the tasks.

➤ You call one of the overloads of the static method `Task.Run`. Those methods create and start the tasks. This is a simplified wrapper for `TaskFactory.StartNew`.

➤ You can call one of the continuation methods. Those are `Task.WhenAll`, `Task.WhenAny`, `TaskFactory.ContinueWhenAll`, `TaskFactory.ContinueWhenAny`.

`TaskFactory.StartNew` offers a great deal of flexibility. When you create a new task, you need to specify at least the method or function that you want to run as a task. In addition, you can specify options for creating the task, a cancelation token, and a scheduler that queues tasks into threads. (Schedulers are discussed in the next section, and cancellation will be discussed later in this chapter in the "Working with Cancellations" section.)

`TaskCreationOptions` enumeration describes the options for creating tasks. Table 7-9 describes the options.

TABLE 7-9: System.Threading.Tasks.TaskCreationOptions Members

MEMBER NAME	DESCRIPTION
None	Default behavior.
PreferFairness	Tasks should be scheduled in a fair manner. This is just a hint and the intended result is that tasks scheduled sooner will have a better chance to be run sooner, and tasks scheduled later will be more likely to be run later.
LongRunning	This is used to specify that the task will take a long time to complete. This is just a hint and the result will be oversubscription. Oversubscription allows the scheduler to create more threads to run the tasks than the available number of hardware threads.
AttachedToParent	The newly created task is attached to the parent task in the hierarchy.

MEMBER NAME	DESCRIPTION
DenyChildAttach	Specifies that no child tasks are allowed to be attached to the current task. If you attempt to attach a child task to this newly created task, an `InvalidOperationException` will be thrown.
HideScheduler	Specifies that the current scheduler should not be used when creating new tasks from this newly created task. Those new tasks should use `Default` as the current scheduler when they are created.

This enumeration is decorated with the `FlagsAttribute`, meaning that these options can be combined.

Now take a moment to look at some code that deals with tasks. Consider the following code snippet. It is a variation of the code you saw in the first section, but instead of calling one I/O and one computing-intensive method, you call the same computing method 32 times.

```
class Program {

    const int NUMBER_OF_ITERATIONS = 32;

    static void Main(string[] args) {

        // We are using Stopwatch to time the code
        Stopwatch sw = Stopwatch.StartNew();

        // Run the method
        RunSequential();

        // Print the time it took to run the application.
        Console.WriteLine("We're done in {0}ms!", sw.ElapsedMilliseconds);

    }

    static void RunSequential() {

        double result = 0d;

        // Here we call same method several times.
        for (int i = 0; i < NUMBER_OF_ITERATIONS; i++) {
            result += DoIntensiveCalculations();
        }

        // Print the result
        Console.WriteLine("The result is {0}", result);

    }

    static double DoIntensiveCalculations() {

        // We are simulating intensive calculations
        // by doing nonsens divisions and multiplications
```

```
        double result = 10000d;
        var maxValue = Int32.MaxValue >> 4;
        for (int i = 1; i < maxValue; i++) {
            if (i % 2 == 0) {
                result /= i;
            }
            else {
                result *= i;
            }
        }
        return result;
    }


}
```

Running this code results in the following output:

```
The result is 22.0386557304958
We're done in 41860ms!
```

As you can see it takes approximately 42 seconds to run this code sequential. You should improve that time by using tasks. First, you must replace the call to RunSequential with a call to RunTasks. Add the RunTasks method to your code that should look like this:

```
static void RunTasks() {

    double result = 0d;

    Task[] tasks = new Task[NUMBER_OF_ITERATIONS];

    // We create one task per iteration.
    for (int i = 0; i < NUMBER_OF_ITERATIONS; i++) {
        tasks[i] = Task.Run(() => result += DoIntensiveCalculations());
    }

    // Print the result
    Console.WriteLine("The result is {0}", result);
}
```

By running the application on a machine with eight cores, you get the following result:

```
The result is 2.75483196631197
We're done in 10115ms!
```

There are two things to notice here. Before telling you what those are, take a minute to see if you can spot them.

Now for the first one: The result is incorrect. Can you guess why?

Secondly, the application is not eight times faster as expected.

COMMON MISTAKES: The Performance Gain Induced by Modern Processors

The reason the application is not eight times faster is because you run the application on an Intel Core I7 processor. This is a quad core with hyper-threading. Quad core means that there are four cores in one silicon chip. Hyperthreading means that every core has two instruction pipelines, but only one execution engine. The operating system sees those as eight different processors. Hyperthreading improves the performance by 30 percent, not 100 percent as expected, whereas every core on the chip improves the performance by 70 percent.

If you didn't guess why the result is incorrect, it is because it is not obvious for an untrained eye. Earlier in this chapter we hinted something about race conditions. That discussion will be deferred once more, but what is happening here is that instead of adding the return value of the method to the result, you overwrite the result with that return value. To solve that you need to make sure that only one task at the time updates the result, or that you read the results of the calculation one at a time. A corrected version of the method looks something like this:

```
static void RunTasksCorrected() {

    double result = 0d;

    Task<double>[] tasks = new Task<double>[NUMBER_OF_ITERATIONS];

    // We create one task per iteration.
    for (int i = 0; i < NUMBER_OF_ITERATIONS; i++) {
        tasks[i] = Task.Run(() => DoIntensiveCalculations());
    }

    // We wait for the tasks to finish
    Task.WaitAll(tasks);

    // We collect the results
    foreach (var task in tasks) {
        result += task.Result;
    }

    // Print the result
    Console.WriteLine("The result is {0}", result);
}
```

After replacing the call in the main method as well and running the application, you get the following result:

```
The result is 22.0386557304958
We're done in 10369ms!
```

Now the result is correct, and the speed up is roughly four times.

> **ADVICE FROM THE EXPERTS: Getting Results from a Task**
>
> It's not actually necessary to call `Task.WaitAll(tasks)` in the code because `task.Result` will block the caller if the task didn't finish the calculation. So if any of the tasks isn't done when you enter the `foreach` loop, the caller will block and wait for the task to finish.

Working with the Scheduler

The work of queuing tasks into threads is done by a component called *task scheduler*, implemented by the `TaskScheduler` class. Normally, you don't work with the scheduler directly. When you start a new task, if you are not specifying any scheduler, it uses a default one.

There is one situation, though, that you need to use the scheduler when you use tasks, and that is when you use tasks in a Windows Forms or WPF application. If you remember from the previous section, the UI can be updated only by the UI thread, so if a task needs to update the UI, it needs to be executed by the UI thread. To achieve that you need to call one of the `StartNew` or `ContinueWith` overloads that takes a `TaskScheduler` parameter and pass `TaskScheduler.FromCurrentSynchronizationContext()` as the value for that parameter. For instance, if you were to use tasks in the Windows Forms application and you want to call the `UpdateLabel` method on the UI thread, you would use the following:

```
Task.Factory.StartNew(UpdateLabel,
CancellationToken.None,
          TaskCreationOptions.None,
          TaskScheduler.FromCurrentSynchronizationContext());
```

By creating the task this way, it will be executed by the UI thread as soon as the UI thread can process it.

Using the Parallel Class

As discussed, the tasks are abstractions representing asynchronous operations run by threads. Although they are lighter than threads, sometimes you just need a better abstraction to do this kind of multitasking work. That is why Microsoft created the `Parallel` class. This class is part of the `System.Threading.Tasks` namespace. This class has three static methods, as outlined in Table 7-10.

TABLE 7-10: System.Threading.Tasks.Parallel Methods

METHOD	DESCRIPTION
For	Similar to a `for` loop but iterations may run in parallel. There are 12 overloads for this method, some of them accepting a `ParallelOptions` parameter, others using `ParallelLoopState` to control the loop.

METHOD	DESCRIPTION
ForEach	Similar to a `foreach` loop but iterations may run in parallel. There are 20 over-loads for this method, some of them accepting a `ParallelOptions` parameter, others using `ParallelLoopState` to control the loop.
Invoke	This method will attempt to run the provided actions in parallel. There are two overloads for this method, both accepting an array of `Actions` delegates to exe-cute. One of the overloads accepts a `ParallelOptions` parameter.

As you can see all three methods mention the possibility of running in parallel, but they don't guarantee it.

`ParallelLoopState` is used as an input parameter for some of the `For` and `ForEach` methods. It has two methods, `Stop` and `Break`, which you can use to prematurely stop a loop from running. If you use `Break` in a `For` method, you are instructing the loop to stop executing all the iterations with an iterator higher than the one of the current iteration.

Now see how the previous example can be implemented with `Parallel.For`:

```
static void RunParallelFor() {

    double result = 0d;

    // Here we call same method several times in parallel.
    Parallel.For(0, NUMBER_OF_ITERATIONS, i => {
        result += DoIntensiveCalculations();
    });

    // Print the result
    Console.WriteLine("The result is {0}", result);

}
```

As you might have guessed, if you run the previous code snippet, you get an erroneous result for the same reason you did before: race conditions. Here is the result:

```
The result is 2.06612397473398
We're done in 10186ms!
```

To solve the problem you must take care of this by using interim results. You can use the following overload of the `Parallel.For` method to solve this problem:

```
public static ParallelLoopResult For<TLocal>(
    int fromInclusive,
    int toExclusive,
    Func<TLocal> localInit,
    Func<int, ParallelLoopState, TLocal, TLocal> body,
    Action<TLocal> localFinally
)
```

Here is a possible solution:

```
static void RunParallelForCorrected() {

    double result = 0d;

    // Here we call same method several times.
    //for (int i = 0; i < NUMBER_OF_ITERATIONS; i++)
    Parallel.For(0, NUMBER_OF_ITERATIONS,
        // Func<TLocal> localInit,
        () => 0d,

        //    Func<int, ParallelLoopState, TLocal, TLocal> body,
        (i, state, interimResult) => interimResult + DoIntensiveCalculations(),

        // Final step after the calculations
        // we add the result to the final result
        // Action<TLocal> localFinally
        (lastInterimResult) => result += lastInterimResult
    );
    // Print the result
    Console.WriteLine("The result is {0}", result);
}
```

By running the application now, you get this result:

```
The result is 22.0386557304958
We're done in 10370ms!
```

Again, you get the correct result and a speedup of four times.

COMMON MISTAKES: When to Use the Parallel Loops

Try to resist the urge to change all your `for` and `foreach` loops into their parallel counterparts. If you do that, you risk breaking your application. As you saw in the simple sample, it was easy to do just that. If you know that the iterations are completely independent of each other and you can avoid race conditions, then by all means, go for it. But chances are high that not all your loops are that simple, so a bit of analysis and testing is always recommended.

NOTE *TPL has another abstraction in the form of Parallel Linq (PLinq) that is also built using tasks and the TPL. This subject is addressed in Chapter 10, "Working with Language Integrated Query (LINQ)."*

Working with Continuations

In some situations you cannot transform everything into tasks without breaking your application. You need to take care of the dependencies imposed by your algorithm. If you have dependencies between tasks such as you can't start step 3 before step 1 and 2 are done, you can use some of the continuations mechanisms available in the TPL. Assume that you have three methods that you need to call in your application. You call them Step1, Step2, and Step3.

The code should look similar to this:

```
class Program {
    static void Main(string[] args) {

        Step1();
        Step2();
        Step3();
    }

    static void Step1() {
        Console.WriteLine("Step1");
    }
    static void Step2() {
        Console.WriteLine("Step2");
    }
    static void Step3() {
        Console.WriteLine("Step3");
    }
}
```

Following are four main scenarios:

➤ Step1, Step2 and Step3 are independent of each other.

➤ Step1 and Step2 are independent of each other, and Step3 can be run only after Step1 finishes.

➤ Step1 and Step2 are independent of each other, and Step3 can be run only after Step1 and Step2 finish.

➤ Step1 and Step2 are independent of each other, and Step3 can be run only after Step1 or Step2 finishes.

If you want to use tasks to implement this functionality, you have different solutions.

For the first case the Main method looks something similar to this:

```
static void Main(string[] args) {

    Parallel.Invoke(Step1, Step2, Step3);
}
```

The result of running the previous code is unpredictable, meaning that the methods can be run in any order, but considering the independent nature of the steps, it shouldn't matter.

For the second case, you need to change the code to use tasks. The result could be something similar to this:

```
static void Main(string[] args) {

    Task step1Task = Task.Run(() => Step1());
    Task step2Task = Task.Run(() => Step2());
    Task step3Task = step1Task.ContinueWith( (previousTask) => Step3());

    Task.WaitAll(step2Task, step3Task);
}
```

The only guarantee you have by running this is that Step3 runs after Step1. Nothing can be said about when Step2 will be executed. The last line of code Task.WaitAll(step2Task, step3Task); guarantees that you are waiting to collect the results. Without it the Main method just returns, and the application might not get a chance to run the tasks. You don't need to wait for Step1 because Step3 starts only after Step1 finishes.

For the third case, the code should look like this:

```
static void Main(string[] args) {

    Task step1Task = Task.Run(() => Step1());
    Task step2Task = Task.Run(() => Step2());
    Task step3Task = Task.Factory.ContinueWhenAll(
            new Task[] { step1Task, step2Task },
            (previousTasks) => Step3());

    step3Task.Wait();
}
```

For this call ContinueWhenAll that takes as a first parameter an array of tasks, and as a second parameter a delegate to run when all the tasks finish. It returns a new task, which you can use to wait for all the tasks to complete. The delegate takes as in parameter the array of tasks it was waiting for.

For the last scenario use the following code:

```
static void Main(string[] args) {

    Task step1Task = Task.Run(() => Step1());
    Task step2Task = Task.Run(() => Step2());
    Task step3Task = Task.Factory.ContinueWhenAny(
            new Task[] { step1Task, step2Task },
            (previousTask) => Step3());

    step3Task.Wait();
}
```

By calling ContinueWhenAny, you create a task that runs the delegate after any task from the list completes. The delegate takes as a parameter the completed task. If the completed task returns something, you can get that value from the previousTask.Result property. This scenario is quite common when you have some redundant services and you care only about the value retrieved by the quickest one.

Programming Asynchronous Applications with C# 5.0

Prior to C# 5.0 to achieve *asynchrony* you had to manually implement this kind of functionality using the `IAsyncResult` and callbacks. The resulting code was hard to follow and error prone. When lambda expressions made their entry in C# 3.0, the code could be made somewhat more compact but still had the same problems as before. It was difficult to both implement and maintain. TPL made possible the birth of another paradigm in .NET: asynchronous programming. In C# 5.0 Microsoft introduced two new language keywords: `async` and `await`.

You can use the `async` modifier to mark a method as asynchronous, and to notify the compiler that the method will have at least an await statement. If your method lacks the `await` statement, the compiler generates a warning.

The `await` operator is applied to a task in an asynchronous method to suspend the execution of the method until the awaited task completes. The task represents ongoing work.

Many of the classes in .NET Framework Library that deal with I/O have been modified by adding to them asynchronous methods to support the `async`/`await` pattern. If you have classes that deal with I/O, you can do the same. See how you can change an existing synchronous method into an asynchronous one. Here you have the `ReadDataFromIO` method:

```
public static double ReadDataFromIO() {
    // We are simulating an I/O by putting the current thread to sleep.
    Thread.Sleep(2000);
    return 10d;
}
```

The asynchronous variant of the method can be implemented as simple as this:

```
public static Task<double> ReadDataFromIOAsync() {
    return Task.Run(new Func<double>(ReadDataFromIO));
}
```

To make a method asynchronous, you must return a `Task` or `Task<TResult>` and add the `Async` suffix to the method name. The suffix is there so the programmers using your library know that the method is the asynchronous counterpart of your synchronous method.

> ### RETURN TYPE OF ASYNCHRONOUS METHODS
>
> When a method is marked with an `async` modifier, it can have one of the following three return types: `void`, `Task`, and `Task<TResult>`. If your synchronous method were returning `void`, you have a choice between `void` and `Task`. If the method is not an event handler, the recommendation is to return `Task`. By returning `Task` you make the method not only asynchronous, but awaitable as well. If your synchronous method were returning something else than `void`, you must change the return type to `Task<TResult>`, so a synchronous method returning `double` returns in the asynchronous variant `Task<double>`.

> **ADVICE FROM THE EXPERTS: To Asynchronize or Not to Asynchronize?**
>
> What you did in the previous sample is a naïve implementation of an asynchronous method, obtained by wrapping the synchronous method inside a task. Just because it is that easy to do it doesn't mean you should transform all your synchronous methods into asynchronous methods, and that all the methods should be transformed like that. This chapter has mentioned I/O operations several times, so if your method deals with I/O then you should consider making your methods asynchronous.

Now it's time to get back to the WPF application from the previous sections and see how you can transform the application from using `ReadDataFromIO` method to using the asynchronous version of it. Recall that the example is a simple WPF application with a button called `btnRun` and a label called `lblResult`.

```
public partial class MainWindow : Window {
    public MainWindow() {
        InitializeComponent();
    }

    private void btnRun_Click(object sender, EventArgs e) {
        lblResult.Content = ReadDataFromIO();
    }

}
```

If you run the application and press the button, the UI freezes for two seconds. You cannot move nor do anything with it. The reason is simple: `btnRun_Click` is run by the UI thread, so the method `ReadDataFromIO` will be run by the UI thread. Before C# 5.0 you had to make use of a `BackgroundWorker` to offload the UI thread. To solve the problem with C# 5.0, the solution is simple:

```
    private async void btnRun_Click(object sender, EventArgs e) {
        lblResult.Content = await ReadDataFromIOAsync();
    }
```

If you run the application now, you can see that the application does not freeze this time and yields the same result.

Take a moment now to analyze what you just did and to understand why it works:

1. You added the `async` reserved word to mark the method as asynchronous. The return type of the method wasn't changed because you need to follow the `EventHandler` delegate signature.

2. You replaced the call to `ReadDataFromIO` with the `await ReadDataFromIOAsync`. This is approximately equivalent with `Task<double> task = ReadDataFromIOAsync();` `lblResult.Content = task.Result;`.

3. When you call `ReadDataFromIOAsync`, .NET Framework runs the code until the method will be blocked by an I/O operation. At that point the framework saves the state of the method, wraps it in a task, and returns to the calling method.

4. The calling method continues to run until it needs the result. In this case that's right away, but it is completely possible to save the task, do some more synchronous work, and then call `await task` later, blocking the calling method.

5. When the compiler sees the `await` keyword, it rewrites the method to do what you just described.

If you have an application and a library that makes use of some asynchronous methods, you can change them as well. Take a moment to see how the code can change if you do not call the `ReadDataFromIO` directly from the event handler, but instead call it several times via another method, updating several labels. So using the previous example, you add an extra label called `lblResult2`.

The code might look like this:

```
public partial class MainWindow : Window {
    public MainWindow() {
        InitializeComponent();
    }

    private void btnRun_Click(object sender, EventArgs e) {
        GetData();
    }

    private void GetData() {
        lblResult.Content = ReadDataFromIO();
        lblResult2.Content = ReadDataFromIO();
    }

}
```

To make it asynchronous, you need first to transform `GetData`. One possible implementation would be this:

```
private async Task GetDataAsync() {
    lblResult.Content = await ReadDataFromIOAsync();
    lblResult2.Content = await ReadDataFromIOAsync();
}
```

As you can see, the `async` modifier was added to the method, and the name was changed by adding the *Async* suffix to give an indication to the developers using the method that this is an asynchronous method. The return type was changed from `void` to `Task`, and you used the asynchronous variant of the `ReadDataFromIO` method, `ReadDataFromIOAsync`, together with the `await` keyword.

If you run the application now, you can see that the application won't freeze. After two seconds you get the first result, and after another two seconds you get the second result.

The reason for that is because you block the calling method in the first `await` and then call the second method and `await` for it. One way to improve this code will be to rewrite the `GetDataAsync` as follows:

```
private async Task GetDataAsync() {
    var task1 = ReadDataFromIOAsync();
    var task2 = ReadDataFromIOAsync();

    // Here we can do more processing
    // that doesn't need the data from the previous calls.

    // Now we need the data so we have to wait
    await Task.WhenAll(task1, task2);

    // Now we have data to show.
    lblResult.Content = task1.Result;
    lblResult2.Content = task2.Result;
}
```

In this case, you call `ReadDataFromIOAsync` the first time, and when it blocks, it wraps the call in a `Task<double>` and returns the control to `GetDataAsync`. Then `GetDataAsync` method calls the second `ReadDataFromIOAsync`, and when that one blocks as well, it will wrap the call in another `Task<double>` and returns the control back to `GetDataAsync`. Then you might do some more processing that doesn't require the data you just asked for asynchronously. When you need the data, you can `await` for it blocking the calling method. After you get the data, the calling method gets unblocked. The method unwraps the result from the tasks by calling `task.Result`.

BEST PRACTICES: Dealing with Multiple Await Statements

You could have implemented the `GetDataAsync` as follows:

```
private async Task GetDataAsync() {
    var task1 = ReadDataFromIOAsync();
    var task2 = ReadDataFromIOAsync();

    lblResult.Content = await task1;
    lblResult2.Content = await task2;
}
```

This implementation and the previous one would have been almost identical. From the end result standpoint, they are equivalent, but calling `await` two times forces the compiler to rewrite the method twice, when you just need both values for the method to complete.

For more in-depth information about asynchronous programming in C# 5.0, consult the links in the "Additional Reading and Resources" section at the end of this chapter.

> **NOTE** *Asynchronous methods are meant to be nonblocking operations, meaning that the calling method will not block the current thread while waiting on the awaited task to finish. Using* `async` *and* `await` *doesn't create additional threads, because the asynchronous method doesn't run on its own thread. More information about threads and asynchronous operations can be found on the "Additional Reading and Resources" section.*

EXPLORING ADVANCED MULTITHREADING PROGRAMMING TOPICS

Multithreaded programing is hard—much harder than single-threaded programing—for several reasons:

➤ It introduces some "strange" behavior, caused because several threads can update the same piece of data at the same time.

➤ Is not as easy to follow and understand.

➤ It is not as predictable; although, you have to guarantee the same result.

➤ It is not as easy to debug, making it harder to find bugs.

➤ It is harder to test.

➤ The list can continue.

As stated before, one of the most common problems is called race condition. This happens when two threads try to update the same data. Here's a simple example. Assume that you have one variable called `sharedData` and two threads, and both of them want to run the following instruction: `sharedData++`, which is executed by the CPU in the following way:

1. Read `sharedData` in a register.

2. Add `1` to the value in the register.

3. Write the new value from the register back into `sharedData` variable.

Why is that important to know? Because if it would have been only one instruction, the CPU would have executed that once, and no error can be introduced here. That is called *atomic operation*. But when you have a multithreaded application, the scheduler can interrupt the current thread at any time, and that might result in an error. Here's how:

1. `sharedData` has an initial value of `0`.

2. The first thread runs the first instruction, reading the value `0`.

3. The second thread runs the first instruction, reading the value `0`. On a single-core machine, this can happen when the scheduler interrupts the first thread and schedules the second thread. In a multicore machine this is a common situation because the threads can be scheduled on different cores.

4. The first thread increments the value to 1.

5. The first thread writes back the value 1 into `sharedData`.

6. The second thread increments the value to 1. Now the value should have been 2, but the value that the second thread has is the "old" value of 0.

7. The second thread writes back the value 1 into `sharedData`.

As explained, this kind of behavior can happen even if you run your application on a machine with one core, but it is more likely to manifest itself if you run it on a machine with several cores. To avoid this kind of problem, you must ensure that only one thread can access a shared variable at any given time.

The best way to deal with share data is not to share it. If you do need to share data, make it in a read-only kind of way. Sometimes, this might not be feasible because the data is big. If that is the case, try to isolate the data and make sure you access it in a controlled way. If this is not possible either, make sure you synchronize access to the data using different mechanisms. In conclusion, the order to consider sharing data is as follows:

1. Don't share.

2. Make data read-only.

3. Isolate the data in smaller modules.

4. Use synchronization mechanisms.

Microsoft provides several classes that deal with this. There are classes that deal with signaling, classes that deal with mutual exclusion, classes that deal with cancellations, and classes that deal with concurrent collection. Most of them are discussed in the remainder of this section.

Synchronizing Resources

If you recall, earlier in this chapter the discussion about signaling was deferred, and now is the time to discuss it. Signaling is used as a communication mechanism between threads. In .NET there are two kinds of signaling mechanisms: synchronization events and barriers.

> **COMMON MISTAKES: Disambiguating Event**
>
> Synchronization events should not be confused with the C# events.

Synchronization Events

Synchronization events are objects that can be in one of two states: signaled and nonsignaled. If a thread needs something to be done by another thread, it can use a synchronization event and interrogate the state of the event as a communication mechanism. If it is signaled, it continues the execution; if not, it blocks the execution, waiting for the event to be signaled. When the other thread finishes its work, it signals the event, unblocking the waiting thread or threads. Synchronization events are implemented by two classes: `EventWaitHandle` and `CountdownEvent`.

EventWaitHandle Class

This class represents a thread synchronization event. `EventWaitHandle` is defined in the `System .Threading` namespace, and Table 7-11 lists the most common methods.

TABLE 7-11: System.Threading.EventWaitHandle Methods

METHOD	DESCRIPTION
EventWaitHandle	Constructor. This method has four different overloads. At minimum you need to specify if the event should be signaled, and if the event should be reset manually or automatically using the `EventResetMode` enumeration.
Dispose	This is the method from the `IDisposable` interface. You need to call this method to ensure that the OS resources are freed when this object is not needed anymore.
Reset	Sets the state of the event to nonsignaled state, causing threads to block.
Set	Sets the state of the event to signaled state. One or more waiting threads will be able to proceed. If the event were created as `AutoReset`, only one thread will be enabled to call `WaitOne` without being blocked. Or if there are threads already blocked as a result of a call to `WaitOne`, only one thread will be unblocked, and then the event will be again nonsignaled until the `Set` method is called again. If the event was created as `ManualReset`, the event will be signaled until `Reset` is called on this event.
WaitOne	Blocks the current thread if the event is nonsignaled. When this event is signaled, if it was created as `AutoReset`, it unblocks the thread and resets the event back in the nonsignaled state.

You can find a complete list of methods and properties in the "Additional Reading and Resources" section at the end of this chapter.

Here's an example of using this class. And to be more precise, you can see how to correct the thread pool solution to be sure that you are not trying to read the result of the calculation before the calculation is actually completed. The original method looked like this:

```
static void RunInThreadPool() {

    double result = 0d;

    // Create a work item to read from I/O
    ThreadPool.QueueUserWorkItem((x) => result += ReadDataFromIO());
```

```
    // Save the result of the calculation into another variable
    double result2 = DoIntensiveCalculations();
    // Wait for the thread to finish

    // TODO: We will need a way to indicate
    // when the thread pool thread finished the execution

    // Calculate the end result
    result += result2;

    // Print the result
    Console.WriteLine("The result is {0}", result);

}
```

A possible solution using signaling looks like this:

```
static void RunInThreadPoolWithEvents() {

    double result = 0d;

    // We use this event to signal when the thread is don executing.
    EventWaitHandle calculationDone =
            new EventWaitHandle(false, EventResetMode.ManualReset);

    // Create a work item to read from I/O
    ThreadPool.QueueUserWorkItem((x) => {
        result += ReadDataFromIO();
        calculationDone.Set();
    });

    // Save the result of the calculation into another variable
    double result2 = DoIntensiveCalculations();

    // Wait for the thread to finish
    calculationDone.WaitOne();

    // Calculate the end result
    result += result2;

    // Print the result
    Console.WriteLine("The result is {0}", result);
}
```

The previous code does the following:

1. The code first creates an `EventWaitHandle` object in the nonsignaled state.

2. The code then queues a new work item. After you get the first result, you signal the event to indicate that the calculation is done.

3. In the main thread, you call the second method.

4. After the second method returns, you need to wait for the first calculation to be done, by waiting on the event to get signaled.

5. When you get the signal, you know that you have the result, so you can just calculate the final result and show it.

.NET provides two classes that inherit from `EventWaitHandle`: `AutoResetEvent` and `ManualResetEvent`. Both classes have only one constructor and no methods or properties of their own defined. In both cases the constructor takes one boolean parameter specifying if the event is initially signaled. `AutoResetEvent` class constructor creates an `EventWaitHandle` and sets the mode to `EventResetMode.AutoReset`. The `ManualResetEvent` class constructor sets the mode parameter to `EventResetMode.ManualReset`.

CoundownEvent Class

.NET 4 introduced a new class called `CoundownEvent`, defined in the `System.Threading` namespace. The usage scenario is straightforward: You need to wait for a predefined number of threads to finish their work. Before .NET this was implemented by using several `EventWaitHandle` objects and calling the `WaitHandle.WaitAll` method. As this is a common scenario, Microsoft decided to implement this functionality in .NET. Tables 7-12 and 7-13 list the most common methods and properties of `CoundownEvent`.

TABLE 7-12: System.Threading.CountdownEvent Methods

METHOD	DESCRIPTION
CountdownEvent	Constructor that accepts as parameter an integer value called count, representing the number of signals it needs to receive before it becomes signaled.
AddCount	Two overloads. Increments the `CountdownEvent`'s current count by one, or by a specified value. If the `CountdownEvent` object is already set, then this method can throw an `InvalidOperationException`.
Dispose	This is the method from the `IDisposable` interface. You must call this method to ensure that the OS resources are freed when this object is not needed anymore.
Reset	Two overloads. Resets the `CurrentCount` to the value of `InitialCount` or to a specified value.
Signal	Two overloads. Registers a signal with the `CountdownEvent`, decrementing the value of `CurrentCount` by one or by a specified value.
TryAddCount	Two overloads. Attempts to increment `CurrentCount` by one or by a specified value. This method won't throw an exception as `AddCount` does. It returns `true` or `false` to indicate the success or failure of the operation.
Wait	Six overloads. Blocks the current thread until the `CountdownEvent` is set. The overloads are used to call the method with a cancellation token and/or with a timeout.

TABLE 7-13: System.Threading.CountdownEvent Properties

PROPERTY	DESCRIPTION
CurrentCount	Read-only property that returns the number of remaining signals required to set the event.
InitialCount	Read-only property that returns the numbers of signals initially required to set the event.
IsSet	Read-only property that returns true if the event is set.
WaitHandle	Read-only property that returns a WaitHandle used to wait for the event to be set.

You can find a complete list of methods and properties in the "Additional Reading and Resources" section at the end of this chapter.

The CoundownEvent does not inherit from WaitHandle like almost all other synchronization classes, instead has a property called WaitHandle that will return a WaitHandle instance. That instance can be used wherever a WaitHandle is needed.

Barriers

In a multithreaded scenario, there are situations when you spawn several threads and you want to make sure that they arrive all at a certain point before you can continue the execution of your code. One common example for this scenario is as follows: A group of friends decide to travel by cars from point A to point C, via point B. They want to start traveling together from point A and stop at point B; then they plan to start together again to travel and meet at the final point C. Some of them might even decide that they don't want to go anymore and return back home.

Before looking at a possible implementation, you need to look at what .NET can offer to solve this kind of problems. One way would be to use the Countdown event, but it is not actually modeling what you need! .NET 4 introduced a new class called System.Threading.Barrier that deals with exactly such situations. Tables 7-14 and 7-15 list some of the methods and properties of the class.

TABLE 7-14: System.Threading.Barrier Methods

METHOD	DESCRIPTION
Barrier	Constructor. Initializes a new instance of the Barrier class. This method has two overloads, both taking as a parameter the number of participants. The second overload takes as an extra parameter an Action that will be run after all the participants have arrived at the barrier on one phase.
AddParticipant	Send a notification to the Barrier that there will be one more participant.
AddParticipants	Send a notification to the Barrier that there will be several more participants.
Dispose	This is the method from the IDisposable interface. You must call this method to ensure that the OS resources are freed when this object is not needed anymore.

METHOD	DESCRIPTION
RemoveParticipant	Sends a notification to the `Barrier` that there will be one less participant.
RemoveParticipants	Sends a notification to the `Barrier` that there will be fewer participants.
SignalAndWait	Six overloads. Signals that a participant has reached the barrier and waits for all other participants to reach the barrier as well. The overloads are used to call the method with a cancellation token and/or with a timeout.

TABLE 7-15: System.Threading.Barrier Properties

PROPERTY	DESCRIPTION
CurrentPhaseNumber	Read-only property that returns the number of the barrier's current phase.
ParticipantCount	Read-only property that returns the total number of participants in the barrier.
ParticipantsRemaining	Read-only property that returns the number of participants in the barrier that haven't arrived yet.

You can find a complete list of methods and properties in the "Additional Reading and Resources" section at the end of this chapter.

CODE LAB | **Using barriers [Chapter7\BarrierSample\Program.cs]**

Consider the following code snippet that uses the `Barrier` class:

```
static void Main(string[] args) {
    var participants = 5;

    Barrier barrier = new Barrier(participants + 1,
        // We add one for the main thread.
        b => { // This method is only called when all the paricipants arrived.
            Console.WriteLine("{0} paricipants are at rendez-vous point {1}.",
                            b.ParticipantCount -1, // We substract the main thread.
                            b.CurrentPhaseNumber);
        });

    for (int i = 0; i < participants; i++) {
        var localCopy = i;
        Task.Run(() => {
            Console.WriteLine("Task {0} left point A!", localCopy);
            Thread.Sleep(1000 * localCopy + 1); // Do some "work"
            if (localCopy % 2 == 0) {
                Console.WriteLine("Task {0} arrived at point B!", localCopy);
                barrier.SignalAndWait();
            }
            else {
```

```
                    Console.WriteLine("Task {0} changed its mind and went back!",
                                localCopy);
                    barrier.RemoveParticipant();
                    return;
                }
                Thread.Sleep(1000 * (participants - localCopy)); // Do some "more work"
                Console.WriteLine("Task {0} arrived at point C!", localCopy);
                barrier.SignalAndWait();
            });
        }

        Console.WriteLine("Main thread is waiting for {0} tasks!",
                barrier.ParticipantCount - 1);
        barrier.SignalAndWait(); // Waiting at the first phase
        barrier.SignalAndWait(); // Waiting at the second phase
        Console.WriteLine("Main thread is done!");
    }
```

In this sample you create a barrier to keep track of the participants that arrived at the meeting points. You have to initialize the barrier with the number of participants plus one. The extra participant is used by the main thread.

Then you create one task per participant. The statement `var localCopy = i` captures the value of the iterator, so you avoid problems that might appear. Just to make the scenario more interesting, every other task will "change its mind" and go back, but not before informing the others. The main thread is calling `barrier.SignalAndWait` twice, once for each phase.

Running the previous sample yields the following result:

```
Main thread is waiting for 5 tasks!
Task 4 left point A!
Task 2 left point A!
Task 0 left point A!
Task 3 left point A!
Task 1 left point A!
Task 0 arrived at point B!
Task 1 changed its mind and went back!
Task 2 arrived at point B!
Task 3 changed its mind and went back!
Task 4 arrived at point B!
3 paricipants are at rendez-vous point 0.
Task 4 arrived at point C!
Task 2 arrived at point C!
Task 0 arrived at point C!
3 paricipants are at rendez-vous point 1.
Main thread is done!
```

Using Locking Mechanisms

One way to deal with data sharing is mutual exclusion. *Mutual exclusion* ensures that only one thread at a time can access a shared resource. If another thread tries to gain access to the same resource, it will be blocked while the first thread works with the shared resource. Instead of trying to control all the code paths that lead to a specific data region, you control the code regions that are trying to access that piece of data. Mutual exclusion is implemented in .NET in several ways: monitors, mutexes, semaphores, reader-writer locks, and some lock-free implementations. This section describes using monitors and some lock-free implementations.

Monitors

Monitors are synchronization primitives used to synchronize access to objects. They are implemented in .NET in the `System.Threading.Monitor` class. The `Monitor` class is used in conjunction with reference types, not value types, to ensure that only one thread can access that object at the time. The class exposes only static methods that take as a first parameter the object you want to take the lock on. At any given time at most one thread can place a lock on an object by calling the `Monitor.Enter` static method. If another thread will call `Monitor.Enter` before the first thread called `Monitor.Exit`, that second thread will be blocked until the first thread calls `Monitor.Exit`. In .NET all objects have a field that holds a reference to the thread that acquired a lock on the object, a ready list with all the threads that want to acquire the lock, and a waiting list with all the threads waiting for the object to get a notification via `Pulse` or `PulseAll` methods.

The class exposes several static methods, some of which are listed in Table 7-16.

TABLE 7-16: System.Threading.Monitor Methods

METHOD	DESCRIPTION
Enter	Acquires an exclusive lock on a specified object. If the lock were already acquired by another thread, the current thread will be placed in the ready queue and will block its execution until the thread that owns the object releases the lock.
Exit	Releases an exclusive lock on the specified object.
IsEntered	Returns `true` if the current thread holds the lock on the specified object. This method was introduced in .NET 4.5.
Pulse	Notifies the thread in the waiting queue that the locked object's state changed, in effect moving the thread from the waiting queue to the ready queue.
PulseAll	Notifies all waiting threads that the locked object's state changed, in effect moving all the threads from the waiting queue to the ready queue.
TryEnter	Attempts to acquire an exclusive lock on the specified object. This method has six overloads enabling you to specify a timeout as well.
Wait	Releases the exclusive lock on the object and blocks the current thread until it reacquires the lock. The current thread will be placed on the waiting queue, and it will wait there for another thread to call `Pulse` or `PulseAll` so it can resume its execution.

Wait, Pulse, and PulseAll can be called only by the thread that owns the lock on the object. Here's some simple code using a monitor:

```
object syncObject = new object();
Monitor.Enter(syncObject);

// Code updating some shared data

Monitor.Exit(syncObject);
```

This code creates a new object to be used specifically for locking. You acquire the lock by calling Monitor.Enter. You execute the code that accesses the shared data. You then release the lock by calling the Monitor.Exit.

Although this is a complete piece of code, it does not account for the fact that the code that updates the shared data might throw an exception. If that happens, the lock won't be released, leading to a *deadlock*. To solve this problem you can change the code as follows:

```
object syncObject = new object();

Monitor.Enter(syncObject);

try {
    // Code updating some shared data
}
finally {
    Monitor.Exit(syncObject);
}
```

In this way you make sure that even if the code throws an exception, the lock it is still released. The C# language provides a shortcut instruction for this called lock. The previous snippet can be written with lock as follows:

```
object syncObject = new object();

lock (syncObject) {
    // Code updating some shared data
}
```

Lock-Free Alternatives

Locking is both dangerous and resource-intensive. Sometimes, you just need to perform simple operations, and you need to make sure that they are atomic. To solve this kind of problem, .NET offers a class called Interlocked, defined in the System.Threading namespace. The class has only static methods, and all the represent atomic operations, meaning they will be performed without being interrupted by the scheduler. Those methods are listed in the Table 7-17.

COMMON MISTAKES: Using References with Monitors

As mentioned, monitors work only with reference objects, not value objects. The reason is simple. Value objects are copied when they are sent as parameters. The result will be that the lock will be acquired on one object, but when you call release you will be on another object. When you call `Exit` on an object that you never called `Enter` on, .NET will throw an exception.

The best practice to deal with locks is the one shown earlier. You have to create an object that will be used only for this purpose. If you have to deal with legacy code, or if you look for samples on the Internet, you might find code acquiring a lock on `this` reference. The code looks like this:

```
lock (this) {
    // Code updating some shared data
}
```

Although this is a perfectly valid C# code snippet, and indeed acquires and releases a lock on the current object, this code has a latent error that can manifest itself at any time. Where might the error come from? See the following code snippet:

```
public class LockThisBadSample {
    public void OneMethod() {
        lock (this) {
            // Do Something here
        }
    }
}

public class UsingTheLockedObject {
    public void AnotherMethod(){
        LockThisBadSample lockObject = new LockThisBadSample();
        lock (lockObject) {
            // Do something else
        }
    }
}
```

As you can see `AnotherMethod` acquires a lock on `lockObject`, which is this reference inside the `OneMethod` call. Because you don't have control over all the code that would like to acquire locks on the objects, this can easily lead to deadlocks.

The lesson here is to avoid `lock(this)` even if you see online samples using this kind of programming, and MSDN is no exception.

TABLE 7-17: System.Threading.Interlocked Methods

METHOD	DESCRIPTION
Add	Adds two 32-bit or 64-bit integers and replaces the first integer with the sum, as an atomic operation.
CompareExchange	Compares the first and third parameters for equality and, if they are equal, replaces the value of the first parameter with the second parameter.
Decrement	Decrements a specified variable and stores the result, as an atomic operation.
Exchange	Sets an object to a specified value and returns a reference to the original object, as an atomic operation.
Increment	Increments a specified variable and stores the result, as an atomic operation.
Read	Loads a 64-bit value as an atomic operation and returns it to the caller. This is only necessary on 32-bit Platforms.

Working with Concurrent Collections

The collections defined in `System.Collections` and `System.Collections.Generic` were not implemented to be thread-safe. They were implemented to be fast. Prior to .NET 4 if you needed a thread-safe collection, you had to implement it by yourself. In .NET 4 Microsoft introduced new collections that are thread-safe. They are all defined in the `System.Collections.Concurrent` namespace. Except `ConcurrentDictionary`, all concurrent collection classes implanted by Microsoft implement the `IProducerConsumerCollection` interface. This interface requires a class that implements it to provide the method listed in Table 7-18.

TABLE 7.18: System.Collections.Concurrent.IProducerConsumerCollection Interface

METHOD	DESCRIPTION
CopyTo	Copies the elements of the `IProducerConsumerCollection` object into an `Array`, starting at the specified location.
ToArray	Returns a new array containing all the elements in the `IProducerConsumerCollection`.
TryAdd	Tries to add an object to the `IProducerConsumerCollection`.
TryTake	Tries to remove and return an object from the `IProducerConsumerCollection`.

The concurrent collection classes available in .NET are listed in Table 7-19.

TABLE 7.19: System.Collections.Concurrent Classes

CLASS	DESCRIPTION
BlockingCollection<T>	Implements the IProducerConsumerCollection<T> interface, providing blocking and bounding capabilities.
ConcurrentBag<T>	Represents a thread-safe collection of objects.
ConcurrentDictionary <TKey, TValue>	Represents a thread-safe version of the Dictionary <TKey, TValue> class.
ConcurrentQueue<T>	Represents the thread-safe version of the Queue<T> class.
ConcurrentStack<T>	Represents the thread-safe version of the Stack<T> class.

Working with Cancellations

One thing mentioned several times but never talked about in this chapter is how to cancel an ongoing operation. Prior to .NET 4 the ways to cancel an ongoing operation were unsafe. They included aborting threads, interrupting threads, or even abandoning operations you weren't interested in anymore. Although this worked most of the time, cancellations were the source of many errors. .NET 4 introduced cancellations as first-class citizens of the .NET library. The cancellations provided in .NET are cooperative cancellations, meaning that you can send a cancellation request to another thread, or task, but it is their choice to honor the request. Cancellation capabilities are implemented using one class, CancellationTokenSource, and one struct, CancellationToken, and works as follows:

1. If a thread wants to have the capability to cancel subsequent operations, it creates a CancellationTokenSource object.

2. When a cancellable asynchronous operation starts, the calling thread passes a CancellationToken obtained via the Token property of the CancellationTokenSource object. Cancelable asynchronous operation means either an operation that has support for cancellations or a new thread or that will be created by the current thread. This is normally expressed in the form of one or several overloaded methods accepting a CancellationToken parameter. By sending a CancellationToken you won't allow the operation to initiate the cancellation. This can be done only via the CancellationTokenSource object.

3. If the parent thread wants to cancel the ongoing cancelable operations, it calls Cancel on the CancellationTokenSource object.

4. All ongoing operations might use the CancelationToken sent as a parameter to check if a cancellation is pending and respond accordingly. Note that ignoring the cancellation request is a perfect valid option.

You can find more information about cancellations in the "Additional Reading and Resources" section at the end of this chapter.

You can find a practical example about how to use cancellations in the following Code Lab.

CODE LAB: **Using barriers with cancellations**
[Chapter7\BarrierWithCancellationSample\Program.cs]

Earlier in this chapter you saw an example in which barriers were used to coordinate the arrival of several threads at the same point. But what happens if you want to cancel the trip? The next code sample does just this.

```
static void Main(string[] args) {
    var participants = 5;

    // We create a CancellationTokenSource to be able to initiate the cancellation
    var tokenSource = new CancellationTokenSource();
    // We create a barrier object to use it for the rendez-vous points
    var barrier = new Barrier(participants,
        b => {
            Console.WriteLine("{0} paricipants are at rendez-vous point {1}.",
                        b.ParticipantCount,
                        b.CurrentPhaseNumber);
        });

    for (int i = 0; i < participants; i++) {
        var localCopy = i;
        Task.Run(() => {
            Console.WriteLine("Task {0} left point A!", localCopy);
            Thread.Sleep(1000 * localCopy + 1); // Do some "work"
            if (localCopy % 2 == 0) {
                Console.WriteLine("Task {0} arrived at point B!", localCopy);
                barrier.SignalAndWait(tokenSource.Token);
            }
            else {
                Console.WriteLine("Task {0} changed its mind and went back!",
                            localCopy);
                barrier.RemoveParticipant();
                return;
            }
            Thread.Sleep(1000 * localCopy + 1);
            Console.WriteLine("Task {0} arrived at point C!", localCopy);
            barrier.SignalAndWait(tokenSource.Token);
        });
    }

    Console.WriteLine("Main thread is waiting for {0} tasks!",
                    barrier.ParticipantsRemaining - 1);
    Console.WriteLine("Press enter to cancel!");
    Console.ReadLine();
    if(barrier.CurrentPhaseNumber < 2){
        tokenSource.Cancel();
        Console.WriteLine("We canceled the operation!");
    }
    else{
```

```
            Console.WriteLine("Too late to cancel!");
        }
        Console.WriteLine("Main thread is done!");
    }
```

Code Lab Analysis

The code starts by creating a `CancellationTokenSource` and a `Barrier`. The participant count for this barrier will be the same as the number of participants because you want to use the main thread for the cancellation.

Next, the code creates one task per participant. As before, the code makes every other task change its mind and remove itself from the barrier.

The code then calls `SignalAndWait`, which sends a cancellation token from the `CancellationTokenSource`.

The main thread now calls `Console.ReadLine` instead of waiting on the barrier to wait for the user input. When the user presses Enter, the code looks first to see if everyone arrived at the destination. It finds this out by querying the value of the `CurrentPhaseNumber` property of the barrier object. If this is 2, it means that everyone passed through the first and second phase, so there is no need to cancel the operation.

Finally, the code calls `tokenSource.Cancel`, which sends cancellation signals to all objects waiting on the barrier object, effectively unblocking them and canceling the remainder of the operation.

SUMMARY

This chapter described how to work with different technologies to improve the performance of applications.

First, the chapter looked at threads and how they are created and started. Unfortunately, threads are resource-consuming, but one way to circumvent this is to use threads from the thread pool. The thread pool has a pool of pre-created threads that can pick up work items placed in a queue by the application.

With .NET 4 Microsoft introduced the Task Parallel Library. Tasks represent an asynchronous unit of work. A task can be created and started in one operations via `Task.Run` or `Task.Factory.StartNew` methods. Tasks can be started as well as continuations of other tasks by calling one of the `ContinueWith`, or `WhenAnll`/`WhenAny` methods. One more class introduced by .NET 4 is the `Parallel` class, which abstracts away tasks' creation and makes it easier to deal with loops or running or parallel invocation of methods.

C# 5.0 took the tasks concepts further, by making asynchronous programming in .NET a first-class citizen, via `async`/`await` keywords. The chapter also looked at some of the advanced topics in multi-threading applications such as synchronization events, barriers, different locking mechanisms, and the lock-free alternatives offered by the `Interlocked` class.

Finally, the chapter looked at the concurrent collections that implement a thread-safe version of the most common collections, and it looked at ways to cancel ongoing operations with cancellation tokens.

CHAPTER TEST QUESTIONS

Read each question carefully and select the answer or answers that represent the best solution to the problem. You can find the answers in Appendix A, "Answers to Chapter Test Questions."

1. You are a developer at company xyx. You have been asked to improve the responsiveness of your WPF application. Which solution best fits the requirements?

    a. Use the `BackgroundWorker` class.

    b. Use the `LongRunningMethod` class.

    c. Run the method in the UI thread.

    d. Use the `WorkInBackground` class.

    e. None of the above.

2. How do you execute a method as a task?

    a. Create a new `Task` object, and then call the `Start` method on the newly created object.

    b. Create the task via the `Task.Run` method.

    c. Create the task via the `Task.Factory.StartNew` method.

    d. All the above.

    e. None of the above.

3. Which of the following is not a locking mechanism?

    a. Monitor

    b. Semaphore

    c. Mutex

    d. `async`

4. How can you schedule work to be done by a thread from the thread pool?

    a. You create a new object of type `ThreadPool`, and then you call the `Start` method.

    b. You call the `ThreadPool.Run` method.

    c. You call the `ThreadPool.QueueUserWorkItem` method.

    d. You create a new thread and set its property `IsThreadPool` to `true`.

    e. You call `ContinueWith` on a running thread from the thread pool.

5. Which of the following are methods of the `Parallel` class?

   a. Run

   b. Invoke

   c. For

   d. ForEach

   e. Parallel

6. Which method can you use to cancel an ongoing operation that uses `CancelationToken`?

   a. Call `Cancel` method on the `CancelationToken`

   b. Call `Cancel` method on the `CancelationTokenSource` object that was used to create the `CancelationToken`

   c. Call `Abort` method on the `CancelationToken`

   d. Call `Abort` method on the `CancelationTokenSource` object that was used to create the `CancelationToken`

7. Which method would you call when you use a barrier to mark that a participant reached that point?

   a. Signal

   b. Wait

   c. SignalAndWait

   d. RemoveParticipant

   e. JoinParticipant

8. What code is equivalent with `lock(syncObject){…}`?

   a. `Monitor.Lock(syncObject) {…}`

   b. `Monitor.TryEnter(syncObject) {…}`

   c. `Monitor.Enter(syncObject);   try{…} finally{`
      `Monitor.Exit(syncObject); }`

   d. `Monitor.Lock(syncObject);   try{…} catch{`
      `Monitor.Unlock(syncObject); }`

9. In a multithreaded application how would you increment a variable called `counter` in a lock free manner? Choose all that apply.

   a. `lock(counter){counter++;}`

   b. `counter++;`

   c. `Interlocked.Add(ref counter, 1);`

   d. `Interlocked.Increment (counter);`

   e. `Interlocked.Increment (ref counter);`

10. Which method will you use to signal and `EventWaitHandle`?

    a. `Signal`

    b. `Wait`

    c. `Set`

    d. `Reset`

    e. `SignalAndWait`

ADDITIONAL READING AND RESOURCES

Here are some additional useful resources to help you understand the topics presented in this chapter:

Parallel Processing and Concurrency in the .NET Framework
    `http://msdn.microsoft.com/en-us/library/hh156548.aspx`
Thread Class
    `http://msdn.microsoft.com/en-us/library/system.threading.thread.aspx`
Threading in C# by Joseph Albahari
    `http://www.albahari.com/threading/`
Asynchronous Programming Patterns
    `http://msdn.microsoft.com/en-us/library/jj152938.aspx`
Consuming the Task-based Asynchronous Pattern
    `http://msdn.microsoft.com/en-us/library/hh873173.aspx`
BackgroundWorker Class
    `http://msdn.microsoft.com/en-us/library/4852et58.aspx`
Threading Model
    `http://msdn.microsoft.com/en-us/library/ms741870.aspx`
Task Class
    `http://msdn.microsoft.com/en-us/library/system.threading.tasks.task.aspx`
Asynchronous Programming with Async and Await
    `http://msdn.microsoft.com/en-us/library/hh191443.aspx`
Asynchronous Programming with Async and Await and Threads
    `http://msdn.microsoft.com/en-us/library/hh191443.aspx#BKMK_Threads`
Parallel Programming team blog
    `http://blogs.msdn.com/b/pfxteam/`
EventWaitHandle Class
    `http://msdn.microsoft.com/en-us/library/system.threading.eventwaithandle.aspx`
CountdownEvent Class
    `http://msdn.microsoft.com/en-us/library/system.threading.countdownevent.aspx`
Barrier Class
    `http://msdn.microsoft.com/en-us/library/system.threading.barrier.aspx`
Cancellation in Managed Threads
    `http://msdn.microsoft.com/en-us/library/dd997364.aspx`

CHEAT SHEET

This cheat sheet is designed as a way for you to quickly study the key points of this chapter.

Threads

➤ Create a thread object by sending to the constructor a delegate that will be the thread's main method.

➤ Start the thread by calling explicitly the start method on the thread object.

➤ To use the thread pool, call `ThreadPool.QueueUserWorkItem` or `ThreadPool.RegisterWaitForSingleObject`.

Tasks

➤ Create a task object by sending to the constructor a delegate that will be the tasks main method. Start the task by calling explicitly the start method on the task object.

➤ Call one of the `Task.Run` static methods and send as parameter a delegate that will be tasks main method. The task is started automatically.

➤ Call one of the `Task.Factory.StartNew` static methods and send as parameter a delegate that will be the task's main method. The task is started automatically.

Locks

➤ Use `Monitor.Enter` or `Monitor.TryEnter` to acquire a lock, and use `Monitor.Exit` to release the lock.

➤ Use the `lock` statement in C#.

Cancellations

➤ Use `CancellationTokenSource` objects to control cancelable operations.

➤ Use the `CancellationToken` obtained from a `CancellationTokenSource` object via the `Token` property to start a cancelable operation

➤ Call `Cancel` on the `CancellationTokenSource` object to initiate the cancellation.

➤ Inside the cancelable operation stop what you were doing to cancel the operation.

async/await

➤ These are two new keywords introduced in C# 5.0

➤ `async` marks a method as asynchronous, effectively telling the compiler that the method will have an await instruction in the body. If you don't have any `await` instruction in the method body, the compiler will issue a warning.

➤ `await` blocks the execution of the current method, waiting for the awaited operation to complete.

BackgroundWorker

➤ Wire the long-running method that you need executed via the `DoWork` event.

➤ Start the operation by calling `RunWorkerAsync`.

➤ To find out when the long operation is done, subscribe to the `RunWorkerCompleted` event.

➤ To get information about the progress of the operation, subscribe to the `ProgressChanged` event.

Task continuation

➤ Continue a task by invoking `ContinueWith`, `WhenAll`, or `WhenAny` methods.

REVIEW OF KEY TERMS

asynchrony Operations that are run in a nonblocking fashion. When a method needs to call another method that potentially can block, instead of calling that method directly you can apply different techniques to avoid the blocking of the calling method.

Asynchronous Pattern Model (APM) When using this pattern, a method is split in two parts, a `Begin` and an `End` part. The begin part is responsible to prepare the call and to return the caller right away, and the end part is the one called to get back the result. The method was run in a thread from the thread pool. It is not recommended to use this approach for new development; instead use the new TAP.

atomic operation An operation that will be run at once without being interrupted by the scheduler.

deadlock Occurs when two or more threads try to acquire a lock on a resource that one of the other threads has locked already; neither of them can make more progress. There are four conditions that need to be fulfilled and that lead to a deadlock: mutual exclusion, hold and wait, no preemption, and circular wait.

Event-based Asynchronous Pattern (EAP) This pattern requires a method to be suffixed with `Async` and provide events and delegates to signal when the method finished or failed. It is not recommended for new development to use this approach; instead use the new TAP.

fork-join pattern The process of spawning another thread from the current thread (fork) to do something else while the current threads continue their work and then to wait for the spawned thread to finish its execution (join).

multithreading The capability of an operating system, or a hardware platform to have several threads of execution at the same time.

mutual exclusion Mutual exclusion is the problem, first solved by Edsger W. Dijkstra, of ensuring that two threads can't be in the same critical section at the same time.

race condition Occurs when two or more threads access shared data, writing at the same time. If the access to data is for read purposes only, there is no problem. But when several threads try to write, one thread might overwrite the data written by another thread, not taking in consideration the change.

scheduler A component of the operating system that ensures that threads are given access to the CPU in a fair manner, avoiding situations when a thread monopolizes the CPU.

task A unit of work. It normally represents an asynchronous operation that is part of a bigger problem.

Task Parallel Library (TPL) A .NET library created by Microsoft that tries to abstract away and simplify the code that deals with threads.

Task-based Asynchronous Pattern (TAP) A pattern based on a single method that returns `Task` or `Task<Result>` objects that represent the asynchronous work in progress. This is the recommended pattern for the new development.

thread The smallest unit of execution that can be independently scheduled by the operating system.

thread pool The thread pool represents a pool of precreated threads that can be used by the tasks, or to queue work items, or to run asynchronous I/O operations.

EXAM TIPS AND TRICKS

You can print the Review of Key Terms and the Cheat Sheet for this chapter to help you study. You can find these files in the ZIP file for this chapter at `www.wrox.com/remtitle.cgi?isbn=1118612094` on the Download Code tab.

Creating and Using Types with Reflection, Custom Attributes, the CodeDOM, and Lambda Expressions

WHAT YOU WILL LEARN IN THIS CHAPTER

- ➤ Using the `System.Reflection` namespace
- ➤ Reading and creating custom attributes
- ➤ Generating code using the CodeDOM namespace
- ➤ Understanding lambda expressions

WROX.COM CODE DOWNLOADS FOR THIS CHAPTER

You can find the code downloads for this chapter at www.wrox.com/remtitle .cgi?isbn=1118612094 on the Download Code tab. The code is in the chapter08 download and individually named according to the names throughout the chapter.

This chapter has a mix of topics that will be covered on the exam, and these four topics do not directly relate to each other. The first three topics cover features that can be used to examine, customize, or generate C# code, while the last topic explains how to write shorthand syntax for your existing methods. It is especially important to understand the concept of lambda expressions because not only will you see them used extensively in Chapter 10, "Working with Language Integrated Query (LINQ)," but you will see questions on the test that use lambda expressions and you could be asked what the result of the expression would be.

Table 8-1 introduces you to the exam objectives covered in this chapter.

TABLE 8-1: 70-483 Exam Objectives Covered in This Chapter

OBJECTIVE	CONTENT COVERED
Create and use types	*Reflection*. This includes finding, executing, and creating types at run time.
	Attributes. This includes creating, applying, and reading attributes that can be used to change the behavior of your class.
	The CodeDOM. This includes creating code generators.
	Lambda expressions. This is shorthand syntax for creating methods without the normal method declaration syntax.

USING THE SYSTEM.REFLECTION NAMESPACE

Reflection refers to the ability to examine code and dynamically read, modify, or invoke behavior for an assembly, module, or type. A *type* is any class, interface, array, value type, enumeration, parameter, generic type definition, and open or closed constructed generic types. You can use the classes in the System.Reflection namespace and the System.Type class to discover the assembly name, the namespace, the properties, the methods, the base class, and plenty of other metadata about a class or variable.

The System.Reflection namespace contains numerous classes that can be used to read metadata or dynamically invoke behavior from a type. Table 8-2 lists some of the frequently used classes in the System.Reflection namespace.

TABLE 8-2: Commonly Used Classes in the System.Reflection Namespace

TYPE	DESCRIPTION
Assembly	Represents a DLL or EXE file and contains properties for the Assembly name, classes, modules, and other metadata language run-time application.
EventInfo	Represents an event defined in your class and contains properties such as the event name.
FieldInfo	Represents a field defined in your class and contains properties such as whether the field is public or private.
MemberInfo	Abstracts the metadata about a class and can represent an event, a field, and so on.
MethodInfo	Represents a method defined in your class and can be used to invoke the method.

TYPE	DESCRIPTION
Module	The module is a file that composes the assembly. This is usually a DLL or EXE file.
ParameterInfo	Represents a parameter declaration for a method or a constructor. This allows you to determine the type of parameter, its name, as well as other properties.
PropertyInfo	Represents a property defined in your class and contains properties such as the property name and type.

Reflection is a powerful feature and can be used with some design patterns such as the Factory or Inversion of Control design patterns. These design patterns are more advanced topics and won't be covered in the test, but it is important to understand the concept of reflection and its capabilities for the test.

Assembly Class

An *assembly* is essentially a compiled piece of code that is typically a DLL or EXE file. You can use the Assembly class to load the assembly, read metadata about the assembly, and even create instances of the types contained in the assembly. Table 8-3 lists frequently used properties for an Assembly.

TABLE 8-3: Commonly Used System.Reflection.Assembly Properties

Property	Description
CodeBase	Returns the path for the assembly
DefinedTypes	Returns a collection of the types defined in this assembly
ExportedTypes	Returns a collection of the public types defined in this assembly
FullName	Returns the name of the assembly
GlobalAssemblyCache	Returns a boolean value indicating whether the assembly was loaded from the global assembly cache
ImageRuntimeVersion	Returns the version of the Common Language Runtime (CLR) for the assembly
Location	Returns the path or UNC location of the assembly
Modules	Returns a collection that contains the modules in this assembly
SecurityRuleSet	Returns a value that indicates which set of security rules the Common Language Runtime enforces for the assembly

The following code sample loads the `System.Data` assembly and writes some of the assembly's properties to the Output window:

```
Assembly myAssembly = Assembly.Load("System.Data, Version=4.0.0.0, Culture=neutral,
PublicKeyToken=b77a5c561934e089");

Debug.WriteLine("CodeBase: {0}", myAssembly.CodeBase);
Debug.WriteLine("FullName: {0}", myAssembly.FullName);
Debug.WriteLine("GlobalAssemblyCache: {0}", myAssembly.GlobalAssemblyCache);
Debug.WriteLine("ImageRuntimeVersion: {0}", myAssembly.ImageRuntimeVersion);
Debug.WriteLine("Location: {0}", myAssembly.Location);
```

The preceding code produces the following output:

```
CodeBase: file:///C:/Windows/Microsoft.Net/assembly/GAC_32/System.Data/
v4.0_4.0.0.0__b77a5c561934e089/System.Data.dll
FullName: System.Data, Version=4.0.0.0, Culture=neutral,
PublicKeyToken=b77a5c561934e089
GlobalAssemblyCache: True
ImageRuntimeVersion: v4.0.30319
Location: C:\Windows\Microsoft.Net\assembly\GAC_32\System.Data\
v4.0_4.0.0.0__b77a5c561934e089\System.Data.dll
```

Table 8-4 lists the frequently used methods for an Assembly.

TABLE 8-4: Commonly Used System.Reflection.Assembly Methods

METHOD	DESCRIPTION
CreateInstance(String)	Creates an instance of the class by searching the assembly for the class name
GetCustomAttributes(Boolean)	Returns an array of objects that represent the custom attributes for this assembly
GetExecutingAssembly	Returns an `Assembly` object for the currently running program
GetExportedTypes	Returns the public classes defined in this assembly
GetModule	Returns the specified module in this assembly
GetModules()	Returns all the modules that are part of this assembly
GetName()	Returns the `AssemblyName` for this assembly
GetReferencedAssemblies	Returns an array of `AssemblyName` objects that represent all referenced assemblies
GetTypes	Returns an array of `Type` object defined in this assembly
Load(String)	Loads an assembly given the long form of its name

LoadFile(String)	Loads the contents of an assembly file given a file path
LoadFrom(String)	Loads an assembly given its file name or path
ReflectionOnlyLoad(String)	Loads an assembly but you can only perform reflection on the types defined in the assembly
UnsafeLoadFrom	Loads an assembly bypassing some security checks

The GetExecutingAssembly method is a static method that enables you to get a reference to the currently executing code. The GetExportedTypes and GetTypes methods are all used to get references to the types defined in the assembly. (The System.Type class will be explained in more detail in the next section.) The difference between GetExportedTypes and GetTypes is that the GetExportedTypes returns only the types that are public. The following code snippet displays all the types defined in the currently executing assembly:

```
Assembly myAssembly = Assembly.GetExecutingAssembly();

Type[] myAssemblysTypes = myAssembly.GetTypes();

foreach (Type myType in myAssemblysTypes)
{
    Debug.WriteLine(string.Format("myType Name: {0}", myType.Name));
}
```

The Modules property or the GetLoadedModules, GetModules, and GetModule methods return the list of modules or a specific module defined in the assembly. A *module* is a file that composes the Assembly. This is usually a single DLL or EXE file. The following code lists all the modules defined in the System.Data assembly:

```
Assembly myAssembly = Assembly.Load("System.Data, Version=4.0.0.0, Culture=neutral,
                                    PublicKeyToken=b77a5c561934e089");

Module[] myAssemblysModules = myAssembly.GetModules();

foreach (Module myModule in myAssemblysModules)
{
    Debug.WriteLine(string.Format("myModule Name: {0}", myModule.Name));
}
```

The output for the preceding code snippet is as follows:

```
myModule Name: System.Data.dll
```

The preceding code snippet used the Load method to load the System.Data assembly into memory. Because the assembly was loaded using the Load method, you can then execute code within the assembly. If you do not need to execute code, you can use the ReflectionOnlyLoad method.

You can also load an assembly by calling the LoadFrom or LoadFile methods. Both methods take a file path as a parameter. To understand the difference between LoadFrom and LoadFile, you need to understand the concept of *context* and the different types of context there are. Think of the context as where reflection searches for the assembly. An assembly can be in one of three contexts or no context at all:

➤ The first context is the *load context*, which contains the assemblies found by probing. *Probing* is the process of looking in the GAC, the host assembly store, the folder of the executing assembly, or the private bin folder of the executing assembly to find the assembly.

➤ The second context is the *load-from* context. This contains the assemblies located in the path passed into the `LoadFrom` method.

➤ The third context is the *reflection-only* context, which contains the assemblies loaded with the `ReflectionOnlyLoad` and `ReflectionOnlyLoadFrom` methods.

ADVICE FROM THE EXPERTS: The Disadvantages of Using LoadFrom

There are a few disadvantages of using the `LoadFrom` method, and using `Load` is recommended. First, if there is already an assembly loaded with the same identity, then this assembly is returned, not the one found in the file path. If an assembly of the same identity is found in the probing path but in a different location, an exception can occur. Third, you must have `FileIOPermissionAccess.Read` and `FileIOPermissionAccess.PathDiscovery` permissions to the file path. `LoadFile` is different in that it can load the specific file passed in the parameter, but you still need the correct file permissions to load the assembly. You would use the `LoadFile` when there are two assemblies with the same identity in different folders on the computer.

Once you have an assembly loaded you can then create instances of the classes defined in the assembly. To create an instance of a class, use the `CreateInstance` method. The following code creates an instance of the `DataTable` and prints the number of rows to the Output window:

```
Assembly myAssembly = Assembly.Load("System.Data, Version=4.0.0.0, Culture=neutral,
                                     PublicKeyToken=b77a5c561934e089");

DataTable dt = (DataTable)myAssembly.CreateInstance("System.Data.DataTable");

Debug.Print("Number of rows: {0}", dt.Rows.Count);
```

COMMON MISTAKES: Working with the CreateInstance Method

The `CreateInstance` method will not throw an exception if you pass in a type name that is not found in the assembly. The return value will be null, so be sure to check that the name is correct.

The `GetReferencesAssemblies` is used to discover the references for the assembly. This can be helpful when troubleshooting deployment issues. The following code prints all the referenced assemblies for the `System.Data` assembly:

```
Assembly myAssembly = Assembly.Load("System.Data, Version=4.0.0.0, Culture=neutral,
                                    PublicKeyToken=b77a5c561934e089");

AssemblyName[] referencedAssemblyNames = myAssembly.GetReferencedAssemblies();

foreach (AssemblyName assemblyName in referencedAssemblyNames)
{
    Debug.WriteLine("Assembly Name: {0}", assemblyName.Name);
    Debug.WriteLine("Assembly Version: {0}", assemblyName.Version);
}
```

The preceding code will produce the following results:

```
Assembly Name: mscorlib
Assembly Version: 4.0.0.0
Assembly Name: System
Assembly Version: 4.0.0.0
Assembly Name: System.Xml
Assembly Version: 4.0.0.0
Assembly Name: System.Configuration
Assembly Version: 4.0.0.0
Assembly Name: System.Transactions
Assembly Version: 4.0.0.0
Assembly Name: System.Numerics
Assembly Version: 4.0.0.0
Assembly Name: System.EnterpriseServices
Assembly Version: 4.0.0.0
Assembly Name: System.Core
Assembly Version: 4.0.0.0
```

The `GetCustomAttributes` and `GetCustomAttributesData` will be explained later in this chapter in the "Read and Create Custom Attributes" section. But for now just realize that you can use the `Assembly` class to get the list of custom attribute classes defined in an assembly.

The System.Type Class

The `System.Type` class represents a class, interface, array, value type, enumeration, parameter, generic type definitions, and open or closed constructed generic types. For the most part, you usually use a `Type` to get information about a class contained in an assembly. You can obtain a reference to a type in two ways. You can use the `typeof()` keyword and pass in the name of the type:

```
System.Type myType = typeof(int);
```

Or you can use the `GetType()` method on an instance of the type:

```
int myIntVariable = 0;
System.Type myType = myIntVariable.GetType();
```

Both of these examples create an instance of a type class for the `int` type. After you have a reference to the type, you can then examine the properties. Table 8-4 lists commonly used properties for the `System.Type` class.

TABLE 8-4: Commonly Used Properties of the System.Type Class

PROPERTY	DESCRIPTION
Assembly	Returns the `Assembly` in which the type is declared
AssemblyQualifiedName	Returns a string which is the assembly-qualified name of the `Type`, which includes the name of the assembly from which the `Type` was loaded
BaseType	Return a `Type` from which the current `Type` inherits
FullName	Returns a string which is the fully qualified name of the `Type`, including the namespace of the `Type` but not the assembly
IsAbstract	Returns a boolean value indicating whether the `Type` is abstract
IsArry	Returns a boolean value indicating whether the `Type` is an array
IsClass	Returns a boolean value indicating whether the `Type` is a class rather than a value type or interface
IsEnum	Returns a boolean value indicating whether the current `Type` represents an enumeration
IsInterface	Returns a boolean value indicating whether the `Type` is an interface
IsNotPublic	Returns a boolean value indicating whether the `Type` is not declared public
IsPublic	Returns a boolean value indicating whether the `Type` is declared as public
IsSerializable	Returns a boolean value indicating whether the `Type` is serializable
IsValueType	Returns a boolean value indicating whether the `Type` is a value type
Name	Returns the name of the type
Namespace	Returns the namespace of the current type

The following code creates an instance of an `int` variable, obtains a reference to the `int` type, and writes some of its properties to the Output window:

```
int myIntVariable = 0;
System.Type myType = myIntVariable.GetType();
```

```
Debug.WriteLine("AssmeblyQualifiedName: {0}", myType.AssemblyQualifiedName);
Debug.WriteLine("FullName: {0}", myType.FullName);
Debug.WriteLine("IsValueType: {0}", myType.IsValueType);
Debug.WriteLine("Name: {0}", myType.Name);
Debug.WriteLine("Namespace: {0}", myType.Namespace);
```

The preceding code produces the following output:

```
AssmeblyQualifiedName: System.Int32, mscorlib, Version=4.0.0.0, Culture=neutral,
PublicKeyToken=b77a5c561934e089
FullName: System.Int32
IsValueType: True
Name: Int32
Namespace: System
```

The System.Type class also has methods that you can use to get the properties, methods, constructors, interfaces, events and any other metadata about the type. Table 8-5 lists some of the methods of the type class.

TABLE 8-5: Commonly Used Methods of the System.Type Class

NAME	DESCRIPTION
GetArrayRank	When the type represents an array, this returns the number of dimensions in an Array.
GetConstructor(Type[])	Searches for a public instance constructor whose parameters match the types in the specified array and returns a ConstructorInfo object.
GetConstructors()	Returns an array of ConstructorInfo objects for all the public constructors defined for the current Type.
GetEnumName	When the type represents an enumeration, this returns the name of the element that has the specified value.
GetEnumNames	When the type represents an enumeration, this returns the all of the names of the members.
GetEnumValues	When the type represents an enumeration, this returns an array of the values of the enumeration.
GetField(String)	Searches for the public field with the specified name.
GetFields()	Returns all the public fields of the current Type.
GetInterface(String)	Returns the interface with the specified name.
GetMember(String)	Returns the public member with the specified name.
GetMembers()	Returns all public members of the current Type.

continues

TABLE 8-5 *(continued)*

NAME	DESCRIPTION
GetMethod(String)	Returns the public method with the specified name.
GetMethods()	Returns all the public methods of the current Type.
GetProperties()	Returns all the public properties of the current Type.
GetProperty(String)	Returns the public property with the specified name.
GetTypeArray	Returns all the types of objects in the specified array.
InvokeMember(String, BindingFlags, Binder, Object, Object[])	Executes a method using the specified binding constraints and matching the specified argument list.

GetArrayRank

When the Type object represents an array, the GetArrayRank method returns the number of dimensions in the array. The following code creates a three-dimensional array and prints the array rank to the Output window:

```
int[,,] myIntArray = new int[5,6,7];
Type myIntArrayType = myIntArray.GetType();
Debug.Print("Array Rank: {0}", myIntArrayType.GetArrayRank());
```

The preceding code prints the following to the Output window:

```
Array Rank: 3
```

GetConstructors

The GetConstructors method returns an array of ConstructorInfo objects that you can use to get information about all the constructors of the type. The following code prints the constructors and the parameters for a System.DataTable object to the Output window:

```
DataTable myDataTable = new DataTable();
Type myDataTableType = myDataTable.GetType();
ConstructorInfo[] myDataTableConstructors = myDataTableType.GetConstructors();

for(int i = 0; i <= myDataTableConstructors.Length - 1; i++)
{
    ConstructorInfo constructorInfo = myDataTableConstructors[i];
    Debug.Print("\nConstructor #{0}", i + 1);

    ParameterInfo[] parameters = constructorInfo.GetParameters();
    Debug.Print("Number Of Parameters: {0}", parameters.Length);

    foreach (ParameterInfo parameter in parameters)
    {
```

```
            Debug.Print("Parameter Name: {0}", parameter.Name);
            Debug.Print("Parameter Type: {0}",
                        parameter.ParameterType.Name);
        }
    }
```

The preceding code produces the following output:

```
Constructor #1
Number Of Parameters: 0

Constructor #2
Number Of Parameters: 1
Parameter Name: tableName
Parameter Type: String

Constructor #3
Number Of Parameters: 2
Parameter Name: tableName
Parameter Type: String
Parameter Name: tableNamespace
Parameter Type: String
```

GetEnumName, GetEnumNames, and GetEnumValues

When the `Type` object represents an enumeration, the `GetEnum` methods enable you to determine all the names and values within an enumeration. For example, the following is a custom enumeration with three members:

```
private enum MyCustomEnum
{
    Red = 1,
    White = 2,
    Blue = 3
}
```

The following code writes all the names in the enumeration to the Output window:

```
Type myCustomEnumType = typeof(MyCustomEnum);

string[] enumNames = myCustomEnumType.GetEnumNames();

foreach (string enumName in enumNames)
{
    Debug.Print(string.Format("Name: {0}", enumName));
}
```

The preceding code displays the following in the Output window:

```
Name: Red
Name: White
Name: Blue
```

You can obtain the values for the enumeration by using the `GetEnumValues` method. The following code prints all the enumerations values to the Output window:

```
Type myCustomEnumType = typeof(MyCustomEnum);

Array enumValues = myCustomEnumType.GetEnumValues();
foreach (object enumValue in enumValues)
{
    Debug.Print(string.Format("Enum Value: {0}", enumValue.ToString()));
}
```

The preceding code produces the following output:

```
Enum Value: Red
Enum Value: White
Enum Value: Blue
```

> **COMMON MISTAKES: The Value Is the Same as the Name**
>
> Note that the value is the same as the name, not the numbers 1, 2, or 3.

You can also use the `GetEnumName` method to retrieve the name. The following displays all the members by using the underlying value of the enumeration.

```
Type myCustomEnumType = typeof(MyCustomEnum);

for (int i = 1; i <= 3; i++)
{
    string enumName = myCustomEnumType.GetEnumName(i);
    Debug.Print(string.Format("{0}: {1}", enumName, i));
}
```

The preceding code produces the following output.

```
Red: 1
White: 2
Blue: 3
```

GetField and GetFields

A *field* is a variable defined in a class or struct. The `GetField` method is used to get a `FieldInfo` object for one field. The `GetFields` method returns an array of `FieldInfo` objects. The `GetFields` method can also return the fields from inherited classes. When you call `GetFields`, you pass in the `BindingFlags` enumeration to specify the scope of fields that you want it to return. For example, the following class contains five fields all with different scope:

```
class ReflectionExample
{
    private string _privateField = "Hello";
    public string _publicField = "Goodbye";
    internal string _internalfield = "Hola";
```

```
        protected string _protectedField = "Adios";
        static string _staticField = "Bonjour";
}
```

You can use `GetFields` to get the values of these variables regardless of the scope.

```
ReflectionExample reflectionExample = new ReflectionExample();
Type reflectionExampleType = typeof(ReflectionExample);

FieldInfo[] fields = reflectionExampleType.GetFields(BindingFlags.Public |
                                        BindingFlags.Instance |
                                        BindingFlags.Static |
                                        BindingFlags.NonPublic |
                                        BindingFlags.FlattenHierarchy);

foreach (FieldInfo field in fields)
{
    object fieldValue = field.GetValue(reflectionExample);

    Debug.WriteLine(string.Format("Field Name: {0}, Value: {1}", field.Name,
                fieldValue.ToString()));
}
```

The preceding code produces the following output:

```
Field Name: _privateField, Value: Hello
Field Name: _publicField, Value: Goodbye
Field Name: _internalfield, Value: Hola
Field Name: _protectedField, Value: Adios
Field Name: _staticField, Value: Bonjour
```

When calling `GetFields`, you use the `BindingFlags` enumeration and can specify more than one value by using the bitwise operator.

ADVICE FROM THE EXPERTS: Declaring Variables as Private

Even if you declare a variable as private, the user of your class can still read the value of the field using reflection, so be careful what you put in these variables, especially if you store passwords or sensitive data.

The `FieldInfo` object also has a `SetValue` method that enables you to change the value of the field, even if it is private or protected. To demonstrate, add the following `get` accessor to the `ReflectionExample` class:

```
public string PrivateField
{
    get { return privateField; }
}
```

The following code changes the value of the `privateField` variable and prints its value to the Output window:

```
ReflectionExample reflectionExample = new ReflectionExample();
Type reflectionExampleType = typeof(ReflectionExample);

reflectionExampleType.GetField("privateField", BindingFlags.NonPublic |
            BindingFlags.Instance).SetValue(reflectionExample, "My New Value");

Debug.Print("Private Field Value: {0}",
            reflectionExample.PrivateField);
```

The preceding code produces the following output:

```
Private Field Value: My New Value
```

GetProperty and GetProperties

The `GetProperty` and `GetProperties` methods are similar to the `GetField` and `GetFields` methods because they enable you to get the properties, get their value, or set their value. The difference is that you use a `PropertyInfo` object instead of the `FieldInfo` object, and you can access only properties instead of fields. The `PropertyInfo` object has `GetValue` and `SetValue` methods just like the `FieldInfo` object and works the same way.

GetMethod and GetMethods

The `GetMethod` and `GetMethods` methods enable you to obtain information about a method for a type. After you have a reference to the method, you can execute the method by calling the `Invoke` method of the `MethodInfo` class. You can also execute the method by calling the `InvokeMember` method of the `Sytem.Type` class and pass in the name of the method and its parameters.

Add the following method to the `ReflectionExample` class:

```
public double Multiply(double x, double y)
{
    return x * y;
}
```

The following code calls the `Multiply` method and prints the return value to the Output window:

```
ReflectionExample reflectionExample = new ReflectionExample();
Type reflectionExampleType = typeof(ReflectionExample);

MethodInfo methodInfo = reflectionExampleType.GetMethod("Multiply");

double returnValue = (double)methodInfo.Invoke(reflectionExample,
                                      new object[] { 4, 5 });

Debug.Print("Return Value: {0}", returnValue);
```

Notice that you pass parameters to the method by creating an array of objects and passing it as the second parameter to the `Invoke` method. The preceding code prints "`Return Value: 20`" to the Output window.

When using the InvokeMember method of the System.Type class, the syntax is as follows:

```
ReflectionExample reflectionExample = new ReflectionExample();
Type reflectionExampleType = typeof(ReflectionExample);

double returnValue = (double)reflectionExampleType.InvokeMember("Multiply",
        BindingFlags.InvokeMethod,
        null,
        reflectionExample,
        new object[] { 4, 5 });

Debug.Print(string.Format("Return Value: {0}", returnValue));
```

The second parameter is BindingFlags.InvokeMethod, which triggers the InvokeMember method to invoke the method.

REAL-WORLD CASE SCENARIO **Using reflection to map a table's columns to the properties of a class**

A common pattern in a C# application is to map the columns in a table to the properties of a class. You can use reflection to create a shared utility method that can set the properties of your class to the value of the columns in your table and only have to write this code once for all your classes. This can save you a lot of time. For this exercise, you will need a database with a table called Person and a class that already contains a property for each column. Figure 8-1 displays the design of the table in SQL Server Enterprise Manager.

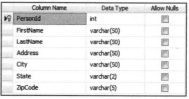

FIGURE 8-1: Table design in SQL Server Enterprise Manager

The following code is your class definition:

```
class Person
{
    public int PersonId { get; set; }
    public string FirstName { get; set; }
    public string LastName { get; set; }
    public string Address { get; set; }
    public string City { get; set; }
    public string State { get; set; }
    public string ZipCode { get; set; }
}
```

Solution

1. Create a class called ReflectionExample and add the following method:

```
public static bool LoadClassFromSQLDataReader(object myClass, SqlDataReader dr)
{
    if (dr.HasRows)
    {
        dr.Read();

        Type typeOfClass = myClass.GetType();
```

```
            for (int columnIndex = 0; columnIndex <= dr.FieldCount - 1; columnIndex++)
            {
                //Get the name of the column
                string columnName = dr.GetName(columnIndex);

                //Check if a property exists that matches that name.
                PropertyInfo propertyInfo = typeOfClass.GetProperty(columnName);

                if (propertyInfo != null)
                {
                    //Set the value to the value in the SqlDataReader
                    propertyInfo.SetValue(myClass, dr.GetValue(columnIndex));
                }
            }

            return true;
        }
        else
        {
            return false;
        }
    }
```

This method takes an instance of a class and a `SqlDataReader` as a parameter. It first checks if the `SqlDataReader` has rows, and if it does it positions the cursor on the first record. Then it gets the type for `myClass` using the `GetType` method. Next, it loops around for each column in the `SqlDataReader`. In the loop it first gets the column name and then tries to retrieve the property from the object with that name. If the property exists, the value of the property is set to the data in the column.

2. Now you can add the `GetPerson` method to the `Person` class to use this method:

```
public bool GetPerson(int personId)
{
    //Open the connection to the database.
    SqlConnection cn = new
        SqlConnection("Server=(local);Database=Reflection;Trusted_Connection=True;");
    cn.Open();

    //Retrieve the record.
    SqlCommand cmd = new SqlCommand(
        string.Format("SELECT * FROM Person WHERE PersonId = {0}", personId), cn);

    SqlDataReader dr = cmd.ExecuteReader(CommandBehavior.CloseConnection);

    return ReflectionExample.LoadClassFromSQLDataReader(this, dr);
}
```

Be aware, though, that when using reflection there is a performance hit because there is extra processing going on to resolve all the references. You need to take this into account when deciding whether to use reflection.

READ AND CREATE CUSTOM ATTRIBUTES

Attributes enable you to define metadata for a class, a property, or a method. The class, property, or method is referred to as the *target* of the attribute. Reflection can then be used to read these attributes dynamically and change how the target behaves. Attributes are contained in square brackets "[ ]" above the target and can be stacked on top of each other when multiple attributes are needed to define the target. For example, if you want to make a class serializable, you need to add the [Serializable()] attribute above the class declaration:

```
[Serializable()]
public class MyClass
{
    …
}
```

The Serializable attribute is actually a class defined in the .NET Framework that inherits from System.Attribute. The System.Attribute class is an abstract class that is the base class for all custom attributes. This section explains how to read attributes using reflection and then create your own custom attributes.

Read Attributes

In the previous section you learned about the System.Reflection namespace and the numerous classes defined in the namespace that let you read the metadata about the classes within an assembly. An assembly has a GetCustomAttributes method that enables you to enumerate through all the custom attributes classes contained in the assembly or filter the specific type of attribute you would like to retrieve. The following code block iterates through all the referenced assemblies for the currently executing assembly and prints the custom attributes class names and properties to the Output window:

```
Assembly assembly = Assembly.GetExecutingAssembly();

AssemblyName[] assemblyNames = assembly.GetReferencedAssemblies();

foreach (AssemblyName assemblyName in assemblyNames)
{
    Debug.WriteLine("\nAssembly Name: {0}", assemblyName.FullName);

    Assembly referencedAssembly = Assembly.Load(assemblyName.FullName);

    object[] attributes = referencedAssembly.GetCustomAttributes(false);

    foreach (object attribute in attributes)
    {
        Debug.WriteLine(\nAttribute Name: {0}",
                                    attribute.GetType().Name);

        //Get the properties of this attribute
        PropertyInfo[] properties = attribute.GetType().GetProperties();
```

```
        foreach (PropertyInfo property in properties)
        {
            Debug.WriteLine("{0} : {1}", property.Name,
                                    property.GetValue(attribute));
        }
    }
}
```

The following text is a partial list of the output from the preceding code. The currently executing assembly referenced three assemblies: mscorlib, System.Data, and System. Each has their own set of custom attribute classes.

```
Assembly Name: mscorlib, Version=4.0.0.0, Culture=neutral,
            PublicKeyToken=b77a5c561934e089

Attribute Name: StringFreezingAttribute
TypeId : System.Runtime.CompilerServices.StringFreezingAttribute

...

Assembly Name: System.Data, Version=4.0.0.0, Culture=neutral,
            PublicKeyToken=b77a5c561934e089

Attribute Name: AllowPartiallyTrustedCallersAttribute
PartialTrustVisibilityLevel : VisibleToAllHosts
TypeId : System.Security.AllowPartiallyTrustedCallersAttribute

Attribute Name: CLSCompliantAttribute
IsCompliant : True
TypeId : System.CLSCompliantAttribute

Attribute Name: RuntimeCompatibilityAttribute
WrapNonExceptionThrows : True
TypeId : System.Runtime.CompilerServices.RuntimeCompatibilityAttribute

...

Assembly Name: System, Version=4.0.0.0, Culture=neutral,
            PublicKeyToken=b77a5c561934e089

Attribute Name: ComVisibleAttribute
Value : False
TypeId : System.Runtime.InteropServices.ComVisibleAttribute
```

Notice that the GetCustomAttributes method returns an array of objects. This is because each attribute is its own class. The first attribute in the mscorlib assembly is the StringFreezingAttribute. This is a class that inherits from System.Attribute and can have its own properties and methods. As you read through the preceding output, you can see that each attribute class has its own custom properties and also the properties of the System.Attribute class.

Create Attributes

To create your own custom attribute, you need to create a class that inherits from the `System` `.Attribute` abstract class:

```
class MyCustomAttribute : System.Attribute
{
}
```

> **BEST PRACTICES: Naming Custom Attribute Classes**
>
> When naming a custom attribute class, it should always have `Attribute` at the end of its name. When using the custom attribute, you reference it by the name and exclude the `Attribute` part.

After you declare your class, you can then add properties and enumerations to the class just like any other class. For this example, you add one enumeration and three properties:

```
public enum MyCustomAttributeEnum
{
    Red,
    White,
    Blue
}

public bool Property1 { get; set; }
public string Property2 { get; set; }
public MyCustomAttributeEnum Property3 { get; set; }
```

The next step is to define the scope of the attribute. For this example you limit the scope of this attribute so that the target can be only a class or a struct. To do this you use the `System.AttributeUsage` custom attribute. This attribute is applied to the class:

```
[System.AttributeUsage(AttributeTargets.Class | AttributeTargets.Struct)]
class MyCustomAttribute : System.Attribute
{
    ...
}
```

Now you can use this attribute when defining a class. Create a new class named `MyTestClass`. Above the `class` declaration add the following code:

```
[MyCustom(Property1 = true, Property2 = "Hello World", Property3 =
MyCustomAttribute.MyCustomAttributeEnum.Red)]
class MyTestClass()
{
}
```

Notice that the name of the attribute is `MyCustom`, not `MyCustomAttribute`. To set the properties of the attribute, you pass the values to the constructor as named parameters. You could have also added a constructor to the `MyCustomAttribute` class with three parameters and then set the property values in the body of the constructor.

Now that you have the class with a custom attribute, you can use reflection to read the attribute values. The following code can read the custom attributes for the `MyTestClass`:

```
Type myTestClassType = typeof(MyTestClass);

MyCustomAttribute attribute =
(MyCustomAttribute)myTestClassType.GetCustomAttribute
(
                                       typeof(MyCustomAttribute),
                                       false
                         );

Debug.WriteLine("Property1: {0}", attribute.Property1);
Debug.WriteLine("Property2: {0}", attribute.Property2);
Debug.WriteLine("Property3: {0}", attribute.Property3);
```

The preceding code produces the following output:

```
Property1: True
Property2: Hello World
Property3: Red
```

REAL-WORLD CASE SCENARIO **Using custom attributes**

In the previous Real-World Case Scenario, you learned how to use reflection to map the value of the columns in a table to the properties in a class. This works great as long as the names of the columns in the table match the names of the properties in the class. But if for some reason they do not match, you may want to map a column to a property of a different name. A custom attribute is a great way to handle this situation. Try creating it now, before looking at the solution provided.

Solution

1. Add a class to the project and name it `DataMappingAttribute`. Because this attribute should be used only for classes, set the `AttributeTarget` property to `Class`. You also want to use this attribute for more than one column, so you need to set the `AllowMultiple` property of the `AttributeUsage` class to true.

```
[System.AttributeUsage(AttributeTargets.Class, AllowMultiple=true)]
class DataMappingAttribute : System.Attribute
{
}
```

2. Add two string properties called `ColumnName` and `PropertyName`. When implemented, these properties contain the column name that maps to the property name:

```
public string ColumnName { get; set; }
public string PropertyName { get; set; }
```

3. Add a constructor to the attribute class that takes the column and property names as parameters and sets the property value:

```
public DataMappingAttribute(string columnName, string propertyName)
{
    ColumnName = columnName;
    PropertyName = propertyName;
}
```

4. Open the `Person` class that was created in the previous Real-World Case Scenario, change the name of the `FirstName` property to **FName**, and change the **LastName** property to LName. Add the `DataMapping` attributes above the class name, and set the appropriate mappings for the first and last name columns\properties:

```
[DataMapping("FirstName", "FName")]
[DataMapping("LastName", "LName")]
class Person
{
    ...
}
```

5. Open the `ReflectionExample` class, and modify the `LoadClassFromSqlDataReader` method to the following:

```
public static bool LoadClassFromSQLDataReader(object myClass, SqlDataReader dr)
{
    if (dr.HasRows)
    {
        dr.Read();

        Type typeOfClass = myClass.GetType();

        object[] dataMappingAttributes =
            typeOfClass.GetCustomAttributes(typeof(DataMappingAttribute), false);

        for (int columnIndex = 0; columnIndex <= dr.FieldCount - 1; columnIndex++)
        {
            //Get the name of the column.
            string columnName = dr.GetName(columnIndex);

            //Check if a property exists that matches that name.
            PropertyInfo propertyInfo = null;

            //Check if an attribute exists that maps this column to a property.
            foreach (DataMappingAttribute dataMappingAttribute in
                                    dataMappingAttributes)
            {
                if (dataMappingAttribute.ColumnName == columnName)
                {
                    propertyInfo =
                        typeOfClass.GetProperty(dataMappingAttribute.PropertyName);
                    break;
                }
            }
```

```
            //The the property was mapped explicitly then try to find a
            //property with the same name as the column.
            if (propertyInfo == null)
            {
                propertyInfo = typeOfClass.GetProperty(columnName);
            }

            //If you found a property then set its value.
            if (propertyInfo != null)
            {
                //Set the value to the value in the SqlDataReader
                propertyInfo.SetValue(myClass, dr.GetValue(columnIndex));
            }
        }

        return true;
    }
    else
    {
        return false;
    }
}
```

You can now see the power of attributes and how they can help control the flow of your application.

GENERATE CODE USING THE CODEDOM NAMESPACE

The Code Document Object Model, *CodeDOM*, is a set of classes in the .NET Framework that enables you to create code generators. A code generator is a program that can write your code for you. The CodeDOM is an object model that contains classes that represent properties, methods, classes, boolean logic, parameters, and any other type of code element you can write in your program. You can use the CodeDOM classes to write your code generically and then have it generated in C#, VB.NET, or JScript.

Have you ever written classes that have properties that map to a table? This can be tedious and time-consuming. This is a great example of when you would want to use the CodeDOM to generate this code for you automatically. You can create a program that reads the columns from a table in a database and creates a class that contains a column for each property. This section explains the classes within the CodeDOM namespace and shows you how to generate code for classes, properties, and methods, and even generate looping structures and if statements.

Generate Code Using the CodeDOM Namespace

The classes in the CodeDOM model the code statements, such as an if statement or variable declaration. You can write a code generator using the CodeDOM classes and then generate your code in either C#, VB.NET, or JScript. The CodeDOM classes are great for automating repetitive coding tasks or enforcing patterns within your projects. This section will demonstrate how to create a class file using the CodeDOM that contains fields, properties, and methods.

The typical structure of a class within C# contains the following elements:

➤ Text file that contains the code for the class

➤ Set of using statements

➤ Namespace declaration

➤ Class name declaration

➤ Set of fields and properties

➤ Set of methods, which contain logic with looping structures and logical expressions such as if and switch statements

The CodeDOM namespace contains classes that enable you to create a structure called a CodeDOM Graph that models these elements. Table 8-6 lists some of the classes you can use in the CodeDOM namespace.

TABLE 8-6: Commonly Used Classes in the CodeDOM Namespace

NAME	DESCRIPTION
CodeArgumentReferenceExpression	Represents a reference to the value of an argument passed to a method
CodeAssignStatement	Represents an assignment statement
CodeBinaryOperatorExpression	Represents an expression that consists of a binary operation
CodeCastExpression	Represents an expression that casts to another data type or interface
CodeComment	Represents a comment
CodeCompileUnit	Provides a container for a CodeDOM, which contains the declarations, namespace, class, and components of your class
CodeConditionStatement	Represents a conditional statement, typically represented as an if statement
CodeConstructor	Represents a declaration of an instance constructor
CodeFieldReferenceExpression	Represents a reference to a field

continues

TABLE 8-6 *(continued)*

NAME	DESCRIPTION
`CodeIterationStatement`	Represents a `for` statement or other looping structure
`CodeMemberEvent`	Represents a declaration for an event
`CodeMemberField`	Represents a declaration for a field
`CodeMemberMethod`	Represents a declaration for a method
`CodeMemberProperty`	Represents a declaration for a property
`CodeMethodInvokeExpression`	Represents an expression that invokes a method
`CodeMethodReturnStatement`	Represents a return value statement
`CodeNamespace`	Represents a namespace declaration
`CodeNamespaceImport`	Represents a namespace import directive
`CodeObjectCreateExpression`	Represents an expression that creates a new instance of a type
`CodeParameterDeclarationExpression`	Represents a parameter declaration for a method, property, or constructor
`CodePropertyReferenceExpression`	Represents a reference to the value of a property
`CodePropertySetValueReferenceExpression`	Represents the value argument of a property `set` method
`CodeRegionDirective`	Specifies the name and mode for a code region
`CodeSnippetCompileUnit`	Represents a literal code fragment that can be compiled
`CodeSnippetStatement`	Represents a statement using a literal code fragment
`CodeThisReferenceExpression`	Represents a reference to the current local class instance
`CodeThrowExceptionStatement`	Represents a statement that throws an exception
`CodeTryCatchFinallyStatement`	Represents a `try`, `catch`, and `finally` block

NAME	DESCRIPTION
CodeTypeConstructor	Represents a static constructor for a class
CodeTypeDeclaration	Represents a declaration for a class, structure, interface, or enumeration
CodeTypeDelegate	Represents a delegate declaration
CodeVariableDeclarationStatement	Represents a variable declaration
CodeVariableReferenceExpression	Represents a reference to a local variable

As you can see from the list of classes in Table 8-6, the CodeDOM has classes for every type of statement you can make in the .NET Framework. You can then choose to have the code rendered in the language of your choice. For example, look at the following class and then later in the chapter you will use the CodeDOM to generate this class:

```csharp
using System;
using System.Collections.Generic;
using System.Linq;
using System.Text;
using System.Threading.Tasks;

namespace Reflection
{
    class Calculator
    {
        private double x;
        private double y;

        public double X
        {
            get { return this.x; }
            set { this.x = value; }
        }

        public double Y
        {
            get { return this.y; }
            set { this.y = value; }
        }

        public double Divide()
        {
            if (this.Y == 0)
            {
                return 0;
            }
            else
            {
                return this.X / this.Y;
            }
```

```
        }

        public double Exponent(double power)
        {
            return Math.Pow(this.X, power);
        }
    }
}
```

This is a simple class called `Calculator` that is in the `Reflection` namespace, contains two fields, two properties, and two methods. The following sections demonstrates which classes in the CodeDOM you should use to create the class dynamically.

CodeCompileUnit

The `CodeCompileUnit` class is the top-level class that is the container for all other objects within the class you want to generate. Think of this as the class that represents the file that contains your code. The following code is used to create an instance of the `CodeCompileUnit` class:

```
CodeCompileUnit codeCompileUnit = new CodeCompileUnit();
```

CodeNamespace and CodeNamespaceImport

The next step is to add the namespace. The `CodeNamspace` class is used to represent the namespace. The constructor takes the namespace as the parameter.

```
CodeNamespace codeNamespace = new CodeNamespace("Reflection");
```

Now that you have a namespace, you can append the `using` statements. Normally, when you create a class file, the using statements are above the namespace declaration, but they still work if you add them after the namespace. The `CodeNamespaceImport` class is used to define the namespace you would like to import. In C# you use the `using` keyword, but in VB.NET you would use the `imports` keyword. By using the CodeDOM, you don't have to worry about the correct keyword.

```
codeNamespace.Imports.Add(new CodeNamespaceImport("System"));
codeNamespace.Imports.Add(new CodeNamespaceImport("System.Collections.Generic"));
codeNamespace.Imports.Add(new CodeNamespaceImport("System.Linq"));
codeNamespace.Imports.Add(new CodeNamespaceImport("System.Text"));
codeNamespace.Imports.Add(new CodeNamespaceImport("System.Threading.Tasks"));
```

The preceding code produces the following output:

```
namespace Reflection
{
    using System;
    using System.Collections.Generic;
    using System.Linq;
    using System.Text;
    using System.Threading.Tasks;
}
```

CodeTypeDeclaration

The next step is to declare the class. This is done by using the `CodeTypeDeclaration` class.

```
CodeTypeDeclaration targetClass = new CodeTypeDeclaration("Calculator");
targetClass.IsClass = true;
targetClass.TypeAttributes = TypeAttributes.Public;

//Add the class to the namespace.
codeNamespace.Types.Add(targetClass);
```

The preceding code creates an instance of the `CodeTypeDeclaration` class and sets the `IsClass` attribute to `true`, which tells the .NET Framework to generate a class declaration. The `TypeAttributes` property enables you to define attributes such as `public`, `private`, and `static`. These can be combined using the bitwise operator (|). After the class is defined, you need to add it to the `Types` collection of the namespace. The preceding code produces the following output:

```
public class Calculator
{
}
```

CodeMemberField

The next step is to add the fields to the class. This is done by using the `CodeMemberField` class. You simply create an instance of the class and set its `Name` property, set the `Type` property, and add it to the `Members` collection of the `CodeTypeDeclaration` object. The following code creates two fields, _x and _y, both of which are declared as a `double`:

```
CodeMemberField xField = new CodeMemberField();
xField.Name = "x";
xField.Type = new CodeTypeReference(typeof(double));
targetClass.Members.Add(xField);

CodeMemberField yField = new CodeMemberField();
yField.Name = "y";
yField.Type = new CodeTypeReference(typeof(double));
targetClass.Members.Add(yField);
```

The preceding code produces the following output:

```
private double x;
private double y;
```

CodeMemberProperty

The next step is to create the properties for the x and y fields. You use a `CodeMemberProperty` class to create a property and generate the `get` and `set` methods. The following code creates the X and Y properties in the `Calculator` class:

```
//X Property
CodeMemberProperty xProperty = new CodeMemberProperty();

xProperty.Attributes = MemberAttributes.Public | MemberAttributes.Final;
```

```
xProperty.Name = "X";
xProperty.HasGet = true;
xProperty.HasSet = true;
xProperty.Type = new CodeTypeReference(typeof(System.Double));

xProperty.GetStatements.Add(new CodeMethodReturnStatement(
    new CodeFieldReferenceExpression(new CodeThisReferenceExpression(), "x")));

xProperty.SetStatements.Add(new CodeAssignStatement(
    new CodeFieldReferenceExpression(new CodeThisReferenceExpression(), "x"),
                        new CodePropertySetValueReferenceExpression()));
targetClass.Members.Add(xProperty);

//Y Property
CodeMemberProperty yProperty = new CodeMemberProperty();
yProperty.Attributes = MemberAttributes.Public | MemberAttributes.Final;
yProperty.Name = "Y";
yProperty.HasGet = true;
yProperty.HasSet = true;
yProperty.Type = new CodeTypeReference(typeof(System.Double));

yProperty.GetStatements.Add(new CodeMethodReturnStatement(
    new CodeFieldReferenceExpression(new CodeThisReferenceExpression(), "y")));

yProperty.SetStatements.Add(new CodeAssignStatement(
    new CodeFieldReferenceExpression(new CodeThisReferenceExpression(), "y"),
                        new CodePropertySetValueReferenceExpression()));

targetClass.Members.Add(yProperty);
```

The `CodeMemberProperty` class has two properties (`HasGet` and `HasSet`) that you need to set to `true` so the code generator can create the `Get` and `Set` accessors. The `GetStatements` collection property is used to add the code to the `Get` accessor. In this example, the `Get` method returns the `this.x` field. The `CodeThisReferenceExpression` class is used because in C# you use `this`; in VB you use `Me`. The code generator knows which keyword to use when you generate the code. The `SetStatements` collection property contains the code to set the `this.x` field. In this instance you need to create a `CodeAssignStatement` along with the `CodePropertySetValueReferenceExpression`. The preceding code produces the following output:

```
public double X
{
    get
    {
        return this.x;
    }
    set
    {
        this.x = value;
    }
}
public double Y
{
    get
```

```
        {
            return this.y;
        }
        set
        {
            this.y = value;
        }
    }
}
```

CodeMemberMethod

The next step is to create the `Divide` method. To create methods using the CodeDOM, you need to use the `CodeMemberMethod` class. The following code creates an instance of the `CodeMemberMethod` class, names the method `Divide`, sets the return type to `double`, and sets its attributes to public and final. If you want to set other attributes, such as static, virtual, or new, you can use the bitwise operator to concatenate the attributes.

```
CodeMemberMethod divideMethod = new CodeMemberMethod();
divideMethod.Name = "Divide";
divideMethod.ReturnType = new CodeTypeReference(typeof(double));
divideMethod.Attributes = MemberAttributes.Public | MemberAttributes.Final;
```

Now that the method signature is defined, you need to create the code for the body of the method. The `Divide` method checks if the `Y` property is `0` and either returns `0` or the quotient. `If` logic is created by using the `CodeConditonStatement` class.

```
CodeConditionStatement ifLogic = new CodeConditionStatement();

ifLogic.Condition = new CodeBinaryOperatorExpression(
    new CodeFieldReferenceExpression(
        new CodeThisReferenceExpression(), yProperty.Name),
    CodeBinaryOperatorType.ValueEquality,
    new CodePrimitiveExpression(0));

ifLogic.TrueStatements.Add(new CodeMethodReturnStatement(
    new CodePrimitiveExpression(0)));

ifLogic.FalseStatements.Add(new CodeMethodReturnStatement(
    new CodeBinaryOperatorExpression(
        new CodeFieldReferenceExpression(
            new CodeThisReferenceExpression(), xProperty.Name),
        CodeBinaryOperatorType.Divide,
        new CodeFieldReferenceExpression(
            new CodeThisReferenceExpression(), yProperty.Name))));

divideMethod.Statements.Add(ifLogic);
```

As you can see the `CodeConditonStatement` class has a `Condition` property that is a `CodeBinaryOperatorExpression` class. This class is used to create a binary expression. In this example the expression equates to `(this.Y == 0)`. The `CodeBinaryOperatorExpression` class also has a `TrueStatements` and a `FalseStatements` property that enables you to create the code that will be written for the true and false conditions. The preceding code creates the following output:

```
public double Divide()
{
    if ((this.Y == 0))
    {
        return 0;
    }
    else
    {
        return (this.X / this.Y);
    }
}
```

CodeParameterDeclarationExpression and CodeMethodInvokeExpression

The next step is to create the `Exponent` method. This method takes a parameter called `power` and returns `this.Y` raised to that power.

```
CodeMemberMethod exponentMethod = new CodeMemberMethod();

exponentMethod.Name = "Exponent";
exponentMethod.ReturnType = new CodeTypeReference(typeof(double));
exponentMethod.Attributes = MemberAttributes.Public | MemberAttributes.Final;

CodeParameterDeclarationExpression powerParameter =
    new CodeParameterDeclarationExpression(typeof(double), "power");
exponentMethod.Parameters.Add(powerParameter);

CodeMethodInvokeExpression callToMath = new CodeMethodInvokeExpression(
    new CodeTypeReferenceExpression("System.Math"),
    "Pow",
    new CodeFieldReferenceExpression(new CodeThisReferenceExpression(),
        xProperty.Name), new CodeArgumentReferenceExpression("power"));

exponentMethod.Statements.Add(new CodeMethodReturnStatement(callToMath));

targetClass.Members.Add(exponentMethod);
```

You use the `CodeParameterDeclarationExpression` class to create the `power` parameter. The `CodeMethodInvokeExpression` class is used to call a method and pass a parameter to the method. The preceding code produces the following output:

```
public double Exponent(double power)
{
    return System.Math.Pow(this.X, power);
}
```

CodeDOMProvider

The last step is to generate the class file. You use the `CodeDOMProvider` class to create the file in either C#, VB, or JScript. This class has a method called `GenerateCodeFromCompileUnit` that takes a `CodeCompileUnit`, `TextWriter`, and `CodeGeneratorOptions` class as parameters. The `CodeGeneratorOptions` class has properties that enable you to control the formatting of your automatically generated code. The following sample tells the compiler to use single-line spacing between the member declarations. Setting the `BracingStyle` property to "C" places the brackets, {}, on separate lines.

```
CodeDOMProvider provider = CodeDOMProvider.CreateProvider("CSharp");

CodeGeneratorOptions options = new CodeGeneratorOptions();
options.BlankLinesBetweenMembers = false;
options.BracingStyle = "C";

using (StreamWriter sourceWriter = new StreamWriter(@"c:\CodeDOM\Calculator." +
                                                    provider.FileExtension))
{
    provider.GenerateCodeFromCompileUnit(codeCompileUnit, sourceWriter, options);
}
```

LAMBDA EXPRESSIONS

Lambda expressions are shorthand syntax for creating an anonymous methods. What's an anonymous method? Well, an *anonymous method* is essentially a method without a name. What good is a method without a name? Well, when writing methods that are small and used in limited scope, you can write an anonymous method without going through the trouble of creating the method signature. Also, you can pass an anonymous method to other methods to dynamically change how those methods behave. This concept is extremely important to understand before tackling the concept of LINQ. Lambda expressions are used everywhere in LINQ.

Delegates

Before exploring lambda expressions start with the basics. A *delegate* is a type that references a method. When you declare a delegate, you specify the signature of the method that you want to reference. For example, create a new class called `LambdaExpressions` and add the following method that takes a string parameter and writes it to the console window:

```
static void WriteToConsoleForward(string stringToWrite)
{
    Console.WriteLine("This is my string: {0}", stringToWrite);
}
```

If you want to reference this method, first create a delegate that has the same signature.

```
delegate void MyFirstDelegate(string s);
```

Notice that the return type is `void` and the parameter's type is `string` which matches the signature of the `WriteToConsoleForward` method. Now that you have a delegate, you need to associate a variable of this type to the method.

```
MyFirstDelegate myFirstDelegate = new
    MyFirstDelegate(LambdaExpressions.WriteToConsoleForward);
```

The `myFirstDelegate` variable essentially holds a reference to the method. You can now call the method by using the `myFirstDelegate` variable and passing in a parameter.

```
myFirstDelegate("Hello World");
```

Now create a second method that takes a string as a parameter and writes the string backward to the console.

```
static void WriteToConsoleBackwards(string stringToWrite)
{
    char[] charArray = stringToWrite.ToCharArray();
    Array.Reverse(charArray);

    Console.WriteLine("This is my string backwards: {0}",
                                    new string(charArray));
}
```

Both methods have the same signature, so you can create a single delegate to reference either method. Now create another method that takes the delegate as a parameter and calls the method.

```
static void WriteToConsole(MyFirstDelegate myDelegate, string stringToWrite)
{
    myDelegate(stringToWrite);
}
```

Now you can call the `WriteToConsole` method and pass in the method as a parameter.

```
WriteToConsole(LambdaExpressions.WriteToConsoleForward, "Hello World");

WriteToConsole(LambdaExpressions.WriteToConsoleBackwards, "Hello World");
```

The preceding two lines of code produce the following output:

```
This is my string: Hello World
This is my string backwards: dlroW olleH
```

ADVICE FROM THE EXPERTS: Covariance and Contravariance

Something to note about delegates are the concepts of covariance and contravariance. *Covariance* enables you to have a method with a more derived return type than the delegate's return type. So the delegate's return type could be a base class, and the method's return type can be a type that inherits from the base class. *Contravariance* permits parameter types that are less derived than the delegate's parameter types. So the delegate's parameters can be a base class, but the method's parameters can be a class that is derived from the base class.

Anonymous Methods

Anonymous methods are similar to delegates except you don't have to create the method. You still create the delegate, but you can assign the method all within the same line of code.

```
MyFirstDelegate forward = delegate(string s2)
    {
        Console.WriteLine("This is my string: {0}", s2);
    };


forward("Hello World");
```

The preceding code creates a delegate variable called `forward`, and it references the body of a method. The method can have as many lines as you want. One difference between an anonymous method and a delegate is that you can reference local variables that are not passed as parameters. For example, the following sample creates a delegate that has no parameters. It then creates a local variable and an anonymous method that uses the variable.

```
delegate void MyAnonymousMethod();

static void Main(string[] args)
{
    string myLocalString = "Hello World";

    //Create an anonymous method using the local variable.
    MyAnonymousMethod forward = delegate()
    {
        Console.WriteLine(string.Format("This is my string: {0}", myLocalString));
    };

    forward();
}
```

This method produces the same output as the previous method. As you can see, programmatically these methods produce the same output, but anonymous methods involve less coding.

Lambda Expressions

Lambda expressions enable you to create an anonymous function using shorthand syntax. Consider the following:

```
delegate double square(double x);

static void Main(string[] args)
{
    square myLambdaExpression = x => x * x;
    Console.WriteLine("X squared is {0}", myLambdaExpression(5));
}
```

The lambda expression is x => x * x. When reading the code, you would say x *goes to* x times x. The => is called the *goes to operator*. The left side of the goes to operator evaluates to the input parameters of your method. The body of your method goes on the right side of the goes to operator. In this instance the method can square whatever number is passed into the method. If you need to pass multiple parameters, you use the following syntax:

```
delegate bool GreaterThan(double x, double y);

static void Main(string[] args)
{
    GreaterThan gt = (x, y) => x > y;
    Console.WriteLine("Is 6 greater than 5. {0}", gt(6, 5));
}
```

The preceding code produces the following output:

```
Is 6 greater than 5. True
```

When the method contains only a single expression, it is referred to as an *expression lambda*. When you need multiple statements in the body of the method it is referred to as a *statement lambdas*. Statement Lambdas are contained in brackets, {}. The following is a lambda expression for the WriteToConsoleBackward method:

```
s =>
    {
        char[] charArray = s.ToCharArray();
        Array.Reverse(charArray);
        Console.WriteLine("This is my string to write backwards: {0}",
                                    new string(charArray));
    };
```

You can also use a lambda expression to pass a function to a method. The following uses a lambda expression to call the WriteToConsole method:

```
WriteToConsole(x => Console.WriteLine("This is my string {0}", x), "Hello World");
```

As you can see, the syntax requires less typing as you go from delegate, to anonymous function, to lambda expressions.

SUMMARY

This chapter described a number of topics, starting with reflection. Reflection is a powerful feature in the .NET Framework that enables you to examine all types within an assembly, create instances of classes, invoke methods, read attributes, and perform many other useful operations within your code.

Attributes are metadata that can be applied to a class, a method, or a property. You can use reflection to read attributes and dynamically change the behavior of your application.

You can create custom attribute classes and associate them with your own classes, properties, or methods. Custom attributes are created by creating a class that inherits from the System.Attribute class.

The Code Document Object Model (CodeDOM) is the object model provided by the .NET Framework that enables you to generate code dynamically in either C#, VB, or JScript. Learning the types in the `System.CodeDOM` namespace is useful when you want to automate tedious tasks or compile code programmatically.

Lambda expressions are shorthand syntax for creating anonymous functions. Anonymous functions are small methods without a signature. Lambda expressions are used extensively in LINQ.

CHAPTER TEST QUESTIONS

Read each question carefully and select the answer or answers that represent the best solution to the problem. You can find the answers in Appendix A, "Answers to Chapter Test Questions."

1. You are given an assignment to create a code generator to automate the task of creating repetitive code. Which namespace contains the types needed to generate code?

    a. `System.Reflection`

    b. CodeDom

    c. Reflection

    d. `System.CodeDom`

2. Which code can create a lambda expression?

    a. `delegate x = x => 5 + 5;`

    b. `delegate MySub(double x);  MySub ms = delegate(double y) {     y * y;  }`

    c. `x => x * x;`

    d. `delegate MySub();    MySub ms = x * x;`

3. You are consulting for a company called Contoso and are taking over an application that was built by a third-party software company. There is an executable that is currently not working because it is missing a DLL file that is referenced. How can you figure out which DLL files the application references?

    a. Create an instance of the `Assembly` class, load the assembly, and iterate through the `ReferencedAssemblies` property.

    b. Create an instance of the `Assembly` class, load the assembly, and call the `GetReferencedAssemblies` method.

    c. Create an instance of the `Assembly` class, load the assembly, and iterate through the `Modules` property.

    d. Create an instance of the `Assembly` class, load the assembly, and call the `GetModulesReferenced` method.

4. You are a developer for a finance department and are building a method that uses reflection to get a reference to the type of object that was passed as a parameter. Which syntax can be used to determine an object's type?

   a. `Type myType = typeof(myParameter);`

   b. `Object myObject = myParameter.GetType(object);`

   c. `Object myObject = typeof(myParameter);`

   d. `Type myType = myParameter.GetType();`

5. You are asked to create a custom attribute that has a single property, called `Version`, that allows the caller to determine the version of a method. Which code can create the attribute?

   a.
```
class MyCustomAttribute :System.Reflection.Attribute
{          public string Version { get; set; }     }
```

   b.
```
class MyCustomAttribute : System.Attribute
{          public string Version { get; set; }     }
```

   c.
```
class MyCustomAttribute : System.AttributeUsage
{          public string Version { get; set; }     }
```

   d.
```
class MyCustomAttribute : System.ClassAttribute
{          public string Version { get; set; }     }
```

6. Which class in the `System.Reflection` namespace would you use if you want to determine all the classes contained in a DLL file?

   a. `FileInfo`

   b. `Assembly`

   c. `Type`

   d. `Module`

7. Which method of the `Assembly` class allows you to get all the public types defined in the `Assembly`?

   a. `DefinedTypes`

   b. `Types`

   c. `GetExportedTypes`

   d. `GetModules`

8. Which property of the `Assembly` class returns the name of the assembly?

   a. `Name`

   b. `FullyQualifiedName`

   c. `Location`

   d. `FullName`

9. Which method of the `Assembly` class returns an instance of the current assembly?

    a. `GetExecutingAssembly`

    b. `GetAssembly`

    c. `GetCurrentAssembly`

    d. `Assembly`

10. Which syntax will `Load` an `Assembly`? (Choose all that apply)

    a. `Assembly.Load("System.Data, Version=4.0.0.0, Culture=neutral, PublicKeyToken=b77a5c561934e089");`

    b. `Assembly.LoadFrom(@"c:\MyProject\Project1.dll");`

    c. `Assembly.LoadFile(@"c:\MyProject\Project1.dll");`

    d. `Assembly.ReflectionOnlyLoad(("System.Data, Version=4.0.0.0, Culture=neutral, PublicKeyToken=b77a5c561934e089");`

11. Which method should you call if you want the .NET Framework to look in the load-context to load an `Assembly`?

    a. `ReflectionOnlyLoad`

    b. `LoadFrom`

    c. `Load`

    d. `LoadFromContext`

12. Which method should you call if you want the .NET Framework to look in the load-from context?

    a. `ReflectionOnlyLoad`

    b. `LoadFrom`

    c. `Load`

    d. `LoadFromContext`

13. Which line creates an instance of a `DataTable` using reflection?

    a. `myAssembly.CreateInstance("System.Data.DataTable");`

    b. `DataTable.GetType();`

    c. `typeof("System.Data.DataTable");`

    d. `myType.CreateInstance("System.Data.DataTable");`

14. Which class would you create if you wanted to determine all the properties contained in a class using reflection?

   a. `Assembly`

   b. `Class`

   c. `Property`

   d. `Type`

15. How can you determine if a class is public or private?

   a. Create an instance of the `Type` class using the `typeof` keyword and then examine the `IsPublic` property of the `Type` variable.

   b. Create an instance of the `Type` class using the `typeof` keyword and then examine the `IsPrivate` property of the `Type` variable.

   c. Create an instance of the class within a `try catch` block and catch the exception if you cannot create an instance of the class.

   d. Create an instance of the class and check the `IsPublic` property.

16. Which class in the `System.Reflection` namespace is used to represent a field defined in a class?

   a. `PropertyInfo`

   b. `FieldInfo`

   c. `Type`

   d. `EventInfo`

17. Which property of the `Type` class can you use to determine the number of dimension for an array?

   a. `GetDimension`

   b. `GetRank`

   c. `GetDimensions`

   d. `GetArrayRank`

18. Which statement will returns a private, instance field called `"myPrivateField"` using reflection? Assume the `myClass` variable is an instance of a class.

   a. `myClass.GetType().GetField("myPrivateField", BindingFlags.NonPublic | BindingFlags.Instance)`

   b. `myClass.myPrivateField`

   c. `myClass.GetType().GetField("myPrivateField")`

   d. `myClass. GetType().GetField("myPrivateField", BindingFlags.NonPublic & BindingFlags.Instance)`

19. Which method of the `MethodInfo` class can be used to execute the method?

a. `Execute`

b. `Invoke`

c. `Call`

d. `Load`

20. Which statement uses reflection to execute the method and passes in two parameters given the following code block?

```
MyClass myClass = new MyClass();
MethodInfo myMethod = typeof(MyClass).GetMethod("Multiply");
```

a. `myMethod.Execute(myClass, new object[] { 4, 5 });`

b. `myMethod.Execute(MyClass, new object[] { 4, 5 });`

c. `myMethod.Invoke(myClass, new object[] { 4, 5 });`

d. `myMethod.Invoke(MyClass, new object[] { 4, 5 });`

ADDITIONAL READING AND RESOURCES

Here are some additional useful resources to help you in your understanding of the topics presented in this chapter:

Complete list of Microsoft's System.Reflection namespace classes
http://msdn.microsoft.com/en-us/library/system.reflection(v=vs.110).aspx
Microsoft's Attribute Reference
http://msdn.microsoft.com/en-us/library/z0w1kczw(v=vs.110).aspx
Microsoft's CodeDOM Quick Reference
http://msdn.microsoft.com/en-us/library/f1dfsbhc.aspx
Microsoft's Lambda Expression description
http://msdn.microsoft.com/en-us/library/bb397687(v=vs.110).aspx
Code Project.com (a great reference site with a sample of reflection, CodeDOM, and lambda expressions)
http://www.codeproject.com/
StackOverflow.com (a great reference site for sample code)
http://www.StackOverflow.com

CHEAT SHEET

This cheat sheet is designed as a way for you to quickly study the key points of this chapter.

Reflection

➤ There are two ways to get a reference to the `Type` object, using `typeof()` or the `.GetType()` method on an object.

➤ You can use the `System.Reflection.Assembly` class to examine the types within an EXE file or DLL file.

➤ The `Assembly.Load` method loads an assembly into memory and enables you to execute code.

➤ The `Assembly.ReflectionOnlyLoad` method loads the assembly into memory, but you cannot execute any code.

➤ The `Assembly.CreateInstance` method creates an instance of a type.

➤ The `System.Type` class represents a class, interface, array, value type, enumeration, parameter, generic type definitions, and open or closed constructed generic types.

➤ The `Type.GetProperty` method returns a `PropertyInfo` object and enables you to set or get a property's value.

Attributes

➤ Attributes enable you to create metadata for a class, a property, or a method.

➤ Attributes are contained in square brackets `[]` just above the target.

➤ Custom attributes must inherit from the `System.Attribute` class.

Code Document Object Model (CodeDOM)

➤ The CodeDOM is a set of classes that enables you to create code generators.

➤ The `System.CodeDom.CodeCompileUnit` class is the top-level class; this is the container for all other object within the class you want to generate.

➤ The `System.CodeDom.CodeDOMProvider` class generates the class file in either C#, VB, or JScript.

Lambda expressions

➤ Lambda expressions are shorthand syntax for anonymous functions.

➤ A delegate is a type that references a method.

➤ Covariance enables you to have a method with a more derived return type than the delegate's return type.

➤ Contravariance permits parameter types that are less derived than the delegate type.

➤ The `=>` in a lambda expression is referred to as "goes to."

REVIEW OF KEY TERMS

anonymous method Enables you to associate a block of code with a delegate without declaring the method signature.

assembly A compiled piece of code in a DLL or EXE file.

attribute Enables you to associate metadata with assemblies, types, methods, properties, and so on.

Code Document Object Model (CodeDOM) Enables the developer to generate code in multiple languages at run time based on a single code set.

context When loading an assembly using reflection, the context is where reflection searches for the assembly.

contravariance Permits parameter types that are less derived than the delegate's parameter types.

covariance Enables you to have a method with a more derived return type than the delegate's return type.

delegate A type that references a method.

expression lambda A lambda expression that contains only one statement for the body.

Expression Tree Code in a tree-like structure where each node is an expression.

field A variable defined in a class or struct.

lambda expression Shorthand syntax for an anonymous method that can be associated with a delegate or expressions tree.

load context When loading an assembly using reflection, this context contains the assemblies found by probing.

load-from context When loading an assembly using reflection, this context contains the assemblies located in the pat passed into the `LoadFrom` method.

module A file that composes an assembly. Typically this is the DLL or EXE file.

probing The process of looking in the GAC, the host assembly store, the folder of the executing assembly, or the private bin folder of the executing assembly to find an assembly.

reflection Provides classes that can be used to read metadata or dynamically invoke behavior from a type.

reflection-only context When loading an assembly using reflection, this is the context that contains the assemblies loaded with the `ReflectionOnlyLoad` and `ReflectionOnlyLoadFrom` methods.

statement lambda A lambda expression with more than one statement in the body of the expression.

target The class, property, or method that contain metadata defined by an attribute.

type Any class, interface, array, value type, enumeration, parameter, generic type definition, and open or closed constructed generic type.

EXAM TIPS AND TRICKS

The Review of Key Terms and the Cheat Sheet for this chapter can be printed off to help you study. You can find these files in the ZIP file for this chapter at `www.wrox.com/remtitle.cgi?isbn=1118612094` on the Download Code tab.

Working with Data

WHAT YOU WILL LEARN IN THIS CHAPTER

- ➤ Working with data collections
- ➤ Consuming data
- ➤ Performing I/O operations
- ➤ Understanding serialization

WROX.COM CODE DOWNLOADS FOR THIS CHAPTER

You can find the code downloads for this chapter at `www.wrox.com/remtitle .cgi?isbn=1118612094` on the Download Code tab. The code is in the chapter09 download and individually named according to the names throughout the chapter.

Managing data is an essential part of most applications, and understanding all the options available to you is critical when studying for the test, but also for advancing your career as a developer. The first section in this chapter will explain the concept of arrays and collections. These are two options you have for managing sets of data in C#.

The second section, on consuming data, discusses accessing databases using ADO.NET, the ADO.NET Entity Framework, and WCF Data Services. ADO.NET is a set of classes in the .NET Framework that enables you to connect to a database, retrieve data, execute stored procedures, add, update, and delete records. The ADO.NET Entity Framework is an object relational mapping tool that provides a graphical user interface that generates the code for you to perform the operations against a database using ADO.NET. WCF Data Services is a feature in .NET that exposes an ADO.NET Entity Framework model so that it can be accessed over the web or an intranet.

The third section reviews I/O operations and the many choices available for reading and writing files. It also demonstrates how to read and write files asynchronously to create responsive applications during long running processes.

The final section discusses serialization and how to convert an object into binary format, XML, or JSON. This allows you to easily transform a record, or records, in a database to a format that could be used by another system or persisted to disk as a file.

Table 9-1 introduces you to the exam objectives covered in this chapter.

TABLE 9-1: 70-483 Exam Objectives Covered in This Chapter

OBJECTIVE	CONTENT COVERED
Perform I/O operations	This includes reading-and-writing files and streams either synchronously or asynchronously.
Consume data	This includes retrieving, adding, updating, and deleting data from a database. This also includes using the ADO.NET Entity Framework and WCF Data Services to expose a database to other systems.
Serialize and deserialize data	This includes how to serialize and deserialize data using binary, custom, XML, JSON, and Data Contract serialization.
Store data in and retrieve data from collections	This includes data using arrays and collections

WORKING WITH DATA COLLECTIONS

Understanding how to manipulate a series of data is critical for all types of developers. For example, drop-down lists require a set of data, reading records from a database requires a set of data, and reading a file requires storing a set of data in memory. There are many different terms peoples use to describe a series of data such as *arrays*, *sets*, *collections*, *lists*, *dictionaries*, or *queues*. They all are used to store a series of data in memory, and each offers functionality for appending, searching, and sorting the data. This section explains arrays and collections and the differences between the two. Arrays are the most primitive type in C#, with limited functionality, while collections is a general term that encompasses lists, dictionaries, queues, and other objects.

Arrays

An *array* is the most basic type used to store a set of data. An array contains elements, and they are referenced by their index using square brackets, [ ]. The following example creates a single dimensional array of integers:

```
int[] mySet = new int[5];

mySet[0] = 1;
mySet[1] = 2;
mySet[2] = 3;
mySet[3] = 4;
mySet[4] = 5;
```

When you create an array, you must specify the number of elements the array can contain. In the previous example the number of elements is 5. You can also create a multidimensional array using the following syntax:

```
int[,] mySet = new int[3, 2];

mySet[0, 0] = 1;
mySet[0, 1] = 2;
mySet[1, 0] = 3;
mySet[1, 1] = 4;
mySet[2, 0] = 5;
mySet[2, 1] = 6;
```

COMMON MISTAKES: Arrays Are Zero Based

Arrays in C# are zero based. So if you have an array with two elements, the first index is 0 and the second is 1. You may see a question regarding this in the exam.

The preceding code created a two-dimensional array with three elements in the first dimension and two elements in the second dimension. Conceptually, this is like having a table with rows and columns. The preceding code could be represented by the table shown in Figure 9-1.

1	2
3	4
5	6

FIGURE 9-1: Two-dimensional array

EXAM TIPS AND TRICKS: Declaring Multidimensional Arrays

You may see a question regarding how to declare an multidimensional array, so be sure to know that when you declare the array, the type is first and the number of dimensions is specified on the left side of the equals sign when the array is initialized.

You can create 3, 4, or 5, or up to 2,147,483,647 dimensions. You simply need to declare the variable with the number of dimensions and initialize the size of each dimension.

All arrays inherit from the base class `System.Array`. This class contains properties and methods that are useful when working with arrays. The two most commonly used properties of an array are `Length` and `Rank`. The `Length` property indicates the total number of elements in all dimensions of the array. The `Rank` property indicates the number of dimension in the array. These properties are helpful when determining the bounds of an array when doing `for` or `while` loops.

The `Clone` method is used to make a *shallow copy* of the array, while the `CopyTo` method copies the elements of the array to another array.

ADVICE FROM THE EXPERTS: Understanding Shallow Copies

It is important to understand the concept of a shallow copy. When cloning an array with reference types, you can inadvertently change the original array if you do not understand the concept of a shallow copy. Consider the following example:

```
Person[] orginal = new Person[1];

orginal[0] = new Person() { Name = "John" };

Person[] clone = (Person[])orginal.Clone();

clone[0].Name = "Mary";

Debug.WriteLine("Original name " + orginal[0].Name);
Debug.WriteLine("Clone name " + clone[0].Name);
```

In this example, the `Name` property of the first element in the clone is changed to `"Mary"`. So what would you expect the output would be? You might be surprised to learn that the output is the following:

```
Original name Mary
Clone name Mary
```

A shallow copy contains the reference to the original element in the original array. Now what would you expect the output to be given the following code?

```
Person[] orginal = new Person[1];

orginal[0] = new Person() { Name = "John" };

Person[] clone = (Person[])orginal.Clone();

clone[0] = new Person() { Name = "Bob" };

Debug.WriteLine("Original name " + orginal[0].Name);
Debug.WriteLine("Clone name " + clone[0].Name);
```

You might be surprised to learn that the output is the following:

```
Original name John
Clone name Bob
```

Notice that this time the names are different because in the cloned array the reference in the first element was replaced, but it didn't replace the reference in the first array.

Collections

Collections is a generic term for special classes in C# that are more flexible than arrays. These classes enable you to dynamically add or subtract elements after they have been initialized, associate keys for elements, automatically sort the elements, and allows for elements to be different types or type specific. Some of the classes are `List`, `List<T>`, `Dictionary`, `Dictionary<T>`, `Stack`, and `Queue`. These classes all have slightly different functionality and are explained in detail in next few sections.

The namespaces for the collection classes are `System.Collections`, `System.Collections.Generic`, and `System.Collections.Concurrent`. The classes in the `System.Collections.Concurrent` namespace are for performing safe operations for accessing the items from multiple threads and are not covered in this section of the book.

System.Collections

The `System.Collections` namespace contains classes for use when you do not have the same type of elements stored within the collection. These collections can mix `int`, string, classes, or structs within the same collection. Table 9-2 lists the types in the `System.Collections` namespace. Each of these types is discussed in more detail in the following sections.

TABLE 9-2: System.Collections

COLLECTION NAME	DESCRIPTION
ArrayList	Creates a collection whose size is dynamic and can contain any type of object
HashTable	Creates a collection with a key\value pair whose size is dynamic and contains any type of object
Queue	Creates a collection that is first-in-first-out for processing
SortedList	Creates a collection of key\value pairs whose elements are sorted by the key value
Stack	Creates a collection that is last-in-first-out for processing

ArrayList

An `ArrayList` is a class that enables you to dynamically add or remove elements to the array. This is different from the simple array, which does not enable you to change the dimensions after it is initialized. The `ArrayList` class is useful when you don't know the number of elements at the time of creation and also if you want to store different types of data in the array. In the `Array` examples, all elements of the `mySet` array had to be an `int`. An `ArrayList` has an `Add` method that takes an object as a parameter and enables you to store any type of object. The following code creates an `ArrayList` object and adds three elements of different types to the `ArrayList`:

```
ArrayList myList = new ArrayList();
```

```
myList.Add(1);
myList.Add("hello world");
myList.Add(new DateTime(2012, 01, 01));
```

Tables 9-3 and 9-4 list the most common properties and methods of the `System.Collections`
`.ArrayList` class.

TABLE 9-3: Common System.Array Properties

PROPERTY	DESCRIPTION
Capacity	Gets or sets the number of elements in the ArrayList
Count	Gets the number of actual elements in the ArrayList
Item	Gets or sets the element at the specified index

TABLE 9-4: Common System.Array Methods

METHOD	DESCRIPTION
Add	Adds an element at the end of the ArrayList
AddRange	Adds multiple elements at the end of the ArrayList
BinarySearch	Searches the sorted ArrayList for an element using the default comparer and returns the index of the element
Clear	Removes all the elements from the ArrayList
Contains	Determines if an element is in the ArrayList
CopyTo	Copies the ArrayList to a compatible one-dimensional array
IndexOf	Searches the ArrayList and returns the index of the first occurrence within the ArrayList
Insert	Inserts an element into the ArrayList at a specific index
Remove	Removes an element from the ArrayList
RemoveAt	Removes an element from the ArrayList by index
Reverse	Reverses the order of the elements in the ArrayList
Sort	Sort the elements in the ArrayList

In addition to the `Add` method, an `AddRange` method enables you to add multiple elements with one call. You can use an `Insert` method, which enables you to add an element in a specific location in the array, and a `Remove` method, which enables you to remove an element from the array. These few methods enable easier maintenance compared to a simple array type.

You can also use the Sort method, which enables you to sort the elements in the array. Consider the following example for a simple sorting exercise:

```
ArrayList myList = new ArrayList();

myList.Add(4);
myList.Add(1);
myList.Add(5);
myList.Add(3);
myList.Add(2);

myList.Sort();

foreach (int i in myList)
{
    Debug.WriteLine(i.ToString());
}
```

The preceding code can print the numbers in order to the Output window. But, what if you want to store a custom object in the array list that wasn't a simple type? For example, say you have a custom class with an ID property that stores the unique identifier for this object:

```
class MyObject
{
    public int ID{ get; set; }
}
```

Now if you were to create an ArrayList, add five instances of this class, and then call the Sort method, what do you think would happen?

```
ArrayList myList = new ArrayList();

myList.Add(new MyObject() { ID = 4 });
myList.Add(new MyObject() { ID = 1 });
myList.Add(new MyObject() { ID = 5 });
myList.Add(new MyObject() { ID = 3 });
myList.Add(new MyObject() { ID = 2 });

myList.Sort();
```

If you were to execute this code, you would get an exception on the line that calls the Sort method: Failed to Compare Two Elements in the Array. This is because the Sort method does not know what it is supposed to sort on. To fix this you can implement the *IComparable* interface in the MyObject class. The IComparable interface enables the class to be sorted.

The IComparable interface has one method called CompareTo, which takes one parameter, the object that you want to compare. The CompareTo method returns either a number less than zero, zero, or greater than zero. Less than zero indicates that the current instance is higher in the sort order; zero indicates that the two objects are equal; and greater than zero indicates that the second object is higher in the sort order.

```
class MyObject : IComparable
{
    public int ID{ get; set; }

    public int CompareTo(object obj)
    {
        MyObject obj1 = obj as MyObject;
        return this.ID.CompareTo(obj1.ID);
    }
}
```

In the preceding example, the ID property is used to sort the MyObject type. Because the ID property is defined as an int, you can use its CompareTo method to determine which object is higher in the hierarchy. If you were to execute the previous code, it would work without error.

Another common use of arrays and array lists is the ability to search the array. You can use a simple for or foreach loop to find a specific element in the array, or you can use the much quicker BinarySearch method. In order to use the BinarySearch method, you must have already sorted the elements in the ArrayList, either by calling the Sort method or explicitly adding them to the ArrayList in order; otherwise, you get unexpected results. The BinarySearch method returns the index of the element if it is found. If it is not found, it returns a negative number.

```
ArrayList myList = new ArrayList();

myList.Add(new MyObject() { ID = 4 });
myList.Add(new MyObject() { ID = 1 });
myList.Add(new MyObject() { ID = 5 });
myList.Add(new MyObject() { ID = 3 });
myList.Add(new MyObject() { ID = 2 });

myList.Sort();
int foundIndex = myList.BinarySearch(new MyObject() { ID = 4 });

if (foundIndex >= 0)
{
    Debug.WriteLine(((MyObject)myList[foundIndex]).ID.ToString());
}
else
{
    Debug.WriteLine("Element not found");
}
```

EXAM TIPS AND TRICKS: BinarySearch Prerequisites

The two important points to remember about the BinarySearch method are that the ArrayList must be sorted and the elements in the ArrayList must implement the IComparable interface.

Hashtable

A `Hashtable` enables you to store a key\value pair of any type of object. The data is stored according to the hash code of the key and can be accessed by the key rather than the index of the element. The following sample creates a `Hashtable` and stores three elements with different keys. You can then reference the elements in the `Hashtable` by its key.

```
Hashtable myHashtable = new Hashtable();

myHashtable.Add(1, "one");
myHashtable.Add("two", 2);
myHashtable.Add(3, "three");

Debug.WriteLine(myHashtable[1].ToString());
Debug.WriteLine(myHashtable["two"].ToString());
Debug.WriteLine(myHashtable[3].ToString());
```

The preceding code will produce the following output:

```
one
2
three
```

Queue

A `Queue` is a first-in-first-out collection. Queues can be useful when you need to store data in a specific order for sequential processing. The following code will create a `Queue`, add three elements, remove each element, and print its value to the Output window:

```
Queue myQueue = new Queue();

myQueue.Enqueue("first");
myQueue.Enqueue("second");
myQueue.Enqueue("third");

int count = myQueue.Count;
for (int i = 0; i < count; i++)
{
    Debug.WriteLine(myQueue.Dequeue());
}
```

Notice that instead of an `Add` method, there is an `Enqueue` method that adds the element to the `Queue`. To `Dequeue` method is used to remove an element from the `Queue`. You can't reference an element by index or key; all you can do is add, remove, or peek at the value that is on the top of the `Queue`. The `Peek` method returns the value at the top of the `Queue` but does not remove it from the `Queue`.

> **EXAM TIPS AND TRICKS: Pay Attention to the Queue Methods**
>
> You will often see a question regarding a queue on the test. Remember that you use `Enqueue` and `Dequeue`, rather than `Add` and `Remove`. Or, the test may have a question regarding a list that must be processed as first-in-first-out and ask which collection class is best suited to perform this operation.

SortedList

A `SortedList` is a collection that contains key\value pairs but it is different from a `Hashtable` because it can be referenced by the key or the index and because it is sorted. The elements in the `SortedList` are sorted by the `IComparable` implementation of the key or the `IComparer` implementation when the `SortedList` is created. The following code creates a `SortedList`, adds three elements to the list, and then prints the elements to the Output window:

```
SortedList mySortedList = new SortedList();

mySortedList.Add(3, "three");
mySortedList.Add(2, "second");
mySortedList.Add(1, "first");

foreach (DictionaryEntry item in mySortedList)
{
    Debug.WriteLine(item.Value);
}
```

The preceding code produces the following output:

```
first
second
third
```

> **COMMON MISTAKES: SortedList Order of Elements**
>
> Notice that the order of the elements was printed based on the order of the key, not the order they were added to the list. The type of variables passed to the key parameter must all be comparable with each other. If you try to add an element with an integer for a key and then add a second element with a string for a key, you would get an error because the two cannot be compared. If your list contains elements with different types for the key, use a `Hashtable`.

Stack

A `Stack` collection is a last-in-first-out collection. It is similar to a `Queue` except that the last element added is the first element retrieved. To add an element to the stack, you use the `Push` method. To remove an element from the stack, you use the `Pop` method. The following code creates a `Stack` object, adds three elements, and then removes each element and prints the value to the Output window:

```
Stack myStack = new Stack();

myStack.Push("first");
myStack.Push("second");
myStack.Push("third");

int count = myStack.Count;
for (int i = 0; i < count; i++)
{
    Debug.WriteLine(myStack.Pop());
}
```

The preceding code produces the following output:

```
third
second
first
```

You cannot access the elements in the stack by an index. All you can do is add, remove, or peek at the next element on the stack.

EXAM TIPS AND TRICKS: Pay Attention to the Stack Methods

A question about a `Stack` is another class that Microsoft likes to put on the exam. Just remember that `Push` and `Pop` are used instead of `Add` and `Remove`. Remember also that you can `Peek` at the next element, but you cannot reference an element by index.

System.Collections.Generic

The `System.Collections.Generic` namespace contains classes that are used when you know the type of data to be stored in the collection and you want all elements in the collection to be of the same type. Table 9-5 lists the types in the `System.Collections.Generic` namespace. These types are described in detail in the following sections.

TABLE 9-5: System.Collections.Generic

COLLECTION NAME	DESCRIPTION
Dictionary<TKey, TValue>	Creates a collection of key\value pairs that are of the same type
List<T>	Creates a collection of objects that are all the same type
Queue<T>	Creates a first-in-first-out collection for objects that are all the same type
SortedList<TKey, TValue>	Creates a collection of key\value pairs that are sorted based on the key and must be of the same type
Stack<T>	Creates a collection of last-in-first-out object that are all of the same type

---

BEST PRACTICES: Use Generic Type Whenever Possible

It is considered best practice to use a collection from the `Generic` namespace because they provide type-safety along with performance gains compared to the non-generic collections.

Dictionary

A `Dictionary` type enables you to store a set of elements and associate a key for each element. The key, instead of an index, is used to retrieve the element from the dictionary. This can be useful when you want to store data that comes from a table that has an Id column. You can create an object that holds the data and use the record's Id as the key.

The following example creates a class called `MyRecord`, which represents a record in a table that has three columns. A `Dictionary` is used to store multiple instances of this class. After the dictionary is loaded, you can then retrieve the elements from the dictionary using the key rather than an index.

```
class MyRecord
{
    public int ID { get; set; }
    public string FirstName { get; set; }
    public string LastName { get; set; }
}

static void Sample1()
{
    Dictionary<int, MyRecord> myDictionary = new Dictionary<int, MyRecord>();

    myDictionary.Add(5, new MyRecord() { ID = 5,
                                FirstName = "Bob",
                                LastName = "Smith" });

    myDictionary.Add(2, new MyRecord() { ID = 2,
                                FirstName = "Jane",
                                LastName = "Doe" });

    myDictionary.Add(10, new MyRecord() { ID = 10,
                                FirstName = "Bill",
                                LastName = "Jones" });

    Debug.WriteLine(myDictionary[5].FirstName);
    Debug.WriteLine(myDictionary[2].FirstName);
    Debug.WriteLine(myDictionary[10].FirstName);
}
```

The preceding code will write `"Bob"`, `"Jane"`, and `"Bill"` to the Output window.

If you want to know how many elements are in the `Dictionary` object, you use the `Count` property, unlike an `Array`, which has a `Length` property.

Table 9-6 lists the most common methods of the `System.Collections.ArrayList` class.

TABLE 9-6: Common System.Collections.Generic.Dictionary Methods

METHOD	DESCRIPTION
Add	Adds a key and value to the dictionary
Clear	Removes all the keys and values in the dictionary

METHOD	DESCRIPTION
ContainsKey	Returns true if the dictionary contains the specified key
ContainsValue	Returns true if the dictionary contains the specified value
Remove	Removes the element with the specified key

The `Dictionary` object has an `Add` method to add elements to the dictionary, a `Remove` method to remove an element, and a `Clear` method to remove all the elements from the `Dictionary`. There is also a `ContainsKey` and `ContainsValue` method that allows you to determine if an element exists in the `Dictionary` before trying to reference it.

> **BEST PRACTICES: Be Aware of Dictionary Exceptions**
>
> If you reference an element in a `Dictionary` by its key and the key isn't found, you will get an exception. It is always good practice to check the `ContainsKey` method before retrieving an element from the `Dictionary`.

List

A `List` class is a strongly typed collection of objects. It is similar to an `ArrayList` except all elements of the `List` must be of the same type. It is different from a `Dictionary` because there is no `Key`, and elements are referenced by index. When you declare the `List` object, you specify the type of elements it can contain.

```
List<int> myList = new List<int>();
```

When you add elements to the list, they must be of that type, or you get an error. The preceding code created a `List` object that can contain only `int` values.

```
myList.Add(1);
myList.Add(2);
myList.Add(3);
```

> **EXAM TIPS AND TRICKS: Know the Differences Between the Collections**
>
> You may see a question asking you which type of collection class to use based on a specific set of requirements. Remember the following points:
>
> 1. Generic collections are used when you have the same type for all elements.
> 2. `Lists` and `ArrayLists` are referenced by index and do not have a key.
> 3. `Dictionaries`, `SortedLists`, and `Hashtables` have a key\value pair.
> 4. `Queues` and `Stacks` are used when you have a specific order of processing.

The `SortedList<TKey, TValue>`, `Queue<T>`, and `Stack<T>` types are the same as their counterpart in the `System.Collections` namespace except that when you create the object, you must specify the type of data for the key or elements, and all elements must be of the same type.

Custom Collections

In addition to the standard collections provided by .NET, you can create your own custom strongly typed collections. Strongly typed collections are useful because they do not incur the performance hit due to *boxing* and *unboxing*. To create your own custom collection, you can inherit from the `CollectionBase` class. Tables 9-7 and 9-8 list the commonly used properties and method of the `CollectionBase` class.

TABLE 9-7: System.Collections.CollectionBase Properties

PROPERTY	DESCRIPTION
Capacity	Gets or sets the number of elements the collection can contain
Count	Returns the number of elements in the dictionary
InnerList	Gets an `ArrayList` containing the elements in the collection
List	Get an `IList` containing the elements in the collection

TABLE 9-8: System.Collections.CollectionBase Methods (Partial List)

METHOD	DESCRIPTION
Clear	Clears the elements from the collection
OnInsert	Enables you to perform custom processing before inserting a new element
OnRemove	Enables you to perform custom processing before removing an element
OnSet	Enables you to perform custom processing before setting a value in the collection
RemoveAt	Removes the element at the specified index

There are not `Add`, `Insert`, `Sort`, or `Search` methods in the base class. When you implement your class, you need to implement whichever methods you want to add, insert, sort, or search items within the collection.

For example, say you have a `Person` class with a few properties:

```
class Person
{
    public int PersonId { get; set; }
    public string FName { get; set; }
```

```
    public string LName { get; set; }
    public string Address { get; set; }
    public string City { get; set; }
    public string State { get; set; }
    public string ZipCode { get; set; }
}
```

You can then create a person collection class that inherits from the `CollectionBase` class. The following code creates a custom collection class for the `Person` class and creates `Add`, `Insert`, and `Remove` methods and creates a strongly typed *indexer*. The indexer is used when you reference the collection by index, such as `myCollection[index]`.

```
class PersonCollection : CollectionBase
{
    public void Add(Person person)
    {
        List.Add(person);
    }
    public void Insert(int index, Person person)
    {
        List.Insert(index, person);
    }
    public void Remove(Person person)
    {
        List.Remove(person);
    }
    public Person this[int index]
    {
        get
        {
            return (Person)List[index];
        }

        set
        {
            List[index] = value;
        }
    }
}
```

Now that you have a strongly typed `PersonCollection` class, you can use it in your code:

```
static void Main(string[] args)
{
    PersonCollection persons = new PersonCollection();

    persons.Add(new Person() {
        PersonId = 1,
        FName = "John",
        LName = "Smith" });

    persons.Add(new Person()
    {
        PersonId = 2,
        FName = "Jane",
```

```
            LName = "Doe" });

        persons.Add(new Person()
        {
            PersonId = 3,
            FName = "Bill Jones",
            LName = "Smith" });

        foreach (Person person in persons)
        {
            Debug.WriteLine(person.FName);
        }

    }
```

The preceding code creates an instance of the `PersonCollection` class, adds three objects to the class, and then enumerates through the collection and prints the element's value to the Output window.

REAL-WORLD CASE SCENARIO   **Populating a drop-down list from a generic list**

One of the most common uses of `ArrayLists`, `Lists`, or `Dictionaries` is to populate a drop-down list in a Windows Form or Web Form. Create an ASP.NET web page with a drop-down list. Next, create a class with an `Id` and a `Name` and then create a `List<T>` object and populate the drop-down list with the items in the list.

Solution

1. Create a new Empty Web Application using Visual Studio 2012. Add a new Web Form to the project and drag a drop-down list control onto the Web Form. The name of the drop-down list will default to `DropDownList1`.

2. Add a class to the application that contains the following code:

```
public class MyRecord
{
    public int Id { get; set; }
    public string Name { get; set; }
}
```

This class has an `Id` property and a `Name` property. The `Id` will be stored in the `Value` attribute of the drop-down `ListItem`. The `Name` property will be set to the text of the `ListItem` in the drop-down list.

3. Add the following code to the `Page_Load` event in the code behind the page of the Web Form:

```
List<MyRecord> myRecordList = new List<MyRecord>();

myRecordList.Add(new MyRecord() { Id = 1, Name = "John" });
myRecordList.Add(new MyRecord() { Id = 2, Name = "Sue" });
myRecordList.Add(new MyRecord() { Id = 3, Name = "Jack" });
```

```
DropDownList1.DataSource = myRecordList;
DropDownList1.DataTextField = "Name";
DropDownList1.DataValueField = "Id";
DropDownList1.DataBind();
```

This code creates a generic list object called `myRecordList`. This list can only contain object that are of the type `MyRecord`. Next, three items are added to the list using the `Add` method. Next, the `DataSource` property of the drop-down list control is set to the `myRecordList`. Now that the control knows where to get the data from, you need to tell it which property should be used as the text and as the value for the list items. The `DataTextField` property must be set to the `Name` property of the `MyRecord` class. The `DataValueField` property specifies which property should be used for the value field; in this instance, the `Id` property. The last step is to call the `DataBind` method, which generates the HTML for a drop-down list control and creates a `ListItem` for each element in the `myRecordList` object.

CONSUMING DATA

This section explains how to retrieve data from a database using ADO.NET, the Entity Framework, or a WCF Data Service. Many applications store information in a database and retrieve the data using one of these methods, and then store the data in memory using the arrays or collections.

Working with ADO.NET

ADO.NET is a set of classes in the .NET Framework that enables you to connect to a database; insert, update, select, or delete records from a table; execute store procedures; or perform data definition language statements. Almost all applications use databases, so you must understand the concepts surrounding ADO.NET.

The ADO.NET types are located in the `System.Data` namespace. There are numerous base classes and interfaces defined in this namespace that a data provider must implement to allow ADO.NET to access a database. For example, the `System.Data.SqlClient` namespace contains the types that implement the ADO.NET base classes and interfaces to connect to a SQL Server database. Oracle, MySQL, and other major database systems all have their own namespace and classes that implement the ADO.NET base classes and interfaces. This enables you to use consistent syntax across all databases. This section uses the classes defined in the `System.Data.SqlClient` namespace.

Connection

A *connection object* is used to open up a line of communication with a database. The `SqlConnection` object is used to connect to a SQL Server database. This class, along with any provider's connection class, inherits from the `System.Data.Common.DBConnection` class. Table 9-9 lists the most common properties for the `DBConnection` class.

TABLE 9-9: Common System.Data.Common.DBConnection Properties

PROPERTY	DESCRIPTION
ConnectionString	Gets or sets the string used to open a connection to a database
ConnectionTimeout	Gets the time in seconds that the system should wait while establishing a connection to the database before generating an error
Database	Gets the name of the database
DataSource	Gets the name of the database server
ServerVersion	Gets the server version for the database
State	Gets a string that represents the state of the connection such as Open or Closed

The most important property to take note of is the ConnectionString property. This tells the connection object which server and database to connect to. For SQL Server a connection string has the following syntax.

```
Server=myServerAddress;Database=myDataBase;User Id=myUsername;Password=myPassword;
```

ADVICE FROM THE EXPERTS: Connection Strings

Each provider has slight variations on the settings within the connection string. http://www.ConnectionStrings.com is a great resource for determining the different syntax for connection strings for many different types of databases.

Table 9-10 lists the most important methods for the DBConnection class.

TABLE 9-10: System.Data.Common.DBConnection Methods (Partial List)

METHOD	DESCRIPTION
BeginTransaction	Begins a database transaction
Close	Closes the connection to the database
GetSchema	Returns a DataTable that contains the schema information for the data source
Open	Opens the database connection using the connection string

The Open method is used to establish a connection to the database. After you have a connection, you can then use this object along with the other ADO.NET objects to execute commands against the database. The following code creates an instance of the `SqlConnection` object, sets the `ConnectionString` property, and opens a connection to the database:

```
SqlConnection cn = new SqlConnection();
cn.ConnectionString = "Server=myServerAddress;Database=myDataBase;
                       User Id=myUsername;Password=myPassword;";
cn.Open();
```

Command

A `Command` object is used to execute statements against a database. You can execute insert, update, delete, select, or stored procedures using the command object. The `System.Data.Common.DBCommand` class is the base class for all provider `Command` classes. The `System.Data.SqlClient.SqlCommand` class is SQL Server's implementation of the `DBCommand` class.

ExecuteNonQuery Method

The `ExecuteNonQuery` method is used to execute statements against the database that do not return resultsets. For example, an insert, update, or delete statement does not return any records. They simply execute the statement against a table. The following code demonstrates how to execute an `insert` statement against the database:

```
SqlConnection cn = new SqlConnection();
cn.ConnectionString = "Server=myServerAddress;Database=myDataBase;
                       User Id=myUsername;Password=myPassword;";
cn.Open();

SqlCommand cmd = new SqlCommand();
cmd.Connection = cn;
cmd.CommandType = CommandType.Text;
cmd.CommandText = "INSERT INTO Person (FirstName, LastName) " +
                  "VALUES ('Joe', 'Smith')";
cmd.ExecuteNonQuery();

cn.Close();
```

Notice the three properties of the command object that had to be set before calling the `ExecuteNonQuery` method. The first is the `Connection` property. This must be set to an open connection. This tells the command object what database to use when executing the text contained in the `CommandText` property. In this sample you use inline SQL, which is why the `CommandType` property is set to `CommandType.Text`.

If you used a stored procedure to insert a `Person` record, you would need to change the `CommandType` to `CommandType.StoredProcedure` and set the `CommandText` to the name of the stored procedure. For example, assume you have the following stored procedure that inserts a record into the `Person` table:

```
CREATE PROCEDURE PersonInsert
    @FirstName varchar(50),
    @LastName varchar(50)
AS
BEGIN
    INSERT INTO PERSON (FirstName, LastName) VALUES (@FirstName, @LastName)
END
```

The following code executes the stored procedure and passes in the `@FirstName` and `@LastName` parameters:

```
SqlConnection cn = new SqlConnection();
cn.ConnectionString = "Server=myServerAddress;Database=myDataBase;
                       User Id=myUsername;Password=myPassword;";
cn.Open();

SqlCommand cmd = new SqlCommand();
cmd.Connection = cn;
cmd.CommandType = CommandType.StoredProcedure;
cmd.CommandText = "PersonInsert";
cmd.Parameters.Add(new SqlParameter("@FirstName", "Joe"));
cmd.Parameters.Add(new SqlParameter("@LastName", "Smith"));
cmd.ExecuteNonQuery();
```

The `Command` object has a `Parameters` property that you use to pass parameters to the stored procedure. Also note that the `ExecuteNonQuery` method returns the number of rows affected by the query. In this example, 1 is returned, but if you have an `Update` or `Delete` statement, you can determine the number of records affected by the query using the return value.

ExecuteReader Method

Use the `ExecuteReader` method to retrieve results from the database such as when you use a `Select` statement. The `ExecuteReader` returns a `DBDataReader` object. The `DBDataReader` object is another class defined in ADO.NET. A `DBDataReader` object is a forward-only resultset that remains connected to the database the entire time the reader is open. Forward-only means that you can traverse only through the records once, and you cannot move the cursor back to any previous record. The following code prints all the records in the `Person` table to the output window using a `DBDataReader` object. The return object is declared as a `SqlDataReader` because that is SQL Server's implementation of the `DBDataReader` class.

```
SqlConnection cn = new SqlConnection();
cn.ConnectionString = "Server=myServerAddress;Database=myDataBase;
                       User Id=myUsername;Password=myPassword;";
cn.Open();

SqlCommand cmd = new SqlCommand();
cmd.Connection = cn;
cmd.CommandType = CommandType.Text;
cmd.CommandText = "SELECT * FROM Person";
SqlDataReader dr = cmd.ExecuteReader();

if (dr.HasRows)
{
    while (dr.Read())
    {
        Debug.WriteLine(string.Format("First Name: {0} , Last Name: {1}",
                                dr["FirstName"], dr["LastName"]));
    }
}
dr.Close();
cn.Close();
```

You must call the Close method on the DBDataReader object and then close the Connection object. If you don't you can be left with orphaned open connections, which can hurt performance. The ExecuteReader method is overloaded and can take a parameter of type CommandBehavior that tells ADO.NET to close the connection automatically when the reader is closed.

> **BEST PRACTICES: Closing Connections in C#**
>
> There are two ways to close a connection in C#. First is to call the Close method, and second is to use a using statement. A using statement defines a scope for the object that is declared and automatically disposes of the object once the object is out of scope. The syntax for a using statement that defines a scope for a connection is as follows:
>
> ```
> using (SqlConnection cn = new SqlConnection())
> {
>
> }
> ```
>
> The open and close brackets, {}, define the scope for the connection. When the connection is disposed, it is closed.

Table 9-11 lists commonly used properties of the DBDataReader class.

TABLE 9-11: Commonly used Properties for System.Data.Common.DBDataReader

PROPERTY	DESCRIPTION
FieldCount	Returns the number of columns on the current row.
HasRows	Returns a boolean indicating if the reader has any rows.
IsClosed	Returns a boolean indicating if the reader is closed.
Item[Int32]	This is an indexer that returns the column based on the index.
Item[String]	This is an indexer that returns the column based on the name of the column.

There isn't a Count property for the number of rows in the resultset. The only way to get the count is to traverse through the datareader. The indexers, which are the Item properties, return an object. They enable you to get the value of a column either by column index or by name. It is up to you to cast the object to the right type when using the indexers.

> **COMMON MISTAKES: null Versus DBNull.Value**
>
> Be aware that if a column contains a null value, the object returned from the indexer is not null; it is DBNull.Value. This can be the cause of many bugs if you do not understand the difference between the two.

Table 9-12 lists commonly used methods for the DBDataReader class.

TABLE 9-12: Commonly used method for the System.Data.Common.DBDataReader

METHOD	DESCRIPTION
Close	Closes the object
GetBoolean	Returns the value of the specified column as a boolean
GetByte	Returns the value of the specified column as a byte
GetChar	Returns the value of the specified column as a character
GetDateTime	Returns the value of the specified column as a DateTime object
GetDecimal	Returns the value of the specified column as a Decimal object
GetDouble	Returns the value of the specified column as a double object
GetFieldType	Returns the data type of the specified column
GetFieldValue<T>	Returns the value of the specified column as a type
GetFloat	Returns the value of the specified column as a single object
GetGuid	Returns the value of the specified column as a GUID
GetInt16	Returns the value of the specified column as a 16-bit integer
GetInt32	Returns the value of the specified column as a 32-bit integer
GetInt64	Returns the value of the specified column as a 64-bit integer
GetName	Returns the name of the specified column given the ordinal position
GetOrdinal	Returns the ordinal position of a column given the column name
GetSchemaTable	Returns a DataTable that describes the column metadata
GetString	Returns the value of the specified column as a string
GetValue	Returns the value of the specified column as an object
GetValues	Populates an array of objects with the values of the columns
NextResult	Moves the cursor to the next resultset in the reader
IsDBNull	Returns a boolean to indicate if the specified column contains a null value
Read	Advances the cursor to the next record

Numerous GetTYPE methods enable you to use a column index to get the value from the data reader and casts the value to the specified type. This works only with column indexes and not names. If the order in your SELECT clause changes, your indexes must also change.

The Read method moves to the next record in the resultset if it exists. It returns true if there is another record and false after it reaches the end of the resultset. There is also a HasRows property, which returns a boolean to tell you if there are rows in the resultset.

BEST PRACTICES: Prevent Errors When Reading a Records

It is always good practice to check the HasRows property before calling the Read method because if there aren't any rows in the resultset and you call the Read method, you get an exception.

When retrieving data from a database, you can save trips by executing multiple SELECT statements in a single call. The DBDataReader has the capability to hold multiple resultsets in a single object. To move to the next resultset, you simply call the NextResult method.

The GetSchemaTable method returns a DataTable that contains the metadata about the columns in the DBDataReader. The returned table with the schema has a row for each column that contains columns for the column name, the column type, the column size, the ordinal position, whether it is an Identity column, and whether the column enables nulls. If all you need is the schema for a query rather than the data, you can call the ExecuteDataReader method and pass in CommandBehavior.SchemaOnly.

ExecuteScalar Method

The ExecuteScalar method is used when you know that your resultset contains only a single column with a single row. This is great when your query returns the result of an aggregate function such as SUM or AVG. The following code calls the ExecuteScalar method and returns the Count of records in the Person table:

```
SqlConnection cn = new SqlConnection();
cn.ConnectionString = "Server=myServerAddress;Database=myDataBase;
                       User Id=myUsername;Password=myPassword;";
cn.Open();

SqlCommand cmd = new SqlCommand();
cmd.Connection = cn;
cmd.CommandType = CommandType.Text;
cmd.CommandText = "SELECT COUNT(*) FROM Person";
object obj = cmd.ExecuteScalar();

Debug.WriteLine(string.Format("Count: {0}", obj.ToString()));

cn.Close();
```

The ExecuteScalar method always returns an object, so it is up to you to cast this value to the right type when you want to use the value.

ExecuteXmlReader Method

The `ExecuteXmlReader` method returns an `XMLReader`, which enables you to represent the data as XML. The following code returns the data from the `Person` table into an `XmlReader` object:

```
SqlConnection cn = new SqlConnection();
cn.ConnectionString = "Server=myServerAddress;Database=myDataBase;
                       User Id=myUsername;Password=myPassword;";
cn.Open();

SqlCommand cmd = new SqlCommand();
cmd.Connection = cn;
cmd.CommandType = CommandType.Text;
cmd.CommandText = "SELECT * FROM Person FOR XML AUTO, XMLDATA";
System.Xml.XmlReader xml = cmd.ExecuteXmlReader();

cn.Close();
```

The SQL statement was changed and included the FOR XML AUTO, XMLDATA clause. The XML result for this query follows:

```
<Schema name="Schema1" xmlns="urn:schemas-microsoft-com:xml-data"
 xmlns:dt="urn:schemas-microsoft-com:datatypes">
  <ElementType name="Person" content="empty" model="closed">
    <AttributeType name="PersonId" dt:type="i4"/>
    <AttributeType name="FirstName" dt:type="string"/>
    <AttributeType name="LastName" dt:type="string"/>
    <AttributeType name="Address" dt:type="string"/>
    <AttributeType name="City" dt:type="string"/>
    <AttributeType name="State" dt:type="string"/>
    <AttributeType name="ZipCode" dt:type="string"/>
    <attribute type="PersonId"/>
    <attribute type="FirstName"/>
    <attribute type="LastName"/>
    <attribute type="Address"/>
    <attribute type="City"/>
    <attribute type="State"/>
    <attribute type="ZipCode"/>
  </ElementType>
</Schema>
<Person xmlns="x-schema:#Schema1" PersonId="1" FirstName="John" LastName="Smith"
Address="123 First Street" City="Philadelphia" State="PA" ZipCode="19111"/>
```

Notice that the schema is returned along with the data in this example.

DataSet, DataTable, and DataAdapter

Another way to retrieve results from a database is to use `DataSets` and `DataTables`. A `DataTable` is similar to a `DBDataReader` except that it is disconnected from the database; you can move the cursor back and forth; and you can update data in the `DataTable`, reconnect to the database, and commit the changes. A `DataSet` is a container for one or more `DataTables`. You can execute a SQL statement that returns multiple resultsets, and each can be contained in the `DataSet`. You can then filter, sort, or update the data in memory. The `DataAdapter` is the object used to populate a `DataSet` or `DataTable` and also the reconnect to the database to perform insert, update, or delete commands.

The following code uses a `DataSet` to retrieve the data from the `Person` table and write all the records to the Output window:

```
SqlConnection cn = new SqlConnection();
cn.ConnectionString = "Server=myServerAddress;Database=myDataBase;
                       User Id=myUsername;Password=myPassword;";
cn.Open();

SqlDataAdapter da = new SqlDataAdapter("SELECT * FROM Person", cn);

DataSet ds = new DataSet();
da.Fill(ds, "Person");

cn.Close();

foreach (DataRow row in ds.Tables[0].Rows)
{
    Debug.WriteLine(string.Format("First Name: {0} , Last Name: {1}",
                         row["FirstName"], row["LastName"]));
}
```

In this example, the constructor of the `SqlDataAdapter` was passed the SQL statement to execute when calling the `Fill` method. The `Fill` method is used to populate the `DataSet`. Notice that after the `Fill` method was called that the `Connection` was closed, but the `DataSet` was still available for use. You cannot do this with a `DBDataReader` because it is connected to the database.

The `DataSet` object has a `Tables` property that you can use to reference the `DataTable` objects returned from your query. In this example there was only one resultset returned, so you can reference it by using the zero index of the `Tables` property. `DataTables` has a `Rows` property, which contains a collection of `DataRow` objects that contains the records. You can reference the records by row index or enumerate through them with a loop. The `Rows` collection also has a `Count` property, which can tell you the number of rows in the `DataTable`. This is also a different from the `DBDataReader` because you can move back and forth between rows.

The `DataAdapter` class enables you to insert, update, or delete rows after you have changed the underlying `DataTable` in your dataset. The following example shows you how to use the `DataAdapter` to insert records into a database.

CODE LAB **Use a DataAdapter to add a record to a table [ADONETSamples.cs]**

The following code demonstrates how to use a `DataAdapter` to add a new record to a table. You must have a database with a table named Person with a PersonId, FirstName, and LastName column.

```
SqlConnection cn = new SqlConnection();
cn.ConnectionString = "Server=myServerAddress;Database=myDataBase;
                       User Id=myUsername;Password=myPassword;";
cn.Open();

SqlDataAdapter da = new SqlDataAdapter("SELECT * FROM Person", cn);

//Create the insert command
```

```
SqlCommand insert = new SqlCommand();
insert.Connection = cn;
insert.CommandType = CommandType.Text;
insert.CommandText = "INSERT INTO Person (FirstName, LastName) VALUES (@FirstName,
                      @LastName)";

//Create the parameters
insert.Parameters.Add(new SqlParameter("@FirstName", SqlDbType.VarChar, 50,
                                        "FirstName"));
insert.Parameters.Add(new SqlParameter("@LastName", SqlDbType.VarChar, 50,
                                        "LastName"));

//Associate the insert command with the DataAdapter.
da.InsertCommand = insert;

//Get the data.
DataSet ds = new DataSet();
da.Fill(ds, "Person");

//Add a new row.
DataRow newRow = ds.Tables[0].NewRow();
newRow["FirstName"] = "Jane";
newRow["LastName"] = "Doe";
ds.Tables[0].Rows.Add(newRow);

//Update the database.
da.Update(ds.Tables[0]);

cn.Close();
```

Code Lab Analysis

The DataAdapter has an InsertCommand property that must be set to a DBCommand object. The DBCommand object can be associated with a stored procedure or dynamic SQL. In this sample the insert command is associated with dynamic SQL. This is accomplished by setting the CommandType to CommandType.Text and the CommandText to a valid INSERT statement. Notice that the INSERT statement has two parameters, @FirstName and @LastName. You have to add these parameters to the DBCommand's Parameters property and specify the column name that should be used for that parameter. In this example the column names are FirstName and LastName respectively.

The code sample uses the NewRow method of the DataTable object to obtain a reference to a DataRow object that has all the fields in the table. After you set the value of the columns, you can then add the DataRow to the DataTable using the DataTable.Rows.Add method. Calling the Update method of the DataAdapter can trigger ADO.NET to look at any added, updated, or deleted records and call the corresponding command. In this example only records were added so that the InsertCommand is called.

The next code lab demonstrates how to use the DeleteCommand and UpdateCommand.

Update and delete records using the DbDataAdapter [ADONETSamples.cs]

This code lab will demonstrate how to use the `UpdateCommand` property of a `DbDataAdapter` object to update a record, and also how the use the `DeleteCommand` property of a `DbDataAdapter` to delete a record.

```csharp
SqlConnection cn = new SqlConnection();
cn.ConnectionString = "Server=myServerAddress;Database=myDataBase;
                       User Id=myUsername;Password=myPassword;";
cn.Open();

SqlDataAdapter da = new SqlDataAdapter("SELECT * FROM Person", cn);

//Create the update command
SqlCommand update = new SqlCommand();
update.Connection = cn;
update.CommandType = CommandType.Text;
update.CommandText = "UPDATE Person SET FirstName = @FirstName, LastName = @LastName
                      WHERE PersonId = @PersonId";

//Create the parameters
update.Parameters.Add(new SqlParameter("@FirstName", SqlDbType.VarChar, 50,
                                       "FirstName"));
update.Parameters.Add(new SqlParameter("@LastName", SqlDbType.VarChar, 50,
                                       "LastName"));
update.Parameters.Add(new SqlParameter("@PersonId", SqlDbType.Int, 0, "PersonId"));

//Create the delete command
SqlCommand delete = new SqlCommand();
delete.Connection = cn;
delete.CommandType = CommandType.Text;
delete.CommandText = "DELETE FROM Person WHERE PersonId = @PersonId";

//Create the parameters
SqlParameter deleteParameter = new SqlParameter("@PersonId", SqlDbType.Int, 0,
                                                "PersonId");
deleteParameter.SourceVersion = DataRowVersion.Original;
delete.Parameters.Add(deleteParameter);

//Associate the update and delete commands with the DataAdapter.
da.UpdateCommand = update;
da.DeleteCommand = delete;

//Get the data.
DataSet ds = new DataSet();
da.Fill(ds, "Person");

//Update the first row
ds.Tables[0].Rows[0]["FirstName"] = "Jack";
ds.Tables[0].Rows[0]["LastName"] = "Johnson";
```

```
//Delete the second row.
ds.Tables[0].Rows[1].Delete();

//Updat the database.
da.Update(ds.Tables[0]);

cn.Close();
```

Code Analysis

Notice that the `UpdateCommand` and `DeleteCommand` properties are set to different command objects that contain the logic for updating and deleting records. The `DbDataAdapter` logic will automatically execute the command object according to which function it should perform. Be sure to put the right logic in your command objects, because the `DbDataAdapter` is just going to execute the command; it does not check that it actually does the correct work.

Working with the ADO.NET Entity Framework

The *ADO.NET Entity Framework* is a set of classes within the .NET Framework that also enables you to add, insert, update, and delete data within a database. The Entity Framework has a graphical user interface that enables you to drag and drop objects from a database onto a design surface. This is called an *Object-Relational Mapping tool*, or *ORM tool*. There are many different ORM tools on the market. The Entity Framework and LINQ to SQL are just two examples that Microsoft has created for use within Visual Studio. There are other vendors that create ORM tools for other databases and other languages such as NHibernate, CakePHP, and ActiveRecord, just to name a few.

The sample code in this section uses the Northwinds database, which is a sample database provided by CodePlex.com. You can download the database from `http://northwinddatabase.codeplex.com/` and restore the backup file to your SQL Server.

Create an Entity Framework Model

At the core of the Entity Framework is the Model. The Model contains all of the classes that represent an object in the database. Follow these steps to create an Entity Framework Model by mapping the Northwinds database:

1. Launch Visual Studio 2012.
2. Click New Project from the Start Page.
3. Select Console Application from the list of installed C# templates.
4. Name the project **NorthwindsConsole**, and click the OK button.
5. Right-click the project in the Solution Explorer, click Add. Then select New Item from the pop-up menu.
6. Select ADO.NET Entity Data Model from the list of installed C# templates.
7. Change the Name to **NorthwindsModel**, and click the Add button. The Entity Data Model Wizard appears.

8. Because you already have the database, select the Generate from Database option. This approach is called Database First. An alternative approach is called Model First, which enables you to create all your classes in the model first and then generate a database from the model.

9. Click the Next button. The next page asks for the database connection.

10. Click the New Connection button. The Choose Data Source dialog appears.

11. Select Microsoft SQL Server from the list of data sources, and click the Continue button. The Connection Properties dialog appears.

12. Enter the name of the server where you created the Northwinds database.

13. You can either use Windows Authentication or a SQL Server Authentication to connect to the database. If you select SQL Server Authentication, you need to enter a valid SQL Login and Password.

14. Select the Northwinds database from the Select or Enter a Database Name list.

15. Click the OK button. This brings you back to the Entity Data Model Wizard. By default the connection string will be stored in an `app.config` file within your project.

16. Click the Next button. This screen enables you to select the objects in the database that you want to map. Select the check boxes next to Tables, Views, and Stored Procedures from the list, and leave the other settings unchanged. Click the Finish button.

The Entity Data Model Wizard automatically generates the Model (see Figure 9-2).

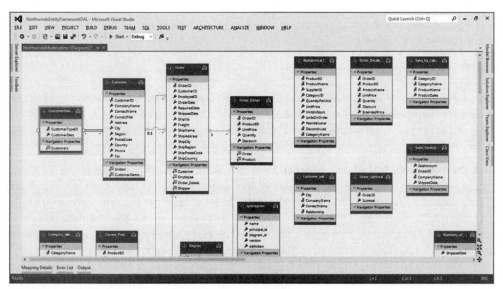

FIGURE 9-2: Northwinds Model - Entity Framework Designer

The NorthwindsModel.edmx file was added to your project in the Solution Explorer. This file is the graphical representation of all the classes that were created to represent the objects in the database.

Click the arrow next to the NorthwindsModel.edmx file in the Solution Explore to view all the files that were created for you.

Notice the file called NorthwindsModel.tt. This is a *Text Transformation Template Toolkit* file, also known as a T4 template. A *T4 template* file is used to automatically generate code within Visual Studio. T4 templates are a mixture of text blocks and control statements that enable you to generate a code file. Click the arrow next to the NorthwindsModel.tt file to expand the list of files generated by this template. A file was created for each table, view, and stored procedure that returns a resultset.

Click the Category.cs file. This file contains a class that maps to the Category table in the Northwinds database. There is a property for each column in the table. There is also a property called `Products`, which is of type `ICollection<Product>`. The reason why this property was created is because there is a foreign key in the Products table that references the Category table. Categories can have many products associated with it. The Entity Framework Wizard was smart enough to recognize this and generated these properties for you.

Click the Category_Sales_for_1997.cs file. This maps to the Category_Sales_for_1997 view in the database. The class file that was generated maps to the columns in the query of the view.

Click the CustOrderHist_Results.cs file. This class was created to represent the columns that are returned from the `CustOrderHist` stored procedure. The `CustOrderHist` stored procedure is defined as follows:

```
CREATE PROCEDURE [dbo].[CustOrderHist] @CustomerID nchar(5)
AS
SELECT ProductName, Total=SUM(Quantity)
FROM Products P, [Order Details] OD, Orders O, Customers C
WHERE C.CustomerID = @CustomerID
AND C.CustomerID = O.CustomerID
AND O.OrderID = OD.OrderID
AND OD.ProductID = P.ProductID
GROUP BY ProductName
```

This procedure returns two columns: `ProductName` and `Total`. Notice that the `CustOrderHist_Result` class has two properties, `ProductName` and `Total`. So as you can see, the Entity Data Model Wizard saves you from writing these classes and is smart enough to read the definition of a view or a stored procedure to create a class that can be used to represent the resultset of either.

Now click the NorthwindsModel.Context.tt file in the Solution Explorer. This is the T4 Template for the `Context` object. Think of the `Context` object as the class that represents the entire database. If you click the arrow next to the NorthwindsModel.Context.tt file, you can see one file, NorthwindsModel.Context.cs. This is the class that was created by the T4 Template. Open the NorthwindsModel.Context.cs file by clicking it. The class name is NorthwindsEntities and has properties for each table contained in the database. The properties are generic `DbSet` types, which is a collection of the each type that represents a table or view. A few of the properties that were created are listed here:

```
public DbSet<Category> Categories { get; set; }
public DbSet<CustomerDemographic> CustomerDemographics { get; set; }
public DbSet<Customer> Customers { get; set; }
public DbSet<Employee> Employees { get; set; }
public DbSet<Order_Detail> Order_Details { get; set; }
```

The stored procedures are created as methods. After the properties are defined, there is a list of methods that have the same name as the stored procedures in the database. Any parameters to the stored procedures are parameters to the method. If a store procedure returns a resultset, the return value of the method is an `ObjectResult` collection of that type. For example, the `CustOrderHist` stored procedure is created as the following method:

```
public virtual ObjectResult<CustOrderHist_Result> CustOrderHist(string customerID)
{
    var customerIDParameter = customerID != null ?
        new ObjectParameter("CustomerID", customerID) :
        new ObjectParameter("CustomerID", typeof(string));

    return ((IObjectContextAdapter)this).ObjectContext.ExecuteFunction
            <CustOrderHist_Result>("CustOrderHist", customerIDParameter);

}
```

The `CustOrderHist_Result` class is the type for the return set. The stored procedure had one string parameter for the customer ID, so the method has one parameter for the customer ID. To call the stored procedure, the `ExecuteFunction` method is called, which is a method contained in the `NorthwindEntities` base class, `DbContext`. The `DbContext` class is defined in the `System.Data .Entity` namespace, and this is like an ADO.NET connection object on steroids. This class has methods for executing commands against the database and behind the scenes is using ADO.NET to do the heavy lifting. The gory details are spared from you, and everything is automatically generated by running the wizard.

Select Records

Now that you have a Model, you can use it to make calls to the database without having to know anything about SQL syntax. Follow the next set of instructions to select the records from the Category table, and print them to the Output window.

Open the `Program.cs` file in the designer, and add the following using statements:

```
using System.Diagnostics;
```

Add the following code to the `Main` method:

```
using (NorthwindsEntities db = new NorthwindsEntities())
{
    var categories = from c in db.Categories
                        select c;

    foreach (Category category in categories)
    {
        Debug.WriteLine(string.Format("CategoryId: {0}, CategoryName: {1}",
                                category.CategoryID,
                                category.CategoryName));
    }
}
```

Run the project and the following will be printed to the Output window:

```
CategoryId: 1, CategoryName: Beverages
CategoryId: 2, CategoryName: Condiments
CategoryId: 3, CategoryName: Confections
CategoryId: 4, CategoryName: Dairy Products
CategoryId: 5, CategoryName: Grains/Cereals
CategoryId: 6, CategoryName: Meat/Poultry
CategoryId: 7, CategoryName: Produce
CategoryId: 8, CategoryName: Seafood
```

As you can see it took only a few lines of code to get the records, and you didn't have to write any SQL queries. Everything is handled for you by the Entity Framework. In this example the db variable is declared as a `NorthwindsEntities` type. A LINQ query is used to retrieve the data from the database and retrieve the results in the `categories` variable. Notice that you write the query using C# syntax. The Entity Framework classes know how to convert that to a SQL query for you behind the scenes. When the data is retrieved, you can then enumerate through the `categories` to write each record to the Output window.

Earlier it was pointed out that the Products table had a foreign key to the Categories table. The `Product` class that is generated by the Entity Data Model Wizard created a property to represent this relationship.

```
public virtual Category Category { get; set; }
```

The following code sample shows you how to write a LINQ query to join the two tables and write the product name and the category name to the Output window:

```
using (NorthwindsEntities db = new NorthwindsEntities())
{
    var products = from c in db.Categories
                   join p in db.Products on c.CategoryID equals p.CategoryID
                   select p;

    foreach (Product product in products)
    {
        Debug.WriteLine(string.Format("ProductName: {0}, CategorName: {1}",
                        product.ProductName,
                        product.Category.CategoryName));
    }
}
```

In this example instead of selecting the `Category` object, it selects the `Products` object. The Entity Framework retrieves the correct columns and populate the properties of the `Products` class, and as you can see, it also populates the `Category` property, which is a `Categories` class.

Insert Records

Inserting records into a database with the Entity Framework is simple. The following code sample inserts a record in the `Categories` table:

```
using (NorthwindsEntities db = new NorthwindsEntities())
{
    Category category = new Category()
```

```
    {
        CategoryName = "Alcohol",
        Description = "Happy Beverages"
    };

    db.Categories.Add(category);
    db.SaveChanges();
}
```

This code created an instance of the Category class and initialized its properties. It then added the object to the Categories property of the NorthwindsEntities. The SaveChanges() method is then called to add the record to the database. Again, there was no SQL syntax needed; the Entity Framework handled all that behind the scenes.

Update Records

Updating records is just as trivial. The following code sample retrieves the Category with the name Alcohol, changes its description, and then updates the record in the database:

```
Category category = db.Categories.First(c => c.CategoryName == "Alcohol");
category.Description = "Happy People";
db.SaveChanges();
```

Delete Records

You can also delete records by using just a few lines of code.

```
using (NorthwindsEntities db = new NorthwindsEntities())
{
    Category category = db.Categories.First(c => c.CategoryName == "Alcohol");
    db.Categories.Remove(category);
    db.SaveChanges();
}
```

In Entity Framework 5.0 you use the Remove method. In previous versions the method was called DeleteObject.

Call a Stored Procedure

As previously shown, all the stored procedures were created as methods in the NorthwindsEntities class by the Entity Data Model Wizard. To call a stored procedure, you simply need to call the method. The following code sample calls the CustOrderHist stored procedure, passes in a customer ID, and then prints the orders to the Output window:

```
using (NorthwindsEntities db = new NorthwindsEntities())
{
    var custOrderHist = db.CustOrderHist("ALFKI");

    foreach (CustOrderHist_Result result in custOrderHist)
    {
        Debug.WriteLine(string.Format("ProductName: {0}, Total: {1}",
                                      result.ProductName, result.Total));
    }
}
```

As you can see, all the heavy lifting is done for you by the Entity Framework, but it is still important to understand what is going on behind the scenes with ADO.NET to become a more complete developer.

Creating WCF Data Services

WCF Data Services is a component of the .NET Framework that enables you to access a database over the web or an intranet using a URI. In previous versions of .NET, this was called ADO.NET Data Services. You can select, filter, add, update, and even delete data using a URI and query string parameters. The WCF Data Services use the *Open Data Protocol*, OData, which is a web protocol that uses HTTP. For example, the following request can be made to a WCF Data Service that exposes the Categories table from the Northwinds database.

```
http://localhost/WcfDataService1.svc/Categories?$filter=CategoryName eq 'Beverages'
```

In this example, `Categories` specifies the entity to return, and the `filter` parameter in the querystring is used to find the category with the name 'Beverages'. In the example the filter is set to `CategoryName eq 'Beverages'`. The spaces are allowed in the query string. You can choose to have the data returned as either XML, in which case it follows the *OData ATOM* Format (the XML representation of data returned from an OData query), or *JavaScript Object Notation*, JSON (a lightweight data-interchange format). By default the data is returned as XML. The following XML shows the response for the preceding call to the WCF Data Service:

```xml
<?xml version="1.0" encoding="utf-8" ?>
<feed xml:base="http://localhost:5000/WcfDataService1.svc/"
 xmlns=http://www.w3.org/2005/Atom
 xmlns:d=http://schemas.microsoft.com/ado/2007/08/dataservices
 xmlns:m="http://schemas.microsoft.com/ado/2007/08/dataservices/metadata">
<id>http://localhost:5000/WcfDataService1.svc/Categories</id>
<title type="text">Categories</title>
<updated>2013-01-01T23:54:24Z</updated>
<link rel="self" title="Categories" href="Categories" />
<entry>
<id>http://localhost:5000/WcfDataService1.svc/Categories(1)</id>
<category term="NorthwindsModel.Category"
 scheme="http://schemas.microsoft.com/ado/2007/08/dataservices/scheme" />
<link rel="edit" title="Category" href="Categories(1)" />
<title />
<updated>2013-01-10T23:54:24Z</updated>
<author>
<name />
</author>
<content type="application/xml">
<m:properties>
<d:CategoryID m:type="Edm.Int32">1</d:CategoryID>
<d:CategoryName>Beverages</d:CategoryName>
<d:Description>Soft drinks, coffees, teas, beers, and ales</d:Description>
<d:Picture m:type="Edm.Binary">FRwvA…</d:Picture>
</m:properties>
</content>
</entry>
</feed>
```

Notice that the columns have been returned as elements in the m:properties element along with the data.

Create a WCF Data Service

Creating a WCF Data Service involves creating a web application, creating an ADO.NET Entity Framework model for the database and then exposing the model by adding a WCF Data Service file to your web application.

1. Launch Visual Studio 2012, and select New Project from the Start Page.

2. Select Empty ASP.NET Web Application from the list of installed C# templates.

3. Change the name of the site to **NorthwindsWCFDataService** and click the OK button.

4. Right-click the project in the Solution Explorer, click Add, and then select New Item from the pop-up menu. Steps 5 through 14 create an ADO.NET Entity Data Model for the Northwinds database just as you did in the previous exercise.

5. Select ADO.NET Entity Data Model from the list of installed C# templates.

6. Change the Name to **NorthwindsModel** and click the Add button. The Entity Data Model Wizard appears.

7. Select the Generate from Database option; click the Next button. The next page asks for the database connection.

8. Click the New Connection button. The Choose Data Source dialog appears.

9. Select Microsoft SQL Server from the list of data sources, and click the Continue button. The Connection Properties dialog appears.

10. Enter the name of the server where you created the Northwinds database.

11. You can either use Windows Authentication or a SQL Server Authentication to connect to the database. If you select SQL Server Authentication, you have to enter a valid SQL Login and Password.

12. Select the Northwinds database from the Select or Enter A Database Name list.

13. Click the OK button. This brings you back to the Entity Data Model Wizard. By default, the connection string will be stored in a Web.config file within your project.

14. Click the Next button. This screen enables you to select the objects in the database that you want to map. Select the check boxes next to Tables, Views, and Stored Procedures from the list, and leave the other settings unchanged. Click the Finish button.

15. The Entity Data Model appears in Visual Studio's designer. Save your changes, and then close the window in the designer.

16. Right-click the project in the Solution Explorer, click Add, and then select New Item from the pop-up menu.

17. Choose WCF Data Service from the list of Installed C# Web templates.

18. Name the file **NorthwindsService.svc,** and click the Add button. Visual Studio creates the NorthwindsService class.

```
public class NorthwindsService : DataService
                     < /* TODO: put your data source class name here */ >
{
    // This method is called only once to initialize service-wide policies.
    public static void InitializeService(DataServiceConfiguration config)
    {
        // TODO: set rules to indicate which entity sets and service
        //       operations are
        //          visible, updatable, etc.
        // Examples:
        // config.SetEntitySetAccessRule("MyEntityset",
        //                              EntitySetRights.AllRead);
        // config.SetServiceOperationAccessRule("MyServiceOperation",
        //                                  ServiceOperationRights.All);
        config.DataServiceBehavior.MaxProtocolVersion =
                                    DataServiceProtocolVersion.V3;
    }
}
```

The NorthwindsService inherits from the `DataService` class, which expects an Entity Framework model as the type. Notice the `/* TODO:` code that was automatically generated.

19. Replace the commented TODO text with the name of the Entity Data Model that you created during steps 5 through 14. It should be `NorthwindsEntities`.

20. Remove the commented code in the `InitializeService` method.

21. Add the following line in the `InitializeService` method:

```
config.SetEntitySetAccessRule("Categories", EntitySetRights.AllRead );
```

This line of code defines which entities are available for the web service. In this example only the `Categories` entity is exposed. Your class should contain the following code:

```
public class NorthwindsService : DataService< NorthwindsEntities >
{
    // This method is called only once to initialize service-wide policies.
    public static void InitializeService(DataServiceConfiguration config)
    {
        config.SetEntitySetAccessRule("Categories", EntitySetRights.AllRead);
        config.DataServiceBehavior.MaxProtocolVersion =
                                    DataServiceProtocolVersion.V3;
    }
}
```

22. Click the Run button to start debugging. You should get the following XML response:

```
<?xml version="1.0" encoding="UTF-8"?>
<service xmlns:atom=http://www.w3.org/2005/Atom
         xmlns="http://www.w3.org/2007/app"
```

```
                           xml:base="http://localhost:8999/NorthwindsService.svc/">
     <workspace>
       <atom:title>Default</atom:title>
         <collection href="Categories">
           <atom:title>Categories</atom:title>
         </collection>
     </workspace>
   </service>
```

This lists the entities that are exposed by this service; for this example only the Categories entity is exposed.

23. Append `Categories` to the URL in the browser and press Enter.

```
http://localhost:8999/NorthwindsService.svc/Categories
```

You should now get an XML response that lists all the records in the Categories table. If you were to append `"?$filter=CategoryName eq 'Beverages'"` to the URL in the browser and click enter, you would get only the Category with the name Beverages. The `$filter` is an OData query option. The WCF Data Services also support the following query options, as shown in Table 9-13.

TABLE 9-13: OData Query Options

OPTION	DESCRIPTION
`$orderby`	Sets the sort order for the returned data.
	Example: `$orderby=CategoryName,CategoryId`
`$top`	Set the number of entities to include in the returned data.
	Example: `$top=10`
`$skip`	Specifies the number of entities to skip before returning data.
	Example: `$skip=10`
`$filter`	Defines an expression that filters the entities.
	See Table 9-14 through Table 9-18 for `OData` filter options.
`$expand`	Specifies which related entities are returned in the data.
	Example: `$expand=Products`
`$select`	Specifies which properties (columns) in the returned data.
	Example: `$select=CategoryName,CategoryId`
`$inlinecount`	Requests the count of entities returned from the query.

Table 9-14 lists the keywords for use with the `$filter` query option.

TABLE 9-14: OData $filter Query Options

OPTION	DESCRIPTION
Eq	Equal
Ne	Not equal
Gt	Greater than
Ge	Greater than or equal to
Lt	Less than
Le	Less than or equal to
And	Logical and
Or	Logical or
Not	Logical not
()	Precedence grouping
Add	Addition ($filter=Cost Add 5 Gt 100)
Sub	Subtraction ($filter=Cost Sub 5 Gt 100)
Mul	Multiplication ($filter=Cost Mul 5 Gt 1000)
Div	Division ($filter=Cost Div 5 Gt 100)
Mod	Remainder ($filter=Cost Mod 2 Eq 0)

In addition to the operators, there are also specific functions that can be used for string, dates, math, and type (see Tables 9-15 through 9-18).

TABLE 9-15: OData $filter string Functions

FUNCTION	DESCRIPTION
bool substring(string p0, string p1)	Returns true if p0 is in p1
bool endswith(string p0, string p1)	Returns true if p0 ends with p1
bool startswith(string p0, string p1)	Returns true if p0 starts with p1
int length(string p0)	Returns the length of p0

FUNCTION	DESCRIPTION
`int indexof(string p0, string p1)`	Returns the first character index of `p0` that contains `p1`
`string replace(string p0, string p1, string replace)`	Searches `p0` for `p1` and replaces it with `replace`
`string substring(string p0, int pos)`	Returns the substring of `p0` from position `pos`
`string substring(string p0, int pos, int length)`	Returns the substring of `p0` from position `pos` for the specified length of characters
`string tolower(string p0)`	Returns `p0` in lowercase
`string toupper(string p0)`	Returns `p0` in uppercase
`string trim(string p0)`	Removes leading and trailing whitespace
`string concat(string p0, string p1)`	Concatenates strings `p0` and `p1`

TABLE 9-16: OData $filter date Functions

FUNCTION	DESCRIPTION
`int day(DateTime p0)`	Returns the day of the date time
`int hour(DateTime p0)`	Returns the hour of the date time
`int minute(DateTime p0)`	Returns the minute of the date time
`int month(DateTime p0)`	Returns the month of the date time
`int second(DateTime p0)`	Returns the second of the date time
`int year(DateTime p0)`	Returns the year of the date time

TABLE 9-17: OData $filter math Functions

FUNCTION	DESCRIPTION
`double round(double p0)`	The nearest integral value to the parameter value, following the rules defined in IEEE754-2008
`decimal round(decimal p0)`	The nearest integral value to the parameter value, following the rules defined in IEEE754-2008

continues

TABLE 9-17 *(continued)*

FUNCTION	DESCRIPTION
`double floor(double p0)`	The largest integral value less than or equal to the parameter value, following the rules defined in IEEE754-2008
`decimal floor(decimal p0)`	The largest integral value less than or equal to the parameter value, following the rules defined in IEEE754-2008
`double ceiling(double p0)`	The smallest integral value greater than or equal to the parameter value, following the rules defined in IEEE754-2008
`decimal ceiling(decimal p0)`	The smallest integral value greater than or equal to the parameter value, following the rules defined in IEEE754-2008

TABLE 9-18: OData $filter type Functions

FUNCTION	DESCRIPTION
`bool isOf(type p0)`	Returns true if the entity is of type p0
`bool IsOf(expression p0, type p0)`	Returns true if p0 is of type p1

In addition to filtering with the `$filter` syntax, OData also enables you to specify a primary key value in `()`to select a record based on its primary key. The following URI returns the `Category` with the primary key of 1:

```
http://localhost:8999/NorthwindsService.svc/Categories(1)
```

The following URI returns the `CategoryName` of the `Category` with a primary key of 1:

```
http://localhost:8999/NorthwindsService.svc/Categories(1)/CategoryName
```

Create a Client Application That Uses WCF Data Services

The section creates a client application that consumes the WCF Service. This is similar to the section that described how to create an ADO.NET Entity Framework model and showed you how to select, add, update, and delete records. This section creates a console application that references the Northwinds WCF Data Service and performs all the CRUD operations on the data.

1. Open the NorthwindsWCFDataService project in Visual Studio 2012 that was created in the last section.

2. Select File, click Add, and then select New Project from the menu.

3. Select Console Application from the list of installed templates.

4. Name the project **NorthwindsClient** and click the OK button.

5. Right-click the References of the NorthwindsClient project in the Solution Explorer, and select Add Service Reference from the pop-up menu.

6. Click the arrow next to the button that says Discover, and select Services in Solution.

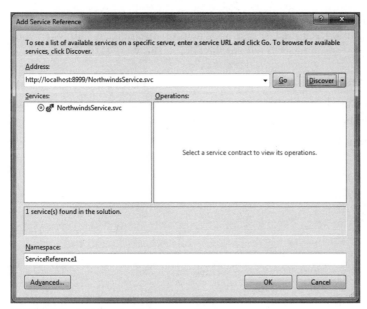

FIGURE 9-3: Add Service Reference dialog

7. Change the Namespace to **NorthwindsServiceReference**, and click the OK button.

8. Open the Program.cs file in the console application, and add the following `using` statements:

```
using NorthwindsClient.NorthwindsServiceReference;
using System.Diagnostics;
using System.Data.Services.Client;
using System.Net;
```

9. Add the following code to the `Main` method. Note that the port number will vary based on your local server. In this sample the port number was 8999, but it will most likely be different for your project.

```
NorthwindsEntities db = new NorthwindsEntities(new
    Uri("http://localhost:8999/NorthwindsService.svc/"));

var categories = from c in db.Categories
                 select c;

foreach (Category category in categories)
```

```
    {
        Debug.WriteLine(string.Format("CategoryId: {0}, CategoryName: {1}",
                          category.CategoryID, category.CategoryName));
    }
```

10. Set the console application as the startup project and run the application.

Notice that the code to query the database was the same as it was when querying directly against the ADO.NET Entity Framework model in the last section. The only difference is that when you create the NorthwindsEntities object, you need to pass in the URI of the WCF Data Service.

Add Records Using WCF Data Services

The next few lines of code can be used to add a record to the Categories table in the Northwinds database. Replace the code in the Main method with the following:

```
NorthwindsEntities db = new NorthwindsEntities(new
                        Uri("http://localhost:8999/NorthwindsService.svc/"));

//Create a category
Category category = new Category()
{
    CategoryName = "Alcohol",
    Description = "Happy Beverages"
};

db.AddToCategories(category);
DataServiceResponse response = db.SaveChanges();

if (response.First().StatusCode == (int)HttpStatusCode.Created)
{
    Debug.WriteLine("New CategoryId: {0}", category.CategoryID);
}
else
{
    Debug.WriteLine("Error: {0}", response.First().Error.Message);
}
```

There are a couple things to note here that are different from when you added a record using the ADO.NET Entity Framework. First, a method called AddToCategories was created in the NorthwindsEntities class. This is used to add records to the Categories table. Second, the SaveChanges method returns a DataServiceResponse object. This object has a list of responses from the server. In this example, you use the first response's StatusCode property to determine if the record were successfully added. If you run this code as-is, you get an error: "An Error Occurred While Processing This Request." This is because you did not allow the creation of Category records when you set up the security in the WCF Data Service. To allow add, update, and delete capability to the Categories table, you need to open the NorthwindsService.svc.cs file in the WCF Data Service project. Change the InitializeService method to the following:

```
public static void InitializeService(DataServiceConfiguration config)
{
    config.SetEntitySetAccessRule("Categories", EntitySetRights.AllRead |
```

```
                                                 EntitySetRights.AllWrite );
    config.DataServiceBehavior.MaxProtocolVersion = DataServiceProtocolVersion.V3;
}
```

The `SetEntitySetAccessRule` has an additional permission, `EntitySetRights.AllWrite`. This allows a client to add, update, or delete records in the table. If you run the project again, it adds the new Category record and prints the newly added `CategoryId` to the Output window.

Update Records Using WCF Data Services

The following code updates a Category record using the WCF Data Service. Replace the code in the Main method with the following:

```
NorthwindsEntities db = new NorthwindsEntities(new
                        Uri("http://localhost:8999/NorthwindsService.svc/"));

Category category = db.Categories.Where(c => c.CategoryName ==
                                        "Alcohol").FirstOrDefault();

category.Description = "Happy People";

db.UpdateObject(category);

db.SaveChanges();
```

This code uses a lambda expression to retrieve the Category entity from the service. The code then changes the Description property and calls the `UpdateObject` method of the `NorthwindsEntities` object. This marks the object to be updated when `SaveChanges` is called.

Delete Records Using WCF Data Services

The following code deletes a record from the Category table:

```
NorthwindsEntities db = new NorthwindsEntities(new
                        Uri("http://localhost:8999/NorthwindsService.svc/"));

Category category = db.Categories.Where(c => c.CategoryName ==
                                        "Alcohol").FirstOrDefault();
db.DeleteObject(category);
db.SaveChanges();
```

This time you needed to call the `DeleteObject` method instead of the `Remove` method when using the ADO.NET Entity Framework.

Request Data as JSON in a Client Application

By default, the data returned from a WCF Data Service is in XML format. You can, however, send the header "`Accept: application/json;odata=verbose`" in the HTTP request to return the data in JSON format. The following code creates a request using the `WebRequest` object in the `System.Net` namespace:

```
HttpWebRequest req =
(HttpWebRequest)WebRequest.Create("http://localhost:8999/NorthwindsService.svc/
```

```
                            Categories(1)?$select=CategoryID,CategoryName,Description");

    req.Accept = "application/json;odata=verbose";

    using (HttpWebResponse resp = (HttpWebResponse)req.GetResponse())
    {
        Stream s = resp.GetResponseStream();
        StreamReader readStream = new StreamReader(s);

        string jsonString = readStream.ReadToEnd();

        Debug.WriteLine(jsonString);

        resp.Close();
        readStream.Close();
    }
```

This code creates a request that selects the Category record with the primary key of 1 and selects the `CategoryId`, `CategoryName`, and `Description` properties. The `req.Accept = "application/json;odata=verbose"` line tells the WCF Data Service to return the data as JSON. When you execute this code, it prints the following to the Output window. Line breaks are added to make it easier to read.

```
{
  "d":
  {
    "__metadata":
    {
      "id":"http://localhost:8999/NorthwindsService.svc/Categories(1)",
      "uri":"http://localhost:8999/NorthwindsService.svc/Categories(1)",
      "type":"NorthwindsModel.Category"
    },
    "CategoryID":1,
    "CategoryName":"Beverages",
    "Description":"Soft drinks, coffees, teas, beers, and ales"
  }
}
```

PERFORMING I/O OPERATIONS

I/O operations refer to reading and writing files to and from storage. Files are stored in directories, and the .NET Framework provides a set of classes for copying, moving, deleting, or checking for the existence of files or directories. A file is an ordered and named collection of bytes that has been saved to storage. When working with files, you use a *stream*. A stream is an in-memory object used to represent the sequence of bytes in a file. Special reader and writer classes enables working with encoded streams. This section first reviews the basic types that represent files and directories, then reviews the different types of streams, and finally reviews the different types of readers and writers. All the types for performing these I/O operations can be found in the `System.IO` namespace.

Files and Directories

Table 9-19 lists the classes defined for working with files and directories.

TABLE 9-19: File and Directory Classes

CLASS NAME	DESCRIPTION
File	A static class that provides methods for creating, copying, deleting, moving, and opening files
FileInfo	Provides for creating an instance of a class that provides methods for creating, copying, deleting, moving, and opening files
Directory	A static class that provides methods for creating, moving, deleting, and enumerating through the files in a directory
DirectoryInfo	Provides for creating an instance of a class that provides methods for creating, moving, deleting, and enumerating through the files in a directory
Path	A static class that provides methods for obtaining information or manipulating a file or directory name using a string variable

The File and FileInfo class are similar except that the File class is static and contains only methods in which the FileInfo class enables you to create an instance that represents a file, so it has properties and methods. Table 9-20 lists some of the properties for the FileInfo class. Note that the File class does not have properties because it is a static class.

TABLE 9-20: FileInfo Properties

PROPERTY NAME	DESCRIPTION
Directory	Gets an instance of a DirectoryInfo object for the parent directory
DirectoryName	Gets a string for the directory's full path
Exists	Returns a boolean indicating if the file exists
IsReadOnly	Returns a boolean indicating if the file is read-only
Length	Returns the size in bytes of the file
Name	Gets the name of the file

The FileInfo object, unlike the File object, inherits from the System.IO.FileSystemInfo object, which contains properties for the attributes, the creation time, the extension, the full name, the last access time, and the last write time of the file.

The constructor of the `FileInfo` class takes a string parameter that contains the path and name of the file. This is the only constructor for the `FileInfo` object. The following code sample creates an instance of a `FileInfo` object and writes the name of the file to the Output window:

```
FileInfo fileInfo = new FileInfo(@"c:\Chapter9Samples\HelloWorld.txt");
Debug.WriteLine(fileInfo.Name);
```

> **COMMON MISTAKES: FileInfo Does Not Open a File**
>
> The file was not "opened,"; the instance is simply enabling you to get information about the file. There are methods that enable you to open and change the contents of the file, but simply creating an instance of a `FileInfo` object does not open the file.

The methods for the `File` and `FileInfo` class are similar. The methods for the `File` class take parameters to a file path where the methods for the `FileInfo` class use the instance rather than parameters. Table 9-21 lists some of the common methods between the `File` and `FileInfo` class. Be aware that the parameters are different based on whether you use a `File` or `FileInfo` object.

TABLE 9-21: File and FileInfo Methods

METHOD NAME	DESCRIPTION
AppendAllText	Creates a `StreamWriter` that can be used to append text to the file
CopyTo (FileInfo) Copy (File)	Copies the file
Create	Creates the file
Decrypt	Decrypts the file that was encrypted by the current account
Delete	Deletes the file
Encrypt	Encrypts the file so only the account used to encrypt the file can decrypt it
MoveTo	Moves a file to a different directory
Open	Returns a `FileStream` object for read, write, or read\write access
Replace	Replaces the content of a file with the contents from another file
SetAccessControl	Applies access control list entries by a `FileSecurity` object

The `Directory` and `DirectoryInfo` classes are similar to the `File` and `FileInfo` classes except they handle directories rather than files. The `Directory` class is a static object and the `DirectoryInfo` class enables the creation of an instance of the class. The `DirectoryInfo` class inherits from the

`System.IO.FileSystemInfo` object, and just like the `FileInfo` object, it contains the same properties for the attributes, the creation time, the extension, the full name, the last access time, and the last write time of the directory. The properties for the `DirectoryInfo` class are listed in Table 9-22.

TABLE 9-22: DirectoryInfo Properties

PROPERTY NAME	DESCRIPTION
Exists	Returns a boolean indicating if the directory exists
Name	Gets the name of the `DirectoryInfo` instance
Parent	Returns a `DirectoryInfo` object of the parent directory
Root	Returns a `DirectoryInfo` object of the root directory

The `Directory` and `DirectoryInfo` object have similar methods that perform the same operation; the only difference is that because the `Directory` object is static, the methods take parameters to the directories to manipulate, and the `DirectoryInfo` object manipulates the directory for the instance. Table 9-23 lists some of the common methods between the `Directory` and `DirectoryInfo` object.

TABLE 9-23: Directory and DirectoryInfo Methods

METHOD NAME	DESCRIPTION
Create (DirectoryInfo) CreateDirectory (Directory)	Creates the directory
Delete	Deletes the directory
GetAccessControl	Returns a `DirectorySecurity` object that encapsulates the access control list entries for the current directory
GetDirectories	Returns a `DirectoryInfo` array of the subdirectories in the current directory
GetFiles	Returns a `FileInfo` array of the files in the current directory
GetFileSystemInfos	Returns a `FileSystemInfo` array of the files and directories in the current directory
MoveTo (DirectoryInfo) Move (Directory)	Moves a directory
SetAccessControl	Applies access control list entries described by a `DirectorySecurity` object to the current directory

The following code writes all the directories and all the files in the c drive to the Output window:

```
//DirectoryInfo
DirectoryInfo directoryInfo = new DirectoryInfo(@"c:\");

//Directories
Debug.WriteLine("Directories");
foreach (FileInfo fileInfo in directoryInfo.GetFiles())
{
    Debug.WriteLine(fileInfo.Name);
}

//Files
Debug.WriteLine("Files");
foreach (DirectoryInfo di in directoryInfo.GetDirectories())
{
    Debug.WriteLine(di.Name);
}
```

Streams

Streams are classes used to contain the contents of a file. Table 9-24 lists the different types of streams available in the .NET Framework.

TABLE 9-24: Streams

CLASS NAME	DESCRIPTION
FileStream	Reads and writes files
IsolatedStorageFileStream	Reads and writes files in isolated storage
MemoryStream	Reads and writes data to memory
BufferedStream	Used to store a block of bytes in memory to cache data
NetworkStream	Reads and writes data over a network socket
PipeStream	Reads and writes data over an anonymous or named pipes
CryptoStream	Used to link data streams to cryptographic transformations

A `FileStream` can be used to read, write, open, and close files. The following example creates a new file, writes the numbers 1 through 10 in the file, and then closes the file:

```
FileStream fileStream = new FileStream(@"c:\Chapter9Samples\Numbers.txt",
                        FileMode.Create, FileAccess.Write, FileShare.None);

for(int i = 0; i < 10; i++)
{
    byte[] number = new UTF8Encoding(true).GetBytes(i.ToString());
```

```
        fileStream.Write(number, 0, number.Length);
    }

    fileStream.Close();
```

In this example, the `FileStream` constructor takes four parameters, the path to the file, the file mode, the file access, and the file share. The `FileMode` enumeration values are listed in Table 9-25. The `FileMode` enumeration determines whether you create, open, or truncate a file.

> **EXAM TIPS AND TRICKS: Know the Options when Opening a File**
>
> Be sure to pay attention to these options because it is likely that you will be asked a question about the `FileMode`, `FileAccess`, or `FileShare` enumerations.

TABLE 9-25: FileMode Enumeration

VALUE	DESCRIPTION
Append	Opens a file if it exists and seeks to the end of the file, or creates a new file if it doesn't exist. This can be used only with `FileAccess.Write`.
CreateNew	Creates a new file. If the file already exists, an exception is thrown.
Create	Creates a new file. If the file already exists it will be overwritten. If the file exists and is hidden, an exception is thrown.
Open	Opens a file. If the file does not exist, an exception is thrown.
OpenOrCreate	Opens a file if it exists or creates a new file if it does not exist.
Truncate	Opens an existing file and truncates the data in the file. If the file does not exist, an exception is thrown.

The `FileAccess` enumeration determines what you can do with the stream after it is created (see Table 9-26).

TABLE 9-26: FileAccess Enumeration

VALUE	DESCRIPTION
Read	Read access to the file
Write	Write access to the file
ReadWrite	Read-and-write access to the file

The `FileShare` enumeration determines the type of access other streams can have on this file at the same time you have it open (see Table 9-27).

TABLE 9-27: FileShare Enumeration

VALUE	DESCRIPTION
None	Does not enable another stream to open the file
Read	Enables subsequent opening of the file for reading only
Write	Enables subsequent opening of the file for writing
ReadWrite	Enables subsequent opening of the file for reading or writing
Delete	Enables for subsequent deletion of the file
Inheritable	Makes the file handle inheritable by child processes

When creating or opening a file, the process must have the correct permissions to the file or directory to perform the specified operation. The `System.Security.Permissions` `.FileIOPermissionAccess` enumeration contains the types of permissions for a file or directory (see Table 9-28).

TABLE 9-28: FileIOPermissionAccess Enumeration

VALUE	DESCRIPTION
NoAccess	No access to a file or directory
Read	Read access to a file or directory
Write	Write access to a file or a directory
Append	Access to append data to a file or directory. Append access also includes the ability to create a new file or directory
PathDiscovery	Access to the information about the path
AllAccess	Append, Read, Write, and PathDiscovery provide access to the file or directory

The stream classes are used for reading or writing byte arrays. The next section will discuss using reader and writer classes to manipulate arrays of binary values, arrays of characters, or strings.

Readers and Writers

Readers and writers are classes in the `System.IO` namespace that read or write encoded characters to and from streams. Table 9-29 lists the common types of readers and writers in the `System.IO` namespace.

TABLE 9-29: Reader and Writer Classes (Partial List)

CLASS	DESCRIPTION
BinaryReader, BinaryWriter	Used for reading and writing binary values
StreamReader, StreamWriter	Used for reading and writing characters by using an encoded value to convert the characters to and from bytes
StringReader, StringWriter	Used for reading and writing characters to and from strings
TextReader, TextWriter	Abstract classes for other readers and writers that read-and-write character or strings

The `StreamReader` and `StringReader` both inherit from the `TextReader` abstract class. The `StreamWriter` and `StringWriter` both inherit from the `TextWriter` class.

The `StreamReader` class is used to read character input in a particular encoding. The default encoding is UTF-8. You can use a `StreamReader` to read a standard text file. Table 9-30 lists some of the methods for the `StreamReader` class.

TABLE 9-30: StreamReader Methods (Partial List)

METHOD NAME	DESCRIPTION
Close	Closes the stream reader and underlying stream
Peek	Returns the next character in the stream but does not move the character position
Read()	Returns the next character in the stream and moves the character position by one
Read(Char[], Int32, Int32) ReadBlock(Char[], Int32, Int32)	Reads the specified number of characters into the byte array
ReadLine	Reads a line of characters and returns a string
ReadToEnd	Reads all characters from the current position to the end of the file and returns a string

The `StreamReader` provides methods for reading character by character, line by line, or an entire file in one call. The `Read` and `ReadBlock` methods return characters and character arrays; the `ReadLine` and `ReadToEnd` methods return strings. The following code opens a file with the following content:

```
abc
123
456
789
```

The code first writes the contents character by character to the Output window, line by line to the Output window, and then writes the entire contents to the Output window:

```
StreamReader streamReader = new StreamReader(@"c:\Chapter9Samples\Numbers.txt");
Debug.WriteLine("Char by Char");
while (!streamReader.EndOfStream)
{
    Debug.WriteLine((char)streamReader.Read());
}

streamReader.Close();

streamReader = new StreamReader(@"c:\Chapter9Samples\Numbers.txt");
Debug.WriteLine("Line by line");
while (!streamReader.EndOfStream)
{
    Debug.WriteLine(streamReader.ReadLine());
}

streamReader.Close();

streamReader = new StreamReader(@"c:\Chapter9Samples\Numbers.txt");
Debug.WriteLine("Entire file");
Debug.WriteLine(streamReader.ReadToEnd());
```

The preceding code prints the following to the Output window:

```
Char by Char
a
b
c


1
2
3


4
5
6


7
8
9
Line by line
abc
123
456
789
Entire file
abc
123
456
789
```

The `StringReader` class is similar to the `StreamReader` class, except that instead of reading a file you read a string. The constructor of the `StringReader` class takes a string as a parameter. This is not a path to a file but just a regular string that contains text. The `StringReader` then enables you read the string character by character, line by line, or the entire string. The following code writes the contents of a string character by character to the Output window:

```
StringReader stringReader = new StringReader("Hello\nGoodbye");
int pos = stringReader.Read();
while (pos != -1)
{
    Debug.WriteLine("{0}", (char)pos);
    pos = stringReader.Read();
}
stringReader.Close();
```

The `StreamWriter` class is similar to a `Stream` except that a `StreamWriter` is for characters of a particular encoding, and a `Stream` is designed for byte input and output. You can use the `StreamWriter` class to write data to a file. The `StreamWriter` has `Write` and `WriteLine` methods used to write to the stream in memory. The `StreamWriter` has a property called `AutoFlush` that, when set to `true`, can write to store when the `Write` method is called and when set to `false` can write to storage when the `Flush` method is called or the `StreamWriter` is closed. The following code creates a `StreamWriter` and writes a string, a boolean value, and an integer to the file:

```
StreamWriter streamWriter = new
                    StreamWriter(@"c:\Chapter9Samples\StreamWriter.txt");

streamWriter.WriteLine("ABC");
streamWriter.Write(true);
streamWriter.Write(1);

streamWriter.Close();
```

In this example, the constructor is passed a path to a file. If the file does not exist, it is created; if it does exist it is overwritten. Be aware that you can also pass a `Stream` object to the constructor. The sample code uses both the `WriteLine` and `Write` methods to write to the file. The character representation of nonstring or char values will be written. The boolean value `true` is written as "True" in the file.

You can use the `BinaryWriter` class to write primitive types in binary or strings in a specific coding. The following code writes the same data as the last exercise but writes it in binary format:

```
FileStream fileStream = new FileStream(@"c:\Chapter9Samples\BinaryWriter.txt",
    FileMode.Create);
BinaryWriter binaryWriter = new BinaryWriter(fileStream);

binaryWriter.Write("ABC");
binaryWriter.Write(true);
binaryWriter.Write(1);

binaryWriter.Close();
```

The `BinaryWriter` class requires a `Stream` object be passed to the constructor; you cannot pass a string that points to a file path. If you open the BinaryWriter.txt file created in this exercise, you would see the values in binary format.

If you need to read a binary file, you use a `BinaryReader` class to read the data. The following code reads the file created in the previous exercise:

```
FileStream fileStream = new FileStream(@"c:\Chapter9Samples\BinaryWriter.txt",
    FileMode.Open);
BinaryReader binaryReader = new BinaryReader(fileStream);

string abs = binaryReader.ReadString();
bool b = binaryReader.ReadBoolean();
int i = binaryReader.ReadInt32();

binaryReader.Close();
```

Asynchronous I/O Operations

The `Stream`, `Reader`, and `Writer` classes all provide the ability to read or write files asynchronously. This can be helpful when you want to return processing back to the user interface while you are performing a time-consuming operation on a large file. In C# there are two new keywords used when dealing with asynchronous processing: *async* and *await*.

The `async` keyword is a method modifier that enables the method to use the `await` keyword and also enables a calling method to this function using the `await` keyword. The `await` keyword is used when calling a method to suspend execution in that method until the awaited task completes. For example, suppose you have a Windows forms application that has a button that performs a long-running task. You can modify the button click event signature with the `async` modifier and then call the long-running method using the `await` keyword. This allows the long-running process to run, but also allows the user to navigate to different parts of your application, so the system does not appear to be locked up.

```
private async void button1_Click(object sender, EventArgs e)
{
    this.Text = "Started";

    await MyLongRunningProcess();

    this.Text = "Finished";
}
```

In the preceding example the caption of the form is changed to `"Started"` when the button is clicked. When the `MyLongRunningProcess` method is called, the method is executed, but processing is returned to the main thread until the `MyLongRunningProcess` method finishes executing. After it is done, the form's caption is changed to `"Finished"`.

You can use the asynchronous methods for file I/O in a similar manner. The following code sample searches all files in a given folder and searches for a specific string in the file. If the file contains the string, its name is written to an output file. When the process is complete, the output file is shown in the default text viewer.

```csharp
private async void button1_Click(object sender, EventArgs e)
{
    this.Text = "Searching...";

    string outputFileName = @"c:\Test\FoundFiles.txt";

    await SearchDirectory(@"c:\Chapter9Samples", "A", outputFileName);

    this.Text = "Finished";

    Process.Start(outputFileName);
}

private static async Task SearchDirectory(string searchPath, string searchString,
    string outputFileName)
{
    StreamWriter streamWriter = File.CreateText(outputFileName);

    string[] fileNames = Directory.GetFiles(searchPath);
    await FindTextInFilesAsync(fileNames, searchString, streamWriter);

    streamWriter.Close();
}

private static async Task FindTextInFilesAsync(string[] fileNames, string
    searchString, StreamWriter outputFile)
{
    foreach (string fileName in fileNames)
    {
        if (fileName.ToLower().EndsWith(".txt"))
        {
            StreamReader streamReader = new StreamReader(fileName);

            string textOfFile = await streamReader.ReadToEndAsync();
            streamReader.Close();

            if (textOfFile.Contains(searchString))
            {
                await outputFile.WriteLineAsync(fileName);
            }
        }
    }
}
```

Each method is modified with the `async` keyword. This enables you to call asynchronous methods within the method using the `await` keyword. If you don't use the `async` keyword but have an `await` command in the method, you get a compile error. The potentially time-consuming operation is the reading of the file. The `StreamReader`'s `ReadToEndAsync` method is called with the `await` command. Execution does not continue in this method until the entire file is read, but the calling method can continue to execute.

UNDERSTANDING SERIALIZATION

Serialization is the process of transforming an object into a form that can either be persisted to storage or transferred from one application domain to another. When transforming the object you are serializing the object; when reading it back, you are deserializing the object. You can serialize an object to a disk, to a stream, to memory, or over a network. Two common formats for passing objects between systems are XML and JSON. You've seen samples of these in the section about WCF DataServices. As you remember, by default, in WCF Data Services an object is returned as XML. There was also a later sample that showed how to return the object as JSON. The objects were serialized to either XML or JSON before being transferred to the client. The .NET Framework has classes that support binary, XML, and JSON, and you can even create your own custom serialization, as discussed in the following sections.

Binary Serialization

The `BinaryFormatter` object is used to serialize and deserialize an object. This is found in the `System.Runtime.Serialization.Formatters.Binary` namespace. The two main methods you need to be concerned about are the `Serialize` and `Desearialize` methods. You can use the `BinaryFormatter` along with a `FileStream` to read and write your objects to disk. Remember, the `FileStream` is an object used to read and write data to and from disk as byte arrays. For a class to be serialized, you must add the `[Serializable]` attribute to the top of the class. The following example creates a class called `Person` and makes it serializable:

```
[Serializable]
class Person
{
    private int _id;
    public string FirstName;
    public string LastName;

    public void SetId(int id)
    {
        _id = id;
    }
}
```

If you want to persist this object's data to storage, you can create an instance of the `BinaryFormatter` object and call its `Serialize` method.

```
Person person = new Person();
person.SetId(1);
person.FirstName = "Joe";
person.LastName = "Smith";

IFormatter formatter = new BinaryFormatter();
Stream stream = new FileStream("Person.bin", FileMode.Create, FileAccess.Write,
    FileShare.None);
formatter.Serialize(stream, person);
stream.Close();
```

Be aware that even the private field will be persisted to the disk. You can restore the state of the object by reading the `Person.bin` file and deserializing the file.

```
stream = new FileStream("Person.bin",FileMode.Open,FileAccess.Read,FileShare.Read);
Person person2 = (Person)formatter.Deserialize(stream);
stream.Close();
```

If you execute the code and view the `person2` object in the Watch window, you can see that all the fields retain their value, even the private `_id` field. If you want to prevent the private field from being persisted, you can add the `[NonSerialized]` attribute before the field declaration.

```
[Serializable]
class Person
{
    [NonSerialized]
    private int _id;
    public string FirstName;
    public string LastName;

    public void SetId(int id)
    {
        _id = id;
    }
}
```

When serializing the object, the `_id` field will be skipped. If you were to run the code again and serialize the object and deserialize the object and view `person2` in the Watch window, you would notice the `_id` is 0.

XML Serialization

XML serialization is just as simple to implement as binary serialization. You use the `XmlSerializer` class in the `System.Xml.Serialization` namespace. One difference between the `XmlSerializer` and `BinaryFormatter` is that the `XmlSerializer` serializes only public properties and fields. You also do not need to use the `[Serializable]` attribute when declaring the class. Also, the class must be public. The following code serializes the `Person` object:

```
Person person = new Person();
person.SetId(1);
person.FirstName = "Joe";
person.LastName = "Smith";

XmlSerializer xmlSerializer = new XmlSerializer(typeof(Person));
StreamWriter streamWriter = new StreamWriter("Person.xml");
xmlSerializer.Serialize(streamWriter, person);
```

The code produces the following file:

```
<?xml version="1.0" encoding="utf-8"?>
<Person xmlns:xsi="http://www.w3.org/2001/XMLSchema-instance"
    xmlns:xsd="http://www.w3.org/2001/XMLSchema">
  <FirstName>Joe</FirstName>
  <LastName>Smith</LastName>
</Person>
```

If you want to ignore a property, use the `[XmlIgnore]` attribute before the property. The following code would ignore the `FirstName` property when serializing the object to XML:

```
[XmlIgnore]
public string FirstName;
```

You can use the following code to read the XML back into an object:

```
XmlSerializer xmlSerializer = new XmlSerializer(typeof(Person));
FileStream fs = new FileStream("Person.xml", FileMode.Open);
Person person = (Person)xmlSerializer.Deserialize(fs);
```

JSON Serialization

JSON is similar to XML except it is less verbose. JSON looks like a name\value pair but also enables one-to-many relationships such as when you have an invoice object and invoice details. You need to do a little more coding with JSON because you must explicitly put an attribute before each property or field that you want to be serialized. In addition you need to add the `[DataContract]` attribute before the declaration of the class. The following code demonstrates how to change the code for the `Person` class to allow for JSON serialization:

```
[DataContract]
public class Person
{
    [DataMember]
    private int _id;
    [DataMember]
    public string FirstName;
    [DataMember]
    public string LastName;

    public void SetId(int id)
    {
        _id = id;
    }
}
```

To ignore a field or property, you simply do not put the `[DataMember]` attribute in front of its declaration. To serialize an object to JSON, use the `DataContractJsonSerializer` class. This class is in the `System.Runtime.Serialization.Json` namespace. The following code serializes the `Person` object to JSON:

```
Person person = new Person();
person.SetId(1);
person.FirstName = "Joe";
person.LastName = "Smith";

Stream stream = new FileStream("Person.json", FileMode.Create);
DataContractJsonSerializer ser = new DataContractJsonSerializer(typeof(Person));
ser.WriteObject(stream, person);
stream.Close();
```

Instead of calling a `Serialize` method, you call the `WriteObject` method. The JSON for the `Person` object is:

```
{
    "FirstName":"Joe",
    "LastName":"Smith",
    "_id":1
}
```

The code to read the JSON back to the object follows:

```
Person person = new Person();

Stream stream = new FileStream("Person.json", FileMode.Open);
DataContractJsonSerializer ser = new DataContractJsonSerializer(typeof(Person));
person = (Person)ser.ReadObject(stream);
stream.Close();
```

Custom Serialization

There are two methods for customizing the serialization processes. The first is to add an attribute before a custom method that manipulates the object's data during and upon completion of serialization and deserialization. You can use four attributes to accomplish this: `OnDeserializedAttribute`, `OnDeserializingAttribute`, `OnSerializedAttribute`, and `OnSerializingAttribute`. Adding this attribute before a method declaration fires this method during or after the serialization or deserialization process. The following code can be added to the `Person` class to customize the serialization logic:

```
[OnSerializing()]
internal void OnSerializingMethod(StreamingContext context)
{
    FirstName = "Bob";
}

[OnSerialized()]
internal void OnSerializedMethod(StreamingContext context)
{
    FirstName = "Serialize Complete";
}

[OnDeserializing()]
internal void OnDeserializingMethod(StreamingContext context)
{
    FirstName = "John";
}

[OnDeserialized()]
internal void OnDeserializedMethod(StreamingContext context)
{
    FirstName = "Deserialize Complete";
}
```

If you run the code for any of the serializer objects and put breakpoints in each method, you can see when each method is called. This enables you to customize the input or output in case you have enhancements to your objects in later versions, and properties are missing from your persisted files.

The second option for customizing the serialization process is to implement the ISerializable interface. The ISerializable interface has one method that you must implement called GetObjectData. This method is called when the object is serialized. You must also implement a special constructor that will be called when the object is deserialized. The following code changes the Person object, so it implements the ISeriliazable interface:

```
[Serializable]
public class Person : ISerializable
{
    private int _id;
    public string FirstName;
    public string LastName;

    public void SetId(int id)
    {
        _id = id;
    }

    public Person() { }

    public Person(SerializationInfo info, StreamingContext context)
    {
        FirstName = info.GetString("custom field 1");
        LastName = info.GetString("custom field 2");
    }

    public void GetObjectData(SerializationInfo info, StreamingContext context)
    {
        info.AddValue("custom field 1", FirstName);
        info.AddValue("custom field 2", LastName);
    }
}
```

First, take a look at the GetObjectData method. This has a parameter of type SerializationInfo, which enables you to customize the name and data that will be written to the stream. In this example, the value of the FirstName field is written to "custom field 1" and the value of the LastName field is written to "custom field 2". If you were to serialize this code as JSON, the output would be as follows:

```
{
    "custom_x0020_field_x0020_1":"Joe",
    "custom_x0020_field_x0020_2":"Smith"
}
```

When the data is deserialized, the constructor is called. Here you call methods on the SerializationInfo object to get the value based on the custom name you gave the field. Notice that the value for "custom field 1" is set to the FirstName property, and the value for "custom field 2" is set to the LastName property.

ADVICE FROM THE EXPERTS: Use Attributes Instead of ISerializable

Using the four attributes is considered the best practice rather than implementing the ISerializable interface. It is also easier to implement. The attribute methods allow you to manipulate the underlying object before or after serialization or deserialization. Implementing the ISerializable interface intercepts the serialization\deserialization process and can have unexpected results when working with objects that inherit from other object that need to be serialized or deserialized.

SUMMARY

Working with data collections is a fundamental concept that you must learn not only for the test, but also to become a better programmer. This chapter explained the difference between simple arrays and collections and elaborated on the different reasons for why you would choose one class over another. The main classes to know for the test are Arrays, Lists, ArrayLists, Stacks, HashTables, and Queues. You should also know about the generic version of these classes that are available when you have a set of data that must be of the same type.

Consuming data using ADO.NET, the ADO.NET Entity Framework, and WCF Data Services is another concept that is fundamental for building an application that interacts with a database. ADO.NET is the core technology in the .NET Framework that contains the classes that communicate with a database. The Entity Framework allows you to generate a majority of the code using a designer that is needed to communicate with a database. ADO.NET is used behind the scenes in the ADO.NET Entity Framework. WCF Data Services is a layer on top of an ADO.NET Entity Framework model that allows you to access a database via the Internet or an intranet using query string parameters in a URL.

Many applications still use files to exchange data between systems so understanding the many choices you have in the .NET Framework for reading and writing files is important. The .NET Framework has classes that allow you to determine the properties of a file or folder, and also for reading and writing files to disk, in memory, or over a network pipe.

Serialization is the concept of transforming an object and its data into another form such as XML, JSON, or a binary format. The .NET Framework has classes that can accomplish this with very little code or you can implement your own custom serialization.

This chapter covered a lot of material, so it might be a good idea to review it a few times. You might have plenty of questions about the material covered in this chapter, so be sure to walk through all the sample code and get a good understanding of the concepts that have been discussed. Many times on the test you will see specific syntax questions about a particular object, so you must know method and property names. In addition to this chapter, review the articles listed in the "Additional Reading and Resources" section at the end of this chapter. Not only must you understand these concepts for the test, but you will see these concepts when you work with real-world applications.

CHAPTER TEST QUESTIONS

Read each question carefully and select the answer or answers that represent the best solution to the problem. You can find the answers in Appendix A, "Answers to Chapter Test Questions."

1. Which object does the variable `mySet` inherit from?

    ```
    Int[] mySet  = new int[5];
    ```

    a. `System.Collection`

    b. `System.Collection.List`

    c. `System.Array`

    d. None, this is a value type.

2. Which type should you use to store objects of different types but do not know how many elements you need at the time of creation?

    a. `Collection`

    b. `List<T>`

    c. `Stack<T>`

    d. `ArrayList`

3. If you create a custom class that is going to be used as elements in a `List` object and you want to use the `Sort` method of the `List` object to sort the elements in the array, what steps must you take when coding the custom class?

    a. Inherit from the `ICompare` interface. Implement the `Comparable` method.

    b. Inherit from the `IComparable` interface. Implement the `CompareTo` method.

    c. Inherit from the `System.Array` class. Override the `Sort` method.

    d. Inherit from the `List` class. Implement the `Sort` method.

4. Which collection would you use if you need to process the items in the collection on first-in-first-out order?

    a. `HashTable`

    b. `Queue`

    c. `Stack`

    d. `List`

5. Which collection would you use if you need to process the items in the collection on a last-in-first-out order?

    a. `HashTable`

    b. `Queue`

    c. `Stack`

    d. `List`

6. Which collection would you use if you need to quickly find an element by its key rather than its index?

    a. `Dictionary`

    b. `List`

    c. `SortedList`

    d. `Queue`

7. Which ADO.NET object is used to connect to a database?

    a. `Database`

    b. `Connection`

    c. `Command`

    d. `DataAdapter`

8. Which properties of an ADO.NET Command object must you set to execute a stored procedure?

    a. `CommandTypeStoredProcedureNameParameters`

    b. `IsStoredProcedureCommandTypeStoredProcedureNameParameters`

    c. `CommandTypeCommandTextParameters`

    d. `IsStoredProcedureCommandTextParameters`

9. Which `Command` object's method would you use to execute a query that does not return any results?

    a. `ExecuteNonQuery`

    b. `ExecuteDataReader`

    c. `ExecuteScalar`

    d. `Execute`

10. Which `Command` object's method would you use to execute a query that returns only one row and one column?

    a. `ExecuteNonQuery`

    b. `ExecuteDataReader`

    c. `ExecuteScalar`

    d. `Execute`

11. Which ADO.NET object is a forward only cursor and is connected to the database while the cursor is open?

    a. DBDataReader

    b. DataSet

    c. DataTable

    d. DataAdapter

12. Which ADO.NET Command object's property would you use when a query returns the SUM of a column in a table?

    a. ExecuteNonQuery

    b. ExecuteDataReader

    c. ExecuteScalar

    d. Execute

13. Which ADO.NET object is a fully traversable cursor and is disconnected from the database?

    a. DBDataReader

    b. DataSet

    c. DataTable

    d. DataAdapter

14. Which method of a DataAdapter is used to populate a DataSet?

    a. Populate

    b. Fill

    c. Load

    d. DataSets[0].Fill

15. Which property of an ADO.NET DataAdapter is used to insert records in a database?

    a. InsertText

    b. InsertType

    c. InsertCommand

    d. InsertDataTable

16. Which ADO.NET Command object's property would you use when a query returns the SUM of a column in a table?

    a. ExecuteNonQuery

    b. ExecuteDataReader

    c. ExecuteScalar

    d. Execute

17. When using the ADO.NET Entity Framework you create a `Model` that represents the object in the database. What class does the `Model` inherit from?

    a. `DBContext`

    b. `DBSet`

    c. `Model`

    d. `Connection`

18. How are stored procedures represented in the ADO.NET Entity Framework?

    a. A class is created with the same name as the stored procedure, and the `Execute` method is implemented.

    b. A method is added to the Model that is the same name as the stored procedure.

    c. Stored procedures cannot be called from the ADO.NET Entity Framework.

    d. A method is created in the entity class for the table in the stored procedure.

19. Which code uses the ADO.NET Entity Framework to add a record to the database?

    a.

```
using (NorthwindsEntities db = new NorthwindsEntities())
{
    Category category = new Category()
    {
        CategoryName = "Alcohol",
        Description = "Happy Beverages"
    };

    db.Categories.Add(category);
    db.SaveChanges();
}
```

    b.

```
using (NorthwindsEntities db = new NorthwindsEntities())
{
    Category category = new Category()
    {
        CategoryName = "Alcohol",
        Description = "Happy Beverages"
    };

    db.Categories.Add(category);
    db.InsertRecords ();
}
```

    c.

```
using (NorthwindsEntities db = new NorthwindsEntities())
{
    Category category = new Category()
```

```
    {
        CategoryName = "Alcohol",
        Description = "Happy Beverages"
    };

    db.Categories.Insert (category);
    db.SaveChanges();
}
```

d.

```
using (NorthwindsEntities db = new NorthwindsEntities())
{
    Category category = new Category()
    {
        CategoryName = "Alcohol",
        Description = "Happy Beverages"
    };

    db.Categories.Insert(category);
    db.InsertRecords();
}
```

20. Which code uses the ADO.NET Entity Framework to update a record in the database?

a.

```
Category category = db.Categories.First(c => c.CategoryName == "Alcohol");
category.Description = "Happy People";
db.UpdateRecords ();
```

b.

```
Category category = db.Categories.First(c => c.CategoryName == "Alcohol");
category.Description = "Happy People";
db.Categories.UpdateRecords();
```

c.

```
Category category = db.Categories.First(c => c.CategoryName == "Alcohol");
category.Description = "Happy People";
db.SaveChanges();
```

d.

```
Category category = db.Categories.First(c => c.CategoryName == "Alcohol");
category.Description = "Happy People";
db.Categories.SaveChanges();
```

ADDITIONAL READING AND RESOURCES

Here are some additional useful resources to help you understand the topics presented in this chapter:

Microsoft WCF Data Services Documentation
> `http://msdn.microsoft.com/en-us/library/cc668792.aspx`

Open Data Protocol
> `http://www.odata.org`

Open Data Protocol Filter Options
> `http://www.odata.org/developers/protocols/`
> `uri-conventions#FilterSystemQueryOption`

NHibernate
> `http://nhforge.org`

Microsoft's Entity Framework
> `http://msdn.microsoft.com/en-us/data/ef.aspx`

Julie Lerman's blog (Entity Framework Guru)
> `http://thedatafarm.com/blog/`

Microsoft's Collection Reference
> `http://msdn.microsoft.com/en-us/library/ybcx56wz(v=vs.110).aspx`

Connection String
> `http://www.connectionstrings.com`

JSON Reference
> `http://www.json.org`

CHEAT SHEET

This cheat sheet is designed as a way for you to quickly study the key points of this chapter.

Arrays and collections

➤ Arrays all inherit from the System.Array type.

➤ There are numerous collection types that are similar to arrays, but they offer much more flexibility for manipulating the data contained in the collection.

➤ ArrayList, HashTable, Queue, SortedList, and Stack are all in the System.Collections namespace.

➤ Dictionary<TKey, TValue>, List<T>, Queue<T>, SortedList<TKey, TValue>, and Stack<T> are all in the System.Collections.Generic namespace.

➤ The generic collection classes are used when you want all objects to be of the same type.

➤ Queues are first-in-first-out.

➤ Stacks are last-in-first-out.

➤ You can implement the IComparable interface to control how two objects are compared.

➤ A Dictionary object stores a key\value pair.

➤ Custom collections inherit from the CollectionBase class.

ADO.NET

➤ ADO.NET is a set of classes used to execute commands on a database.

➤ A Command object is used to call a stored procedure or execute a dynamic SQL statement.

➤ The Command's ExecuteNonQuery method is used to execute nonresult-returning queries such as an INSERT or UPDATE command.

➤ A DBDataReader object is a read-only, forward-only cursor connected to the database.

➤ The Command's ExecuteScalar method is used to return a single value from a database such as when a query returns a SUM or COUNT.

➤ The Command's ExecuteXMLReader method returns the data represented as XML. Use the FOR XML clause in SQL Server to select the data as XML.

➤ A DataSet is a disconnected resultset and can contain one or more DataTables. A DataAdapter is used to fill a DataSet.

➤ A DataAdapter can be used with a DataSet to add, update, or delete records in a database.

ADO.NET Entity Framework

➤ The Entity Framework is an ORM tool that masks the syntax for using ADO.NET to communicate with a database.

➤ An Entity Framework Model contains the classes that represent the objects in a database.

➤ Stored procedures are methods on an Entity Framework Model.

WCF Data Services

➤ WCF Data Services enables you to access a database over the web or an intranet.

➤ WCF Data Services uses the OData protocol.

➤ WCF Data Services returns data in OData ATOM format but also can return data in JSON format.

➤ You can query data in a database by passing parameters in the URL's query string.

File I\O

➤ `File` and `FileInfo` object are used to determine properties about a file and also perform operations on a file.

➤ A `Stream` is used to represent the contents of a file in memory and can be used to write data to a file or read data from a file.

➤ A `BinaryReader` and `BinaryWriter` are used for reading and writing binary values.

➤ A `StreamReader` and `StreamWriter` are used for reading and writing characters by using an encoded value to convert the characters to and from bytes.

➤ The default character encoding for a `StreamReader` and `StreamWriter` is UTF-8.

➤ You can use a `StreamReader` to read a file character by character, line by line, or the entire file at once.

➤ The `StringReader` and `StringWriter` is used to read and write string data.

➤ The `async` and `await` keywords are used to perform asynchronous operations.

➤ The `async` keyword must modify a method signature for it to use the `await` keyword.

➤ The `await` command kicks off the method but returns processing back to the calling method until the method completes.

Serialization

➤ Serialization is the process of transforming an object's data to persisted storage or to transfer the object from one domain to another.

➤ The `BinaryFormatter` is used to perform binary serialization.

➤ The `XmlSerializer` is used to perform XML serialization.

➤ The `DataContractJsonSerializer` is used to perform JSON serialization.

➤ There are two ways to customize serialization, using attributes or implementing the `ISerializable` interface.

REVIEW OF KEY TERMS

ADO.NET A set of classes in the .NET Framework that enables you to connect to a database, retrieve data, execute stored procedures, add, update, or delete records in a table.

ADO.NET Entity Framework An object relational mapping tool that provides a graphical user interface that generates to code to perform operations against a database using ADO.NET

array The most basic type used to store a set of data.

async Indicates that the method, lambda expression, or anonymous method is asynchronous.

await Suspends the execution of a method until the awaited task completes.

boxing/unboxing Boxing is the process of converting a value type to a reference type. Unboxing is the process of converting a reference type to a value type.

collection A generic term that encompasses lists, dictionaries, queues, stacks, hash tables, and other objects that can contain sets of data.

connection object An object in ADO.NET that allows you to open and execute commands against a database.

IComparable interface A class that implements the `IComparable` interface can be sorted when used in a collection or array.

indexer A method that is used when referencing an element in an array or collection by using square brackets, `[]`, and its index.

JSON JavaScript Object Notation is a lightweight data-interchange format.

Object Relational Mapping (ORM) A computer software term for tools that convert data between type systems using an object oriented programming language.

OData ATOM The XML representation of data returned from an OData query.

Open Data Protocol (OData) A web protocol for querying and updating data through the Internet or intranet.

shallow copy Creating a new copy of an object that copies all value types and copies object references for reference types.

serialization The process of converting an object into a stream of bytes that can be stored or transmitted.

stream An abstract class that provides a generic view of a sequence of bytes.

Text Transformation Template Toolkit (T4 Template) A file that contains text blocks and control statements that enable to you to generate a code file.

WCF Data Services Enables you to use OData to expose and consume data over the web or an intranet.

EXAM TIPS AND TRICKS

The Review of Key Terms and the Cheat Sheet for this chapter can be printed to help you study. You can find these files in the ZIP file for this chapter at `www.wrox.com/remtitle.cgi?isbn=1118612094` on the Download Code tab.

10

Working with Language Integrated Query (LINQ)

WHAT YOU WILL LEARN IN THIS CHAPTER

➤ Understanding query expressions

➤ Understanding method-based LINQ queries

➤ Utilizing LINQ to XML

WROX.COM CODE DOWNLOADS FOR THIS CHAPTER

You can find the code downloads for this chapter at www.wrox.com/remtitle .cgi?isbn=1118612094 on the Download Code tab. The code is in the chapter10 download and individually named according to the names throughout the chapter.

Language Integrated Query (LINQ) is a language feature in the .NET Framework that enables you to use common syntax to query data in a collection, an XML document, a database, or any type that supports the IEnumerable<T> or IQueryable<T> interface. Prior to LINQ, a developer needed to learn different syntax depending on the source of the data. If the source were a database, you needed to learn SQL. If the source were an XML document, you needed to learn XQuery. If the source were an array or a collection, you would write a looping structure, such as a foreach loop, that would enumerate through the items in the collection and filter them appropriately. LINQ enables you to use common syntax regardless of what the source is.

In this chapter, you learn two different styles of syntax for LINQ. Query expressions are the first style, and method-based queries are the second. They are functionally equivalent, which can sometimes be confusing when you first learn LINQ because you can write the code two different ways and it does the exact same thing. The last section discusses LINQ to XML, which enables you to create XML documents without having to write all the tags that normally would be required when working with XML.

Table 10-1 introduces you to the exam objectives covered in this chapter.

TABLE 10-1: 70-483 Exam Objectives Covered in This Chapter

OBJECTIVE	CONTENT COVERED
Query and manipulate data and objects using LINQ	*Writing query expressions and method-based queries using LINQ.* Topics covered include projection, joining and grouping collections, the take and skip methods, and aggregate methods. You will also learn how to create, and modify data structures by using LINQ to XML.

UNDERSTANDING QUERY EXPRESSIONS

As you saw in the introduction to this chapter, *Language Integrated Query* is a language feature in the .NET Framework that enables you to use common query syntax to query data in a collection, an XML document, a database, or any type that supports the `IEnumerable<T>` or `IQueryable<T>` interface. There are two forms of syntax that perform LINQ queries. The first is a query expression, which is discussed in this section. The second are method-based queries, which are discussed in the next section. Functionally, they do the exact same thing; the only difference is the syntax. You must decide which syntax you prefer, but the compiler does not care.

> **ADVICE FROM THE EXPERTS: Query Expressions versus Method-Based Queries**
>
> The compiler converts query expressions to method-based expressions when your assembly is compiled. Query expressions are sometimes easier to read, so you may choose to standardize on that syntax, but be aware that you cannot perform all the operations using query expressions that you can using method-based queries such as a `Count` or `Sum`.

Query expressions search through data stored in an array, a collection, or any type that supports the `IEnumerable<T>` or `IQueryable<T>` interfaces. The syntax for a query expression is similar to the syntax when working with SQL. Before getting into the details about query expressions, you first take a look at the code needed to search data in objects prior to LINQ. For example, suppose you have an array with the numbers 1 through 10. If you want to retrieve all the even numbers from the array, your code would look something like the following:

```
int[] myArray = new int[10] { 1, 2, 3, 4, 5, 6, 7, 8, 9, 10 };
int[] evenNumbers = new int[5];
int evenIndex = 0;

foreach (int i in myArray)
{
    if (i % 2 == 0)
```

```
        {
            evenNumbers[evenIndex] = i;
            evenIndex++;
        }
    }

    foreach (int i in evenNumbers)
    {
        Debug.WriteLine(i);
    }
```

LINQ query expressions enable you to perform "queries" against the array with syntax similar to SQL except it is C# syntax and the order of the elements is different. The benefit of a query expression is less coding and more readability. The following code performs a LINQ query against the array to return only even numbers:

```
    int[] myArray = new int[10] { 1, 2, 3, 4, 5, 6, 7, 8, 9, 10 };

    var evenNumbers = from i in myArray
                      where i % 2 == 0
                      select i;

    foreach (int i in evenNumbers)
    {
        Debug.WriteLine(i);
    }
```

A few things need explaining here. First, the evenNumber variable is declared as a var. A variable defined as var is called an *implicitly typed variable*. This means that the compiler determines the type of variable based on the expression on the right side of the initialization statement. In this sample the compiler knows that the items in the evenNumbers variable are int. It is common practice to declare the results of a LINQ query expression as a var variable.

The second thing to notice is the from clause syntax. In this example, the from clause contains i in myArray. The compiler implicitly knows what type i is based on the type of myArray. This is functionally equivalent to the foreach(int i in myArray) statement. The variable i represents an item in the array as it is enumerated.

The third thing to notice is that the where clause is second and the select clause is third. This is the opposite of SQL syntax. When writing LINQ queries, even if you query a database, the where clause precedes the select clause. The fourth thing is that the where clause contains C# syntax for filtering the data, which means you use the equivalence operator (==) instead of equals (=). This essentially tells the compiler to evaluate each element in the array and return the items that meet this condition.

EXAM TIPS AND TRICKS: Query Expression Syntax

You may see a question on the exam that features the different clauses in a query expression, and you will be asked to put the clauses in the correct order.

Finally, notice that the `select` clause returns the variable `i`. This actually means as the code enumerates through the array it should return all elements that meets the `where` condition. If you were to step through this code, you would notice something different from what you might expect. When you start stepping through the code and get to the `foreach` statement, you can notice that execution keeps transferring from the `foreach` statement back to the `where` clause in the LINQ query. This is because the LINQ query isn't actually executed until the `evenNumbers` variable is used. This is called *deferred execution*. If you were to add a watch statement to the `evenNumbers` variable, you would notice that it doesn't actually store the results. It executes any time the elements are enumerated. If the source of the data changed and you enumerated the elements again, it would pick up the changes. For example, examine the following code:

```
int[] myArray = new int[10] { 1, 2, 3, 4, 5, 6, 7, 8, 9, 10 };

var evenNumbers = from i in myArray
                  where i % 2 == 0
                  select i;

foreach (int i in evenNumbers)
{
    Debug.WriteLine(i);
}

myArray[1] = 12;

foreach (int i in evenNumbers)
{
    Debug.WriteLine(i);
}
```

In the preceding example, the second element in the array, which contains the number 2, is replaced with the number 12 after the first `foreach` loop. When the `evenNumbers` variable is enumerated the second time, the number 12 is written to the Output window along with the other even numbers.

Filtering

Filtering data is done by using the `where` clause in a query expression. Because you are writing in C#, you must use the and (`&&`) and or (`||`) operators when making complex statements. In the previous examples, the `where` clause contained the boolean expression `i % 2 == 0`. This is referred to as a predicate. The *predicate* is the comparison statement that is executed against each element in the sequence. The following example returns all event numbers that are greater than 5:

```
int[] myArray = new int[10] { 1, 2, 3, 4, 5, 6, 7, 8, 9, 10 };

var evenNumbers = from i in myArray
                  where i % 2 == 0 && i > 5
                  select i;

foreach (int i in evenNumbers)
{
    Debug.WriteLine(i);
}
```

You can have multiple `where` clauses in your query expression. This is the same as having multiple expressions in the `where` clause using the `&&` operator. The following code produces the same result as the preceding code:

```
int[] myArray = new int[10] { 1, 2, 3, 4, 5, 6, 7, 8, 9, 10 };

var evenNumbers = from i in myArray
                  where i % 2 == 0
                  where i > 5
                  select i;

foreach (int i in evenNumbers)
{
    Debug.WriteLine(i);
}
```

> **EXAM TIPS AND TRICKS: Multiple where Clauses**
>
> You typically would not use multiple `where` clauses in your code. Instead, you would just separate your clauses by the `&&` operator. However, for the test you may see a question using this syntax, so you need to be aware that multiple `where` clauses is the equivalent of using the `&&` operator.

If you had a complex filter condition that needed precedence operators, you would use parentheses, `()`, just as you would in a regular `if` statement. But be aware that if your query expression contains two `where` clauses, each is executed separately and are considered `and` expressions.

Also be aware that you can call a function in your statement to make your code more readable. The following code sample calls a method called `IsEvenAndGT5` and passes in the current element while enumerating through the array:

```
static void RetrieveEvenNumberGT5V3()
{
    int[] myArray = new int[10] { 1, 2, 3, 4, 5, 6, 7, 8, 9, 10 };

    var evenNumbers = from i in myArray
                      where IsEvenAndGT5(i)
                      select i;

    foreach (int i in evenNumbers)
    {
        Debug.WriteLine(i);
    }
}

static bool IsEvenAndGT5(int i)
{
    return (i % 2 == 0 && i > 5);
}
```

The last point to be aware of regarding the `where` clause is that it can appear anywhere in your query expression as long as it is not the first or last clause.

Ordering

You can sort the results of your query by using the `orderby` clause in your query. You can order ascending or descending just as you would in a SQL statement. The following code sorts the even elements in descending order:

```
int[] myArray = new int[10] { 1, 2, 3, 4, 5, 6, 7, 8, 9, 10 };

var evenNumbers = from i in myArray
                  where i % 2 == 0
                  orderby i descending
                  select i;

foreach (int i in evenNumbers)
{
    Debug.WriteLine(i);
}
```

You can also order by more than one property by separating your conditions with a comma. The following example uses a class that contains a `City` and `State` property. The query returns the elements sorted first by state and then by city alphabetically.

```
class Hometown
{
    public string City { get; set; }
    public string State { get; set; }
}

static void OrderByStateThenCity()
{
    List<Hometown> hometowns = new List<Hometown>()
    {
        new Hometown() { City = "Philadelphia", State = "PA" },
        new Hometown() { City = "Ewing", State = "NJ" },
        new Hometown() { City = "Havertown", State = "PA" },
        new Hometown() { City = "Fort Washington", State = "PA" },
        new Hometown() { City = "Trenton", State = "NJ" }
    };

    var orderedHometowns = from h in hometowns
                           orderby h.State ascending, h.City ascending
                           select h;

    foreach (Hometown hometown in orderedHometowns)
    {
        Debug.WriteLine(hometown.City + ", " + hometown.State);
    }
}
```

The preceding code produces the following results:

```
Ewing, NJ
Trenton, NJ
Fort Washington, PA
```

```
Havertown, PA
Philadelphia, PA
```

The default order in an `orderby` clause is ascending, and you can omit this keyword.

Projection

The `select` clause can return the object in the sequence or return a limited number of properties from the object in the sequence. Selecting a limited number of properties or transforming the result into a different type is referred to as *projection*. For example, assume you have a `Person` call declared with the following properties:

```
class Person
{
    public string FirstName { get; set; }
    public string LastName { get; set; }
    public string Address1 { get; set; }
    public string City { get; set; }
    public string State { get; set; }
    public string Zip { get; set; }
}
```

Now suppose you need to write a query that only returns the `LastName` of each `Person` in a `List` of `Person` objects:

```
List<Person> people = new List<Person>()
{
    new Person()
    {
        FirstName = "John",
        LastName = "Smith",
        Address1 = "First St",
        City = "Havertown",
        State = "PA",
        Zip = "19084"
    },
    new Person()
    {
        FirstName = "Jane",
        LastName = "Doe",
        Address1 = "Second St",
        City = "Ewing",
        State = "NJ",
        Zip = "08560"
    },
    new Person()
    {
        FirstName = "Jack",
        LastName = "Jones",
        Address1 = "Third St",
        City = "Ft Washington",
        State = "PA",
        Zip = "19034"
    }
```

```
                };

var lastNames = from p in people
                select p.LastName;

foreach (string lastName in lastNames)
{
    Debug.WriteLine(lastName);
}
```

The `select` clause selects `p.LastName` instead of the entire `p` object. The compiler determines that the result should be a list of strings, based on the type of the property selected. This is one example of projection. You selected a single property and returned a list of strings from the query.

Now suppose that you needed to return the `FirstName` and `LastName` properties. The following query creates an *anonymous type* that contains just a `FirstName` and `LastName` property. An anonymous type is an object with read-only properties that is not explicitly declared.

```
var names = from p in people
            select new { p.FirstName, p.LastName };

foreach (var name in names)
{
    Debug.WriteLine(name.FirstName + ", " + name.LastName);
}
```

You can also explicitly name the properties of an anonymous type using the following syntax:

```
var names = from p in people
            select new { First = p.FirstName, Last = p.LastName };

foreach (var name in names)
{
    Debug.WriteLine(name.First + ", " + name.Last);
}
```

In the preceding example, the properties of the anonymous type are named `First` and `Last`. Visual Studio's IntelliSense can recognize these properties, which appear in the drop-down lists when you use the anonymous type.

Joining

You can use the `join` clause to combine two or more sequences of objects similar to how you join tables in a SQL statement. The following sample joins two separate lists on a common property called `StateId`:

```
class Employee
{
    public string FirstName { get; set; }
    public string LastName { get; set; }
    public int StateId { get; set; }
}
```

```
class State
{
    public int StateId { get; set; }
    public string StateName { get; set; }
}
static void Join()
{
    List<Employee> employees = new List<Employee>()
    {
        new Employee()
        {
            FirstName = "John",
            LastName = "Smith",
            StateId = 1
        },
        new Employee()
        {
            FirstName = "Jane",
            LastName = "Doe",
            StateId = 2
        },
        new Employee()
        {
            FirstName = "Jack",
            LastName = "Jones",
            StateId = 1
        }
    };

    List<State> states = new List<State>()
    {
        new State()
        {
            StateId = 1,
            StateName = "PA"
        },
        new State()
        {
            StateId = 2,
            StateName = "NJ"
        }
    };

    var employeeByState = from e in employees
                          join s in states
                            on e.StateId equals s.StateId
                          select new { e.LastName, s.StateName };

    foreach (var employee in employeeByState)
    {
        Debug.WriteLine(employee.LastName + ", " + employee.StateName);
    }
}
```

The `join` clause uses the `equals` keyword instead of =. This is because you can join fields only based on equivalence unlike SQL where you can use > or < signs. Using the keyword `equals` is supposed to make it clearer that the operation is equivalence.

EXAM TIPS AND TRICKS: Equals versus "="

You may see a question on the exam that displays four different `join` clauses, and you will be asked which is correct. Be sure to remember that a `join` clause must use the `equals` keyword and not the = operator.

Outer Join

Now suppose you need to perform an *outer join*. An outer join selects all elements from one sequence even if there is not a matching element in the second sequence. In SQL this is referred to as a RIGHT OUTER JOIN or a LEFT OUTER JOIN. In SQL, if you want all the rows from the table on the right side of the JOIN clause, you use a RIGHT OUTER JOIN; if you want all the rows from the table on the left side of the join, you use LEFT OUTER JOIN. This scenario happens often when writing database queries. For example, if you have a table that contains a foreign key that is nullable and you want to join to the table with the primary key, you would use an OUTER JOIN clause to ensure you select all records, even if the column is NULL.

To accomplish this same functionality in a query expression, you need to use the `group join` keyword and the `DefaultIfEmpty` method. A `group join` enables you to combine two sequences into a third object. For example, suppose you added another `Employee` object to the `employees` list in the previous example, but the `StateId` for your new object does not exist in the `states` list.

```
new Employee()
{
    FirstName = "Sue",
    LastName = "Smith",
    StateId = 3
}
```

The following query selects all the elements from the `employees` list even if there is not a match in the `states` List:

```
var employeeByState = from e in employees
                      join s in states
                        on e.StateId equals s.StateId into employeeGroup
                      from item in employeeGroup.DefaultIfEmpty( new State
                                                                   {StateId = 0,
                                                                    StateName = ""})
                      select new { e.LastName, item.StateName };

foreach (var employee in employeeByState)
{
    Debug.WriteLine(employee.LastName + ", " + employee.StateName);
}
```

The joined lists are combined into an object called `employeeGroup`. This is done by using the `into` keyword. There is also a second `from` clause that can create a new instance of a `State` object with a `StateId` of `0` and a `StateName` of `""` when there is not a match found on `StateId`. If you use an `into` clause, you can no longer reference the variable declared on the right side of the on statement in your `select` clause. You instead use the variable that was used to enumerate the values of the new sequence, in this example that is the `item` variable. The `select` clause needs to be changed to use the `item` variable rather than the `s` variable to get the state name.

COMMON MISTAKES: Left Joins Only

For query expressions, you can perform only left joins, so the order of the sequences is important in your `from` clause.

Composite Keys

There may be instances where you need to perform your join on a *composite key*. A composite key contains multiple properties that you need for the purpose of a join. To accomplish this, you create two anonymous types with the same properties and compare the anonymous types. For example, change the `Hometown` class to have a `CityCode` property, and change the `Employee` class to contain the `City` and `State` and remove the `StateId`:

```
class Hometown
{
    public string City { get; set; }
    public string State { get; set; }
    public string CityCode { get; set; }
}

class Employee
{
    public string FirstName { get; set; }
    public string LastName { get; set; }
    public string City { get; set; }
    public string State { get; set; }
}
```

The following query joins a List of `Hometown` objects and `Employee` objects using their `City` and `State` properties:

```
static void CompositeKey()
{
    List<Employee> employees = new List<Employee>()
    {
        new Employee()
        {
            FirstName = "John",
            LastName = "Smith",
            City = "Havertown",
            State = "PA"
```

```csharp
        },
        new Employee()
        {
            FirstName = "Jane",
            LastName = "Doe",
            City = "Ewing",
            State = "NJ"
        },
        new Employee()
        {
            FirstName = "Jack",
            LastName = "Jones",
            City = "Fort Washington",
            State = "PA"
        }
    };

    List<Hometown> hometowns = new List<Hometown>()
    {
        new Hometown()
        {
            City = "Havertown",
            State = "PA",
            CityCode = "1234"
        },
        new Hometown()
        {
            City = "Ewing",
            State = "NJ",
            CityCode = "5678"
        },
        new Hometown()
        {
            City = "Fort Washington",
            State = "PA",
            CityCode = "9012"
        }
    };

    var employeeByState = from e in employees
                      join h in hometowns
                      on new { City = e.City, State = e.State } equals
                          new { City = h.City, State = h.State }
                      select new { e.LastName, h.CityCode };

    foreach (var employee in employeeByState)
    {
        Debug.WriteLine(employee.LastName + ", " + employee.CityCode);
    }
}
```

The join creates two anonymous types with the same properties. The equivalence is determined by matching all properties of the anonymous type.

Grouping

Often, you need to group items to determine the count of elements or the sum of a particular property when working with a sequence of objects. For example, you may need to produce a report that displays the count of employees by state. You can use the `group` clause in a query expression to group by a particular property to accomplish this requirement. For example, the following code creates a List of `Employee` objects and then executes a query to group them by `State`. The count of the employees by state can then be written to the Output window.

```
static void Group()
{
    List<Employee> employees = new List<Employee>()
    {
        new Employee()
        {
            FirstName = "John",
            LastName = "Smith",
            City = "Havertown",
            State = "PA"
        },
        new Employee()
        {
            FirstName = "Jane",
            LastName = "Doe",
            City = "Ewing",
            State = "NJ"
        },
        new Employee()
        {
            FirstName = "Jack",
            LastName = "Jones",
            City = "Fort Washington",
            State = "PA"
        }
    };

    var employeesByState = from e in employees
                           group e by e.State;

    foreach (var employeeGroup in employeesByState)
    {
        Debug.WriteLine(employeeGroup.Key + ": " + employeeGroup.Count());

        foreach (var employee in employeeGroup)
        {
            Debug.WriteLine(employee.LastName + ", " + employee.State);
        }
    }
}
```

In this sample there isn't a `select` clause. This is because a `group` clause returns an `IGrouping<TKey, TElement>` collection. This object is a collection that contains a property for the key that the sequence is grouped by. There are two `foreach` loops in this sample. The first enumerates through the `IGrouping` collection and writes the `Key` property and the `Count` of elements for the `State` to the Output window. The inner `foreach` loop writes the elements that make up the group to the Output window. The output for the previous sample is as follows:

```
PA: 2
Smith, PA
Jones, PA
NJ: 1
Doe, NJ
```

You can add logic in your `group by` clause to group by anything. The following example groups even and odd number and then prints the count and sum of each group to the Output window:

```
static void GroupV2()
{
    int[] myArray = new int[10] { 1, 2, 3, 4, 5, 6, 7, 8, 9, 10 };

    var groupedNumbers = from i in myArray
                         group i by (i % 2 == 0 ? "Even" : "Odd");

    foreach (var groupNumber in groupedNumbers)
    {
        Debug.WriteLine(groupNumber.Key + ": " + groupNumber.Sum());
        foreach(var number in groupNumber)
        {
            Debug.WriteLine(number);
        }
    }
}
```

In the preceding example, the `group by` clause contains a conditional statement that returns the string `"Even"` or `"Odd"` and groups the number appropriately. The preceding code produces the following result:

```
Odd: 25
1
3
5
7
9
Even: 30
2
4
6
8
10
```

You can use a `select` clause when grouping sequences, but you must include an `into` clause in your `group` clause. Suppose in the last example you wanted to select the key and the sum of even or odd numbers in the query. The following code can accomplish this:

```
static void GroupV3()
{
    int[] myArray = new int[10] { 1, 2, 3, 4, 5, 6, 7, 8, 9, 10 };
```

```
var groupedNumbers = from i in myArray
                     group i by (i % 2 == 0 ? "Even" : "Odd") into g
                     select new { Key = g.Key, SumOfNumbers = g.Sum() };

foreach (var groupNumber in groupedNumbers)
{
    Debug.WriteLine(groupNumber.Key + ": " + groupNumber.SumOfNumbers);
}
}
```

The variable g is of type `IGrouping<TKey, TElement>` and you can use that in your `select` clause. The `select` clause creates an anonymous type with two properties: `Key` and `SumOfNumbers`. The preceding code produces the following output:

```
Odd: 25
Even: 30
```

Understanding Method-Based LINQ Queries

The previous section discusses query expressions, which is the syntax used to perform LINQ queries using a shorthand query syntax. You can also perform the same queries using method-based LINQ queries. They are functionally equivalent; the only difference is the syntax.

Method-based queries are actually extension methods found in the `System.Linq` namespace. These methods extend any variable that implements the `IEnumerable<T>` or `IQueryable<T>` interface. Method-based queries take a lambda expression as a parameter, which represents the logic to be performed while enumerating through the sequence. Recall the first example for the query expression syntax:

```
int[] myArray = new int[10] { 1, 2, 3, 4, 5, 6, 7, 8, 9, 10 };

var evenNumbers = from i in myArray
                  where i % 2 == 0
                  select i;
```

This code selects all the even numbers in an array. The equivalent method-based query follows:

```
int[] myArray = new int[10] { 1, 2, 3, 4, 5, 6, 7, 8, 9, 10 };

var evenNumbers = myArray.Where(i => i % 2 == 0);
```

The variable i represents the element in the array, and the code on the right of the *goes to* operator (=>) represents the logic to be performed while enumerating through the array. These two code examples produce the exact same results; again, you must decide which syntax you are more comfortable with.

Filtering

Filtering is done by using the `Where` method as you've seen in the previous examples. You pass a lambda expression to the `Where` method that returns a boolean value to return only the elements that meet the true condition.

```
myArray.Where(i => i % 2 == 0)
```

You still use the and (&&) and or (||) operators for complex conditions because the lambda expression is C# syntax.

```
var evenNumbers = myArray.Where(i => i % 2 == 0 && i > 5);
```

If you need precedence operators, you can chain the `Where` clauses. This is equivalent to having multiple `where` clauses in a query expression.

```
var evenNumbers = myArray.Where(i => i % 2 == 0).Where(i => i > 5);
```

And you can also call a function that returns a boolean.

```
var evenNumbers = myArray.Where(i => IsEvenAndGT5(i));
```

Ordering

You can order the elements in a sequence by using the `OrderBy` or the `OrderByDescending` methods. The following code orders all the even numbers in an array descending:

```
var evenNumbers = myArray.Where(i => i % 2 == 0).OrderByDescending(i => i);
```

If you need to order by more than one field, you chain the methods using a `ThenBy` or `ThenByDescending` method. The following example orders by `State` and then by `City`:

```
static void MethodBasedOrderByStateThenCity()
{
    List<Hometown> hometowns = new List<Hometown>()
    {
        new Hometown() { City = "Philadelphia", State = "PA" },
        new Hometown() { City = "Ewing", State = "NJ" },
        new Hometown() { City = "Havertown", State = "PA" },
        new Hometown() { City = "Fort Washington", State = "PA" },
        new Hometown() { City = "Trenton", State = "NJ" }
    };

    var orderedHometowns = hometowns.OrderBy(h => h.State).ThenBy(h => h.City);

    foreach (Hometown hometown in orderedHometowns)
    {
        Debug.WriteLine(hometown.City + ", " + hometown.State);
    }
}
```

Projection

You can project the result by using the `Select` method. The following code selects only the `LastName` property of a list of `Person` objects:

```
static void MethodBasedProjectionV1()
{
    List<Person> people = new List<Person>()
    {
        new Person()
        {
```

```
                    FirstName = "John",
                    LastName = "Smith",
                    Address1 = "First St",
                    City = "Havertown",
                    State = "PA",
                    Zip = "19084"
                },
                new Person()
                {
                    FirstName = "Jane",
                    LastName = "Doe",
                    Address1 = "Second St",
                    City = "Ewing",
                    State = "NJ",
                    Zip = "08560"
                },
                new Person()
                {
                    FirstName = "Jack",
                    LastName = "Jones",
                    Address1 = "Third St",
                    City = "Ft Washington",
                    State = "PA",
                    Zip = "19034"
                }
            };

        var lastNames = people.Select(p => p.LastName);

        foreach (string lastName in lastNames)
        {
            Debug.WriteLine(lastName);
        }
    }
```

You can create an anonymous type similar to how you do it with a query expression. The only difference is you use a lambda expression. The following creates an anonymous type with just the FirstName and LastName properties:

```
static void MethodBasedProjectionV2()
{
    List<Person> people = new List<Person>()
    {
        new Person()
        {
            FirstName = "John",
            LastName = "Smith",
            Address1 = "First St",
            City = "Havertown",
            State = "PA",
            Zip = "19084"
        },
        new Person()
        {
```

```
                    FirstName = "Jane",
                    LastName = "Doe",
                    Address1 = "Second St",
                    City = "Ewing",
                    State = "NJ",
                    Zip = "08560"
                },
                new Person()
                {
                    FirstName = "Jack",
                    LastName = "Jones",
                    Address1 = "Third St",
                    City = "Ft Washington",
                    State = "PA",
                    Zip = "19034"
                }
            };

            var names = people.Select(p => new { p.FirstName, p.LastName });

            foreach (var name in names)
            {
                Debug.WriteLine(name.FirstName + ", " + name.LastName);
            }
        }
```

You can also explicitly name the anonymous type properties by using the following syntax:

```
var names = people.Select(p => new { First = p.FirstName, Last = p.LastName });
```

The preceding sample created an anonymous type with a `First` and `Last` property rather than `FirstName` and `LastName`.

There is also a `SelectMany` method that you can use to flatten two sequences into one sequence similar to how a join works. The following flattens a list of `Employees` and a list of `States` and returns the combination of the two:

```
static void MethodBasedProjectionV4()
{
    List<Employee> employees = new List<Employee>()
    {
        new Employee()
        {
            FirstName = "John",
            LastName = "Smith",
            StateId = 1
        },
        new Employee()
        {
            FirstName = "Jane",
            LastName = "Doe",
            StateId = 2
        },
        new Employee()
```

```
            {
                FirstName = "John",
                LastName = "Smith",
                StateId = 1
            }
        };

        List<State> states = new List<State>()
        {
            new State()
            {
                StateId = 1,
                StateName = "PA"
            },
            new State()
            {
                StateId = 2,
                StateName = "NJ"
            }
        };

        var employeeByState = employees.SelectMany(e => states.Where(s =>
                e.StateId == s.StateId).Select(s => new { e.LastName, s.StateName }));

        foreach (var employee in employeeByState)
        {
            Debug.WriteLine(employee.LastName + ", " + employee.StateName);
        }
    }
```

Joining

The Join method enables you to join two sequences together using a common property or set of properties. The following code joins a List of Employee and State objects using the StateId property:

```
static void MethodBasedJoin()
{
    List<Employee> employees = new List<Employee>()
    {
        new Employee()
        {
            FirstName = "John",
            LastName = "Smith",
            StateId = 1
        },
        new Employee()
        {
            FirstName = "Jane",
            LastName = "Doe",
            StateId = 2
        },
        new Employee()
        {
            FirstName = "John",
```

```
                LastName = "Smith",
                StateId = 1
            }
        };

        List<State> states = new List<State>()
        {
            new State()
            {
                StateId = 1,
                StateName = "PA"
            },
            new State()
            {
                StateId = 2,
                StateName = "NJ"
            }
        };

        var employeeByState = employees.Join(states,
                                    e => e.StateId,
                                    s => s.StateId,
                                    (e, s) => new { e.LastName, s.StateName });

        foreach (var employee in employeeByState)
        {
            Debug.WriteLine(employee.LastName + ", " + employee.StateName);
        }
    }
```

The `employees` list is considered the *outer sequence*. The first parameter to the `Join` method is the sequence you want to join to: `states`. This is referred to as the *inner sequence*. The second parameter is the key property of the of the outer sequence. The third parameter is the key property of the inner sequence. By default an equivalence comparison will be used to join the two sequences. The fourth parameter is a lambda expression that creates the anonymous type for the result. In this sample you create a new type with `LastName` and `StateName` properties. When joining two sequences it can be more readable to use a query expression rather than the `Join` method.

Outer Join

An outer join is created by using the `GroupJoin` method. The following sample performs a left join using a List of `Employee` and `State` objects. If no matching state is found in the `State` list, the `StateName` will be blank.

```
static void MethodBasedOuterJoin()
{
    List<Employee> employees = new List<Employee>()
    {
        new Employee()
        {
            FirstName = "John",
            LastName = "Smith",
            StateId = 1
        },
```

```
        new Employee()
        {
            FirstName = "Jane",
            LastName = "Doe",
            StateId = 2
        },
        new Employee()
        {
            FirstName = "Jack",
            LastName = "Jones",
            StateId = 1
        },
        new Employee()
        {
            FirstName = "Sue",
            LastName = "Smith",
            StateId = 3
        }
    };

    List<State> states = new List<State>()
    {
        new State()
        {
            StateId = 1,
            StateName = "PA"
        },
        new State()
        {
            StateId = 2,
            StateName = "NJ"
        }
    };

    var employeeByState = employees.GroupJoin(states,
            e => e.StateId,
            s => s.StateId,
            (e, employeeGroup) => employeeGroup.Select(s => new
                {
                    LastName = e.LastName, StateName = s.StateName
                }).DefaultIfEmpty(new
                    {
                        LastName = e.LastName,StateName = ""
                    })).SelectMany(employeeGroup => employeeGroup);

    foreach (var employee in employeeByState)
    {
        Debug.WriteLine(employee.LastName + ", " + employee.StateName);
    }
}
```

The `employees` list is the outer sequence and the `states` list is the inner sequence. The first parameter to the `GroupJoin` method is the inner sequence. The second parameter is the `Key` property for the outer sequence, and the third parameter is the `Key` property for the inner sequence. The fourth parameter is where it is tricky. Recall in the query expression section that when creating an outer join, you needed to include the `into` keyword to create a variable that would contain the results of the join:

```
var employeeByState = from e in employees
                      join s in states
                        on e.StateId equals s.StateId into employeeGroup
                      from item in employeeGroup.DefaultIfEmpty( new State
                                                                 {StateId = 0,
                                                                  StateName = ""})
                      select new { e.LastName, item.StateName };
```

When using the `GroupJoin` method, you simply name the variable when creating the lambda expression in the fourth parameter:

```
var employeeByState = employees.GroupJoin(states,
        e => e.StateId,
        s => s.StateId,
        (e, employeeGroup) => employeeGroup.Select(s => new
            {
                LastName = e.LastName, StateName = s.StateName
            }).DefaultIfEmpty(new
                {
                    LastName = e.LastName,StateName = ""
                })).SelectMany(e => e);
```

You can then use the `Select` method to enumerate through the values in the `employeeGroup` object and use the `DefaultIfEmpty` method when no match is found between the two sequences. Finally, you need to call the `SelectMany` method to return the sequence of objects. This can be quite confusing when dealing with complex structures so the query expression syntax might be more to your liking than the method-based syntax. The preceding code produces the following results:

```
Smith, PA
Doe, NJ
Jones, PA
Smith,
```

Composite Keys

You can use a composite key by creating anonymous types when defining your keys in the `Join` parameters. The following code joins on two fields to match the data between two sequences:

```
static void MethodBasedCompositeKey()
{
    List<Employee> employees = new List<Employee>()
    {
        new Employee()
        {
            FirstName = "John",
            LastName = "Smith",
            City = "Havertown",
            State = "PA"
        },
```

```
        new Employee()
        {
            FirstName = "Jane",
            LastName = "Doe",
            City = "Ewing",
            State = "NJ"
        },
        new Employee()
        {
            FirstName = "Jack",
            LastName = "Jones",
            City = "Fort Washington",
            State = "PA"
        }
    };

    List<Hometown> hometowns = new List<Hometown>()
    {
        new Hometown()
        {
            City = "Havertown",
            State = "PA",
            CityCode = "1234"
        },
        new Hometown()
        {
            City = "Ewing",
            State = "NJ",
            CityCode = "5678"
        },
        new Hometown()
        {
            City = "Fort Washington",
            State = "PA",
            CityCode = "9012"
        }
    };

    var employeeByState = employees.Join(hometowns,
                            e => new { City = e.City, State = e.State },
                            h => new { City = h.City, State = h.State },
                            (e, h) => new { e.LastName, h.CityCode });

    foreach (var employee in employeeByState)
    {
        Debug.WriteLine(employee.LastName + ", " + employee.CityCode);
    }
}
```

The second and third parameters create an anonymous type with two properties. LINQ compares all properties of the two types when doing its equivalence test.

Grouping

The `GroupBy` method can be used to group by one or more fields. This is equivalent to using the `group` keyword when creating a query expression. The following code groups a List of `Employee` objects by `State`:

```
static void MethodBasedGroupV1()
{
    List<Employee> employees = new List<Employee>()
    {
        new Employee()
        {
            FirstName = "John",
            LastName = "Smith",
            City = "Havertown",
            State = "PA"
        },
        new Employee()
        {
            FirstName = "Jane",
            LastName = "Doe",
            City = "Ewing",
            State = "NJ"
        },
        new Employee()
        {
            FirstName = "Jack",
            LastName = "Jones",
            City = "Fort Washington",
            State = "PA"
        }
    };

    var employeesByState = employees.GroupBy(e => e.State);

    foreach (var employeeGroup in employeesByState)
    {
        Debug.WriteLine(employeeGroup.Key + ": " + employeeGroup.Count());

        foreach (var employee in employeeGroup)
        {
            Debug.WriteLine(employee.LastName + ", " + employee.State);
        }
    }
}
```

The `GroupBy` method returns an `IGrouping<TKey, TElement>` collection, which can be enumerated to perform aggregate functions on the elements in the group or enumerate through the elements in each group.

If you need to group by more than one field, you would create an anonymous type as a parameter to the `GroupBy` method. For example, the following code will group by the `City` then the `State` properties:

```
var employeesByState = employees.GroupBy(e => new { e.City, e.State });
```

The following results are printed to the Output window:

```
{ City = Havertown, State = PA }: 1
Smith, PA
{ City = Ewing, State = NJ }: 1
Doe, NJ
{ City = Fort Washington, State = PA }: 1
Jones, PA
```

The { City = Havertown, State = PA } is printed to the Output window because that is now the key. The key was created as an anonymous type with two properties.

Aggregate Functions

Aggregate functions enable you to quickly compute the average, sum, count, max, or min on a sequence. For example, if you had a list of items that represent line items on an invoice you could quickly compute the total for the invoice by using the Sum method. These functions are only available as method-based queries but can be used in a query expression. The following code samples show the query expression syntax and the equivalent method-based syntax for the aggregate functions.

count

Query expression:

```
int count = (from i in myArray
              where i % 2 == 0
              select i).Count();
```

Method-based query:

```
int count = myArray.Where(i => i % 2 == 0).Count();
```

Alternatively, you could write the query expression as follows if you want to defer the execution of the query:

```
var evenNumbers = from i in myArray
                  where i % 2 == 0
                  select i;

int count = evenNumbers.Count();
```

If you were to step through the code for the query expression, you would notice that when you execute the int count = evenNumbers.Count() statement that execution jumps to the where i % 2 == 0 statement five times before setting the value of the count variable. This way of coding the query could be useful if you want to return the count of items and also enumerate through the query results in a later statement. Be aware that the query is executed every time you execute the aggregate function or enumerate through the result.

average

Query expression:

```
double average = (from i in myArray
                  where i % 2 == 0
                  select i).Average();
```

Method-based query:

```
double average = myArray.Where(i => i % 2 == 0).Average();
```

sum

Query expression:

```
int sum = (from i in myArray
           where i % 2 == 0
           select i).Sum();
```

Method-based query:

```
int sum = myArray.Where(i => i % 2 == 0).Sum();
```

min

Query expression:

```
int min = (from i in myArray
           where i % 2 == 0
           select i).Min();
```

Method-based query:

```
int min = myArray.Where(i => i % 2 == 0).Min();
```

max

Query expression:

```
int max = (from i in myArray
           where i % 2 == 0
           select i).Max();
```

Method-based query:

```
int max = myArray.Where(i => i % 2 == 0).Max();
```

first and last

There are two other functions that enable you to find the first or last element in your sequence. These are also only available as methods but can be used by a query expression. These functions can be helpful when you want to find the first or last element in a sequence that meets a specific condition, such as the first even number in an array. The syntax for the `First` and `Last` method is shown in the following examples.

first

Query expression:

```
int first = (from i in myArray
             where i % 2 == 0
             select i).First();
```

Method-based query:

```
int first = myArray.Where(i => i % 2 == 0).First();
```

last

Query expression:

```
int last = (from i in myArray
            where i % 2 == 0
            select i).Last();
```

Method-based query:

```
int last = myArray.Where(i => i % 2 == 0).Last();
```

Concatenation

The Concat method enables you to concatenate two sequences into one. This is similar to how a UNION clause works in a SQL statement. The following example combines two Lists of Employee objects and prints the combined sequence to the Output window:

```
static void Concat()
{
    List<Employee> employees = new List<Employee>()
    {
        new Employee()
        {
            FirstName = "John",
            LastName = "Smith"
        },
        new Employee()
        {
            FirstName = "Jane",
            LastName = "Doe"
        },
        new Employee()
        {
            FirstName = "Jack",
            LastName = "Jones"
        }
    };

    List<Employee> employees2 = new List<Employee>()
    {
        new Employee()
        {
            FirstName = "Bill",
            LastName = "Peters"
        },
        new Employee()
        {
            FirstName = "Bob",
            LastName = "Donalds"
```

```
        },
        new Employee()
        {
            FirstName = "Chris",
            LastName = "Jacobs"
        }
    };

    var combinedEmployees = employees.Concat(employees2);

    foreach (var employee in combinedEmployees)
    {
        Debug.WriteLine(employee.LastName);
    }
}
```

The preceding code prints all six last names to the Output window. Be aware that the type for each list does not need to be the same. You can combine different types by selecting an anonymous type from each sequence that contains the same properties. The following code combines a List of `Employee` and `Person` objects and creates a new anonymous type that just contains a `Name` property:

```
static void ConcatV2()
{
    List<Employee> employees = new List<Employee>()
    {
        new Employee()
        {
            FirstName = "John",
            LastName = "Smith"
        },
        new Employee()
        {
            FirstName = "Jane",
            LastName = "Doe"
        },
        new Employee()
        {
            FirstName = "Jack",
            LastName = "Jones"
        }
    };

    List<Person> people = new List<Person>()
    {
        new Person()
        {
            FirstName = "Bill",
            LastName = "Peters"
        },
        new Person()
        {
            FirstName = "Bob",
            LastName = "Donalds"
        },
```

```
        new Person()
        {
            FirstName = "Chris",
            LastName = "Jacobs"
        }
    };

    var combinedEmployees = employees.Select(e => new { Name =
            e.LastName }).Concat(people.Select(p => new { Name = p.LastName }));

    foreach (var employee in combinedEmployees)
    {
        Debug.WriteLine(employee.Name);
    }
}
```

Skip and Take

You can partition sequences by using the Skip or Take methods. The Skip method enables you to pass in a number and returns all elements in the sequence after that number. For example, the following code skips the first element in the Employee List.

```
var newEmployees = employees.Skip(1);
```

You can use the Take method to limit the number of elements returned from the sequence. The following code returns only the top two elements from the Employee List object.

```
var newEmployees = employees.Take(2);
```

These two methods can be useful when paging through the results of a query and displaying them on a screen one page at a time. If you show 10 elements at a time and want to display the third page, you would use the following syntax.

```
var newEmployees = employees.Skip(20).Take(10);
```

Distinct

The Distinct method returns the distinct list of values in the returned sequence. This is useful when you want to remove duplicates from a sequence. The following code returns the distinct list of numbers from an array:

```
int[] myArray = new int[] { 1, 2, 3, 1, 2, 3, 1, 2, 3 };

var distinctArray = myArray.Distinct();

foreach (int i in distinctArray)
{
    Debug.WriteLine(i);
}
```

The preceding code prints 1, 2, 3 to the Output window.

CODE LAB   Distinct with custom classes

The Distinct method behaves differently when the underlying object is a custom class. Consider the following code:

```
class State : IEquatable<State>
{
    public int StateId { get; set; }
    public string StateName { get; set; }

    public bool Equals(State other)
    {
        if (Object.ReferenceEquals(this, other))
        {
            return true;
        }
        else
        {
            if (StateId == other.StateId && StateName == StateName)
            {
                return true;
            }
            else
            {
                return false;
            }
        }
    }

    public override int GetHashCode()
    {
        return StateId.GetHashCode() ^ StateName.GetHashCode();
    }
}
static void DistinctCodeLab()
{
    List<State> states = new List<State>()
    {
        new State(){ StateId = 1, StateName = "PA"},
        new State() { StateId = 2, StateName = "NJ"},
        new State() { StateId = 1, StateName = "PA" },
        new State() { StateId = 3, StateName = "NY"}
    };

    var distintStates = states.Distinct();

    foreach (State state in distintStates)
    {
        Debug.WriteLine(state.StateName);
    }
}
```

Code Lab Analysis

The `State` class must implement the `IEquatable<T>` interface, because the `Distinct` method uses the default equality comparer when determining if two objects are equivalent. The `IEquatable<T>` interface has one method you must override, called `Equals`. In this example, the `StateId` and `StateName` properties are being used to determine equivalence. You must also override the `GetHashCode` method and return the hash code based on the properties in your object. When you execute the `DistinctCodeLab` method, only three states are printed to the Output window. If the `State` class didn't implement the `IEquatable<T>` interface, then all for states would be printed to the window, which you wouldn't expect.

Utilizing LINQ to XML

LINQ to XML enables you to easily convert a sequence into an XML document. Remember, you can use LINQ to query any sequence regardless of the source. As long as the sequence supports the `IEnumerable<T>` or `IQueryable<T>` interface, you can use a LINQ query expression to convert the sequence to XML. This can be useful when transferring data between two systems.

The following example converts a List of `Employee` objects to XML:

```
static void LINQToXML()
{
    List<Employee> employees = new List<Employee>()
    {
        new Employee()
        {
            FirstName = "John",
            LastName = "Smith",
            StateId = 1
        },
        new Employee()
        {
            FirstName = "Jane",
            LastName = "Doe",
            StateId = 2
        },
        new Employee()
        {
            FirstName = "Jack",
            LastName = "Jones",
            StateId = 1
        }
    };

    var xmlEmployees = new XElement("Root", from e in employees
            select new XElement("Employee", new XElement("FirstName", e.FirstName),
                                            new XElement("LastName", e.LastName)));

    Debug.WriteLine(xmlEmployees);
}
```

The output of the preceding code follows:

```
<Root>
  <Employee>
    <FirstName>John</FirstName>
    <LastName>Smith</LastName>
  </Employee>
  <Employee>
    <FirstName>Jane</FirstName>
    <LastName>Doe</LastName>
  </Employee>
  <Employee>
    <FirstName>Jack</FirstName>
    <LastName>Jones</LastName>
  </Employee>
</Root>
```

The `XElement` class is found in the `System.Xml.Linq` namespace. The first parameter to the constructor is the name of the element. The second parameter is a *ParamArray*, which means you can pass a variable number of arguments to the constructor. In this example, you pass a LINQ query expression that returns the list of employees.

SUMMARY

Language Integrated Query (LINQ) is a feature in the .NET Framework that enables you to query different data sources, such as a collection or a database, with common syntax. It may take a bit of time to understand the different forms of syntax in LINQ, but once learned it will make you a more efficient programmer. The two forms of syntax are query expressions and method-based queries. As stated throughout this chapter, both syntaxes are functionally equivalent. Query expressions can be more readable, but they do not offer all of the capabilities of method-based queries. Method-based queries require you to understand lambda expressions, which sometimes can be harder to read.

LINQ to Objects, LINQ to SQL, and LINQ to XML all refer to the ability to query a data source such as a collection, a database, or an XML document. You can also use LINQ to query data in an ADO.NET Entity Framework model. LINQ replaces the need for you to learn specific SQL or XQuery syntax and allows you to use a handful of keywords to manipulate your data. You are sure to see some questions in the exam regarding LINQ or questions that use LINQ syntax, so be sure to understand all of the keywords described in this chapter.

CHAPTER TEST QUESTIONS

The following questions are similar to the types of questions you will find on Exam 70-483. Read each question carefully and select the answer or answers that represent the best solution to the problem. You can find the answers in Appendix A, "Answers to Chapter Test Questions."

1. Which answer has the correct order of keywords for a LINQ query expression?

   a. `select, from, where`

   b. `where, from, select`

   c. `from, where, select`

   d. `from, select, where`

2. Which `where` clause can select all integers in the `myList` object that are even numbers given the following `from` clause?

   ```
   from i in myList
   ```

   a. `where myList.Contains(i % 2)`

   b. `where i % 2 = 0`

   c. `where i % 2 == 0`

   d. `where i % 2 equals 0`

3. Which line of code executes the LINQ query?

   ```
   [1]     var result = from i in myArray
   [2]                       order by i
   [3]                       select i
   [4]     foreach(int i in result)
   [5]     { …}
   ```

   a. Line 1

   b. Line 2

   c. Line 3

   d. Line 4

4. Which method can you use to find the minimum value in a sequence?

   a. `(from i in myArray select i).Min()`

   b. `from i in myArray select Min(i)`

   c. `from Min(i) in myArray select i`

   d. `from i in Min(myArray) select i`

5. Which methods can you use to find the first item in a sequence?

    a. Min

    b. First

    c. Skip

    d. Take

6. Which where clause returns all integers between 10 and 20?

    a. where i >= 10 and i <= 20

    b. where i >= 10 && i <= 20

    c. where i gt 10 and i lt 20

    d. where i gt 10 && i lt 20

7. Which clause orders the state and then the city?

    a. orderby h.State
        orderby h.City

    b. orderby h.State thenby h.City

    c. orderby h.State, h.City

    d. orderby h.State, thenby h.City

8. Which statement selects an anonymous type?

    a. select { h.City, h.State }

    b. select h

    c. select new { h.City, h.State }

    d. select h.City, h.State

9. Which on statement joins two sequences on the StateId property?

    a. on e.StateId equals s.StateId

    b. on e.StateId = s.StateId

    c. on e.StateId == s.StateId

    d. on e.StateId.Equals(s.StateId)

10. Which two keywords must you use in a join clause to create an outer join?

    a. groupby, into

    b. into, DefaultIfEmpty

    c. new, DefaultIfEmpty

    d. into, groupby

11. Which `join` clause uses a composite key?

    a. `on new { City = e.City, State = e.State } equals new { City = h.City, State = h.State }`

    b. `on e.City = h.City && e.State = h.State`

    c. `on e.City = h.City and e.State = h.State`

    d. `on e.City equals h.City and e.State equals h.State`

12. Which statement groups a sequence by the `State` property?

    a. `groupby e.State`

    b. `group e.State`

    c. `group e by e.State`

    d. `groupby e.State in states`

13. Which answers return the count of all even numbers?

    a. `myArray.Where(i => i % 2 == 0).Count()`

    b. `myArray.Count(i => i % 2 == 0)`

    c. `myArray.Count(i =>).Where(i % 2 == 0)`

    d. `myArray.Count(Where(i => i % 2))`

ADDITIONAL READING AND RESOURCES

Here are some additional useful resources to help you understand the topics presented in this chapter:

Microsoft LINQ Official Documentation

    `http://msdn.microsoft.com/en-us/library/vstudio/bb397926.aspx`

LINQPad

    `http://www.linqpad.net/`

LINQ Wiki

    `http://en.wikipedia.org/wiki/Language_Integrated_Query`

LINQ on Code Project

    `http://www.codeproject.com/KB/linq/`

▶ CHEAT SHEET

This cheat sheet is designed as a way for you to quickly study the key points of this chapter.

Language Integrated Query LINQ

➤ Any object that implements the `IEnumerable<T>` or `IQueryable<T>` interface can be queries using LINQ.

➤ The results of a LINQ query are normally returned to a variable of type `var`, which is an implicitly typed variable.

Query expression

➤ A query expression contains a `from` clause and can contain a `select`, `groupby`, `order by`, `where`, or `join` clause

➤ Joins are always equivalence based for LINQ queries.

➤ The execution of a query does not occur until the result is enumerated. You can force execution of the query by using an aggregate function.

➤ The code in the `where` clause of a query expression is the predicate.

➤ Multiple `where` clauses use the `and` operator.

➤ The `orderby` clause is used in query expressions to sort the results on one or more properties.

➤ You can create a new type on the fly in the `select` clause of a query expression with a limited number of properties from the original object. This is referred to as projection.

➤ You use the keyword `equals` in a `join` clause.

➤ To create an outer join, you include an `into` clause in your join, and also call the `DefaultIfEmpty` method to set the properties on the object when no match was found between the two sequences.

➤ A `join` clause can contain an anonymous type to create a composite key.

➤ The group by clause returns an `IGrouping<TKey, TElement>` collection.

Method-based queries

➤ Method-based queries and query expressions are interchangeable and produce the same results. The only difference is the syntax.

➤ Method-based query use lambda expressions as parameters to the methods.

➤ You can use the `SelectMany` method to flatten two sequences into one sequence similar to how a join works.

➤ You can use the `GroupJoin` method create outer joins when using method-based queries.

➤ You can concatenate two sequences by using the `Concat` method.

➤ You can use the `Skip` method to skip a specific number of elements in a sequence.

➤ You can use the `Take` method to return a limited number of elements from a sequence.

➤ You can use the `Distinct` method to return the distinct list of elements from a sequence.

LINQ to XML

➤ You can use the XElement class in a LINQ to XML query to return the result of a query in XML.

REVIEW OF KEY TERMS

anonymous type A type created with read-only properties without having to write the code to declare the class.

composite keys Contains multiple properties that you need for the purpose of a join.

deferred execution Execution of a LINQ query is deferred until the result is enumerated or by calling a function on the result.

Goes To operator The Goes To operator is the => signs in a lambda expression.

implicitly typed variable A variable that has its type determined by the expression on the right side of the initialization statement. Use the keyword var to declare an implicitly typed variable.

inner sequence When using the method-based Join function, this refers to the sequence passed into the Join method as a parameter.

Language Integrated Query (LINQ) A set of features that extends powerful query capabilities to C#.

method-based query A feature of LINQ that uses extension methods on types that implement the IEnumerable<T> or IQuerable<T> interface to query the data.

outer join Selects all elements from one sequence when joined to another sequence even if there is not a match on the joined property.

outer sequence When using the method-based Join function, this refers to the sequence calling the Join method.

ParamArray A parameter to a method that enables you to pass an unknown number of parameter to the method.

predicate The code executed in a where clause for a query expression.

projection Selecting a subset of properties from a type that creates a new anonymous type.

query expression A feature of LINQ that enables you to query any type that implements the IEnumerable<T> or IQueryable<T> interface by using syntax that is easy to comprehend.

EXAM TIPS AND TRICKS

The Review of Key Terms and the Cheat Sheet for this chapter can be printed to help you study. You can find these files in the ZIP file for this chapter at www.wrox. com/remtitle.cgi?isbn=1118612094 on the Download Code tab.

11

Input Validation, Debugging, and Instrumentation

WHAT YOU WILL LEARN IN THIS CHAPTER

- ➤ Understanding validation input
- ➤ Using regular expressions
- ➤ Managing data integrity
- ➤ Using preprocessor directives and symbols
- ➤ Using the Debug and Trace classes
- ➤ Tracing, logging, and profiling

WROX.COM CODE DOWNLOADS FOR THIS CHAPTER

You can find the code downloads for this chapter at www.wrox.com/remtitle
.cgi?isbn=1118612094 on the Download Code tab. The code is in the chapter11
download and individually named according to the names throughout the chapter.

This chapter explains several topics that at first may seem unrelated. It starts by discussing
input validation techniques that a program can use to protect itself from bad values entered by
the user.

After the data has entered the program, you still need to manage the data so that it doesn't
become corrupted by incorrect calculations. A useful method to do this is to use preprocessor
directives to include testing code during debug builds, but to exclude it from release builds.

That same technique of using preprocessor directives is also useful for studying the program's
activities and performance. It enables you to include or exclude code that traces execution,
logs progress, and profiles the application's performance during the appropriate releases.

This chapter introduces all these topics: input validation, managing data integrity, tracing, logging, profiling, and preprocessor directives that you can use to determine which of those activities occur in various program builds.

Table 11-1 introduces you to the exam objectives covered in this chapter.

TABLE 11-1: 70-483 Exam Objectives Covered in This Chapter

OBJECTIVE	CONTENT COVERED
Debug applications and implement security	*Validate application input.* This includes using string methods and regular expressions to validate inputs.
	Debug an application. This includes creating and using preprocessor directives, and using the `Debug` and `Trace` classes to follow program execution and watch for unexpected values.
	Implement diagnostics. This includes tracing, using the profiler, writing to event logs, and using performance counters.

INPUT VALIDATION

It's hard enough debugging an application when it contains correct data. It's even harder if the data it works with is incorrect. If the data is wrong, how can you tell whether invalid results are caused by buggy code or incorrect data?

As is the case with bugs in code, mistakes in data are easiest to correct if you detect them quickly. Ideally you can catch incorrect data as soon as the user enters it. At that point if you can figure out why the data is incorrect, then you can ask the user to fix it.

The following sections describe methods you can use to validate inputs to detect incorrect data.

Avoiding Validation

Before discussing ways to validate data, it's worth taking a moment to discuss ways to avoid validation.

If the user cannot enter an incorrect value, you don't need to write code to validate the value. C# programs can use lots of different kinds of controls, and many of those let you restrict the user's input to valid values.

For example, suppose the program needs the user to enter an integer value between 1 and 10. You could let the user type the value into a `TextBox`. In that case, the code would need to check the value to make sure the user didn't enter 100, 0, –8, or ten. However, if the program makes the user select the value from a `TrackBar`, the user cannot select an invalid value. You can set the `TrackBar`'s `Minimum` and `Maximum` properties and the control does all the validation work for you.

Not only does this save you the trouble of writing and debugging the validation code, it also saves you the trouble of figuring out what to do if the user enters an invalid number. You don't need to display a message box to the user, and the user's work flow isn't interrupted by the message box.

Many controls enable the user to select values of specific types such as colors, dates, files, folders, fonts, numbers, a single item from a list, and multiple items from a list. Whenever you build a program and plan to let the user type something into a TextBox, you should ask yourself whether there is some control that would let the user select the value instead of typing it.

Triggering Validations

Realistically controls can't help the user select every possible value. To select an arbitrary phone number, a program would probably need to let the user select each digit one at a time, a painfully tedious process. Making the user select an arbitrary name would be even worse.

In cases like these a program should let the user type data but then it must validate the result. The program should verify that the phone number follows the format required by the program's locale. It can't do too much validation for a name but can at least verify that it is not blank.

All this begs the question, "When should the program validate data entered by the user?" Should it validate each keystroke? Should it validate when the user enters a value and then moves to a new field? Or should it validate all the values on a form after the user enters all the data and clicks OK?

The answer depends on how often a particular event occurs and how intrusive the validation is. For example, when the user types a value in a TextBox, many keystrokes occur. It would be extremely annoying if the program interrupted the user between every keystroke with an error message.

Instead the program may simply ignore invalid keystrokes. For example, the MaskedTextBox control enables you to specify a mask that the text must match. In the United States you could set the mask to (999)000-0000 to require that the text match a 10-digit phone number format. The user must enter a digit or space for places corresponding to the 9s and must enter a digit for places corresponding to the 0s. The parentheses and dash character are displayed by the control but the user cannot change them. If the user types any other character, the control ignores it.

The MaskedTextBox can't prevent all invalid inputs. For example, the user could enter (000)000-0000, which is not a valid phone number.

For another example, suppose the user must enter a floating point value such as 1.73. The program can't use a TrackBar, ScrollBar, or other control to let the user select a value because those controls select only integers, so you can let the user type a value into a TextBox. While the user types a floating-point value, there are times when the value may not be valid; it might be part of a possible valid value. For example, the value "–." is not a valid floating point number but "–.1" is. In that case, the program shouldn't interrupt the user with an error message after "–." has been typed. Instead it must wait until the user finishes typing.

When the user moves to a new field, the program can validate the user's input more fully. In a Windows Forms application, you can use a TextBox's Validating event to validate its value when focus moves to another control that has CausesValidation property set to true. The Validating event provides a parameter of type CancelEventArgs that has a Cancel property. If you set this property to true, the program cancels the event that moved focus to this control. This traps the user in the field that set e.Cancel to true until the user fixes the input problem.

> **NOTE** *The form refuses to close as long as a control's* Validating *event sets* e.Cancel *to* true; *although the form closes if focus never reaches that control. The fact that the form sometimes closes and sometimes doesn't makes using* e.Cancel *even more confusing for the user.*

Trapping the user in a field disrupts the user's workflow and forces the user to take immediate action. If the user types "head down" without looking at the screen, it could be a while before the user notices that focus is stuck in the control with the problem.

A better approach, and one taken by many websites these days, is to mark the control so that users can see that it contains an error but to let users continue using other parts of the form until they decide to fix the problem. For example, the program might change a TextBox's background color to yellow, change its foreground color to red, or display an asterisk next to it.

Later when users click the OK button or otherwise try to accept the values on the form, the code can revalidate the values and display error messages if appropriate.

The following list summarizes the three stages of input validation ranging from most frequent and least intrusive to least frequent and most intrusive:

1. **Keystroke validation:** The program can ignore any keystrokes that don't make sense, but be sure to allow values that could turn into something that makes sense as "–." could turn into "–.123". Optionally, you could mark the field as containing an invalid value as long as you don't interrupt the user.

2. **Field validation:** When focus leaves a field, the program can validate its contents and flag invalid values. Now if the field contains "–." it is invalid. The program should display an indicator that the value is invalid but should not force the user to correct it yet.

3. **Form validation:** When the user tries to accept the values on the form, the program should validate all values and display error messages if appropriate. This is the only place where the program should force the user to fix values.

> **NOTE** *Form validation is also the only place where the program can perform cross-field validations where the value of one field depends on the values in other fields. For example, the ZIP code 02138 is in Cambridge, MA. If the user enters this ZIP code but the state AZ, something is wrong. Either the ZIP code is incorrect or the state is incorrect (or both).*

The following section describes specific methods for validating data to ensure that it meets required formats.

Validating Data

After you decide when to validate the user's inputs, you still need to know how to perform the actual validation. The following sections describe two approaches: using built-in functions and using regular expressions.

Using Built-in Functions

One of the most basic *data validations* is to verify that the user entered a required value. If the value should be entered in a `TextBox`, the program can simply check its length. For example, the following code checks the `emailTextBox` control to see if its contents are blank:

```
if (emailTextBox.Text.Length == 0)
{
    // The email field is blank. Display an error message.
    ...
}
```

For some other types of controls, the program must look at different control properties to see if the user has made a selection. For example, a `ListBox` or `ComboBox` uses its `SelectedIndex` and `SelectedItem` properties to indicate the user's selection. To see if the user has made a selection, the code should check whether `SelectedIndex == -1` or `SelectedItem == null`.

> **NOTE** *In normal selection mode, after a* `ComboBox` *or* `ListBox` *has selected an item, the user cannot deselect all items. The user can select a different item but cannot deselect all items. You can ensure that the user makes a selection by selecting a default value when the form loads. Then you don't need to verify that the user has made a selection because you know there must be a selection.*

If the field is not blank, the program may need to perform additional validation to determine whether the field makes sense. For example, the value `test` isn't a valid e-mail address.

C# and the .NET Framework provide several built-in methods for performing additional data validation. Perhaps the most useful of these are the `TryParse` methods provided by built-in data types such as `int`, `float`, and `DateTime`. The `TryParse` methods attempt to parse a string value and return true if they succeed. The following code checks whether the `costTextBox` contains a valid currency value:

```
decimal cost;
if (!decimal.TryParse(costTextBox.Text,
    NumberStyles.Currency,
    CultureInfo.CurrentCulture,
    out cost))
{
    // Cost is not a valid currency value. Display an error message.
    ...
}
```

The `NumberStyles` enumeration and the `CultureInfo` class are in the `System.Globalization` namespace, so this code assumes the program has included that namespace with a `using` statement.

Note that some values may not make sense now, but they must still be allowed because later they may make sense. For example, as was mentioned earlier, the value "–." is not a valid floating point number but "–.1" is, so the program must allow "–." while the user is typing.

However, the value "– –" is not a legal part of a floating-point value, so you don't need to allow that. Most programs just ignore the issue and don't try to validate the entry until the user accepts the form.

If you want to validate partial values, however, you may turn a partial entry into a full entry. In this example, you can add "0" to the end of the string. Then the text "–.0" is a valid floating point value, but the text "– –0" is not.

Using String Methods

A program can use the `string` data type's `Length` property to determine whether the `string` is blank. That lets you easily decide whether the user has left a required field blank on a form.

The `string` class also provides several methods that are useful for performing more complicated string validations. Table 11-2 summarizes the most useful of those methods.

TABLE 11-2: Useful String Validation Methods

METHOD	PURPOSE
Contains	Returns `true` if the string contains a specified substring. For example, you could use this to determine whether an e-mail address contains the @ character.
EndsWith	Returns `true` if the string ends with a specified substring.
IndexOf	Returns the location of a specified substring within the string, optionally starting the search at a particular position.
IndexOfAny	Returns the location of any of a specified set of characters within the string, optionally starting at a particular position.
IsNullOrEmpty	Returns `true` if the string is `null` or blank.
IsNullOrWhitespace	Returns `true` if the string is `null`, blank, or contains only whitespace characters such as spaces and tabs.
LastIndexOf	Returns the last location of a specified substring within the string, optionally starting the search at a particular position.
LastIndexOfAny	Returns the last location of any of a specified set of characters within the string, optionally starting at a particular position.
Remove	Removes characters from the string. For example, you can remove the – characters from the phone number 234-567-8901 and then examine the result to see if it makes sense.
Replace	Replaces instances of a character or substring with a new value.
Split	Returns an array containing substrings delimited by a given set of characters. For example, you could split the phone number 234-567-8901 into its pieces and examine them separately.

METHOD	PURPOSE
StartsWith	Returns true if the string starts with a specified substring.
Substring	Returns a substring at a specified location.
ToLower	Returns the string converted to lowercase. This can be useful if you want to ignore the string's case.
ToUpper	Returns the string converted to uppercase. This can be useful if you want to ignore the string's case.
Trim	Returns the string with leading and trailing whitespace characters removed.
TrimEnd	Returns the string with trailing whitespace characters removed.
TrimStart	Returns the string with leading whitespace characters removed.

With enough work, you can use these string methods to perform all sorts of validations. For example, suppose the user enters a phone number of the format (234)567-8901. You could use the Split method to break this into the pieces 234, 567, and 8901. You can then verify that Split returned three pieces and that the pieces have the necessary lengths.

Although you can use the string methods to perform just about any validation, sometimes that can be hard because the validations can be complex. For example, (234)567-8901 is not the only possible U.S. phone number format. You might also want the program to allow 234-567-8901, 1(234)567-8901, 1-234-567-8901, +1-234-567-8901, 234.567.8901, and other formats.

Phone numbers for other countries, e-mail addresses, postal codes, serial numbers, and other values can also require complicated validations. You can perform all these by using the string class's methods, but sometimes it can be difficult. In those cases you can often use the regular expressions described in the following section to validate the more complex structure that these entities hold.

Using Regular Expressions

Regular expressions provide a flexible language for a pattern in strings. Regular expressions let a program determine whether an entire string matches a *pattern* (a regular expression used for matching parts of a string), find pieces of a string that match a pattern, and replace parts of a string with new values.

The System.Text.RegularExpressions.Regex class provides the objects that a program can use to work with regular expressions. Using the Regex class is fairly complicated, so this section describes only its most common and useful operations.

Table 11-3 summarizes the Regex class's most useful methods.

TABLE 11-3: Useful Regex Methods

METHOD	PURPOSE
IsMatch	Returns true if a regular expression matches a string.
Match	Searches a string for the first part of it that matches a regular expression.
Matches	Returns a collection giving information about all parts of a string that match a regular expression.
Replace	Replaces some or all the parts of the string that match a pattern with a new value. This is more powerful than the string class's Replace method.
Split	Splits a string into an array of substrings delimited by pieces of the string that match a regular expression.

Many of the methods described in Table 11-3 have multiple overloaded versions. In particular, many take a string as a parameter and can optionally take another parameter that gives a regular expression. If you don't pass the method a regular expression, the method uses the expression you passed the object's constructor.

The Regex class also provides static versions of these methods that take both a string and a regular expression as parameters. For example, the following code validates the text in a TextBox and sets its background color to give the user a hint about whether the value matches a regular expression. (Don't worry about the regular expression just yet. Regular expressions are described shortly.)

```
private void ValidateTextBox(TextBox txt, bool allowBlank, string pattern)
{
    // Assume it's invalid.
    bool valid = false;

    // If the text is blank, allow it.
    string text = txt.Text;
    if (allowBlank && (text.Length == 0)) valid = true;

    // If the regular expression matches the text, allow it.
    if (Regex.IsMatch(text, pattern)) valid = true;

    // Display the appropriate background color.
    if (valid) txt.BackColor = SystemColors.Window;
    else txt.BackColor = Color.Yellow;
}
```

The code assumes the value is invalid, so it sets the variable valid to false.

Next, if the allowBlank parameter is true and the text is blank, the code sets valid to true.

The code then uses the Regex class's static IsMatch method to determine whether the regular expression matches the text. If the expression matches the text, the code sets valid to true.

Finally, the code sets the TextBox's background color to SystemColors.Window if the text is valid or yellow if the text is invalid. This gives the user a visible indication when the text is invalid without interrupting the user.

Table 11-3 lists only five methods, whereas Table 11-2 lists 18 methods provided by the `string` class, so you might think the `Regex` class isn't as useful. The power of the `Regex` class comes from the flexibility of the regular expression language.

> **NOTE** *There are a few different regular expression languages used by different programming languages and environments. These languages are similar but not identical, so it's easy to be confused and use the wrong syntax. If you find that an expression doesn't do what you think it does, be sure you're using the right syntax for C#.*
>
> *In particular, if you use the Internet to find an expression to match some standard format such as UK phone numbers or Canadian postal codes, be sure the website where you found the expressions uses the syntax required by C#.*

A regular expression is a combination of literal characters and characters that have special meanings. For example, the sequence `[a-z]` means the `Regex` object should match any single character in the range "a" through "z."

Regular expressions can also include special character sequences called *escape sequences* that represent some special value. For example, the sequence `\b` matches a word boundary and `\d` matches any digit 0 through 9.

Sometimes a program needs to use a character as itself even though it looks like a special character. For example, the `[` character normally begins a range of characters. If you want to use `[` itself, you "escape" it by adding a `\` in front of it as in `\[`. For example, the somewhat confusing sequence `[\[-\]]` matches the range of characters between `[` and `]`.

> **BEST PRACTICES: Avoiding Too Many \ Characters**
>
> Remember that strings inside C# code also treat `\` as a special character. For example, `\t` represents a tab and `\n` represents newline.
>
> To add a `\` inside a string in C#, you must escape it by adding another `\` in front of it as in `\\`. This can become maddeningly confusing. For example, to put the already confusing regular expression pattern `[\[-\]]` in C# code, you would need to use `[\\[-\\]]`.
>
> A much simpler method is to use a string literal that starts with the `@` character. For example, the following code creates a string named `pattern` that contains the text `[\[-\]]`.
>
> ```
> string pattern = @"[\[-\]]";
> ```

The most useful pieces of a regular expression can be divided into character escapes, character classes, anchors, grouping constructs, quantifiers, and alternation constructs. The following sections describe each of these. See the links in the "Additional Reading and Resources" section later in this chapter for information about other features of regular expressions.

Character Escapes

Table 11-4 lists the most useful regular expression character escapes.

TABLE 11-4: Useful Character Escapes

CHARACTER	MEANING
\t	Matches tab
\r	Matches return
\n	Matches newline
\nnn	Matches a character with ASCII code given by the two or three octal digits *nnn*
\xnn	Matches a character with ASCII code given by the two hexadecimal digits *nn*
\unnnn	Matches a character with Unicode representation given by the four hexadecimal digits *nnnn*

Character Classes

A *character class* matches any one of a set of characters. Table 11-5 describes the most useful character class constructs.

TABLE 11-5: Useful Character Class Constructs

CONSTRUCT	MEANING
[*chars*]	Matches a single character inside the brackets. For example, [aeiou] matches a lowercase single vowel.
[^*chars*]	Matches a single character that is not inside the brackets. For example, [^aeiouAEIOU] matches a single nonvowel character such as x, 7, or &.
[*first-last*]	Matches a single character between the character *first* and the character *last*. For example, [a-zA-Z] matches any lowercase or uppercase letter.
.	A wildcard that matches any single character except \n. (To match a period, use the \. escape sequence.)

CONSTRUCT	MEANING
\w	Matches a single word character. Normally this is equivalent to [a-zA-Z_0-9].
\W	Matches a single nonword character. Normally this is equivalent to [^a-zA-Z_0-9].
\s	Matches a single whitespace character. Normally this includes space, form feed, newline, return, tab, and vertical tab.
\S	Matches a single nonwhitespace character. Normally this matches everything except space, form feed, newline, return, tab, and vertical tab.
\d	Matches a single decimal digit. Normally this is equivalent to [0-9].
\D	Matches a single character that is not a decimal digit. Normally this is equivalent to [^0-9].

Anchors

An anchor, or atomic zero-width assertion, represents a state that the string must be in at a certain point. Anchors do not consume characters. For example, the ^ and $ characters represent the beginning and ending of a line or the string, depending on whether the Regex object is working in single-line or multiline mode.

Table 11-6 describes the most useful anchors.

TABLE 11-6: Useful Anchors

ANCHOR	MEANING
^	Matches the beginning of the line or string
$	Matches the end of the string or before the \n at the end of the line or string
\A	Matches the beginning of the string
\z	Matches the end of the string
\Z	Matches the end of the string or before the \n at the end of the string
\G	Matches where the previous match ended
\B	Matches a nonword boundary

REGEX OPTIONS

A program can specify regular expression options in three ways.

First, it can pass an options parameter to a `Regex` object's pattern matching methods such as `IsMatch`. The options are defined by the `RegexOptions` enumeration.

Second, it can use the syntax `(?options)` to include *inline options* in a regular expression. Here, `options` can include any of the values i, m, n, s, or x. (These are described shortly.) If the list begins with a - character, the following options are turned off. The options remain in effect until a new set of inline options reset their values.

Third, it can use the syntax `(?options:subexpression)` in a regular expression. In this case, `options` is as before and `subexpression` is part of a regular expression during which the options should apply.

Table 11-7 describes the available options.

TABLE 11-7: Regular Expression Options

OPTION	MEANING
i	Ignore case.
m	Multiline. Here ^ and $ match the beginning and ending of lines.
s	Single line. Here, . matches all characters including \n. (See the entry for . in Table 11-5.)
n	Explicit capture. Do not capture unnamed groups. See the section "Grouping Constructs" for more information on groups.
x	Ignore unescaped whitespace in the pattern and enable comments after the # character.

For more information on these options, see "Regular Expression Options" at `http://msdn.microsoft.com/library/yd1hzczs.aspx`.

Grouping Constructs

Grouping constructs let you define groups of matching pieces of a string. For example, in a U.S. phone number with the format 234-567-8901, you could define groups to hold the pieces 234, 567, and 8901. The program can later refer to those groups either with code or later inside the same regular expression.

For example, consider the expression `(\w)\1`. The parentheses create a numbered group that, in this example, matches a single word character. The `\1` refers to numbered group 1. That means this regular expression matches a word character followed by itself. If the string is "book," this pattern would match the "oo" in the middle.

There are several kinds of groups, some of which are fairly specialized and confusing. The two most common are numbered and named groups.

To create a numbered group, simply enclose a regular subexpression in parentheses, as shown in the previous example (\w)\1. Note that the group numbering starts with 1, not 0.

To create a named group, use the syntax (?<name>subexpression) where name is the name you want to assign to the group and subexpression is a regular subexpression. For example, the expression (?<twice>\w)\k<twice> is similar to the previous version except the group is named twice. Here, the \k makes the expression match the substring matched by the named group that follows, in this case twice.

Quantifiers

Quantifiers make the regular expression engine match the previous element a certain number of times. For example, the expression \d{3} matches any digit exactly three times. Table 11-8 describes regular expression quantifiers.

TABLE 11-8: Quantifiers

QUANTIFIER	MEANING
*	Matches the previous element 0 or more times
+	Matches the previous element 1 or more times
?	Matches the previous element 0 or 1 times
{n}	Matches the previous element exactly n times
{n,}	Matches the previous element n or more times
{n,m}	Matches the previous element between n and m times (inclusive)

If you follow one of these with ?, the pattern matches as few times as possible. For example, the pattern bo+ matches b followed by 1 or more occurrences of the letter o, so it would match the "boo" in "book." The pattern bo+? also matches b followed by 1 or more occurrences of the letter o, but it matches as few letters as possible, so it would match the "bo" in "book."

Alternation Constructs

Alternation constructs use the | character to allow a pattern to match either of two subexpressions. For example, the expression (yes|no) matches either yes or no.

Useful Regular Expressions

The following code shows one way you could validate a TextBox to see if it contains a 7-digit U.S. phone number:

```
// Perform simple validation for a 7-digits US phone number.
private void phone7TextBox_TextChanged(object sender, EventArgs e)
{
    const string pattern = @"^\d{3}-\d{4}$";
```

```
    bool valid = false;

    string text = phone7TextBox.Text;
    if (text.Length == 0) valid = true;

    if (Regex.IsMatch(text, pattern)) valid = true;

    if (valid) phone7TextBox.BackColor = SystemColors.Control;
    else phone7TextBox.BackColor = Color.Yellow;
}
```

The code first defines a constant named `pattern` to hold the regular expression that the text should match. This pattern's pieces mean the following:

PIECE OF PATTERN	DESCRIPTION
^	Matches the start of the string, so the phone number must start at the beginning of the string.
\d	Match any digit.
{3}	Repeat the previous (match any digit) three times. In other words, match three digits.
–	Match the – character.
\d	Match any digit.
{4}	Match 4 digits.

This is a simple 7-digit phone number format and allows several illegal phone numbers such as 111-1111 and 000-0000.

The code then initializes the boolean variable `valid` to `false`.

If the text entered by the user is blank, the code sets `valid` to `true`. Next if the text matches the pattern, the code sets `valid` to `true`.

After it has performed those checks, the code sets the `TextBox`'s background color to the system's control color if the value is valid or to yellow if the value is invalid.

The following list describes several useful regular expressions.

➤ `^[2-9][0-9]{2}-\d{3}$`: This pattern matches a 7-digit U.S. phone number more rigorously. The exchange code at the beginning must match the pattern NXX where N is a digit 2–9 and X is any digit 0–9.

➤ `^[2-9][0-8]\d-[2-9][0-9]{2}-\d{3}$`: This pattern matches a 10-digit U.S. phone number with the format NPA-NXX-XXXX where N is a digit 2-9, P is a digit 0–8, A is any digit 0–9, and X is any digit 0–9.

➤ `^([2-9][0-8]\d-)?[2-9][0-9]{2}-\d{3}$`: This pattern matches a U.S. phone number with an optional area code. The part of the pattern `([2-9][0-8]\d-)?` matches an area code. The question mark at the end means the part inside the parentheses can appear 0 or 1 times. The rest of the pattern is similar to the earlier pattern that matches a 7-digit U.S. phone number.

➤ `^\d{5}(-\d{4})?$`: This pattern matches a US ZIP code with optional +4 as in `12345` or `12345-6789`.

➤ `^[A-Z]\d[A-Z] \d[A-Z]\d$`: This pattern matches a Canadian postal code with the format A#A #A# where A is any capital letter and # is any digit.

➤ `^[a-zA-Z0-9._%+-]+@[a-zA-Z0-9._%+-]+\.[a-zA-Z]{2,4}$`: This pattern matches an e-mail address. The sequence `[a-zA-Z0-9._%+-]` matches letters, digits, underscores, %, +, and -. The plus sign after it means one of those characters must appear one or more times. Next, the pattern matches the @ symbol. The pattern then matches another letter 1 or more times, followed by a ., and then between 2 and 4 letters. For example, this matches `RodStephens@CSharpHelper.com`. This pattern isn't perfect but it matches most valid e-mail addresses.

Notice that all these patterns begin with the beginning-of-line anchor ^ and end with the end-of-line anchor $. That makes the pattern to match the entire string not just part of it. For example, the pattern `^\d{5}(-\d{4})?$` matches complete strings that look like ZIP codes such as `12345`. Without the ^ and $, it would match strings that contain a string that looks like a ZIP code such as `test12345value`.

Using Sanity Checks

After the program verifies that a value has a reasonable format, it can perform basic *sanity checks* to see whether it makes sense. If the user enters a cost of $1 trillion dollars for a notebook, wants to order 1 million pencils, or has the e-mail address `a@a.com`, something may be wrong. The program can look for this kind of suspicious value and display a message asking the user if the value is correct.

Sometimes these unusual values are correct, so the program should give the user a way to allow them if possible. Your company may not provide 1 million pencils, but if it can that would probably be a lucrative sale.

> **NOTE** Names can be particularly tricky because they can contain almost anything. You can't even count on a name to have a minimum number of letters or to contain both consonants and vowels. Some tricky first names include Sy, Ly, Su, and Gd, and some difficult last names include Ng, Bt, and O. You may even encounter people who use only a single name; although in that case some programs just ask the user to make something up for a last name even if it's only Nothing.

REAL-WORLD CASE SCENARIO | **New order form**

Make a new order form similar to the one shown in Figure 11-1.

FIGURE 11-1: A new order form contains many validations.

Give the form the following field validations:

➤ **First and last name:** These are required. For a sanity check, these should consist of an uppercase letter followed by any number of lowercase letters. That can be followed by a hyphen, apostrophe, or space, and then the whole thing can repeat. For example, O'Neil, Mary Ann, and Jones-Smythe should all be allowed.

➤ **Street:** This is required but has no other validation.

➤ **City and ZIP:** This is a small local business, so the program should allow only the three cities with specific ZIP codes: Programmeria (13370, 13371, and 13372), Bugsville (13375 and 13376), and Abend (13376, 13377, 13378, and 13379).

➤ **State:** The program should allow only FL.

➤ **Items** If any field in a row is present, all are required. As a sanity check, description should contain at least six characters. Unit cost is currency and quantity is an integer. If unit cost and quantity are both present, calculate the row's total. As sanity checks, unit cost should be between $0.01 and $1,000.00, and quantity should be between 1 and 100.

➤ **Grand total:** If any row has a total, calculate the grand total.

Only enable the OK button if the order is complete with all contact fields filled in and at least one row filled in.

When the user clicks OK, make the user confirm any values that violate their sanity checks.

Solution

This example has three kinds of validation. First, as the user types, it changes each field's background color to indicate whether the current value is valid. It doesn't try to restrict the user so, for example, it allows the user to type invalid characters in a numeric field. It just flags the value as invalid.

Second, when the user clicks OK, the program checks the fields and refuses to close the form if any values are invalid.

Finally, when the user clicks OK and all the fields contain valid values, it checks for unusual values such as prices greater than $1,000.00, or name with only one character. If it finds unusual values, the program warns the user and asks if it should continue.

The following steps walk through the solution:

1. Build the form as shown in Figure 11-1. Because there are only three choices for city, it should be a ComboBox. Given a choice for city, there are only a few choices for ZIP code so that should also be a ComboBox. By using ComboBoxes, the program prevents the user from entering invalid values.

2. All the other fields are TextBoxes. Those that the user doesn't enter (the row totals and the grand total) are read-only. Because the state must be FL, it is also read-only. Set the ReadOnly property for those TextBoxes to true.

3. The program begins with the following setup code:

```
using System.Globalization;
using System.Text.RegularExpressions;
...
// Regular expressions for validation.
private const string namePattern = @"^([A-Z][a-z]*[-' ]?)+$";

// Sanity check bounds.
private const int minNameLength = 3;
private const int minDescrLength = 6;
private const decimal minUnitCost = 1.00m;
private const decimal maxUnitCost = 1000;
private const int minQuantity = 1;
private const int maxQuantity = 100;

// ZIP codes for different cities.
private string[][] zips =
{
    new string[] { "13370", "13371", "13372" },            // City 0
    new string[] { "13375", "13376" },                     // City 1
    new string[] { "13376", "13377", "13378", "13379" },   // City 2
};

// Colors for valid and invalid fields.
private Color validColor = SystemColors.Window;
private Color invalidColor = Color.Yellow;

// An array holding the item row TextBoxes.
private TextBox[,] rowTextBoxes;
```

The code starts by including the `System.Globalization` namespace it needs to parse currency values and then including the `System.Text.RegularExpressions` namespace it needs to use regular expressions easily.

It then defines several values that it uses in validations. The first is a regular expression pattern to validate names. The pattern matches an uppercase letter followed by any number of lowercase letters and then a hyphen, apostrophe, or space. It repeats this group at least one time. The pattern as a whole is anchored to the beginning and ending of the text, so all the text must be matched by the pattern.

The code defines some constants to use for sanity checking. It then creates an array of arrays that holds the allowed ZIP codes for the three cities that the program allows.

The last pieces of initialization code define colors to use for fields containing valid and invalid values, and an array to hold the `TextBoxes` that hold information about the items in the order.

The following code shows the program's `Load` event handler and the event handler that executes when the user clicks Cancel:

```
// Get ready.
private void Form1_Load(object sender, EventArgs e)
{
    // Select a city so there's always a selection.
    cityComboBox.SelectedIndex = 0;

    // Initialize the array of item row TextBoxes.
    rowTextBoxes = new TextBox[,]
    {
        { descrTextBox1, unitCostTextBox1, quantityTextBox1, totalTextBox1 },
        { descrTextBox2, unitCostTextBox2, quantityTextBox2, totalTextBox2 },
        { descrTextBox3, unitCostTextBox3, quantityTextBox3, totalTextBox3 },
        { descrTextBox4, unitCostTextBox4, quantityTextBox4, totalTextBox4 },
    };
}

// Just close the form.
private void cancelButton_Click(object sender, EventArgs e)
{
    Close();
}
```

The `Load` event handler selects the first choice in the city `ComboBox`, so a city is always selected. Because a city is always selected and all the selections are valid, the program never needs to validate this entry.

The event handler also initializes the array of `TextBoxes` representing the order items.

The Cancel button simply closes the form.

The following code shows some of the program's validation methods. They are enclosed in `#region` and `#endregion` directives, so it's easy to hide the validation code.

```
#region Field Validation Methods

// Validate a TextBox.
private void ValidateTextBoxPattern(TextBox txt, bool allowBlank, string pattern)
{
```

```
        // Assume it's invalid.
        bool valid = false;

        // Check for allowed blank.
        string text = txt.Text;
        if (allowBlank && (text.Length == 0)) valid = true;

        // If the regular expression matches the text, allow it.
        if (Regex.IsMatch(text, pattern)) valid = true;

        // Display the appropriate background color.
        if (valid) txt.BackColor = validColor;
        else txt.BackColor = invalidColor;
    }

// Validate a TextBox containing a currency value.
// Return true if the TextBox's value is valid.
private bool ValidateTextBoxCurrency(TextBox txt, bool allowBlank,
    out decimal value)
{
        // Assume it's invalid.
        bool valid = false;

        // Check for allowed blank.
        string text = txt.Text;
        if (allowBlank && (text.Length == 0)) valid = true;

        // If it contains a currency value, allow it.
        if (decimal.TryParse(text, NumberStyles.Currency,
                CultureInfo.CurrentCulture, out value))
            valid = true;

        // Display the appropriate background color.
        if (valid) txt.BackColor = validColor;
        else txt.BackColor = invalidColor;

        return valid;
    }

// Validate a TextBox containing an integer.
// Return true if the TextBox's value is valid.
private bool ValidateTextBoxInteger(TextBox txt, bool allowBlank, out int value)
{
        // Assume it's invalid.
        bool valid = false;

        // If the text is blank and blank is allowed, allow it.
        string text = txt.Text;
        if (allowBlank && (text.Length == 0)) valid = true;

        // If it contains a currency value, allow it.
        if (int.TryParse(text, out value)) valid = true;

        // Display the appropriate background color.
```

```csharp
    if (valid) txt.BackColor = validColor;
    else txt.BackColor = invalidColor;

    return valid;
}

// Validate the entries for a row.
// Return true if the row is valid.
private bool ValidateRow(int row)
{
    // If every field is blank, it's valid.
    if ((rowTextBoxes[row, 0].Text.Length == 0) &&
        (rowTextBoxes[row, 1].Text.Length == 0) &&
        (rowTextBoxes[row, 2].Text.Length == 0))
    {
        rowTextBoxes[row, 0].BackColor = validColor;
        rowTextBoxes[row, 1].BackColor = validColor;
        rowTextBoxes[row, 2].BackColor = validColor;

        // Clear the total.
        rowTextBoxes[row, 3].Clear();
        return true;
    }

    // Some fields are non-blank so all are required.
    bool descrIsValid = (rowTextBoxes[row, 0].Text.Length > 0);
    if (descrIsValid) rowTextBoxes[row, 0].BackColor = validColor;
    else rowTextBoxes[row, 0].BackColor = invalidColor;

    // Validate unit cost.
    decimal unitCost;
    bool unitCostIsValid =
        ValidateTextBoxCurrency(rowTextBoxes[row, 1], false, out unitCost);

    // Validate quantity.
    int quantity;
    bool quantityIsValid =
        ValidateTextBoxInteger(rowTextBoxes[row, 2], false, out quantity);

    // If unit cost and quantity are present, calculate total cost.
    if (unitCostIsValid && quantityIsValid)
    {
        decimal total = unitCost * quantity;
        rowTextBoxes[row, 3].Text = total.ToString("C");
    }
    else rowTextBoxes[row, 3].Clear();

    // Enable or disable the OK button.
    EnableOkButton();

    // Return true if all fields are valid.
    return (descrIsValid && unitCostIsValid && quantityIsValid);
}

#endregion Field Validation Methods
```

The `ValidateTextBoxPattern` method examines a `TextBox` and sets its background color to `validColor` or `invalidColor` depending on whether it matches a regular expression.

The `ValidateTextBoxCurrency` method validates a `TextBox` to see if it contains a currency value. It sets the control's background color appropriately and returns true if the `TextBox` contains a valid currency value. If it contains a valid value, the method also returns the value through the parameter `value`.

The `ValidateTextBoxInteger` method is similar to `ValidateTextBoxCurrency` except it determines whether a `TextBox` contains an integer instead of a currency value.

The `ValidateRow` method validates a row of `TextBoxes` that represents an order item. If all the `TextBoxes` are blank, the row is valid.

If any field in the row is nonblank, every field is required and the method validates each appropriately. If the unit cost and quantity are both valid, the method calculates and displays the row's total.

The method finishes by calling the `EnableOkButton` method, which are described next.

The `Changed` event handlers for the `TextBoxes` on each row call the `ValidateRow` method to determine whether the values in their rows are valid.

The following code shows the `EnableOkButton` method:

```
// Enable the OK button if all fields are okay.
private void EnableOkButton()
{
    // Assume all fields are okay.
    bool valid = true;

    // See if the contact fields are okay.
    if (firstNameTextBox.Text.Length == 0) valid = false;
    if (lastNameTextBox.Text.Length == 0) valid = false;
    if (streetTextBox.Text.Length == 0) valid = false;

    // See if all item fields are okay.
    foreach (TextBox txt in rowTextBoxes)
        if (txt.BackColor == invalidColor)
        {
            valid = false;
            break;
        }

    // Calculate the grand total.
    CalculateGrandTotal();

    // Make sure at least one item row has values in it.
    if (grandTotalTextBox.Text.Length == 0) valid = false;

    // If the values are valid, calculate the grand total.
    CalculateGrandTotal();

    // Enable or disable the button.
    okButton.Enabled = valid;
}
```

This method enables or disables the form's OK button depending on whether all the form's fields hold valid values. It begins by validating the first name, last name, and street fields. (The city and ZIP code ComboBoxes always have valid selections, so it doesn't need to validate them.)

The code checks the TextBoxes in the item rows. If any of those TextBoxes has the invalid background color, the form's entries are invalid.

The code then calls the CalculateGrandTotal method (which is described next) to calculate a grand total if possible. If the grand total value is blank, there is no row with a valid unit cost and quantity, so the form's fields are not valid.

The method enables the OK button if all the field values are valid.

The following code shows the CalculateGrandTotal method:

```
// Calculate the grand total if possible.
private void CalculateGrandTotal()
{
    // See if any row has a total.
    if ((totalTextBox1.Text.Length == 0) &&
        (totalTextBox2.Text.Length == 0) &&
        (totalTextBox3.Text.Length == 0) &&
        (totalTextBox4.Text.Length == 0))
    {
        grandTotalTextBox.Clear();
        return;
    }

    // Add up the item totals.
    decimal grandTotal = 0;
    for (int row = 0; row < 4; row++)
    {
        if (rowTextBoxes[row, 3].Text.Length > 0)
            grandTotal += decimal.Parse(
                rowTextBoxes[row, 3].Text, NumberStyles.Currency);
    }

    // Display the grand total.
    grandTotalTextBox.Text = grandTotal.ToString("C");
}
```

If all the item rows have a blank total, none of them have valid unit costs and quantities. In that case, the method blanks the grand total TextBox.

If any item row has a total, the method adds up the totals and displays the grand total.

Each of the controls has an appropriate event handler to set its background color to indicate whether the control holds a valid value. For example, the following code shows how the first name TextBox validates changes:

```
private void firstNameTextBox_TextChanged(object sender, EventArgs e)
{
    ValidateTextBoxPattern(firstNameTextBox, false, namePattern);
    EnableOkButton();
}
```

This code uses `ValidateTextBoxPattern` to set the control's background color appropriately. It then calls `EnableOkButton` to enable or disable the OK button.

The other fields perform similar but appropriate validation. For example, the quantity `TextBoxes` use `ValidateTextBoxInteger` to determine whether they contain valid integer values.

The city `ComboBox` is somewhat different from the other fields. When the user selects a city, the following code executes:

```
private void cityComboBox_SelectedIndexChanged(object sender, EventArgs e)
{
    zipComboBox.Items.Clear();
    foreach (string zip in zips[cityComboBox.SelectedIndex])
        zipComboBox.Items.Add(zip);
    zipComboBox.SelectedIndex = 0;
}
```

This code copies the ZIP codes for the selected city into the ZIP code `ComboBox`. It then selects the first ZIP code, so there is always one selected.

When the user clicks the OK button, the following code performs final validations:

```
// Make sure the form is complete.
private void okButton_Click(object sender, EventArgs e)
{
    // Perform validations that require fixing.
    string message = "";
    TextBox focusTextBox = null;
    if (firstNameTextBox.Text.Length == 0)
    {
        message += "First name cannot be blank.\n";
        if (focusTextBox == null) focusTextBox = firstNameTextBox;
    }
    if (lastNameTextBox.Text.Length == 0)
    {
        message += "Last name cannot be blank.\n";
        if (focusTextBox == null) focusTextBox = lastNameTextBox;
    }
    if (streetTextBox.Text.Length == 0)
    {
        message += "Street cannot be blank.\n";
        if (focusTextBox == null) focusTextBox = streetTextBox;
    }
    if (grandTotalTextBox.Text.Length == 0)
    {
        message += "At least one item row must be entered.\n";
        if (focusTextBox == null) focusTextBox = descrTextBox1;
    }

    // See if any of these failed.
    if (message.Length > 0)
    {
        // Remove the final \n.
        message = message.Substring(0, message.Length - 1);
```

```
            // Display the message.
            MessageBox.Show(message, "Invalid Data",
                MessageBoxButtons.OK, MessageBoxIcon.Error);
            focusTextBox.Focus();
            return;
        }

        // Perform sanity checks.
        if (firstNameTextBox.Text.Length < minNameLength)
        {
            message += "The first name is unusually short.\n";
            if (focusTextBox == null) focusTextBox = firstNameTextBox;
        }
        if (lastNameTextBox.Text.Length < minNameLength)
        {
            message += "The last name is unusually short.\n";
            if (focusTextBox == null) focusTextBox = lastNameTextBox;
        }
        if (streetTextBox.Text.Length < minNameLength)
        {
            message += "The street name is unusually short.\n";
            if (focusTextBox == null) focusTextBox = streetTextBox;
        }
        for (int row = 0; row < 4; row++)
        {
            SanityCheckRow(row, ref message, ref focusTextBox);
        }

        // See if any sanity checks failed.
        if (message.Length > 0)
        {
            // Compose the question.
            message = "Some fields contain unusual values.\n\n" +
                message + "\nDo you want to continue anyway?";

            // Display the message and let the user decide whether to continue.
            if (MessageBox.Show(message, "Continue?",
                MessageBoxButtons.YesNo, MessageBoxIcon.Question) == DialogResult.Yes)
            {
                // Continue anymway.
                Close();
            }
            else
            {
                // Let the user edit the data.
                focusTextBox.Focus();
            }
        }
    }
}
```

The code first performs mandatory validations. It verifies that the first name, last name, and street are not blank and that there is a grand total. As it checks these conditions, it builds a message describing any problems. If any of these conditions are not met, the program displays the message, sets focus to the first control that had a problem, and returns.

If the form passes its mandatory checks, the code performs sanity checks. It verifies that the first name, last name, and street have certain minimum lengths. For each item row, the code calls the `SanityCheckRow` method to see if its values make sense. As with the mandatory checks, the code builds a message describing any problems it finds. If any of the sanity checks finds problems, the method displays the messages describing them and asks the user if it should continue anyway. If the user clicks Yes, the form closes. (In a real application, the program would probably save the order information to a database.)

The following code shows the `SanityCheckRow` method:

```
// Perform sanity checks for a row.
// If a field fails its checks, add a message to the message string
// and set focus to that field (if focus isn't already set somewhere else).
private void SanityCheckRow(int row, ref string message, ref TextBox focusTextBox)
{
    // Either every field is present or every field is blank.
    // If the description is blank, returnu true.
    if (rowTextBoxes[row, 0].Text.Length == 0) return;

    // Check the description.
    if (rowTextBoxes[row, 0].Text.Length < minDescrLength)
    {
        message += "Description " + (row + 1) + " is unusually short.\n";
        if (focusTextBox == null) focusTextBox = rowTextBoxes[row, 0];
    }

    // Check the unit price.
    decimal price = decimal.Parse(
        rowTextBoxes[row, 1].Text, NumberStyles.Currency);
    if ((price < minUnitCost) || (price > maxUnitCost))
    {
        message += "Unit price " + (row + 1) + " is unusual.\n";
        if (focusTextBox == null) focusTextBox = rowTextBoxes[row, 1];
    }

    // Check the quantity.
    int quantity = int.Parse(rowTextBoxes[row, 2].Text);
    if ((price < minUnitCost) || (price > maxUnitCost))
    {
        message += "Quantity " + (row + 1) + " is unusual.\n";
        if (focusTextBox == null) focusTextBox = rowTextBoxes[row, 1];
    }
}
```

This method checks the row's description, unit cost, and quantity to see if they make sense. In any value is suspicious, the code adds a message to the string that will be displayed to the user.

This may seem like a lot of code, but the form contains quite a few fields that have different requirements and sanity checks. Giving the user the best possible experience sometimes takes work.

Managing Data Integrity

Some programmers validate the user's inputs and then assume that the data is correct forevermore. This is usually a big mistake. Even if the user enters correct data, the data can later be corrupted by incorrect calculations as it passes through the system. If the program isn't constantly on the lookout for invalid data, mistakes can sneak in and go unnoticed until long after they were introduced, making it extremely hard to figure out what part of the system caused the mistake.

There are a couple of actions you can take to help prevent this kind of data corruption. Two of these are using database validations and using assertions.

Using Database Validations

If a program uses a database, you can add checks and constraints to the database to prevent it from allowing invalid data. For example, if the database requires that an address has a ZIP code that includes exactly five decimal digits, there is no way the program can insert a record without a ZIP code or with the ZIP code 2812H.

Modern databases can ensure that a field isn't blank, has a certain format, has a unique value, and even has certain relationships with other fields in the same or other records. If these kinds of standard database validations aren't sufficient, you can write custom validation code that the database can execute when a value is created or modified.

Making the database validate its data can prevent the program from saving invalid data and is important, but in some sense it's also a last resort. Many programs perform a considerable amount of work with data before it is saved to a database, so there are opportunities for the data to become corrupted between the user's input and the database.

Programs also use data stored in the database later to perform calculations and that provides other opportunities for the data to become corrupted. Finally, some programs don't use databases at all.

Using Assertions

Another precaution you can take to manage the data's integrity as it passes through the system is to use assertions. An *assertion* is a piece of code that makes a particular claim about the data and that interrupts execution if that claim is false.

One way to make assertions is to simply use an `if` statement to test the data and then throw an exception if the data seems invalid. The following code shows an example:

```
if (!Regex.IsMatch(zip, @"^\d{5}$"))
    throw new FormatException("ZIP code has an invalid format.");
```

This code uses the `Regex` class's static `IsMatch` method to determine whether the string variable `zip` contains a value that matches a five-digit ZIP code format. If the `zip` contains an invalid value, the code throws a `FormatException`.

To make this kind of assertion easier, the .NET Framework provides the `System.Diagnostics.Debug` class. This class's `Assert` method tests a boolean value and throws an exception if it is `false`. The following code is roughly equivalent to the previous code that uses an `if` statement:

```
Debug.Assert(Regex.IsMatch(zip, @"^\d{5}$"));
```

If an assertion fails, the program displays a dialog similar to the one shown in Figure 11-2.

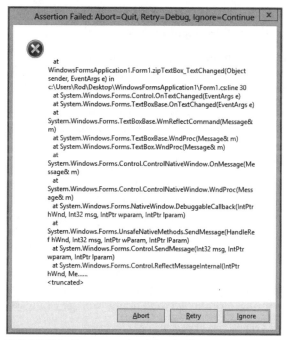

FIGURE 11-2: If an assertion fails, the Debug.Assert method displays a dialog that includes a stack trace showing where the assertion failed.

If you click Abort, the program ends. If you click Retry, Visual Studio pauses the program's execution at the `Assert` statement, so you can try to figure out what went wrong. If you click Ignore, the program continues executing after the `Assert` statement.

Overloaded versions of the `Assert` method let you indicate a message that the dialog should display in addition to the stack trace.

The dialog shown in Figure 11-2 is one big difference between throwing your own exceptions and using the `Assert` statement. Another big difference is that the `Assert` statement executes only in debug releases of a program. In release builds, the `Assert` statement is completely ignored. While you are testing the program, the assertion will help you locate bugs. When you compile a release build and give it to end users, the users won't see the intimidating dialog shown in Figure 11-2.

> **NOTE** *To select a debug or release build, open the Build menu and select Configuration Manager. In the Active Solution Configuration drop-down, select Debug or Release.*

This means the program must be prepared to continue running even if an assertion fails. The program must have a way to work around invalid data or else it will fail in a release build.

If a failed assertion means the program cannot reasonably continue, the program should throw an exception and stop instead of using an assertion that will be skipped in release builds.

For example, suppose a retailer sales program needs to print a customer invoice and a customer has ordered 1,000 pairs of sunglasses. That is a suspiciously large order, so the program can flag it by using an assertion. For instance, it might assert that the number of items ordered is less than 100.

In debug builds, the assertion fails, so you can examine the data to see if the order actually does need 1,000 pairs of sunglasses or if the data has become corrupted. In release builds, this assertion is skipped, so the program prints the invoice for 1,000 pairs of sunglasses. This is an unusual order, but it could actually happen—and you'll make a fair amount of profit.

In contrast, suppose the order doesn't contain a customer address. In that case, the program cannot print a meaningful invoice, so it should not try. The invoice printing code could either catch this error, display an error message, and stop trying to print the invoice, or it could throw an exception and let code higher up in the call stack deal with the problem. Unlike the case of the unusual order size, the program cannot successfully print the invoice, so it may as well give up.

You can use assertions anywhere in the program where you think the data might become corrupted. One particularly good location for assertions is at the beginning of any method that uses the data. For example, the following code shows how an invoice printing method might validate its inputs:

```
private void PrintInvoice(string customerName, string customerAddress,
    List<OrderItem> items)
{
    // Validate inputs.
    // Validate customer name.
    if (string.IsNullOrWhiteSpace(customerName))
        throw new ArgumentNullException("Customer name is missing.");
    // Validate customer address.
    if (string.IsNullOrWhiteSpace(customerAddress))
        throw new ArgumentNullException("Customer address is missing.");
    // Validate item quantities and unit prices.
    foreach (OrderItem item in items)
    {
        Debug.Assert(item.Quantity <= 100,
            "OrderItem " + item.Description +
            ", quantity is larger than 100.");
        Debug.Assert(item.UnitPrice <= 100,
            "OrderItem " + item.Description +
            ", unit price is larger than $100.00.");
    }

    // Print the invoice.
    ...
}
```

This method starts with data validation code. First, it verifies that the customer's name and address are not blank. If either of those values is blank, the method cannot print a useful invoice, so it throws an exception.

Next, the method loops through the order's items and validates their quantities and unit costs. For each item, the code asserts that the item's quantity is at most 100 and its unit cost is at most $100.00. If either of those assertions fails in a debug build, executing stops, so you can try to determine if the data has been corrupted or if this is just an unusual order. In a release build, these assertions are ignored, so the program prints the invoice even if an item's quantity or unit price is unusually large.

Another good place for assertions is at the end of any method that manipulates the data. At that point the code can verify that the changes made by the method make sense.

For example, suppose a method sorts a list of customer records, so they are ordered with those having the largest delinquent balances coming first. Before it returns the newly order list, the method can run through the list and verify that the customers are in their proper order.

> **NOTE** Programmers sometimes resist putting data validation code at the end of their methods because they can't visualize the code making a mistake. That's natural because they just wrote the code, and if it contained a mistake, they would have fixed it.
>
> Of course, if programmers were right and none of their modules contained bugs, the program as a whole wouldn't contain bugs, and that's rarely the case for non-trivial programs.
>
> One way to encourage programmers to add these sorts of validations is to write the validation code before writing the rest of the method. At that point, the programmer doesn't have the preconception that the code is perfect so is more likely to validate the data thoroughly.

Because assertions are ignored in release builds, the program's performance doesn't suffer even if you add a lot of assertions to a method. Even if the validations never detect an error, at least you'll have some reason to believe the code is correct. Validation code is worth the effort if for no other reason than peace of mind.

DEBUGGING

Visual Studio provides good tools for interactively debugging an application. Breakpoints, watches, and the ability to step through the code let you study the application as it runs. You set breakpoint conditions, hit counts, and filters to further refine how breakpoints work.

These are important techniques that every programmer should know, but they are not part of the C# language, so they aren't covered here. Instead the sections that follow describe techniques you can use to make your C# code help debug a program. They explain how to use compiler directives to determine which pieces of code are executed and which are ignored.

Preprocessor Directives

Preprocessor directives tell the C# compiler how to process pieces of code. They let a program exclude pieces of code from compilation, define symbols to use in managing compiled code, and group pieces of code for convenience.

The following sections describe the C# preprocessor directives.

#define and #undef

The #define directive defines a preprocessor symbol or conditional compilation symbol for the module that contains the directive. Later you can use the #if and #elif preprocessor directives to see if the symbol is defined.

Note that you cannot assign a value to the symbol, so it isn't comparable to a C# variable or constant. All you can do is define or undefine the symbol and see if it has been defined.

You can also use Visual Studio to define symbols for an entire project. To do so, open the Project menu and select Properties. In the project's property pages, select the Build tab and enter the names of any symbols you want to define in the Conditional Compilation Symbols text box.

The #undef directive undefines a previously defined preprocessor symbol.

Both the #define and #undef directives must appear in a module before any nondirective statement in a module. Because these statements must go at the beginning of the file, you normally don't use #undef to undefine a symbol that you had just created with #define. Usually #undef is more useful for undefining a symbol that you created by using the project's property pages.

#if, #elif, #else, and #endif

The #if, #elif, #else, and #endif directives work much like the C# if, else, and else if statements do, but they test preprocessor symbols instead of boolean expressions. Because you cannot assign a value to a preprocessor symbol, these statements merely test whether a symbol exists.

The #if and #elif directives determine whether a symbol exists and include their code in the compilation if it does. If the symbol does not exist, the code following the directive is completely omitted from the compilation.

If none of the symbols in a series of #if and #elif directives exists, the code following the #else directive (if it exists) is included in the compilation.

For example, suppose a module begins with the following #define statements:

```
// Debug levels. Level 2 gives the most information.
#define DEBUG1
//#define DEBUG2
```

This code defines the two preprocessor symbols: DEBUG1 and DEBUG2. The second is commented out, so only DEBUG1 is defined.

Now suppose the module later includes the following method:

```
        private void VerifyInternetConnections()
        {
#if DEBUG2
```

```
                // Display lots of debugging information.
                ...
#elif DEBUG1
                // Display some debugging information.
                ...
#else
                // Display minimal debugging information.
                ...
#endif

                // Verify the connections.
                ...
        }
```

The `#if` directive looks for the symbol DEBUG2. That symbol's definition is commented out, so the following code is ignored.

Next, the `#elif` directive looks for the symbol DEBUG1. That symbol's definition is not commented out, so the symbol exists. The code following the `#elif` directive is included in the compilation, and the program displays some debugging information.

If neither DEBUG2 nor DEBUG1 were defined, the `#else` directive would include its code, and the program would display minimal debugging information.

You can use the logical operators `!`, `&&`, and `||` to combine symbols in an expression. For example, the directive `#if DEBUG1 && DEBUG2` includes its code if both of the symbols DEBUG1 and DEBUG2 are defined.

You can also use the relational operators `!=` and `==` to compare the existence of two symbols. The directive `#if DEBUG1 == DEBUG2` includes its code if both DEBUG1 and DEBUG2 are defined or both are undefined.

The special values `true` and `false` represent a symbol's existence. For example, the following statements are all equivalent:

```
#if DEBUG1
#if DEBUG1 == true
#if DEBUG1 != false
```

Similarly, the following statements are equivalent:

```
#if !DEBUG1
#if DEBUG1 != true
#if DEBUG1 == false
```

Finally, you can use parentheses to group symbols and make complex expressions easier to understand.

> **NOTE** *Visual Studio immediately grays out any code that is not included in the current compilation. For example, if a piece of code follows the* `#if DEBUG1` *directive and* DEBUG1 *is not defined, the code is grayed out. This lets you easily see which code will be included in the compilation and which will not.*

#warning and #error

The `#warning` directive generates a warning that appears in Visual Studio's Error List. Visual Studio's code editor also highlights the warning by default with a squiggly green underline.

One use for this is to flag code that is included in a `#ifdef` directive but that is obsolete. For example, consider the following code:

```
#if OLD_METHOD
#warning Using obsolete method to calculate fees.
    ...
#else
    ...
#endif
```

If the symbol `OLD_METHOD` is defined, the code adds the warning to the Error List and includes whatever code is appropriate. If the symbol is not defined, the program includes the code after the `#else` directive and does not include the warning.

The `#error` directive is somewhat similar to the `#warning` directive except it generates an error instead of a warning. Like a warning, the error appears in Visual Studio's Error List. Unlike a warning, the error prevents Visual Studio from successfully building the program. Visual Studio's code editor also highlights the error by default with a squiggly red underline.

#line

The `#line` directive enables you to change the program's line number and optionally the name of the file that is reported in warnings, errors, and stack traces. For example, the following code displays a stack trace with a modified line number and filename:

```
#line 10000 "Geometry Methods"
        Console.WriteLine("********** " + Environment.StackTrace);
```

This stack trace would indicate that the `Console.WriteLine` statement is at line 10000 in the file "Geometry Methods."

Changing the line numbering information in this way can be confusing, so you should use this method sparingly. One reason you might want to do this is if you want to keep a section of code's line numbering even if you insert other lines of code before it.

The `#line default` directive restores the lines that follow to their original numbering. In that case, the lines that were renumbered by a previous `#line` directive are counted normally.

The `#line hidden` directive hides the following lines from the debugger until the next `#line` directive. If you step through the code, the debugger jumps over those lines.

#region and #endregion

As their names imply, the `#region` and `#endregion` directives create a region in the code that you can expand or collapse to hide code in the code editor. Figure 11-3 shows the code editor displaying a piece of code that defines three regions. The first two, which are named Sales Routines and Billing Routines, are expanded. The third, which is named Graphical Routines, is collapsed to hide the code it contains. Click the + or - sign to the left to expand or collapse a region.

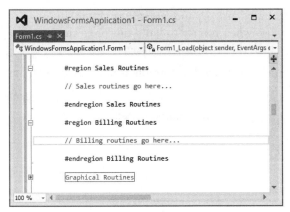

FIGURE 11-3: You can use regions to hide blocks of code to make a file easier to read.

Every #region must end with a corresponding #endregion. You can nest a region inside #if directives, but you cannot make a region that overlaps part of an #if directive.

A region can, however, overlap part of a method. For example, a region could start outside of the LocateCustomer method and end in the middle of it. If you collapsed that region, the code would be confusing to read, so you should probably not make a region that overlaps methods in that way.

You can follow the #region and #endregion directives with an optional name. If you follow the #region directive with a name, the code editor displays it when you collapse the region. In Figure 11-3 the Graphical Routines region is collapsed, and the code editor is displaying its name.

The names following the #region and #endregion directives are just strings that the code editor ignores, so they can contain any characters. The text after an #endregion directive doesn't need to match the text after the corresponding #region directive; although, to make the code as readable as possible, you may want to make them the same.

#pragma warning

The #pragma directive gives special instructions to the compiler, potentially enabling you to create new preprocessor instructions. The C# compiler supports two #pragma directives: #pragma warning and #pragma checksum.

The #pragma warning directive can enable and disable specific warnings. For example, consider the following class definition:

```
private class OrderItem
{
    public string Description;
    public int Quantity = 0;
    public decimal UnitPrice = 0;
}
```

This code defines three public fields: `Description`, `Quantity`, and `UnitPrice`. It initializes `Quantity` and `UnitPrice` but not `Description`, so when you try to build this program, Visual Studio flags the line that declares `Description` with the following warning:

Field 'WindowsFormsApplication1.Form1.OrderItem.Description' is never assigned to, and will always have its default value null.

The following code shows how you can use a `#pragma` directive to hide that warning:

```
            private class OrderItem
            {
#pragma warning disable 0649
                public string Description;
#pragma warning restore 0649
                public int Quantity = 0;
                public decimal UnitPrice = 0;
            }
```

The first `#pragma` directive disables warning number 0649, which is the "never assigned to" warning. (More on how to find the warning number shortly.)

The second `#pragma` directive re-enables the warning. Warnings are displayed for a reason, so it's not a good idea to turn them off without a good reason. Re-enabling the warning lets Visual Studio flag other uninitialized variables so that you can fix them.

Before you can disable a warning, you need to figure out its number. Unfortunately, the Error List displays the warning message, but not its number. To find the number, build the program and then look in the Output window. Somewhere buried in the copious compilation output you should find the warning and its number.

Figure 11-4 shows the Output window after building a program that contains several warnings. The first warning, Using Obsolete Method to Calculate Fees, was created by a `#warning` directive and has number 1030.

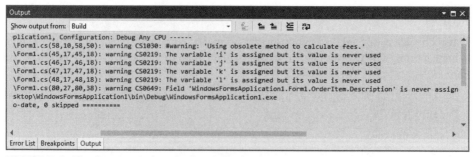

FIGURE 11-4: The Output window displays information about warnings including their numbers.

The next three warnings are about variables that are initialized but never used. Their warning number is 0219.

The final warning, which says the `Description` field is never assigned, has warning number 0649.

#pragma checksum

The `#pragma checksum` directive generates a checksum for a file. Normally, the compiler generates a checksum for a file and puts it in the program database (PDB) file, so the debugger can compare the file it is debugging to the source file. For ASP.NET applications, however, the checksum represents the generated source file rather than the original `.aspx` file, so this solution doesn't work.

The `#pragma checksum` directive enables you to explicitly specify a checksum for the file. The following shows the syntax.

```
#pragma checksum "filename" "{guid}" "bytes"
```

Here `filename` is the name of the file, `guid` is the file's globally unique identifier (GUID), and `bytes` is a string giving an even number of hexadecimal digits specifying the checksum.

This is a specialized directive, so it is not covered further here. For more information, see the online C# reference page `http://msdn.microsoft.com/library/ms173226.aspx`.

Predefined Compiler Constants

Earlier this chapter explained how you can use the `#define` and `#undef` directives to define and undefine conditional compilation symbols. By default, Visual Studio also predefines two other symbols: DEBUG and TRACE. You can use these symbols and the `#if`, `#elif`, `#else`, and `#endif` directives to include or exclude code from a build just as you can with symbols that you define.

Normally, DEBUG is defined in debug builds and TRACE is defined in both debug and release builds, but you can change that behavior.

To determine which kind of build Visual Studio will create, open the Build menu, and select Configuration Manager to display the Configuration Manager, as shown in Figure 115. Use the Active Solution Configuration drop-down on the upper left to select a debug or release build. The drop-down also includes a New option that lets you define a new build type.

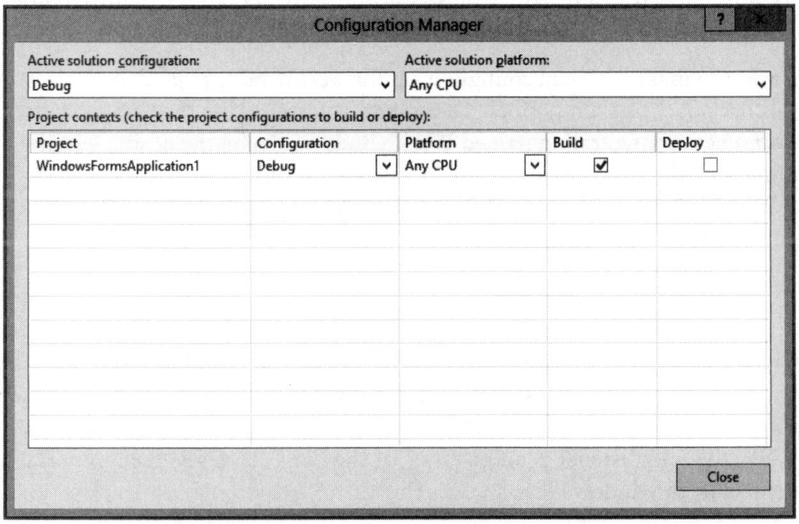

FIGURE 11-5: Use the Configuration Manager to select a debug or release build.

Next, open the Project menu and select Properties to display the project's property pages. On the Build tab, as shown in Figure 11-6, check or uncheck the Define DEBUG Constant and Define TRACE Constant boxes to determine whether those constants are defined. You can also add new constants of your own in the Conditional Compilation Symbols text box. (You can also use the Build page's Configuration drop-down to select a configuration to modify; although, that doesn't change the currently active configuration so it can be a bit confusing.)

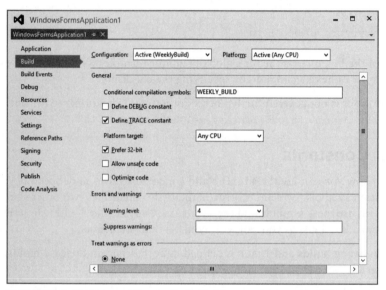

FIGURE 11-6: You can use the project's Build property page to define conditional compilation constants.

The DEBUG and TRACE symbols, and symbols that you define in the Debug property page, are saved with the current configuration. Later if you use the Configuration Manager to select a different configuration, its settings will apply.

For example, suppose you want to make a special configuration for weekly builds that defines the TRACE and WEEKLY_BUILD symbols but not the DEBUG symbol. To do that, you would use the Configuration Manager to define and select a new configuration named WeeklyBuild. Then on the project's Build property page, you would uncheck the DEBUG box and add **WEEKLY_BUILD** to the Conditional Compilation Symbols text box. Now whenever you select the WeeklyBuild configuration, Visual Studio defines the TRACE and WEEKLY_BUILD symbols.

Debug and Trace

Earlier this chapter explained that a program can use the Debug.Assert method to test assertions in the code and that this method is ignored in release builds. Actually, the Debug class and the closely related Trace class do more than merely verify assertions. They provide services that send messages to listener objects. By default, the only listener is an instance of the DefaultTraceListener class, which sends messages to the Output window.

The following section says more about the Debug and Trace classes. The section after that one describes listeners in greater detail.

Debug and Trace Objects

Earlier this chapter said that the Debug class's methods are ignored in release builds. It's actually not the build that controls this behavior but the predefined DEBUG symbol. By default, that symbol is defined in debug builds and not in release builds; although, as was noted earlier, you can use the Build property page to change that behavior. As was mentioned earlier, you can also create your own configurations that may or may not define the DEBUG symbol.

You can also use the #define and #undef directives to define or undefine the DEBUG symbol. For example, you can define the symbol in a particular module to make the program execute the Debug.Assert method even in release builds for that module only.

The Trace class, which is also defined in the System.Diagnostics namespace, is similar to the Debug class except its behavior is controlled by the TRACE symbol. By default, both the debug and release builds define the TRACE symbol.

The Debug and Trace classes provide many of the same methods. Table 11-9 summarizes the classes' most useful methods.

TABLE 11-9: Useful Debug and Trace Methods

METHOD	PURPOSE
Assert	Checks a boolean condition and throws an exception if it is not true.
Fail	Emits a failure message to the object's listeners. Normally, the effect is similar to the way Assert throws an exception.
Flush	Flushes output to the listeners.
Indent	Increases the indent level by 1. This lets you make output displayed by the Write and WriteLine methods easier to read. For example, you could have a recursive method indent the output, so you can tell which method call is displaying different messages.
Unindent	Decreases the indent level by 1. If a method indents its output, it should probably unindent the output when it finishes.
Write	Writes a message to the object's listeners.
WriteIf	If an indicated boolean expression is true, this method writes a message to the object's listeners.
WriteLine	Writes a message followed by a new line to the object's listeners.
WriteLineIf	If an indicated boolean expression is true, this method writes a message followed by a new line to the object's listeners.

Listeners

Both the `Debug` and `Trace` classes have a `Listeners` collection that holds references to listener objects. Initially, these collections hold a reference to a `DefaultTraceListener` object, but you can change that if you like. To remove the `DefaultTraceListener`, call the `Listeners` collection's `Remove` method passing it the `DefaultTraceListener` object.

To direct output to other locations, add an appropriate trace listener object to the `Listeners` collection. The following list describes some of the other trace listener classes that you might use:

➤   `ConsoleTraceListener`: Sends output to the Console window.

➤   `EventLogTraceListener`: Sends output to an event log.

➤   `TextWriterTraceListener`: Sends output to a stream such as a `FileStream`. This lets you write output into any file.

For example, the following code shows how a program might create a `TextWriterTraceListener` to log `Trace` output to the file `TraceFile.txt`.

```
using System.IO;
using System.Diagnostics;

private void Form1_Load(object sender, EventArgs e)
{
    // Create the trace output file.
    Stream traceStream = File.Create("TraceFile.txt");

    // Create a TextWriterTraceListener for the trace output file.
    TextWriterTraceListener traceListener =
        new TextWriterTraceListener(traceStream);
    Trace.Listeners.Add(traceListener);

    // Write a startup note into the trace file.
    Trace.WriteLine("Trace started " + DateTime.Now.ToString());
}
```

When the form loads, this code creates a stream associated with the file `TraceFile.txt`. It then uses that stream to create a `TextWriterTraceListener` that will write into the file. The `Load` event handler finishes by writing a message into the file indicating the time the trace started.

As the program works, it can write other messages into the file. The following code shows how the program might add trace information while processing an order:

```
private void processOrderButton_Click(object sender, EventArgs e)
{
    // Log an order processing message.
    Trace.WriteLine("Processing order");

    // Log the order's data.
    Trace.Indent();
    Trace.WriteLine("CustomerId: " + CustomerId);
    Trace.WriteLine("OrderId: " + OrderId);
    Trace.WriteLine("OrderItems:");
```

```
Trace.Indent();
foreach (OrderItem item in OrderItems)
    Trace.WriteLine(item.ToString());
Trace.Unindent();
Trace.WriteLine("ShippingAddress: " + ShippingAddress);
Trace.Unindent();

// Process the order.
...
}
```

The code starts by adding a message saying that it is processing an order. It then indents the trace output and displays the order's information. It displays the customer and order IDs. It indents the trace again and displays the order's items. After displaying the items, the code unindents to get back to the main order level of indentation, and displays the order's shipping address. Finally, after displaying all the order information, the code unindents again to return to the original indentation level. It then does whatever is necessary to process the order.

When the program stops, it can use the following code to flush any buffered text to the trace file:

```
private void Form1_FormClosing(object sender, FormClosingEventArgs e)
{
    // Flush the trace output.
    Trace.WriteLine("Trace stopped " + DateTime.Now.ToString());
    Trace.Flush();
}
```

This code writes the current date and time into the file and flushes the output. If the program doesn't flush the output before ending, any buffered output will be lost.

The following text shows some sample output describing a single order:

```
Trace started 4/1/2014 10:43:19 AM
Processing order
    CustomerId: 1310
    OrderId: 112980
    OrderItems:
        6 x White copy paper, ream
        1 x Pencils, dozen box
        6 x White copy paper, ream
    ShippingAddress: 123 Main St, East Zephyr NH 01293
Trace stopped 4/1/2014 10:47:19 AM
```

By using a TextWriterTraceListener, you can make a program keep a complete log of its activities.

There are a couple of useful modifications you can make to this technique. First, you can open the file for appending instead of creating it as in the previous example. That lets the trace file keep records of past program runs instead of overwriting the file each time.

You can also allow sharing when you open the file. That lets other programs such as Microsoft Word open the file in read-only mode, so you can take a peek at the file while the program is still running. If you do this, you should call the Trace or Debug object's Flush method each time you write something into the file that you may want to peek at. In the previous example, you would probably want to flush the output after opening the file and after writing an order's information into it.

> **NOTE** *If you set the* `Trace` *or* `Debug` *object's* `AutoFlush` *property to* `true`, *then the object automatically flushes its output after every write.*

The following code shows one way you could open the trace file to append new text at the end of the file if it exists and allowing other programs to read the file.

```
Stream traceStream = File.Open("TraceFile.txt",
    FileMode.Append, FileAccess.Write, FileShare.Read);
```

For information on building your own listener class, see "TraceListener Class" at http:// msdn.microsoft.com/library/system.diagnostics.tracelistener.aspx.

Programming Database Files

When you build a debug release, Visual Studio creates a program database file that contains debugging information about the program. The debugger uses this information to let you debug the application.

You can use the project's property pages to control the amount of information that Visual Studio includes in the PDB file. To do that, select the Project menu's Properties command to open the project's property pages. On the Build tab, click Advanced. On the Advanced Build Settings dialog, use the Debug Info drop-down to select full, pdb-only, or none.

The "full" setting, which is the default for debug builds, creates a fully debuggable program.

The "pdb-only" setting, which is the default for release builds, creates a PDB file so exception messages can include information about where the error occurred. Visual Studio doesn't include the `Debuggable` attribute, however, that makes the code debuggable.

The "none" setting makes Visual Studio not create the PDB file.

If you create a compiled executable, you can still debug it if you have the correct PDB file available. Note that the PDB file is tied to a specific build, and will let you debug only that particular build. Due to the way builds are created, a PDB file cannot debug an executable from a different build even if you haven't changed the code.

To debug a compiled executable, place the PDB file in the same directory as the executable. Next, use Visual Studio to open the executable file and run it. If a `Debug` or `Trace` object's `Assert` or `Fail` method causes an exception, you can click the Retry button on the resulting dialog to debug the program.

The moral of the story is, if you want to debug an executable program after you build it, save its PDB file, and be sure you can figure out which PDB file goes with which version of the executable program.

INSTRUMENTING APPLICATIONS

Instrumenting a program means adding features to it to study the program itself. Usually that means adding code to monitor performance, record errors, and track program execution. With good instrumentation, you can tell what an application is doing and identify performance bottlenecks without stepping through the code in the debugger.

The following sections discuss some ways you can instrument a program to understand its behavior and performance.

Tracing

Tracing is the process of instrumenting a program, so you can track what it is doing. Earlier sections in this chapter explained how to use the Debug and Trace classes to add tracing to a program. By placing calls to Debug and Trace methods in key routines, you can follow the program's execution through those routines. In addition to making the program tell you what it is doing, you can add the current time to messages to get an idea of how fast the program is running at different points.

Logging and Event Logs

Logging is the process of instrumenting a program, so it records key events. For example, in an order processing system, you might want to keep a record of an order's major steps such as order creation, fulfillment, shipping, billing, and payment received.

As earlier sections explained, you can add listeners to the Debug or Trace classes to write messages into files. You could use that technique to log important events into files. The Debug and Trace classes are usually used for tracing not logging, however. In particular, most developers want logging to occur even if the DEBUG and TRACE symbols are not defined.

Instead of using Debug and Trace to log events, the program can write event records into an ordinary text file. This has the advantage of simplicity, and anyone can easily read a text file.

> **NOTE** *Often it is useful to make the amount of logging information recorded configurable, either by using preprocessor symbols or through configuration files. Then if the program is having problems, you can increase the amount of information it saves, so you can study the problem.*
>
> *For example, when it creates a new customer order, a program might normally record only the new order's ID. If you set a configuration flag, it might also log the customer's contact information. If you set a different flag, it might also log all the order's data including information about the order items.*
>
> *When things are running smoothly, you can omit most of this information to save space in the log file, but you can increase the amount of information saved when necessary, so you can troubleshoot problems.*

Another option is to write event information into the system log files. The WriteToEventLog program, which is shown in Figure 11-7 and available for download, demonstrates writing into the system event logs. Enter an event source name, event ID number, and event description of your choosing. The log name should be one of Application, Security, or System. When you have entered the values, click Write to create the log entry.

FIGURE 11-7: The WriteToEventLog program writes messages into the system event logs.

The following code shows how the program works:

```
using System.Diagnostics;
...
// Write an event log entry.
private void writeButton_Click(object sender, EventArgs e)
{
    string source = sourceTextBox.Text;
    string log = logTextBox.Text;
    string message = eventTextBox.Text;
    int id = int.Parse(idTextBox.Text);

    // Create the source if necessary. (Requires admin privileges.)
    if (!EventLog.SourceExists(source))
        EventLog.CreateEventSource(source, log);

    // Write the log entry.
    EventLog.WriteEntry(source, message,
        EventLogEntryType.Information, id);

    MessageBox.Show("OK");
}
```

The code first gets the values you entered on the form. It then uses the EventLog class's SourceExists method to see if the source you entered is defined. If the source has not yet been defined, the code uses the CreateEventSource method to create it. Note that CreateEventSource requires administrative privilege.

Next, the code uses the WriteEntry method to create the event log entry. This method has several overloaded versions. The one used here takes as parameters the source name, entry description, entry type, and ID number.

Figure 11-8 shows the Event Viewer displaying some log entries created by this program. In this figure the third entry is selected, so the General tab at the bottom of the viewer displays that entry's message text, "Created New Order 120193."

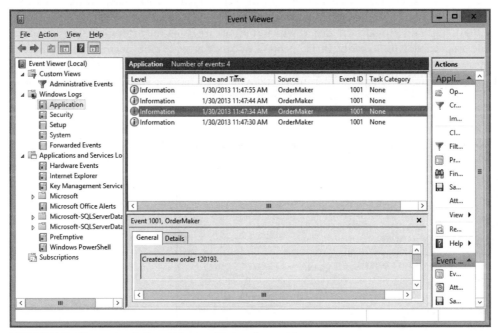

FIGURE 11-8: The system's Event Viewer displays log entries.

The system event logs provide a central place to view messages, so they can be particularly handy if you want to monitor several applications all in one place.

Profiling

Profiling is the process of gathering information about a program to study its speed, memory, disk usage, or other performance characteristics. There are two basic approaches to profiling a program: using a profiler and instrumenting the code by hand.

Using a Profiler

Automatic *profilers* can take several approaches to profiling an application. Some profilers instrument the source code to add timing statements to some or all the program's methods. Others instrument the compiled code. Still others use CPU sampling, periodically peeking at the program's state of execution and building up a statistical model of the amount of time the program spends in each method.

Visual Studio's Premium and Ultimate editions include profiling tools that you can use to measure an application's performance.

Some of the profiler's features require elevated privileges, so when you're ready to use it, start Visual Studio as an administrator. (One way to do that is to right-click the Visual Studio application and select Run As Administrator.)

To start, load a project, open the Analyze menu, and select Launch Performance Wizard to see the wizard shown in Figure 11-9. The CPU Sampling method periodically checks the program's state to see what it is doing. This provides an idea of which routines are using the most CPU time without slowing the program down too badly. Instrumented code may provide more accurate information but adds instrumentation in the compiled code, so it slows the program down. The .NET Memory Allocation option uses sampling to gather information about memory usage. The Resource Contention Data option is used to study concurrency issues in multithreaded applications. For now, just pick CPU Sampling and click Next.

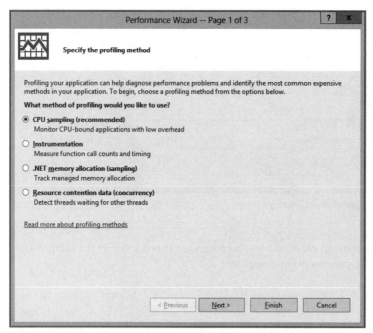

FIGURE 11-9: The Performance Wizard lets you study an application's memory of CPU usage.

The wizard's next page lets you pick the application that you will profile. Leave the currently loaded project selected and click Next.

The wizard's final page says it is ready to collect performance information. Leave the Launch Profiling After the Wizard Finishes box checked and click Finish.

After the wizard closes, the program launches with the profiler running. (It may take several seconds for the profiler start, so be patient.) When the program appears, exercise the features that you want to profile. Because the sampling method takes data periodically, it may miss some fast method calls. To get the best data, exercise the features you're studying several times.

When you finish, close the program normally and the profiler analyzes the data and presents results similar to those shown in Figure 11-10. The panels shown in Figure 11-10 show the hot path, the most often used call path, and the methods that were sampled the most often.

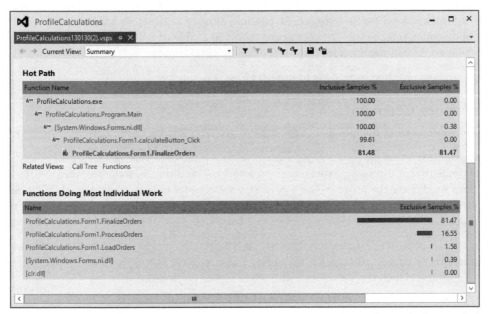

FIGURE 11-10: The profiler's output lets you see the most active call path, the methods sampled most often, and other statistics.

Other views of the report let you see information for modules, methods, all call paths, lines of code, and other categories. See "Beginners Guide to Performance Profiling" at http://msdn.microsoft .com/library/ms182372.aspx for a more comprehensive introduction to using the profiler.

Profiling by Hand

You can profile a program by hand by inserting statements into the source code that record the program's state and the current or elapsed time. For example, the following code shows how a method can use the Stopwatch class provided by the .NET Framework to time itself:

```
private void PerformCalculations()
{
    Stopwatch stopwatch = new Stopwatch();
    stopwatch.Start();

    // Perform the calculations here.
    ...

    Console.WriteLine("Time: " +
        stopwatch.Elapsed.TotalSeconds.ToString("0.00") +
        " seconds");
}
```

When the method starts, it creates a `Stopwatch` object and calls its `Start` method to begin timing. The method does whatever it needs to do and then uses the `Stopwatch`'s `Elapsed` property to see how much time has passed. The code converts the elapsed time into seconds and displays the result.

This technique is effective if you need to study only one or two key methods, but it has some drawbacks. If you don't know where the program is spending most of its time, it's hard to know where to put the profiling code. You can use preprocessor symbols to enable or hide this code when you don't need it, but that could still require a lot of code.

Another approach to profiling by hand is to use performance counters.

Using Performance Counters

Performance counters track operations system wide to give you an idea of the computer's activity.

For example, suppose an image processing program scans a directory every minute. It takes any image files it finds in that directory, processes them somehow, and then moves them into a different directory. You could make the program use a performance counter to keep track of each file it processed. Then you can use the system's Performance Monitor tool to see the counter changing as the program executes.

Before you can use a custom performance counter, you need to make one. If you run Visual Studio with administrator privileges, you can use the Server Explorer built in to Visual Studio to create new performance counters. Open the View menu and select Server Explorer.

> **NOTE** *You can also use C# code to create performance counters. For instructions, see the article "How to: Create Custom Performance Counters" at* `http://msdn` `.microsoft.com/library/5e3s61wf.aspx.`

Expand your computer's entry, right-click Performance Counters, and select Create New Category. Figure 11-11 shows the Server Explorer on the left and the Performance Counter Builder dialog on the right.

Enter a new category name and description. Then use the New button to add new counters to the category. When you finish, click OK.

Figure 11-11 shows two performance counters being created. The first has type `NumberOfItems32`, which represents the total number of some event that is counted by a program. The second counter has type `RateOfCountsPerSecond32`, which tracks the current number of items per second. When a program increments this counter, the counter automatically updates the counts per second value.

To use a performance counter in a program, create a `System.Diagnostics.PerformanceCounter` object for the counter. The following code shows how a program could create `PerformanceCounter` objects for the two performance counters created in Figure 11-11:

```
private PerformanceCounter totalImages, imagesPerSecond;

private void Form1_Load(object sender, EventArgs e)
{
```

```
totalImages = new PerformanceCounter();
totalImages.CategoryName = "ImageProcessor";
totalImages.CounterName = "Images processed";
totalImages.MachineName = ".";
totalImages.ReadOnly = false;

imagesPerSecond = new PerformanceCounter();
imagesPerSecond.CategoryName = "ImageProcessor";
imagesPerSecond.CounterName = "Images per second";
imagesPerSecond.MachineName = ".";
imagesPerSecond.ReadOnly = false;
}
```

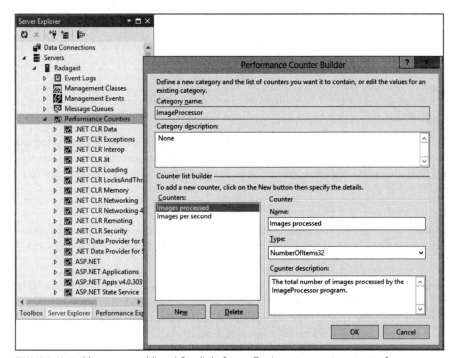

FIGURE 11-11: You can use Visual Studio's Sever Explorer to create new performance counters.

This code first creates a PerformanceCounter object. It sets the object's CategoryName and CounterName to the values used to create the counter in Figure 11-11. The code sets the MachineName to "." to indicate the local computer. It then sets ReadOnly to false to allow the program to modify the counter's value.

The code then repeats those steps to create a second PerformanceCounter object.

Having created the PerformanceCounter objects, the program can increment them when it performs whatever action you want to count.

Suppose the ImageProcessor program periodically examines a directory to see if it contains image files. When it finds a file, the program calls the following `ProcessImageFile` method:

```
private void ProcessImageFile(string filename)
{
    // Process the file.
    ...

    // Increment the performance counters.
    totalImages.Increment();
    imagesPerSecond.Increment();
}
```

This method does whatever it needs to do to the file. It then calls the performance counter objects' `Increment` methods to increment the counters.

That's all you need to do to create and use the performance counters. Now you need to use the system's Performance Monitor tool to see the results.

To start the Performance Monitor in Windows 8, open the Control Panel, and use the navigation bar to go to Control Panel ⇨ All Control Panel Items ⇨ Performance Information And Tools. Click the Advanced Tools link and then click Open Performance Monitor.

In the tree view on the Performance Monitor's left, expand Monitoring Tools and select Performance Monitor. In the graph that appears on the right, click the + sign to add performances counters to the graph. Select the performances counters that you want to view and click Add. After you have selected the counters, click OK.

Figure 11-12 shows the Performance Monitor displaying the two counters used by this example. The steadily increasing curve that wraps around from the right to left edge of the graph represents the Images Processed counter. The curve that wiggles up and down represents the Images Per Second counter.

The graph uses a Y-axis that ranges from 0 to 100 so often you'll want to scale the counters' values. In Figure 11-12, the program has been running for a while so Images Processed is scaled by a factor of 0.1, so its value would fit on the graph. The Images per Second value is scaled by a factor of 10, so the program is actually processing between 0 and approximately 6 image files per second.

To scale a counter, right-click the graph and select Properties. On the properties dialog, select the Data tab, click the counter that you want to scale, and set its Scale value to the scale factor that you want. When you finish, click OK.

Performance counters are fairly complicated and `NumberOfItems32` and `RateOfCountsPerSecond32` are only two of many counter types. For more information on performance counters, see the "Additional Reading and Resources" listed later in this chapter.

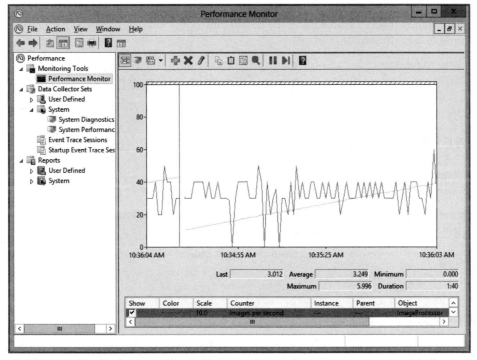

FIGURE 11-12: The Performance Monitor lets you view performance counters graphically.

SUMMARY

This chapter described ways you can protect a program from incorrect data and study a program's behavior.

Input validation techniques enable you to validate the user's input before processing. Useful techniques include using methods provided by the `string` class and using regular expressions. Of course, you can avoid validation entirely if you use controls such as `ComboBox` and `DateTimePicker`, so the user cannot select invalid values.

Even after the program reads the user's inputs, it must manage the data's integrity as it moves through the program. The `Debug.Assert` statement lets the program detect unexpected or incorrect values within the program.

Preprocessor symbols and directives enable you to determine what code is included in a program compilation. Using these you can compile extensive data validation code only for debug builds much as the `Debug.Assert` statement is ignored except in debug builds.

The chapter finished by discussing different ways you can instrument applications and study a program's performance. These include using the `Debug` and `Trace` classes, profilers, hand-coded instrumentation, and performance counters.

By using all these techniques, you can protect the program from invalid user inputs and watch for unexpected changes in the data during processing. You can also monitor the program's performance to see what it is doing and how efficiently it is running.

CHAPTER TEST QUESTIONS

Read each question carefully and select the answer or answers that represent the best solution to the problem. You can find the answers in Appendix A, "Answers to Chapter Test Questions."

1. If the user is typing data into a `TextBox` and types an invalid character, which of the following actions would be inappropriate for the program to take?

    a. Change the `TextBox`'s background color to indicate the error.

    b. Silently discard the character.

    c. Display an asterisk next to the `TextBox` to indicate the error.

    d. Display a message box telling the user that there is an error.

2. If the user types an invalid value into a `TextBox` and moves focus to another `TextBox`, which of the following actions would be inappropriate for the program to take?

    a. Force focus back into the `TextBox` that contains the error.

    b. Change the first `TextBox`'s background color to indicate the error.

    c. Change the first `TextBox`'s font to indicate the error.

    d. Display an asterisk next to the first `TextBox` to indicate the error.

3. If the user enters some invalid data on a form and then clicks the form's Accept button, which of the following actions would be appropriate for the program take?

    a. Change the background color of `TextBoxes` containing invalid values to indicate the errors.

    b. Display a message box telling the user that there is an error.

    c. Do not close the form until the user corrects all the errors.

    d. All the above.

4. Which of the following methods returns `true` if a regular expression matches a string?

    a. `Regex.Matches`

    b. `Regex.IsMatch`

    c. `Regexp.Matches`

    d. `String.Matches`

5. Which of the following regular expressions matches the Social Security number format ###-##-#### where # is any digit?

   a. `^###-##-####$`

   b. `^\d3-\d2-\d4$`

   c. `^\d{3}-\d{2}-\d{4}$`

   d. `^[0-9]3-[0-9]2-[0-9]4$`

6. Which of the following regular expressions matches a username that must include between 6 and 16 letters, numbers, and underscores?

   a. `^[a-zA-Z0-9_]?{6}$`

   b. `^[a-zA-Z0-9_]{6,16}$`

   c. `^[A-Z0-9a-z_]?$`

   d. `^\w{16}?$`

7. Which of the following regular expressions matches license plate values that must include three uppercase letters followed by a space and three digits, or three digits followed by a space and three uppercase letters?

   a. `(^\d{3} [A-Z]{3}$)|(^[A-Z]{3} \d{3}$)`

   b. `^\d{3} [A-Z]{3} [A-Z]{3} \d{3}$`

   c. `^\w{3} \d{3}|\d{3} \w{3}$`

   d. `^(\d{3} [A-Z]{3})?$`

8. Which of the following statements about assertions is true?

   a. The `Debug.Assert` method is ignored in release builds.

   b. The program must continue running even if a `Debug.Assert` method stops the program.

   c. When an assertion fails in debug builds, the `Debug.Assert` method lets you halt, debug the program, or continue running.

   d. All the above.

9. Which of the following statements about the `Debug` and `Trace` classes is true?

   a. The `Debug` class generates messages if DEBUG is defined. The `Trace` class generates messages if both DEBUG and TRACE are defined.

   b. The `Debug` class generates messages if DEBUG is defined. The `Trace` class generates messages if TRACE is defined.

   c. The `Debug` and `Trace` classes both generate messages if DEBUG is defined.

   d. The `Debug` and `Trace` classes both generate messages if TRACE is defined.

10. Which of the following statements about builds is true by default?

    a. Debug builds define the DEBUG symbol.

    b. Debug builds define the TRACE symbol.

    c. Release builds define the DEBUG symbol.

    d. Release builds define the TRACE symbol.

    e. Release builds define the RELEASE symbol.

11. Which of the following statements about PDB files is false?

    a. You need a PDB file to debug a compiled executable.

    b. You can use a PDB file to debug any version of a compiled executable.

    c. The "full" PDB file contains more information than a "pdb-only" PDB file.

    d. If you set the PDB file type to None, Visual Studio doesn't create a PDB file.

12. Which of the following statements about tracing and logging is false?

    a. Tracing is the process of instrumenting a program to track what it is doing.

    b. Logging is the process of making the program record key events in a log file.

    c. You can use DEBUG and TRACE statements to trace or log a program's execution.

    d. A program cannot write events into the system's event logs, so you can see them in the Event Viewer.

13. Which of the following methods would probably be the easiest way to find bottlenecks in a program if you had no idea where to look?

    a. Use an automatic profiler.

    b. Instrument the code by hand.

    c. Use performance counters.

    d. Set breakpoints throughout the code and step through execution.

14. What of the following is the best use of performance counters?

    a. To determine which of a program's methods use the most CPU time.

    b. To determine how often a particular operation is occurring on the system as a whole.

    c. To determine how often a particular operation is occurring in a particular executing instance of a program.

    d. To find the deepest path of execution in a program's call tree.

ADDITIONAL READING AND RESOURCES

Here are some additional useful resources to help you understand the topics presented in this chapter:

.NET Framework Regular Expressions
> http://msdn.microsoft.com/library/hs600312.aspx

Regular Expression Language - Quick Reference
> http://msdn.microsoft.com/library/az24scfc.aspx

Character Classes in Regular Expressions
> http://msdn.microsoft.com/library/20bw873z.aspx

Regular Expression Options
> http://msdn.microsoft.com/library/yd1hzczs.aspx

C# Preprocessor Directives
> http://msdn.microsoft.com/library/ed8yd1ha.aspx

John Robbins' Blog, PDB Files: What Every Developer Must Know
> http://www.wintellect.com/CS/blogs/jrobbins/archive/2009/05/11/
> pdb-files-what-every-developer-must-know.aspx

TraceListener Class
> http://msdn.microsoft.com/library/system.diagnostics.tracelistener.aspx

Tracing and Instrumenting Applications in Visual Basic and Visual C#
> http://msdn.microsoft.com/library/aa984115.aspx

Beginners Guide to Performance Profiling
> http://msdn.microsoft.com/library/ms182372.aspx

Find Application Bottlenecks with Visual Studio Profiler
> http://msdn.microsoft.com/magazine/cc337887.aspx

An Introduction To Performance Counters
> http://www.codeproject.com/Articles/8590/An-Introduction-To-Performance-Counters

How to: Create Custom Performance Counters
> http://msdn.microsoft.com/library/5e3s61wf.aspx

PerformanceCounter Class
> http://msdn.microsoft.com/library/system.diagnostics.performancecounter.aspx

CHEAT SHEET

This cheat sheet is designed as a way for you to quickly study the key points of this chapter.

Input validation

➤ Use `TrackBar`, `ComboBox`, `ListBox`, `DateTimePicker`, `FolderBrowserDialog`, and other controls to avoid validation if possible.

➤ Make frequent validations (such as during keystrokes) provide nonintrusive feedback (such as changing the field's background color).

➤ Do not trap the user in a field until its value is entered correctly.

➤ Remember that some values (such as "–.") may be invalid but may be part of a valid value (such as "–.0").

➤ When the user tries to accept a form, validate all fields. Refuse to accept the form if there are invalid values. Warn the user if there are unusual values.

Validating data—built-in validation functions

➤ Use string length to check for missing values.

➤ Initialize a `ComboBox` or `ListBox` so that it always has a valid selection.

➤ Use `TryParse` to validate data types such as `int` or `decimal`.

➤ String methods that can help with validation include `Contains`, `EndsWith`, `IndexOf`, `IndexOfAny`, `IsNullOrEmpty`, `IsNullOrWhitespace`, `LastIndexOf`, `LastIndexOfAny`, `Remove`, `Replace`, `Split`, `StartsWith`, `Substring`, `ToLower`, `ToUpper`, `Trim`, `TrimEnd`, and `TrimStart`.

Validating data—regular expressions

➤ Table 11-3 summarizes the useful Regex methods `IsMatch`, `Matches`, `Replace`, and `Split`.

➤ Use string literals (beginning with the @ character) to make it easier to use regular expressions that contain escape characters.

➤ For example, the following code checks whether the variable `phone` contains a value that matches a 7-digit U.S. phone number pattern:

```
if (Regex.IsMatch(phone, @"^\d{3}-\d{4}$")) ...
```

➤ Table 11-10 summarizes some of the most useful regular expression components.

TABLE 11-10: Useful Regular Expression Components

ITEM	PURPOSE
\	Begins a special symbol such as \n or escapes the following character
^	Matches the beginning of string or line
$	Matches the end of string or line

ITEM	PURPOSE
\A	Matches the beginning of string (even if in multiline mode)
\Z	Matches the end of string (even if in multiline mode)
*	Matches the preceding 0 or more times
+	Matches the preceding 1 or more times
?	Matches the preceding 0 or 1 times
.	Matches any character
[abc]	Matches any one of the characters inside the brackets
[^abc]	Matches one character that is not inside the brackets
[a-z]	Matches one character in the range of characters
[^a-z]	Matches one character that is not in the range of characters
x|y	Matches x or y
(pattern)	Makes a numbered match group
(?<name>expr)	Makes a named match group
\2	Refers to previously defined group number 2
\k<name>	Refers to previously defined group named name
{n}	Matches exactly n occurrences
{n,}	Matches n or more occurrences
{n,m}	Matches between n and m occurrences
\b	Matches a word boundary
\B	Matches a nonword boundary
\d	Matches a digit
\D	Matches a nondigit
\f	Matches a form-feed
\n	Matches a newline
\r	Matches a carriage return
\s	Matches whitespace (space, tab, form-feed, and so on)
\S	Matches nonwhitespace

continues

TABLE 11-10 *(continued)*

ITEM	PURPOSE
\t	Matches a tab
\v	Matches a vertical tab
\w	Matches a word character (includes underscore)
\W	Matches a nonword character

➤ Use sanity checks to look for unusual values.

Managing data integrity

➤ After you validate user inputs, the code must still protect the data as it is processed.

➤ Use Debug.Assert statements to validate data as it moves through the program.

Debugging

➤ Use the #define and #undef directives to define and undefined preprocessor symbols.

➤ Use the #if, #elif, #else, and #endif directives to determine what code is included in the program depending on which preprocessor symbols are defined.

➤ Use #warning and #error to add warnings and errors to the Error List.

➤ Use #line to change a line number and optionally the name of the file as reported in errors.

➤ Use #region and #endregion to make collapsible code regions.

➤ Use #pragma warning disable *number* and #pragma warning restore *number* to disable and restore warnings.

➤ The DEBUG and TRACE compiler constants are predefined. Normally, DEBUG is defined in debug builds, and TRACE is defined in debug and release builds.

➤ Calls to Debug and Trace class methods are ignored if the symbols DEBUG and TRACE are not defined, respectively.

➤ Useful Debug and Trace methods include Assert, Fail, Flush, Indent, Unindent, Write, WriteIf, WriteLine, and WriteLineIf.

➤ You can add listeners to the Debug and Trace objects. Standard listeners write messages to the Output window, event logs, and text files.

Program Database files

➤ You need a PDB file to debug a compiled executable.

Instrumenting applications

➤ Tracing means instrumenting the program to trace its progress. You can use `Debug` and `Trace` for tracing.

➤ Logging means recording key events. Methods for logging include writing into a text file, using `Debug` and `Trace` with a listener that writes into a text file, and writing in an event log.

➤ Profiling means gathering information about a program to study characteristics such as speed and memory usage. Methods for profiling include using a profiler, instrumenting the code by hand, and using performance counters.

REVIEW OF KEY TERMS

assertion A piece of code that makes a particular claim about the data and that throws an exception if that claim is false. In C# you can use the `System.Diagnostics.Debug.Assert` method to make assertions.

character class A regular expression construction that represents a set of characters to match.

conditional compilation constant A predefined symbol created by Visual Studio that you can use with the `#if`, `#elif`, `#else`, and `#endif` directives to determine what code is included in the program. These include DEBUG and TRACE, which are normally defined in debug and release builds, respectively.

data validation Program code that verifies that a data value such as a string entered by the user makes sense. For example, the program might require that a value be nonblank, that a monetary value be a valid value such as $12.34 not "ten," or that an e-mail address contain the @ symbol.

escape sequence A sequence of characters that have special meaning, for example, in a regular expression.

inline options Options set in a regular expression by using the syntax `(?imnsx)`.

instrumenting Adding features to a program to study the program itself.

logging The process of instrumenting a program, so it records key events.

pattern A regular expression used for matching parts of a string.

performance counter A system-wide counter used to track some type of activity on the computer.

profiler An automated tool that gathers performance data for a program by instrumenting its code or by sampling.

profiling The process of instrumenting a program to study its speed, memory, disk usage, or other performance characteristics.

regular expression An expression in a regular expression language that defines a pattern to match. Regular expressions let a program match patterns and make replacements in strings.

sanity check A test on data to see if the data makes sense. For example, if a user enters the cost of a ream of paper as $1e10.00, that might be a typographical error, and the user may have meant $100.00. Sometimes the user might actually have intended an unusual value, so the program must decide whether to reject the value or ask the user whether the value is correct.

tracing The process of instrumenting a program so that you can track what it is doing.

EXAM TIPS AND TRICKS

The Review of Key Terms and the Cheat Sheet for this chapter can be printed off to help you study. You can find these files in the ZIP file for this chapter at www.wrox .com/remtitle.cgi?isbn=1118612094 on the Download Code tab.

12

Using Encryption and Managing Assemblies

WHAT YOU WILL LEARN IN THIS CHAPTER

- ➤ Understanding encryption
- ➤ Using symmetric encryption
- ➤ Using asymmetric encryption
- ➤ Signing and hashing data
- ➤ Creating strong name assemblies
- ➤ Deploying assemblies in the GAC

WROX.COM CODE DOWNLOADS FOR THIS CHAPTER

You can find the code downloads for this chapter at www.wrox.com/remtitle .cgi?isbn=1118612094 on the Download Code tab. The code is in the chapter12 download and individually named according to the names throughout the chapter.

When you deal with sensitive data, you must protect it from unauthorized access or modification, and for that you need to use techniques such as encryption, digital signatures, and hashing of data. One application of digital signatures and hashing of data used often by .NET is with strong name assemblies.

This chapter begins by going through different technologies that you can use to ensure privacy, integrity, and authenticity of your data. You will look at both symmetric and asymmetric algorithms. In the second part of this chapter you will look in details at how you can ensure the integrity of you assemblies by using digital signatures.

Table 12-1 introduces you to the exam objectives covered in this chapter.

TABLE 12-1: 70-483 Exam Objectives Covered in This Chapter

OBJECTIVE	CONTENT COVERED
Perform symmetric and asymmetric encryption	*Choose an appropriate encryption algorithm.* This includes discussing the symmetric and asymmetric algorithms.
	Manage and create certificates. This includes working with different kind of certificates and certificates store.
	Implement key management. This includes discussing the options available in .NET to store the encryption keys.
	Implement the `System.Security` namespace. This includes discussing the classes and interfaces available in the `System.Security` namespace.
	Hash data. This includes discussing the options available to hash data and to create digital signatures.
	Encrypt streams. This includes using the `CryptoStream` class to encrypt streams
Manage assemblies	*Version assemblies.* This includes choosing a versioning scheme for the assembly.
	Sign assemblies using strong names. This includes signing the assemblies from Visual Studio, as well as using the `sn.exe`.
	Implement side-by-side hosting. This includes discussing techniques you can use to have different version of the same assembly on the same machine at the same time.
	Put an assembly in the global assembly cache. This includes using different tools to deploy the assemblies in the global assembly cache.

USING ENCRYPTION

Encryption is the process of transforming plain data in a way that makes it harder for an unauthorized person to make sense of it. The encrypted data is called *ciphertext*. *Decryption* is the reverse process, meaning that having the ciphertext, you must apply a transformation to it to get back the original information. The harder it is to decrypt the ciphertext, the better the algorithm. You might have reacted to saying "harder" to make sense of it instead of saying "impossible." The reason for that is because any encrypted data can be decrypted eventually, but some algorithms are so complicated that it can take a long time (such as hundreds of years) to decrypt the data, so the information is useless. *Cryptography* is the practice and study of encryption and decryption techniques.

Romans used simple algorithms such as transposition. They replaced every letter with another one, like the next one in the alphabet, or the one found three positions after the current one. But this was just a simple algorithm. To decrypt the message, you only had to figure out the algorithm used (transposition in this example) and the algorithm parameters (how many positions were used for the transposition). In time the algorithms evolved, making it harder and harder to decrypt the data. A notable effort before computers appeared was the German machine Enigma that used an electromechanical rotor cipher to encrypt and decrypt secret messages.

With the invention of computers, the encryption became more and more advanced, and with today's technologies the algorithms are open because their parameters are the ones improving the security of any encrypted data. Today's encryption techniques make heavy use of mathematics.

Sometimes you might not need to hide the data, but to make sure that the data is not tampered with, or that the data comes from the right source. If you want to ensure that the data is not tampered with, you can use a *Secured Hash Algorithm* (SHA), whereas for authenticity of the data you can use a *Message Authentication Code* (MAC) algorithm. So let's assume that you want to send an order to a supplier. To make sure that the order doesn't get altered on its way to the supplier, you can add the SHA signature to the message. If you want to guarantee the identity of the sender of the order as well as the integrity of the order, then you would use a MAC.

Choosing an Appropriate Encryption Algorithm

You saw that encryption and decryption protect data from unauthorized access. Encryption can be done in two ways. One way is called *symmetric encryption*, or *shared secret*, and the second one is called *asymmetric encryption* or *public key*. (Both types of encryption are described in more detail in the following sections.)

Microsoft implemented some of the existing algorithms in .NET, which are implemented in three ways:

➤ **Managed classes (in .NET):** The class name for those is the algorithm name suffixed with `Managed`, for instance `RijndaelManaged` is the managed class that implements the Rijndael algorithm. The managed implementations are somewhat slower than the other implementations and are not certified by the Federal Information Processing Standards (FIPS).

➤ **Wrapper classes around the native Cryptography API (CAPI) implementation:** The class name for those is the algorithm name suffixed with `CryptoServiceProvider`, for instance `DESCryptoServiceProvider` is the wrapper class that implements the Data Encryption Standard (DES) algorithm. The CAPI implementations are suitable for older systems, but they are no longer being developed.

➤ **Wrapper classes around the native Cryptography Next Generation (CNG) API implementation:** The class name for those is the algorithm name suffixed with `CNG`, for instance `ECDiffieHellmanCng` is the wrapper class that implements the Elliptic Curve Diffie-Hellman (ECDH) algorithm. CNG algorithms require a Windows Vista or newer operating system.

All cryptography classes are defined in the `System.Security.Cryptography` namespace and are part of the core .NET library.

Symmetric Encryption

As mentioned symmetric encryption is also known as shared secret encryption, and that is because the encryption of the data is done with an encryption key, a byte array, and the same key is used to decrypt the data. The symmetric algorithms rely on the fact that only an authorized person has access to the encryption key. The main drawback of the symmetric encryption is that if the encryption key becomes compromised, the data will not be secured.

The symmetric algorithms that come with .NET use a chaining mode called *cipher block chaining*. This kind of algorithm works in the following way. If the data is bigger than a predefined size, called *block size*, the data is split in blocks of that predefined size. The first block is encrypted using a random block of data of the same size, called *initialization vector* (IV), and the encryption key. The next block is encrypted using the result of the previous encrypted block instead of the IV and the same encryption key, and so on until it reaches the last block. The block size is determined by the algorithm used. If the last block is less than that size, it will be padded with data so it will have the same size as the size used by the algorithm. To decrypt the cipher text, you must have the IV and the key. The IV doesn't need to be kept secret, but the private key does. You will see later in this chapter how the encryption key can be handled.

.NET Framework implements five different symmetric algorithms, as shown in Table 12-2.

TABLE 12-2: Symmetric Algorithms Implemented in .NET

ALGORITHM SHORT NAME	DESCRIPTION
Aes	Advanced Encryption Standard (AES). There are two classes implementing this algorithm: `AesManaged` and `AesCryptoServiceProvider`.
DES	Data Encryption Standard algorithm implemented by `DESCryptoServiceProvider`.
RC2	Rivest Cipher (or Ron's code) algorithm implemented by `RC2CryptoServiceProvider`.
Rijndael	Rijndael algorithm implemented by `RijndaelManaged`.
TripleDES	Triple Data Encryption Standard (DES) algorithm implemented by `TripleDESCryptoServiceProvider`.

All the classes mentioned in Table 12-2 inherit from the `System.Security.Cryptography .SymmetricAlgorithm` class. This class contains properties and methods that are useful when working with symmetric algorithms. Tables 12-3 and 12-4 list the properties and methods of that class.

TABLE 12-3: System.Security.Cryptography.SymmetricAlgorithm Properties

PROPERTY	DESCRIPTION
BlockSize	Gets or sets the size of the block used by the cryptographic operation. The block size is specified in bits and represents the basic unit of data that can be encrypted or decrypted in one operation. Messages longer than the block size are split into blocks of this size; messages shorter than the block size are padded with extra bits until they reach the size of a block. The algorithm used determines the validity of the block size.

PROPERTY	DESCRIPTION
FeedbackSize	Gets or sets the size of the feedback size used by the cryptographic operation. The feedback size represents the amount of data in bits that is fed back to the next encryption or decryption operation. The feedback size must be lower than the block size.
IV	Gets or sets the IV. Whenever you create a new instance of a symmetric algorithm, the IV is set to a new random value. You can generate one as well by calling the GenerateIV method. The size of the IV property must be the same as the BlockSize property divided by eight.
Key	Gets or sets the secret key used by the algorithm. The secret key has to be the same for both encryption and for decryption. For a symmetric algorithm to be successful, the secret key must be kept secret. The valid key sizes are specified by the particular symmetric algorithm implementation and are listed in the LegalKeySizes property.
KeySize	Gets or sets the size of the secret key used by the symmetric algorithm. The valid key sizes are specified in bits by the particular symmetric algorithm implementation and are listed in the LegalKeySizes property.
LegelBlockSizes	Gets the block sizes in bits that are accepted by the algorithm.
LegalKeySizes	Gets the key sizes in bits that are accepted by the algorithm.
Mode	Gets or sets the mode for operation of the algorithm. See the System.Security.Cryptography.CipherMode enumeration for a description of specific modes.
Padding	Gets or sets the padding mode used by the algorithm. See the System.Security.Cryptography.PaddingMode enumeration for a description of specific modes.

TABLE 12-4: System.Security.Cryptography.SymmetricAlgorithm Methods

METHOD	DESCRIPTION
Clear	Releases all resources used by the SymmetricAlgorithm class. You need to call this method to clear all the resources allocated by the algorithm to ensure that no sensitive data remains in the memory when you finish with the cryptographic object. Do not rely on garbage collector to clear the data.

continues

TABLE 12-4 *(continued)*

METHOD	DESCRIPTION
`Create()`	This static method creates a new cryptographic using the default algorithm, which in .NET 4.5 is `RijndaelManaged`.
`Create(String)`	This static method creates a new cryptographic object using the specified cryptographic algorithm. The name of the algorithm can be either one of the names on the left column of Table 12-2 or the name of the type itself, with or without the namespace. `Aes` corresponds to the `AesCryptoServiceProvider` algorithm. If you want to use the managed version of the algorithm, you need to specify `AesManaged`.
`CreateDecryptor()`	Creates a decryptor object using the `Key` and `IV` currently set in the properties.
`CreateDecryptor(Byte[], Byte[])`	Creates a decryptor object using the `Key` and `IV` values specified as parameters.
`CreateEncryptor()`	Creates an encryptor object using the `Key` and `IV` currently set in the properties.
`CreateEncryptor(Byte[], Byte[])`	Creates an encryptor object using the `Key` and `IV` properties specified as parameters.
`GenerateIV`	Generates a random `IV` to be used by the algorithm. Normally there is no need to call this method.
`GenerateKey`	Generates a random `Key` to be used by the algorithm. The secret key has to be the same for both encryption and for decryption. For a symmetric algorithm to be successful, the secret key must be kept secret. The valid key sizes are specified by the particular symmetric algorithm implementation and are listed in the `LegalKeySizes` property.
`ValidKeySize`	Returns `true` if the specified key size is valid for this specific algorithm.

The workflow of encrypting plain text into chipper text is straightforward:

1. Create a symmetric algorithm object by calling the `Create` method of the `SymmetricAlgorithm` class setting the optional string parameter to the name of the wanted algorithm.

2. If you want you can set a key and an IV, but this is not necessary because they are generated by default.

3. Create an encryptor object by calling the `CreateEncryptor` method. Again, you can choose to send the key and the IV as parameters to this method or use the default, generated one.

4. Call the `TransformFinalBlock` method on the encryptor, which takes as input a byte array, representing the plain data, the offset where to start the encryption from, and the length of the data to encrypt. It returns the encrypted data back.

The code should look like this:

```
byte[] EncryptData(byte[] plainData, byte[] IV, byte[] key) {

    SymmetricAlgorithm cryptoAlgorythm = SymmetricAlgorithm.Create();
    ICryptoTransform encryptor = cryptoAlgorythm.CreateEncryptor(key, IV);
    byte[] cipherData = encryptor.TransformFinalBlock(plainData, 0,
                                                  plainData.Length);

    return cipherData;
}
```

The workflow of decrypting chipper text to get back the plain text is straightforward as well:

1. Create a symmetric algorithm object by calling the `Create` method of the `SymmetricAlgorithm` class setting the optional string parameter to the name of the same algorithm used for encryption.

2. If you want you can set a key and an IV, but this is not necessary now because you can set them on the next step.

3. Create a decryptor object by calling `CreateDecryptor` method. You must now set the key and the IV by sending them as parameters to this method, if you didn't do it in the previous step. The key and the IV must be the same as the ones used for encryption.

4. Call the `TransformFinalBlock` method on the decryptor, which takes as input a byte array, which is the chipper data, the offset where to start the decryption from, and the length of the data to decrypt, and it returns the plain data back.

The code should look like this:

```
byte[] DecryptData(byte[] cipherData, byte[] IV, byte[] key) {

    SymmetricAlgorithm cryptoAlgorythm = SymmetricAlgorithm.Create();
    ICryptoTransform decryptor = cryptoAlgorythm.CreateDecryptor(key, IV);
    byte[] plainData = decryptor.TransformFinalBlock(cipherData, 0,
                                                  cipherData.Length);

    return plainData;
}
```

The biggest challenge of symmetric encryption algorithms is to keep the key secret. If the data doesn't have to leave the machine, you must save it somehow in a safe place so that only you can get access to it when you need to decrypt the data. You see later in this chapter in the "Implementing Key Management" section how to solve that.

If you need to send the data across the wire, make sure that the other party has the key as well. Transmitting the key needs to be done securely so that no unauthorized person gets access to it; otherwise, the whole data becomes compromised.

> **ADVICE FROM THE EXPERTS: Working with Symmetric Algorithms**
>
> By using the abstract base class `SymmetricAlgorithm` instead of the concrete classes and calling the factory method `Create`, you have good flexibility in your system. If later the requirements for your encryption change and you need to use a different algorithm, the only thing that you need to do, in principle, is to change the name of the algorithm.

Asymmetric Encryption

An alternative to symmetric encryption is to use asymmetric encryption. The main reason to use asymmetric encryption is to avoid sharing the encryption key, which is considered a vulnerability. Asymmetric encryption uses two mathematically related keys that complement each other, such as whatever is encrypted with one key can be decrypted only with the other key. One key is made public, and is known as the *public key*, by the receiving party, so whoever wants to transmit secured data can encrypt the data. Make sure at the same time only the receiving party can decrypt the data by using the other key, known as the *private key*. (The mathematics behind generating the two keys is outside the scope of this book.)

The main disadvantage of the asymmetric encryption is that it is slower than the symmetric encryption, but the biggest advantage is that there is no need to have a shared secret for the algorithm to work.

.NET Framework implements five different symmetric algorithms, as shown in Table 12-5.

TABLE 12-5: Asymmetric Algorithms Implemented in .NET

ALGORITHM SHORT NAME	DESCRIPTION
DSA	Digital Signature algorithm. Used to create digital signatures that help protect the integrity of data. There is one class implementing this algorithm: `DSACryptoServiceProvider`. Use DSA only for compatibility with legacy applications and data.
ECDiffieHellman	Elliptic Curve Diffie-Hellman algorithm implemented by `ECDiffieHellmanCng`.
ECDsa	Elliptic Curve Digital Signature Algorithm (ECDSA) algorithm implemented by `ECDsaCng`.
RSA	RSA algorithm implemented by `RSACryptoServiceProvider`.

In .NET all classes that implement an asymmetric algorithm inherit from `System.Security` `.Cryptography.AsymmetricAlgorithm`.

The workflow of encrypting data using asymmetric encryption follows:

1. Obtain the public key of the receiver.

2. Create a new asymmetric encryption object.

3. Set the public key.

4. Encrypt the data.

5. Send the data to the receiver.

The workflow of decrypting data using asymmetric encryption follows:

1. Get the data from the sender.

2. Create a new asymmetric encryption object.

3. Set the private key.

4. Decrypt the data.

If the data were changed or it not encrypted using the corresponding public key, a `CryptographicException` will be thrown.

There are two ways to handle the keys. The first is to send the key directly; the second is to save the keys in a cryptographic service provider container. How to handle the key will be discussed later in this chapter in the "Implementing Key Management" section. To see how those two are implemented, look at the code lab at the end of this section.

One common scenario is to use asymmetric encryption to exchange the keys needed for symmetric encryption using the following workflow:

1. Both parties generate a public/private key pair.

2. The parties exchange the public keys.

3. Each party generates a symmetric key that can use the encrypt data.

4. Each party encrypts the symmetric key using an asymmetric algorithm and the other party's public key.

5. Each party sends the encrypted key to the other party.

6. Each party decrypts the key using the same asymmetric algorithm and their own private key to obtain the symmetric key generated by the other party.

7. They start exchanging data using the same symmetric algorithm and the keys from previous step.

Another common scenario is to use the asymmetric encryption to digitally sign data, ensuring in this way both the authenticity and the identity.

Stream Encryption

As discussed in Chapter 9, "Working with Data," streams represent a file, an I/O device, or a communication channel and can perform three fundamental operations:

➤ **Read**: You can transfer data from the stream into a data structure.

➤ **Write**: You can transfer data to the stream from a data structure.

➤ **Seek**: You can change the current position within the stream where the next read-or-write operation operates.

One important property of streams in .NET is that they can be chained by feeding the output data from a stream into the input of another stream. Sometimes you might want to encrypt the data the goes through those streams, in order to ensure the privacy or integrity of the data. You can either encrypt the data before it is sent through the stream, or you can just chain the streams so one of them will be in charge of encryption. Remember that one of the streams classes presented in Chapter 9 was `CryptoStream`, which you can use to encrypt or decrypt data coming through it.

The workflow of encrypting streams is straightforward:

1. Create a symmetric algorithm object by calling the `Create` method of the `SymmetricAlgorithm` class, setting the optional string parameter to the name of the wanted algorithm.

2. If you want you can set a key and an IV, but this is not necessary because they will be generated by default.

3. Create an encryptor object by calling `CreateEncryptor` method. Again, you can choose to send the key and the IV as parameters to this method or use the default generated one.

4. Create a `CryptoStream` object. The constructor of `CryptoStream` expects three parameters. The first parameter is the stream where you send the encrypted data; the second one is the encryptor you created in the previous step; and the third one is the stream operation mode, which in this case is `Write`.

5. Write data to the `CryptoStream` object either calling one of the `Write` methods exposed by `CryptoStream`, by using a `StreamWriter`, or by chaining it to another stream.

6. When you finish, clear the `CryptoStream` object of all the sensitive data by calling the `Clear` method, and then dispose of the object.

The code should look like this:

```
byte[] EncryptString(string plainData, byte[] IV, byte[] key) {

    SymmetricAlgorithm cryptoAlgorythm = SymmetricAlgorithm.Create();
    ICryptoTransform encryptor = cryptoAlgorythm.CreateEncryptor(key, IV);
    byte[] cipherData = new byte[0];

    using (MemoryStream msEncrypt = new MemoryStream()) {
        using (CryptoStream csEncrypt = new CryptoStream(msEncrypt,
                                            encryptor,
                                            CryptoStreamMode.Write)) {
            StreamWriter swEncrypt = new StreamWriter(csEncrypt);
```

```
                  swEncrypt.Write(plainData);
                  swEncrypt.Close();
                  csEncrypt.Clear();
                  cipherData = msEncrypt.ToArray();
              }
          }
          return cipherData;
      }
```

The workflow of decrypting streams is straightforward as well:

1. Create a symmetric algorithm object by calling Create method of the SymmetricAlgorithm class, setting the optional string parameter to the name of the same algorithm used for encryption.

2. If you want you can set a key and an IV, but this is not necessary now because you can set them on the next step.

3. Create a decryptor object by calling CreateDecryptor method. You now have to set the key and the IV by sending them as parameters to this method if you didn't do it in the previous step. The key and the IV must be the same as the ones used for encryption.

4. Create a CryptoStream object. The constructor of CryptoStream expects three parameters. The first parameter is the stream where to send the encrypted data; the second one is the decryptor you created in the previous step; and the third one is the stream operation mode, which in this case is Read.

5. Read data from the CryptoStream object either calling one of the Read methods exposed by CryptoStream, by using a StreamReader or by chaining it to another stream.

6. When you finish, clear the CryptoStream object of all the sensitive data by calling the Clear method, and then dispose of the object.

The code should look like this:

```
      string DecryptString(byte[] cipherData, byte[] IV, byte[] key) {

          SymmetricAlgorithm cryptoAlgorythm = SymmetricAlgorithm.Create();
          ICryptoTransform decryptor = cryptoAlgorythm.CreateDecryptor(key, IV);
          string plainText = string.Empty;

          using (MemoryStream msDecrypt = new MemoryStream(cipherData)) {
              using (CryptoStream csDecrypt = new CryptoStream(msDecrypt,
                                                 decryptor,
                                                 CryptoStreamMode.Read)) {
                  StreamReader srDecrypt = new StreamReader(csDecrypt);

                  plainText = srDecrypt.ReadToEnd();
                  srDecrypt.Close();
                  csDecrypt.Clear();
              }
          }
          return plainText;
      }
```

> **ADVICE FROM THE EXPERTS: Chaining Streams to Encrypt and Compress Data**
>
> One common scenario is to encrypt and compress the data that is sent via a network. The order in which you do that is important for two reasons. First, compressing text is more effective than compressing binary data, resulting in less data to encrypt. Second, you have to apply the transformations in reverse order, meaning that if you first compress and then encrypt the data on the sender side, you must first decrypt data and then decompress it on the receiver side.

Hashing Data

Hashing is the process of mapping binary data of a variable length to a fixed size binary data. Applying the same hash function to two identical data structures yields the same result. Hashing functions are used in several scenarios:

➤ **Indexing data:** Instead of matching the data when the index key is a variable length, calculate the hash value of the index key and locate that instead. The hash value resulting from a data structure is usually shorter than the original value, so when searching for a shorter amount of data, the search time will be shorter as well. It is possible that two or more index keys can yield the same hash value. In this situation the indexing algorithm uses a technique called *hash bucket*, where all the index keys having the same hash value are grouped together. The kind of hashing used in this scenario has nothing to do with cryptography, but it is worth mentioning.

➤ **Data integrity:** Data integrity is used to ensure that the data reaches the destination unchanged. The sender computes a cryptographic hash of the data that wants to send, and then the sender sends the data, the hash, and information about the technique used to compute the hash to the receiver. The receiver can apply the same algorithm to the data, and it will compare the resulting hash with the one received. If they are the same, it means that the data wasn't changed after the hash was computed. This doesn't guarantee that the data is not changed, though. If someone wants to change the message, the only thing that person will have to do is to compute the hash of the new message and send that instead.

➤ **Data authenticity:** Data authenticity is used when a receiver wants to make sure that the data is coming from the right sender and that it is not changed on its way. It works in this way: The sender computes a cryptographic hash and signs it with its own private key. The receiver hashes the data again and then decrypts the received signature, uses the senders' public key to decrypt the signature, and verifies that is the same as the hash.

➤ **Password storage:** Storing a password in plain text is an unsecure technique, and if the data store becomes compromised, all the passwords will be compromised as well. To protect the passwords, they are usually hashed, and instead of saving the password, you save the hash of the password. When someone attempts to log in, you can hash the entered password and verify that the two hashes are the same.

The strength of the cryptographic hash is that it is improbable that two different inputs generate the same hash. Two passwords that are not the same and differ little from each other can produce two completely different hashes.

There are two kind of hashing algorithms: with or without a key. The algorithms without keys are used only to calculate secure hashes for data to ensure integrity, whereas the keyed algorithms are used together with a key as a MAC for both integrity and authenticity.

.NET Framework comes with implementations for different algorithms, as shown in Table 12-6.

TABLE 12-6: Hash Algorithms Implemented in .NET

ALGORITHM SHORT NAME	DESCRIPTION
SHA1	Implementation of SHA algorithm with a resulting hash size of 160 bits
SHA256	Implementation of SHA algorithm with a resulting hash size of 256 bits
SHA512	Implementation of SHA algorithm with a resulting hash size of 512 bits
SHA384	Implementation of SHA algorithm with a resulting hash size of 384 bits
MD5	Implementation of MD5 hash algorithm
RIPEMD160	Implementation of RIPEMD hash algorithm

In .NET all hashing algorithms inherit from the `System.Security.Cryptography.HashAlgorithm` abstract class. Tables 12-7 and 12-8 list the properties and methods of the `HashAlgorithm` class.

TABLE 12-7: System.Security.Cryptography.HashAlgorithm Properties

PROPERTY	DESCRIPTION
`CanReuseTransform`	Read-only property that returns `true` if the current transform can be reused
`CanTransformMultipleBlocks`	Read-only property that returns `true` if multiple blocks can be transformed
`Hash`	Read-only property that returns the calculated hash code
`HashSize`	Read-only property that returns, in bits, the size of the computed hash code
`InputBlockSize`	Read-only property that returns the size of the input block
`OutputBlockSize`	Gets the size of the output block

DIFFERENT FAMILIES OF HASH ALGORITHMS

There are several families of hash algorithms:

➤ **Message Digest (MD), with different versions such as MD2, MD4, and the current one called MD5:** The resulting hash size for MD5 is 128 bits. Choose this algorithm only if you work with legacy applications. Use instead `SHA256` or `SHA512` because they offer better security and performance. Implementations of this algorithm must inherit from the `System.Security.Cryptography.MD5` abstract class. There are two concrete implementations in .NET 4.5: the CAPI implementation in the `MD5CryptoServiceProvider` class and the CNG one in the `MD5Cng` class.

➤ **RACE Integrity Primitives Evaluation Message Digest (RIPEMD):** This family of algorithms has resulting hash sizes of 128, 160, 256, and 320 bits. The version implemented in .NET is the one with the hash size of 160 bits. Choose this algorithm only if you work with legacy applications. Use instead SHA256 or SHA512 because they offer better security and performance. Implementations of this algorithm must inherit from the `System.Security.Cryptography` `.RIPEMD160` abstract class. There is only one implementation of this algorithm in .NET 4.5, the managed one in the `RIPEMD160Managed` class.

➤ **SHA-1 is the second implementation of the Secure Hash Algorithm designed by National Security Agency (NSA).** The first implementation was called SHA-0, but it proved to have errors, which were corrected by SHA-1. The resulting hash size for SHA-1 is 160 bits. Implementations of this algorithm must inherit from the `System.Security.Cryptography.SHA1` abstract class. There are three concrete implementations in .NET 4.5: the managed implementation in the `SHA1Managed` class, the CAPI implementation in the `SHA1CryptoServiceProvider` class, and the CNG one in the `SHA1Cng` class.

➤ **SHA-2 is the third implementation of SHA by NSA, which addresses some of the vulnerabilities found in SHA-1.** This family of algorithms has resulting hash sizes of 224, 256, 384, and 512 bits. .NET is not implementing the 224 bit hash size version of the algorithm. Implementations of this algorithm must inherit from the `System.Security.Cryptography.SHA256` for the 256-bit size hash, the `System.Security.Cryptography.SHA384` for the 384 bits size hash, and the `System.Security.Cryptography.SHA512` for the 512-bit size hash abstract classes. All three versions are implemented as managed, CAPI wrappers and CNG wrappers.

TABLE 12-8: System.Security.Cryptography.HashAlgorithm Methods

METHOD	DESCRIPTION
Clear	Releases all resources used by the HashAlgorithm class.
ComputeHash(Byte[])	Calculates the hash for the a byte array.
ComputeHash(Stream)	Calculates the hash for the a Stream object.
ComputeHash(Byte[], Int32, Int32)	Calculates the hash for a region of a byte array.
Create()	This static method creates a new cryptographic using the default algorithm, which in .NET 4.5 is SHA1.
Create(String)	This static method creates a new hash algorithm object using the specified algorithm. The name of the algorithm can be either one of the names on the left column of Table 12-6 or the name of the type itself, with or without the namespace.
TransformBlock	Calculates the hash for the specified region of the inputBuffer byte array and copies the result to the specified region of the outputBuffer byte array.
TransformFinalBlock	Calculates the hash for the specified region of the inputBuffer byte array.

Normally, you use only Create and the ComputeHash methods. TransformBlock and TransformFinalBlock methods are used when you want to compute the hash for portions of your data.

BEST PRACTICES: Implementing Your Own Algorithm

If you check the online documentation on MSDN for the HashAlgorithm class, you can notice three extra methods not mentioned on the Table 12-8. They are HashCore, HashFinal, and Initialize. All three methods are abstract methods that need to be implemented by the implementers of the hash algorithm. This is the way Microsoft implemented the existing algorithms. Although it sounds tempting, you should not start implementing your own hash algorithms if this is not what your main business is. You should instead use the existing implementations.

The keyed hashing algorithms inherit from the System.Security.Cryptography .KeyedHashAlgorithm class, which has only one extra property compared with the HashAlgorithm class, as shown in Table 12-9.

TABLE 12-9: System.Security.Cryptography.KeyedHashAlgorithm Properties

PROPERTY	DESCRIPTION
Key	Read/write property representing the key to be used by the hash algorithm. If you attempt to change the key after the hashing has begun, a `CryptographicException` is thrown.

The workflow of hashing data is as follows:

1. Create a hashing algorithm object.

2. Set the hashing key if the algorithm used is a keyed one.

3. Call the `ComputeHash` method.

4. Save the hash of the data.

The code should look something like this:

```
string ComputeHash(string input)
{
    HashAlgorithm sha = SHA256.Create();
    byte[] hashData = sha.ComputeHash(Encoding.Default.GetBytes(input));
    return Convert.ToBase64String(hashData);
}
```

The workflow of verifying a hash for data follows:

1. Create a hashing algorithm object using the same algorithm you used for hashing the data.

2. If a hashing keyed algorithm was used, set the key to the same value used for hashing.

3. Extract the original hash of the data.

4. Call the `ComputeHash` method.

5. Compare the extracted hash with the computed one. If they are the same, it means that the data wasn't changed.

```
bool VerifyHash(string input, string hashValue) {

    HashAlgorithm sha = SHA256.Create();
    byte[] hashData = sha.ComputeHash(Encoding.Default.GetBytes(input));
    return Convert.ToBase64String(hashData) == hashValue;
}
```

Managing and Creating Certificates

Although the communication might seem secure at times, when two parties communicate, they need to make sure that they are talking with the right partner. For instance, when you want to do a bank transaction via the Internet, you need to make sure that you are on your bank site and not on some website that is spoofing the identity of your bank. You also want to know that the communication is secured. For web applications there are two protocols that solve this problem: *Transport Layer Security* (TLS) and *Secure Socket Layer* (SSL).

COMMON MISTAKES: Avoiding Convert.ToBase64String

The `Convert.ToBase64String` transforms the input byte array into a string-encoded `base64`. There is no need to use this function. The only reason we use it here is just to make it easier to compare the result of the hashing functions. The alternative would have been to write a function that compares two arrays if they are the same in both length and content. The way the two previous methods are used resembles the following code:

```
public static void Run() {

    string input = "Data to be hashed!";
    string hash = ComputeHash(input);
    bool sameHash = VerifyHash(input, hash);

    Console.WriteLine("Input:{0}", input);
    Console.WriteLine("Hash: {0}", hash);
    Console.WriteLine("Same hash: {0}", sameHash);
}
```

The output of this code should look exactly like the one in Figure 12-1.

FIGURE 12-1: Output of string hashing

Both encrypt data and ensure data authenticity. For authenticity they use *Public Key Infrastructure* (PKI) (the infrastructure needed to handle digital certificates). PKI uses a notion called *Certificate Authority* (CA). A CA is an entity that issues digital certificates. Digital certificates bind a public key with an identity. By doing this, when two parties wants to communicate and the sending party wants to make sure that it talks with the right party, the sending party can use PKI to verify the identity of the receiving party.

The principle is simple. You can either choose to trust the other party directly, but this might become cumbersome if you have to do that for every party, or you can choose to trust a third party instead that only verifies the identity of different entities. This second choice is a hierarchic one, meaning the number of entities you choose to trust is limited. Those entities can verify the identity of other entities, which become trusted entities and so on, until one of them will trust the entity you want to communicate with and confirm its identity.

The top-level certificates that you choose to trust are called root certificates. Normally, you won't add any root certificates. They come with your Windows installation or via Windows Updates. If you want to see which roots certificates your computer is set up to trust by default, go to Control Panel and open the Internet Options dialog. From there open the Content tab, and press the Certificates button; then choose the Trusted Root Certification Authorities tab. A dialog similar with the one in Figure 12-2 appears. As you can see, the list is long, but it can save you a lot of trouble if you want to have secure communication.

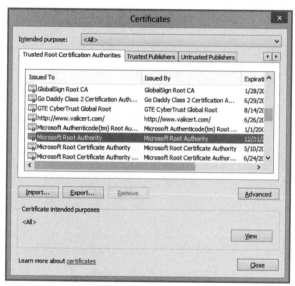

FIGURE 12-2: The root certificate authorities list

If a site now wants to guarantee its identity, it must verify only its identity with one of the entities you chose to trust. One example is Microsoft. On your computer, as you can see in the previous figure, there is a Root Certificate Authority called *GTE CyberTrust Global Root*. If you point your browser to https://www.microsoft.com (note the *https*) and you want to see the certificate of the site and go to the Certification Path tab, a dialog similar with the one in Figure 12-3 appears.

As you can see, www.microsoft.com is trusted by Microsoft Secure Server Authority, which is trusted by Microsoft Internet Authority, which is trusted by GTE CyberTrust Global Root, which you can choose to trust, as one of your Root Certificate Authorities.

The standard used by the PKI is X.509, which specifies the format the PKIs, the *Certificate Revocation List* (CLR), attributes for the certificates, and how to validate the certificate path.

.NET Framework implements the X.509 standard, and all the classes needed to create and manage the certificates are defined in the System.Security.Cryptography.X509Certificates namespace. If you have a certificate with the private key installed locally, you can use it to decrypt data encrypted with the corresponding public key.

FIGURE 12-3: SSL certificate info
for Microsoft.com

> **NOTE** Microsoft offers a tool called `Makecert.exe` (Certificate Creation Tool) that can you can use to create certificates. You can find more information about this tool in the "Additional Reading and Resources" section at the end of this chapter.

To work with certificates programmatically, you can use the `X509Certificate2` class.

Certificates use the notion of *certificate stores*, which are the places where the certificates are securely kept. In .NET stores are implemented in the `X509Store` class. Windows offers two store locations represented by the `StoreLocation` enumeration. The possible values are shown in Table 12-10.

TABLE 12-10: System.Security.Cryptography.X509Certificates.StoreLocation

MEMBER NAME	DESCRIPTION
`CurrentUser`	Represents the certificate store used by the current user
`LocalMachine`	Represents the certificate store common to all users on the local machine

Windows offers eight predefined stores represented by the `StoreName` enumeration. The possible values are shown in Table 12-11.

TABLE 12-11: System.Security.Cryptography.X509Certificates.StoreName

MEMBER NAME	DESCRIPTION
AddressBook	Certificate store for other users
AuthRoot	Certificate store for third-party CAs
CertificateAuthority	Certificate store for intermediate CAs
Disallowed	Certificate store for revoked certificates
My	Certificate store for personal certificates
Root	Certificate store for trusted root CAs
TrustedPeople	Certificate store for directly trusted people and resources
TrustedPublisher	Certificate store for directly trusted publishers

X509Store class offers a string property called Name, which you can use if you want to create your own store.

The following program shows how you can use the X509Store to show the X509Certificates information similar to the one in Figure 12-2.

```
using System;
using System.Security.Cryptography.X509Certificates;

namespace Encryption {
    class CertificateTest {

        static void Main() {

            X509Store store = new X509Store(StoreName.Root,
                                     StoreLocation.LocalMachine);
            store.Open(OpenFlags.ReadOnly);

            Console.WriteLine("Friendly Name\t\t\t\t\t Expiration date");
            foreach (X509Certificate2 certificate in store.Certificates) {
                Console.WriteLine("{0}\t{1}", certificate.FriendlyName
                                    , certificate.NotAfter);
            }
            store.Close();
        }

    }
}
```

This small program starts by opening in read-only mode the root store from the local machine and then prints the name and the expiration date of all the certificates in there.

> **NOTE** *Figure 12-2 includes two more fields, called Issued To and Issued By. If you want to obtain this information, it is part of the* Subject *and* Issuer *property, respectively. Those are of type* X509DistinguishedName. *From there you must extract the value of the Common Name (CN) attribute.*

Implementing Key Management

Sometimes you might just need to keep data safely without thinking too much about the algorithm used or how it is implemented. For example, in order for an encryption algorithm to be effective, you will need to protect the shared secret for a symmetric algorithm, and the private key for an asymmetric algorithm.

To solve this kind of problems, .NET Framework offers in the System.Security.Cryptography namespace one static class named ProtectedData. This class has two static methods: Protect and Unprotect. As the name implies, the first one is used to encrypt the data, and the second one is used to decrypt the data.

Their signatures are as follows:

```
public static byte[] Protect(
    byte[] userData,
    byte[] optionalEntropy,
    DataProtectionScope scope
)
public static byte[] Unprotect(
    byte[] encryptedData,
    byte[] optionalEntropy,
    DataProtectionScope scope
)
```

As you can see, both methods accept three parameters. The first parameter represents the data to by encrypted (userData) or decrypted (encryptedData); the second one is called optionalEntropy, and it is used to increase the complexity of the encrypted data; and the last one is called scope and is of type DataProtectionScope. The scope parameter specifies who can decrypt the data. The values it can take are: DataProtectionScope.CurrentUser and DataProtectionScope.LocalMachine. First, one specifies that only the current user can decrypt the encrypted data, and the second one specifies that any logged-in user on the local machine will be able to decrypt the data.

Protect returns the encrypted data, and Unprotect returns the unencrypted data.

REAL-WORLD CASE SCENARIO Encrypt data using the ProtectData class

Use the ProtectedData class to write a method called ProtectString that takes a string in clear text and encrypts it so that only the current user can decrypt it.

Solution

A possible solution might look like this:

```
byte[] ProtectString(string data) {

    byte[] userData = System.Text.Encoding.Default.GetBytes(data);
    byte[] encryptedData = ProtectedData.Protect(userData, null,
                                  DataProtectionScope.CurrentUser);
    return encryptedData;
}
```

First you convert the string into a byte array, and then you call the `ProtectedData.Protect` method to encrypt the data.

Choosing When to Use Which

Microsoft recommends the following algorithms to be used in the following situations:

- ➤ For data privacy, use Aes.
- ➤ For data integrity, use HMACSHA256 or HMACSHA512.
- ➤ For digital signatures, use RSA or ECDsa.
- ➤ For key exchange, use RSA or ECDiffieHellman.
- ➤ For random number generation, use RNGCryptoServiceProvider.
- ➤ For generating a key from a password, use Rfc2898DeriveBytes.

You can find a link to more information about the Cryptography Model on MSDN in the "Additional Reading and Resources" section.

CODE LAB   **Using the RSA asymmetric algorithm [Chapter12\Asymmetric\RSASample.cs]**

Consider the following complete piece of code:

```
using System;
using System.Text;
using System.Security.Cryptography;

namespace EncryptionSamples.Asymmetric
{
    public class RSASample
    {
        public static void Main() {

            string keyContainerName = "MyKeyContainer";
            string clearText = "This is the data we want to encrypt!";
            CspParameters cspParams = new CspParameters();
```

```csharp
            cspParams.KeyContainerName = keyContainerName;

            RSAParameters publicKey;
            RSAParameters privateKey;

            using (var rsa = new RSACryptoServiceProvider(cspParams)) {

                rsa.PersistKeyInCsp = true;
                publicKey = rsa.ExportParameters(false);
                privateKey = rsa.ExportParameters(true);

                rsa.Clear();
            }

            byte[] encrypted = EncryptUsingRSAParam(clearText, publicKey);
            string decrypted = DecryptUsingRSAParam(encrypted, privateKey);

            Console.WriteLine("Asymmetric RSA - Using RSA Params");
            Console.WriteLine("Encrypted:{0}", Convert.ToBase64String(encrypted));
            Console.WriteLine("Decrypted:{0}", decrypted);

            Console.WriteLine("Asymmetric RSA - Using Persistent Key Container");
            encrypted = EncryptUsingContainer(clearText, keyContainerName);
            decrypted = DecryptUsingContainer(encrypted, keyContainerName);

            Console.WriteLine("Encrypted:{0}", Convert.ToBase64String(encrypted));
            Console.WriteLine("Decrypted:{0}", decrypted);

        }

        static byte[] EncryptUsingRSAParam(string value, RSAParameters rsaKeyInfo)
        {
            using (RSACryptoServiceProvider rsa = new RSACryptoServiceProvider())
            {
                rsa.ImportParameters(rsaKeyInfo);
                byte[] encodedData = Encoding.Default.GetBytes(value);
                byte[] encryptedData = rsa.Encrypt(encodedData, true);

                rsa.Clear();
                return encryptedData;
            }
        }

        static string DecryptUsingRSAParam(byte[] encryptedData,
                                    RSAParameters rsaKeyInfo) {
            using (RSACryptoServiceProvider rsa = new RSACryptoServiceProvider())
            {
                rsa.ImportParameters(rsaKeyInfo);
                byte[] decryptedData = rsa.Decrypt(encryptedData, true);
                string decryptedValue = Encoding.Default.GetString(decryptedData);

                rsa.Clear();
                return decryptedValue;
            }
        }
```

```
static byte[] EncryptUsingContainer(string value, string containerName)
{
    CspParameters cspParams = new CspParameters();
    cspParams.KeyContainerName = containerName;
    using (var rsa = new RSACryptoServiceProvider(cspParams))
    {
        byte[] encodedData = System.Text.Encoding.Default.GetBytes(value);
        byte[] encryptedData = rsa.Encrypt(encodedData, true);

        rsa.Clear();
        return encryptedData;
    }
}

static string DecryptUsingContainer(byte[] encryptedData, string container)
{
    CspParameters cspParams = new CspParameters();
    cspParams.KeyContainerName = container;
    using (var rsa = new RSACryptoServiceProvider(cspParams))
    {
        byte[] decryptedData = rsa.Decrypt(encryptedData, true);
        string decryptedValue = Encoding.Default.GetString(decryptedData);

        rsa.Clear();
        return decryptedValue;                    }
    }
}
}
```

Code Lab Analysis

Start by generating new encryption keys pair, by creating a new instance of the RSACryptoServiceProvider and not specifying any keys. This object won't be used for encryption or decryption, only to get or create the keys. Because you send the cspParams as a parameter and set the PersistKeyInCsp property to true (which is true by default, anyway, you are just being explicit), specify that you want the keys to be saved in a container called MyKeyContainer. When you run the code second time, it uses the keys that exist in that container. By setting PersistKeyInCsp property to false, when you call the Clear method, the parameter is removed from the container.

By calling ExportParameters on the RSA object, you can export the parameters necessary to re-create the public key (when you invoke it with false as a parameter) or both keys (when you invoke it with true as a parameter).

Now examine the EncryptUsingRSAParam method, which takes two parameters: the string to encrypt and an RSAParameters value needed to create the public key.

1. Create a new instance of RSACryptoServiceProvider that implements the RSA algorithm.

2. Call ImportParameters that takes as a parameter the RSAParameters value exported earlier, which can generate the public key.

3. The call to the System.Text.Encoding.Default.GetBytes method transforms the input value from a string into a byte array, so you can prepare it for the Encrypt method.

4. Call `Encrypt` to encrypt the data. The second parameter is to be set to `false` only if you run your application on a version of Windows prior to Windows XP; otherwise, set it to `true`.

5. Call `Clear` to remove any sensitive data from memory and return the encrypted data in a byte array format.

Now examine the `DecryptUsingRSAParam` method, which takes two parameters: the encrypted data as a byte array and an `RSAParameters` value needed to create the public and private key.

1. Create a new instance of `RSACryptoServiceProvider` that implements the RSA algorithm.

2. Call `ImportParameters` that takes as a parameter the `RSAParameters` value exported earlier, which can generate the public and private key. You don't need the public key here, but it will be created anyway.

3. Call `Decrypt` to decrypt the data. The second parameter is to be set to `false` only if you run your application on a version of Windows prior to Windows XP; otherwise, set it to `true`.

4. The call to the `System.Text.Encoding.Default.GetString` method is transforming the input value from a byte array into the decrypted string.

5. Call `Clear` to remove any sensitive data from memory and return the decrypted string.

`EncryptUsingContainer` and `DecryptUsingContainer` works in exactly the same manner with the only difference that instead of sending `RSAParamaters` that are used to generate the keys, you use the same Crypto Service Provider container that you used when you generated the keys.

MANAGING ASSEMBLIES

Compiling projects results in executable files, generally known as *assemblies*. Assemblies are the building blocks of every .NET applications. They are the fundamental unit for deployment, versioning, reuse, and security.

What Is an Assembly?

An assembly contains *Intermediate Language* (IL), metadata, and resources. IL is the result of compiling the source code files into a common language that the *Common Language Runtime* (CLR) understands. CLR has a component called a *Just In Time* (JIT) compiler that compiles the IL code into binary code to run it on a specific platform, such as Windows. An assembly can be a single-file assembly or a multifile assembly. Because Visual Studio can generate only single-file assemblies, this book does not cover the multifile assembly, but you can find additional information in the "Additional Reading and Resources" section at the end of this chapter.

An assembly is obtained by compiling a project. The resulting assembly could be a process assemblies (EXE files) or library assemblies (DLL files); the only difference between the two of them is the presence of the main entry point in process assemblies. The main entry point indicates which method should be called when the application is started, aka the `Main` method.

Because an assembly is the unit of deployment of any .NET application, if you want to split your application in smaller units of deployment to make it more manageable and reusable by different products, you need to split the functionality into different assemblies. Every assembly can then represent a module in your application, which can be updated independent of the other projects. The simplest way to implement this kind of modularization is to create different projects, where one project is one module, and group those into one big solution. To differentiate between different versions of the same assembly, you need to use Assembly Versions.

Understanding Assembly Versions

Software evolves, and the way to mark that is by creating new versions, with every new version adding new features, fixing bugs, or being a complete rewrite of the software, hopefully for the better.

The .NET assembly version is implemented as a string, normally made up of four numeric parts separated by dots: Major, Minor, Build number, and Revision. For instance, the current version of .NET is known as 4.5. This is the marketing version number, or what the customers get to see. Instead, the assemblies that were released with this version have the following version string embedded: `4.0.30319.17929`, where 4 represents the Major number, 0 the Minor number, 30319 the Build number, and 17929 the Revision. If you choose to have a version number that is in another format, the compiler generates an error. The recommendation is to use the number format to give the assembly version a meaning.

> **ADVICE FROM THE EXPERTS: Versioning Your Assemblies**
>
> Choose the versioning scheme carefully because this can help you in the long run. If you use the recommended way with numbers, it is much easier to decide which version is newer based on the version number. The way to think about the different parts of the version follows.
>
> The Revision is normally a random number used to differentiate two versions that have the same build number. Normally, you must set a new number every time you check in and your project is built.
>
> The Build number is a number that normally increases every day, while you are working on a certain version of your product. This is done normally every night by your nightly build process.
>
> The Minor number is increased with every public release of your product. Normally, two versions of the same assembly having the same major number, but different minor numbers are backward compatible—although this is not always the case. Backward compatibility means that when replacing an assembly with a newer version of the same assembly, the system will still work. The way to achieve this is by adding new features, but never removing existing features or changing the public face of the existing ones.
>
> The Major number is increased every time when you have a major release of your product, either by changing existing features or rewriting the entire application.

You can set the version of your assembly in two ways. First is via your project settings. Right-click your project settings and choose Properties. On the Assembly property page, press the Assembly Information button. A dialog similar to the one in Figure 12-4 appears. The four Assembly Version fields represent the aforementioned parts of the assembly version.

The second way to set the version is to go directly and edit the AssemblyInfo.cs file. To find the file, you have to click the project for which you want to change the version, and then expand the property node, as shown in Figure 12-5.

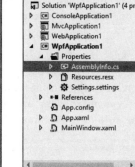

FIGURE 12-4: Assembly Information dialog   **FIGURE 12-5:** Opening the AssemblyInfo.cs file

At the end of the file, you can find a line resembling the following code:

```
[assembly: AssemblyVersion("2.1.42.15")].
```

As explained in Chapter 8, "Creating and Using Types with Reflection, Custom Attributes, the CodeDOM, and Lambda Expressions," this is an attribute implemented in the `AssemblyVersionAttribute` applied to the assembly that specifies which version the assembly should have.

The Assembly Version is ignored by CLR unless it is used together with the strong names. Strong names are covered in the next section.

USING DIFFERENT KINDS OF VERSIONS

Referring to Figure 12-4, you can see two kinds of versions: Assembly Version and File Version. The corresponding attribute for the file version is called `AssemblyFileVersionAttribute`.

continues

continued

The CLR doesn't use the File Version. This information is something that has a meaning for you or your product. Normally, the marketing department cares about the File Version. Although the File Version is normally specified in the same format as the assembly version with a Major, Minor, Build, and Revision number, you can have any string you want. If you use a different format, though, the compiler emits a harmless warning. You cannot set the File Version to a string via the Assembly Information window. You must do it in code by passing the value to the `AssemblyFileVersionAttribute` attribute.

.Net Framework offers a third attribute for versioning called the `AssemblyInformationalVersionAttribute`. This is plain text and is normally the value of your product version. If you don't set it, it will have the value of `AssemblyVersionAttribute`.

To see the values of the `AssemblyFileVersionAttribute` and the `AssemblyInformationalVersionAttribute`, you can compile your assembly, using Windows Explorer navigate to the output folder, and then right-click the assembly. Then choose the Property menu to bring up the file properties window, and choose the Details tab. A dialog similar to the one in Figure 12-6 should appear.

FIGURE 12-6: File and product version information

The value of the `AssemblyFileVersionAttribute` is represented by the value of the `File Version` property and the value of `AssemblyInformationalVersionAttribute` is represented by the value of the `Product Version` property.

Signing Assemblies Using Strong Names

One of the major problems developers were facing prior to .NET was the DLL hell. DLL stands for dynamic linked library, and it was a way to share code and optimize the space an application takes on the disk. The problem that the DLL hell refers to could appear when different applications used the same library. If they were compiled against different version of the same library, the one that was installed last would override the existing DLL. If there were compatibility issues between different versions of the same assembly, one application started to act erratic, or even refused to start. .NET solved this problem by introducing a new concept called *side-by-side versioning*. For this to work, you must make a distinction between different versions of the same assembly, while assuring that the two different versions are coming from the same source.

In .NET the name of the assembly consists of four parts:

➤ The friendly name

➤ The version

➤ The culture

➤ The public key token

The friendly name is what you previously called the library name. In the normal situation, this is the name of the assembly file without the extension, so if your assembly file were called `ProgrammingCSharp.dll`, then the assembly-friendly name would be ProgrammingCSharp.

The version is the Assembly Version discussed in the previous section.

The culture represents the culture of the assembly. The culture is used when you want to localize your application for different markets. To localize your application, you create one assembly containing the code and one assembly for each region you want your application to be localized for. The localized assemblies contain only resources for that specific region such as translated strings or specific images. The executable assembly always has the culture set to neutral. If you try to set it to something else, an error will be generated by the complier. Globalization and localization are outside the scope of this exam, but if you want to know more about this, please see the "Additional Reading and Resources" section for a link to the MSDN list of articles about this subject.

For an assembly to have a strong name, it needs to be signed with a public/private pair of keys using the techniques discussed in the previous section. The private key is used to digitally sign the assembly, whereas the public key is used to verify the signature. The Public Key Token is a 64-bit hash of the assembly public key. The reason that the .NET uses a hash of the signature instead of the signature itself is to save space because the signature is much bigger than 64 bits. An assembly that is not digitally signed can have the Public Key Token set to `null`.

As mentioned earlier, to sign an assembly, you need a pair of public/private keys. You can generate those keys in two ways. The first way is to create the file via Visual Studio. To do that, you right-click the project and then choose Properties. On the properties page, choose the Signing tab. There, check the Sign the Assembly check box, as shown in Figure 12-7.

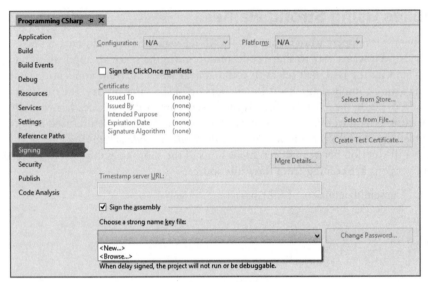

FIGURE 12-7: The Signing tab in Visual Studio 2012

When you do that, a dialog similar to the one shown in Figure 12-8 appears.

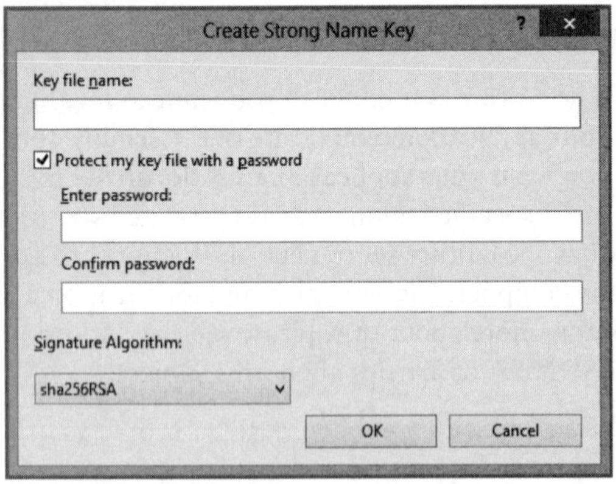

FIGURE 12-8: Create Strong Name Key dialog

As you can see, there you can specify the name of the key file, a password that you can use to protect the private key in the file, and the algorithm to be used for the signature. The choices for the algorithm are sha256RSA and sha1RSA. After you create the file, it will be added to your project. When your project is opened by another user, or by you on another machine, you must to introduce the password you just set in the previous step.

BEST PRACTICES: Signing Assemblies

It is recommend that you use a strong password for the key file and make the password available only for a few selected developers—or even better, for the person responsible for the deployment of your applications. If the password is compromised, it will be easy for someone else to create assemblies and distribute them as if they come from you. To keep the password secret but still have other developers working with your application, you must use Delay sign only. Delay sign is outside the scope of this exam. For extra information about the Delay sign process, look at the "Additional Reading and Resources" section.

The second way to generate a key is to use the sn.exe program. To do that, you need to open the Developer Command Prompt for VS2012. From the command line, run the following:

```
sn.exe -k myFile.snk
```

The command output should look similar to the one in Figure 12-9.

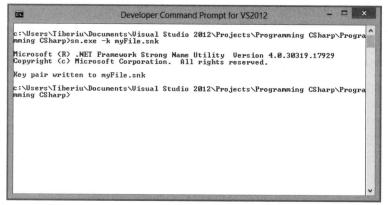

FIGURE 12-9: Sn.exe output

After you generate the file, instead of choosing <New...> in Visual Studio on the Signing tab, you need to choose <Browse...> and choose the newly created file. The downside of using sn.exe is that you cannot specify the password, but sn.exe is used in the delay sign scenario, to extract the public key from the file, or to sign the assembly before the deployment. You can find more information about sn.exe in the "Additional Reading and Resources" section.

NOTE Delay signing is not required for the exam but you should to read the article specified in the "Additional Reading and Resources" section about this subject.

When an assembly needs to be digitally signed, the compiler signs the assembly using the private key and embeds the public key in the assembly for later verification by other assemblies that refer to it. The next step is to hash the public key to create the Public Key Token, and embed that one as well into the assembly.

In conclusion, the assembly name is not only the filename or the friendly name. The complete name of an assembly is known as the *Fully Qualified Name* (FQN). For instance the FQN of the System assembly in .NET 4.5 is

```
System, Version=4.0.0.0, Culture=neutral, PublicKeyToken=b77a5c561934e089
```

Implementing Side-by-Side Versioning

Strong naming would have only little value without the power of running side-by-side different versions of the same assembly. Consider the following scenario.

In your organization there are two teams working on two different products, but both of them need to use some common functionality. As mentioned earlier, the best way to deal with this kind of situation is to move the common code into a separate project, creating a separate assembly that can be used by both teams. Everything works fine; they deploy their products, and there is only one copy of the common assembly per machine, instead of having one per product. After a while the first team might need some additional functionality to be added into the common assembly, but the second team is "not there yet." Without the side-by-side versioning, you must keep a copy of the assembly private for every installation. With two products this might be an acceptable solution, but if you have more products, or if you are a third-party vendor, then it will become much harder to maintain this kind of solution.

Side-by-side versioning works only with strong name assemblies because it requires them to be deployed into the *Global Assembly Cache* (GAC). GAC is covered in the next section. But for now, see how side-by-side versioning works.

When you add a reference to an assembly, information about the referred assembly is added to the manifest file of the assembly. The manifest is embedded into the assembly as part of the metadata. Inside the manifest file every referenced assembly is represented by a block resembling the following code:

```
// Metadata version: v4.0.30319
.assembly extern mscorlib
{
  .publickeytoken = (B7 7A 5C 56 19 34 E0 89 )                    // .z\V.4..
  .ver 4:0:0:0
}
.assembly extern CommonFunctionality
{
  .ver 1:0:0:0
}
.assembly 'Programming CSharp Assembly'
{ ... }
```

The first .assembly extern line represents the reference to the mscorlib assembly, which is referenced by default by all .NET applications because this one contains all the definitions for all the base data types in .NET. The version of the assembly is 4.0.0.0 and the Public Key Token is (B7 7A 5C 56 19 34 E0 89). The second .assembly extern represents a reference to an assembly called CommonFunctionality that has version 1.0.0.0 and is not signed. If the second assembly would have been signed as well, the manifest information would have been something like this:

```
// Metadata version: v4.0.30319
.assembly extern mscorlib
{
  .publickeytoken = (B7 7A 5C 56 19 34 E0 89 )                      // .z\V.4..
  .ver 4:0:0:0
}
.assembly extern CommonFunctionality
{
  .publickeytoken = (48 27 85 37 58 E3 97 63 )                      // H'.7X..c
  .ver 1:0:0:0
}
.assembly 'Programming CSharp Assembly'
{ …}
```

This information is shown using the Intermediate Language Disassembler (ildasm.exe) application. To see that, open the Developer Command Prompt for VS2012 and go the output folder of your assembly (normally *<Your Project Folder>*\bin\Debug). From there type **ildasm.exe** *<Your assembly name>***.exe**. The command output should look similar with the one in Figure 12-10.

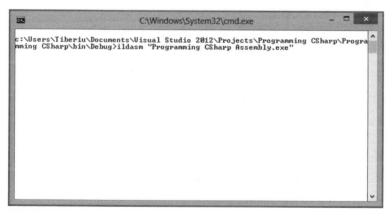

FIGURE 12-10: Invoking ildasm.exe

This opens the IL DASM application, as shown in Figure 12-11.

From there you can double-click the MANIFEST node to open the manifest file, as shown in Figure 12-12.

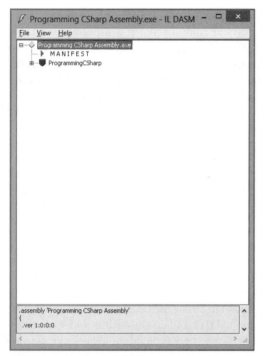

FIGURE 12-11: The IL DASM main application window

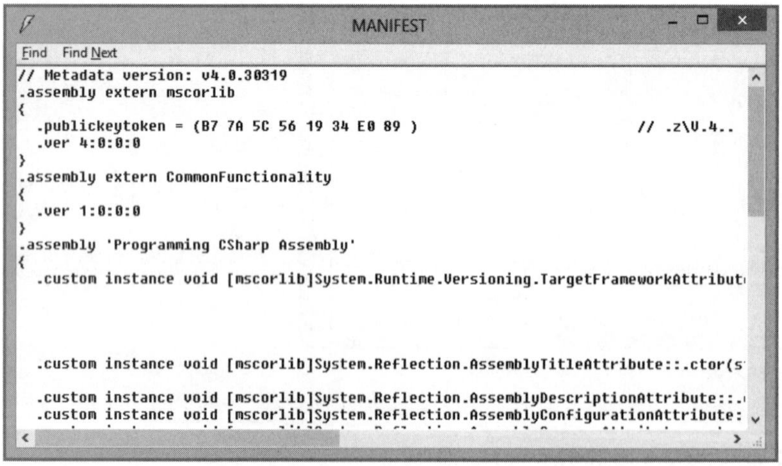

FIGURE 12-12: The IL DASM MANIFEST window

Now when you try to run the application, the run time tries to locate the right assemblies for you.

If an assembly is not signed, CLR looks into the local folder of the application to try to find an assembly based only on the assembly name and assembly filename, ignoring the assembly version.

If the assembly is signed, CLR first tries to see if there are any policies specified for that particular assembly that can instruct CLR to use a different version. This process of replacing an assembly without requiring to recompile the assemblies that use it is called *binding redirection*. After the version is established, CLR first looks in the GAC for that particular version of the assembly, and if it is not there, it looks in the local folder of the application to try to find the right assembly. When the CLR finds the assembly, it verifies the digital signature of the assembly to ensure that the assembly wasn't tampered with. If the CLR finds the assembly but doesn't find the right version for it or the signature doesn't match, it throws a `System.IO.FileLoadException`. If the CLR cannot find the assembly, a `System.IO.FileNotFoundException` is thrown.

> **NOTE** *Two different exceptions are thrown.* `FileLoadException` *is only thrown if the CLR doesn't find the right version of a signed assembly or the assembly was tampered with.* `FileNotFoundException` *is thrown if the assembly is not found at all.*

How CLR does probing on the local folders is outside the scope of this exam, but you can find a link on the "Additional Reading and Resources" section.

PROCESSOR ARCHITECTURE

Since .NET 2.0, Microsoft added the processor architecture to the assembly name, which is optional. This means that you can have two identical versions of the same assembly that differ only by the `ProcessorArchitecture` attribute. The values permitted for the `ProcessorArchitecture` are described by the `System.Reflection.ProcessorArchitecture` enumeration. The values and their meaning are shown in Table 12-12.

TABLE 12-12: System.Reflection.ProcessorArchitecture Members

MEMBER NAME	DESCRIPTION
None	Not specified or unknown
MSIL	Processor independent
X86	A 32-bit Intel processor
IA64	A 64-bit Intel processor only
Amd64	A 64-bit AMD processor only
Arm	An ARM processor

The processor architecture attribute is shown only if it has a value different than `None`, so if the `System` assembly that you saw earlier would set the `ProcessorArchitecture` to `MSIL`, the assembly name would have been

```
System, Version=4.0.0.0, Culture=neutral,
    PublicKeyToken=b77a5c561934e089, ProcessorArchitecture=MSIL
```

Adding Assemblies to the Global Assembly Cache

As mentioned earlier, only signed assemblies can be placed in the GAC, but what is the GAC?

If your application is a non-.NET application and uses dynamic link libraries, it looks for them either on the folder that the application was installed on or on the folders specified in the `PATH` environment variable. If you want to see the value of the `PATH` environment variable, open the Developer Command Prompt for VS2012 and run the following commend:

```
set PATH
```

This outputs something similar with the text shown in Figure 12-13.

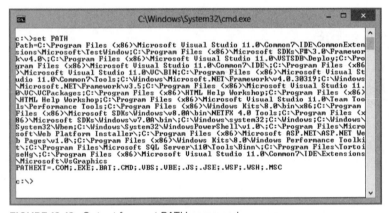

FIGURE 12-13: Output from set PATH command

Instead, .NET uses the concept of GAC, which is an assembly repository that acts as a cache for shared libraries. The location of the GAC is *<Your Windows Installation Folder>*\assembly. If you want to see which assemblies are in your GAC, you can open Windows Explorer and navigate to this folder, and you see something resembling Figure 12-14.

As you can see, the list shows all the aforementioned attributes of an assembly: Assembly Name, Version, Culture, Public Key Token, and Processor Architecture. The empty Culture means that this is the neutral culture, whereas the empty Processor Architecture means NONE for the processor architecture. There is no empty Public Key Token because only strong named (digitally signed) assemblies can be deployed on the GAC.

Before talking about how to add assemblies to GAC, you'll first explore the advantages of using the GAC.

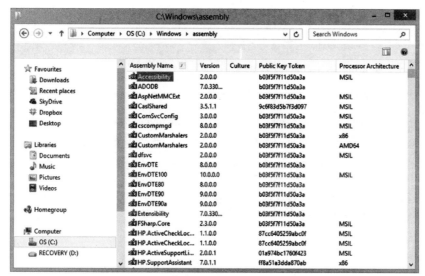

FIGURE 12-14: The GAC view from Windows Explorer

First, two advantages already mentioned are side-by-side versioning and sharing of assemblies. If an assembly is already loaded in memory, the CLR does not load it again.

Another advantage is that the assembly signature is verified before it is installed on the GAC, so when the assembly will be loaded by the CLR when it is executed, it skips verification improving the startup time of your application.

Last is the possibility to precompile the assemblies, so they won't need to be compiled by the JIT compiler every time you load them, as discussed at the beginning of this section. This can speed up the startup process even more. To do that you must run a utility called ngen.exe (Native Image Generator), which is outside the scope of this book, but as always you can find more information in the "Additional Reading and Resources" section.

You can install an assembly in the GAC in two ways.

First, use an installer that can do this. This is the preferred way. By using the installer you ensure that the installation is atomic, meaning that it either succeeds to install all the components or none at all, and it gives you the possibility to uninstall it later in the same manner. When an assembly is installed this way, the installer adds the assembly if is not there, or if it is there, it increases the reference count only, making sure that the assembly won't be uninstalled if it is still used when you uninstall the application.

The second way is to use the utility called gacutil.exe, which can be run as follows:

```
gacutil.exe [options] [assemblyName | assemblyPath | assemblyListFile]
```

Table 12-13 shows the most common parameters for the gacutil.exe. For a complete reference, refer to the "Additional Reading and Resources" section.

TABLE 12-13: gacutil.exe Usage

OPTION	DESCRIPTION
/i	Adds an assembly to the GAC.
/u	Removes an assembly from the GAC.
/l [assemblyName]	Lists all the assemblies in the GAC. Specifying the `assemblyName` parameter will list only the assemblies matching that name.
/r	Traces references to an assembly by increasing a counter on every install and decreasing the counter on uninstall. Specify this option with the `/i`, `/il`, `/u`, or `/ul` options. If an assembly is traced, it will be removed from GAC only when the counter is 0.

SUMMARY

In this chapter you learned how to encrypt sensitive data in your application using both symmetric and asymmetric algorithms. You looked at some of the existing algorithms, how you can manage and create certificates, and how to manage the encryption keys. Then you looked at how to hash data to ensure that the information is not modified and you ended by looking at how you can encrypt streams of data.

In this chapter you learned as well about assemblies, what they are, and how you can create strong-named assemblies to use several side-by-side versions. You then looked at the options available to add an assembly to the GAC, and how you can create a WINMD assembly.

CHAPTER TEST QUESTIONS

The following questions are similar to the types of questions you will find on Exam 70-483. Read each question carefully and select the answer or answers that represent the best solution to the problem. You can find the answers in Appendix A, "Answers to Chapter Test Questions."

1. You are a developer at company xyx. You have been asked to implement a method to safely save and restore data on the local machine. What kind of algorithm best fits the requirements?

   a. Symmetric algorithm

   b. Asymmetric algorithm

   c. Hashing algorithm

   d. X509Certificate

   e. None of the above

2. You are a developer at the company xyx. You have been asked to implement a method to safely send data to another machine. What kind of algorithm best fits the requirements?

   a. Symmetric algorithm

   b. Asymmetric algorithm

   c. Hashing algorithm

   d. X509Certificate

   e. None of the above

3. You are a developer at the company xyx. You have been asked to implement a method to handle password encryption without offering the possibility to restore the password. What kind of algorithm best fits the requirements?

   a. Symmetric algorithm

   b. Asymmetric algorithm

   c. Hashing algorithm

   d. X509Certificate

   e. None of the above

4. Which of the following code snippets will you use to calculate the secure hash of a byte array called `userData`? If you already have created an algorithm object called `sha`.

   a. `userData.GetHashCode(sha);`

   b. `sha.ComputeHash(userData);`

   c. `sha.GetHash(userData);`

   d. `sha.EncryptHash(userData);`

5. Which of the following code snippets will you use to encrypt an array called `userData` that can be decrypted by anyone logged in on the current machine, and without using any entropy?

   a. `ProtectedData.Protect(userData, null,`
   `DataProtectionScope.CurrentUser);`

   b. `ProtectedData.Protect(userData, null,`
   `DataProtectionScope.LocalMachine);`

   c. `ProtectedData.Encrypt(userData, null,`
   `DataProtectionScope.CurrentUser);`

   d. `ProtectedData.Unprotect(userData, null,`
   `DataProtectionScope.LocalMachine);`

6. Which of the following code will you use to encrypt an array called `encryptedData` that can be encrypted by the current user, and without using any entropy?

    a. `ProtectedData.Unprotect(encryptedData, null, DataProtectionScope.CurrentUser);`

    b. `ProtectedData.Protect(encryptedData, null, DataProtectionScope.LocalMachine);`

    c. `ProtectedData.Decrypt(encryptedData, null, DataProtectionScope.CurrentUser);`

    d. `ProtectedData.Unprotect(encryptedData, null, DataProtectionScope.LocalMachine);`

7. What describes a strong name assembly?

    a. Name

    b. Version

    c. Public key token

    d. Culture

    e. Processor Architecture

    f. All the above

8. How can you deploy a strong named assembly?

    a. By running gacutil.exe

    b. By creating an installer

    c. By running asm.exe

    d. By copying the file to the `Bin` folder of the application

    e. By running regsvcs.exe

9. How can you deploy a private assembly?

    a. By running gacutil.exe

    b. By adding a reference to the assembly in Visual Studio

    c. By copying the file in the `Bin` folder of the application

    d. By copying the file in `C:\Windows` folder

10. What is a strong name assembly?

    a. An assembly with the name marked as bold

    b. An assembly with a major and minor version specified

    c. An assembly with a full version specified

    d. An assembly with the culture info specified

    e. A signed assembly

ADDITIONAL READING AND RESOURCES

Here are some additional useful resources to help you understand the topics presented in this chapter:

Cryptography Model

    `http://msdn.microsoft.com/en-us/library/0ss79b2x.aspx`

Makecert.exe (Certificate Creation Tool)

    `http://msdn.microsoft.com/en-us/library/bfsktky3.aspx`

Working with Assemblies

    `http://msdn.microsoft.com/en-us/library/8wxf689z.aspx`

Globalization and Localization

    `http://msdn.microsoft.com/en-us/library/hh965328.aspx`

Delay signing of an assembly

    `http://msdn.microsoft.com/en-us/library/t07a3dye.aspx`

Ngen.exe (Native Image Generator)

    `http://msdn.microsoft.com/en-us/library/6t9t5wcf(v=vs.110).aspx`

Sn.exe (Strong Name Tool)

    `http://msdn.microsoft.com/en-us/library/k5b5tt23(v=vs.110).aspx`

How CLR Locates Assemblies

    `http://msdn.microsoft.com/en-us/library/yx7xezcf.aspx`

Gacutil.exe (Global Assembly Cache Tool)

    `http://msdn.microsoft.com/en-us/library/ex0ss12c.aspx`

CHEAT SHEET

This cheat sheet is designed as a way for you to quickly study the key points of this chapter.

Choosing an encryption algorithm

➤ If you need to encrypt data that is used locally, or you have a secure way to distribute the encryption key, use the symmetric encryption.

➤ If you don't have a secure way to send the encryption key data between parties, then asymmetric encryption is recommended.

➤ If you need only to ensure integrity of the data, use a hashing algorithm.

➤ If you need to ensure both integrity and authenticity, choose a MAC algorithm.

Symmetric encryption

➤ Based on a common key called shared secret.

➤ It needs an initialization vector (IV) that doesn't need to be secret but is used to encrypt the first block of data.

➤ You use it by instantiating a symmetric algorithm object and then calling `CreateEncryptor` or `CreateDecryptor`.

➤ The encryptor/decryptor is then used with either by calling directly the `TransformFinalBlock` method or by sending it to a `CryptoStream`.

Asymmetric encryption

➤ It is based on a pair of complementary keys. Encrypted data with one key can be decrypted only with the other key.

➤ One key is kept secret and is called a *private key*; the other one is made available to anyone that wants to encrypt data, or verify encrypted data, and it is called a *public key*.

Hashing

➤ Mapping binary data of a variable length to a fixed size binary data, called *hash*.

➤ When you need to make sure that data is not modified while transferred, you can calculate the cryptographic hash and send it together with the data to be verified by the receiving party.

➤ The two commonly used algorithms are SHA256 and SHA512 with resulting hashes of 256 and 512 bits, respectively (32 and 64 bytes).

Key management

➤ Symmetric keys can be exchanged using asymmetric algorithms.

➤ Asymmetric private keys can be secured either by using certificates or by using Crypto Service Providers containers.

Assembly version

➤ An assembly version is specified by four parts: Major, Minor, Build, and Revision.

Strong name

➤ An assembly that is digitally signed is called a *strong named assembly*.

➤ A strong name has five parts: Friendly Name, Version, Culture, Public Key Token, and Processor Architecture.

GAC

➤ Stands for *Global Assembly Cache*.

➤ A repository to share .NET assemblies.

➤ Only strong named assemblies can be deployed on the GAC.

➤ Several versions of the same assembly can be deployed on the GAC at the same time.

REVIEW OF KEY TERMS

assembly An assembly is the unit of reuse, deployment, versioning, and security.

asymmetric encryption (public key) A cryptographic algorithm that uses two complementary keys, one for encryption and one for decryption. Data encrypted with the public key can only be decrypted using the private key.

Certificate Authority (CA) An entity that issues digital certificates.

Certificate Revocation List (CRL) A list of digital certificates that has been revoked for various reasons. You shouldn't use a certificate if it is revoked.

certificate stores A special storage location on your computer, used to store encryption certificates.

Common Language Runtime (CLR) CLR is the component of .NET Framework responsible for running .NET applications and managing their running environment.

cryptography The practice and study of techniques for secure communication.

decryption The process of decoding previously encrypted data so that it can be used by your application.

encryption The process of encoding data so that it cannot be read by an unauthorized person.

Global Assembly Cache (GAC) GAC is a machine-wide code cache.

hash bucket A data structure that holds items that share the same hash value.

hashing Used to map data structures of variable length, to fixed size data structures. Hashing the same data using the same algorithm will always yield the same hash value.

initialization vector (IV) A data array used by the encryption algorithms to encrypt the first data block. The IV doesn't need to be kept secret.

Intermediate Language (IL) The result of compiling a .NET application from source code.

Just In Time compiler (JIT) A component of the .NET that transforms the IL into binary code that can be run on the target platform.

Message Authentication Code (MAC) A family of cryptographic algorithms used to provide data integrity and authenticity.

private key The public and private keys are a pair of complementary keys used together in the asymmetric encryption. Data encrypted with the private key can only be decrypted using the public key, and data encrypted with the public key can only be decrypted using the private key.

public key See *private key.*

Public Key Infrastructure (PKI) The infrastructure needed to handle digital certificates.

Secured Hash Algorithm (SHA) A family of cryptographic algorithms used to calculate hashes published by NIST.

Secure Socket Layer (SSL) A cryptographic protocol used for secure communication over the Internet.

symmetric encryption (shared secret) A cryptographic algorithm that uses the same key for both encryption and decryption of data.

Transport Layer Security (TLS) A cryptographic protocol used for secure communication over the Internet, the successor of SSL.

EXAM TIPS AND TRICKS

The Review of Key Terms and the Cheat Sheet for this chapter can be printed to help you study. You can find these files in the ZIP file for this chapter at www.wrox .com/remtitle.cgi?isbn=1118612094 on the Download Code tab.

Answers to Sample Test Questions

CHAPTER 1: INTRODUCING THE PROGRAMMING IN C# CERTIFICATION

Chapter 1 has no chapter test questions.

CHAPTER 2: BASIC PROGRAM STRUCTURE

1. You want to declare an integer variable called `myVar` and assign it the value `0`. How can you accomplish this?

    b. `myVar = 0;`

2. You need to make a logical comparison where two values must return true in order for your code to execute the correct statement. Which logical operator enables you to achieve this?

    d. `&&`

3. What kind of result is returned in the condition portion of an `if` statement?

    a. Boolean

4. What are the keywords supported in an `if` statement?

    b. `if`, `else`, `else if`

5. In the following code sample, will the second `if` structure be evaluated?

```
bool condition = true;

if(condition)
```

```
if(5 < 10)
    Console.WriteLine("5 is less than 10);
```

   a.   Yes

6.   If you want to iterate over the values in an array of integers called `arrNumbers` to perform an action on them, which loop statement enables you to do this?

   a.   `foreach (int number in arrNumbers){}`

7.   What is the purpose of `break;` in a switch statement?

   b.   It causes the code to exit the switch statement.

8.   What are the four basic repetition structures in C#?

   c.   `for, foreach, while, do-while`

9.   How many times will this loop execute?

```
int value = 0;
do
{
    Console.WriteLine (value);
} while value > 10;
```

   b.   1 time

CHAPTER 3: WORKING WITH THE TYPE SYSTEM

1.   What is the maximum value you can store in an `int` data type?

   d.   4,294,967,296

2.   True or false: Double and float data types can store values with decimals.

   a.   True

3.   Which declaration can assign the default value to an `int` type?

   b.   `int myInt = new int();`

4.   True or false: structs can contain methods.

   a.   True

5.   What is the correct way to access the `firstName` property of a struct named `Student`?

   a.   `string name = Student.firstName;`

6.   In the following enumeration, what will be the underlying value of Wed?

```
enum Days {Mon = 1, Tue, Wed, Thur, Fri, Sat, Sun};
```

   b.   3

7.   What are two methods with the same name but with different parameters?

   a.   Overloading

8. What is the parameter in this method known as?

```
public void displayAbsoluteValue(int value = 1)
```

    b. Optional

9. When you create an abstract method, how do you use that method in a derived class?

    b. You must override the method in your derived class.

10. How do you enforce encapsulation on the data members of your class?

    a. Create private data members.

    c. Use public properties.

11. Boxing refers to:

    b. Converting a value type to a reference type

12. What is one advantage of using named parameters?

    a. You can pass the arguments in to the method in any order using the parameter names.

13. What is an advantage of using Generics in .NET?

    b. Generics enable you to create classes that accept the type at creation time.

14. What does the <T> designator indicate in a generic class?

    c. It is a placeholder that will contain the object type used.

15. How are the values passed in generic methods?

    b. They are passed by reference.

CHAPTER 4: USING TYPES

1. To parse a string that might contain a currency value such as $1,234.56, you should pass the `Parse` or `TryParse` method which of the following values?

    c. `NumberStyles.Currency`

2. Which of the following statements is true for widening conversions?

    d. All of the above.

3. Which of the following statements is true for narrowing conversions?

    b. The source and destination types must be compatible.

4. Assuming `total` is a `decimal` variable holding the value 1234.56, which of the following statements displays `total` with the currency format $1,234.56?

    c. `Console.WriteLine(total.ToString("c"));`

5. Which of the following statements generates a string containing the text "Veni, vidi, vici "?

    c. `String.Format("{2}, {0}, {3}", "vidi", "Venti", "Veni", "vici")`

6. If `i` is an `int` and `l` is a `long`, which of the following statements is true?

    a. `i = (int)l` is a narrowing conversion.

7. Which of the following methods is the best way to store an integer value typed by the user in a variable?

    d. `TryParse`

8. The statement `object obj = 72` is an example of which of the following?

    c. Boxing

9. If `Employee` inherits from `Person` and `Manager` inherits from `Employee`, which of the following statements is valid?

    a. `Person alice = new Employee();`

10. Which of the following is not a `String` method?

    c. `StopsWith`

11. Which of the following techniques does not create a `String` containing 10 spaces?

    d. Use the String class's Space method passing it 10 as the number of spaces the string should contain.

12. Which of the following statements can you use to catch integer overflow and underflow errors?

    a. `checked`

13. Which of the following techniques should you use to watch for floating point operations that cause overflow or underflow?

    c. Check the result for the value `Infinity` or `NegativeInfinity`.

CHAPTER 5: CREATING AND IMPLEMENTING CLASS HIERARCHIES

1. Which the following statements about the `base` keyword is false?

    c. The `base` keyword lets a constructor invoke a different constructor in the same class.

2. Which the following statements about the `this` keyword is false?

    b. A constructor can use a `this` statement and a `base` statement if the `base` statement comes first.

3. Suppose you have defined the `House` and `Boat` classes and you want to make a `HouseBoat` class that inherits from both `House` and `Boat`. Which of the following approaches would not work?

    a. Make `HouseBoat` inherit from both `House` and `Boat`.

4. Suppose the `HouseBoat` class implements the `IHouse` interface implicitly and the `IBoat` interface explicitly. Which of the following statements is false?

    b. The code can use a `HouseBoat` object to access its `IBoat` members.

5. Which of the following is not a good use of interfaces?

    d. To reuse the code defined by the interface.

6. Suppose you want to make a `Recipe` class to store cooking recipes and you want to sort the `Recipes` by the `MainIngredient` property. In that case, which of the following interfaces would probably be most useful?

    b. `IComparable`

7. Suppose you want to sort the `Recipe` class in question 6 by any of the properties `MainIngredient`, `TotalTime`, or `CostPerPerson`. In that case, which of the following interfaces would probably be most useful?

    c. `IComparer`

8. Which of the following statements is true?

    c. A class can inherit from at most one class and implement any number of interfaces.

9. A program can use the `IEnumerable` and `IEnumerator` interfaces to do which of the following?

    a. Use `MoveNext` and `Reset` to move through a list of objects.

10. Which of the following statements about garbage collection is false?

    d. Before destroying an object, the GC calls its `Dispose` method.

11. Which of the following statements about destructors is false?

    c. Destructors are inherited.

12. If a class implements `IDisposable`, its `Dispose` method should do which of the following?

    d. All of the above.

13. If a class has managed resources and no unmanaged resources, it should do which of the following?

    b. Implement `IDisposable` and not provide a destructor.

14. If a class has unmanaged resources and no managed resources, it should do which of the following?

    a. Implement `IDisposable` and provide a destructor.

CHAPTER 6: WORKING WITH DELEGATES, EVENTS, AND EXCEPTIONS

1. Which of the following is a valid delegate definition?

    d. `private delegate void MyDelegate(float x);`

2. Which of the following statements is *not* true of delegate variables?

    a. You need to use a cast operator to execute the method to which a delegate variable refers.

3. If the `Employee` class inherits from the `Person` class, covariance lets you do which of the following?

 b. Store a method that returns an `Employee` in a delegate that represents methods that return a `Person`.

4. If the `Employee` class inherits from the `Person` class, contravariance lets you do which of the following?

 c. Store a method that takes a `Person` as a parameter in a delegate that represents methods that take an `Employee` as a parameter.

5. In the variable declaration `Action<Order> processor`, the variable `processor` represents which of the following?

 b. Methods that take an `Order` object as a parameter and return `void`.

6. In the variable declaration `Func<Order> processor`, the variable `processor` represents which of the following?

 a. Methods that take no parameters and return an `Order` object.

7. Suppose F is declared by the statement `Func<float, float> F`. Then which of the following correctly initializes F to an anonymous method?

 d. `F = delegate(float x) { return x * x; };`

8. Suppose the variable `note` is declared by the statement `Action note`. Then which of the following correctly initializes `note` to an expression lambda?

 c. `note = () => MessageBox.Show("Hi");`

9. Suppose the variable `result` is declared by the statement `Func<float, float> result`. Which of the following correctly initializes `result` to an expression lambda?

 d. Both a and c are correct.

10. Which of the following statements about statement lambdas is false?

 b. A statement lambda cannot return a value.

11. Suppose the `MovedEventHandler` delegate is defined by the statement `delegate void MovedEventHandler()`. Which of the following correctly declares the `Moved` event?

 d. Both b and c are correct.

12. Suppose the `Employee` class is derived from the `Person` class and the `Person` class defines an `AddressChanged` event. Which of the following should you *not* do to allow an `Employee` object to raise this event?

 b. Create an `OnAddressChanged` method in the `Employee` class that raises the event.

13. Which of the following statements subscribes the `myButton_Click` event handler to catch the `myButton` control's `Click` event?

 a. `myButton.Click += myButton_Click;`

14. Suppose the `Car` class provides a `Stopped` event that takes as parameters `sender` and `StoppedArgs` objects. Suppose also that the code has already created an appropriate `StoppedArgs` object named `args`. Then which of the following code snippets correctly raises the event?

    c. `if (Stopped != null) Stopped(this, args);`

15. Which of the following statements about events is false?

    c. If an object subscribes to an event once and then unsubscribes twice, its event handler throws an exception when the event is raised.

16. Which of the following statements about inheritance and events is false?

    a. A derived class can raise a base class event by using code similar to the following:

`if (base.EventName != null) base.EventName(this, args);`

17. Which of the following statements about exception handling is true?

    a. You can nest a `try-catch-finally` block inside a `try`, `catch`, or `finally` section.

18. Which of the following methods can you use to catch integer overflow exceptions?

    d. Either b or c.

19. Which of the following returns `true` if variable `result` holds the value `float.PositiveInfinity`?

    d. All of the above.

20. Which of the following statements about throwing exceptions is false?

    b. If you rethrow the exception `ex` with the statement `throw`, the exception's call stack is reset to start at the current line of code.

21. Which of the following should you *not* do when building a custom exception class?

    c. Make it implement `IDisposable`.

CHAPTER 7: MULTITHREADING AND ASYNCHRONOUS PROCESSING

1. You are a developer at company xyx. You have been asked to improve the responsiveness of your WPF application. Which solution best fits the requirements?

    a. Use the `BackgroundWorker` class.

2. How do you execute a method as a task?

    d. All the above.

3. Which of the following is not a locking mechanism?

    d. `async`

4. How can you schedule work to be done by a thread from the thread pool?

    c. You call the `ThreadPool.QueueUserWorkItem` method.

    d. You create a new thread and set its property

5. Which of the following are methods of the `Parallel` class?

    b. `Invoke`

    c. `For`

    d. `ForEach`

6. Which method can you use to cancel an ongoing operation that uses `CancelationToken`?

    b. Call `Cancel` method on the `CancelationTokenSource` object that was used to create the `CancelationToken`

7. Which method would you call when you use a barrier to mark that a participant reached that point?

    c. `SignalAndWait`

8. What code is equivalent with `lock(syncObject){…}`?

    c. `Monitor.Enter(syncObject);   try{…} finally{   Monitor.Exit(syncObject); }`

9. In a multithreaded application how would you increment a variable called `counter` in a lock free manner? Choose all that apply.

    c. `Interlocked.Add(ref counter, 1);`

    e. `Interlocked.Increment (ref counter);`

10. Which method will you use to signal and `EventWaitHandle`?

    c. `Set`

CHAPTER 8: CREATING AND USING TYPES WITH REFLECTION, CUSTOM ATTRIBUTES, THE CODEDOM, AND LAMBDA EXPRESSIONS

1. You are given an assignment to create a code generator to automate the task of creating repetitive code. Which namespace contains the types needed to generate code?

    d. System.CodeDom

2. Which code can create a lambda expression?

    c. `x => x * x;`

3. You are consulting for a company called Contoso and are taking over an application that was built by a third-party software company. There is an executable that is currently not working because it is missing a DLL file that is referenced. How can you figure out which DLL files the application references?

    b. Create an instance of the `Assembly` class, load the assembly, and call the `GetReferencedAssemblies` method.

4. You are a developer for a finance department and are building a method that uses reflection to get a reference to the type of object that was passed as a parameter. Which syntax can be used to determine an object's type?

    d. `Type myType = myParameter.GetType();`

5. You are asked to create a custom attribute that has a single property, called `Version`, that allows the caller to determine the version of a method. Which code can create the attribute?

    b. `class MyCustomAttribute : System.Attribute    {       public string Version { get; set; }    }`

6. Which class in the `System.Reflection` namespace would you use if you want to determine all the classes contained in a DLL file?

    b. `Assembly`

7. Which method of the `Assembly` class allows you to get all the public types defined in the `Assembly`?

    c. `GetExportedTypes`

8. Which property of the `Assembly` class returns the name of the assembly?

    d. `FullName`

9. Which method of the `Assembly` class returns an instance of the current assembly?

    a. `GetExecutingAssembly`

10. Which syntax will `Load` an `Assembly`?

    a. `Assembly.Load("System.Data, Version=4.0.0.0, Culture=neutral, Public KeyToken=b77a5c561934e089");`

    b. `Assembly.LoadFrom(@"c:\MyProject\Project1.dll");`

    c. `Assembly.LoadFile(@"c:\MyProject\Project1.dll");`

    d. `Assembly.ReflectionOnlyLoad(("System.Data, Version=4.0.0.0, Culture=neutral, PublicKeyToken=b77a5c561934e089");`

11. Which method should you call if you want the .NET Framework to look in the load-context to load an `Assembly`?

    c. `Load`

12. Which method should you call if you want the .NET Framework to look in the load-from context?

    b. `LoadFrom`

13. Which line creates an instance of a `DataTable` using reflection?

    a. `myAssembly.CreateInstance("System.Data.DataTable");`

14. Which class would you create if you wanted to determine all the properties contained in a class using reflection?

    d. `Type`

15. How can you determine if a class is public or private?

    a. Create an instance of the `Type` class using the `typeof` keyword and then examine the `IsPublic` property of the `Type` variable.

16. Which class in the `System.Reflection` namespace is used to represent a field defined in a class?

    b. `FieldInfo`

17. Which property of the `Type` class can you use to determine the number of dimension for an array?

    d. `GetArrayRank`

18. Which statement will returns a private, instance field called `"myPrivateField"` using reflection? Assume the `myClass` variable is an instance of a class.

    a. `myClass.GetType().GetField("myPrivateField", BindingFlags.NonPublic | BindingFlags.Instance)`

19. Which method of the `MethodInfo` class can be used to execute the method?

    b. `Invoke`

20. Which statement uses reflection to execute the method and passes in two parameters given the following code block?

```
MyClass myClass = new MyClass();
MethodInfo myMethod = typeof(MyClass).GetMethod("Multiply");
```

    c. `myMethod.Invoke(myClass, new object[] { 4, 5 });`

CHAPTER 9: WORKING WITH DATA

1. Which object does the variable `mySet` inherit from?

```
Int[] mySet  = new int[5];
```

    c. `System.Array`

2. Which type should you use to store objects of different types but do not know how many elements you need at the time of creation?

    d. `ArrayList`

3. If you create a custom class that is going to be used as elements in a `List` object and you want to use the `Sort` method of the `List` object to sort the elements in the array, what steps must you take when coding the custom class?

   b. Inherit from the IComparable interface.Implement the `CompareTo` method.

4. Which collection would you use if you need to process the items in the collection on first-in-first-out order?

   b. `Queue`

5. Which collection would you use if you need to process the items in the collection on a last-in-first-out order?

   c. `Stack`

6. Which collection would you use if you need to quickly find an element by its key rather than its index?

   a. `Dictionary`

   c. `SortedList`

7. Which ADO.NET object is used to connect to a database?

   b. `Connection`

8. Which properties of an ADO.NET Command object must you set to execute a stored procedure?

   c. `CommandTypeCommandTextParameters`

9. Which `Command` object's method would you use to execute a query that does not return any results?

   a. `ExecuteNonQuery`

10. Which `Command` object's method would you use to execute a query that returns only one row and one column?

   c. `ExecuteScalar`

11. Which ADO.NET object is a forward only cursor and is connected to the database while the cursor is open?

   a. `DBDataReader`

12. Which ADO.NET `Command` object's property would you use when a query returns the SUM of a column in a table?

   c. `ExecuteScalar`

13. Which ADO.NET object is a fully traversable cursor and is disconnected from the database?

   c. `DataTable`

14. Which method of a `DataAdapter` is used to populate a `DataSet`?

   b. `Fill`

15. Which property of an ADO.NET DataAdapter is used to insert records in a database?

    c. `InsertCommand`

16. Which ADO.NET `Command` object's property would you use when a query returns the SUM of a column in a table?

    c. `ExecuteScalar`

17. When using the ADO.NET Entity Framework you create a `Model` that represents the object in the database. What class does the `Model` inherit from?

    a. `DBContext`

18. How are stored procedures represented in the ADO.NET Entity Framework?

    b. A method is added to the Model that is the same name as the stored procedure.

19. Which code uses the ADO.NET Entity Framework to add a record to the database?

    a.

```
using (NorthwindsEntities db = new NorthwindsEntities())
{
    Category category = new Category()
    {
        CategoryName = "Alcohol",
        Description = "Happy Beverages"
    };

    db.Categories.Add(category);
    db.SaveChanges();
}
```

20. Which code uses the ADO.NET Entity Framework to update a record in the database?

    c.

```
Category category = db.Categories.First(c => c.CategoryName == "Alcohol");
category.Description = "Happy People";
db.SaveChanges();
```

CHAPTER 10: WORKING WITH LANGUAGE INTEGRATED QUERY (LINQ)

1. Which answer has the correct order of keywords for a LINQ query expression?

    c. from, where, select

2. Which `where` clause can select all integers in the `myList` object that are even numbers given the following `from` clause?

```
from i in myList
```

    c. `where i % 2 == 0`

3. Which line of code executes the LINQ query?

```
[1]     var result = from i in myArray
[2]                         order by i
[3]                         select i
[4]     foreach(int i in result)
[5]     { …}
```

   d. Line 4

4. Which method can you use to find the minimum value in a sequence?

   a. `(from i in myArray select i).Min()`

5. Which methods can you use to find the first item in a sequence?

   b. `First`

   d. `Take`

6. Which `where` clause returns all integers between 10 and 20?

   b. `where i >= 10 && i <= 20`

7. Which clause orders the state and then the city?

   c. `orderby h.State, h.City`

8. Which statement selects an anonymous type?

   c. `select new { h.City, h.State }`

9. Which `on` statement joins two sequences on the `StateId` property?

   a. `on e.StateId equals s.StateId`

10. Which two keywords must you use in a join clause to create an outer join?

   b. `into, DefaultIfEmpty`

11. Which `join` clause uses a composite key?

   a. `on new { City = e.City, State = e.State } equals new { City = h.City, State = h.State }`

12. Which statement groups a sequence by the `State` property?

   c. `group e by e.State`

13. Which answers return the count of all even numbers?

   a. `myArray.Where(i => i % 2 == 0).Count()`

   b. `myArray.Count(i => i % 2 == 0)`

CHAPTER 11: INPUT VALIDATION, DEBUGGING, AND INSTRUMENTATION

1. If the user is typing data into a `TextBox` and types an invalid character, which of the following actions would be inappropriate for the program to take?

    d. Display a message box telling the user that there is an error.

2. If the user types an invalid value into a `TextBox` and moves focus to another `TextBox`, which of the following actions would be inappropriate for the program to take?

    a. Force focus back into the `TextBox` that contains the error.

3. If the user enters some invalid data on a form and then clicks the form's Accept button, which of the following actions would be appropriate for the program take?

    d. All the above.

4. Which of the following methods returns `true` if a regular expression matches a string?

    b. `Regex.IsMatch`

5. Which of the following regular expressions matches the Social Security number format ###-##-#### where # is any digit?

    c. `^\d{3}-\d{2}-\d{4}$`

6. Which of the following regular expressions matches a username that must include between 6 and 16 letters, numbers, and underscores?

    b. `^[a-zA-Z0-9_]{6,16}$`

7. Which of the following regular expressions matches license plate values that must include three uppercase letters followed by a space and three digits, or three digits followed by a space and three uppercase letters?

    a. `(^\d{3} [A-Z]{3}$)|(^[A-Z]{3} \d{3}$)`

8. Which of the following statements about assertions is true?

    d. All the above.

9. Which of the following statements about the `Debug` and `Trace` classes is true?

    b. The `Debug` class generates messages if `DEBUG` is defined. The `Trace` class generates messages if `TRACE` is defined.

10. Which of the following statements about builds is true by default?

    a. Debug builds define the `DEBUG` symbol.

    b. Debug builds define the `TRACE` symbol.

    d. Release builds define the `TRACE` symbol.

11. Which of the following statements about PDB files is false?

    b. You can use a PDB file to debug any version of a compiled executable.

12. Which of the following statements about tracing and logging is false?

> **d.** A program cannot write events into the system's event logs, so you can see them in the Event Viewer.

13. Which of the following methods would probably be the easiest way to find bottlenecks in a program if you had no idea where to look?

> **a.** Use an automatic profiler.

14. What of the following is the best use of performance counters?

> **b.** To determine how often a particular operation is occurring on the system as a whole.

CHAPTER 12: USING ENCRYPTION AND MANAGING ASSEMBLIES

1. You are a developer at company xyx. You have been asked to implement a method to safely save and restore data on the local machine. What kind of algorithm best fits the requirements?

> **a.** Symmetric algorithm

2. You are a developer at the company xyx. You have been asked to implement a method to safely send data to another machine. What kind of algorithm best fits the requirements?

> **b.** Asymmetric algorithm

3. You are a developer at the company xyx. You have been asked to implement a method to handle password encryption without offering the possibility to restore the password. What kind of algorithm best fits the requirements?

> **c.** Hashing algorithm

4. Which of the following code snippets will you use to calculate the secure hash of a byte array called `userData`? If you already have created an algorithm object called `sha`.

> **b.** `sha.ComputeHash(userData);`

5. Which of the following code snippets will you use to encrypt an array called `userData` that can be decrypted by anyone logged in on the current machine, and without using any entropy?

> **b.** `ProtectedData.Protect(userData, null, DataProtectionScope.`
> `LocalMachine);`

6. Which of the following code will you use to encrypt an array called `encryptedData` that can be encrypted by the current user, and without using any entropy?

> **a.** `ProtectedData.Unprotect(encryptedData, null, DataProtectionScope.`
> `CurrentUser);`

7. What describes a strong name assembly?

   f. All the above

8. How can you deploy a strong named assembly?

   a. By running gacutil.exe

   b. By creating an installer

   d. By copying the file to the `Bin` folder of the application

9. How can you deploy a private assembly?

   b. By adding a reference to the assembly in Visual Studio

   c. By copying the file in the `Bin` folder of the application

10. What is a strong name assembly?

   e. A signed assembly

INDEX

M

W